Sedimentary Processes in the Intertidal Zone

Geological Society Special Publications

Series Editors

A. J. FLEET

A. C. MORTON

A. M. ROBERTS

GEOLOGICAL SOCIETY SPECIAL PUBLICATION NO. 139

Sedimentary Processes in the Intertidal Zone

EDITED BY

K. S. BLACK
St Andrews University, UK

D. M. PATERSON
St Andrews University, UK

AND

A. CRAMP
University of Wales, Cardiff, UK

1998

Published by

The Geological Society

London

THE GEOLOGICAL SOCIETY

The Society was founded in 1807 as The Geological Society of London and is the oldest geological society in the world. It received its Royal Charter in 1825 for the purpose of 'investigating the mineral structure of the Earth'. The Society is Britain's national society for geology with a membership of around 8500. It has countrywide coverage and approximately 1500 members reside overseas. The Society is responsible for all aspects of the geological sciences including professional matters. The Society has its own publishing house, which produces the Society's international journals, books and maps, and which acts as the European distributor for publications of the American Association of Petroleum Geologists, SEPM and the Geological Society of America.

Fellowship is open to those holding a recognized honours degree in geology or cognate subject and who have at least two years' relevant postgraduate experience, or who have not less than six years' relevant experience in geology or a cognate subject. A Fellow who has not less than five years' relevant postgraduate experience in the practice of geology may apply for validation and, subject to approval, may be able to use the designatory letters C Geol (Chartered Geologist).

Further information about the Society is available from the Membership Manager, The Geological Society, Burlington House, Piccadilly, London W1V 0JU, UK. The Society is a Registered Charity, No. 210161.

Published by The Geological Society from:
The Geological Society Publishing House
Unit 7, Brassmill Enterprise Centre
Brassmill Lane
Bath BA1 3JN
UK
(*Orders*: Tel. 01225 445046
Fax 01225 442836)

First published 1998

The publishers make no representation, express or implied, with regard to the accuracy of the information contained in this book and cannot accept any legal responsibility for any errors or omissions that may be made.

British Library Cataloguing in Publication Data
A catalogue record for this book is available from the British Library.

ISBN 1-86239-013-4

Distributors

USA
AAPG Bookstore
PO Box 979
Tulsa
OK 74101-0979
USA
(*Orders*: Tel. (918) 584-2555
Fax (918) 560-2652)

Australia
Australian Mineral Foundation
63 Conyngham Street
Glenside
South Australia 5065
Australia
(*Orders*: Tel. (08) 379-0444
Fax (08) 379-4634)

India
Affiliated East-West Press PVT Ltd
G-1/16 Ansari Road
New Delhi 110 002
India
(*Orders*: Tel. (11) 327-9113
Fax (11) 326-0538)

Japan
Kanda Book Trading Co.
Tanikawa Building
3-2 Kanda Surugadai
Chiyoda-Ku
Tokyo 101
Japan
(*Orders*: Tel. (03) 3255-3497
Fax (03) 3255-3495)

Typeset by Aarontype Ltd, Unit 47, Easton Business Centre, Felix Road, Bristol BS5 0HE, UK

Printed by The Alden Press, Osney Mead, Oxford, UK

Contents

Preface

Broad intertidal sand and mudflats fringe the coastlines of many countries in mid-latitude, meso- and macro-tidal environments. These areas form extensive low-slope flats and are usually associated with a shore-connected marsh system. Despite the extreme conditions of periodic exposure to air and variations in salinity, these coastal deposits are one of the most productive natural ecosystems on Earth, with a gross primary productivity equal to many more familiar terrestrial systems. Intertidal flats form an integral and important part of coastal systems, which have for centuries been usefully exploited by humans for communication, transportation, waste disposal, power generation and amenity development. They provide an indispensable feeding ground for many species of shorebirds, play a vital role in protecting the shoreline against erosion by wave action, and they act as both a source and sink to sediments and pollutants and are therefore intrinsically related to the ecological 'health' of the system as well as its geomorphology. It is thus important that we monitor these environments, and build up a comprehensive picture of the dynamic processes that have produced and now modify them. Interactions are complex, and many parameters and processes control the behaviour of sediments in inter-tidal areas (Fig. 1). These sediments are subject to atmospheric and oceanographic forces as well as changing biological and sedimentological interactions, on a variety of spatial and temporal scales. It is only through development of a greater understanding and a solid knowledge base that we will be able to manage these sensitive environments effectively and efficiently.

The scientific drive behind this Special Publication is the LISP-UK (Littoral Investigation of Sediment Properties) project – a multi-disciplinary, multi-institutional study of the intertidal mudflats seaward of the village of Skeffling in the Humber Estuary, UK. The LISP-UK project was funded by the National Environment Research Council (NERC) as part of its Land Ocean Interaction Study (LOIS). The origin and motivation for LISP-UK itself can be traced back some time. The concept of LISP was first devised in 1987 by a group of Canadian scientists with an interest in the intertidal mudflat environment of the Bay of Fundy, Nova Scotia. It was borne from the perception of the genuine complexity of such environments. They recognized that such complexity necessitated a multi-disciplinary approach, and this resulted in a series of interrelated experiments on the physics, chemistry and biology of the sediments during the summer of 1989. They thus established a scientific and logistical framework within which future estuarine sedimentary research programmes could operate. Intertidal science had become a truly interdisciplinary affair.

In particular, the Canadian study established unequivocally that under natural conditions, the behaviour of intertidal (and subtidal) sediments is greatly influenced by biotic factors (DABORN, G. R. (ed.) 1991. *Littoral Investigation of Sediment Properties, Minas Basin, 1989*, Final Report, ACER, Acadia University, ACER publication 17), and this continues to be an emerging consensus amongst many unrelated studies from a variety of different intertidal environments. Such biogenic influences extend to both cohesive and non-cohesive sediments although the phenomenon is more easily demonstrated with the more predictable non-cohesive sediments. These studies have two important consequences. Firstly, measurements made in the laboratory intended to represent the erosion of sediments *in situ* must be interpreted with caution since extrapolation from the laboratory to the field may be misleading. It is difficult to maintain or duplicate natural conditions within test sediments and it is, therefore, preferable to make measurements *in situ*. Secondly, the understanding of sediment behaviour under natural conditions is most likely

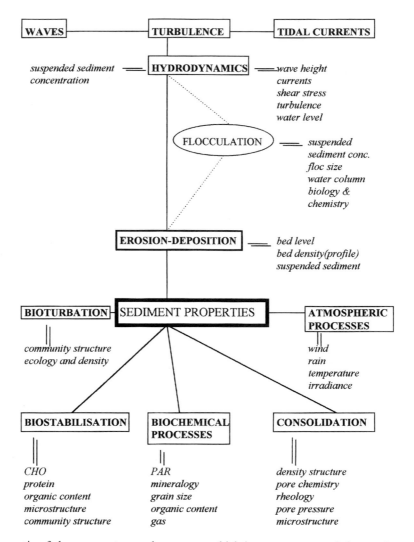

Fig. 1. Schematic of the parameters and processes which interact to control the erosion and deposition of (cohesive) inter-tidal sediments (processes = bold face, parameters = italic font). Courtesy of Black and Paterson, 1996, *Terra Nova* **8**, 304–307.

to be advanced by an interdisciplinary approach to the subject. The examination of sediment behaviour while taking account of the environmental and biological status of the site is one of the recent challenges in sedimentological research. The cross-discipline philosophy of the Canadian experience was adopted by a group of British scientists, and LISP-UK was born to further the same goals. The number of multi-disciplinary papers in this Publication, from both within and outside the LISP study, bears strong witness to the virtue of this approach. Overall the volume brings together the work of geoscientists, chemists and biologists working on the intertidal zones of European and North American estuaries and coasts.

This volume is arranged in two parts. Part I comprises papers relating to the LISP-UK study, while Part II comprises results of European and North American studies. Although intertidal science has a comparatively long history, there has been little in the way of a dedicated overview of the many physical, chemical and biological processes for some years. This publication is therefore timely, and should be of use to scientists and engineers, municipal authorities with a responsibility for shoreline management, and environmental agencies and consultancy organizations concerned with estuarine and coastal sedimentary processes.

The Organizing Committee is grateful for the assistance provided by the Joint Nature Conservation Council, the Challenger Society for Marine Science, the European Commission and the Society for Underwater Technology.

The topics covered in the volume included work completed within the LISP-UK programme, together with contributions derived from the European Community-funded MAST III and Environment Research Programmes (INTRMUD Contract MAS3-CT95-0022 and PRO-MAT Contract EV5V-CT94-0411, respectively).

The editors are particularly grateful for the organizational assistance provided by Irene Taylor, Sarah Lee, Steve Shayler and Damon O'Brien. Syd and Norma Barton together with their staff at Burlington House provided trouble-free catering and refreshment. The Linnean Society is thanked for provision of their library. In addition, the editors thank all those who peer reviewed the contributions which appear in this Special Publication.

Further information (abstract volume etc.) about the meeting from which this volume arose can be found on the World Wide Web at:

http://www.st-and.ac.uk/ksb2/conference/booklet.htm.

K. S. Black
D. M. Paterson
A. Cramp

LISP-UK Littoral Investigation of Sediment Properties: an introduction

K. S. BLACK & D. M. PATERSON

Gatty Marine Laboratory, St Andrews University, East Sands, Fife KY16 8LB, UK

Abstract: The Humber estuary on the east coast of England was selected as the study area by the UK Natural Environment Research Council (NERC) as the focus of the Land Ocean Interaction Study (LOIS) Community Research Programme. LISP-UK stands for Littoral Investigation of Sediment Properties, and is a Special Topic funded directly by LOIS. LISP-UK is concerned with the dynamics of sediment transport to and from the intertidal mudflats within the Humber estuary. This paper describes the historical, scientific and logistical basis of LISP, and provides the regional setting of the mudflat field area as a preface to LISP-related papers appearing in this volume.

The Humber estuary and its land and sea hinterland were chosen as the study area for the largest and most ambitious Community Research Project mounted to date by the Natural Environment Research Council (NERC). The rationale for choosing the east coast of England was based on its susceptibility to change and particularly to rising sea-level. The east coast is in the main a lower, 'softer' coastline than the west coast. It is also a region where isostatic rebound may not keep pace with rising sea-level and where coastal erosion in some areas (e.g. the Holderness coast) is an acute problem. In addition, the Humber estuary has a significant pollution problem and receives input associated with 20% of England living within its catchment area.

LOIS – the Land Ocean Interaction Study – aims to quantify the exchange, transformation and storage of materials through the Humber and its estuary and to determine how these vary in time and space. The Plymouth Marine Laboratory (PML) co-ordinated LOIS on behalf of NERC and provided a framework within which smaller projects in a variety of geographic environments (river basin, estuarine and coastal, continental shelf and shelf edge) were integrated. LOIS has a planned six year duration commencing 1992.

LOIS funded a Special Topic (#122) within its Rivers Atmospheres Estuaries and Coasts Study (**RACS**) section to examine the dynamics of sediment transport to and from the intertidal mudflats within the Humber estuary. This was the LISP-UK programme.

Origination

The original concept of LISP was devised in 1987 by a group of Canadian scientists with an interest in the intertidal environment of the Bay of Fundy, Nova Scotia (Daborn 1991). It was developed from the recognition of the complexity of such environments. Figure 1, in the Preface to this Special Publication, reveals the myriad processes to which natural mudflat sediments are subject. Clearly, a multidisciplinary approach, utilizing expertise of scientists from a number of specialist fields e.g. sedimentology, fluid dynamics, micro- and macro-biology, geochemistry, is necessary in order to derive a more integrated understanding of the behaviour of these deposits. The Canadians demonstrated both the virtue of an inter-disciplinary approach and the feasability and scientific advantages of *in situ* study. Their philosophy, and to an extent their logistical operations, were adopted by a small group of British scientists with similar interests, and in 1992 LISP-UK came into being.

LISP-UK

The project began in August 1994, and was completed in June 1997. Altogether it involved over 50 scientists from a number of UK universities, as well as Government and private institutions in both the UK and Canada. The project was co-ordinated centrally from St Andrews University with assistance from a Steering Committee comprising individuals from a number of UK universities. LOIS provided funding directly to LISP to cover travel and subsistence costs for all participating scientists.

The formal objectives of LISP are outlined below.

(1) To assess the relative importance of hydrodynamic, sedimentary, biological and atmospheric processes in determining shear strength, erosion rate and critical erosion shear stress of cohesive intertidal sediments *in situ.*

BLACK, K. S. & PATERSON, D. M. 1998. LISP-UK Littoral Investigation of Sediment Properties: an introduction. *In*: BLACK, K. S., PATERSON, D. M. & CRAMP, A. (eds) *Sedimentary Processes in the Intertidal Zone.* Geological Society, London, Special Publications, **139**, 1–10.

(2) To obtain realistic values of critical erosion shear stress and erosion rate suitable for numeric simulation.

(3) To develop a quantified simulation model of cohesive sediment behaviour.

(4) To compare and evaluate different techniques now available for *in situ* and laboratory measurement of shear strength, erosion rate and critical erosion shear stress.

(5) To stimulate development of interdisciplinary research on cohesive sediments, utilising resources at research institutions principally in the UK.

As the LOIS programme was undertaken in the Humber estuary, a natural choice of field site for LISP was the broad, tidal mudflats within Spurn Bight on the north shore of the estuary

(53°38.5′N, 0°4.25′E; Fig. 1). The precise location was an area to the south of Skeffling village known locally as Skeffling Clays, which had suitable access and a sufficient shore area for large numbers of scientists to work. In addition, a flood prevention Pumping Station at the marsh edge, with toilet facilities, bench space, electricity and fresh water was made available to LISP by the UK Environment Agency.

The main experimental phase of LISP took place over the first three weeks of April 1995. An intensive and comprehensive field-based study encompassing a full Spring–Neap tidal cycle was completed by scientists at four different locations along a 2.2 km shore-normal transect (Figs 2 and 3). This experimental configuration provided downshore changes in sub-aerial exposure and sediment textural properties. During

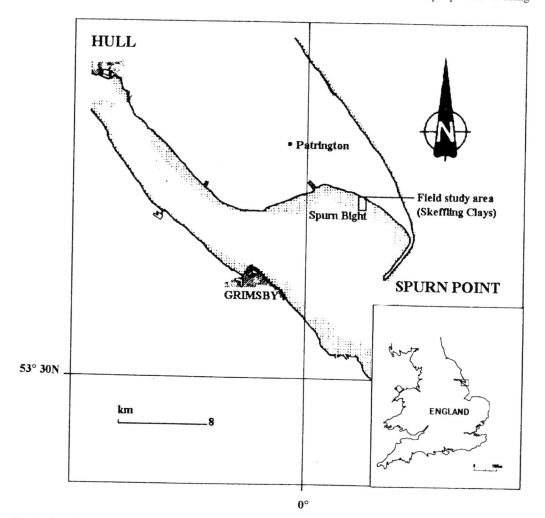

Fig. 1. Location map of the field study area, Skeffling Clays, Humber estuary, UK.

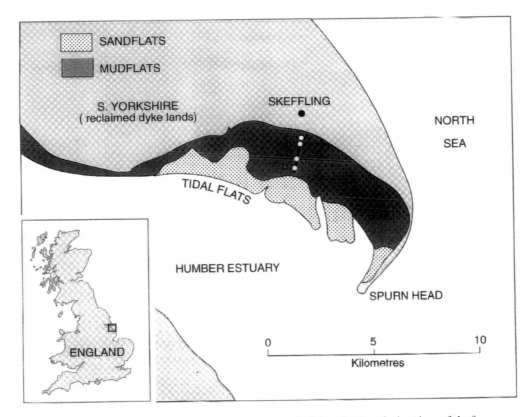

Fig. 2. Detail of the LISP transect (diagram courtesy of Dr Carl Amos). Note the locations of the four experimental stations along the transect (A–D).

this time scientists lived in Hull and worked daily at the field site, either from a shore base or from a shallow draft barge anchored over the mid tidal flat. LISP also provided full logistic support including a mobile field laboratory, which was sited close to the marsh edge at Skeffling. Boat launching facilities at Spurn Point were available to inflatable craft courtesy of the Yorkshire Wildlife Trust. The flat keel barge, which could beach directly on top of the mudflat at low tide, operated each day out of Grimsby. Whilst many of the experiments were conducted *in situ*, the facilities at the LOIS Laboratory at Hull University were also used extensively by LISP scientists.

A secondary study of mudflat properties was made over an entire year from 04/95–04/96. The objective of this study was to sample the mudflat monthly to examine longer term variability in certain properties. These included bulk density, bed level, particle size, microalgal pigments and bacterial biomass, sedimentary carbohydrate, carbon indices (total, organic, inorganic, carbonate), and nitrogen and sulphur.

Characteristics of the field study area

A brief overview only of the specific field study area is presented here. The historical evolution and present-day geomorphology of the Humber system, and hydrography of the tidal waters in the estuary and across the mudflats are reported in various symposia (e.g. Denman 1979; De Boer 1981; Gameson 1982a, b; Pethick 1988; Catt 1990).

Intertidal geomorphology

The total intertidal width from the marsh edge to low Spring tide level at Skeffling is approximately *c.* 4 km. The lowermost 1.5 km of this region comprises clean fine, non-cohesive sands. Moving progressively inshore, the substratum becomes more muddy until at the marsh edge, and across the marsh surface, sand grains are rarely present. The LISP study was concerned only with cohesive sediment transport processes and hence the field area was limited to above the mid-tide datum (Fig. 2).

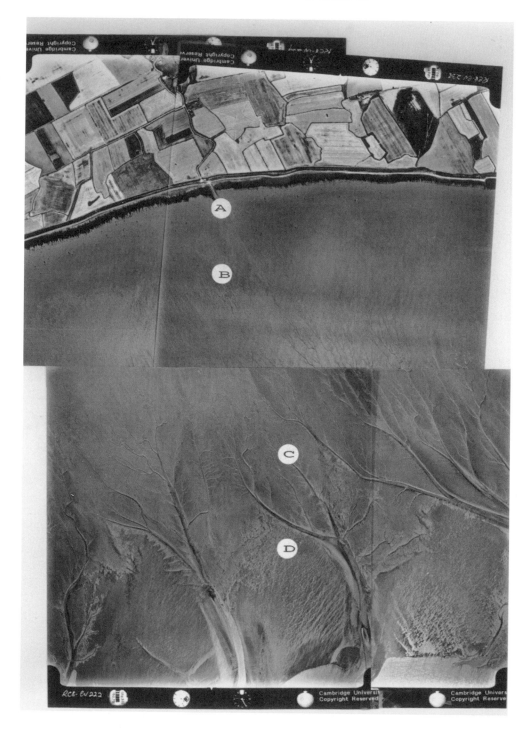

Fig. 3. Montage of aerial photographs (courtesy of Cambridge Aerofilms) of the study area (Skeffling Clays). The photographs were taken *c.* 14.30 hrs on Saturday 16 September 1978, at approximately mid-tide (low water @ 11.40 hrs). The four transect stations are indicated. Scale: the distance from station A to station D is *c.* 2180 m.

Table 1. *Location and drying heights of the four experimental LISP stations*

	Drying height (mCD)	Horizontal distance from shore (m)	Grid reference
Station A	5.2–6.0 m	0–200 m	53688, 41804
Station B	5.1 m	585 m	53683, 41774
Station C	4.3 m	1528 m	53653, 41684
Station D	3.56 m	2181 m	53269, 41623

An approximately shore-normal transect was established from the marsh edge to about *c.* 2.2 km onto the mudflat. Four experimental stations (A, B, C and D) were fixed along this line at which scientists could reference their positions and conduct experiments. Drying heights and location information of these stations are contained in Table 1. In certain instances, extra stations were established in between the four primary stations.

The relation of the tide curve recorded at Immingham Port to the station heights during the field study period is shown in Fig. 4.

The nature of the down-shore profile is shown in Fig. 5, revealing a gently sloping gradient from the marsh edge to station D. The marsh surface has in comparison quite a steep gradient, and a ridge (probably created by sedimentation as the flood water slows dramatically at this point) adjacent to the marsh front is a persistent feature. A 3D survey of mudflat elevation reveals a general NE–SW trend to the surface

on a macro-scale (Fig. 6), which is consistent with the slope of the entire intertidal region (Admiralty Chart No. 1130).

The mudflat profile controls, to a first order, small-scale topography like ridges, furrows and erosional/depositional features. Between stations A and B, the mudflat surface is relatively flat and featureless, and is observed to pond water following tidal emersion (Fig. 7). Just beyond station B the mudflat surface becomes obviously steeper, dropping *c.* 0.15 m over 200 m horizontal distance. This regions corresponds to a shore-normal 'mud wave' field shown in Fig. 8 and just visible on an aerial photograph of the area (Fig. 3). The link between gradient and the formation and presence of mud waves is unclear. Dyer (pers comm.) has suggested they may be formed by counter-rotating secondary helical motions in the flow. Streaks of rougher surface water which follow the underlying bed morphology are often seen as the tide ebbs. The mud waves do not form into a dendritic drainage

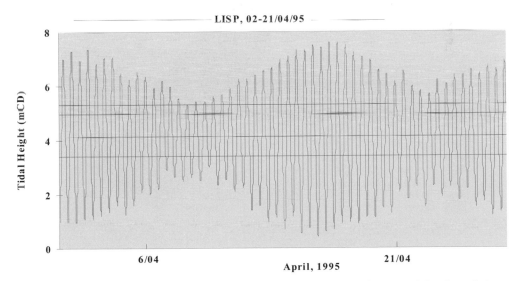

Fig. 4. Recorded tidal variation at Immingham port (south shore of the Humber estuary) for the period 01–30 April 1995. Elevation at the field site preceeds that at Immingham by *c.* 20 minutes. The duration of the LISP field study (02–21 April) and the elevations of the four transect stations are shown.

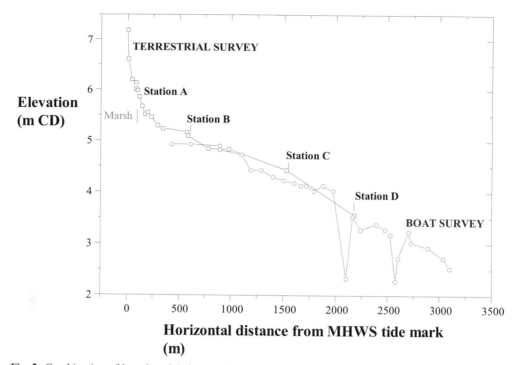

Fig. 5. Combination of boat-based (echo sounder) and terrestrial (electronic distance meter) bathymetric data sets down the LISP transect to 3100 m offshore.

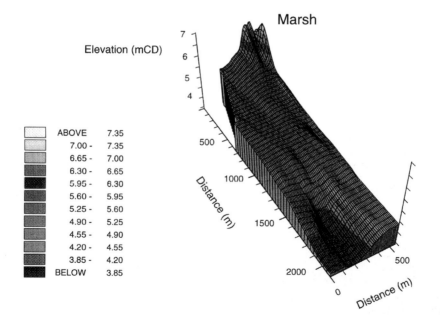

Fig. 6. 3D contour plot of the mudflat surface down the LISP transect to Station D (swath *c.* 500 m wide). Diagram created using the software package UNIMAP 2000. The original data (polar form) were converted into *x-y* co-ordinates and interpolation on a 200(N–S) × 50(W–E) grid was performed using a bi-linear UNIMAP routine. Note the elevation of the marsh surface is improperly represented in the top left corner due to insufficient data points to provide a sensible interpolation.

Fig. 7. View looking North towards the marsh mid-way between station B and station A.

Fig. 8. View looking north across the mudflat from just beyond station B (c. 650 m offshore). The ridge–runnel pattern is aligned normal to the shore. The mud waves have a length of 0.5–1.5 m and a trough depth of 0.1–0.3 m. The majority of runnels do not form into a dendritic drainage network on this area of the mudflat.

Fig. 9. South facing view of a young drainage channel towards the marsh mid-way between stations B and C. The drainage channel is *c*. 1.5 m wide and 1 m deep. The floor of the channel is covered in a thin (5 cm) layer of fluid mud, which overlies a comparatively firm substratum. It also contains many dead bivalve shells.

pattern, but are disconnected, parallel ridges and runnels. The gradient steadily increases towards stations C and D. Data from a bathymetric survey suggest almost a step feature to the bed height *c*. 1100 m from shore. A 0.2 m drop in bed height over 80 m horizontal distance was recorded. This elevation appears to be approximately the point at which drainage channels begin to incise the mudflat surface. A young channel typically found here is shown in Fig. 9. These channels vary in size but are generally shallow (<1 m) and broad (1–2 m). Channels generally grow in size as they traverse the lower intertidal region, however it is interesting to note that the two channels recorded with the echo sounder have incised to about the same depth (Fig. 5).

Characteristics of the bed particles

X-ray diffraction analysis reveals that the particle composition across the muddy portion of Spurn Bight is relatively constant (Table 2). The dominant clay mineral is illite with lesser amounts of chlorite and calcite. Quartz is measurable in the silt (2–63 μm) fraction in the range 14–24% across all stations.

Table 3 summarizes some of the physical properties of the surficial sediments (top-most 1 cm) at the four stations. Although across the entire transect the sediments are all nominally cohesive in nature, some general trends, as one might expect, are evident. The onshore fining in inorganic particle size and the commensurate increase in organic carbon content are

Table 2. *Summary of the mineralogical composition of the mud (<2 μm) fraction. Analysis courtesy of J. Herniman, Department of Earth Sciences, University of Wales, Cardiff*

	Station			
	A	B	C	D
Illite	58.50	68.10	61.50	55.40
Kaolinite	24.50	16.80	19.40	23.40
Chlorite	15.00	13.70	17.20	19.10
Calcite	2.00	1.40	1.90	2.50

Table 3. *Selected physical sediment properties at each of the four transect stations*

	%			Mode (μm)	C_{org} (%)	Particle density (gcm^{-3})	Bulk density (gcm^{-3})
	Sand	Silt	Clay				
A	9.39	59.00	31.61	22.28	1.56	2.62	1.70
B	15.92	59.66	25.39	45.59	1.44	2.52	1.88
C	22.51	51.69	25.80	72.46	1.10	2.57	1.68
D	23.13	52.71	24.16	83.71	0.68	2.71	1.45

Textural parameters were determined using a Laser Particle Sizer; organic carbon content was determined by titrimetric assay; particle and bulk density were determined volumetrically. Samples were collected during July 1995.

clear. A more detailed sampling of particle size changes across the intertidal zone is shown in Fig. 10. Note the slight increase in sand content between stations B and C. These data broadly fit with both the British Geological Survey sediment distribution maps of Spurn Bight (Sheets Spurn 53°N–00°W and Humber Trent 53°N–02°W) and the survey of McQuillan *et al.* (1969), which show a slightly coarser substratum in this area. This has been loosely attributed to tidal processes wherein maximum current speeds across the mudflat occur at this datum (McQuillan *et al.* 1969). The generally higher bulk density at station B (Table 3) may be related to the coarser nature of the sediments, as sand particles in a muddy sediment increase drainage and promote compaction (Delo, 1988). Notwithstanding this, trends in bulk density down the transect (and also many other variables) are not consistent and vary considerably throughout the year, particu-

larly following periods when wind waves scour the mudflat surface.

Data banking

A LISP WorldWideWeb site was constructed to bank data centrally from all participants. This may be found at *http://www.st-and.ac.uk/~ksb2/lisp/intro.htm* (contact KSB for the user-name and password). The site was conceived as a useful data storage area to which all participants would have access. It has been set up to enable downloading of data only. It is not possible to view or edit any of the data files. Under the data conventions of LOIS, data from all participants have been submitted to the British Oceanographic Centre for final archiving and dissemination via CD-ROM. The password protection will be removed on 1 May 1998.

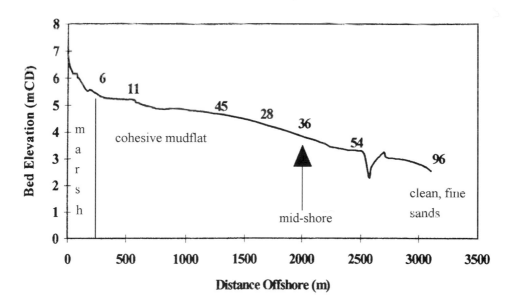

Fig. 10. Percentage of sand (particles >63 μm in diameter) in surface scrapes down the LISP transect.

This is LOIS publication number 401 of the LOIS Community Research Programme, carried out under a Special Topic Award from the Natural Environment Research Council.

References

CATT, J. A. 1990. Geology and relief. *In*: ELLIS, S. & CROWTHER, D. R. (eds) *Humber Perspectives: a Region Through the Ages.* Hull University Press.

DABORN, G. R. 1991 (ed.) 1991. *Littoral Investigation of Sediment Properties, Minas Basin*, 1989, Final Report, ACER, Acadia University, ACER Publication 17.

DE BOER, G. 1979. History and general features of the estuary. *In*: *The Humber Estuary*: a selection of papers on present knowledge of the estuary and its future potential given at two symposia arranged by the Humber Advisory Group and the University of Hull. NERC Publications Series C, **20**, 1–4.

DELO, E. A. 1988. *Estuarine Muds Manual.* Hydraulics Research, Wallingford, UK, Report SR 164.

DENMAN, N. E. 1979. Physical characteristics of the Humber. *In*: *The Humber Estuary*: a selection of papers on present knowledge of the estuary and its future potential given at two symposia arranged by the Humber Advisory Group and the University of Hull. NERC Publications Series C, **20**, 5–9.

GAMESON, A. L. H. 1982*a* Description of estuary and surveys. *In*: GAMESON, A. L. H. (ed.) *The Quality of the Humber Estuary: a Review of the Results of Monitoring* 1961–1981. Report of the Humber Estuary Committee, published by the Yorkshire Water Authority, Chapter 1.

——1982*b*. Physical characteristics. *In*: GAMESON, A. L. H. (ed.) *The Quality of the Humber Estuary: a Review of the Results of Monitoring 1961–1981.* Report of the Humber Estuary Committee, published by the Yorkshire Water Authority, Chapter 2.

MCQUILLAN, R., ARNOLD, S. E., TULLY, M. C. & HULL, J. H. 1969. *Cruise Report Humber Investigations 1968.* Institute of Geological Sciences Report 69/3. Institute of Geological Sciences, London.

PETHICK, J. S. 1988. The physical characteristics of the Humber. *In*: *A Dynamic Estuary: Man, Nature and the Humber.* Hull University Press, 31–55.

The typology of intertidal mudflats

K. R. DYER

Institute of Marine Studies, University of Plymouth, Plymouth PL4 8AA, UK

Abstract: A descriptive typology of intertidal mudflats is presented as the first stage of the development of a quantitative classification. This categorizes the various attributes of intertidal mudflats in terms of readily visible parameters. Mudflats are present in a wide range of tidal situations, and from exposed to sheltered from high wave energy. They can show morphological profiles indicative of erosion and deposition; concave upwards or convex upwards respectively. Their slopes can also vary widely, with some mudflats being several kilometres in width, and they possess characteristic bedforms. The sediments range from being comparatively hard to extremely soft, with complementary variations in their organic contents and biological assemblages. The relationships between these factors are shown to be distinctive of the mudflat type.

Intertidal mudflats fringe many thousands of kilometres of the world's coastlines and protect them from inundation with only modest defences. They are present in a wide variety of situations, ranging from high to low tidal range, within sheltered estuaries and inlets, on coasts exposed to considerable wave effects, and at all latitudes. Though mudflats are composed of a mixture of sand and mud, the mud content is sufficiently high for the sediment to exhibit cohesive properties. They are bounded in many areas by lower lying sandflats, and above high water neap tide by a zone where marsh vegetation grows. Their fauna can range from being quite diverse, to almost monospecific. However, an important characteristic is that there is a very intense coupling of biological, sedimentary and physical processes. For instance, diatom growth on the mud surface can inhibit erosion, and macrophytic growth can aid trapping of sediment. Because of this there is likely to be considerable seasonal variation in the suspended sediment concentrations as the plants grow and die. High concentrations of mud in suspension increase the effective viscosity of the fluid, and attenuate the waves, which are then less able to erode the sediment.

Mudflats are naturally backed by saltmarshes, but their morphology and the processes that act upon them are quite different (Pethick 1984). There is an extensive literature on saltmarshes, but their dependence on the fronting mudflats and the fluxes of energy, sediments and chemicals that cross them is often scarcely mentioned. In contrast, mudflats are poorly researched, because of the difficulty of access onto such soft substrates, the fact that access tends to destroy the features being investigated and that disturbance can take a long time to heal.

Salt marsh vegetation becomes established above high water neap tides, and there is a floral zonation which is controlled by the duration of inundation occurring during the lunar cycle. At low latitudes the same zonation occurs with different species of mangroves. Mudflats and saltmarshes are very sensitive to changes in sea level and there is potential for considerable land loss, risk of flooding and loss of life. They are 'reclaimed' for agriculture, or for industrial and domestic purposes, often being used for waste disposal. This poses problems for environmental managers of habitat loss, with the value of those habitats having only recently been fully appreciated. Many intertidal areas are protected because of migrating and overwintering birds, which feed on the in-fauna. Where the mudflats are backed by dykes, or by development, rising sea level will involve them in the 'coastal squeeze', whereby their width gradually reduces, and their characteristics change.

Many saltmarshes and mudflats appear to be accreting at the same rate as sea level rises, thereby suggesting that an equilibrium exists between the dynamic forcing and the sedimentary response. However, the timescales and timelags involved in this are unknown. Their response to changing sea level, climate and anthropogenic pressure cannot be predicted, other than in very general terms. To improve on that capability is an important objective, and this depends upon an understanding that explains the reasons for the observed differences between mudflats. At the moment there is not a classification scheme, nor a typology, of mudflats to aid definition of the hierarchy in the relative importances of the underlying processes, or provide concepts that can be tested against examples to improve understanding. This is needed to provide a framework within which models and management strategies can be constructed. Such classifications exist for saltmarshes, e.g. the maturation sequence (Frey &

DYER, K. R. 1998. The typology of intertidal mudflats. *In*: BLACK, K. S., PATERSON, D. M. & CRAMP, A. (eds) *Sedimentary Processes in the Intertidal Zone.* Geological Society, London, Special Publications, **139**, 11–24.

Basan 1978), and the accretionary sequence of Stevenson *et al.* (1986). Nevertheless, there are some concepts that need to be included in such a development.

This paper presents a typology for mudflats that has been derived from the experience and comparisons of the collaborators in the EU MAST III funded project INTRMUD 'The morphodynamics of intertidal mudflats'. It is presented here for wider discussion and modification into a more rigorous classification.

Mudflat processes

Morphological profiles

In general terms the intertidal width will be greater in areas of high tidal range than in areas of small range (Hayes 1975; Dieckmann *et al.* 1987), but there are wide variations which indicate that there are other controls, such as tidal currents and waves. The average slope can be about 1:1000, so that widths of several kilometres are frequent. There is a useful division of the intertidal into: a lower mudflat which occurs between low tide spring tides and low tide neaps, a middle flat between low tide neaps, and high tide neaps; and an upper flat between high tide neaps and the lower salt marsh. The level at which the lower salt marsh starts depends on several factors (Pethick 1984), including the sediment type, deposition rates, wave activity and

climate. Consequently, the unvegetated upper mudflat may only have a small relief, 0.3 m in the Wash (Pethick 1984), but its width could be of the order of 300 m. It has been shown that there are two end members in the hypsographic curve across the mudflats (Kirby 1992). The overall elevational profile is concave upwards and the mean flat level is below the mean tide level in situations where there is overall erosion, or a deficit in the amount of sediment input. In this case the maximum slope will be towards the upper part of the mudflat, often with a small cliff appearing at the junction with the saltmarsh, because of the extended period at about high water when wave erosion can be active. In contrast, a convex profile, with the maximum slope closer to low water mark, occurs where there is deposition, an increase in the input of sediment, and progradation. Examples of these profiles are shown in Fig.1.

The different approaches to characterization of the cross flat profile shapes have been discussed by Mehta *et al.* (1996). An expression by Lee (1995) and Lee & Mehta (1997) considers wave action as the most significant process and the height h at a distance y is given by:

$$h = Fy\,e^{-\beta y} + h_0\,e^{4k(y_0-y)}(y/y_0)^2 \qquad (1)$$

where h_0, y_0 define the offshore coordinates of the profile, k is a mean wave-attenuation coefficient for the profile, F is the bottom slope at $y = 0$, and β determines the offshore extent of

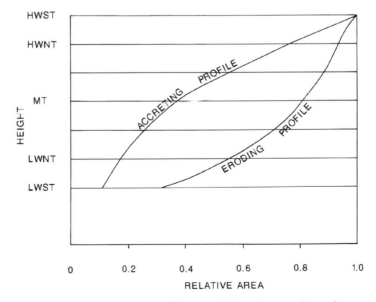

Fig. 1. Diagrammatic representation of a convex shore profile showing accretion and a concave profile showing erosion.

the combined influence of slope at the shoreline and scour due to wave breaking. Between them, β and k specify the rate of change of slope shorewards of the low water line. Equation (1) can be fitted iteratively to the observed profiles, using β and k as free variables or fitting parameters, though with sufficient wave measurements k could be estimated independently. High values of k are associated with the concave erosional profile, and as k approaches zero the profile becomes accretionary. Fitting to a large number of profiles has given ranges for the variables, but there is considerable overlap in the ranges for erosional and accretionary situations. Within these overlaps are included the influence of characteristics, such as the sediment erodibility, that have been omitted from equation (1).

As an alternative approach Mehta *et al.* (1996) consider a stability number which compares the stabilizing factors characterizing the resistance to erosion against those which destabilize and create erosion. They develop the equation:

$$S = 1 - \alpha_{sed} F_{st} (\beta_1 F_{tc} + \beta_2 F_{WV})^{-1} \qquad (2)$$

where F_{st} is the sediment resistance to erosion, α_{sed} is a factor that relates to the sediment supply, such that a value of 1 implies no sediment supply, F_{tc} and F_{WV} are the two erosional factors relating to tidal currents and waves, respectively, with a relative weighting so that $\beta_1 + \beta_2 = 1$. An accreting profile is thus given by $S < 0$ and an eroding profile by $S > 0$. This approach introduces a greater number of variables, with the difficulty of specifying quantitative values for them, though the concept is scientifically appealing.

Mudflats appear to undergo cycles of erosion and deposition. It is possible to see both types of profile occuring simultaneously on different parts of the flats (e.g. Wang 1983), and there can be seasonal changes in the relative extents of erosion and deposition due to wave activity. A concave profile on the upper part of the flats frequently occurs where the flats are constrained by dykes or other defence structures. The water depth and consequent wave activity are relatively high at high water, often with reflection of waves providing additional energy, thereby limiting deposition on the upper flat.

Accretion on the mudflats occurs because of shoreward transport due to the settling lag of suspended sediment (Postma 1961), with the main centres of accumulation on the saltmarshes close to the highest spring tide level and at about mid tide. The sediment deposited at mid tide level is normally consolidated, or underconsolidated, and soft, with a high moisture content (low bulk density). Since density is correlated to

a reasonable degree with the critical erosion shear strength, these soft muds are prone to erosion during storms. When the mudflat is in stable equilibrium, with little deposition or erosion, the muds tend to become somewhat overconsolidated because of atmospheric effects during exposure.

Erosion seems to be indicated first by the presence of gravel or shell cheniers at the edge of the marsh (Greensmith & Tucker 1976). They migrate landwards and the marsh is re-exposed at their trailing edge, where it becomes susceptible to active erosion with the formation of small cliffs and mud mounds. Once erosion starts the water depth becomes relatively greater, and wave attenuation becomes concentrated on a narrower zone of the mudflat. The waves are then even more competent at eroding the sediment until a level is reached in the consolidated sediment where the density and erosion threshold is sufficiently high to limit further erosion. The mud that is revealed is overconsolidated, and any coarser material, pebbles and shells are left on the surface.

The overall sedimentary context of the mudflat will be important in determining the supply of muddy sediment. This will control the lateral extent of the mudflats and the relative proportions of mud to other sedimentary material. Adjacent to the turbidity maximum in estuaries where high concentrations of suspended mud are available, mudflats containing little silt or sand can occur. Where there is no mud available, or where the wave agitation is sufficient to winnow away the mud, then sand flats are likely to be present. When both are available, a mixed sand and mud flat may occur. In the Wash (Evans 1965), there is a lower sandflat exposed to strong alongshore tidal currents, and also an upper sand flat exposed to wave action, with mud at about mid-tide level.

There are a number of processes that need to be considered which may control the erodability of the mud and the development of the profile shape.

Exposure

Across the mudflat there are large variations in atmospheric exposure. On the upper flats there is a duration of submergence that varies from 0 to $c.\,2.5\,hr$, whereas on the lower flats there are durations of exposure of $c.\,0\text{--}2.5\,hr$. During exposure to the atmosphere the sediment surface undergoes heating, and drying out by evaporation caused by sunlight and wind. This decreases the surface moisture content, and the consequent increase in the threshold erosion characteristics of the mud inhibits erosion during the next inundation (Amos *et al.* 1988). In contrast, when exposed rainfall will increase the surface moisture content and may actually cause erosion of the surface through pitting and run-off. Diatoms on the sediment surface

photosynthesize and produce large amounts of extra-cellular polysaccharides (EPS). These mucal substances also tend to stabilize the sediment against erosion (Grant 1988; Paterson 1989; Paterson *et al.* 1990).

One particular feature of the tides is that there are coastlines where high water at spring tides

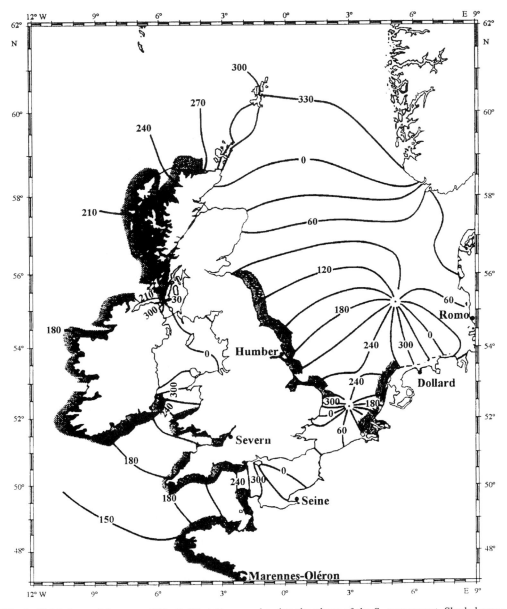

Fig. 2. Tidal chart of the seas of North West Europe, showing the phase of the S_2 component. Shaded areas are where the S_2 phase is $90°-270°$ and where low water spring tide occurs 0900–1500 hrs. The unshaded areas are where the phase is $270°-90°$ and where high water spring tide occurs 0900–1500. The names are for the mudflats being investigated as part of the INTRMUD project.

always occurs at around midday, and others where low water occurs at that time. The timing is governed by the relative phases of the lunar semi-diurnal constituent M_2 and the solar semi-diurnal constituent S_2, such that spring tide low water occurs between 0900 and 1500 hr when the phase is between 90° and 270°. Conversely, when the phase is between 270° and 90° high water occurs at those times. Figure 2 shows that there are significant differences between parts of the British coast and the coast of the continent east of Cherbourg. In North-western Europe the areas with high tide at mid-day are macro or hypertidal, whereas those with low tide at mid-day are mesotidal. Conceivably, these differences will be reflected in the sediment characteristics and biological patterns.

Waves

Bed friction attenuates waves, and high suspended sediment concentrations cause additional viscous attenuation, so that non-breaking waves can lose 93–96% of their energy over the flat. This tends to limit erosion, since a balance can be established between the concentrations and the effect they have on reducing the bed shear stresses. The resulting solitary waves induce oscillatory currents that are strongest in a shoreward direction (Wells & Coleman 1981),

with the net result that suspended sediment is carried towards the upper flats by the process of settling lag. Despite this, even small waves in the very shallow water at the edge of the tide can suspend material and carry it shorewards as the tide rises (Anderson 1983). Concentrations can reach in excess of $1\,\mathrm{g\,l^{-1}}$ near this tidal edge (Christie *et al.* 1996). Changes in the cross shore morphological profile will cause changes in the degree of wave attenuation with tidal level and provide a complex feedback situation.

The duration of wave attack at any level on the flats is a combination of the effects of wave attenuation and the relationship between the slope of the shore and the shape of the tidal curve (Carr & Graf 1982; Kirby 1992). At high and low tide, wave attack can last a relatively long time, but at mid-tide it is of limited duration as the rate of change of water level is greatest.

Wave action can transport both mud and sand, but the sand deposits while the mud is still in suspension and results in a laminated or layered sediment of clean sand, and mud without sand. The mud layers appear to be formed during calm periods when exposure and drying produces a fairly homogeneous firm mud. During storms, however, the surface is eroded and a thin sand layer deposited before the next mud layer. This process can be enhanced when the waves act together with tidal currents. The sediments on the flats of Portishead Bay (Fig. 3) are an

Fig. 3. A layered, partly-consolidated mudflat in Portishead Bay, Severn Estuary, being revealed by erosion. The mud layers are *c.* 5 cm thick, of intermediate density and separated by millimetre thick layers of very fine sand.

example. Whether the layers are annual or shorter term remains to be determined. Upon erosion the layers form blocks, which are eventually abraded into mud-balls (a process that is hard to parameterize in mud models). On mudflats it is the short period locally generated wind waves that can be the most erosive. Consequently, it is the angle of the mudflat to the prevailing winds that is likely to be significant, rather than fetch, though both may need to be considered in the definition of exposed and sheltered situations.

Sediment

There are large differences in the sediment structure and density between and across mudflats, which become most marked when one tries to walk on them. Soft mud is generally homogeneous, with indications that sedimentation is rapid. High suspended sediment concentrations and sedimentation rates are detrimental to filter feeding animals, and detritus feeding creatures become most numerous. The biology tends to be rather poor with a predominance of worms. However, the organic content is generally high, often in excess of 5%, and there is the tendency for anaerobic conditions and the production of gas. Nevertheless, X-ray analysis often shows traces of annual banding, relating to the degree of biological activity. Mudflats with a slower rate of deposition have time to consolidate normally so that the vertical gradient of density is much more rapid. The sediment is better oxygenated and supports a greater species diversity, with macrofauna being more abundant. This situation benefits filter feeding organisms, which themselves can enhance the sedimentation rate by the creation of faeces and pseudo-faeces. Bioturbation tends to obliterate annual variations and can maintain a high moisture content in the sediment, yet stabilizing it by the production of mucus. Erosion removes the surface layer to a depth that is determined by the ambient fluid shear stress, leaving an overconsolidated substrate. Consequently, surface moisture content, or bulk density, is a good measure of whether the mudflats are depositing or eroding, and it is linked to the biological factors.

Bedforms

The direction and strength of the flood and ebb flows across the flats are mainly governed by the surface water slopes and friction. On wide flats the currents tend to be shore-normal because the tidal wave travels faster along shore in deep water than in the shallows. The surface water gradients are therefore towards or away from the shore. On narrower flats the tidal currents are directed sub-parallel to the shore. In high tidal ranges the flooding tide can come in with a bore-like front edge at velocities in excess of $50 \, \text{cm s}^{-1}$, since the volume flow required to cover the flats is initially very high. As water depth increases, the velocities diminish. The velocities are greatest in the small channels, up which the water has to flow to flood the flats further shorewards. This is sufficient to create erosion. At high water, low velocities occur and suspended sediment can settle, but wind effects can create significant shore-parallel and shore-normal flows. On the ebb tide the water flow accelerates as the water shallows, and further erosion can take place. Residual circulations can be complex (e.g. Evans & Collins 1976) and may be controlled by the channel patterns, and by wave induced mean flows. The net sediment transport is thus likely to vary with tidal range and wave conditions.

Generally, the tidal wave acts as a standing wave with a progressive component and the maximum velocities in deep water occur close to the time of mean sea level. The lower mud flats will therefore be subjected to high velocities sub-parallel to the shore and to winnowing of fine grained sediment. Consequently, the lower flats tend to be more sandy, and current ripples and irregular dunes can occur.

Where waves are active the upper flats are likely to be planar, but crossed with channels originating from the saltmarshes. These carry water during low tide and can cut across features that appear to be related to the dynamics of the flats themselves. On some flats there is a zone of shore-normal ridges and troughs (or runnels) at mid-tide level (Fig. 4). They typically have a wavelength of c. 3 m and are tens of metres long. They have a height of 20–40 cm. Water is often trapped in the troughs throughout the low tide and the substrate remains soft, not drying out to the same extent as on the ridges. The temperature of the trapped water can rise considerably during this time. The mechanism of formation of the features is unknown at the moment, but during the ebb tide, lanes of rippled and smooth water have been observed located over the ridges and troughs, respectively, which suggest the presence of organized helical secondary flows. These could produce a regular spatial distribution of bed shear stresses. However, it is unclear whether these effects are causing the bedforms or being caused by them. Towards the upper flats, the ridges and runnels are of low amplitude and towards the lower flats, they become more

Fig. 4. Shore-normal ridge and runnel features developed on the mudflats of the Humber estuary at mid-tide level. The wavelength of the features is c. 3–5 m, their height is c. 30 cm and their length is in excess of 10 m.

irregular. Similar features are shown for the mid-tide zone on Korean mudflats by Frey *et al.* (1989) and on the Chinese coast by Wang & Eisma (1988). The latter observations suggest that the features are a conduit for the transport of fluid muds and temporary deposition sites. Somewhat similar features have been described as mud mounds (Greensmith & Tucker 1965), rills (Pethick 1992), or spurs and grooves (Allen & Pye 1992). However, these occur on the upper mudflats and appear to be formed by dissection of the marsh surface. It has been suggested that they are a sedimentary device for dissipating wave energy and limiting erosion (Pethick 1992). Certainly they tend to be obscured by sediment cover during calm periods, and exposed by wind wave erosion.

Wide mudflats are crossed by channels, which are numerous, small and sinuous in shallow water in the upper zone, and which become of a lower order, deeper and more widely spaced in the middle flats. They are often floored by a layer of sand, shells and small pebbles, or reach the underlying harder substrate. They alter their position by the process of meander erosion and point-bar deposition (Bridges & Leeder 1976). On the lower flats these channels become much wider and straighter, with gentle rather than steep sided slopes. The larger channels can carry water throughout the ebb tide, but the smaller ones empty late in the tide.

On steep flats, gullies are present which have a V-shaped cross-section, but without a flat floor. These are short in length and are associated with active erosion of the mudflats, though they may be a means of limiting depositional progradation at mid-tide levels. Slumping can also occur where the slopes have become oversteepened by erosion at their base, or by excessive deposition at the top of the slope.

Biology

The intertidal mudflats are dynamic environments characterized by large horizontal and vertical gradients. The biota also shows patterns of zonation in response to these gradients. The upper flats are affected by the period of emersion, rather than the immersion, and the flora and fauna have to be adapted to cope with drastic changes in temperature and salinity. The lower levels are less affected by atmospheric processes. The sediment is richly organic and supports an active food web, at the upper end of which is the birdlife when the flats are exposed and fish when they are covered. In general, where the sedimentation rate and the suspended sediment concentration are high, worms tend to predominate over bivalves, which prefer better consolidated substrates and clearer water. The growth of macrophytes is generally limited to

Table 1. *Typology of intertidal mudflats*

Type	Tide range	Wave energy	Sed.	Slope	Zone	Sed. dens.	Channels	Gullies	Slumps	Planar	Bedforms	Cliff	High org. cont.	Worms	Bivalves	Macrophy	Microphy
1A	Macrotidal	High	Surplus	Flat	Upper	Inter.	×			×							×
					Middle	Soft	×						×				×
					Lower	Inter.							×	×			×
1B			Deficit	Flat	Upper	Hard					×						
					Middle	Inter.		×			×			×	×	×	
					Lower	Inter.					o	×			×		
2A		Low	Surplus	Steep	Upper	Soft	×			×			×				×
					Middle	Soft		×					×		×		×
					Lower	Soft		×	×						×		×
2B			Deficit	Steep	Upper	Inter.			×			×					
					Middle	Soft		×	×		o				×		
					Lower	Soft		×							×	×	
3A	Mesotidal	High	Surplus	Flat	Upper	Inter.				×							×
					Middle	Soft	×			×			×	×			×
					Lower	Inter.	×			×			×	×			×
3B			Deficit	Steep	Upper	Hard				×							
					Middle	Inter.					o			×	×	×	
					Lower	Inter.		×				×			×		
4A		Low	Surplus	Flat	Upper	Inter.				×			×				×
					Middle	Soft		×		×			×	×	×		×
					Lower	Soft								×	×		×
4B			Deficit	Steep	Upper	Hard		×		×							
					Middle	Inter.						×		×	×	×	
					Lower	Inter.		×		×				×	×		
5A	Microtidal	High	Surplus	Steep	Upper	Inter.		×		×			×	×			
					Middle	Inter.				×			×	×			
					Lower	Inter.				×					×		
5B			Deficit	Steep	Upper	Hard				×							
					Middle	Hard				×		×		×	×		
					Lower	Hard				×					×		
6A		Low	Surplus	Steep	Upper	Soft				×			×				
					Middle	Soft				×			×	×	×	×	
					Lower	Inter.				×							
6B			Deficit	Steep	Upper	Hard						×			×		
					Middle	Hard				×					×	×	
					Lower	Inter.				×					×		

harder substrates where sedimentation is limited, or where erosion is taking place. Many organisms are effective in modifying the physical and biochemical properties of their environment, and can both stabilize and destabilize it. Filter feeding in-fauna remove particles from the water and create faeces and pseudo-faeces. Deposit feeding in-fauna process the sediment, oxygenating it and altering its shear strength. Microbiota produce webs, mats and glues which stabilize the sediment. Thus there is an important biological feedback on the sedimentary environment.

Typology

A classification of mudflats would need to be based on the above processes and include quantified definitions and limiting conditions. At the moment there are not precise definitions for all of the terms, and there is a lack of detailed comparative data from a wide range of mudflats. Thus we are looking initially for a typology; a group of simple qualitative descriptors that can be used over a wide range of mudflats to establish some conceptual patterns that can then be quantified with detailed measurements. Once quantification is possible we will be able to move from a typology to a classification.

It is sensible to start from the basis of the geographical situation, and the external driving parameters which are imposed on the mudflat and to which it has to respond. Then we can consider the characteristics of the mudflat which reveal its response to these influences and the possible interactions between them. The proposed typology is shown in Table 1, with indication of when a particular feature is present.

Tidal range

Wells (1983) has described examples of mudflats from micro, meso and macro-tidal coastlines, and has distinguished several unifying characteristics; extreme wave attenuation, high suspended sediment concentration, and the rapid migration and shifting of soft muds. He also points out that there is simultaneous erosion and deposition at different locations along the shoreline, as well as stabilization of some areas with the welding of mudshoals to the shoreline. However, there are distinguishing features. Alexander *et al.* (1991) show that the macrotidal Korean mudflats do not have the well developed dendritic drainage patterns that are present on North Sea mudflats. Thus there are likely to be differences in

mudflat characteristics based on tidal range. It is convenient to categorize the tidal conditions into macro-, meso- and micro-tidal, according to the definition of Davies (1964).

Wave energy

Mudflats on open coasts are more exposed to wave action than those within an estuary. However, locally generated waves can be more important than swell, and the dominant factor is likely to be the relationship of the mudflat to the wind direction. Fetch is generally limited in the estuarine situation, and the maximum waves are likely to approach at an angle to the coastline, rather than directly onshore, as is more likely in an open coastal situation. The intermittency of storms and wave effects may give significant differences, particularly when the changes are seasonal, as in monsoonal areas. However, they can not be considered separately here. The definition of the terms high and low wave energy in Table 1 is thus very qualitative, and is based on fetch and exposure to the prevailing winds. In a micro-tidal situation where wave activity is high, the muddy sediment will be winnowed away, and it is possible that mudflats will be very limited in extent.

Sediment supply

Sediment supply ultimately depends on the entire sediment budget for the flat area. It can be defined in terms of the average suspended sediment concentration at some relevant nearshore site, but most often insufficient data are available. Since the shape of the mudflat profile shows whether erosion or deposition is taking place, and much of the sediment will originate from local recycling, a surplus will be considered to equate to an overall convex profile, and a deficit to a concave profile. Since a mudflat profile may show both erosion and deposition as it changes its form to adjust to changing forces, more detail may be required, but this may be partly apparent in the bedform characteristics and biology.

Steepness

The slope or steepness of the mudflat will affect the cross shore velocities during the tide. It depends upon the tidal range and the mudflat width. The boundary between flat and steep is taken at about 1:750. Thus a wide mudflat in a

macrotidal situation will be flat, and high velocities will develop on flood and ebb as the tidal
front crosses the mudflat. Similarly a narrow
mudflat would be steep and more subjected to
shore parallel tidal currents. Since these terms
are relative, a wide microtidal mudflat would be
of very low slope, but narrower than one of the
same slope in macrotidal conditions. Wide, low
slope mudflats are more likely to develop drainage channels than steeper ones.

Zones

It is convenient to consider the mudflat in three
zones defined according to the lunar tidal range
variations, as stated earlier. They have different
exposure durations, bedforms, sediment characteristics and biological communities, and will
respond somewhat differently to the driving
forces (Klein 1975). In many areas the upper
flats may be missing because of flood defence
measures, and in some the lower flats may be
sandy because of high tidal current action.

Sediment density

The density can be readily measured in bulk
samples as moisture, or water content, or as
bulk density in syringe samples. However, the
top few centimetres of the sediment may be
ephemeral, and may be underlain by much more
resistant, higher density material, and an average value needs to be considered for the overall
mudflat response. In this case a good qualitative
measure of density is how far one sinks in when
walking on the mud. For Table 1, a depth of
10 cm is taken as being the critical depth
separating hard and intermediate density mud,
and 30 cm is the lower limit of soft mud.
Experience has shown that these limits generally
equate to mean bulk densities of about 1300 and
$1200 \, \text{kg m}^{-3}$, respectively. Soft sediment generally seems to result from high rates of sediment
deposition and density can be equated to a
certain extent to the threshold shear strength for
erosion, and also correlates with sand content.

It would also be useful to distinguish whether
the sediment is visibly laminated or not, but this
often appears to agree with hard and soft categories. Percentages of sand, silt and clay may be
diagnostic, but they are often very variable, with
such wide ranges within small areas as to make
differences between mudflats insignificant. However, there is often a trend of increasing mean
size towards low tide mark (e.g. Frey *et al.* 1989,
for the Korean mudflats).

Bedforms

The presence of shore-normal bedforms appears
to be distinctive of high tidal range mudflats and
there are two types; those present at mid-tide
on accreting mudflats (shown with a cross on
Table 1) and those near the salt marsh on the
upper flats of eroding flats (shown as an ○ on
Table 1). The latter have cores of harder material
often with traces of laminations and rootlets,
indicating original deposition under salt marsh
conditions.

Channels show a variety of forms, but are
generally flat bottomed and sinuous, though
sinuosity decreases towards the low tide mark.
They are generally most numerous at the landward edge of the middle zone, where they are a
few centimetres deep and show well developed
dendritic patterns when there are wide flats.
They can become well incised and narrow in the
middle flats, with depths in excess of 2 m, and
with 'hanging valley' tributaries, but they widen
out and become features with much more gentle
relief on the lower flats. It is possible that the
'order' of channels present may relate to mudflat
width. It is also possible that they may be better
developed on mudflats exposed to wave activity,
as they could act as conduits for discharge of
water transported shorewards by Stokes' Drift.

Gullies

Gullies are V-shaped features with very steep
sides and a steep thalweg. They are particularly
well developed in sheltered, narrow, high tidal
range situations (Fig. 5), and normally have
associated slumping.

Planar

Planar flats are typical of the upper flats, where
the long duration of wave action at high water
and low tidal currents prevent formation of bedforms. Their extent appears to increase as the
tidal range diminishes and maximum velocities
are close to or less than the threshold of motion.

Cliffs

Cliff-like features are indicative of erosion. They
can range in height from a few centimetres to of
the order of 1 m. When they are small they often
separate sediment with strongly contrasting density; the contrast indicating a temporal change
from erosion to deposition. Though they occur

Fig. 5. Gullies and slumps developed in the mudflats bordering the Parrett Estuary, a tributary of the Severn. The tidal level is about mid-tide.

most frequently at the junction between the upper flats and the salt marshes, they can occur at other levels on the flats, particularly at about mid tide when progradation is becoming reversed.

Organic content

The organic content of flats can be very variable, but those sediments having low organic content are normally aerobic with olive grey to blue grey colour. Those with high contents tend to be black and anaerobic. A rough division between the two states can be taken at an organic matter content of about 5% determined by loss on ignition, with high organic content indicated above this limit. A useful alternative to this might be consideration of the depth of the surface oxic layer, since a thin oxic layer is likely in rapidly accreting sediment. A thicker layer may suggest current and wave reworking of the sediment, or active bioturbation.

Biology

The main biological communities, which, taken together, are indicative of the variation on mudflats, are the worms, bivalves, macrophytes and microphytobenthos. Some of them will tend to stabilize the sediment, mainly by the production of mucal polysaccharides, whilst others destabilize the sediment by bioturbation. It is difficult to define the dominant community affecting the sediment characteristics, as a small number of bivalves may have a much bigger impact than large numbers of small worms, and they exist together. However, it is relatively easy to estimate the presence of some of the creatures from the surface holes, pits, mounds and trails they produce. The macrophytes Enteromorpha and Zostera can be quantified in terms of areal coverage, though the latter is becoming rare because of pollution. The density of faecal mounds of Arenicola can similarly be counted. Siphon holes and funnels of polychaetes and bi-valves also can be distinctive. The important characteristic of the microphytobenthos is the presence of diatoms. They can normally be distinguished by the colouration of the surface sediment and the slight mounds on which they form.

Consequently in Table 1 the micro-topography is used as an estimate of the biological effects and the dominant family is estimated visually. Worms tend to be dominant in soft sediment and bivalves in intermediate density. Microphytobenthos prefer soft substrates, whereas macrophytes tend to occur where there are pebbles, shells or a harder substrate. Additional quantification may be possible using EPS production, chlorophyll, total biomass and diversity indices.

Colloidal carbohydrate, for instance, appears to correlate with the threshold erosion shear stress (D. Paterson pers. comm.).

Discussion

The typology presented here is obviously only a first attempt to produce a coherent structure for comparison of mudflat characteristics. It is likely to undergo considerable modification when a wider range of examples is considered and when better quantification is possible. However, the intention has been to retain simplicity and encompass the main diagnostic features. Nevertheless, the typology may be used in a predictive sense. For instance, examination of the topographic features and bed characteristics may allow prediction of the fauna, or of the sediment availability on a mudflat.

The Korean mudflats are macrotidal, with widths in excess of 5 km and relatively high though seasonal energy (Wells 1983; Frey *et al.* 1989; Alexander *et al.* 1991). The mid-tide level contains channels and shore-normal bedforms. Accumulation rates at mid-tide are $5-9\,mm\,yr^{-1}$, and decrease to *c.* $1-2\,mm\,yr^{-1}$ both landwards and seawards. Typical sediments contain 1–20% sand, 50–70% silt and 20–30% clay. The sediment surface is relatively firm, with a density of $1200-1300\,kg\,m^{-3}$, but has ephemeral drapes

of soft mud, typically 20 cm thick. There seems to be an abundance of gastropods and bivalves. These flats appear to be good examples of the Type 1a mudflat.

Figure 6 shows the sheltered mudflats at Weir Quay in the Tamar Estuary, UK where the spring tide range reaches 4.5 m. The lower flats are exposed to strong shore parallel flows and the upper flats are constrained by a built-up roadway. Consequently, the flats are relatively steeper than might otherwise be expected. The mud is very soft and rapidly accreting, with a convex profile, though there is evidence of a former erosional cliff at about mid-tide. This flat appears to be an example of Type 2a.

The mudflats of the Dollard Estuary, which was the site of extensive detailed measurements by the INTRMUD group, are mesotidal, but sheltered within the estuary. They are several kilometres in width and the middle mudflats are hard to intermediate, according to the above definition, one of the harder areas having a mean bulk density of $1712.5\,kg\,m^{-1}$, an organic content of 3.53% and a mud content of 16.97% (Mitchener & Feates 1996). The flats are planar with only occasional channels. The dominant biological community is worms, with significant near surface bioturbation. Accumulation appears to be very slow, matching sea-level rise. This mudflat seems to be an example of Type 3b.

Fig. 6. The mudflats developed at Weir Quay on the Tamar Estuary, South England. Note the convex profile and the small cliff feature on the upper slope. The stones in the foreground have been artificially placed.

The mudflats of Surinam described by Wells (1983) have a tidal range of 2 m and are *c.* 3 km wide. The area is moderately exposed. There are small drainage channels and the sediment appears to be soft, with a bulk density of $1030-1300 \, kg \, m^{-3}$. The mudflats appear to be an example of Type 4a.

The mudflats of Louisiana (Wells 1983) have a tidal range of 0.5 m and are of low wave energy. Drainage channels and other bedforms are generally absent, and the sediment bulk density is $1150-1300 \, kg \, m^{-3}$. This appears to be an example of Type 6a mudflats.

The typology has to be used with a certain amount of care, since there is a number of parameters that may be important and which, so far, have not been taken into account. For instance, a separate category of mudflats may be required to explicitly take coastal defence structures on the upper flats into account. Similarly, it is probably sensible to use the typology on sections of the mudflats that are fairly restricted in the longshore direction, because there is considerable lateral non-uniformity that may relate to the detailed local wave exposure, and to cycles of erosion and deposition. These variations generally appear to be on a longshore scale equal to, or somewhat greater than, the mudflat width. The intention here has been to propose the simplest initial set of parameters, and it is an objective of the INTRMUD project to assemble a data base on intertidal mudflats which can clarify the generality of the above typology, and quantify the limiting conditions for the various parameters.

The preparation of this paper is part of EC MAST III project INTRMUD and was funded by the EC under contract MAS3-CT95 0022. The author is grateful for comments on the typology by the Partners in the project, and to D. Paterson for assistance with the preparation of the photographs.

References

ALEXANDER, C. R., NITTROUER, C. A., DEMASTER, D. J., PARK, Y.-A. & PARK, S.-C. 1991. Macrotidal mudflats of the Southwestern Korean coast: a model for interpretation of intertidal deposits. *Journal of Sedimentary Petrology*, **61**, 805–824.

ALLEN, J. R. L. & PYE, K. 1992. Coastal saltmarshes: their nature and importance. *In*: ALLEN, J. R. L. & PYE, K. (eds) *Saltmarshes*. Cambridge University Press, 1–18.

AMOS, C. L., VAN WAGGONER, N. A. & DABORN, G. R. 1988. The influence of sub-aerial exposure on the bulk properties of fine grained sediment from Minas Basin, Bay of Fundy. *Estuarine Coastal Shelf Science*, **27**, 1–13.

ANDERSON, F. E. 1983. The northern muddy intertidal: seasonal factors controlling erosion and deposition – a review. *Canadian Journal of Fisheries and Aquatic Science*, **40**, Supp. 1, 143–159.

BRIDGES, P. H. & LEEDER, M. R. 1976. Sedimentary model for intertidal mudflat channels with examples from the Solway Firth, Scotland. *Sedimentology*, **23**, 533–552.

CARR, A. P. & GRAFF, J. 1982. The total immersion factor and shore platform development: discussion. *Transactions Institute of British Geographers*, N. S. **7**, 240–245.

CHRISTIE, M. C., DYER, K. R., FENNESSY, M. J. & HUNTLEY, D. A. 1996. Field measurements of erosion across a shallow water estuarine mudflat. *In*: DALLY, W. R. & ZEIDLER, R. B. (eds) *Coastal Dynamics '95*. American Society of Civil Engineering, New York, 759–770.

DAVIES, J. L. 1964. A morphogenetic approach to world shorelines. *Zeitshrift für Geomorphologie*, **8**, 127 142.

DIECKMANN, R. OSTERTHUN, M. & PARTENSCKY, H.-W. 1987. Influence of water-level elevation and tidal range on the sedimentation in a German tidal flat area. *Progress in Oceanography*, **18**, 151–166.

EVANS, G. 1965. Intertidal flat sediments and their environment of deposition in the Wash. *Quarterly Journal of Geological Society London*, **121**, 209 245.

—— & COLLINS, M. B. 1976. The transportation and deposition of suspended sediment over the intertidal flats of the Wash. *In*: HAILS, J. & CARR, A. (eds) *Nearshore Sediment Dynamics and Sedimentation*. John Wiley, London, 273–306.

FREY, R. W. & BASAN, P. B. 1978. Coastal salt marshes. *In*: DAVIS, R. A. JR (ed.) *Coastal Sedimentary Environments*. Springer-Verlag, New York, 101–169.

——, HOWARD, J. D., HAN, S.-J. & PARK, B.-K. 1989. Sediments and sedimentary sequences on a modern macrotidal flat, Inchon, Korea. *Journal of Sedimentary Petrology*, **59**, 28 44.

GRANT, J. 1988. Intertidal bedforms, sediment transport, and stabilization by benthic microalgae. *In*: DEBOER, P. L. VAN GELDER, A. & NIO, S. D. (eds) *Tide-Influenced Sedimentary Environments and Facies*. D. Reidel, Amsterdam, 499–510.

GREENSMITH, J. T. & TUCKER, E. V. 1965. Salt marsh erosion in Essex. *Nature*, **206**, 606–607.

—— & ——1976. Dynamic structures in the Holocene chenier plain setting of Essex, England. *In*: HAILS, J. & CARR, A. (eds) *Nearshore Sediment Dynamics and Sedimentation*. John Wiley, London, 251–272.

HAYES, M. O. 1975. Morphology of sand accumulation in estuaries. *In*: CRONIN, L. E. (ed.) *Estuarine Research*, Vol. 2, Academic Press, New York, 3–22.

KIRBY, R. 1992. Effects of sea level rise on muddy coastal margins. *In*: PRANDLE, D. (ed.) *Dynamics and Exchanges in Estuaries and the Coastal Zone*. American Geophysical Union, Washington DC, 313–334.

KLEIN, G. D. 1975. Tidal sedimentation: some remaining problems. *In*: GINSBURG, R. N. (ed.) *Tidal Deposits*. Springer-Verlag, New York, 407–410.

LEE, S.-C. 1995. *Response of mudshore profiles to waves*. PhD Thesis, University of Florida, Gainesville, USA.

—— & MEHTA, A. J. 1997. Equilibrium hypsometry of fine-grained shore profiles. *In*: BURT, N., PARKER, R. & WATTS, J. (eds) *Cohesive Sediments*. John Wiley, Chichester, 429–437.

MEHTA, A. J., KIRBY, R. & LEE, S.-C. 1996. *Some observations on mudshore dynamics and stability*. Report UFL/COEL/MP-96/1, University of Florida, USA.

MITCHENER, H. J. & FEATES, N. G. 1996. *Field measurements of erosional behaviour and settling velocities of intertidal sediments at the Dollard, Netherlands, 21–23 May 1996*. HR Wallingford Report TR 16.

PATERSON, D. M. 1989. Short term changes in the erodability of intertidal cohesive sediments related to the migratory behaviour of epipelic diatoms. *Limnology & Oceanography*, **34**, 223–234.

——, CRAWFORD, R. M. & LITTLE, C. 1990. Subaerial exposure and changes in the stability of intertidal estuarine sediments. *Estuarine Coastal Shelf Sci.*, **30**, 541–556.

PETHICK, J. K. 1984. *An Introduction to Coastal Geomorphology*. Arnold, London.

——1992. Saltmarsh geomorphology. *In*: ALLEN, J. R. L. & PYE, K. (eds) *Saltmarshes*. Cambridge University Press, 41–62.

POSTMA, H. 1961. Transport and accumulation of suspended matter in the Dutch Wadden Sea. *Netherlands Journal Sea Res.*, **1**, 148–190.

STEVENSON, J. C., WARD, L. G. & KEARNEY, M. S. 1986. Vertical accretion in marshes with varying rates of sea level rise. *In*: WOLFE, D. A. (ed.) *Estuarine Variability*. Academic Press, 241–260.

WANG, B. C. & EISMA, D. 1988. Mudflat deposition along the Wenzhou coastal plain in Southern Zhejiang, China. *In*: DEBOER, P. L., VAN GELDER, A. & NIO, S. D. (eds) *Tide-Influenced Sedimentary Environments and Facies*. D. Reidel, Amsterdam, 265–274.

WANG, Y. 1983. The mudflat system of China. *Canadian Journal of Fisheries and Aquatic Science*, **40**, Supp. 1, 160–171.

WELLS, J. T. 1983. Dynamics of coastal fluid muds in low-, moderate-, and high-tide-range environments. *Canadian Journal of Fisheries and Aquatic Science*, **40**, Supp. 1, 130–142.

WELLS, J. T. & COLEMAN, J. M. 1981. Physical processes and fine-grained sediment dynamics, coast of Surinam, South America. *Journal of Sedimentary Petrology*, **51**, 1053–1068.

The stability of a mudflat in the Humber estuary, South Yorkshire, UK

CARL L. AMOS[1], M. BRYLINSKY[2], T. F. SUTHERLAND[3], D. O'BRIEN[4], S. LEE[4] & A. CRAMP[4]

[1] Geological Survey of Canada, P.O. Box 1006, Dartmouth, NS, Canada
[2] Acadia Centre for Estuarine Research, Acadia University, Wolfville, NS, Canada
[3] Martec Limited, 1888 Brunswick Street, Halifax, NS, Canada
[4] Department of Earth Sciences, Cardiff University, Cardiff, UK

Abstract: The stability of a mudflat in the Humber estuary, South Yorkshire, was investigated at seven sites along a shore-normal transect during early spring. This was carried out using the benthic flume Sea Carousel, and from the investigation of surface samples in a laboratory equivalent to the Sea Carousel, the Lab Carousel. A clear trend in erosion threshold [$\tau_c(0)$] was evident, showing two maxima: the greatest on the inner mudflat (0.78 Pa); and a second on the central mudflat (0.75 Pa). We ascribe these maxima to two causes: (1) desiccation of the inner mudflats; and (2) biostabilization by algae of the central flats. Our results suggest that of these factors biostabilization was the dominant one at the time of the study. Most of the variation in erosion rate is explained through the sediment bulk density (ρ_b) and colloidal carbohydrate (DCHO) $[\tau_c(0)] = 0.5[1.93\log_{10}(DCHO + 2.5 \times 10^{-4}\rho_b] + 1.7$; $r^2 = 0.63$. Thus variations in DCHO had $O(10^4)$ greater impact on erosion threshold than equivalent variations ρ_b. The relationship between mean erosion rate (E_m) and current speed (U_y) was similar for all sites and is defined by the exponential function: $E_m = 2.47 \times 10^{-6} \cdot 10^{(3.749U_y)}\,\mathrm{kg\,m^{-2}\,s^{-1}}$. In situ mean still-water settling rates (W_s) were up to $2.46 \times 10^{-3}\,\mathrm{m\,s^{-1}}$, which is up to an order of magnitude faster than was measured in other estuaries at similar suspended sediment concentrations, S. The decay constant, k, for still-water settling appeared to be a linear function of S, and compared favourably with values derived from five Canadian coastal mudflats. Results from Lab Carousel showed that the erosion thresholds were the same as those measured in situ, using Sea Carousel. Furthermore the spatial trends in erosion were the same in both studies with the exception of the innermost sites (A and A/B). Differences are explained by consolidation and desiccation caused by solar radiation which were not simulated in the lab. Mean erosion rates showed a similar exponential relationship with current speed to that determined from Sea Carousel. Lab-derived values of k were much higher than the Sea Carousel ones and indicated much faster sediment settling under laboratory conditions. k was a weak inverse function of applied stress. Values of τ_d derived from Krone's (1962) method yielded threshold values of between 0.03 and 0.32 Pa. These values were $38 \pm 16\%$ of the erosion threshold $\tau_c(0)$.

The evolution and dynamics of intertidal mudflats has received considerable attention due to the complex linkages between physical and biological bed properties (Nowell et al. 1981; Paterson 1989; Paterson & Underwood 1990; Paterson et al. 1990; Dade & Nowell, 1991; Heinzelmann & Wallisch 1991; Yallop et al. 1994). Many questions pertaining to these linkages remain to be answered (Vos et al. 1988; Dade & Nowell 1991). A multidisciplinary project called LISP-UK (Littoral Investigation of Sediment Properties) was established to study factors influencing the stability, growth and productivity of littoral tidal flats, and in particular, to integrate field effort for tidal flat monitoring at common space and time scales.

It was recognized that tidal flat attributes are variable in time and space; that the factors which influence tidal flat evolution vary widely due to atmospheric exposure, tidal inundation and biological production; and that synoptic, in situ measurements and the integration of manipulative experimentation with field monitoring are necessary. The purpose of this study was to determine trends in the erodibility of a mudflat on a transect of the LISP study, and to define those attributes of the tidal flats that appeared to control the measured erodibility. The work was undertaken using the in situ benthic flume Sea Carousel (see later) and a laboratory-equivalent of the in situ flume called Lab Carousel that was housed on site in a container.

AMOS, C. L., BRYLINSKY, M., SUTHERLAND, T. F. ET AL. 1998. The stability of a mudflat in the Humber estuary, South Yorkshire, UK. In: BLACK, K. S., PATERSON, D. M. & CRAMP, A. (eds) Sedimentary Processes in the Intertidal Zone. Geological Society, London, Special Publications, **139**, 25–43.

The study region

The site for LISP-UK was immediately west of Spurn Head, Yorkshire on the Skeffling mudflats (53°37′N; 0°05′E), on a broad tidal flat (3600 m wide) along the northern margin of the estuary (Fig. 1). The inner salt marsh was *c.* 50 m wide and was artificially introduced to fringe a reclamation dyke. The adjacent mudflat was 3000 m wide and sloped seawards at 1:1000 to mean sealevel (MSL). The innermost 200 m of mudflat was smooth; the remainder was furrowed by shore-normal drainage runnels (0.2 m deep and 1–2 m wide) which were crossed by an intricate network of deep creeks. The surface roughness of the mudflat increased seawards to MSL, and gave way to an extensive sandflat that extended to low water. Seven reference sites were established along the mudflat portion of the transect (Fig. 2).

Definitions

Ambiguity often arises regarding the definition of 'erodibility' and 'sedimentation' character. They are not purely synonyms for 'erosion threshold' and 'mass settling rate', respectively, but rather define the attributes that control mudflat response to the stabilizing and destabilizing forces at play. For present purposes, we define erodibility in terms of: the erosion threshold (cohesion) at the sediment surface, $\tau_c(0)$; the erosion threshold as a function of sediment depth, $\tau_c(z)$; the friction coefficient, ϕ; the peak and mean rates of erosion (E_p, E_m) as a function of applied bed shear stress and eroded depth; the trend of erosion as a function of time (erosion type) at a constant applied bed shear stress; the size spectra and modes of transport of material eroded from the bed; and the effect of consolidation time on the erosion threshold.

We define sedimentation character in terms of the critical shear stress for the onset of deposition, τ_d; the mass deposition rate, $\delta M/\delta t$; the concentration decay constant, k; and the still-water mass settling rate, W_s. The decay constant is derived on the assumption that settling takes place as a logarithmic function of settling time (t): $S(t) = -k\ln(t) + S_0$, where S_0 is the starting sediment concentration. The mean still-water mass deposition rate has been derived from the rate of change in suspended

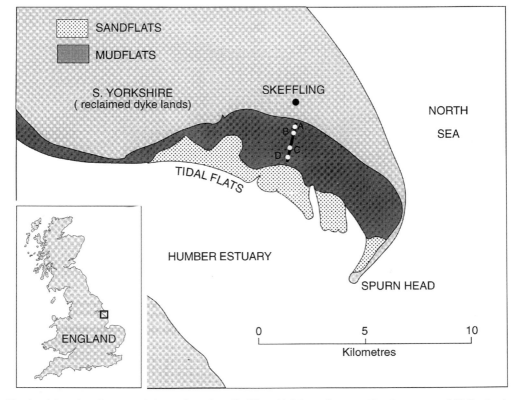

Fig. 1. A location diagram of the study region: Skeffling tidal flats, the outer Humber estuary, NE England.

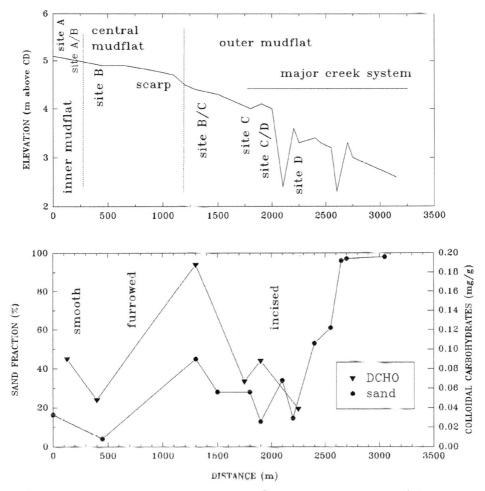

Fig. 2. A profile of the tidal transect across Skeffling tidal flats showing the stations occupied in this study. Also shown are the concentrations of sand and colloidal carbohydrate in the surface sediments.

sediment concentration S within Sea Carousel, and is the product of $S(t)$ and the mass settling rate, $W_s = \delta M/\delta t \cdot 1/S(t)$. The critical threshold for onset of deposition (τ_d) was determined from Krone's (1962) relationship: $\delta M/\delta t = S(t)W_s(1 - \tau_o/\tau_d)$, where τ_o is the applied shear stress. τ_d is determined by measuring the mass settling rate ($\delta M/\delta t$) at a known and finite stress (for $\tau_o < \tau_d$), and solving: $\tau_d = \tau_o/(1 - \{\delta M/\delta t \cdot 1/S(t) \cdot W_s\})$.

Synthetic cores were produced by plotting the applied shear stress (τ_o) against the erosion depth. Eroded depth, z, was derived from Exner's equation: $\gamma_b(1 - P)\delta z/\delta t = h\delta S/\delta t$, where γ_b is the sediment bulk density, P is porosity and h is the flume height. An erosion threshold [$\tau_c(z)$] for a given depth, z, was inferred when erosion ceased, and was equated with the sediment

strength (τ_d) at that depth. The friction coefficient (Φ), which was produced from the synthetic cores, is the arctan of the increase in bed strength (τ_d) with increasing geostatic load (σ): $\Phi = \tan^{-1}(\tau_d/\sigma)$. Conversely, the erosion threshold at any depth was determined from: $\tau_c(z) = \sigma \cdot \tan(\Phi) + \tau_c(0)$. Porosity ($P$) was also defined, and has been derived from the formula: $P = (1 - V_s)$, where $V_s = $ (wet-weight bulk density − water density)/sediment buoyant density.

Instrumentation

Sea Carousel

Sea Carousel is a benthic annular flume designed for field use in intertidal and subtidal settings (Amos *et al.* 1992a, b). The carousel is 1.0 m in radius with an annulus 0.15 m wide and 0.30 m high. Flow in the annulus was induced by rotating a movable lid that was driven by a 0.35 hp DC, digital stepping motor powered from the surface. Eight small paddles, spaced equidistantly beneath the lid, induced a flow of water in the annulus. The Carousel was equipped with three optical backscatter sensors (OBSs; Downing and Beach 1989). Two of these sensors were located non-intrusively on the inner wall of the annulus at heights of 0.03 and 0.18 m above the base. The third OBS detected ambient S outside the annulus. A sampling port is situated in the outer wall of the annulus at a height of 0.2 m above the base. Samples from this port were used to calibrate the OBSs and to determine chlorophyll concentrations in suspension. The lid speed was detected through a shaft encoder resting on the lid. Tangential (U_y) and vertical (U_w) current speeds were detected by a Marsh–McBirney® EM flow meter (model 513) situated about 0.18 m above the bed. Data from all sensors were logged on a Campbell Scientific® CR10 data logger at a rate of 1 Hz. The flume was deployed from a moored boat during tidal inundation of the flats. It was controlled and operated from the surface through underwater cabling.

Lab Carousel

Lab Carousel is an annular flume designed to examine the erosion and settling of natural marine sediments under controlled conditions. It has the exact same dimensions as Sea Carousel and so is directly comparable in terms of flow character, turbulence structure and bed shear stress distribution. The flume is made of clear acrylic so that flow conditions and bed erosion could be clearly observed. Flow is induced by a lid suspended over the water surface from a central shaft. Eight paddles, fixed equidistantly beneath the lid, induce flow. The shaft is turned by a 0.75 Hp Industrial Drive® motor and Focus® controller. Three OBSs are situated at heights of 0.03, 0.10 and 0.20 m above the flume base. A Marsh–McBirney® electro-magnetic flow meter is located in the flume at a height of 0.18 m above the flume bed. The OBS and EM flow meter data are logged on a Campbell Scientific® CR10 data logger and stored on a PC hard-drive.

A Sony® Hi8 video camera was situated near the flume base in order to record erosion and settling processes during each experiment. Lid speed was increased in a series of 5-minute steps until the OBS sensors became saturated. Saturation took place above $S \approx 800\,\mathrm{mg\,l^{-1}}$ which

restricted the experiments to lid speeds less than about $0.4\,\mathrm{m\,s^{-1}}$. At each increment of lid speed, 0.5 l water samples were collected from three ports at the heights of the three OBSs. All samples were analysed for S, chlorophyll, and particulate organic and inorganic matter.

Sampling and sample analysis

Three types of samples were collected from each of the sites occupied by Sea Carousel. The first were short gravity cores of the topmost 30–50 cm of the mudflat. These samples were collected using a Benthos® gravity corer that was ballasted with 200 lbs of lead. The core samples were sealed in wax, maintained vertical, and stored at a temperature less than 10°C. The cores were split, logged, photographed and analysed for: water content; bulk density; Atterburg limits; vane shear strength; grain size; and clay mineralogy. An Eckman grab sample of the sediment surface was taken, from which were collected: two syringe cores that were flash-frozen in liquid nitrogen for SEM analysis of microfabric, and Catscan analysis for bulk density; (after Amos *et al.* 1996*b*); a 100 g surface scrape for grain size analysis; four 1.5 cm diameter, 3 mm deep syringe cores for analysis of water content, organic content, sediment chlorophyll *a*, colloidal carbohydrate and bacterial numbers; and one 1.5 cm diameter, 10 cm deep syringe core for the analysis of sediment nematode numbers. A large-sample (5–10 kg) surface scrape was collected at each site for use in the Lab Carousel.

Results

Sea Carousel results

A total of 19 Sea Carousel deployments were attempted during the course of this study. Thirteen of the 19 deployments were successful. A summary of the results obtained from these stations is given in Table 1. Lid speed was constant at lower levels of flow, but above $0.5\,\mathrm{m\,s^{-1}}$ it was erratic. Consequently, results from these faster-flowing intervals should be treated as suspect. Water samples (500 ml in volume) were pumped from the Sea Carousel about 3 mins into each increment of lid speed. A 5-minute period of still-water mass settling was possible only at stations 13, and 14 (site A) and 5 (site C).

Site A was flat, smooth and ideal for Sea Carousel deployments, however the remaining sites were dominated by slope-parallel ridges

Table 1. *A summary of Sea Carousel stations and corresponding surface erosion thresholds, the computed friction coefficients, and the range of wet-weight sediment bulk densities determined from Catscan analyses of syringe cores (e stands for falling tide; f stands for rising tide). Erosion threshold is derived by using suspended sediment concentration as the index of bed failure*

Station #	Site	Erosion threshold (pa)	Friction coeff. (ϕ)	Bulk density (kg m^{-3})
1	D(e)	–	–	1700–1800
2	D(f)	0.43	34	1700–1800
3	D(e)	0.42	64	1700–1800
4	D(f)	0.32	10	1700–1800
5	C(e)	0.44	3	1500–1700
6	C(f)	–	–	–
7	C/D(e)	0.44	77	1600–1800
8	C/D(f)	0.44	63	1600–1800
9	–	–	–	–
10	B/C(e)	1.22	51	1400–1700
11	B/C(f)	–	–	–
12	B/C(f)	0.19	12	1400–1700
13	A(e)	0.78	6	1800
14	A(f)	0.75	11	1800
15	A(f)	0.77	11	1800
16	–	–	–	–
17	B(e)	0.19	85	1500–1700
18	B(e)	0.19	26	1500–1700
19	B(f)	–	–	–

and runnels *c.* 20 cm deep and 50 cm wide. Leakage from the flume base was possible in regions dominated by these features. A calibrated, time-series of results from site A is shown in Fig. 3. OBS1 and 3 show trends of increasing *S* in harmony with the current time-series of panel A. OBS2, however, shows little change with time as it is outside the annulus and monitors ambient *S*. Raw *S* is uncorrected for dispersion (leakage) and generally agreed with the pumped samples (solid dots). OBS1 and OBS3 have been corrected for dispersion (based on a method outlined in Amos *et al.* 1992a). Panel C illustrates the erosion rate time-series determined from the changes in corrected *S* with time. E_p clearly correspond to the beginning of each increment of lid speed and are short-lived events. This typifies type I erosion wherein bed erosion ceases *c.* 1 minute after application of the eroding flow.

Erosion thresholds and erosion rates. The overall increases in S with time illustrated that bed erosion took place. The surface threshold for this erosion [$\tau_c(0)$] was evaluated from plots of applied bed shear stress against *S*. These results are plotted in Fig. 4 and are listed in Table 1. Results obtained from three stations at site A (13, 14, and 15) yielded $\tau_c(0) = 0.77(\pm 0.01)$ Pa. Friction coefficients were all low ($<11°$) diag-

nostic of low consolidation yet the surface bulk density was the highest of the transect. Mean erosion rate (E_m) showed a strong positive correlation with azimuthal velocity of the form: $E_m = 9.12 \times 10^{-7} \cdot 10^{(5.047 U_y)}$ kg m^{-2} s^{-1}; $r^2 = 0.86$; $n = 20$. Site A/B yielded results very similar to those from site A.

All stations from site B were subject to rapidly changing ambient *S*. This was the result of the passage of turbidity fringe during the period of Sea Carousel deployment which masked the erosion trends. $\tau_c(0)$ was, nevertheless, derived and was a constant 0.19 Pa. The topmost 0.03 mm was rapidly eroded whereas beneath, a substrate of steadily increasing strength with depth was found ($\Phi = 26°-85°$). This was later verified from measures of bulk density illustrated in Fig. 5. There was no clear relationship between peak erosion rate (E_p) and bed shear stress or current speed. The mean erosion rate (E_m) showed only a poor relationship to flow speed.

The mass eroded from site B/C was generally very low. Furthermore, the erosion rate time-series was erratic with no obvious trends with time. The trends in *S* during deployment 12 suggested that erosion was type I. However, the ambient values of *S* varied on a scale of the changes resulting from the erosion process itself. Furthermore, systematic fluctuations in the lower OBS (the origin of which are unknown)

SITE A – 14 APRIL, 1995

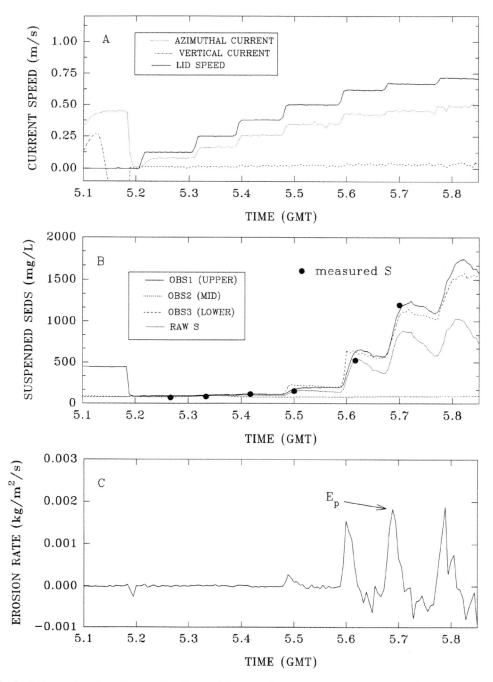

Fig. 3. A time-series of results from Sea Carousel during a deployment at site A on 14 April 1995: (**a**) lid speed, and azimuthal and vertical current speeds; (**b**) suspended sediment concentrations (*S*) monitored within the Sea Carousel (OBS1 and 3) and outside the flume (OBS2), raw *S* (without the correction for leakage), and measured *S* based on filtration of samples pumped from the flume; and (**c**) erosion rate.

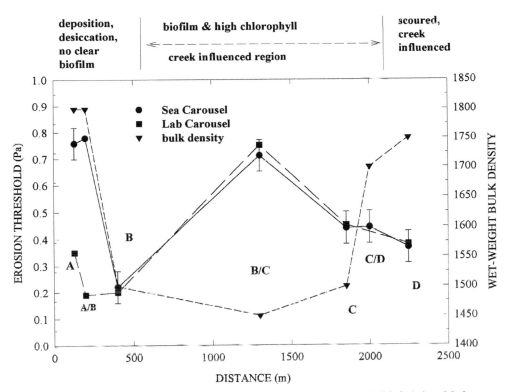

Fig. 4. The erosion thresholds of surface sediments derived from Sea Carousel (solid circles) and Lab Carousel (solid squares) together with bulk density. There is a good correspondence in results between all stations except the inner ones (A and A/B). The departure at the inner sites is interpreted to be the result of solar radiation (and high bulk density) which took place prior to deployment of Sea Carousel, an effect that was not simulated in the Lab Carousel.

masked the erosion trends and the surface erosion thresholds were ambiguous. E_m showed considerable scatter and yielded unreliable estimates of the erosion threshold by the extrapolation of erosion rate to zero. S, by contrast, appeared to increase as a smooth power function of τ_0 and good estimates of the erosion threshold were derived from it (Table 1). These were 1.22 and 0.19 Pa for stations 10 and 12, respectively. Note the large difference in values for the same site which may be related to sediment patchiness, or perhaps boat disturbance of the bed during the survey.

Results from site C showed a well-defined threshold followed by type I erosion, albeit from one station (5). Onset of erosion was characterized by a rapid increase in S. The surface erosion threshold was 0.44 Pa; an intermediate value. Peak erosion rates were relatively constant at 8×10^{-4} kg m^{-2} s^{-1}. Mean erosion rates were amongst the highest in the survey and showed a positive correlation with applied bed shear stress and current speed of the exponential

form: $E_m = 1.45 \times 10^{-5} \cdot 10^{(3.166 U_y)}$ kg m^{-2} s^{-1}, $r^2 = 0.88$; $n = 12$. The still-water settling rate (W_s) at this site $(9.07 \times 10^{-3}$ m/s) was the highest value of the survey, and was approximately three times larger than the values of site A. The friction coefficient for site C was extremely low $(3°)$ and was diagnostic (in this context) of recent deposition.

Bed failure at site C/D (stations 7 and 8) took place early and was manifested by a continuous release of bed material typical of type II erosion. This was apparent at all applied bed shear stresses above the critical. The erosion thresholds for the two sites were intermediate in magnitude being a constant 0.44 Pa. The friction coefficients were amongst the highest recorded from the transect (63–77°) and indicated a stable bed in keeping with the high bulk density of the site (Fig. 4).

Four stations were occupied at site D. Station 1 was abandoned as it was located on a steep-sided creek wall. Station 2 was located on a smooth creek levée that showed evidence of

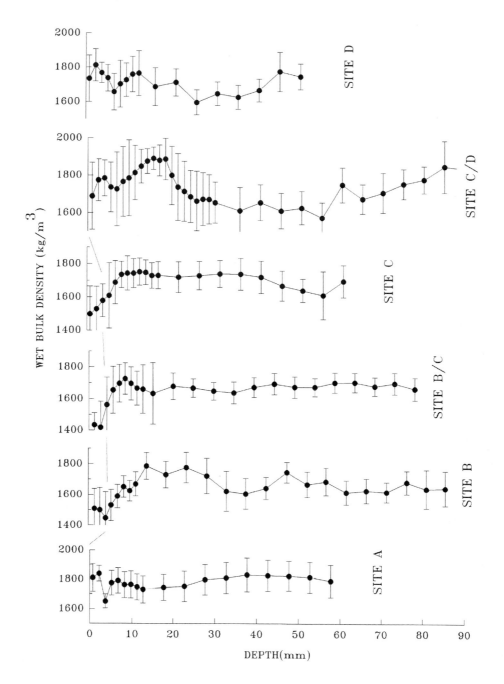

Fig. 5. The bulk density of the surface 9 cm of each site derived from Catscan analyses of syringe cores described in Amos *et al.* (1996*b*). The horizontal bars denote the standard deviation of bulk densities at each level derived from about 14 000 independent measures at each interval. Notice the relatively soft surface layer at sites B, B/C and C corresponding to the region of high colloidal carbohydrate content. Notice also that the greatest changes take place in the topmost 10 mm of the sediment column.

deposition. Station 3 was on 0.2 m-high erosion furrows and leakage from the base of the Carousel was suspected. Station 4 was at the base of a major creek which was composed of fully-saturated, soft sandy material. The erosion of creek levée material produced well-defined asymptotes in S diagnostic of type I erosion. Peak erosion rates were very high; up to 10^{-2} kg m^{-2} s^{-1}. The threshold for erosion was well-defined and intermediate in value (0.43 Pa). The furrowed mudflat also eroded in type I fashion, although decreases in corrected S at each speed increment suggested losses from the base of the Carousel. The erosion threshold for this material (0.42 Pa) was higher than that measured at the levée. The friction coefficient of the furrowed mudflat was also higher ($\Phi = 64°$) than that adjacent to the creek ($\Phi = 34°$), and possessed an apparently in-erodible substrate at a depth of 0.03 mm which may be diagnostic of compacted sediment produced by scouring. The creek bed exhibited an erosion pattern that was transitional between type I and type II; i.e. an initial peak was evident yet erosion continued measurably throughout each increment of applied stress. The peak erosion rates were lower than at other stations (up to 10^{-3} kg m^{-2} s^{-1}) but were continuous in form which is diagnostic of remoulded material (Mehta and Partheniades 1979). The erosion threshold was low [$\tau_c(0) = 0.32$ Pa] as a consequence of the soft, saturated nature of the bed material. The friction coefficient was much lower than that of the creek levée ($\Phi = 10°$) reflecting the highly saturated mobile sand on the creek bed. Mean erosion rates showed exponential trends with flow which were similar to those at the landward sites, though the scatter in results was large.

Bulk density profiles. The bulk density profiles of the surface sediment have been evaluated through Catscan analysis of syringe cores taken from each Sea Carousel site. The results are

plotted in Fig. 5 and presented in Table 2. In general, two layers were recognized: (1) a surface layer, up to 5 mm thick of relatively low bulk density (<1600 kg m^{-3}, present only at sites B, B/C, and C); and (2) a uniform sub-stratum of high bulk density (1600–1900 kg m^{-3}) exhibiting slowly-varying physical properties with depth. A high density surface layer evident at site A (1800 kg m^{-3}) may have resulted from desiccation of surface sediment through solar heating which took place during the tidal exposure at the time of sampling or through drainage (Anderson and Howell 1984). The scatter in bulk density values (horizontal bars around each data point) reflects sediment heterogeneity at each depth interval, not a standard deviation of replicate cores. This scatter was largest near the surface and decreased over the topmost 30 mm where primary consolidation was taking place (Lambe and Whitman 1969) to a near constant value where secondary consolidation appeared to dominate.

Lab Carousel

A bulk sample from site A was split and one half was mixed with seawater collected from Spurn Head pier, and then settled in the Lab Carousel under still-water conditions for 20 hrs (water temperature was 9°C). The second half was settled in local seawater for 44 hrs. As well, insert trays were filled with the remoulded bulk material and stored in seawater for a period of 7 days. The purpose of these experiments was to examine the effects of consolidation time on erosion threshold. Analyses of sites B, C and D were made on material consolidated for 20 hrs. A summary of results is given in Table 3.

Results after 20 hrs of consolidation. Type I erosion prevailed at early stages of the erosion process, with well-defined, short-lived peaks in

Table 2. *A summary of sediment physical properties determined from the Catscan analyses, and erosion threshold [$\tau_c(0)$] determined for (1) the Sea Carousel and (2) Lab Carousel*

Site	Wet bulk density (kg m^{-3})	Porosity (%)	Dry bulk density (kg m^{-3})	$\tau(0)$ 1 (Pa)	$\tau(0)$ 2 (Pa)
Site A	1800	53	1255	0.76	0.35
Site A/B	1800*	53*	1255*	0.78	0.19
Site B	1500	71	769	0.19	0.20
Site B/C	1450	74	688	0.71	0.75
Site C	1500	71	769	0.44	0.45
Site C/D	1700	60	1093	0.44	–
Site D	1750	56	1174	0.37	0.38

* Derived from site A.

Table 3. *A summary of Lab Carousel experiments on bulk samples taken from the Skeffling transect. Unless otherwise stated, the samples were allowed to consolidate for 20 hrs*

Experiment	Site	Settling time (hrs)	W_s (m s^{-3})	Threshold (Pa)	
				Deposition	Erosion
Lab2	Site A	20	–	–	0.35
Lab3	Site A	44	7.78×10^{-3}	–	0.43
Lab5	Site B	100	8.67×10^{-3}	0.03	0.20
Lab6	Site D	20	2.47×10^{-3}	0.23	0.38
Lab7	Site C	20	3.97×10^{-3}	–	0.45
Lab8	Site B/C	20	4.90×10^{-3}	0.32	0.75
Lab9	Site A/B	20	1.64×10^{-3}	0.07	0.19

erosion rate, while type II erosion (continuous) dominated during the later stages. *S* increased as logarithmic or power functions of the applied bed shear stress. The mean erosion thresholds for site A were between 0.35 and 0.43 Pa which is well below those derived from Sea Carousel. The erosion threshold for site A/B was amongst the lowest of those tested ($\tau_c(0) = 0.19$ Pa; Fig. 4) and again was well below *in situ* values. E_p bore no obvious relationship to either applied stress or current speed in either absolute or excess form. Settling rates showed considerable scatter ($1.64–7.78 \times 10^{-3}$ m s^{-1}) but spanned values derived from the Sea Carousel. The threshold for deposition yielded a value of 0.07 Pa which is about 36% of $\tau_c(0)$ for this station.

All remaining stations yielded results that corresponded well with *in situ* values (see Fig. 4). The erosion threshold at site B was 0.20 Pa. Type I erosion prevailed throughout with peak erosion rates of 3×10^{-4} kg m^{-2} s^{-1}. The mean erosion rate (E_m) showed a positive correlation to flow (see later). The still-water mean particle settling rate (W_s) was 2.07×10^{-3} m s^{-1}, and the deposition threshold stress (τ_d) was evaluated as 0.03 Pa i.e. 15% of $\tau_c(0)$.

Site B/C showed a well-defined erosion threshold of 0.75 Pa which was the highest threshold recorded in the Lab Carousel. The mean sediment concentration (*S*) showed a positive correlation with bed shear stress of the form: $E_m = 85\tau_0^{5.214}$ kg m^{-2} s^{-1}, which is unique to this site. This implies that erosion proceeded at a high rate once a surface, more resistant, layer had been broken. The still-water settling rate (W_s) for this site was 4.90×10^{-3} m s^{-1}, which was the highest of the Lab Carousel estimates. $\delta M/\delta t$ for an applied stress of 0.13 Pa was 1.71×10^{-3} kg m^{-2} s^{-1}, which yielded a deposition threshold (τ_d) of 0.32 Pa, i.e. 42% of $\tau_c(0)$.

A clear peak in erosion was evident at early stages of erosion of the site C sample and bed failure was largely type II; erosion rates reached values of 9×10^{-4} kg m^{-2} s^{-1}. The erosion threshold was estimated to be 0.45 Pa which was very close to the Sea Carousel value (0.44 Pa). The still-water settling rate (W_s) for this site was 3.97×10^{-3} m s^{-1}. Peak erosion rates from site D were comparable to those from Sea Carousel (10^{-3} kg m^{-2} s^{-1}). The erosion threshold [$\tau_c(0)$] was well-defined and had a value of 0.38 Pa. This falls within the range derived from Sea Carousel. The mean erosion rate (E_m) was defined in terms of the flow speed: $E_m = 5.56 \times 10^{-6} \cdot 10^{(6.102U_y)}$; $r^2 = 0.53$; $n = 7$. The high exponent demonstrates that this material was more susceptible to erosion than the natural site. The still-water settling rate was evaluated to be 2.47×10^{-3} m s^{-1}, which is approximately three times higher than sites A and A/B (reflecting the sandy nature of the bed material, see Fig. 2). Furthermore, the mean threshold for deposition was 0.23 Pa, thus the ratio $\tau_c(0)$: τ_d was 1.65 which is close to a ratio used in modelling by Diserens *et al.* (1993).

Biological sample analyses

The results of sample analysis for biological parameters are listed in Table 4. There were no consistent trends across the mudflat. Sediment organic contents ranged between 4.3 and 9.2% (Table 4) which is within the range reported by Yingst & Rhoades (1978). Inner tidal flat chlorophyll *a* concentrations were intermediate in value being similar to those reported by Vos *et al.* (1988) but much lower than those reported by Underwood & Paterson (1993). Chlorophyll *a* concentration decreased towards the low water mark. Colloidal carbohydrate concentrations were greatest at site B/C and decreased both landwards and seawards (Fig. 2). Bacteria abundance (reported in Amos *et al.* 1996) were

Table 4. *A summary of the biological properties measured at the Sea Carousel sites*

Site	Organic content (%)	Chlorophyll (µg/g)	Carbohydrate (mg/g)
Site A	3.6	12.1	0.090
Site B	9.2	16.1	0.048
Site B/C	4.3	26.4	0.188
Site C	8.9	8.5	0.067
Site C/D	5.0	16.6	0.088
Site D	5.2	5.3	0.039

within the range normally reported for marine sediments (Dade *et al.* 1990), but showed no obvious relationship to either sediment organic content, chlorophyll *a* or colloidal carbohydrate concentrations.

General interpretations

The variation in erosion threshold

The variation of erosion threshold measured in Sea Carousel across the mudflat showed no systematic trends, but rather two distinct maxima were evident (Fig. 4). The scatter in replication (the standard deviation of three replicates) at any site was less than the variation across the mudflat, so the spatial trends that we describe appear real. The highest threshold was found at the innermost site (A), reflecting the probable effects of solar radiation during subaerial exposure. Recent deposition was evident at site A (as a smooth brown slick absent of bioturbation), yet the bulk density values were higher than those on the middle mudflats perhaps as a result of desiccation (see bulk density values in Table 1). The effect of desiccation, apparent only at site A, was probably the result of two causes: the relatively long duration of exposure (9 hrs); and the cloudy and cold conditions during deployments at all other sites. The second maximum was found on the central mudflat in a region of the highest chlorophyll and carbohydrate contents, but of the lowest surface bulk density (Fig. 4).

The lowest erosion thresholds detected by Lab and Sea Carousels were at site B. This is perhaps reflected in the low surface bulk density detected at this site which may reflect recent deposition. Site B/C showed high erosion thresholds which contrasts with the lowest bulk density of the transect. Here we suspect the dominating role of biostabilization which is evident in the high levels of colloidal carbohydrates [Fig. 2(b)]. The high sand content at this site is not considered to influence erodibility based on results of Torfs

(1995) and Mitchener & Torfs (1996), who showed that below values of about 80%, changes in sand content have little effect on erosion resistance.

There is a good relationship between wet-weight bulk density (ρ_b) and erosion threshold ($\tau_c(0)$) of the form $\tau_c(0) = 7.51 \times 10^{-4}$ ($\rho_b - 1000$), where ρ_b is in $kg\,m^{-3}$. B/C forms an outlier in the above relationship which may be the result of biostabilization by a biofilm that was visible at this site (Paterson this volume). This outlier may be removed by substituting the effects of colloidal carbohydrate (DCHO) for bulk density. Figure 6(a) shows the positive relationship between colloidal carbohydrate and erosion threshold, which has been fitted with the logarithmic form: $\tau_c(0) = 0.73 \log(DCHO) + 1.63$; $r^2 = 0.53$; $n = 13$; however, the scatter in results is large. The predicted variation in the range in values of $\tau_c(0)$ has been evaluated by solving the above relationships for the range in DCHO ($0.0156 - 0.0752\,kg\,m^{-3}$) and ρ_b ($1400 - 1800\,kg\,m^{-3}$) across the transect; variations in DCHO account for a change of 0.50 Pa in $\tau_c(0)$, while variations in ρ_b account for a change of 0.30 Pa in $\tau_c(0)$. DCHO appears to dominate the observed variation in erosion threshold across the intertidal transect, but variations in ρ_b should not be ignored.

Biofilm activity and state of evolution may be quantified in terms of the colloidal carbohydrate content (Sutherland *et al.* in press), which were greatest at site B/C. By combining the variation in colloidal carbohydrate along the transect with those of bulk density the scatter in predicted $\tau_c(0)$ is reduced about 10%:

$$[\tau_c(0)] = 0.5[1.93 \log_{10}(DCHO) + 2.5 \times 10^{-4}\rho_b]$$
$$+ 1.7; \quad r^2 = 0.63 \qquad (1)$$

(Fig. 6(b), where ρ_b and DCHO are expressed in units of $kg\,m^{-3}$). The relative effects of the two variables on bed stability are evaluated by expressing DCHO in the same units as ρ_b (multiplication of DCHO in Table 4 by 0.4 assuming a dry unit weight of 400 $kg\,m^{-3}$;

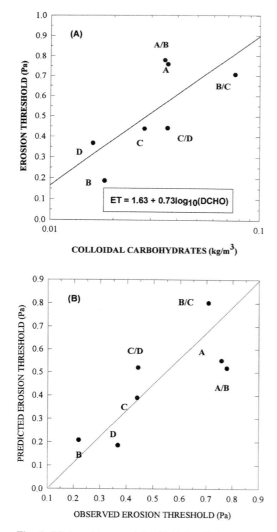

Fig. 6. (a) A scattergram of colloidal carbohydrate (DCHO) within the surface sediments of each site and erosion threshold [$\tau_c(0)$]. The solid line is derived by least squares regression; and (b) the observed erosion threshold plotted against the predicted value derived from an empirical relationship incorporating bulk density (ρ_b in kg m^{-3}) and colloidal carbohydrate (in kg m^{-3}) of the form: $\tau_c(0) = 0.5(2.5 \times 10^{-4}\rho_b + 1.93 \log_{10}(\text{DCHO})) + 1.7$ Pa; $r^2 = 0.63$.

Lambe & Whitman 1969). The trend shown in Fig. 6(b) indicates an increasing resistance to erosion with increasing bulk density and colloidal carbohydrate; a result also found by Underwood & Paterson (1993). The empirical constants in equation (1) suggest that changes in DCHO have O(10^4) greater effect on bed erodibility than equivalent changes in bulk density.

Bed erosion threshold has been shown by Paterson *et al.* (1990) and Christian (1989) to increase with time during exposure due to subaerial effects on mudflats. Although a reversal of this trend takes during the subsequent inundation some effect of exposure may remain, particularly if strong drying has taken place. Our measurements were made on either early rising (f) or late falling (e) of the tide (see Table 1). Replication at each site involved at least one flooding and one ebbing period, yet no systematic difference in erosion thresholds was apparent in results for the two stages of the tide.

In situ *erosion rates from Sea Carousel*

Mean erosion rates (E_m) for all sites occupied by Sea Carousel appeared to follow similar relationships to applied azimuthal current speed (U_y) and takes the exponential form:

$$E_m = 2.47 \times 10^{-6} \cdot 10^{(3.749 U_y)} \text{ kg m}^{-2} \text{ s}^{-1};$$

$$r^2 = 0.55; \quad n = 100 \qquad (2)$$

(see Fig. 7a). Considering the diversity of sites, the correspondence of results is notable. For modelling purposes, equation (2) would be a reasonable representation of the entire mudflat. There appears to be a link between peak and mean erosion rates with the former being about an order of magnitude greater than the latter. Yet we could find no consistent trends in the factors controlling E_p.

Lab Carousel erosion rates

The mean erosion rates derived from each site in Lab Carousel appeared to show reasonable correspondence with current speed and follow a similar trend to that of Sea Carousel. The best-fit regression of all sites is shown in Fig. 7(b). The form of the fit is:

$$E_m = 1.99 \times 10^{-5} \cdot 10^{(3.85 U_y)} \text{ kg m}^{-2} \text{ s}^{-1};$$

$$r^2 = 0.38; \quad n = 52 \qquad (3)$$

The scatter in the Lab Carousel results and erosion rates was higher than that of Sea Carousel. The fact that the Lab Carousel samples were remoulded would favour higher erosion rates due to the breakdown of *in situ* bed strength. By contrast, one might expect less scatter in the laboratory-derived data.

Settling rates and depositional thresholds

The decay constant, k (in units of s^{-1}), is an index of mean settling rate and has been shown in previous studies to be strongly related to S_0

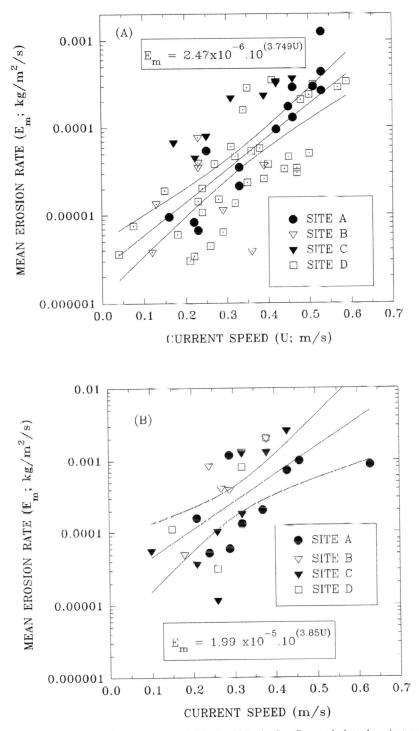

Fig. 7. (a) A scattergram of index current speed ($U_{0.18}$) within the Sea Carousel plotted against mean erosion rate (E_m). There is a good positive correlation that appears to fit all sites across the tidal transect; and (b) a scattergram of index current speed with the Lab Carousel and mean erosion rate. Note that the scatter is larger, but the best-fit line is almost the same as that for the Sea Carousel.

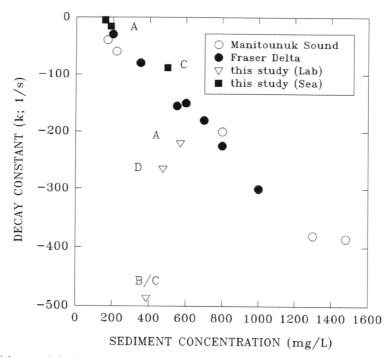

Fig. 8. Initial suspended sediment concentration (S_o) within the Sea and Lab Carousels plotted against the exponential decay constant k, derived from equation $S(t) = -k \ln \delta(t) + S_o$. The Sea Carousel data fall on the inverse linear trends detected in Manitounuk Sound, Northern Canada (Amos *et al.* 1996a) and Fraser Delta, British Columbia (Amos *et al.* 1997). The results from Lab Carousel shows some departure from this trend. Notice site B/C exhibits extremely high settling (large negative value of k) which may be due to the high colloidal carbohydrates at this site (site letters are indicated on the figure).

(Amos *et al.* in press). Figure 8 shows values of k derived from sites A and C in the Sea Carousel, and from samples collected at sites A, B/C and D in the Lab Carousel. The results from Sea Carousel show that k varied as a function of S in a fashion that agreed well with results from Manitounuk Sound, Quebec, Canada (Amos *et al.* 1996a), from the Fraser Delta, British Columbia (Amos *et al.* in press), and from other estuarine sites reported by Amos & Mosher (1985) and Dyer (1986).

The results from Lab Carousel in general indicate faster settling than the *in situ* results. Sites A and D are only slightly greater, whereas site B/C shows extremely rapid settling. Note that this site also exhibits the highest DCHO concentrations (Fig. 2) and also the highest erosion thresholds of the survey (Fig. 4). Bulk density is not a contributing factor to the observed settling as site B/C shows the lowest density of surface material of the transect. Thus the process of flocculation is likely to be more rapid and may be enhanced by the high levels of DCHO.

Lab Carousel experiments showed that settling rates were lowest at site A, were at a maximum at site B/C and generally decreased in a seaward direction (Table 2). Thus settling rate mimics the trends in erosion threshold. This is not unexpected if we assume that flocculation, which enhances settling and consolidation, is itself enhanced by organic matter.

Bed stability and bed physical properties

The physical properties of gravity cores collected at each site were measured at 5 cm depth intervals using standard laboratory techniques reported in Amos *et al.* (1996c). No clear relationship between these physical properties and erodibility was found. Site B had the lowest erosion threshold of all the sites, and also the lowest sand and highest clay contents, which is opposite to the trend one would expect if cohesion was significant. Site B/C was intermediate in terms of sediment texture. Illite, which exhibits strong cohesion, was highest at this site and so may also play a role in stabilizing the surface in association with biostabilization. Water content does not seem to have any bearing on the erodibility of the sediments. Site D had the highest water content along with a high percentage of clay, but it had the same erosion threshold as site C which had one of the lowest water contents.

A comparison between the Lab Carousel and Sea Carousel results

The erosion thresholds measured in Lab Carousel corresponded well with the *in situ* ones measured using Sea Carousel (Fig. 9). This was unexpected as the consolidation time (20 hrs) was chosen for practical reasons only. The erosion threshold of site A material was a well-defined logarithmic function of the consolidation time, t: $\tau(0) = 0.261 \log_{10}(t)$ (Fig. 10). Thus we infer that the age of the surface sediment of the transect was approximately two tidal inundations and that the biofilm, evident at site B/C had re-established itself in Lab Carousel within

20 hrs. The innermost sites A and A/B do not follow the trends of the other stations. We interpret this to be the result of solar radiation of the flats prior to the field deployments.

A comparison of results with other locations

The relationship between erosion threshold and wet-weight bulk density has been proposed by Amos *et al.* (in press) based on Sea Carousel results from five locations across Canada. These results are shown in Fig. 11 together with the results of this study. Notice that, in general, the erosion thresholds for this study conform with Canadian values for sediments of similar bulk density. The form of the best-fit regression line in the figure is: $\tau_c(0) = 5.04 \times 10^{-4} \rho_h$; $r^2 = 0.35$ which is well below the laboratory-derived values proposed by Mitchener & Torfs (1996) and Ockenden & Delo (1988). The over-estimation of laboratory-flume experiments has also been noted by Mitchener & Torfs (1996) though no explanation for the cause is given.

An exception to the above trend was site B/C, which falls well above the results from Canada

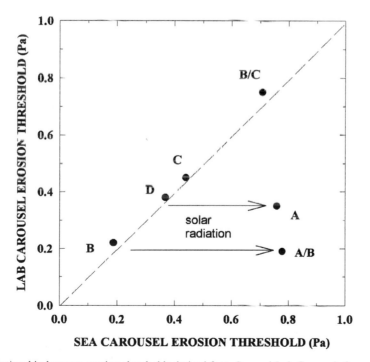

Fig. 9. The relationship between erosion thresholds derived from Sea and Lab Carousels for each deployment site. Notice that there is an almost exact agreement between all but the innermost sites (A and A/B). The differences are attributed to desiccation and strengthening (through solar radiation) in the field because of unusually warm dry weather immediately prior to these deployments.

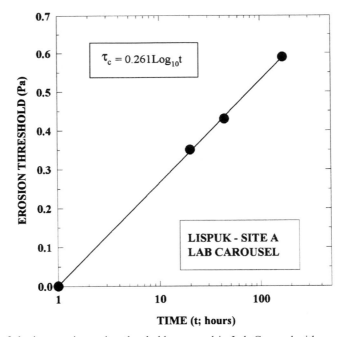

$$\tau_c = 0.261 \text{Log}_{10}t$$

LISPUK - SITE A
LAB CAROUSEL

TIME (t; hours)

Fig. 10. A plot of the increase in erosion threshold measured in Lab Carousel with consolidation time of surface sediment from site A. The flume was filled with sea water from the site and maintained at 10°C; the sediment, which was used within hours of collection, was mixed with the seawater and settled under still-water conditions. Erosion threshold increased logarithmically with time, and had acquired the strength of most field sites within 20 hrs. Below 1 hr consolidation time, the sediment-water interface generated Kelvin-Helmholtz waves indicating it to be a fluid mud, not a solid. For longer settling times, the interface was rigid and eroded as a solid bed.

but is consistent with results of Mitchener & Torfs (1996). The biostabilization of site B/C thus appears exceptional when compared to Canadian examples. This appears particularly so given the time of year of this study (April). Note that some values of bulk density fall below that of water (i.e. positively buoyant). The origin and significance of these buoyant biofilms are discussed by Sutherland *et al.* (in press).

Conclusions

The stability of intertidal muds of the Humber estuary was investigated at seven sites along a transect using the *in situ* benthic flume Sea Carousel. Results were compared with erosion experiments carried out using the Lab Carousel on 'fresh' (2 hrs from collection; 20 hrs consolidation time), remoulded samples from these sites. Finally, results from the Humber estuary were compared with Sea Carousel results from Canada. The following are the main points of conclusion of this study:

(1) Results from Sea Carousel were obtained from 13 stations across the intertidal transect. These showed clear erosion thresholds followed by type I (asymptotically-decaying) erosion rates.

(2) Two maxima in erosion threshold were evident along the transect: (1) the inner mudflat (0.76 ± 0.01 Pa) interpreted to be the result of desiccation on exposure; and (2) the central mudflat (0.71 ± 0.51 Pa) interpreted to be the result of biostabilization.

(3) The Lab Carousel results yielded trends similar to those of the Sea Carousel. As the consolidation time in Lab Carousel was 20 hrs we conclude that the sediments on the tidal flat are of this age. Furthermore, the biofilm present in the field appeared to have regenerated fully in the lab within 20 hrs.

(4) Catscan analysis of syringe cores for bulk density showed that the surface 5 mm of the central mudflat was characterized by sediments of relatively low bulk density ($< 1600 \, \text{kg m}^{-3}$); below this level and at remaining sites the bulk density varied

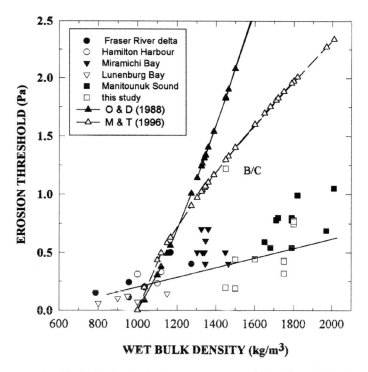

Fig. 11. A scattergram of wet bulk density within the topmost mm's of the sediment bed plotted against erosion threshold derived from Sea Carousel. The results of this study are compared with results from Sea Carousel from Fraser Delta, British Columbia, Canada (Amos *et al.* in press), Hamilton Harbour, Lake Ontario (Amos & Droppo 1996), Miramichi Bay, New Brunswick (Amos and Gibson 1994), Lunenburg Bay, Nova Scotia (Sutherland *et al.* in press), and Manitounuk Sound, Quebec (Amos *et al.* 1996a). All sites fall on a positive linear trend with density except site B/C which is high in colloidal carbohydrate. The trends of Ockenden & Delo (1988) and Mitchener & Torfs (1996) are also plotted. Notice that these two laboratory studies indicate much higher erosion thresholds than were measured in the field at similar densities. The reason for the differences are unknown.

between 1600 and 1900 kg m^{-3}. Standard techniques for measurement of bulk density would be likely to mask this surface layer, with a resulting reduction in the correlation with erosion threshold.

(5) Erosion threshold [$\tau_c(0)$] may be expressed as a function of wet-weight bulk density (ρ_b) and colloidal carbohydrate content (DCHO): $\tau_c(0) = 0.5[1.93 \log_{10}(\text{DCHO}) + 2.5 \times 10^{-4}(\rho_b)] + 1.7$. Thus, changes in DCHO have O(10^4) greater effect on stability than equivalent changes in ρ_b.

(6) Mean erosion rate (E_m) measured in Sea Carousel varied as a power function of current speed (U_y): $E_m = 2.47 \times 10^{-6} \cdot 10^{(3.749 U_y)}$. Similar trends were evident in the Lab Carousel results: $E_m = 1.99 10^{-5} \cdot 10^{(3.85 U_y)}$.

(7) The erosion thresholds of this study were equivalent to those measured in Canadian estuaries on marine sediments of similar bulk density.

(8) The still-water sediment concentration decay constant k, measured in Sea Carousel, varied in proportion with starting sediment concentration S_0 in the same fashion as Canadian counterparts. k measured in Lab Carousel, on the other hand, yielded values greater than the field counterparts, with site B/C showing settling rates three times faster than elsewhere. This we attribute to high levels of DCHO.

(9) The deposition thresholds, measured only in Lab Carousel, varied between 0.03 and 0.32 Pa, and was 38 ± 16% of the erosion threshold. The two thresholds appear to co-vary weakly.

The authors wish to acknowledge the financial support provided by the LISP-UK project through a grant to

Da. Paterson. The coordination of the field program and onsite laboratory facilities as well as accommodation was undertaken by Drs K. Black and D. Paterson. This is LOIS publication number 400 of the LOIS Community Research Programme, carried out under a Special Topic Award from the Natural Environment Research Council.

References

AMOS, C. L. & DROPPO, I. 1996. *The stability of remediated lakebed sediment, Hamilton Harbour, Lake Ontario, Canada.* Geological Survey of Canada Open File Report No. 2276.

——, SUTHERLAND, T. F. & ZEVENHUIZEN, J. 1996*a*. The stability of sublittoral, fine-grained sediments in a subarctic estuary. *Sedimentology*, **43**, 1–19.

——, ——, T. F., RADZIJEWSKI, B. & DOUCETTE, M. 1996*b*. A rapid technique to determine bulk density of fine-grained sediments by X-ray computed tomography. *Journal of Sedimentary Research*, **66**, 1023–1039.

——, BRYLINSKY, M., LEE, S., O'BRIEN, D. 1996*c*. Littoral mudflat stability monitoring, the Humber estuary, S. Yorkshire, England. LISPUK – April 1995. *Geological Survey of Canada Open File Report* 3214: 46p.

—— & GIBSON, A. J. 1994. The stability of dredge material at dumpsite B, Miramichi Bay, New Brunswick, Canada. *Geological Survey of Canada Open File Report No.* 3020.

——, GRANT, G. R., DABORN, G. R., & BLACK, K. 1992*a*. Sea Carousel – a benthic annular flume. *Estuarine Coastal and Shelf Science*, **34**, 557–577.

——, DABORN, G. R., CHRISTIAN, H. A., ATKINSON, A. & ROBERTSON, A. 1992*b*. *In situ* erosion measurements on fine-grained sediments from the Bay of Fundy. *Marine Geology*, **108**, 175–196.

——, FEENEY, T., SUTHERLAND, T. F. & LUTERNAUER, J. L. 1997. The stability and erodibility of fine-grained sediments from the Fraser river delta. *Estuarine Coastal and Shelf Science*, **45**, 507–524.

—— & MOSHER, D. A. 1985. Erosion and deposition of fine-grained sediments from the Bay of Fundy. *Sedimentology*, **32**, 815–832.

ANDERSON, F. E. & HOWELL, B. A. 1984. Dewatering of an unvegetated muddy tidal flat during exposure – desiccation or drainage. *Estuaries*, 7, 225–232.

CHRISTIAN, H. A. 1989. Geomechanics of the Starrs Point tidal flat. *In: Littoral Investigation of Sediment Properties*. Acadia Centre for Estuarine Research Publication No. 17, 113–144.

DADE, W. B. & NOWELL, A. R. M. 1991. Moving muds in the marine environment. *In: Proceedings of Coastal Sediments 1991*. Publ. American Society of Civil Engineers, 54–71.

——, DAVIS, J. D., NICHOLS, P. D., NOWELL, A. R. M., THISTLE, D., TREXLER, M. B. & WHITE, D. C. 1990. Effects of bacterial exopolymer adhesion on the entrainment of sand. *Geomicrobiology Journal* 8, 1–16.

DISERENS, A. P., OCKENDEN, M. C. & DELO, E. A. 1993. Application of a mathematical model to investigate sedimentation at Eastham Dock, Mersey estuary. *In:* MEHTA, A. J. (ed.) *Nearshore and Estuarine Cohesive Sediment Transport.* American Geophysical Union, 486–503.

DOWNING, J. P. & BEACH, R. A. 1989. Laboratory apparatus for calibrating optical suspended solids sensors. *Marine Geology*, **86**, 243–249.

DYER, K. R. 1986. *Coastal and Estuarine Sediment Dynamics.* John Wiley & Sons, 342.

HEINZELMANN, C. & WALLISCH, S. 1991. Benthic settlement and bed erosion. A review. *Journal of Hydraulic Research*, **29**, 355–371.

KRONE, R. B. 1962. *Flume studies in the transport of sediment in estuarial shoaling processes.* Final Report, Hydraulic Engineering Laboratory and Sanitation Engineering Research Laboratory, University of California, Berkeley, USA.

LAMBE, T. W. & WHITMAN, R. V. 1969. *Soil Mechanics.* Wiley, New York.

MEHTA, A. J. & PARTHENIADES, E. 1979. Kaolinite resuspension properties. *Journal of Hydraulics Division.* American Society of Civil Engineers, **104**, 409–416.

MITCHENER, H. & TORFS, H. 1996. Erosion of mud/sand mixtures. *Coastal Engineering*, **29**, 1–25.

NOWELL, A. R. M., JUMARS, P. A. & ECKMAN, J. E. 1981. Effects of biological activity on the entrainment of marine sediments. *Marine Geology*, **42**, 133–153.

OCKENDEN, M. C. & DELO, E. A. 1988. Consolidation and erosion of estuarine mud and sand mixtures – an experimental study. Hydraulics Research Station, Wallingford Report No. SR149.

PATERSON, D. M. 1989. Short-term changes in the erodibility of intertidal cohesive sediments related to the migratory behaviour of epipelic diatoms. *Limnology and Oceanography*, **34**, 223–234.

—— & UNDERWOOD, G. J. C. 1990. The mudflat ecosystem and epipelic diatoms. *Proceedings of the Bristol Naturalists' Society*, **50**, 74–82.

——, CRAWFORD, R. M. & LITTLE, C. 1990. Subaerial exposure and changes in the stability of intertidal estuarine sediments. *Estuarine, Coastal and Shelf Science*, **30**, 541–556.

SUTHERLAND, T. F., AMOS, C. L. & GRANT, J. in press . The effects of buoyant biofilms on the erodibility of sublittoral sediments in a microtidal temperate estuary. *Limnology and Oceanography*.

TORFS, H. 1995. *Erosion of mud/sand mixtures.* Unpublished PhD Thesis, Katholeike Universitiet Leuven.

UNDERWOOD, G. J. C. & PATERSON, D. M. 1993. Seasonal changes in diatom biomass, sediment stability and biogenic stabilization in the Severn estuary. *Journal Marine Biology Association UK*, **73**, 871–887.

VOS, P. C., DE BOER, P. L. & MISDORP, R. 1988. Sediment stabilization by benthic diatoms in intertidal sandy shoals. *In:* DE BOER, P. L. *et al.* (eds) *Tide-Influenced Sandy Environments and Facies.* D. Reidel Publishing Company, 511–526.

YALLOP, M. L., DE WINTER, B., PATERSON, D. M. & STAL, L. J. 1994. Comparative structure, primary production and biogenic stabilization of cohesive and non-cohesive marine sediments inhabited by microphytobenthos. *Estuarine, Coastal and Shelf Science*, **39**, 565–582.

YINGST, J. Y. & RHOADES, D. C. 1978. Seafloor stability in central Long Island Sound: Part II. Biological interactions and their potential importance for seafloor erodibility. *In*: WILEY, M. L. (ed.) *Estuarine Interactions*. Academic Press, 245–260.

Measurements of the turbid tidal edge over the Skeffling mudflats

M. C. CHRISTIE & K. R. DYER

*Institute of Marine Studies, Plymouth University, Drake Circus,
Plymouth PL4 8AA, UK*

Abstract: The effects of wave and current action on the shallow water's edge are quantified, by describing the relationships between velocity, bed shear stress and suspended sediment concentration. Advective processes dominated the sediment fluxes. Wave effects were negligible and high concentrations were generally limited to the first few minutes of covering by the flood tide. Velocities over $0.5 \, \text{m s}^{-1}$ and concentrations above $10 \, \text{g l}^{-1}$ were measured in the advancing water's edge at this time. For depths $<1 \, \text{m}$, there was a linear relationship between concentration and velocity. An apparent erosion threshold occurred at a velocity of $0.2 \, \text{m s}^{-1}$.

Successful environmental management of estuarine intertidal regions depends upon *in situ* measurements to help specify the interactions between the active processes and so allow the development of predictive models.

The processes of erosion, deposition and consolidation are fundamental to cohesive sediment dynamics and their complex inter-relationships are not easily modelled. Accurate descriptions of these processes depend partly upon knowledge of the sediment response to hydrodynamic forcing. The interactions between the sea bed and combinations of waves and currents in shallow water (i.e. depth, $h < 1.0 \, \text{m}$) are particularly important, but not well understood. High suspended sediment concentrations are often found in the shallow edge of the tidal water which flows over a mudflat. The passage of this zone across the intertidal area can potentially deposit large quantities of suspended sediment on the upper mudflat, particularly at slack water. Conversely, waves and currents can cause significant erosion as the shallow tidal waters move across the mudflat. The waves involved in this process are often very small and can cause erosion in just a few centimetres of water (Dyer 1989). There are few field measurements of these shallow water processes due to both the difficulty of working in these locations and a lack of suitable instrumentation.

The POST system was developed to measure sediment fluxes in very shallow water (see Dyer *et al.* 1994 for specifications). POST was deployed on the Skeffling mudflats during the collaborative LISP UK field experiment from 13th to 20th April 1995. The aim was to relate sediment fluxes to physical processes, by measuring the near-bed hydrodynamics and the associated effects on the mudflat. The dominant hydrodynamic processes causing erosion could then be identified and quantified. The measurements focused on the high concentrations found in the leading edge of the tidal waters moving across the mudflat, particularly during the first few minutes of immersion by the advancing flood tide.

Methodology

POST comprised of four miniaturized electromagnetic flowmeters and four compact optical backscatter sensors (OBS), with additional inputs from conventional hydrostatic pressure and CTD instruments. The instruments were designed to measure vertical velocity and concentration profiles to within a few centimetres of the sea bed. POST was deployed from the side of a flat-bottomed boat, at four locations on a rough line ($\approx 197°$) due south of Skeffling. Seven sets of time series measurements were sampled during different tidal conditions, called Record 1–7, respectively, as summarized in Table 1. Burst mean data values were obtained from 3 minutes 47 seconds of time series, comprising 4096 data points (i.e. data recorded at 18 Hz). Variations in the sea surface elevation were calculated from the cross-shore velocity time series using linear wave theory. The significant wave height (H_s) was calculated from four times the RMS amplitude, where H_s was considered to best represent the energy in the wave field, following the approach of Madsen *et al.* (1993). Bed shear stresses due to mean flow, and the combination of waves and currents were calculated, and show the contribution of waves and currents to sediment erosion and advection.

Shear stresses due to the mean flow (τ_o) were calculated from a logarithmic velocity profile approach, thus assuming an approximately constant shear stress with height from the bed. But, in practice, many of the measured velocity

CHRISTIE, M. C. & DYER, K. R. 1998. Measurements of the turbid tidal edge over the Skeffling mudflats. *In:* BLACK, K. S., PATERSON, D. M. & CRAMP, A. (eds) *Sedimentary Processes in the Intertidal Zone.* Geological Society, London, Special Publications, **139**, 45–55.

Table 1. *Position, flow conditions and Record number for all measurements*

Station	Tidal level of station	Tidal conditions during Record	Record nos	Date	GPS position of POST (in Lat. and Long.)
A	High shore	Flood and ebb	2	14/4/95 pm	053°38.423′N
		Flood	3	15/4/95 am	000°04.138′E
B	Upper mid-shore	Ebb	4	18/4/95 pm	053°38.193′N
		Flood	5	19/4/95 am	000°04.091′E
C	Lower mid-shore	Flood	1	13/4/95 pm	053°37.997′N
					000°03.876′E
D	Low shore	Ebb	6	20/4/95 am	053°37.445′N
		Flood	7	20/4/95 pm	000°03.840′E

profiles did not show a logarithmic form. Thus, the mean velocity value from one of the near bed sensors was used to calculate τ_o by fitting an assumed logarithmic profile to this one velocity value, finding the depth mean velocity value, and using a value for the roughness length (z_o) of 0.2 mm (from Soulsby 1997).

Bed shear stresses due the combination of waves and currents (τ_{wc}) were obtained from a parameterization of Huynh-Tanh & Temperville's (1991) kinetic energy and mixing length (KL) model, where eddy viscosity is related to the mean turbulent energy by a length scale. Flow conditions during the POST measurements were considered to be current dominated. This flow description followed a method of Soulsby & Humphery (1990) who used the ratio of the RMS horizontal velocity and the total horizontal velocity to define when the current-related drag coefficient was enhanced by wave activity. The Huynh-Tanh & Temperville (1991) model, chosen as an intercomparison of wave and current interaction models by Soulsby *et al.* (1993), shows good agreement of the Huynh-Tanh & Temperville (1991) method with other model behaviour for current dominated conditions. The time invariant eddy viscosity approach of Grant & Madsen (1979) was not used to describe the wave and current interaction, because Soulsby *et al.* (1993) showed for current dominated conditions the Grant & Madsen (1979) model produced distinctly different results to the other methods.

The shear stress calculations were performed using version 1.0 of H.R. Wallingford's SANDCALC software which uses Fortran routines to parameterize the Huynh-Tanh & Temperville (1991) model.

Regression analysis was used to examine relationships between the measured and calculated variables, such that suspended sediment concentration could be predicted from other physical parameters. The 'least squares' method was used to calculate a straight line (95% confidence) that best fitted the data, where the dependent Y value was a function of the independent X value(s). An 'adjusted' correlation coefficient (R^2) removed any bias in the data, with values tending towards 1 indicating a good fit and a meaningful relationship.

Results

Sea breezes were unable to generate significant local wave activity during deployments of POST. The sea surface was calmest at the beginning and end of mudflat immersion, with significant wave activity usually only occurring as the depth increased. This served to reduce the eroding effects of any wave activity, as the near bed orbital velocities were invariably very small at all stages of immersion.

Water temperature and salinities were measured every 10 min. Salinity values were relatively consistent throughout the study period, with values from *c.* 31 to 33. Water temperatures ranged from 6 to 9°C. Salinity and temperature gradients were not considered to be important in the behaviour of the turbid water's edge.

Mean velocity and concentration

Representative data from the whole study period are described by the following sections, predominantly using Record 2 (see Table 1) for illustration, as this record included both flood and ebb periods. All the figures show data from sensors when completely covered by water. Where appropriate, the sensor heights above the bed are given by the figure legends. There were onshore flows in excess of $0.25\,\mathrm{m\,s^{-1}}$ during the first hour of flood coverage for all records. The mudflat gradient varied between 1:800 to 1:1000 between the neap high water and neap low water marks, such that Stations A–D (see earlier site description paper) were positioned on gently sloping mudflat. The strong onshore flows resulted from the 7 m tidal range and the wide intertidal region. The tidal waters had roughly 6 h to cross c. 5 km of mudflat between low and high water levels, requiring a mean current speed of $0.23\,\mathrm{m\,s^{-1}}$. Maximum flow speeds would thus be expected to occur around the mid-tide level, corresponding to stations C and D.

Typical mean velocity and depth data are shown in Fig. 1. These data were recorded at station A, about two hours either side of the local high water (at 17:42 hrs), from 15:56 to 20:06 hrs. Both the end of the flood, and the beginning of the ebb phase of the tidal cycle were sampled. Maximum current speeds of $0.32\,\mathrm{m\,s^{-1}}$ (towards 035°) were measured at the start of the record. The onshore flow then decreased to a minimum of $0.02\,\mathrm{m\,s^{-1}}$ before high water. As depths increased (i.e. $h > 0.80\,\mathrm{m}$), the current direction veered slowly to the south-east. After high water, the current flowed alongshore ($\approx 145°$) and the flow speed increased to c. $0.40\,\mathrm{m\,s^{-1}}$. This ebb flow remained steady until all the sensors were exposed at c. 20:06 hrs. The corresponding mean concentration data are

shown in Fig. 2. Concentrations peaked at about $0.65\,\mathrm{g\,L^{-1}}$ in shallow water ($h < 0.5\,\mathrm{m}$). Values decreased to c. $0.37\,\mathrm{g\,l^{-1}}$ during the high water period. The change in concentration was extremely marked during the first few minutes of the flood phase. This can be clearly seen in time series from Record 3, obtained at Station A, on the upper mudflat. Approximately three minutes of concentration time series data from the two lowest OBS are shown by Fig. 3. During this time, the leading edge of the flood water flowed steadily onshore at over $0.60\,\mathrm{m\,s^{-1}}$, from 04:14 to 04:22 hrs. The lowest OBS (at 10.5 cm above the bed) was completely covered at 04:14.15 hrs and concentrations exceeded $7.0\,\mathrm{g\,l^{-1}}$ ($h < 0.12\,\mathrm{m}$). These high concentrations decreased in 90 s to below $2.0\,\mathrm{g\,l^{-1}}$ with the continued rise in water level ($h \approx 0.21\,\mathrm{m}$). The second lowest OBS (at 17 cm) was covered at 04:16.08 hrs. OBS 3 at 26 cm above the bed (not shown in Fig. 3) was completely covered at 04:19.09 hrs. Concentrations continued to decrease but at a much lower rate than during the first two minutes of coverage. The high concentrations in the leading water's edge were considered to be from the resuspension of a surface biofilm. This weak layer was considered to be partly the result of deposition during the previous ebb cycle, and the movements of micro organisms and other biological activity during emmersion of the mudflat. Algal layers and

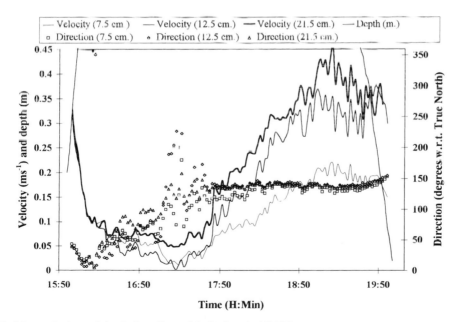

Fig. 1. Mean velocity and depth data. Record 2. Station A, 14/4/95.

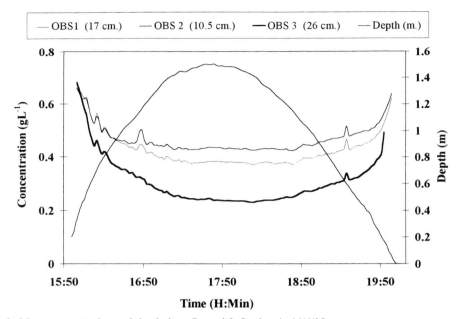

Fig. 2. Mean concentration and depth data. Record 2. Station A, 14/4/95.

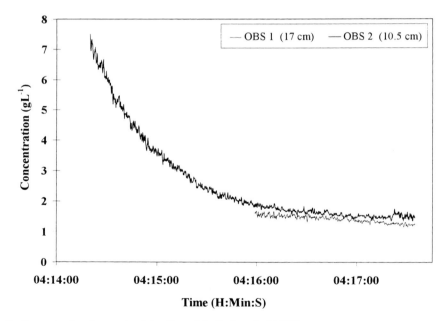

Fig. 3. Concentration time series data. Record 3. Station A, 14/4/95.

other organic debris appeared to be lifted off the sediment surface by the advancing water and it is thought that this suspended material produced the high concentrations within the shallow water's fringe (when $h > 0.25$ m). It is probable that the suspended material would settle at a higher location as the tidal velocities decreased. The rapidly rising water covered the highest OBS (at 39.5 cm above the bed) $c.$ 9 mins after the lowest sensor.

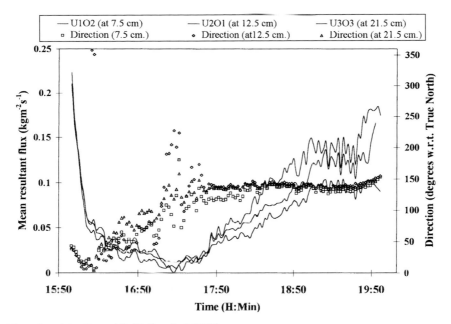

Fig. 4. Mean flux data. Record 2. Station A, 14/4/95.

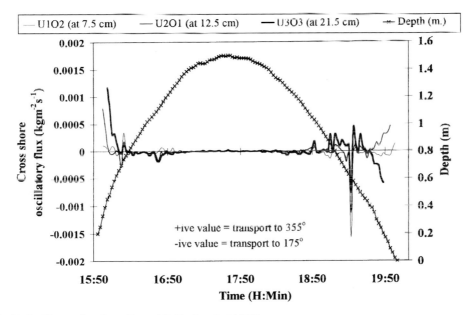

Fig. 5. Oscillatory flux data. Record 2. Station A, 14/4/95.

Sediment fluxes

Typical sediment fluxes (calculated from 3 minutes 47 seconds of time series) are shown by Figs 4 and 5. Generally, for the whole data set, the mean fluxes ($\overline{u}\overline{c}$) were about two orders of magnitude greater than the oscillatory fluxes (calculated directly from the time series as $\overline{u'c'}$), because the tidal currents dominated the erosion and transport of sediment.

The oscillatory flux directions were largely random, and magnitudes were greatest in shallow

water as near-bed wave effects were most significant at these times. There were also peaks in
oscillatory flux in deeper water, as for example at
19:25 hrs in Fig. 5. In this case examination of
the raw time series showed there was an increase
in concentrations, by about $200 \, \text{mg} \, \text{l}^{-1}$ for 25 s,
measured by the lowest three OBS. This type of
concentration variation produced peaks in the
oscillatory flux which were due to advection of
high concentrations passed the sensors. The
surface waves during the study period had a
negligible effect on the net sediment flux.

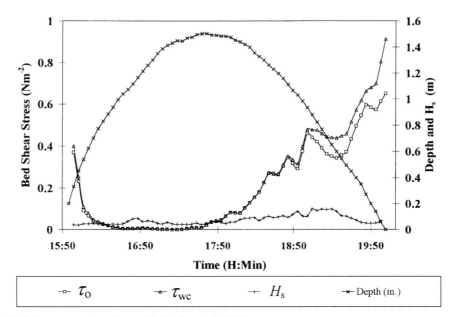

Fig. 6. Bed shear stress data. Record 2. Station A, 14/4/95.

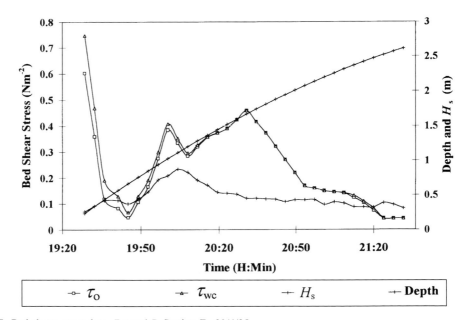

Fig. 7. Bed shear stress data. Record 7. Station D, 20/4/95.

Bed shear stresses

The bed shear stresses were dominated by the mean flows, and the calculated mean values of τ_o and τ_{wc} were very similar, showing that the τ_{wc} values were not significantly enhanced by the wave contribution. Ursell parameters were calculated for the whole data set and these values showed that linear wave theory was suitable for water depths in excess of 0.25 m, remembering that the hydrodynamics were considered to be predominantly current dominated.

Figures 6 and 7 show typical mean bed shear stresses due to currents τ_o and the combination of waves and currents τ_{wc}. The significant wave height (H_s) is also plotted in the same figures. For Record 2 the first twenty minutes of covering were not recorded and Fig. 6 shows shear stresses exceeded 0.4 N m^{-2} during early covering and after high water (at around 18:30 hrs onwards, when ebb flow speeds exceeded 0.25 m s^{-1}). Similar results were also obtained when the first minutes of immersion were measured (i.e. during Records 1, 3, 5 and 7). Figure 7 shows bed shear stresses for Record 7 reached 0.7 N m^{-2} immediately after immersion. Shear stresses of this magnitude would be sufficient to cause erosion of the sediment surface. For all the POST data the bed shear stresses during the early flood covering exceeded the critical shear stress for erosion (τ_c) of about 0.22 N m^{-2} as measured at Skeffling by Williamson (1996) and for much of the time exceeded $\tau_c \approx 0.7$ N m^{-2} as measured by Amos et al. (1996). Erosion was considered to occur when the bed shear stress exceeded τ_c and thus erosion was taken to be limited to the shallow water ($h < 0.5$ m) periods, whilst in deeper water, advective processes dominated.

Linear regression analysis of shallow water data (i.e. $h < 1.0$ m)

Some strong relationships between mean concentration and tidal conditions were identified for all of the flood data. The best expressions for relating concentration to near bed processes were obtained by examining data from the lowest OBS. With distance away from the bed, all relationships became less distinct because of mixing and the time lags between concentration variations in the upper water column and bed shear stresses.

There were simple inverse relationships between mean concentration and depth for all of our data, from both flood and ebb conditions ($h < 1.0$ m). Table 2 summarizes the expressions which varied considerably between the individual tides because of differences in background concentrations and the rate of change of depth, depending on position upon the mudflat. Figure 8 shows a characteristic scatter graph for one of the relationships in Table 2. There were only a few mean concentration points (c. 15) per expression as the shallow water period was relatively short lived. Nonetheless, good R^2 coefficients (≥ 0.830) were obtained for all flood data.

From in situ observations, there was a clear relationship between mean velocity (U) and concentration within 15 cm of the bed. This was particularly apparent for the early stages of the flood phase, with concentrations being directly correlated to flow speed. This relationship could be quantified for each record by simple correlations between concentration and either U, τ_o and τ_{wc} (remembering for the current dominated flow, $\tau_o \approx \tau_{wc}$). Table 3 shows the linear relationships between concentration within 11 cm of the

Table 2. *Linear regressions of mean concentration with depth ($h < 1.0$ m)*

Record nos and station	Dependent variable	Coefficient for the independent variable FLOOD CONDITIONS	Intercept c	Adjusted R^2 value
1C	$C_{24.5}$	−0.259	0.690	0.830
2A	$C_{10.5}$	−2.858	2.245	0.964
3A	$C_{10.5}$	−1.230	1.628	0.964
5B	$C_{7.5}$	−1.157	1.321	0.922
7D	$C_{9.5}$	−0.822	1.045	0.963

Record nos and station	Dependent variable	Coefficient for the independent variable EBB CONDITIONS	Intercept c	Adjusted R^2 value
2A	$C_{10.5}$	−1.972	1.4307	0.606
4B	C_7	−0.935	1.4250	0.918
6D	$C_{9.5}$	−2.980	1.9724	0.876

where C_x is the concentration at a height x cm above the bed.

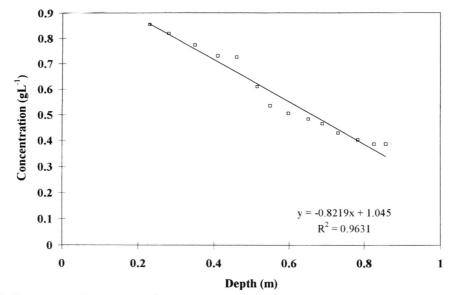

Fig. 8. Concentration depth relationship. Record 7. Station D, 20/4/95.

Table 3. *Linear regressions of concentration and flood flow* (h < 1.0 m)

Tide nos and station	Independent variable	Coefficient for the independent variable	Intercept c	Adjusted R^2 value
3A	U	1.548	0.320	0.950
	τ_o	0.553	0.664	0.979
	τ_{wc}	0.539	0.649	0.979
5B	U	2.253	0.174	0.862
	τ_o	1.747	0.441	0.934
	τ_{wc}	1.707	0.442	0.934
7D	U	1.246	0.307	0.730
	τ_o	1.111	0.465	0.664
	τ_{wc}	1.086	0.465	0.664

bed and the flow parameters U, τ_o and τ_{wc}, obtained during the flood phase ($h < 1.0$ m) of Records 3, 5 and 7 at stations A, B and D across the mudflat. Flood data from Station C (Record 1) were not included in Table 3, as near bed concentrations were not measured because the height of the lowest sensor was at 24.5 cm. Data from Record 2 was also excluded as measurements only started when the water depth exceeded 0.25 m. Significant correlations were not obtained (i.e. $R^2 < 0.600$) between concentration and oscillatory flow, or any of the wave shear stress parameters as wave activity was low.

The clearest association in Table 3 was found to exist for station A and became less distinct with distance offshore. This was due to two factors. The first was simply the accumulation of suspended sediment in the leading edge of the tidal water. The concentrations in the leading water's edge appeared to increase as the water flowed onshore because more material was resuspended (i.e. $\tau_o > \tau_c$) than deposited. Secondly, the larger bedforms lower down the mudflat at stations C and D reduced the relationships between flow and concentration obtained from this data set. Erosion of a surface biofilm by the flood tide would produce the high concentrations measured in the fringe of the rapidly advancing water's edge. This high concentration, longshore band was moved onshore while depths were less than 0.5 m. The larger bedforms served to channel these concentrations, and at stations C and D the maximum concentrations were observed within the channel troughs. However, it was not possible to record these high concentrations as the POST frame had to be placed on top of the channel ridges. Further up the mudflat the bedforms became much smaller and POST was able to measure the high concentrations close to the flat, smooth mudflat. So the data obtained from the upper mudflat better represent the velocities and high concentrations of the leading water's edge.

Data from the ebb phase were sampled at the end of Record 2, and during Records 4 and 6. Concentrations doubled during the last half hour of immersion (when $h < 1.0$ m) for each of these three records. This increase in concentration was consistent for the study period but could not be related clearly to either flow speed or bed shear stresses. Flow speeds varied considerably during the last hour of the ebb tide, and both accelerating and decelerating flows were measured while concentrations increased. The general trend was for flow direction to veer directly offshore as water depths decreased below 1.0 m. The increase in the amount of suspended sediment was not considered to be due to erosion as such, but more simply the result of accumulation and enhanced vertical mixing of near bed suspensions in the shallows at the end of the ebb flow.

Multiple regression analysis of shallow water data

Multiple regression analysis was used in an attempt to identify significant groups of factors that controlled suspended sediment variations. The clearest relationships were again obtained when depths were less than 1.0 m. Near-bed concentrations were correlated against appropriate combinations of mean velocity, depth, wind speed, wave height, orbital velocity, τ_o and τ_{wc}. Good expressions were obtained relating concentration to a combination of H_s/h and wave orbital velocity. Probability (P) values <0.01 indicated both variables were very significant in determining concentration. But, these results do not provide reliable predictions of concentration when small wave conditions prevail. This is because both H_s/h, and orbital velocity were directly related to depth, and were not independent. It was the concentration/depth relationship which produced the strong relationship between concentration, H_s/h and orbital velocity. More data, from periods with larger waves, would help verify if there is a relationship between wave parameters and concentration under wave dominated conditions.

The best expression relating concentration to the local hydrodynamics was simply that between near bed concentration within 10 cm of the bed (i.e. C_{10} in $g\,l^{-1}$) and the mean current

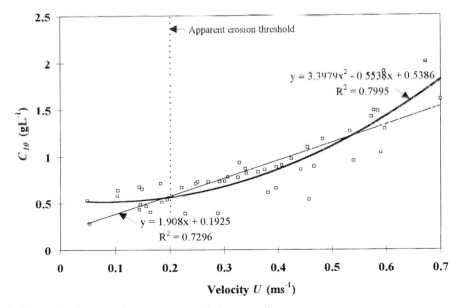

Fig. 9. Scatter plot for general concentration velocity expression.

velocity (in $m s^{-1}$). By taking all the data used for the velocity relationships shown for tides 3, 5 and 7 in Table 3, linear and polynomial expressions were obtained such that:

$$C_{10} = 1.908U + 0.193 \qquad R^2 = 0.730 \qquad (1)$$

or

$$C_{10} = 3.3979U^2 - 0.5538U + 0.5386$$

$$R^2 = 0.799 \qquad (2)$$

The scatter of data for these two relationships is shown by Fig. 9 and the expressions were applicable for shallow ($h < 1.0\,m$) current dominated, flood tide conditions, across the upper half of the mudflat. An apparent erosion threshold was estimated to occur at $c.\,0.2\,m\,s^{-1}$.

Conclusions

(1) During the study period, the sea state was generally calm, and the weather conditions were mild and dry with moderate wind speeds. The flow conditions were predominately current driven and erosion due to wave activity was minimal. This is a slightly unusual result which occurred because of the combination of rapid cross shore flows and the calm sea state. However it is important to realize that storm events and waves would probably play an important role in the morphological dynamics of the intertidal regions, producing much larger bed level changes than typical seasonal variations. These sorts of extreme, episodic conditions were not measured by this study.

(2) The shear stresses were dominated by the mean tidal flows with maximum values of τ_o around $0.7\,N\,m^{-2}$ during the flood phase ($h < 1.0\,m$). Bed shear stresses were at a minimum at slack water.

(3) Any local erosion of the mudflat was largely due to the mean flows, and occurred during the first and last half hour of tidal coverage. Maximum velocities and concentrations were recorded at all sample sites at these times. Maximum flood currents across the mudflat reached $0.60\,m\,s^{-1}$ (during the first few minutes of immersion), and these onshore flows seemed to resuspend any low density surface biofilm. The strong flood currents produced a clearly visible, highly turbid, longshore shallow water fringe (when $h < 0.3\,m$), which was advected onshore over the mudflat. High concentrations also occurred during the ebb phase (when $h < 0.75\,m$, which were attributed to mixing of high concentration near bed suspensions formed by settling over slack water.

(4) Generally for $h < 1\,m$, current speeds were inversely related to depth. Concentrations were directly related to speed, and hence inversely related to depth. Different concentration values occurred for the same current speed at different sites and each expression was site specific.

(5) It was difficult to define a mean expression because of daily environmental variations, different sample locations and the associated changes in the rate of rise of the tide. The most useful overall relationship was simply that between the near-bed concentrations C_{10} (in $g\,l^{-1}$) and the mean tidal flow U (in $m\,s^{-1}$) during the flood phase ($h < 1.0\,m$). Where a simple linear relationship was defined as [equation (1)]: $C_{10} = 1.908U + 0.193$ ($R^2 = 0.730$).

(6) Care must be taken to apply the basic relationships from the regression analysis for the appropriate environmental conditions. Daily variations inevitably produced different reltionships, with changes in one variable altering other factors. The net result can be a marked difference in the response of a mudflat to tidal coverage. A variety of expressions are thus required to comprehensively quantify and model natural intertidal zone sediment dynamics.

(7) For the Skeffling data, there were no correlations between suspended sediment concentration and measured environmental parameters such as sunshine, cloud cover, humidity, temperature, pressure, surface sediment properties (moisture content and shear strength). But, all of these environmental parameters can alter the erosion potential of a mudflat and affect suspended sediment concentrations in shallow water. However, such environmental parameters are generally of less importance than the dominant hydrodynamics and sediment bed properties in determining mudflat morphology. The poor relationships with the environmental parameters were due in part to the limited data available for some of these parameters as well as the complex interdependent relationships which existed between all the variables.

(8) It is postulated that during calm conditions a cross-shore cycle of material was driven by the mean horizontal flows in the Spurn Bight, resulting in slow accretion rates across the upper mudflat. It was thought that wave activity contributed infrequently to the tidal resuspension of sediment. Historically, there has been net accretion over the upper mudflats, with an annual bed level change of about a few millimetres (De Boer 1979). Seasonal variations (particularly in biology) are likely to provide secondary controls on this cycle. Further long term studies would allow the influence of changes in tidal range, season and episodic storm events to be related to the

sediment fluxes and net sediment transport, and accretion rates could be further quantified.

This is LOIS publication number 398 of the LOIS Community Research Programme, carried out under a Special Topic Award from the Natural Environment Research Council.

References

AMOS, C. L., BRYLINSKI, M., LEE, S. & O'BRIEN, D. 1996. *Littoral mudflat stability monitoring, the Humber estuary, S. Yorkshire, England. LISP-UK, April 1995.* Geological Survey of Canada Open file report No. 3214.

DE BOER, G. 1979. History and general features of the estuary. *In: The Humber Estuary* – a selection of papers on present knowledge of the estuary and it's future potential given at two symposia arranged by the Humber Advisory Group and the University of Hull. NERC Publications Series C, Number 20. January 1979, p. 1–4.

DYER, K. R. 1989. Sediment processes in estuaries. future research requirements. *Journal of Geophysical Research*, **94**, 14 327–14 339.

——, CHRISTIE, M. C., GRIFFITHS, J. & QUARTLEY, C. 1994. *Measurement of mud transport in very shallow water.* Energy Technology Support Unit (ETSU) report T/04/00148/REP, on behalf of the Dept of Trade and Industry.

GRANT, W. D. & MADSEN, O. S. 1979. Combined wave and current interaction with a rough bottom. *Journal of Geophysical Research*, **84**, 1797–1808.

HUYNH-TANH, S. & TEMPERVILLE, A. 1991. A numerical model of the rough turbulent boundary layer in combined wave and current interaction. *In:* SOULSBY, R. L. & BETTEES, R. (eds) *Euromech 262 – Sand Transport in Rivers, Estuaries and the Sea.* Balkema, Rotterdam.

MADSEN, O. S., WRIGHT, L. D., BOON, J. D. & CHISHOSLM, T. A. 1993. Wind stress, bed roughness and sediment suspension on the inner shelf during an extreme storm event. *Journal of Continental Shelf Research*, **13**, 1303 1324.

SOULSBY, R. L. 1997. *Dynamics of marine sands: a manual for practical applications.* HR Wallingford Report SR 466, October 1994 (to be published by Thomas Telford publishers).

——, HAMM, L., KLOPMAN, G., MYRHAUG, D., SIMONS, R. R. & THOMAS, G. P. 1993. Wave current interaction within and outside the bottom boundary layer. *Coastal Engineering*, **21**, 41–69.

—— & HUMPHERY, J. D. 1990. Field observations of wave current interaction at the sea bed. *In:* TORMUN, A. & GUDMESTAD, O. T. (eds) *Water Wave Mechanics.* Kluwar Academic Publishers, Netherlands, 413 428.

WILLIAMSON, H. J. 1996. *In situ measurement of shear stress.* LISP-LOIS RACS (C) Special Topic 122. Preliminary Results. Compiled by K. Black and D. Paterson, March 1996.

In situ characterization of suspended particles using focused-beam, laser reflectance particle sizing

D. J. LAW[1,2] & A. J. BALE[1]

[1] *CCMS Plymouth Marine Laboratory, Prospect Place, West Hoe, Plymouth PL1 3DH, UK*
[2] *School of Ocean Sciences, University of Wales, Bangor, Menai Bridge, Gwynedd, LL59 5EY*

Abstract: Measurements of the size distribution of suspended particles were made as part of the LISP (UK) experiment using a novel, *in situ* instrument which employs focused-beam, laser reflectance. Data were acquired over three complete, ebb-flood tidal cycles at two stations possessing different elevations on the intertidal mudflat. The reflectance method, which employs a physical arrangement similar to optical back-scatter sensors for measuring the concentration of suspended particulate matter (SPM), measures sediment particles in the size range 2–1000 μm with negligible disruption to fragile aggregates and can operate over the wide range of SPM concentrations found in estuaries. The results indicated that the median sizes (D_{50}) of particle populations over the intertidal mud flats were relatively constant at 60–100 μm even during mild erosion and resuspension events caused by ebb and flood tides. However, populations with D_{50} values of up to 300 μm were seen at one station within the ridge-runnel systems during resuspension. These large aggregates were attributed to the particularly 'mobile' sediment in that environment and to increased biodeposition. In general, variations in the size characteristics of particles measured *in situ* were consistent with the properties of the underlying substrate. Measured sizes compared well with values determined by direct video-microscope observation.

Intertidal mudflats in estuaries are sites of sediment accumulation, many of which have reached an approximate steady state with respect to sea level following the Flandrian transgression (Dyer 1986). However, on shorter time scales, estuarine mudflats undergo sediment cycling in response to wave, tide (de Jonge & van Beusekom 1995) and seasonal or climatic (Bale et al. 1985; Lucotte & d'Anglejan 1986) influences. There is a pressing need to understand the factors which control the short-term behaviour of estuarine sediments because of their environmental and ecological importance, and because estuaries tend to be industrialized and subject to environmental pressure.

The key factor determining the long-term stability of intertidal mudflats is the dynamic balance between erosion and deposition. Erosion of cohesive sediment is complex, being influenced by both biological and physical factors. As such, the topic has received considerable attention over recent years (Postma 1967; Owen 1976a) and formed a major component of the UK Littoral Investigation of Sediment Properties (LISP) experiment. This paper looks at factors influencing particle resuspension and deposition, and reports our measurements of the size characteristics of suspended particles in relation to current velocity, suspended load, and the physical and biological properties of the sediment. Particle sizes influence sedimentation and transport over intertidal areas and are therefore an important component of sediment dynamics modelling studies.

In natural waters, it is known that particle sizes are not constant but change continuously; either increasing as particles aggregate (Eisma et al. 1991; Fennessy et al. 1994) or decreasing as the aggregates are broken up by turbulent shear. In the estuarine environment, cyclical aggregation and breakage tends to result in fragile entities which are difficult to measure without breaking them into smaller aggregates which no longer reflect the true size distribution of the population (Gibbs & Konwar 1982, 1983; Bale & Morris 1987). Because of this fragile nature, various methods of characterizing size and settling rates, which minimize the disturbance associated with sampling, have been developed. These have included sedimentation tubes, generically known as Owen tubes, which are deployed and recovered horizontally before turning them to the vertical to initiate the settling phase (Owen 1976b; Pejrup & Edelvang 1996), Owen tubes combined with video image-analysis (Dearnaley 1996), various *in situ* camera and video devices (Fennessy et al. 1994; Milligan 1996; Eisma & Kalf 1996; van Leussen & Cornelisse, 1996) and laser diffraction systems (Bale & Morris 1987; Agrawal & Pottsmith

LAW, D. J. & BALE, A. J. 1998. *In situ* characterization of suspended particles using focused-beam, laser reflectance particle sizing. *In*: BLACK, K. S., PATERSON, D. M. & CRAMP, A. (eds) *Sedimentary Processes in the Intertidal Zone*. Geological Society, London, Special Publications, **139**, 57–68.

1994; Gentien *et al.* 1995; Van der Lee this volume). Whilst the advantages of non-disruptive, *in situ* observation of aggregates have been clearly demonstrated (Bale & Morris 1987), none of these devices is capable of rapid, real-time observations at high SPM loads ($>1\,g\,l^{-1}$). In this paper, we describe the characterization of suspended particles over the LISP (UK) sites using a focused-beam reflectance apparatus which is capable of measuring particle sizes *in situ* at particle concentrations up to $50\,g\,l^{-1}$.

Instrumentation

The instrument used in this study was a focused-beam reflectance device produced by Lasentec Inc., (Redmond, WA 98052) which has recently been adapted for direct *in situ* observations in estuaries (Law *et al.* 1997). The instrument measures particle sizes by timing the period of the backscattered pulse generated when a scanning laser beam intersects a particle (Fig. 1). A laser diode and rotating lens provide high power ($2 \times 10^{10}\,W\,m^{-2}$) at the focal point ($0.8 \times 2.0\,\mu m$). As the scanning speed is assumed to be fast ($2\,m\,s^{-1}$) relative to the particle movement, the pulse duration is dependent only on the size of the particle. The instrument sizes particles in the range $2{-}1000\,\mu m$ in 38, logarithmically-sized channels and, using only a single optical window, causes minimal disruption to fragile aggregates. This system provides data in near real time and can work in particle

concentrations up to $50\,g\,l^{-1}$. The sizing method is based only on the period of the back-scattered pulse and not on pulse intensity, so is largely independent of the nature of the particles. The only discrimination employed is based on the 'rise times' of the backscattered signal and acts to exclude signals from particles intersected outside the focal point.

Site and methods

The LISP UK sampling stations were sited along a shore-normal transect within the Spurn Bight, close to Skeffling (Fig. 2). The stations span the region from just below the mean HW mark (Station A) to about the mid tide level (Station D). Because of the requirement for electrical power, our particle size measurements were only made at the two seaward stations (C & D) from a barge which took the ground over low water. Size distributions were measured 10 cm above the bed every few minutes on the ebb until water depth fell below the sensor and again on the flood tide once the water had returned.

Current velocity profiles were measured using an array of 10, Ott current meters (five facing upstream, five facing downstream) attached to a vertical mast at different heights above the bed. The lower sensors (at 10–17 cm elevation) corresponded to the elevation of the particle sizer. The current meters were operated for one minute in every ten and the velocity averaged over the minute (Black pers. comm.). SPM

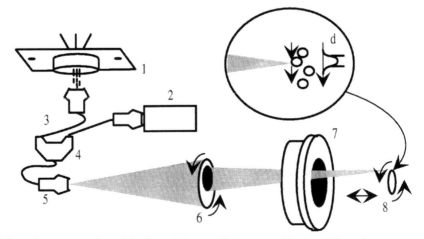

Fig. 1. Schematic representation of the focused-beam reflectance particle sizer. The main components are: (1) laser diode, (2) photo detector, (3) fibre optic link, (4) beam splitter, (5) laser launcher/collector, (6) eccentrically rotating lens, (7) saphire/titanium window and (8) scanning focal point. The inset figure represents the interaction of the laser beam with a particle at the focal point to give a reflected light pulse of duration *d*.

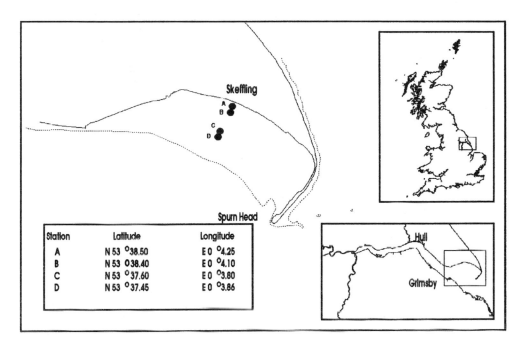

Fig. 2. Map of the Spurn Bight on the north shore of the Humber Estuary showing the location of the LISP stations.

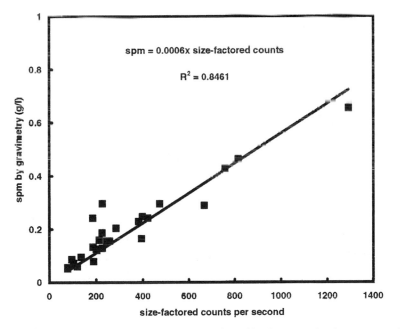

Fig. 3. Multiple regression of the particle sizer counts (number of back-scattered pulses per second) and distribution median size, against gravimetric analyses of suspended solids ($n = 27$) measured by C. Bull (Bangor).

concentrations were derived from a multiple regression of the particle count obtained by the particle sizer with the D_{50} of the size distribution of the particles against gravimetric data (Fig. 3).

Results

Measurements of the size spectra of suspended particles were obtained with the laser reflectance particle sizer at Station C on the 4th and 7th April, and at Station D on the 6th April (Fig. 2). The stations were occupied from about high tide, or just afterwards, through the ebb until the barge grounded shortly after half-tide, at which

time the sediment became exposed. Measurements were resumed when the flood tide had risen sufficiently to inundate the mud and cover the various sensors, and continued until the following high water. Throughout this series of observations the tidal range at the port of Immingham decreased from 5.8 m on the 4th to 3.8 m on the 7th April (bottom panel, Fig. 4). For comparison, the mean spring and neap ranges for Immingham are given as 6.4 m and 3.2 m, respectively. The wind speed measured at Spurn Head was mostly light ($2-4\,\mathrm{m\,s^{-1}}$) on the 4th and 6th, but increased to $8\,\mathrm{m\,s^{-1}}$ on the 7th April (top panel, Fig. 4). The wind direction on the 4th veered from predominantly northerly

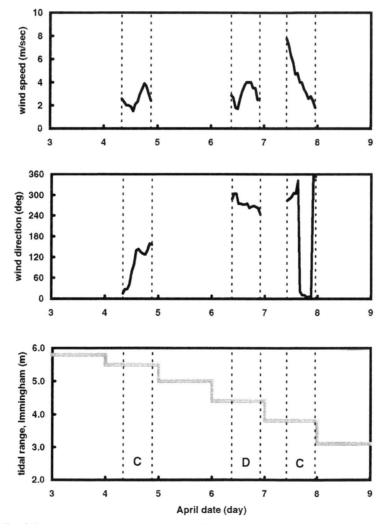

Fig. 4. Details of the wind strength (upper panel) and direction (centre panel) recorded at Spurn Head and the predicted tidal range at Immingham (lower panel) for the three periods in early April when particle size measurements were made on the LISP Stations, C and D.

through to southerly during the course of the day making the study sites mostly sheltered until the end of the day (centre panel, Fig. 4). On the 6th and 7th, the study site was more exposed to the wind which was predominantly from the west or north west, particularly on the 7th when the wind speed was greatest, but the direction became northerly and off-shore toward the latter part of the 7th as the wind speed fell.

Examples of the size spectra obtained at each station arc given in Fig. 5. At Stations C and D on the 4th and 6th April, respectively, the spectra are very similar throughout the tidal cycles and on the two days (top and centre panels, Fig. 5). Particle sizes measured on these days fell in the range $10–300\,\mu m$ with modes centred around $100\,\mu m$. Only at the very end of the ebb on the 4th were different size distributions observed and these tended to contain smaller particles (top panel, Fig. 6) where modes fell to $40\,\mu m$. At Station C on the 7th, the range of spectra measured was much greater; the smallest size distributions were smaller or similar to those measured on the 4th and 6th

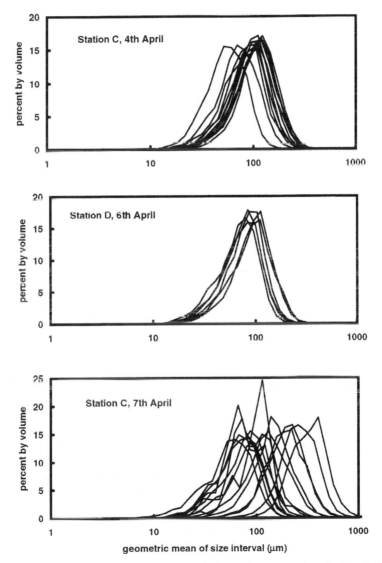

Fig. 5. Examples of particle size spectra obtained at 30 min intervals or approximately 1 in 5 of the measurements. The upper and middle panels are Stations C and D on the flat, intertidal region whereas the lower panel shows data obtained at Station C within the ridge-runnel systems.

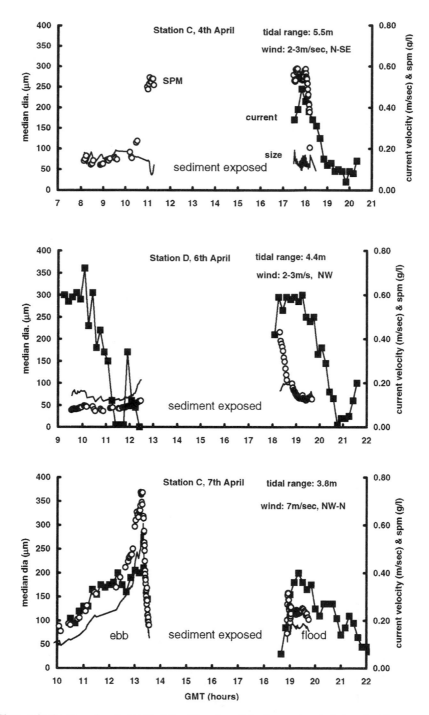

Fig. 6. Changes in the D_{50} values (solid black line) for all particle size spectra plotted against time over each tidal cycle with the corresponding SPM concentrations (open circles) and 1 in 10 min current velocity averages (solid squares). NB: (1) Current velocity data were not available for the ebb tide on the 4th April but SPM concentrations were similar on ebb and flood suggesting that the velocity profile was also symetrical. (2) The D_{50} values on the flood tides at C and D on the 6th and 7th, respectively, are partly masked by SPM data but fall in the range $60–100\,\mu$m on both occasions.

but, co-incident with resuspension on the ebb, much larger particles were present with distributions which ranged from $100-1000\,\mu m$ and modes of $300-400\,\mu m$ (bottom panel, Fig. 5).

The variation in particle size, plotted as D_{50} values, over the tidal cycles and their relation to current velocity and SPM values are summarized in Fig. 6. At Station C on the 4th, the tidal range was 5.0 m and the maximum velocity measured on the flood was $0.5\,m\,s^{-1}$. There was no current data available for the ebb period on the 4th although the concentration of SPM measured towards the end of the ebb increased from $0.15\,g\,l^{-1}$ to $c.\,0.55\,g\,l^{-1}$ indicating that just before the sediment became exposed, it was subject to erosion by increased stress. Throughout this cycle the D_{50} value changed only slightly, ranging mostly from 60 to $80\,\mu m$ but falling to $40\,\mu m$ for a while when SPM concentrations maximized on the ebb. On the flood, the SPM values reached $0.50-0.60\,g\,l^{-1}$ for nearly 1 h but the D_{50} of the size distributions, measured concurrently, ranged only from 50 to $80\,\mu m$.

Station D was the most seaward site. On the 6th April the tidal range was only 4.0 m, although the maximum current velocities were greater than those on the 4th at Station C. At Station D, a peak velocity of $0.6\,m\,s^{-1}$ was recorded on the ebb and flood tides, possibly because of greater water depth there at mid tide compared with Station C. SPM concentrations were low on the ebb, barely exceeding $0.10\,g\,l^{-1}$ except for the last half hour before the sediment became uncovered. Station D exhibited a decoupling of current velocity and tidal elevation. On the ebb the velocity fell to zero almost one hour before the sediment was exposed, although it subsequently increased for a short time in the last half hour. The D_{50} of the particles in suspension fell slightly from $c.\,80$ to $60\,\mu m$ but increased to $120\,\mu m$ as the SPM concentration increased in the last half hour before the sediment was exposed. At this station the initial flood corresponded more closely to the time of maximum currents in the main channel; velocities in the first 10 min increased from 0.4 to $0.6\,m\,s^{-1}$ and stayed at that level for over an hour. Sediment was initially eroded and SPM concentrations of $0.50\,g\,l^{-1}$ were recorded, although levels fell quickly to concentrations below $0.20\,g\,l^{-1}$ even though the current velocity remained high for another hour. The size change in the suspended particles followed the change in SPM concentration with D_{50} values initially rising to $c.\,80\,\mu m$ and levelling off while suspended solids concentrations fell rapidly, reducing to values of $60-70\,\mu m$ once SPM values had minimized.

A second set of data was obtained at Station C on 7th April but the sediment properties recorded at this time were quite different to those obtained on the 4th (bottom panel, Fig. 6). The tidal range on the 7th was 3.8 m, which is close to the tabulated value for the mean neap tide at Immingham, and the ebb and flood peak current values were proportionally lower at $c.\,0.4\,m\,s^{-1}$. However, the erosion of sediment on the ebb on this day was considerably more pronounced and SPM concentrations reached $0.75\,g\,l^{-1}$. The size of the particles was also much more varied than previously; the D_{50} values at high water (10:00 hr) were $c.\,50\,\mu m$ but increased steadily with SPM concentration and current velocity reaching a maximum of $300\,\mu m$ at peak current velocity around 13:15 hr before falling to $50\,\mu m$ as SPM and velocity decreased, shortly before the sediment was exposed. On the flood the current velocity pattern was similar to the ebb but the concentration of SPM only reached $0.35\,g\,l^{-1}$ (compared with $0.75\,g\,l^{-1}$ on the ebb) and the size distribution also fell within the narrow range of $50-100\,\mu m$.

Discussion

One of the most efficient aspects of the LISP (UK) experiment was the collaborative, multi-disciplinary approach which enabled a large number of sediment properties, biotic characteristics and related parameters to be measured at the same site. This approach provided a valuable suite of data with which to evaluate and compare results. Examination of the sediment substrate properties (see Figure 7) indicates that the changes in the concentration and the size characteristics of the suspended particles measured at these stations is broadly consistent with the nature of the sediment in terms of granulometry, bioturbation and erosion thresholds (Widdows *et al.* this volume). Figure 7 (2nd panel down) shows there was a clear gradient of increasing sand content ($>63\,\mu m$) from the shore at Station A seaward which was the opposite of sediment exposure (upper panel, Fig. 7) and is a general feature of intertidal mudflats (Reineck 1967). Furthermore, the numbers of bioturbating organisms measured by Davey and Partridge (this volume) when both animal numbers and their size are taken into account, show a maximum impact at station B and a steady decline to station D (2nd panel up, Fig. 7). Both these factors (and related properties) are reflected in the critical erosion thresholds measured by Widdows *et al.* (this volume) which decreased slightly from Stations

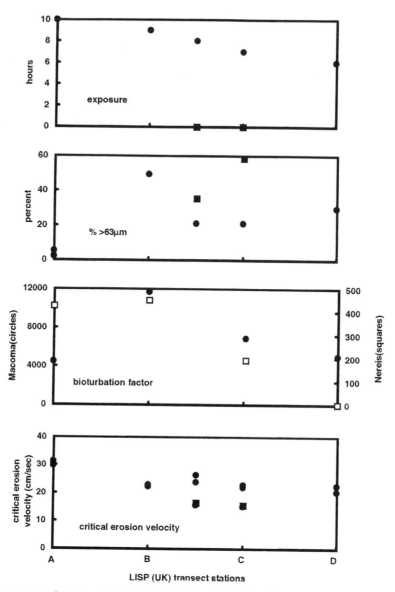

Fig. 7. Sediment properties across the LISP transect. Upper panel is sediment exposure time to air in hours. The panel second from top shows the percentage of sediment >63 μm and the panel second from bottom gives a bioturbation factor generated by taking account of both the numbers and size of Macoma (solid circles) and Nereis (open squares) at each station. The lower panel shows the critical erosion velocity at each station. Solid circles overlaid with crosses represent data for the pools and runnels which exhibit negligible exposure (i.e do not dry), relatively lower silt content and low critical erosion thresholds (i.e are more easily eroded). The bioturbation information is adapted from Davey & Partridge (this volume) and the exposure, silt and erosion measurements were from Widdows *et al.* (this volume).

A to D but decreased markedly at Stations B/C and C in the pools and runnel environments which are also wetter and have higher sand contents than the surrounding ridges.

Although current velocity data were not available for the ebb phase at Station C on the 4th

April, the SPM concentration data (top panel, Fig. 6) implied that the ebb and flood velocities were reasonably symmetrical. At Station D the velocity profile appeared to be more asymmetric; the ebb currents fell to zero well before the sediment became exposed and, although the velocity subsequently increased slightly again, the sediment was disturbed far less than on the flood where the initial velocity was higher (centre panel, Fig. 6). However, despite the erosion and resuspension observed at these sites which, except on the ebb at Station D, gave rise to increased SPM concentrations, the size characteristics remained relatively unchanged, with D_{50} values mostly in the range 60–100 μm, even when SPM concentrations increased 3–4 fold. This implied that under relatively 'tranquil' conditions (i.e. tides falling to neaps and low wind stresses) in this estuary, particularly at the more sandy sites, the size of the 'background' suspended population and the material which was eroded under these conditions had a similar size distribution, with D_{50} values falling in the range 60–70 μm.

The results which are more difficult to rationalize at first are the differences between Station C on the 4th and 7th. On the 7th April, the tidal range at Immingham was only 3.8 m compared with 5.5 m on the 4th and the maximum current velocities were correspondingly lower at 0.4 m s^{-1}. The ebb and flood velocity profiles were symmetrical but, despite the smaller tides, the erosion of sediment on the ebb was much more pronounced than on the 4th, and SPM concentrations reached 0.75 g l^{-1}. The erosion of sediment on the ebb on the 7th was also much greater than on the flood for a similar current speed. The size distribution of the eroded particles was also wider; D_{50} values increased from 50 to 300 μm with increasing SPM concentration, whereas previously, changes in concentration caused by erosion did not change the size distribution noticeably. Three factors may have a bearing; bed morphology, wind speed and wind direction: wind speed early on the 7th was higher (8 m s^{-1}) than on the 4th and the direction (300°) was onshore.

We believe that the differences between these results at Station C are predominantly due to the bed morphology. Whereas Station D was located over a flat, muddy-sand regime, Station C fell at the transition from mud-flat to a pronounced ridge-runnel system (amplitude up to 0.5 m). There is clear evidence of a difference in the substrate properties at station C between the tidal-flats and the ridge-runnel region (see Fig. 7). Even more pronounced was the difference in properties between the ridges, which tended to be harder to erode, and the runnels, which had higher sand and water contents, were more bioturbated and more easily mobilized. From direct observations when the barge grounded over low water, it was clear that the station position on the 7th was within the ridge-runnel systems

whereas, on the 4th, the barge was located over the tidal flat region of Station C.

The difference in erosion response to the currents between ebb and flood at Station C on the 7th is most likely explained by the presence of easily mobilized biodeposits (faeces and pseudo-faeces of suspension feeder such as *Cerastoderma*) produced over high water (Widdows pers. comm.) and microphytobenthic production during air exposure (stabilizing sediment on the flood). Microphytobenthic photosynthetic activity has a marked stabilizing effect on sediment because of the secretion of extracellular polymeric substances (EPS) of which up to 80% are carbohydrates (Smith & Underwood this volume). Table 1 shows carbohydrate values measured by Amos (pers. comm.) along the LISP transect and indicates a gradual decrease in carbohydrate values from about 0.10 mg g^{-1} at Stations A to 0.04 mg g^{-1} at Station D which is broadly consistent with decreasing air exposure. However, much higher concentrations of EPS carbohydrate were measured at Station B/C which may be more indicative of the more productive, but possibly localized, regions within the ridge-runnel systems. The higher EPS carbohydrate levels and increased bioturbation at Station C, and particularly at Station B/C compared with Station D, is consistent with our observations on the 7th where erosion on the flood only generated SPM concentrations of 0.35 g l^{-1} compared with 0.75 g l^{-1} on the ebb.

The morphology of the ridge-runnel system itself may also have an influence on the asymmetric, ebb flood behaviour because, over high water, sedimented material, including biodeposits, would tend to concentrate in the runnel systems where it could be trapped and retained to provide a supply of mobile, easily suspended material during the following ebb tide. Over slack water at low tide, however, the sediment was exposed so similar deposition was not possible.

The size spectra given in Fig. 5 indicate that virtually no material smaller than 10 μm was

Table 1. *Carbohydrate values (Amos, pers. comm.) measured on the LISP transect*

Station	Carbohydrate value (mg g^{-1})
A	0.094
A/B	0.087
B	0.048
B/C	0.188
C	0.067
C/D	0.088
D	0.039

detected. However, it should be remembered that the lower size limit of the laser reflectance systems is 2.0 μm so it would not be expected to detect clay or silt primary particles, if present. Except on the 7th April, when resuspension gave rise to much larger flocs, very little material greater than 300 μm was observed. The 5th and 95th percentiles calculated from the volume distributions were typically 20 and 180 μm, respectively, although on the 7th, the 95th percentiles reached 650 μm coincident with the period of maximum SPM concentration on the ebb. This range of values compared well with floc sizes measured using image-analysis by Fennessy & Dyer (1996) when the same stations were occupied between the 15th and 20th of April. The particles measured then were observed and sized within an *in situ* settling velocity apparatus (INSSEV) and mostly ranged from 30 to 200 μm, although particles up to 300 μm were seen on the 15th April. One factor to note is that, using the image analysis system, typically only 20–100 particles were sized from samples taken, at best, at 30 min intervals whereas, with the laser system, typical particle counts ranged from 4000 to 12 000 per 25 s sample.

Measurements of particle size were also made by Jago et al. (pers. comm.) using a Galai Cis-100, laser-optic, time-of-transition apparatus. D_{50} values reported for these analyses covaried with values obtained in this work but were typically 50–60 μm bigger except during the resuspension event on the 7th April when the D_{50} values measured with this system were not as large as recorded by us. This may have been due to the fact that the samples for these analyses were taken by bucket in which case:

(a) they were surface samples whereas the laser-reflectance instrument was close to the bed and (b) the largest particles may possibly have been broken during sampling although this fails to explain the slightly larger overall sizes recorded at other times. By contrast, the median sizes of suspended sediments suspended within the annular flume of Widdows et al. (this volume) when sized by Coulter Counter ranged from 8 to 22 μm, which clearly indicates the fragile nature of the aggregates and the disruption caused by shear within the flume (>1.5 Pa) combined with the sampling method (syringe) and the effect of the Coulter orifice.

Our measurements at this site cannot be used to infer settling rates directly since advective processes in this environment would completely overwhelm changes in concentration at a station brought about by sedimentation. Furthermore, our size measurements were not made in still conditions. However, since our size distribution data are comparable with INSSEV results and, if we assumed effective densities similar to those derived by Fennessy & Dyer (1996) from their results, our data would be consistent with their sedimentation values.

Statistical comparison of the particle size data obtained in this work with current velocity data is not straightforward because of the discrepancy in the sampling frequency of the respective measurements and the fact that the velocity values were averaged over one minute. However, employing a data-merging routine based on time, a D_{50} size value was extracted which corresponded with each current velocity value for periods where the measurements overlapped. These D_{50} values are plotted against velocity

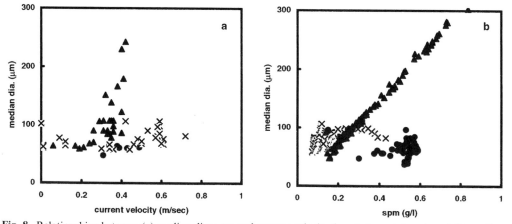

Fig. 8. Relationships between (**a**) median diameter and current velocity for all three data sets and (**b**) median diameter and SPM concentration (solid circles are 4th April, crosses are 6th April and solid triangles are 7th April).

in Fig. 8(a) and against SPM concentration in Fig. 8(b). During these measurements, made predominantly under tranquil environmental conditions, suspended particle size was largely independent of current velocity even though SPM concentrations changed with erosion and deposition [Fig. 8(a)]. Only at Station C on the 7th, which was bioturbated and exhibited low critical erosion thresholds, were both D_{50} and SPM concentration observed to increase significantly with current velocity. However, the relationship between SPM concentration and particle size needs to be viewed cautiously, since both parameters were derived from the same instrument.

Conclusions

(1) Non-disruptive, *in situ* particle size measurements using laser reflectance enabled the size distribution of suspended material to be observed with high temporal resolution in the waters overlying intertidal 'mud' flats during the ebb and flood period of the tidal cycle.

(2) At station D and the tidal flat of station C, the characteristics of the particles were relatively constant, possibly because of reducing tidal currents at the time of this experiment and predominantly tranquil wind/wave conditions. Only on the initial part of the flood were particle concentrations elevated significantly and, at the time of these measurements, this had little or no effect on the particle size distribution.

(3) Significant erosion was experienced within the ridge-runnel environment at Station C which gave rise to localized high SPM concentrations and correspondingly larger particle sizes. This is attributed mainly to biodeposition in the runnels but higher wind stress on that day may have contributed.

(4) With hind-sight, studies of the character istics and behaviour of the suspended particle population, as opposed to those of the eroding population, would be better undertaken over flood-ebb cycles rather than the ebb-flood periods as in this experiment.

(5) The particle sizing apparatus employed in this study is capable of acquiring data at relatively high frequency (order of seconds); progress in the interpretation of processes influencing the size distribution of suspended particles will require parallel measurements of current velocity and hence turbulence at similar or faster sampling rates (cf. POST, Christie & Dyer this volume).

This work was funded by a NERC Research Grant, GR3/09469. The authors are grateful to LOIS RACS(C) and the LISP Steering Group for providing support for D. J. Law during the field work. We are grateful to Colin Jago and Christopher Bull (U. Wales, Bangor) for the current velocity data, gravimetry and particle size data (Galai Cis-100) collected at the same time as this work, and to Carl Amos and colleagues (Bedford Institute) for sediment carbohydrate values. Likewise the bed sediment characteristics and erosion thresholds measured by John Widdows *et al.* (PML) and the characterization of the sediment macrofauna by John Davey and Valerie Partridge have added greatly to our ability to interpret the changes in measured particle size characteristics. The Humber Observatory operated by the School of Geography and Earth Resources at the University of Hull supplied the meteorological data. Our thanks also to Reg Uncles and John Widdows (PML) for their constructive comments on an early draft of this manuscript.

A. J. Bale is the corresponding author for this paper.

References

AGRAWAL, Y. C. & POTTSMITH, H. C. 1994. Laser diffraction particle sizing in STRESS. *Continental Shelf Research*, **14**, 1101–1121.

BALE, A. J., MORRIS, A. W. & HOWLAND, R. J. M 1985. Seasonal sediment movement in the Tamar Estuary. *Oceanologica Acta*, **8**, 1–6.

BALE, A. J. & MORRIS, A. W. 1987. *In situ* measurement of particle size in estuarine waters. *Estuarine, Coastal and Shelf Science*, **24**, 253–263.

CHRISTIE, M. & DYER, K. R. (this volume). Measurements of shallow water erosion over the Skeffling mudflats.

DAVEY, J. & PARTRIDGE, V. (this volume). The macrofauna of the Skeffling mud flats.

DEARNALEY, M. P. 1996. Direct measurements of settling velocities in the Owen tube: a comparison with gravimetric analysis. *Journal of Sea Research*, **36**, 41–47.

DYER, K. R. 1986. Coastal and Estuarine Sediment Dynamics. John Wiley & Sons.

EISMA, D., BERNARD, P., CADEE, G. C., ITTEKKOT, V., KALF, J., LAANE, R., MARTIN, J. M., MOOK, W. G., VAN PUT, A. & SCHUMACHER, T. 1991. Suspended matter particle size in some West-European estuaries; Part 1: particle size distribution. *Netherlands Journal of Sea Research*, **28**, 193–214.

—— & KALF, J. 1996. *In situ* particle (floc) size measurements with the NIOZ *in situ* camera system. *Journal of Sea Research*, **36**, 49–53.

FENNESSY, M. J., DYER, K. R. & HUNTLEY, D. A. 1994. INSSEV: an instrument to measure the size and settling velocity of flocs *in-situ*. *Marine Geology*, **117**, 107–117.

—— & —— 1996. Floc spectra of suspended sediment obtained with INSSEV during tidal advance over the Skeffling mud flats. LISP Preliminary Results. K. Black & D. Paterson (eds), 87–88.

GENTIEN, P., LUNVEN, M., LEHAITRE, M. & DUVENT, J. L. 1995. *In-situ* depth profiling of particle sizes. *Deep-Sea Research*, **42**, 1297–1312.

GIBBS, R. J. & KONWAR, L. N. 1982. Effect of pipetting on mineral flocs. *Environmental Science and Technology*, **16**, 119–121.

—— & ——1983. Sampling of flocs using Niskin bottles. *Environmental Science and Technology*, **17**, 374–375.

DE JONGE, V. N. & VAN BEUSEKOM, J. E. E. 1995. Wind- and tide-induced resuspension of sediment and microphytobenthos from tidal flats in the Ems Estuary. *Limnology and Oceanography*, **40**, 766–778.

LAW, D. J., BALE, A. J. & JONES, S. E. 1997. Adaption of focused beam reflectance measurements to *in situ* particle sizing in estuaries and coastal waters. *Marine Geology*, **140**, 47–59.

VAN LEUSSEN, W. & CORNELISSE, J. M. 1996. The underwater video system, VIS. *Journal of Sea Research*, **36**, 77–81.

LUCOTTE, M. & D'ANGLEJAN, B. 1986. Seasonal control of the Saint Lawrence maximum turbidity zone by tidal-flat sedimentation. *Estuaries*, **9**, 84–94.

MILLIGAN, T. G. 1996. *In situ* particle (floc) size measurements with the Benthos 373 plankton silhouette camera. *Journal of Sea Research*, **36**, 93–100.

OWEN, M. W. 1976a. Problems in the modelling of transport, erosion, and deposition of cohesive sediments. *In*: GOLDBERG, E. D., McCAVE, I. N., O'BRIEN, J. J. & STEELE, J. H. (eds) *The Sea*, Wiley-Interscience, New York, **6**, 513–537.

——1976b. Determination of the settling velocities of cohesive muds. H. R. Wallingford. Report No IT 161.

PEJRUP, M. & EDELVANG, K. 1996. Measurements of in-situ settling velocities in the Elbe estuary. *Journal of Sea Research*, **36**, 109–113.

POSTMA, H. 1967. Sediment transport and sedimentation in the estuarine environment. *In*: LAUF, G. L. (ed.) *Estuaries*. American Association for the Advancement of Science. Publication No. 83, 158–179.

REINECK, H. E. 1967. Layered sediments of tidal flats, beaches, and shelf bottoms of the North Sea. *In*: LAUF, G. L. (ed.) *Estuaries*. American Association for the Advancement of Science. Publication No. 83, 191–206.

SMITH, D. J. & UNDERWOOD, G. J. C. (this volume). *In situ* measurements of exopolymer production by intertidal epipelic diatom-dominated biofilms.

VAN DER LEE, W. T. B. (this volume). Floc size variations within a tidal cycle above an intertidal flat and in a tidal channel.

WIDDOWS, J., BRINSLEY, M. & ELLIOTT, M. (this volume). Use of an *in situ* flume to quantify particle flux (biodeposition rates and sediment erosion) for an intertidal mudflat in relation to changes in current velocity and benthic macrofauna.

Sedimentation on a Humber saltmarsh

SUE L. BROWN

Institute of Terrestrial Ecology, Furzebrook Research Station, Wareham, Dorset BH20 5AS, UK

Abstract: Sediment deposition was measured on two transects down the profile of Skeffling marsh in four short term studies, ranging from two tidal covers to a spring tide cycle, and in longer term studies of four intervals over 18 months. Sedimentation in *Spartina* and bare areas at the same elevation at the marsh front was measured to determine the role of *Spartina* in accretion, and the effect of two levels of stem density on short term deposition was compared.

In terms of sediment deposition per number of tidal inundations at the different elevations, accretion was greatest on the upper parts of the marsh. At lower elevations, subjected to more frequent inundation, deposition generally increased with the number of tidal covers in three of the four short-term studies, although there was evidence of resuspension and/or bedload movement. During an autumn high spring tidal cycle, large amounts of sediment were deposited on the upper marsh (up to 4–5 mm), but very little sediment was retained on the lower marsh and erosion was observed on the bare mud at the marsh edge.

The longer term studies revealed accretion at all sites on the marsh compared with the initial baseline measurements, ranging between 3.2 and 6.3 cm after 18 months, depending upon the transect and elevation. At both transects, accretion was generally continuous at the upper levels, but deposition was more variable in the lower zones, particularly the bare mud at the marsh edge. This area accreted the most during the summer months, but lost material during the winter of 1996–1997 while the upper zones continued to build up.

There was no evidence to suggest that *Spartina* enhances deposition in the pioneer zone at Skeffling. The tide advances rapidly across the expanse of mudflats and scours channels around the vegetation at the marsh edge. *Spartina* is probably more effective as a sediment stabilizer during periods of erosion and any resulting net accretion is likely to be apparent only when measured over longer time scales.

Rates of sediment accretion on UK saltmarshes are critically important in view of rising relative sea level. Sedimentation rates are not uniform throughout a marsh profile and may be influenced by a range of factors, in particular the elevation or age of the marsh and its relationship to the duration of tidal flooding (Richards 1934, Steers 1948; Pethick 1981; Stoddart *et al.* 1989; Adam 1990). Other factors include proximity to overflowing creeks, tidal range, storms, organic matter accumulation, compaction and vegetation cover (Ranwell 1964; Harrison and Bloom 1977; Randerson 1979; Stumpf 1983; Stoddart *et al.* 1989). Variations in sedimentation patterns also occur seasonally (Ranwell 1964) and may be influenced by biotic processes.

A number of models relating sedimentary, tidal and elevational parameters have been developed to describe saltmarsh depositional processes and the rate of marsh growth, over periods from a single tide to long term changes (e.g. Allen 1992; Pye and French 1993).

The simplest models relating accretion to frequency of submergence and vegetation trapping sediment may not be applicable to all marsh types. The classic view of marsh vegetation is that it acts as a baffle and promotes accretion (Ranwell 1972; Pethick 1984), and *Spartina anglica* has been planted extensively during this century to stabilize sediments and protect coastlines. However, physical conditions may be of far greater significance than vegetation cover on the pattern of deposition (Harper 1979) and under certain conditions dense vegetation may increase turbulence. Laboratory flume studies have shown that complex velocity profiles and associated shear stresses develop as the water flow encounters vegetation (Pethick *et al.* 1990), resulting in lower deposition rates than on bare surfaces such as open mudflat (Pethick, in Toft & Maddrell 1995). A small scale laboratory flume study by Gleason *et al.* (1979) found that sand accumulation was a (non-linear) function of *Spartina alterniflora* stem density, but this study may not be representative of many field conditions.

Sediment accretion can be measured at a range of spatial and temporal scales, and it is important to relate them; short-term rates and patterns may not reflect longer term net accretion rates due to factors such as seasonality and storms. This paper describes the results of short

BROWN, S. L. 1998. Sedimentation on a Humber saltmarsh. *In*: BLACK, K. S., PATERSON, D. M. & CRAMP, A. (eds) *Sedimentary Processes in the Intertidal Zone*. Geological Society, London, Special Publications, **139**, 69–83.

term patterns of net deposition and some longer term measurements on Skeffling marsh. The interdisciplinary LISP-UK programme, April 1995 (this volume) on sediment behaviour in the intertidal zone at Skeffling, provided an opportunity to study short term deposition which was continued at different periods during 1996. The aim of this study was to investigate short term net deposition at different elevations and vegetation communities on the marsh surface, following a range of tidal inundations from two tidal covers to a spring tidal cycle; also, to determine the effect of pioneer vegetation (*Spartina anglica*) on deposition by comparing bare and vegetated areas at the marsh front, and adjacent areas of different stem densities at the same elevation. Longer term sediment level changes on the east coast (Norfolk to Lindisfarne) are currently being measured as part of the LOIS (Land Ocean Interaction Study) community programme, and include two transects at Skeffling. Results to date (after 18 months) from these transects are included in this paper for a comparison of deposition measurements over different time scales.

The major areas of saltmarsh at the seaward end of the Humber estuary lie on the north side. In general they are narrow marshes with a patchy distribution along the coast, widening out at Welwick and then becoming a more or less continuous fringe of marsh eastwards towards Spurn Head. Skeffling marsh is relatively steep and narrow, 60–80 m wide, with a band of mixed general saltmarsh community (*Puccinellia maritima* and *Atriplex* (formerly *Halimione*) *portulacoides* dominant, with occasional *Aster tripolium*, *Sueda maritima*, *Spergularia spp.*, *Spartina anglica* and *Salicornia europaea*; hereafter referred to as *Spartina* and *Salicornia*), a middle section of narrow ridges (<1m wide, with mixed vegetation), interspersed with runnels largely bare of vegetation but with occasional patches of *Spartina* and *Salicornia*. The lower section is colonized by a monoculture of *Spartina* which protrudes as tongues of vegetation surrounded by water-filled channels at the marsh front.

Methods

Two transects were set up 500 m apart (Skeffling 'east' and 'west'), perpendicular to the embankment on the saltmarshes, for measurements of sediment level changes under the LOIS programme, and for short term deposition studies detailed here. Zones representing different elevations and plant communities were marked out

with canes. Four zones were marked at Skeffling east, and five zones at Skeffling west where the upper marsh is wider.

Short term measurements

Short term sediment deposition was measured using pre-weighed pairs of high 'wet burst' filter papers: 5.5 cm diameter papers placed on top of 7 cm diameter papers to ensure a clean surface under the top paper. The double filters were secured with three plastic coated paper clips bent at right angles and pinned into the sediment (Fig. 1).

Five replicate filters were laid down in each zone, at positions chosen at random, for each of the experimental periods. In the middle marsh, filters were placed on both ridges and runnels; at the front edge of the marsh, filters were placed on bare and vegetated (*Spartina*) areas to compare deposition on the different substrates.

The experiment was carried out initially in April 1995, in which filter papers were left for 2, 4 and 10 tidal inundations during the spring tidal cycle. The methods were repeated subsequently in July 1996 (2, 4 and 6 tidal inundations); September–October 1996 (left for an entire spring tidal cycle; ten replicates set in each zone to allow for possible losses); and November 1996 (for a 1 week period in the latter half of the spring tidal cycle).

In April 1995, ten replicate filters were also placed in patches of *Spartina* growing at different densities at the same elevation (seawards of the ridge and runnel system), to investigate whether stem density had any measurable effect on net deposition over 2, 4 and 10 tidal inundations.

At the end of each experimental period, the filter papers were lifted carefully, placed in glass tubes and dried at 80°C for 3–4 days. The dry weight of sediment was corrected for the weight of the filters and the salt content of the sediment and filters. Filter paper salt content was 5.7% of the dry weight (range 5.2–6.0% in ten replicate samples). To correct for sediment salt content a range of sediment quantities was used to produce a calibration curve. Ten samples were sonicated with distilled water, centrifuged at 14 000 rpm for 10 min and decanted. This was repeated several times before the samples were re-dried and weighed. Salt content was 3–4% of the sediment dry weight.

Sediment deposition per area of filter was corrected for the area taken up by the paper clip tips and calculated as grams dry weight deposited per 100 cm^2.

Fig. 1. Short term deposition experiment: two double filter papers in *Spartina* (scale: filter paper 7 cm diameter).

Surface scrapes of the top 1 mm of sediment were taken at each zone (four replicates per zone at random positions near each transect) for particle size analysis during the April 1995 study.

Longer term sediment level changes

Two methods were used, depending upon the terrain and vegetation cover. In different plant communities down the marsh profile, and in areas of continuous vegetation, five expanded aluminium plates (15 cm × 15 cm) were buried at random positions along a 5 m line perpendicular to the slope, to a depth of *c*. 10 cm. The plates were left to settle in for 4–6 months before the initial base line measurements were made at the end of September 1995. Measurements were taken every 4 months, by taking five readings from the sediment surface to each plate, using a fine metal ruler (7 mm wide).

In areas such as narrow ridges and tunnels, and at the front edge of the marsh where there are patches of *Spartina* and unvegetated areas at the same elevation, pairs of 1.2 m canes were pushed into the surface 1.2 m apart until they were precisely level at a height of 20–35 cm above the sediment. Five pairs of canes were

used for each vegetation type and for unvegetated areas. From a level placed across the canes, five measurements were taken to the sediment surface at positions initially selected randomly, but subsequently permanent. Results are expressed as mm sediment level change. Significant differences reported in the results refer to $p < 0.05$ or less.

Results

Short term studies

The experiment in April 1995 (Fig. 2) was conducted over high spring tides containing a high suspended sediment load [maximum flood and ebb suspended sediment concentrations of 1.63 and 1.29 g l^{-1}, respectively, in a sample taken 0.25 m above the bottom (Black 1996, unpublished preliminary results)]. Deposition was very variable within each zone, even over very short distances. The two transects also varied, with generally more deposition at Skeffling west than at Skeffling east (12 of 18 estimates of mean deposition in comparable zones were 1.4–4.7 times greater). The uppermost site on each transect experienced just two

(a)

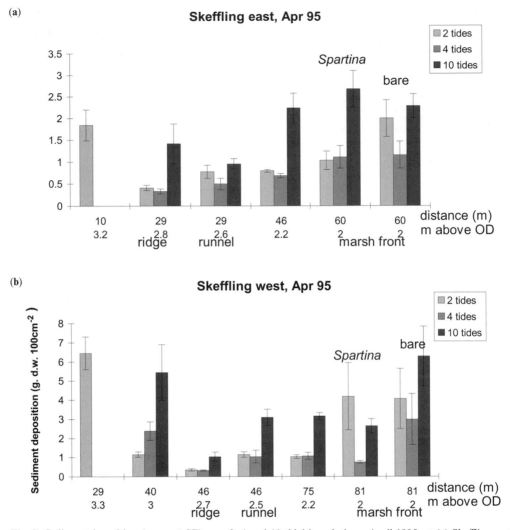

(b)

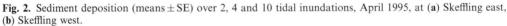

Fig. 2. Sediment deposition (means ± SE) over 2, 4 and 10 tidal inundations, April 1995, at (**a**) Skeffling east, (**b**) Skeffling west.

Table 1. *Particle sizes and percentage less than 3 size categories; range is back-transformed 95% confidence limits from arcsine square root scale*

Sample	Particle size ± SE		Percentage of particles < 2, 20 & 63 μm, upper and lower limits ($p < 0.05$)		
	Mean	Median	% < 2 μm	% < 20 μm	% < 63 μm
Upper marsh	9.00 ± 0.28	9.18 ± 0.25	12.57–13.96	71.90–73.30	90.83–91.61
Ridges	11.52 ± 0.32	13.14 ± 0.31	10.59–11.30	62.71–64.46	89.90–91.24
Runnels	15.30 ± 0.29	17.30 ± 0.32	8.28–8.69	53.54–54.67	84.81–86.06
Spartina	13.63 ± 0.27	15.10 ± 0.35	9.22–9.73	57.22–58.63	86.72–87.41
Marsh front – *Spartina*	13.43 ± 0.14	14.70 ± 0.17	9.94–10.22	57.74–58.32	86.10–86.50
Marsh front – bare	13.50 ± 0.32	15.17 ± 0.57	8.77–9.26	57.19–59.40	87.64–88.45

tidal inundations during the highest tides in which net deposition was significantly greater than over the middle section of the marsh and greater or similar to sedimentation at the marsh front under the same two tidal inundations, producing a u-shaped deposition pattern in profile. At the upper site at Skeffling west, for example, 6.45 ± 0.85 (mean $\pm$ SE) grams dry weight of sediment were deposited per $100 \, cm^2$, equivalent to $0.645 \, kg \, m^2$. At the front edge, $4.128 \pm 1.7 \, g$ dry wt were deposited over two tides (mean value for bare and vegetated areas). The smallest amount of sediment was retained on the ridges in the middle marsh ($0.36 \pm 0.065 \, g$ dry wt), with significantly greater amounts depo-

sited in the runnels ($1.156 \pm 0.146 \, g$ dry wt). The transect at Skeffling west has a wider upper marsh above the ridge and runnel system, and the site 40 m from the embankment near the tidal limit at slack water also retained more deposited sediment than the middle marsh sites, under 2, 4 and 10 tidal covers, with the amount deposited increasing with the number of inundations. The u-shaped sedimentation profile is therefore repeated over four and ten tidal inundations. From the ridge and runnel system seawards, sediment deposition generally increases with distance seawards at both transects. Less sediment was collected from the filters after four tides than after two (although

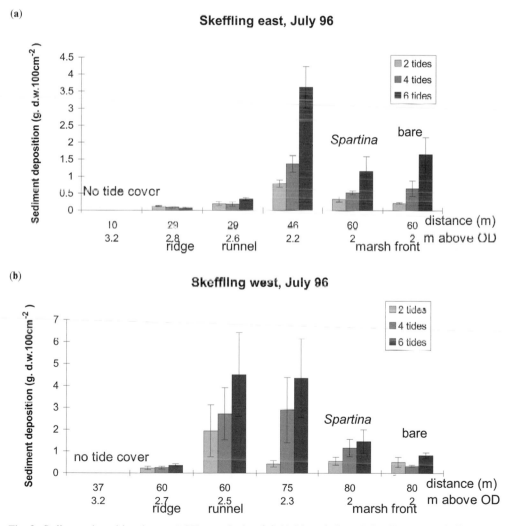

Fig. 3. Sediment deposition (means $\pm$ SE) over 2, 4 and 6 tidal inundations, July 1996, at **(a)** Skeffling east, **(b)** Skeffling west.

the differences were not significant). This observation, and the higher deposition at upper
levels, suggests that a considerable proportion of
deposited sediment may be resuspended or
moved as bedload from the ridge/runnel slope
and the lower marsh during a tidal cycle. After
ten tidal covers over a decreasing tidal range
(springs towards neaps), all zones showed
greater net deposition, particularly on the bare
areas at the marsh edge.

Particle size analysis (volume statistics) of surface scrapes revealed the marsh sediment to be
primarily fine silt with a small proportion of very
fine sand, with 90–98% of all samples <125 μm,
and 84–93% of all samples composed of silt
(<63 μm). A smaller mean particle size was
found on the upper marsh and the top

of the ridges, than in the loosely consolidated
runnels and the lower marsh, reflecting different hydrodynamic conditions and settling rates
of suspended particles carried on the flood
tide. Mean particle size ($\pm$ SE) in the general
saltmarsh vegetation was 9.0 μm $\pm$ 0.28 and
11.5 μm $\pm$ 0.32 on the ridges; compared with
15.3 μm $\pm$ 0.29 in the runnels. On the lower
marsh, particle size was not significantly different between either bare or vegetated areas
(13.5 μm $\pm$ 0.32 and 13.4 μm $\pm$ 0.14, respectively), or sparse and dense *Spartina* cover
(14.0 μm $\pm$ 0.18 and 14.3 μm $\pm$ 0.18, respectively). The upper marsh and ridges also contained correspondingly higher percentages of
particles less than the 2, 20 and 63 μm categories (Table 1).

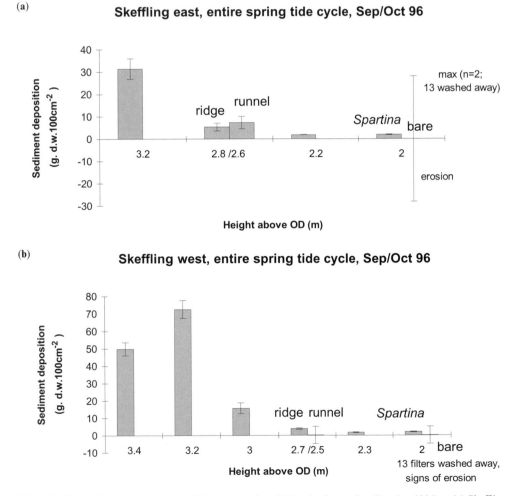

Fig. 4. Sediment deposition (means $\pm$ SE) over a spring tidal cycle, September/October 1996, at (**a**) Skeffling east,
(**b**) Skeffling west.

The July 1996 experiment [2, 4 and 6 tidal covers; Fig. 3] was conducted during calmer conditions than April 1995, with smaller tides. Again, the greatest deposition was just below the limit of the high tides, in this case between 2.2–2.5 m OD in the continuous *Spartina* sward behind the marsh front (2.2–2.3 m OD) and in the runnels at Skeffling west. Above this, only a very shallow covering was observed over the runnels at Skeffling east and the ridges were barely covered at slack water, hence there would be very little suspended sediment to settle out from a very shallow overlying water column. During the three days of the study, net deposition generally increased with the number of tidal inundations.

In September–October 1996, filter papers were left in place for the entire high (autumn equinox) spring tidal cycle (Fig. 4). These tides represent a range of tidal inundations over the zones on the marsh from five tidal covers at the top sites (3.2–3.4 m OD); 12–13 over the ridges and and middle marsh at Skeffling west (2.7–3 m OD); to 24 at the marsh front (2 m OD). Despite the fewer tidal covers at the top of the marsh, the greatest net deposition was measured here, with up to 4–5 mm depth of deposit on the

filter papers. More sediment was deposited at Skeffling west than at Skeffling east, as noted during the spring tide measurements of April 1995. Net deposition decreased towards the marsh front despite the increasing number of tidal inundations. Unfortunately, most filter papers were washed away in the mobile runnels and on the bare mud at the front. Observations indicate that this was not simply a consequence of strong wave action, but that erosion occurred at the marsh front during these big tides; some filters had evidently been washed away during the last few tidal covers as these areas, and those still retaining filter papers, were visible as small 7 cm diameter mounds, protected from erosion by the overlying filter papers (Fig. 5).

In November 1996, filter papers were left for six days during the latter half of the spring tidal cycle (springs to neaps), during which conditions were calmer than in October. The uppermost sites experienced two tides, with six over the top of the ridge systems, increasing to 12 at the marsh front. In general, deposition was similar at all sites below the top site, except behind the marsh front at Skeffling east in the continuous *Spartina* where deposition was greater (Fig. 6). As seen in previous studies where the

Fig. 5. Evidence of erosion in bare patches at the marsh front. Filter paper (left) and on previously washed away (right) show raised sediment mound beneath and clips, initially flush with surface, now raised above (scale: filter paper 7 cm diameter).

(a)

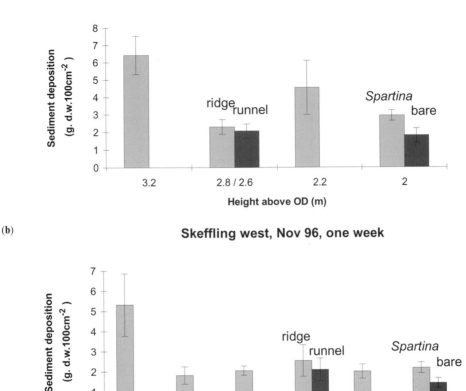

Fig. 6. Sediment deposition (means ± SE) over the latter half of a spring tidal cycle, November 1996 at (a) Skeffling east, (b) Skeffling west.

tidal range was sufficient to reach the higher sites, the greatest net sedimentation occurred on the upper marsh at both transects, from just two tides.

Longer term measurements

Cumulative sediment level changes between October 1995 and March 1997 are shown in Figs 7 and 8, for Skeffling east and west, respectively. After the first winter period, accretion at Skeffling east mirrored the u-shaped pattern seen in some of the short term measurements, followed by a more variable pattern of sedimentation over the summer (Fig. 7). The top site and the ridges show continued accretion with time, but the lower marsh shows fluctua-

tions in sediment levels. Most notably, net accretion occurred on the unvegetated patches at the extreme edge of the marsh up to the summer of 1996, followed by erosion over the following autumn and winter period. The same pattern was seen on the bare front at Skeffling west (Fig. 8), with losses during the autumn and winter, but levels remaining more stable in the adjacent vegetated tongues at the marsh edge and in the runnel systems. Sedimentation at the top sites, down to the ridges, was also similar to Skeffling east in that accretion continued over the measurement period. The net result, after 18 months, was an increase in sediment level of *c.* 3.5–4.5 cm over all sites at Skeffling west, and the middle and lower sites at Skeffling east, with slightly higher sedimentation (5–6 cm) at the highest two sites at Skeffling east.

(a)

Skeffling east, Oct95-Mar97

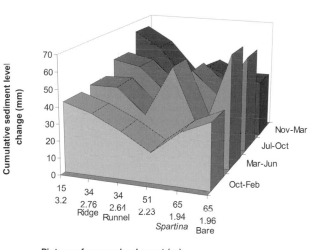

(b)

Skeffling east, Oct95-Mar97

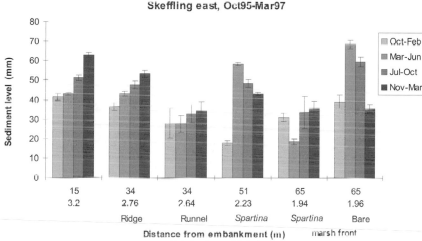

Fig. 7. Sediment level changes from baseline measurements at Skeffling east, October 1995–March 1997 (**a**) 3D display, (**b**) means ± SE.

Spartina *and bare areas at the marsh front*

No consistent differences were found between sedimentation in *Spartina* patches and on adjacent bare patches at the marsh front. The short term studies show either no significant difference, or greater deposition in the vegetation over some periods; but on the bare areas at other times (Fig. 9).

In the continuous sward behind the marsh front, *Spartina* stem density had no effect on net deposition over 2, 4 or 10 tides (Fig. 10).

The longer term studies show greater deposition on the bare mud at the marsh edge than in the vegetation (Fig. 11). At Skeffling east, some of the *Spartina* which was initially healthy and freely draining at low tide during the set up and baseline measurements (Sept/Oct 1995), is now

(a)

Skeffling west, Oct95-Mar97

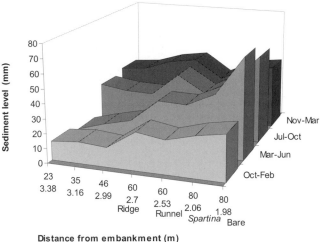

Distance from embankment (m)
Height above OD (m)

(b)

Skeffling west, Oct95-Mar97

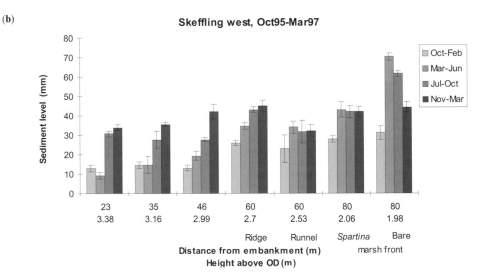

Fig. 8. Sediment level changes from baseline measurements at Skeffling west, October 1995–March 1997 (**a**) 3D display, (**b**) means ± SE.

sitting in waterlogged hollows and the plants appear to be dying back in some areas. The vegetation at the marsh front appears to create erosion hollows as the rapidly advancing tide encounters the tongues and clumps of *Spartina* and swirls around the edges of the vegetation, scouring a channel. This has been demonstrated by establishing an artificial *Spartina* clump using bamboo kebab sticks placed to mimic a typical clump size and stem density, on an area of bare mud at the marsh front. Within a few weeks a

depression began to form around the clump [Fig. 12(a)] which deepened considerably after 18 months to form a waterfilled hollow [Fig. 12(b)]. The bare mud seaward of the marsh is at a higher elevation, impeding drainage from parts of the marsh front on the receding tide. These conditions are also likely to hinder any seaward advance of the *Spartina* at this site. However, since June 1996, there has been consistent erosion of the bare sites, while sediment levels have remained similar in the vegetation. This

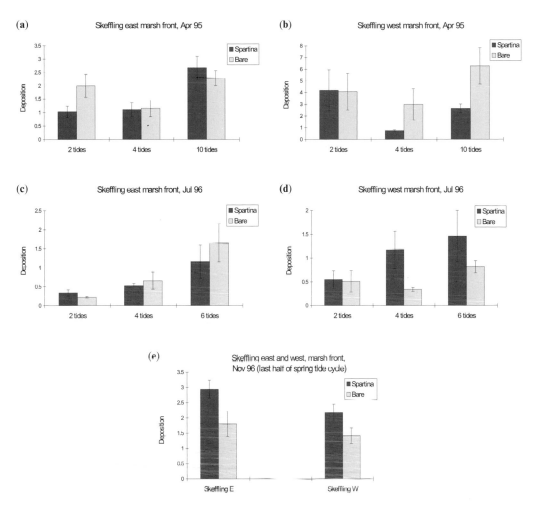

Fig. 9. Sediment deposition (in grams dry wt per 100 cm², means + SE) in *Spartina* and on bare areas at the marsh front during short term studies (a & b) April 1995, (c & b) July 1996, (e) November 1996.

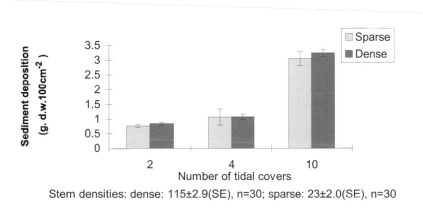

Stem densities: dense: 115±2.9(SE), n=30; sparse: 23±2.0(SE), n=30

Fig. 10. Sediment deposition in two different densities of *Spartina*, April 1995.

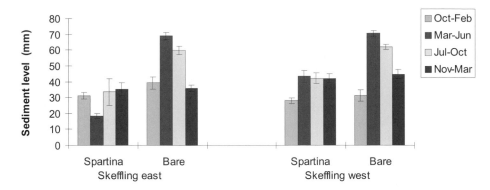

Fig. 11. Sediment level change from baseline measurements (means ± SE) in *Spartina* and on bare mud at the marsh front October 1995–March 1997.

suggests that *Spartina* helps to stabilize sediment during periods of erosion.

Discussion

Although considerable variation in sedimentation was observed over the four short term studies, some general patterns can be described. The greatest deposition generally occurred just below the limit of the high tides, so that in most cases, the upper to mid marsh areas, above the ridge systems, experienced the greatest net deposition over the duration of each experiment. In July, under smaller tides, the highest sedimentation was on the middle to lower marsh areas. Net deposition generally increased with the number of tidal inundations, especially over the calm July tidal cycle, but there is evidence of resuspension or bedload movement as the tide crossed the marsh surface in April. Under more extreme hydrodynamic conditions such as those experienced over the September/October tidal cycle, the front of the marsh was eroded, while accretion at the upper sites (over five tides) was the greatest observed during all of the experiments; an order of magnitude greater than that measured during other periods (two–three tides). These sedimentation patterns would maintain the relatively steep marsh profile of these narrow Humber marshes. The net result would be to produce a profile in which the upper and middle marsh continues to build up, but the lower marsh experiences more variable sedimentation, with cycles of accretion and erosion that in the longer term may prove to be seasonal. This is evident in the longer term measurements in which there has been generally a consistent increase at the upper and middle sites, but a

more variable pattern of sedimentation at the extreme marsh front. The bare areas at the edge of the marsh showed a marked increase in sediment level between March and June 1996, with subsequent erosion over the winter of 1996–1997.

A similar pattern was found by Harper (1979) on a Lincolnshire marsh: the upper marsh accreted slowly and steadily, the central marsh accreted rapidly and the lower marsh displayed erratic fluctuations in level. It should be noted that the top sites in this study were 15 m and 23 m seawards of the embankment, and accretion was not measured in the zone immediately in front of the embankment (i.e. the uppermost marsh zone) as this area is only rarely covered. Ranwell (1964) also reports a similar pattern of sedimentation, with pronounced seasonal cycles. In autumn and winter the extreme seaward edge of the marsh at Bridgewater Bay tended to erode while higher levels were accreting. In spring and early summer there was a reversal of the autumn pattern. There are indications of this occurring at Skeffling, with significant gains to the upper sites in autumn and winter 1996–1997, and losses at the extreme seaward edge; in contrast to spring and early summer 1996, where the upper sites were either lower or similar to the previous winter's levels and the highest deposition was at the bare marsh edge. After just 18 months of long term measurements, it is too early to conclude a seasonal pattern to sedimentation in the Humber, particularly as the period may have experienced some unusual events. The marked increase in sedimentation at the marsh front during spring 1996 may have been enhanced by additional fine material washed out from the severe storm breach of Spurn Head in February 1996 and transported into the

Fig. 12. Tongues of *Spartina* in water-filled hollows at the front edge of Skeffling marsh. In the middle is an artificial clump made from kebab sticks, placed initially in a flat surface to simulate a small *Spartina* patch. After two months (**a**) a hollow is beginning to form, which had deepened considerably after 18 months. (Scale: clump size *c*. 35 cm diameter).

estuary. Some loss of sediment at the marsh front was measured over winter 1996–1997, however an increase (of the order of 3 cm) in sedimentation was observed (from the baseline measurements) over the previous winter. This increase in the pioneer zone was observed at all 33 transects studied in the LOIS programme between Norfolk and Lindisfarne, in spite of the wide geographic range of the transects. The winter of 1995–1996 experienced persistent east winds, which may account for the observed changes. In contrast, little change in sedimentation was observed generally throughout the LOIS area last winter. With just two winter periods, it is not possible to determine the more usual pattern of events. We hope to continue longer term measurements of selected sites set up under LOIS, which should determine any seasonality in sedimentation patterns on east coast saltmarshes.

From observations of tidal limits on the marsh surface against corresponding tide table heights (ignoring meteorological variables), the number of spring tides estimated to have covered the highest sites on each transect during intervals between measurements was as follows: October 1995–February 1996: 7; March–June: 2; July–October: 4; and November 1996–March 1997: 3. The greatest increase in sediment level would be expected in autumn and winter 1995–1996 with seven spring tidal cycles, followed by late summer to autumn 1996 with four spring tidal cycles. Less accretion would be expected in spring 1996 under two spring tidal cycles. This was found to be the case at both transects. Over 18 months, the upper sites accreted 3.4 cm and 6.3 cm of sediment at Skeffling west and east, under c. 16 spring tidal cycles. An average rate of 2.1 mm and 3.9 mm, respectively, per spring tidal cycle would be needed to build up this amount of sediment (ignoring losses due to compaction and any additions from organic input). Weights of sediment deposited in the short term experiments have not been converted to equivalent depth of sediment, however between 2–5 mm of sediment were frequently observed on the filter papers under high spring tides, suggesting that the accretion rates measured during the longer term study could be met by the estimated number of spring tides reaching the upper sites.

There was no evidence to suggest that *Spartina* enhances deposition on this marsh and scouring occurs around the vegetation at the marsh front. In the continuous sward behind the marsh front, *Spartina* stem density had no effect on short term sediment deposition. The pioneer vegetation on Skeffling marsh is probably more important as a sediment stabilizer during periods of erosion, than as a deposition enhancer. Net accretion resulting from sediment stabilization may only be apparent when measured over a longer time scale.

This is LOIS publication number 399 of the LOIS Community Research Programme, carried out under a Special Topic Award from the Natural Environment Research Council. The author thanks A. J. Gray for helpful comments on the manuscript.

References

ADAM, P. 1990. *Saltmarsh Ecology*. Cambridge University Press.

ALLEN, J. R. L. 1992. Tidally influenced marshes in the Severn Estuary, southwest Britain. *In*: ALLEN, L. R. L. and PYE, K. (eds) *Saltmarshes*. Cambridge University Press.

GLEASON, M. L., ELMER, D. A. & PIEN, N. C. 1979. Effects of stem density upon sediment retention by salt marsh cord grass, *Spartina alterniflora* Loisel. *Estuaries*, **2**, 271–273.

GRAY, A. J. 1992. Saltmarsh plant ecology: zonation and succession revisited. *In*: ALLEN, L. R. L. and PYE, K. (eds) *Saltmarshes*. Cambridge University Press.

HARPER, S. A. 1979. Sedimentation on the New Marsh at Gibraltar Point, Lincolnshire. *East Midland Geographer*, **7**, 153–167.

HARRISON, E. Z. & BLOOM, A. L. 1977. Sedimentation rates on tidal salt marshes in Connecticut. *Journal of Sedimentary Petrology*, **47**, 1484–1490.

PETHICK, J. S. 1981. Long-term accretion rates on tidal salt marshes. *Journal of Sedimentary Petrology*, **51**, 571–577.

PETHICK, J. 1984. *An Introduction to Coastal Geomorphology*. Edward Arnold, London.

——, LEGGETT, D. & HUSAIN, L. 1990. Boundary layers under salt marsh vegetation developed in tidal currents. *In*: THOMAS, J. B. (ed.) *Vegetation and Erosion*. John Wiley and Sons, 113–124.

PYE, K. & FRENCH, P. W. 1993. *Erosion and Accretion Processes on British Saltmarshes. Volume Four, Modelling of Saltmarsh and Mudflat processes*. Final Report to Ministry of Agriculture, Fisheries and Food, London. Report ES19B(4).

RANDERSON, P. F. 1979. A simulation model of saltmarsh development and plant ecology. *In*: KNIGHTS, B. and PHILLIPS, A. J. (eds) *Estuarine and Coastal Land Reclamation and Water Storage*. Saxon House, Farnborough, 48–67.

RANWELL, D. S. 1964. *Spartina* salt marshes in southern England II. Rate and seasonal pattern of sediment accretion. *Journal of Ecology*, **52**, 79–94.

——1972. *Ecology of Salt Marshes and Sand Dunes*. Chapman and Hall, London.

RICHARDS, F. J. 1934. The salt marshes of the Dovey estuary. IV. The rates of vertical accretion, horizontal extension and scarp erosion. *Annals of Botany*, **48**, 225–239.

STEERS, J. A. 1948. Twelve years' measurement of accretion on Norfolk salt marshes. *Geological Magazine*, **85**, 163–166.

STODDART, D. R., REED, D. J. & FRENCH, J. R. 1989. Understanding salt-marsh accretion, Scolt Head Island, Norfolk, England. *Estuaries*, **12**, 228–236.

STUMPF, R. P. 1983. The process of sedimentation on the surface of a salt marsh. *Estuarine, Coastal and Shelf Science*, **17**, 495–508.

TOFT, A. R. & MADDRELL, R. J. (eds) 1995. *A Guide to the Understanding and Management of Saltmarshes*. National Rivers Authority. R&D Note 324.

Use of *in situ* flume to quantify particle flux (biodeposition rates and sediment erosion) for an intertidal mudflat in relation to changes in current velocity and benthic macrofauna

JOHN WIDDOWS[1], MARY BRINSLEY[1] & MIKE ELLIOTT[2]

[1] *Plymouth Marine Laboratory, Prospect Place, West Hoe, Plymouth PL1 3DH, UK*
[2] *Department of Biological Sciences, University of Hull, Hull HU6 7RX, UK*

Abstract: A portable *in situ* annular flume was deployed on eight occasions at five stations along a shore normal transect from immediately below the saltmarsh to the mid-tide level of the Skeffling mudflat in the Humber estuary. Both large scale (km) and small scale (m) spatial differences (i.e. between ridges, gullies and pools on ridges) were examined. Biodeposition rates were measured at low current velocities ($5 \, \mathrm{cm \, s^{-1}}$), while sediment resuspension and erosion rates were determined in response to step-wise increases in current velocities between 10 and $50 \, \mathrm{cm \, s^{-1}}$ (equivalent to a range in shear stress from 0.02 to 1.6 Pa). Maximum biodeposition rates ($6.6 \, \mathrm{g \, m^{-2} \, h^{-1}}$) were more than an order of magnitude higher than the mean sedimentation rate in the absence of sediment and biota. There was a significant correlation between biodeposition rate and the density of the suspension feeder *Cerastoderma edule* ($r = +0.90$; $P < 0.05$). The intertidal sites could be separated into three distinct groups on the basis of sediment stability/erodibility. Upper shore sites had the highest stability with critical erosion velocities (u_{crit}) of $30 \, \mathrm{cm \, s^{-1}}$, whereas the pools and gullies were the most easily eroded with u_{crit} of $15 \, \mathrm{cm \, s^{-1}}$. Site differences in sediment erodibility were not significantly correlated with measured physical properties of the sediment (bulk density, moisture content, % POM, % sand) However, there was a significant correlation between sediment erodibility and the density of *Cerastoderma* ($r = +0.89$; $P < 0.01$) and an index of the bioturbation activity of *Macoma balthica* ($r = +0.96$; $P < 0.001$).

The flux of particles across the sediment–water interface of an intertidal mudflat is dependent on a variety of physical, chemical and biological factors including particle size and density, water and organic content, cohesiveness, depositional history, air exposure and the composition of the biological community. Biota can play a particularly important role in mediating material flux at the sediment water interface: (1) by enhancing the process of sedimentation (e.g. biodeposition by suspension feeders and sediment trapping by saltmarsh vegetation), (2) by stabilizing sediments [e.g. microphytobenthos, high densities of epifauna species (e.g. mussels) and tube-building infauna (e.g. polychaetes)] and (3) by destabilizing sediments (e.g. bioturbation caused by the feeding and burrowing activity of deposit feeders). The impact of biota on sediment stability/erodibility has been emphasized by many authors (Rhoads & Boyer 1982; Jumars & Nowell 1984; Paterson 1989; Meadows & Meadows 1991; Davis 1993). However, Meadows & Meadows (1991) concluded that although there is considerable interest and speculation in the literature about biological effects, there was only a limited amount of experimental analysis (field or laboratory based).

There is now a variety of *in situ* techniques for investigating the erosion potential of cohesive marine sediments (reviewed by Black & Paterson 1997), including the large annular flumes deployed from a boat (e.g. Sea Carousel; Amos *et al.* 1992; Maa *et al.* 1993). A smaller, portable, *in situ* annular flume developed at PML (Widdows *et al.* 1998*a*) is similar in principal to the Sea Carousels and enables sediment stability/erodibility of undisturbed cohesive sediments, together with its natural biological community, to be studied in the field under experimentally controlled conditions of increasing current velocity/shear stress.

The primary objectives of this study, which forms part of the multidisciplinary Littoral Investigation of Sediment Properties (LISP-UK), were:

(a) To use a new, portable, *in situ* annular flume to investigate particle flux across sediment–water interface at sites down the Skeffling mudflat, particularly in relation to changes in current velocity/shear stress and the benthic community structure/density of key macrofauna species.

(b) To quantify particle flux in terms of the enhanced sedimentation resulting from suspension feeding activity (i.e. biodeposition), as well as the quantity/quality of resuspended sediment, sediment erodibility and critical erosion velocities.

WIDDOWS, J., BRINSLEY, M. & ELLIOTT, M. 1998. Use of *in situ* flume to quantify particle flux. *In*: BLACK, K. S., PATERSON, D. M. & CRAMP, A. (eds) *Sedimentary Processes in the Intertidal Zone*. Geological Society, London, Special Publications, **139**, 85–97.

Materials and methods

The *in situ* annular flume was deployed on eight occasions at five stations along a 2.2 km shore-normal transect of *c.* 2.2 km from immediately below the saltmarsh (site A; Grid reference TA 368183) to the mid-tide level (site D: Grid reference TA 365164) on Skeffling mudflat near the mouth of the Humber estuary in April 1995. In addition to examining differences in flux measurements and sediment erodibility over this large spatial scale, comparisons were also made over a smaller spatial scale of *c.* 2 m (i.e. between ridges, gullies and pools on ridges).

The annular flume and operating procedures have been described in detail by Widdows *et al.* (1998*a*). In summary, the flume represents a smaller, modified version of the design described by Fukada & Lick (1980). The annular flume (Fig. 1) is constructed of acrylic material with a 64 cm (outer) and 44 cm (inner) diameter, resulting in a 10 cm channel width with a total bed area of $0.17 \, \text{m}^2$, a maximum water depth of 35 cm, a maximum volume of 60 l. Current velocities ranging from 1 to $50 \, \text{cm s}^{-1}$ and bed shear stresses (0.01–2 Pa) are generated by a rotating annular drive plate (a smooth surface without paddles) driven by a 12 V motor, with controller board and data logger, which is powered by two 12 V batteries. The drive plate speed is monitored using an infra-red photo switch and this is recorded every 15 s by the data-logger. An electromagnetic (EM) current flow meter (Valeport Model 800-175) and video-tracking of neutrally buoyant particles have been used to measure free-stream current velo-cities and vertical profiles in the flume and to calibrate the rotation speed of the drive plate. The concentration of suspended particulate matter (SPM) in the flume is monitored at 15 s intervals using an optical back scatter sensor (OBS-3; D & A Instruments) which is calibrated against water samples taken for gravimetric analysis.

The annular flume was placed on an area of flat sediment (recently air-exposed) and was care-fully pushed into the sediment to a depth of between 8 and 10 cm. In order to fill the flume with seawater without disturbing the surficial sediment, a sheet of 'bubblewrap' in the shape of an annulus was carefully placed on the sediment surface and the seawater (collected from Spurn

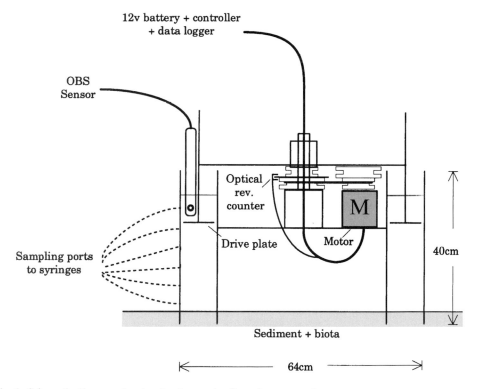

Fig. 1. Schematic diagram showing *in situ* annular flume in cross section.

Point at the mouth of the estuary) gently pumped onto the sheet, which then gradually floated off the sediment surface. After filling the flume with 45 l of seawater, the rotating drive plate and OBS (optical back scatter) sensor were fitted.

There are two phases to the measurement of material flux across the sediment–water interface: Phase I is conducted under conditions of low current velocity (5 cm s^{-1}) and quantifies the clearance rate or the removal of suspended particles from the water column over a period of c. 45–60 min. This process will be enhanced by the suspension feeding activity of benthic macrofauna and their net clearance rate (CR: l h^{-1}) is determined from the difference between the clearance rate in the flume and 'control' (i.e. water column without sediment and benthic fauna). The clearance rate is calculated using the following equation:

$$CR(l h^{-1}) = (\text{litres of water in flume})$$

$$\times (\log_e C_1 - \log_e C_2)$$

$$/(\text{time interval: h})$$

where C_1 and C_2 are the volumes of suspended particles, between 3.2 and 12.1 μm equivalent spherical diameter, at the beginning and end of each time increment (15 min). Water samples are taken by syringe from the middle of the water column in the flume and control. The volumes of suspended particles are determined by means of a Coulter Counter® Multisizer using a 100 μm orifice tube. Clearance rates of suspended particles (phase I) are then calculated from the exponential decline in the suspended particle concentration in the flume compared with the control chamber.

Studies have confirmed that there are no significant differences between the clearance/sedimentation rates in a 'control flume' and a 'control cylinder' within the first 30–45 min. Biodeposition rates are calculated as follows:

Biodeposition rate (g m^{-2} h^{-1})

$$= (\text{net } CR: l h^{-1})(\text{mean SPM})(1/\text{flume area})$$

where mean SPM of Spurn seawater $= 0.052$ g l^{-1} and flume area $= 0.17$ m^2.

Phase II (2.5 h duration) quantifies the sediment resuspension and the sediment erosion rate in response to stepwise increase in current velocity from 10 to 50 cm s^{-1}, in 5 cm s^{-1} increments, each with a duration of 15 min. The relationship between measured free-stream current velocity (i.e 10 cm above the bed) and estimated bed shear stress (based on log vertical profile 1 cm above bed when smooth turbulent flow over

fine-grain cohesive mud) is described by the following equation:

$$\text{Shear stress (Pa)} = 0.0008x^2 - 0.0006x + 0.0052$$

$$(r^2 = 0.99)$$

where $x =$ current velocity (cm s^{-1}).

Calculation of shear stress is based on a log profile of current velocity within 1 cm above the bed. EM current meter measurements and video-tracking of suspended particles show that free-stream current velocities are constant down the water column to within 1 cm of the sediment surface. These observations confirm vertical profiles recorded in annular flumes by previous researchers (e.g. Fukada & Lick 1980; Maa 1990).

During phase II, the resuspension of sediment was determined by frequent monitoring (i.e. 15 s intervals) of the OBS which was calibrated against water samples taken for gravimetric analysis. The nature of the surface sediment and the resuspended particles was also measured in terms of size fractions (by wet sieving for >63 μm diameter and Coulter Counter Multisizer analysis for 2–63 μm), % particulate organic matter (POM; loss on ignition at 450°C), bulk density (mass of wet sediment/volume of wet sediment) and moisture content (mass of water/mass of dry sediment).

At the end of each experimental run, four cores (10 cm × 10 cm × 15 cm depth) were sampled from the area covered by the annular flume. These were sieved through a 0.5 mm mesh, the macrofauna preserved in Rose-Bengal in formalin (8% after dilution) and subsequently sorted, identified and counted.

Statistical analysis of the data was performed using ANOVA, Covariance analysis and Pearson Correlation Matrix (Systat v. 5.03 for Windows and SAS, 1989). Non-parametric multivariate analyses were performed using PRIMER (Plymouth Routines In Multivariate Ecological Research), a suite of computer programmes primarily developed for analysing benthic community abundance data (Clarke 1993).

Results

Physical properties of surface sediments

Eight benthic annular flume experiments were carried out at five stations along the Skeffling mudflat transect between 5th and 13th April 1995. The physical descriptors of the sediments and resuspended sediments at the eight sites are presented in Tables 1 and 2. There was no apparent trend in any of these parameters down

Table 1. *Physical parameters describing surface sediment (2 cm depth) and resuspended sediments at Skeffling sites (mean of n = 3)*

Sites	Grid reference	Distance from saltmarsh (m)	Date	Air exposure (h per tidal cycle)	Moisture content % (g water/g dry sediment)	Bulk density (g/cm³)	% Particulate organic matter	% of sediment >63 µm	Resuspended sediment: median diameter (µm)
A1	TA 368183	2	8/4/95	10	76.5	1.54	7.98	5.2	18
A2	TA 368183	2	10/4/95	10	53	1.65	7.27	2.1	13
B	TA 368180	300	7/4/95	9	44.7	1.72	3.75	49.4	17
B/C ridge	TA 367174	1000	13/4/95	8	65.4	1.58	6.93	21.0	12.5
B/C pool	TA 367174	1000	13/4/95	0	65.7	1.6	5.82	35.3	12
C ridge	TA 366168	1600	5/4/95	7	63.8	1.6	6.63	21.0	22
C gully	TA 366168	1600	5/4/95	0	52.2	1.68	4.62	58.5	8
D ridge	TA 365164	2200	12/4/95	6	65.1	1.58	6.45	29.6	10

Table 2. *Size fractionation of Skeffling surface (2 cm depth) sediment*

Sites	Sampling date	% of total dry weight					
		$>1000\,\mu m$	$<1000\,\mu m$ $>500\,\mu m$	$<500\,\mu m$ $>250\,\mu m$	$<250\,\mu m$ $>125\,\mu m$	$<125\,\mu m$ $>63\,\mu m$	$<63\,\mu m$
A1	8/4/95	0.2	0.3	0.3	0.4	4.0	94.8
A2	10/4/95	<0.1	0.1	0.2	0.2	1.6	97.9
B	7/4/95	0.5	0.6	0.3	2.1	45.9	50.6
B/C ridge	13/4/95	0	0.1	0.1	0.5	20.3	79.0
B/C pool	13/4/95	0.2	0.1	0.2	0.9	33.9	64.7
C ridge	5/4/95	0	0.1	0.2	0.8	19.9	79.0
C gully	5/4/95	0.1	0.1	0.4	2.5	55.4	41.5
D	12/4/95	0	0.2	0.3	1.9	27.2	70.4

the shore, although sites A1 and A2 had the highest % POM and the smallest proportion of large particles ($>63\,\mu m$ diameter).

Suspension feeding activity and biodeposition rates

The activity of suspension feeders can be quantified in terms of clearance rate (i.e. litres cleared of suspended particles per hour), which is converted to biodeposition rates (mg of material deposited as faeces and pseudofaeces per hour; when the SPM has a high inorganic content) by multiplying by the mean SPM concentration during phase I (i.e. 52 mg l^{-1}; Table 3). Note that the variation in control clearance/sedimentation rate during phase I is primarily dependent on the daily variation in the quality and quantity of SPM in the water that is pumped into the flume. Net biodeposition rate is therefore based on the clearance rates in the flume with sediment and

biota (= biodeposition + sedimentation) minus the equivalent clearance rate (= sedimentation) in the control cylinder. Maximum net biodeposition rates (6.61 g m^{-2} h^{-1}) were recorded at sites B/C and C (Table 3) where the suspension feeding cockles (*Cerastoderma edule*) occurred at the highest densities (Table 4). These biodeposition rates were approximately an order of magnitude higher than the natural sedimentation rates in the controls (i.e. 0.66 g m^{-2} h^{-1}; Table 3).

Sediment erosion/resuspension

A representative time-course of suspended particulate matter concentration (SPM, mg l^{-1}) and erosion rate (mg m^{-2} s^{-1}; calculated from ΔSPM × volume of flume/15 s interval/flume area) in response to step wise increases in current velocities (phase II) at site D are illustrated in Figs 2 and 3. Following each increase in current velocity, above the erosion threshold, there

Table 3. *Rates of clearance (l h^{-1}) and sedimentation / biodeposition (g m^{-2} h^{-1}) in the control and flume at sites along the Skeffling intertidal transect in the Humber (April 1995)*

Site	Clearance rate (l h^{-1})			Sedimentation/biodeposition rate (g m^{-2} h^{-1})		
	Control	Flume + biota	Net clearance rate	Control	Flume + biota	Net biodeposition rate
A1	2.9	4.3	1.4	0.89	1.32	0.43
B	6.3	8.9	2.6	1.93	2.72	0.79
B/C ridge	−1.0	9.8	10.8	−0.25	3.00	3.25
B/C pool	13.5	35.1	21.6	4.13	10.74	6.61
C ridge	1.1	18.7	17.6	0.34	5.72	5.38
D	1.3	7.8	6.5	0.40	2.39	1.99

Sedimentation and biodeposition rates (g m^{-2} h^{-1}) are based on litres of water cleared of particles h^{-1} for a mean SPM concentration of 52 mg l^{-1} (water collected from Spurn) and a flume area of 0.17 m^2.
Net clearance rate and net biodeposition rate is the difference between flume and control.
Mean sedimentation rate in control (without sediment & biota) = 0.66 g m^{-2} h^{-1}
(excluding B/C pool control which was abnormally high, due to rapid settlement of resuspended micro-aggregates).

Table 4. *Macrofauna density for Skeffling intertidal mudflat (N m^{-2})*

Species	Site A1	Site A2	Site B	Site B/C ridge	Site B/C pool	Site C ridge	Site C gully	Site D
Date	8/4/95	10/4/95	7/4/95	13/4/95	13/4/95	5/4/95	5/4/95	12/4/95
Macoma balthica	100	200	1575	1500	1375	1525	1325	1225
Cerastoderma edule	0	0	0	(25)‡	50	25	50	25
Retusa obtusa	75	0	25	50	100	100	550	25
Hydrobia ulvae	25	0	0	50	150	25	0	0
Nereis diversicolor	100	300	250	50	300	25	25	25
Nephtys hombergii	25	0	0	225	250	700	300	800
Eteone longa	75	100	125	50	25	0	25	0
Spionidae*	175	75	225	2200	1375	2575	250	(6000)§
Oligochaeta†	75	250	650	1550	550	100	75	25
Total abundance	725	925	2975	5875	4175	5075	2900	2895

* Principally *Pygospio elegans.*
† Principally *Tubificoides benedeii.*
‡ Observed in flume but not sampled in cores.
§ High number of tubes observed in flume but not detected/quantified in cores – data from Davey & Partridge (this volume).

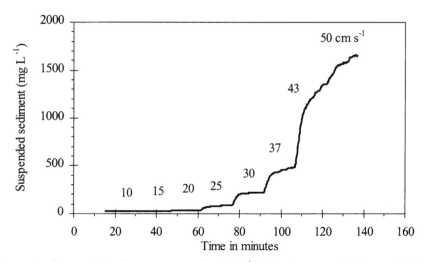

Fig. 2. Time-series of suspended sediment concentration (mg l^{-1}) following a step-wise increase in free-stream current velocities between 10 and 50 cm s^{-1} in the *in situ* flume deployed at Skeffling site D in the outer Humber estuary.

is a rapid increase in sediment resuspension with the maximum erosion rates (ΔSPM/t) occurring within one to two minutes of the step-wise increase in current velocity. At the lower current velocities (i.e. <37 cm s^{-1}) the suspended sediment concentration reaches a quasi-steady state within 5 min of a change in current velocity and the erosion rate peaks (max E) after c. 1–2 min followed by a decay (i.e. type I erosion; Amos *et al.* 1992). In contrast, at 43 and 50 cm s^{-1} there is insufficient time to reach a steady state and there is evidence of a variable and continuous rate of erosion (i.e. type II erosion).

The maximum resuspended sediment concentration and the maximum erosion rates recorded at each current velocity and for each site are presented in Figs 4 and 5, and the maximum values at a current speed of 43 cm s^{-1} in Table 5(a). The relationships describing max SPM vs current velocity and max E vs current velocity (Figs 6 and 7) were analysed by linear regression following log transformation of SPM and erosion rates. These regressions were then compared by covariance analysis and this demonstrated that there were significant differences in the slopes of the regression lines. Calculation of

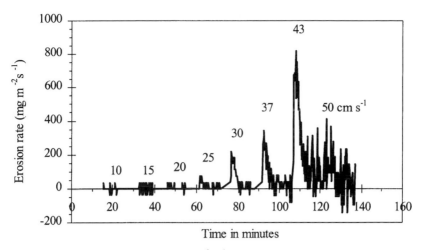

Fig. 3. Time-series of sediment erosion rates ($mg\,m^{-2}\,s^{-1}$) following a step-wise increase in free-stream current velocities between 10 and $50\,cm\,s^{-1}$ at Skeffling site D in the outer Humber estuary.

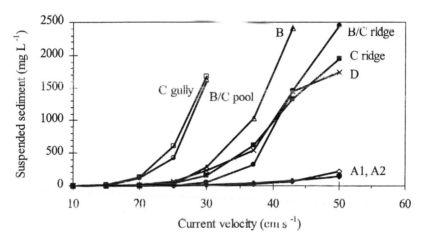

Fig. 4. Relationship between current velocity and maximum concentration of suspended sediment measured using the *in situ* annular flume at eight sites on the Skeffling mudflat.

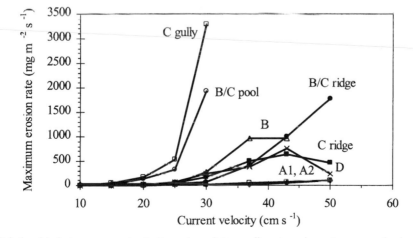

Fig. 5. Relationship between current velocity and maximum sediment erosion rate measured using the *in situ* annular flume at eight sites on the Skeffling mudflat.

Table 5. *Measurements derived from* in situ *annular flume experiments (phase II)*
*(a) Maximum concentration of resuspended sediments and maximum erosion rate at 43 cm s^{-1}
(shear stress = 1.46 Pa)*

Sites	Maximum SPM concentrations (mg l^{-1})	Maximum erosion rate (mg m^{-2} s^{-1})
A1	94	40
A2	85	60
B	2446	948
B/C ridge	1402	872
B/C pool*	1505	1740
C ridge	1305	686
C gully*	1654	3418
D	1356	758

* Experimental run curtailed at 30 cm s^{-1} due to incoming tide.

(b) Critical erosion velocities (u$_{crit}$: mean ± 95% C.I.) or current velocity (x) required to increase suspended sediment concentration (y) above threshold of 10 mg l^{-1}

Sites	Equation	Critical erosion velocity (cm s^{-1})	Critical erosion stress (Pa)
A1	$y = 0.0228e^{0.1944x}$	31.3 ± 2.1	0.70
A2	$y = 0.0112e^{0.2263x}$	29.7 ± 1.8	0.68
B	$y = 0.0053e^{0.3394x}$	22.2 ± 1.9	0.34
B/C Ridge	$y = 0.0011e^{0.3472x}$	26.3 ± 1.3	0.50
B/C Pool	$y = 0.0256e^{0.3816x}$	15.6 ± 1.3	0.18
C Ridge	$y = 0.0151e^{0.2962x}$	21.9 ± 1.6	0.33
C Gully	$y = 0.0304e^{0.3826x}$	15.1 ± 1.4	0.17
D	$y = 0.0339e^{0.2797x}$	20.3 ± 1.8	0.31

(c) Critical erosion velocities (u$_{crit}$: mean ± 95% C.I.) or current velocity (x) required to increase maximum erosion rate (y) above threshold of 20 mg m^{-2} s^{-1} (maximum rate over period of 30 s)

Sites	Equation	Critical erosion velocity (cm s^{-1})	Critical erosion stress (Pa)
A1	$y = 0.2788e^{0.1411x}$	30.2 ± 6	0.72
A2	$y = 0.0465e^{0.2014x}$	30.1 ± 5	0.72
B	$y = 0.0252e^{0.2912x}$	22.9 ± 8	0.34
B/C Ridge	$y = 0.0619e^{0.2429x}$	23.8 ± 3	0.44
B/C Pool	$y = 0.0571e^{0.3568x}$	16.4 ± 3	0.21
C Ridge	$y = 0.0502e^{0.2621x}$	22.8 ± 4	0.34
C Gully	$y = 0.0616e^{0.3729x}$	15.5 ± 3	0.19
D	$y = 0.0601e^{0.2581x}$	22.5 ± 4	0.34

the slope estimates and their associated standard errors for regressions of SPM vs current velocity showed that only site A1 was different from sites B/C pool and C gully at the 5% significance level. However, analysis of the slope estimates and associated standard errors for max E vs current velocity indicated more marked differences. A1 and A2 were significantly lower than B, B/C ridge, C ridge and D ($P < 0.05$), and these groups were both significantly different from sites B/C pool and C gully ($P < 0.05$).

Further analysis of these relationships provided 95% C.I. for the estimated critical erosion velocities (u_{crit}: cm s^{-1}) at a given value of y [Tables 5(b) and 5(c)]. The selected thresholds for determining u_{crit} and critical shear stress were an increase in SPM of >10 mg l^{-1} and an increase in the erosion rates of >20 mg m^{-2} s^{-1}, both of which are readily detected by the OBS sensor in the flume. While the analysis demonstrated that there was little difference between the two approaches for estimating u_{crit} (i.e. ΔSPM and erosion rates with appropriate thresholds of erosion) the SPM data provided narrower 95% C.I. due to the steeper slopes and higher correlation coefficients. The results summarized

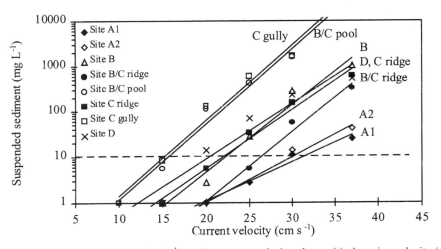

Fig. 6. Linear regressions of log SPM (mg l^{-1}) against current velocity where critical erosion velocity (or shear stress) is defined in terms of the current velocity (or shear stress) inducing an increase in SPM concentration of >10 mg l^{-1}.

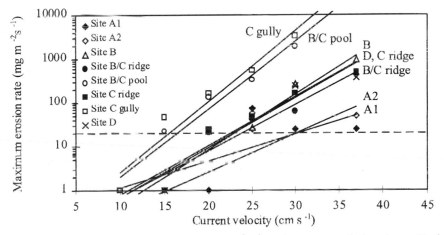

Fig. 7. Linear regressions of log max erosion rates (mg m^{-2} s^{-1}) against current velocity where critical erosion velocity is defined in terms of the current velocity inducing an increase in erosion rate >20 g m^{-2} s^{-1}.

in Tables 5(b) and 5(c) show that the upper shore sites had the highest u_{crit} values (31 cm s^{-1}) and these were significantly higher (ANOVA, $P < 0.05$) than the mid shore sites (u_{crit} of 22–26 cm s^{-1}) and the lowest u_{crit} values were found in the C gully and B/C pool (u_{crit} of 15 cm s^{-1}). To our knowledge this is the first time such data have been replicated and statistically analysed in this manner for the purpose of identifying significant differences amongst sites and of calculating critical erosion velocities with their error estimates.

These various descriptors of sediment erodibility therefore demonstrate that the eight sites fall into three distinct groups: [A1, A2]; [B, B/C ridge, C ridge, D]; [B/C pool, C gully]. For

example, the sites with the highest sediment stability (A1 and A2) were high on the mud-flat above the neap high tide level and just below the saltmarsh (max $E_{50} = 82$ mg m^{-2} s^{-1}; max SPM$_{50} = 231$ mg l^{-1} at 50 cm s^{-1}; $u_{crit} = 31$ cm s^{-1}). In contrast, the lowest sediment stability was associated with the gullies and pools at the mid shore site C (max $E_{30} = 3418$ mg m^{-2} s^{-1}; max SPM$_{30} = 1654$ mg l^{-1} at 30 cm s^{-1}; $u_{crit} = 15.5$ cm s^{-1}).

Macrofauna analysis

Table 4 summarizes the density of the main macrofauna species at the eight sites along the transect. The Skeffling mudflat has an estuarine fauna typical of cohesive muds in the middle/lower part of an estuary. Statistical analysis (ANOVAR) indicated significant differences between sites, although there were no significant differences between the sites in terms of species richness (i.e the number of taxa present). Total macrofauna abundance was significantly lower ($P < 0.001$) at sites A1 and A2 above the HW neap tide level, compared to sites B/C and C ridge. There were significant differences in *Macoma* density between sites ($P < 0.001$), attributable to lower densities at sites A1 and A2, and *Cerastoderma* were absent from the upper sites (A1, A2, B) on the shore. The method of sampling using four $10\,cm \times 10\,cm$ cores is not ideal for sampling the relatively low densities of adult *Cerastoderma* and in future these should be assessed by sampling the total surface sediments within the flume. In addition, spionid tubes at high densities may have a significant biostabilization role, even when animals are no longer present. However, these could not be quantified satisfactorily from the large cores and in future need to be sampled by means of smaller cores which are then gently washed/sieved.

Pearson correlation matrix for physical and biological data

A Pearson correlation matrix was used to highlight the significant correlations between the various physical and biological factors. Clearly, a number of the physical parameters covary (e.g. water content, bulk density, % POM and % $>63\,\mu m$), as well as descriptors of sediment erosion (e.g. u_{crit}, max SPM$_{30}$ and max E_{30}). However, differences in sediment stability/erodibility, measured in terms of u_{crit}, max E_{30} and max SPM$_{30}$, were not significantly correlated with the physical properties of the sediment, or with most of the species comprising the macrofauna community. The Pearson correlation matrix showed a number of important correlations:

(1) A significant correlation between duration of air exposure and u_{crit} ($r = +0.91$; $P < 0.01$), max SPM$_{30}$ ($r = -0.96$; $P < 0.001$) and max E_{30} ($r = -0.92$; $P < 0.01$), but no correlation with water content or bulk density.
(2) A negative correlation between *Cerastoderma edule* density and the duration of air exposure ($r = -0.96$; $P < 0.01$), and a positive correlation between *Cerastoderma* density and biodeposition rate ($r = +0.91$; $P < 0.05$).

(3) A positive correlation between an index of *Macoma* bioturbation activity [i.e. density of the main bioturbator of surface sediments (*Macoma balthica*) × proportion of tidal cycle immersed and available for feeding] and the descriptors of sediment erodibility, u_{crit} ($r = -0.96$; $P < 0.001$), max SPM$_{30}$ ($r = +0.93$; $P < 0.005$) and max E_{30} ($r = +0.88$; $P < 0.05$).
(4) A positive correlation between *Cerastoderma* density and the descriptors of sediment erodibility, u_{crit} ($r = -0.89$; $P < 0.01$), max SPM$_{30}$ ($r = +0.89$; $P < 0.01$) and max E_{30} ($r = +0.85$; $P < 0.05$).
(5) There were also some significant correlations ($P < 0.05$) observed amongst species, Spionids & *Nephtys*, *Nereis* & Oligochaeta, and *Nephtys* & *Eteone*.

The macrofauna were also divided into two broad functional groups (i.e. sediment stabilizers and destabilizers) in an attempt to establish whether there were any significant correlations between measures of sediment stability and the two groups (i.e. 'sediment stabilizers' comprising of tube dwellers such as the Spionid, *Pygospio*, which produces a robust tube, *Nereis*, Oligochaetes; and 'destabilizers' consisting of bioturbators such as *Macoma*, *Cerastoderma*, *Hydrobia*). The simple ratio between the relative abundance of sediment stabilizers and destabilizers was also examined because these functional groups coexist at each site. The only significant correlation observed was between the 'bioturbators' and u_{crit} ($r = -0.78$; $P < 0.05$).

The possible relationships between measures of sediment stability/erodibility and the physical and biological parameters were also investigated using multivariate analyses. Ordination was by non-metric multidimensional scaling (MDS) and relationships were examined by the BIOENV procedure which calculates rank correlations between a similarity matrix thereby defining suites of variables which 'best explain' the results. These analyses demonstrated that u_{crit}, max SPM$_{30}$ and max E_{30} were best explained by air exposure and *Macoma* density.

Discussion

Results from the field deployment of the PML annular flume have clearly demonstrated both large scale (km) and small scale (m) spatial variation in aspects of particle flux (biodeposition rates, erosion rates and the resuspended sediment concentration) across the sediment–water interface along the LISP-UK Skeffling transect. However, there was no simple correlation between sediment flux measurements and the physical properties of the sediment, including bulk density and moisture content, which showed no consistent relationship with the duration of air exposure.

There was, however, a significant correlation between the biodeposition rate and the density of the main suspension feeder on the mudflat, *Cerastoderma edule*. Maximum rates of biodeposition were recorded at Skeffling sites B/C and C (mean of $6 \, \mathrm{g \, m^{-2} \, h^{-1}}$) and these rates were similar to those measured by Smaal *et al.* (1986) at three intertidal mudflats in the Oosterschelde (mean of $6.8 \, \mathrm{g \, m^{-2} \, h^{-1}}$). At Skeffling sites A and B, net biodeposition rates were very low due to the absence of suspension feeding bivalves at upper shore sites which are immersed for less than 4 h per tidal cycle. It is important to note that this biologically enhanced downward flux from the water column to the sediment is only representative of the period around 'slack high water' when the currents are below the critical resuspension velocities for faeces and pseudofaeces (i.e. *c.* $15–20 \, \mathrm{cm \, s^{-1}}$; Widdows *et al.* 1998*b*). Consequently, the majority of biodeposits will be resuspended on the ebb tide. This is consistent with the *in situ* particle size analysis of Law *et al.* (this volume). Larger particle sizes, as well as higher SPM concentrations were recorded on the ebb compared to the flood at the site C (ridge/gully) on 7th April, and this will probably include resuspended faeces and pseudofaeces of the suspension feeder, *Cerastoderma edule*, and the bioturbator, *Macoma balthica*.

Although biodeposition rates were determined at relatively low SPM concentrations (i.e. mean SPM concentration in the flume of $52 \, \mathrm{mg \, l^{-1}}$), in contrast to the higher SPM concentrations recorded over the Skeffling mudflat ($300–800 \, \mathrm{mg \, l^{-1}}$; from Christie & Dyer this volume), the biodeposition rates will not be markedly different at these higher SPM concentrations. Recent studies by Navarro & Widdows (1997) have shown that biodeposition rates are maintained relatively constant over a wide range of seston concentrations, between 100 and $600 \, \mathrm{mg \, l^{-1}}$, due to the gradual reduction in clearance rate by *Cerastoderma* with increasing SPM concentration.

Measurement of sediment stability/erodibility using the *in situ* annular flume indicated that sites on the Skeffling mudflat can be separated into three distinct groups, on the basis of resuspended sediment concentration and maximum erosion rates, as well as critical erosion velocities. Furthermore, analysis of the data also demonstrated significant correlations between these

descriptors of sediment erodibility and *Cerastoderma* density, as well as an index of bioturbation activity, based on the density of *Macoma balthica* and the time available for feeding per tidal cycle (i.e. immersion time). The significant correlation between *Cerastoderma* density and sediment erodibility suggests that the biodeposits and the burrowing activity of this bivalve may provide a significant contribution to sediment erosion/resuspension. Subsequent laboratory experiments (Widdows *et al.* 1998*b*) have also shown that sediment erodibility is highly correlated with the burrowing/feeding activity and the density of *Macoma balthica*. These studies found a marked increase in sediment resuspension with increasing *Macoma* density (0, 250, 500, 1000 and 1500 *Macoma* $\mathrm{m^{-2}}$). For example, at relatively low current velocities ($20 \, \mathrm{cm \, s^{-1}}$) and at the mudflat density of 1000 *Macoma* $\mathrm{m^{-2}}$, sediment resuspension increased >4-fold (from 46 to $190 \, \mathrm{mg \, l^{-1}}$). Penetrometer measurements also showed that the sediment shear strength decreased from 285 to $167 \, \mathrm{N \, m^{-2}}$ with increasing *Macoma* density and feeding activity (Widdows *et al.* 1998*b*). Furthermore, there is close agreement between the values of u_{crit} and max. $\mathrm{SPM_{30}}$ recorded in both field (at sites B/C pool and C gully) and laboratory studies, at densities of 1000–1500 *Macoma* $\mathrm{m^{-2}}$ and when continually immersed. In the field *Macoma* can be observed actively feeding during low tide, when immersed in the pools and gullies.

Other LISP-UK studies using the Sea Carousel (Amos *et al.* this volume) and controlled stress rheometry (Ruddy *et al.* this volume) recorded comparable critical erosion shear stresses at the Skeffling sites, ranging from 0.7 Pa at site A to 0.3 Pa at site D. Furthermore, Amos *et al.* (this volume) using the Sea Carousel found a significant positive correlation between sediment stability and the concentration of microphytobenthos in the surficial sediment (measured in terms of chlorophyll a). These findings are consistent with the results of the present study, but reflect the inverse of the positive relationship between sediment erodibility and bioturbation activity. Microphytobenthos densities will tend to be reduced at lower shore levels, and in the pools and gullies, due to the higher grazing activity of *Macoma* and to a lesser extent *Hydrobia*, whereas they are observed at higher densities on the ridges and at higher shore levels where they are exposed to the light for longer and are less subject to grazing.

Data enabling comparisons between the *in situ* flume results and the *in situ* field measurement of SPM and current velocity are rather limited, but the available evidence suggests that there is good agreement. Vertical profiles of current velocities and SPM concentrations were made from an inflatable boat at mid-ebb tide at site C on 5/4/95 just prior to the deployment of the *in situ* flume (but current meter failure prevented further measurements by PML). Current velocities of $25-33 \text{ cm s}^{-1}$ ($z = 10 \text{ cm}$) and suspended particulates of $300-800 \text{ mg l}^{-1}$ were recorded just prior to air exposure of the tidal mudflat. At these current velocities the flume measurements would predict significant sediment erosion and resuspension from the ridges and particularly the gullies. For example, the range recorded in the flume at site C (i.e. between 25 and 30 cm s^{-1}) was $117-214 \text{ mg l}^{-1}$ on the ridge and $601-1654 \text{ mg l}^{-1}$ in the gully, resulting in a mean and range comparable to the field observations.

Detailed measurements of current velocities and SPM concentrations were made by Christie & Dyer (this volume) at the Skeffling sites using 'POST' (Profiles of Sediment Transport). These results also show good agreement between the *in situ* field and flume data, when comparing the observed net resuspension of sediment at sites A, B, C and D (i.e. difference between SPM at maximum current velocity and residual SPM at slack high water) with that predicted by the *in situ* flume studies.

Conclusions

(1) The eight sites between high-water springs (A) and mid-tide level (D) on the Skeffling intertidal mudflat were separated into three distinct groups on the basis of sediment stability/erodibility. The upper sites (A1 and A2) had the highest stability with significantly high critical erosion velocities (31 cm s^{-1}) and low SPM concentrations and erosion rates. In contrast sites B/C pool and C gully had the lowest sediment stability with low critical erosion velocities (15 cm s^{-1}) and high SPM concentrations and erosion rates. Sites B, B/C ridge, C ridge and D were intermediate with critical erosion velocities in the range 20–26 cm s^{-1}.

(2) Maximum erosion rates and maximum concentration of resuspended sediment showed a similar trend amongst the sites.

(3) Maximum biodeposition rates ($6.61 \text{ g m}^{-2} \text{ h}^{-1}$) were approximately an order of magnitude higher than the mean sedimentation rate ($0.66 \text{ g m}^{-2} \text{ h}^{-1}$) in the absence of suspension feeding macrofauna. There was a significant correlation between the biodeposition rate and the density of *Cerastoderma edule*, the main suspension feeder on the mudflat ($r = 0.91$; $P < 0.05$).

(4) Site differences in sediment stability/erodibility were not significantly correlated with any measured differences in the physical properties of the sediment.

(5) There were significant correlations ($P < 0.05$ to >0.001) between the erodibility, measured in terms of u_{crit}, max SPM$_{30}$ and max E_{30}, and *Cerastoderma edule* density and the level of bioturbation activity by *Macoma balthica*.

(6) Subsequent laboratory studies have confirmed that the feeding/burrowing/bioturbatory activity of *Macoma* significantly enhances sediment erodibility.

We thank Martin Carr for advice and assistance with the statistical analyses, Norman Bowley for constructing the flume and assisting with its field deployment, Colin Barrett for the development of the electronics, and Drs Kevin Black and David Paterson for the organization of the LISP-UK fieldwork. We are also indebted to the Environment Agency for allowing us to use their Skeffling pump station as a base for fieldwork. This is LOIS publication number 217 of the LOIS Community Research Programme, carried out under a Special Topic Award from the Natural Environmental Research Council.

References

AMOS, C. L., GRANT, J., DABORN, G. R. & BLACK, K. 1992. Sea Carousel – a benthic, annular flume. *Estuarine, Coastal and Shelf Science*, **34**, 557–577.

——, BRYLINSKY, M., SUTHERLAND, T. & CRAMP, A. 1998. The stability of a winter-profile mudflat, Humber estuary, Yorkshire, UK. *This volume*.

BLACK, K. S. & PATERSON, D. M. 1997. Measurement of the erosion potential of cohesive marine sediments: A review of current *in situ* technology. *Journal Marine Environmental Engineering*, **4**, 43–83.

CHRISTIE, M. & DYER, K. 1998. Measurements of shallow water erosion over the Skeffling mudflats. *This volume*.

CLARKE, K. R. 1993. Non-parametric multivariate analyses of changes in community structure. *Australian Journal of Ecology*, **18**, 117–143.

DAVEY, J. T. & PARTRIDGE, V. A. 1998. The macrofaunal communities of the Skeffling muds (Humber estuary) with special reference to bioturbation. *This volume*.

DAVIS, W. 1993. The role of bioturbation in sediment resuspension and its interaction with physical shearing. *Journal of Experimental Marine Biology and Ecology*, **171**, 187–200.

FUKADA, M. K. & LICK, W. 1980. The entrainment of cohesive sediment in freshwater. *Journal of Geophysical Research*, **85**, 2813–2824.

JUMARS, P. A. & NOWELL, A. R. M. 1984. Effects of benthos on sediment transport: difficulties with functional grouping. *Continental Shelf Research*, **3**, 115–130.

LAW, J. D., BALE, A. J. & JONES, S. E. 1998. *In situ* characterisation of suspended particles over the LISP (UK) sites using focused beam, laser reflectance particle sizing. *This volume.*

MAA, J. P.-Y. 1990. The bed shear stress of an annular sea-bed flume. *In*: MICHAELIS, W. (ed.) *Estuarine Water Quality Management: Monitoring, Modelling and Research.* Berlin: Springer-Verlag, 271–275.

——, WRIGHT, L. D., LEE, C.-H. & SHANNON, T. W. 1993. VIMS Sea Carousel: a field instrument for studying sediment transport. *Marine Geology*, **115**, 271–287.

MEADOWS, P. S. & MEADOWS, A. 1991. The geotechnical and geochemical implications of bioturbation in marine sedimentary ecosystems. *Symposium of the Zoological Society of London*, **63**, 157–181.

NAVARRO, J. M. & WIDDOWS, J. 1997. Feeding physiology of *Cerastoderma edule* (L.) in response to a wide range of seston concentrations. *Marine Ecology Progress Series*, **152**, 175–186.

PATERSON, D. M. 1989. Short term changes in the erodibility of intertidal cohesive sediment related to the migratory behaviour of epipelic diatoms. *Limnology and Oceanography*, **34**, 223–234.

RHOADS, D. C. & BOYER, L. F. 1982. The effects of marine benthos on physical properties of sediments: a successional perspective, *In*: McCALL, P. L. & TEVESZ, M. J. S. (eds) *Animal–Sediment Relations: the Biogenic Alteration of Sediments.* Plenum Press, New York, 3–52.

RUDDY, G., TURLEY, C. M., JONES, E., TAYLOR, I. & PATERSON, D. M. 1998. The microbial mediation of sediment transport. *This volume.*

SAS. 1989. *User's Guide: Statistics.* SAS Institute, Inc. Cary, NC.

SMAAL, A. C., VERHAGEN, J. H. G., COOSEN, J. & HAAS, H. A. 1986. Interaction between seston quantity and quality and benthic suspension feeders in the Oosterschelde, the Netherlands. *Ophelia*, **26**, 385–399.

WIDDOWS, J., BRINSLEY, M. D., BOWLEY, N. & BARRETT, C. 1998*a*. A benthic annular flume for *in situ* measurement of suspension feeding/biodeposition rates and erosion potential of intertidal cohesive sediment. *Estuarine, Coastal and Shelf Science* (in press).

——, ——, SALKELD, P. N. & ELLIOTT, M. 1998*b*. Use of annular flumes to determine the influence of current velocity and bivalves on material flux at the sediment water interface, (ECSA 1996 Conference, submitted to *Estuaries*).

Pigment fingerprints as markers of erosion and changes in cohesive sediment surface properties in simulated and natural erosion events

K. H. WILTSHIRE[2], T. TOLHURST[1], D. M. PATERSON[1],
I. DAVIDSON[1] & G. GUST[3]

[1] Sediment Ecology Research Group, Gatty Marine Laboratory, University of St Andrews,
St Andrews, Fife KY16 8LB, UK
[2] Present address: Max-Planck-Institute for Limnology, August-Thienemann Strasse 2,
Postfach 165, 24302 Plön, Germany
[3] Technical University of Hamburg-Harburg, Arbeitsbereich Meerestechnik,
Lauenbruch ost 1, DE-21071 Hamburg

Abstract: The pollutant dynamics of estuaries is closely associated with the transport of particulate matter and one problematic area is the quantification of the erosion, deposition and transport of intertidal sediment. The primary event in sediment erosion is the resuspension of surficial layers which are often densely colonized by assemblages of microphytobenthos and bacteria. The dominant microphytobenthos (Bacillariophyceae or diatoms) contain characteristic marker pigments, chlorophyll c and fucoxanthin. To date, few marker compounds have been used to characterize particulate matter and to monitor its transport. This study identifies pigments as useful marker compounds in monitoring erosive events, particularly at low erosion rates. Erosion can either be considered as occurring when the stress at the surface exceeds the threshold strength of the bed or as one side of a deposition/entrainment equilibrium always occurring at the bed surface. The present analysis indicates that an erosion threshold exists and that pigments derived from surface biofilms appear in the water column before the general failure of the bed. The result is a lower yield stress (U^*_{crit}) for biofilm components than for the sediments themselves, supporting the contention that the 'yield stress' of natural sediments has a strong biological component, in addition to purely physical control. Pigment fingerprinting is shown to provide information on the origin of suspended matter, including the suspension and deposition of particles. The potential for using microphytobenthic pigments as indicators of erosion events in laboratory simulations (erosion and respiration chambers) and in the field is discussed.

The erosion, transport, deposition and consolidation (the EDTC cycle) of cohesive material is a problem of international concern (Amos 1995, Burt et al. 1997). There is a basic requirement to understand sediment dynamics and in addition the pollutant dynamics of an estuary is closely linked to the distribution of particulate matter (Wiltshire et al. 1994). Thus, the nature of the sediment supply and the erosive behaviour of intertidal deposits, which act as sources and sinks for sediments in suspension, are critical to understanding the EDTC cycle of estuaries. However, the quantification of the erosion, deposition and transport of intertidal particulate matter remains one of the most difficult and important areas in estuarine research. This goal is hampered by the lack of suitable in situ tracer materials for monitoring the movement of particulate matter. To date, only a few marker compounds have been used in the literature to characterize suspended matter and to monitor its transport. These include mineralogical components (Schwedhelm et al. 1988) and trace metals (Salomons et al. 1987). Apart from the diverse

mixture of mineral components, suspended matter in estuaries contains large amounts of biogenic material. However, biological compounds, apart from carbon, have rarely been used in the characterization of sediment and suspended matter. In aquatic systems, algae constitute a large component of particulate matter either growing in situ (phytoplankton) or arising from the resuspension of benthic forms (microphytobenthos). Algal groups have characteristic pigments (Van den Hoek et al. 1995) and certain assemblages occurring in different water bodies and/or sediments can be differentiated on the basis of their pigment compliment (i.e. pigment fingerprints). Pigment fingerprints determined by HPLC (Gieskes & Kraay 1983; Wright & Jeffrey 1987) can be used to study the composition of assemblages of primary producers in suspended matter in aquatic systems. It has been shown that rivers and estuaries (such as the Elbe, Germany) can therefore be separated into zones using the characteristics of pigments contained in the suspended matter (Wiltshire & Schroeder 1994). In areas where

WILTSHIRE, K. H., TOLHURST, T. & PATERSON, D. M. et al. 1998. Pigment fingerprints as markers of erosion. In: BLACK, K. S., PATERSON, D. M. & CRAMP, A. (eds) Sedimentary Processes in the Intertidal Zone. Geological Society, London, Special Publications, **139**, 99–114.

sediments receive illumination, they are often densely colonized by varied assemblages of microphytobenthos (MacIntyre *et al.* 1996) and attempts have been made to characterize sediments on the basis of pigments from microphytobenthos assemblages (Wiltshire 1992; Cariou-Le Gall & Blanchard 1995). This paper augments these studies by applying the pigment tracer concept to the resuspension of biofilm components by hydrodynamic stress. Novel techniques applied include:

(1) A non-destructive sediment sampling technique (Wiltshire *et al.* 1997) to examine the influence of the erosion process on the fine-structure of the bed and obtain fine sections of sediments for the vertical analyses of pigment distribution.
(2) Pigment analysis (HPLC) in conjunction with the fine-structural analysis by low-temperature scanning electron microscopy (Paterson 1995).
(3) A flow chamber which induces erosion under hydrodynamic conditions similar to those in the field (Gust & Müller 1997).

Experiments were conducted by inducing erosion and analysis of natural ebb/flood water samples carried out. The potential of using microphytobenthic pigment signatures as indicators of the initial erosion events both in the field and in microcosm systems is discussed.

Materials and methods

Erosion experiments were conducted on the north shore of the Eden Estuary while tidal flow studies were carried out in the Ems-Dollard Estuary (Fig. 1). The mudflats of the Eden are relatively short (100–300 m) with a few surface drainage channels running perpendicular to the shore, but no developed ridge/runnel system. The sediment at the sample station was composed of a silt/sand mixture (mean grain size 110 μm) with >30% < 63 μm and displaying cohesive properties. The Dollard site was located on the Heringsplaat, a tidal mud flat, containing 20% <63 μm, opposite the harbour of the German city of Emden. The sample sites were chosen close to a specialized intertidal measurement bridge (Netherlands BOA project bridge, geographical co-ordinates: 09 28 12. 17 06 .32).

Erosion studies

The Microcosm System (MS) erosion device (Gust 1990; Hüttel & Gust 1992) was deployed

(a)

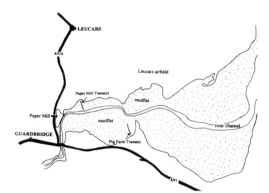

(b)

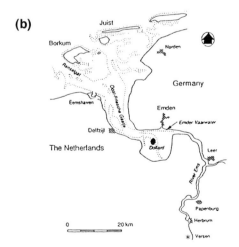

Fig. 1. (a) The UK and the position of the experimental station close to the paper mill. (b) The location of the BOA measuring bridge on the intertidal flats of the Ems Dollard Estuary.

twice on the mid-intertidal sector of the exposed shore to establish a consistent pattern for the erosional properties of the flat, such as erosion thresholds and entrainment rates. Once the erosional properties were understood, detailed pigment analysis was conducted from a further run at a similar station. The MS is relatively small (30 cm diameter) and can be deployed easily in the field. The system consists of a circular test chamber, with a removable lid, housing a stirring disc. Water can be abstracted via an intake located at the axis of disc rotation. The MS generates a spatially homogenous bed shear stress, by controlling two parameters simultaneously: (1) the rotational speed of a stirring disc and (2) the volume of water removed through the rotating axis and re-circulated to the chamber (Gust 1990; Hüttel & Gust 1992). The hydrodynamic characteristics of the chamber have been well-described and in comparative trials of erosion devices the MS has been shown to produce a turbulent intensity spectrum most similar to that of the natural environment (Gust & Müller 1997). The system has been calibrated such that the friction velocity is known [U^* where $U^* = (\tau/\text{rho})^{0.5}$, and τ is bottom stress] for a series of rotational speeds and water abstraction rates at given water depth, and verified by a theoretical model of the chamber flow. Experiments consist of increasing U^* in known steps over a set time period (10 min), standardized for each erosion run. The initial erosion runs were used to

establish the range of steps needed to examine the erosion of biofilm material at higher resolution on the third run when pigment analysis also took place. The MS was either pressed into the sediment *in situ* during the outgoing tide and the tidal water thus entrapped was used as the erosional medium, or gently filled with medium from an isotonic supply. Calculations were corrected for initial suspended particulate matter (SPM) concentrations. Water samples taken from the chamber at regular time intervals were used to determine the SPM and the change in SPM concentration with time was used to calculate erosion rates. The pigment concentrations of the suspended matter in the final run were determined by High Performance Liquid Chromatography (HPLC). Sediment samples were taken using the Cryolander technique (described below) at the time of the erosion run and from the area eroded by the MS system after completion of the run and removal of the chamber.

Sediment samples

All surface sediments were sampled with a Cryolander, a specially developed liquid nitrogen sampler (Fig. 2, Wiltshire *et al.* 1997). The Cryolander (surface area *c.* 20 cm^2) was placed on the sediment surface and liquid nitrogen dribbled onto the absorbent cotton producing nitrogen vapour. When enough vapour had been

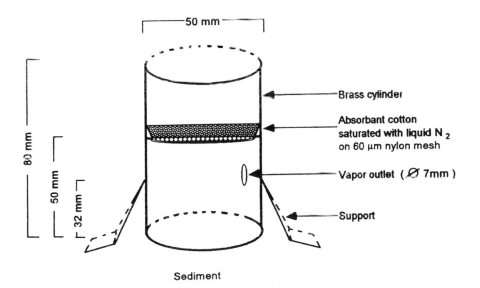

Fig. 2. Schematic diagram of the Cryolander device for the *in situ* freeze sampling of unconsolidated sediments.

produced to freeze the sediment surface, more liquid nitrogen was poured onto the cotton. This procedure was continued until the sediment around the base of the Cryolander was frozen (2–3 mm rim). The Cryolander was then removed with the sediment block attached to the base. This was then detached, placed in a pre-labelled dish and frozen in liquid nitrogen. Samples could then be returned to the laboratory for analysis. The sediment core was cut, while still frozen, into 1 cm^3 blocks, using a diamond lapidary saw. The frozen blocks were placed on a freezing microtome and sectioned at 200 μm intervals. The sediment sections were removed from the microtome blade using a pre-weighed piece of glass fibre filter paper. This was then re-weighed (wet) and placed in an opaque pre-weighed vial and freeze dried for 12 h. Dry weight and water content were calculated and since the volume of sediment was known (surface area × depth of slice) it was possible to calculate the approximate wet bulk density of the upper layers of sediments (Taylor and Paterson in press). For HPLC analysis, 2 ml of acetone was added to the sample, and the material re-frozen at −70°C and stored until required for analysis. A replicate sample block was used to examine the microstructure of the upper sediment layers using low-temperature scanning electron microscopy (LTSEM).

Water samples

Water samples (200 ml) were removed from the microcosm using a syringe-attachment and dispensed into sample bottles (300 ml). 100–200 ml of the sample was filtered through a glass fibre filter (GFF) which was suspended in 2 ml of acetone, in black vials, frozen at −70°C and retained for pigment analyses.

High performance liquid chromatography (HPLC)

The water and sediment samples were analysed for pigments using HPLC, enabling detection of chlorophylls a, b, c1 and c2, chlorophyllides, phaeophorbides, phaeophytins, fucoxanthin, hexanoyl-fucoxanthin, butanoyl- fucoxanthin, diadinoxanthin, zeaxanthin, diatoxanthin, violaxanthin, lutein, b-carotene and a-carotene. Chlorophyll *a* was expressed as an absolute value calculated against a known Chl *a* standard while other pigments (standards not available) were expressed in terms of a ratio against Chl *a*. The suspended matter mixtures for analyses

Table 1. *Solvent gradient used in HPLC analysis*

Time (min)	% A	% B
0	80	20
0.30	80	20
4	55	45
35	0	100
45	0	100
50	80	20

were frozen at −70°C for a minimum of 24 h before use. Samples were extracted by sonication at 0°C for 3 min (14 amperes, ultrasound microtip, Ultrasonics). The extracts were filtered through 0.45 μm cellulose filters and then injected by autosampler straight into a HPLC system consisting of a quaternary high pressure pump system (Perkin Elmer 410), an autosampler (Waters WISP 417) and a diode array detector (Waters 910). The chromatography involved the use of a C30 reversed phase column in conjunction with a simple binary gradient. The flow used was 0.9 ml min^{-1}, and the two solvent systems were: (A) methanol : acetonitrile : water (45% : 20% : 35%) and (B) methanol : acetonitrile:ethyl acetate (30% : 50% : 20%). Running conditions were as described by Villerius *et al.* (1996) and the solvent gradient is given in Table 1.

Low-temperature scanning electron microscopy (LTSEM)

Sediment microstructure was examined using LTSEM (Paterson 1995; Défarge *et al.* 1996). Using this technique, material can be examined while still frozen on the specially-adapted stage of a SEM (Oxford Instruments Cryosystem with Joel 35FC SEM). Freezing the material preserves the structural properties of water within the sample which is of particular importance in biological materials and hydrated sediments. Samples cut from frozen cryolander blocks were mounted on a mechanical stub and examined in the microscope at −180°C. Frozen surface moisture was removed by raising the temperature of the SEM stage to *c.* −90°C which allows unbound surface water to sublimate directly into vacuum in a process known as heat etching (Jeffree & Read 1992). Once completed, samples are coated in gold while being maintained at low-temperature and then examined. A review of LTSEM as applied to sediments can be found in Paterson (1995).

Measurements of natural ebb/flood waters

Samples of the ebb and tidal flood waters in the Ems-Dollard estuary (The Netherlands) were obtained. Sampling was carried out from a bridge constructed in the intertidal of the Ems-Dollard (Fig. 1). The water samples were pumped up from the intertidal water at depths of 10, 15 and 40 cm above the sediment bed, at hourly intervals, using a vacuum pump. 200 ml of sample was filtered through glass fibre filters (GFF) which were then suspended in 2 ml of acetone, in black vials, frozen in liquid nitrogen and retained for pigment analysis. Surface sediment samples were taken by Cryolander immediately after emersion and just prior to immersion. The Cryolander samples were analysed for pigments, water contents, density and microstructure as outlined above.

Results

Erosion experiments: Eden Estuary

The erosion experiments were conducted in the Eden Estuary during low tide when a faint coloration was present at the surface of the sediment, indicative of the presence of micro-organisms. A thin biofilm on the sediment surface consisting mainly of diatoms was confirmed by light microscopy and LTSEM.

Microcosm experiments. The SPM concentrations at given values of U^* for the erosion runs during the field MS deployments are given (Fig. 3). The patterns of erosion in the first two runs (Fig. 3a, b) were very similar. At the onset of MS deployment small surface flocs were observed to erode from the bed. This very limited erosion was not detectable by SPM measurements and may comprise loose surface flocculant material. Further measurable erosion took place after a U^* of 1.4 cm s^{-1} had been reached and significant erosion occurred by a U^* of 2.24 cm s^{-1} in both cases. Peak erosion rates (max mass per unit time) are shown in Table 2. The sediments examined in the third run (used for pigment analysis) were slightly less stable than those from the other runs, showing erosion at $U^* = 1.39$ cm s^{-1} with bed failure at $U^* = 1.51$ cm s^{-1} (peak erosion rate = 343 mg m^{-2} s^{-1}).

Pigment analysis. The appearance of pigment compounds in the water column above the test bed did not follow the pattern determined from SPM concentration and erosion rate (Fig. 4a, b). There was an initial small peak in chlorophyll and suspended matter at the beginning of the experimental run; visual observations indicate that this initial period of erosion consisted of the removal of loose surface particles and pieces of the microphytobenthos biofilm. After this, the chlorophyll concentration was relatively low and constant, until a U^* of 1.4 cm s^{-1} when a pronounced peak in concentration was observed (Fig. 4a, b). This increase in chlorophyll a concentration reflected only a slight increase in the erosion rate of material from the sediment bed as determined by a SPM concentration of 500 mg l^{-1}. The ratios of the major pigments to chlorophyll a (Fig. 5a) demonstrated that fucoxanthin (a marker for diatoms) was the most prominent of the accessory pigments whereas pheophytin (breakdown product) appeared only as erosion increased beyond a U^* of 1.3 cm s^{-1} (Fig. 5a). The material eroded at the beginning of the run was largely fucoxanthin and Chl a while the diatom pigment diadinoxanthin appeared as an important component from above a U^* of 1.2 cm s^{-1}. The peak in Chl a erosion did not show an unusual pigment fingerprint (time 40, Fig. 5a) although the relative proportion of the accessory pigments decreased in relation to Chl a.

Pre- and post-erosion changes to the bed structure. The surface concentration of Chl a within the sediment was reduced by the erosion event in the microcosm (Fig. 5b). The largest difference in concentration appeared to be in the upper 800 μm of the sediments. Analysis of additional pigments showed that fucoxanthin and diadinoxanthin ratios to Chl a were generally higher before the erosion event (Fig. 5b, c). Indeed, diadinoxanthin only appeared at the sediment surface before the erosion event (Fig. 5d).

The density of the sediment also varied before and after erosion with an increase in the average density of the 200 μm sections examined over the upper 2 mm from 1.39 to 1.50 g cm^{-3} after erosion. The expectation that density of the substrata would increase after the erosion of less dense surface material (Taylor and Paterson in press) was supported by statistical analysis of the matched sections (one tailed t-test for matched pairs, $P < 0.05$). The water contents of the upper sediment layers were not found to be significantly different after erosion (Fig. 6a, b). Sediment structure was examined using LTSEM. Before the onset of erosion, an intact biofilm was present on the sediment surface (Fig. 7a). This skin is typical of biofilm assemblages

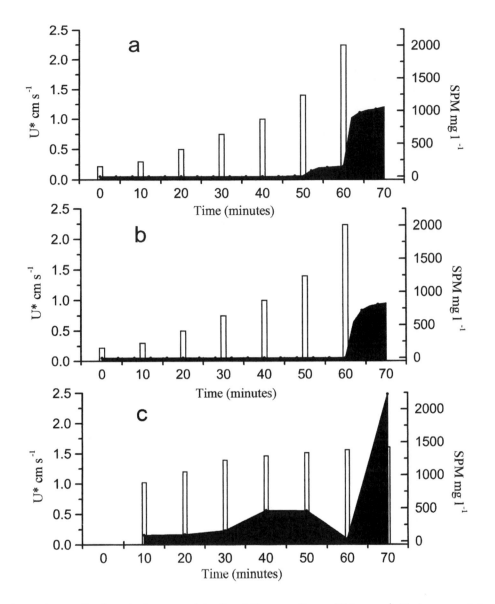

Fig. 3. Erosion profiles from deployments of the Gust MS system. Bars $= U^*$ in cm s^{-1}. Black $=$ suspended particulate matter in mg l^{-1}. (**a**) First deployment. (**b**) Second deployment. (**c**) Third deployment.

Table 2. *Time-averaged erosion rates (10 min period) from* in situ *experiments deploying the Microcosm in the Eden Estuary*

Deployment	Erosion rate (mg m^{-2} s^{-1}), 10 min interval		
	$U^* = 1.4$ cm s^{-1}	$U^* = 1.51$ cm s^{-1}	$U^* = 2.24$ cm s^{-1}
Run 1	0	ND	130
Run 2	23	ND	140
Run 3 (pigment analysis)	48	344	ND

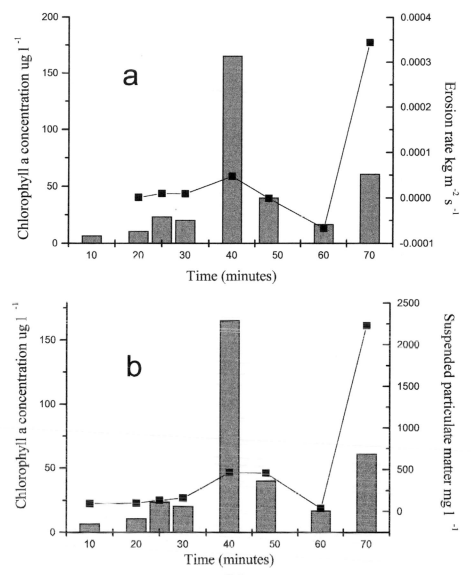

Fig. 4. Detail of erosion from the third microcosm deployment combined with HPLC pigment analysis from the water column during erosion. (**a**) Chlorophyll *a* (bar) against erosion rate (line). (**b**) Chlorophyll *a* (bar) against suspended particulate matter (line).

(Paterson 1995) and overlies the more open card-house structure associated with unconsolidated sediments (Fig. 7f). The surface skin, as represented by LTSEM, amounted to $<10 \mu m$ in depth, and on erosion and release of the diatoms the SPM concentration increased from 100 to $500 \, mg \, l^{-1}$ (Fig. 4b). After erosion, the surface skin was no longer visible and the card-house structure extended to the surface of the sediment (Fig. 7b). The sub-surface layer was porous

with the matrix including mineral grains, organic material and some remaining diatom cells (Fig. 7b).

Tidal flow measurements: Ems-Dollard

Sediment structure. The Ems-Dollard sediments were covered with a dense mat of diatoms as shown by LTSEM (Fig. 7c–f) forming

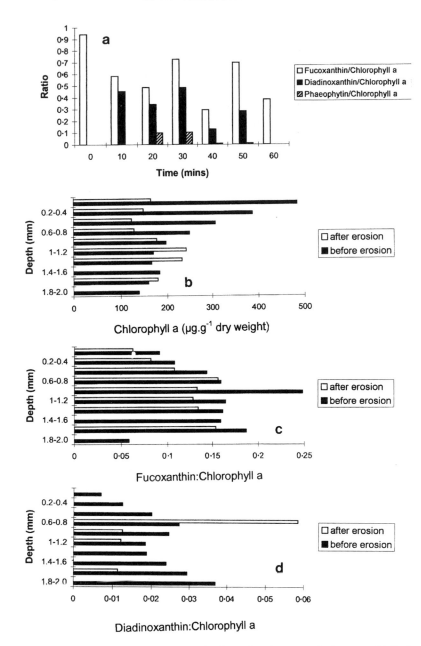

Fig. 5. HPLC analysis of sediments and water samples from the microcosm deployment. (**a**) Ratio of major pigments to Chl *a* with time in the MS water column. (**b–d**) HPLC analysis of depth profiles within the sediments before and after erosion. (**b**) Chlorophyll *a*. (**c**) Ratio of fucoxanthin to chlorophyll *a*. (**d**) Ratio of diadinoxanthin to chlorophyll *a*.

a matrix varying between 40–80 m in depth (Fig. 7f). The erosion of patches of the sediment surface was clearly visible *in situ*. Sections of the diatom mat were peeled off the surface of the sediments by the action of the first incoming waves moving over the mudflat and the sediment underneath became exposed. The surface of the sediment from eroded patches had the characteristic card-house structure of cohesive sediments (Fig. 7e). The water contents and density of the

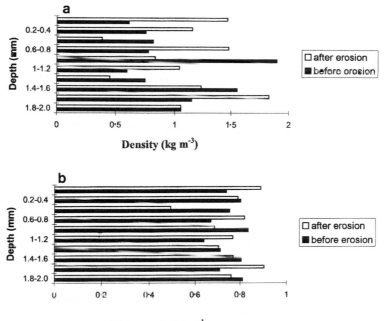

Fig. 6. Sediment dry density (**a**) and sediment water content (**b**) calculated from thin sections of frozen material taken before and after erosion. Solid bars = before erosion, outline bars = after erosion.

upper sediment layers show some variation before and after erosion (Fig. 9). After erosion, the density of the sediment tended to be higher while the water content was significantly lower (one tailed t-test for matched pairs, $P < 0.01$). From these data, it is evident that the surface properties of the exposed sediment have been altered by the removal of surface layers.

Pigment analysis. The Chl a content of the surface layer (0–200 μm) of sediment was markedly reduced by the natural erosion events. Indeed, Chl a could not be measured beneath a depth of 1.4 mm after the erosion event (Fig. 8a). Fucoxanthin showed a similar pattern while the relative amounts of diadinoxanthin to Chl a (Fig. 8c) were higher in the eroded sediment. The typical fingerprints of the upper 200 μm of the sediments before erosion shows the importance of the diatom marker pigment, fucoxanthin, and the smaller amounts of the chlorophyll breakdown product, chlorophyllide (Fig. 9). In comparison, chlorophyllide is more important after erosion and the proportion of fucoxanthin decreases.

Water samples. The chlorophyll concentrations and suspended matter in the water column varied with tidal height (Fig. 10a). The pigment fingerprints of the suspended matter over the tidal inundation indicate that the pigment content varied with the flood and ebb tides (Fig. 10b). In the latter samples, the pigments chlorophyllide, chlorophyll c1 and carotene were present. These pigments were not present in the 11:15 and 14:00 samples (greater tidal height). To investigate the possibility that the results were an artefact of the sampling depths, the pigment signatures for the 14:00 station were sampled at three different depths (surface, 40 cm and 10 cm from the bed) and examined (Fig. 10c). The results suggested that the water column was well-mixed in terms of pigment distribution. There was no consistent pattern of Chl a concentration with tidal height although the maximum value was recorded as the flood tide flowed over the flats (10:15). Chl a varied independently of SPM and reached its second highest value when the SPM concentration was at its slack water minimum (Fig. 10b).

Discussion and conclusions

Algal pigment fingerprint data allow the distinction of different types of particulate matter on large scales in estuarine water bodies (Wiltshire

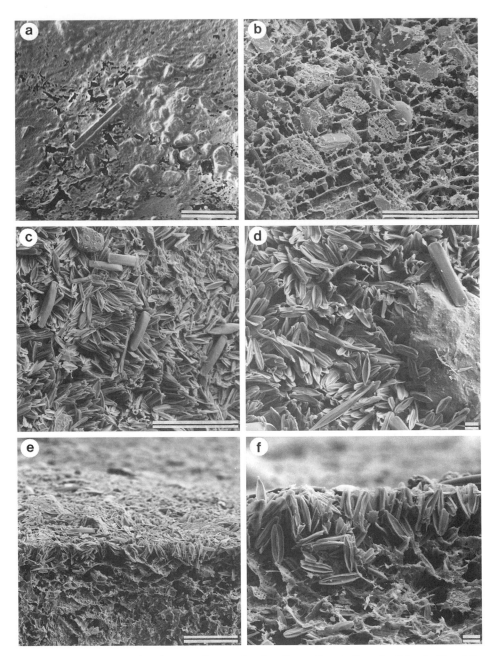

Fig. 7. Low-temperature scanning electron micrographs of surface sediments from the Eden (**a, b**) and Ems Dollard estuaries (**c–f**). (**a**) Surface biofilm on the sediments of the Eden before erosion by the Gust MS system. Note uniform cover of sediment by matrix (Bar marker 100 μm). (**b**) The surface of a similar sediment after the erosion of the biofilm layer. The sediment appears porous with the segregation zones caused during ice crystal formation clearly visible between particulate matter and organic material (Bar marker 100 μm). (**c**) The dense surface biofilm from the Ems Dollard site largely made up of the genus *Nitzschia* (Bar marker 100 μm). (**d**) Detail of the surface biofilm showing the inclusion of a sand grain among the varied diatom assemblage (Bar marker 10 μm). (**e**) Freeze-fracture face through the surface biofilm. The biofilm layer at this point is *c.* 50 μm deep with diatoms ranked in a vertical series at the sediment surface (Bar marker 100 μm). (**f**) Detail of the surface biofilm. Cells of the genus *Nitzschia* arranged on top of the open card-house matrix of the underlying cohesive sediment (Bar marker 10 μm).

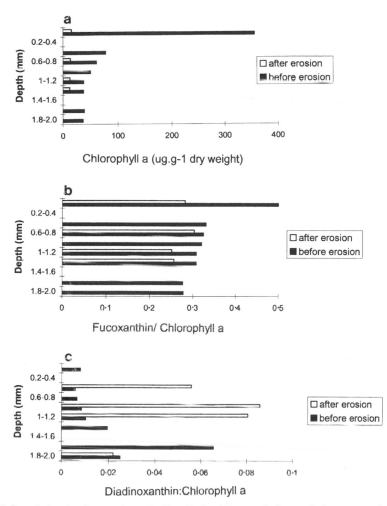

Fig. 8. HPLC analysis of sediments from the Ems Dollard Estuary before and after a natural erosion event. (**a**) Chlorophyll *a*. (**b**) Ratio of fucoxanthin to chlorophyll *a*. (**c**) Ratio of diadinoxanthin to chlorophyll *a*.

et al. 1994) but there have been few studies examining the potential of pigments in the surface layers of intertidal sediments as an indicator of erosion or as a potential marker of sediment transport (see Sutherland 1996). The algae that inhabit sediment in the intertidal zone accumulate in the surface layer to obtain sufficient light for photosynthesis since the sediment euphotic zone may be limited to a few hundred microns (Yallop *et al.* 1994, Kühl *et al.* 1994). This layer is often rich in algae and their associated pigments (Paterson 1995, Wiltshire *et al.* 1997). The dominant algae of these populations are the Bacillariophyceae (or diatoms) which contain characteristic marker pigments such as fucoxanthin and chlorophyll c and pigments have already been used for mapping microalgae distribution in sediments (Wiltshire 1992; Cariou-

le Gall & Blanchard 1995; Paterson *et al.* in review) and to characterize bodies of water (Wiltshire *et al.* 1994).

Using the simulated natural flow conditions in the controlled-stress erosion chamber to mimic natural erosion and deposition, combined with fine-scale analysis of pigment distribution (Cryolander technique; Wiltshire *et al.* 1997), it was shown that the erosion of the microalgal layer can be traced into the water column. This confirms recent laboratory flume studies with diatom cultures by Sutherland (1996) and field work by Humann (1995) which have suggested that surface biofilms have a different threshold for erosion than the associated sediments. These variations in erosive behaviour of biofilms can be determined only by careful analysis of the water column or the remaining sediment since,

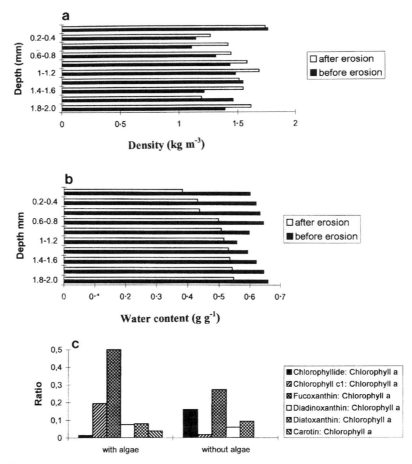

Fig. 9. (a) Sediment dry density and (b) sediment water content calculated from thin sections of frozen material taken before and after erosion. Solid bars = before erosion, outline bars = after erosion. (c) Chlorophyll *a* concentration and the ratio of major pigments to Chl *a* before and after erosion of the surface biofilm layer.

during simulated and natural erosion events, Chl *a* concentration is uncoupled from SPM load. Erosion is a critical phase of the ETDC cycle and is governed by a complex of processes including physical and biological effects (Black 1997, Paterson 1997). Erosion can be considered as taking place when the shear stress at the surface exceeds the inherent strength of the bed (Delo 1988). It is also sometimes suggested that erosion represents one side of a deposition/entrainment equilibrium which is always occurring at the bed surface. Under the latter circumstances, the stress at which the removal of particles first exceeds deposition is the point of interest and no 'threshold' for erosion exists. Data supporting this concept are lacking. Using the MS system in the field, it was clear that an erosion threshold existed and the combined MS/HPLC analysis indicated that

the U^*_{crit} varied between the biofilm (U^*_{crit} Chl $a = 1.4\,\mathrm{cm\,s^{-1}}$) and the underlying bed (U^*_{crit} sediment $= 1.5\,\mathrm{cm\,s^{-1}}$). This supports the work of Sutherland (1996). The results support the contention that the 'yield stress' of natural sediment surfaces has a strong biological component in addition to purely physical aspects.

The Cryolander system allows the fine structure of the sediment surface to be analysed on a scale relevant to surface erosion (Type I erosion, Mehta & Partheniades 1982) and the distribution of biofilm components examined (Taylor & Paterson in press). In addition, the nature of the pigments found in the water column varies through the erosion process probably related to the distribution of pigments with depth in the sediment, for example the depth that breakdown products produced by the algal assemblages accumulate (e.g. phaeophorbides).

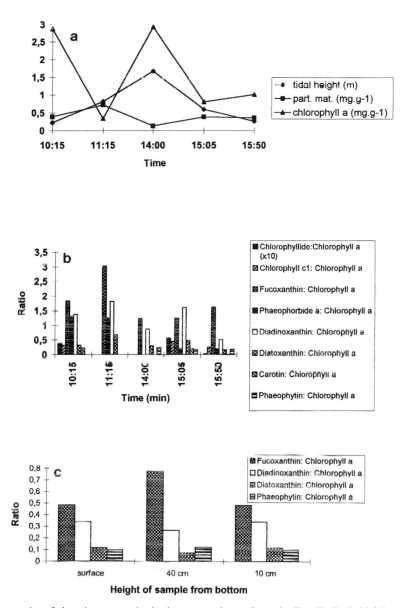

Fig. 10. Time series of changing properties in the water column above the Ems Dollard tidal flats. (**a**) Tidal height, SPM and chlorophyll *a* concentration. (**b**) Ratio of the major pigments to chlorophyll *a*. (**c**) Distribution of pigment ratios with depth in the water column from the surface to the bed at high water.

Pigments in the water column as indicators of biofilm erosion

The increase of pigments in the water column and the corresponding decrease of pigments in the upper 200 μm of the sediments after erosion is reported here for the first time. The discrimination of this pathway required HPLC

and LTSEM studies, which indicated biofilm and pigment loss and the removal of the surface organic layer associated with natural algal biofilms (Underwood & Paterson 1993; Paterson 1995). It was also clear that components of the bed eroded at different times and flow strengths, as evidenced by the pigment fingerprints. There was an initial small peak in chlorophyll and suspended matter at the beginning of the experiment at a U^* of $1\,\mathrm{cm\,s^{-1}}$. This represents the removal of unattached surface flocs, when the MS began to induce stress at the sediment surface. This flocculent layer has been noted in many previous studies and was shown to have a high biogenic load. The peak in chlorophyll concentration after 40 min represented the failure of the surface biofilm (equivalent to a U^* of $1.4\,\mathrm{cm\,s^{-1}}$) as shown by a large increase in the chlorophyll a in the water column. The SPM only varied slightly at lower U^* and eventually increased at a U^* of $1.5\,\mathrm{cm\,s^{-1}}$ (Fig. 3c). The question remains as to whether the biofilm has imparted extra stability on the surface of the sediment or if the initial erosion of the biofilm had little or no impact on the underlying layer. This question is not addressed here but fine scale analysis of the erosion process under controlled conditions may help to illuminate the role of the organic matter, such as extracellular polymeric substances (EPS, Underwood *et al.* 1995) often cited as the mechanism of biogenic stabilisation (Yallop *et al.* 1994; Paterson 1997).

The combination of the MS system, Cryolander and LTSEM techniques allows more detailed analysis of the erosion process than has yet been possible. It was shown that a similar pattern of erosion and similar bed effects were produced in natural and simulated erosion events. Both experimental sites supported biofilms and analysis showed the removal and destruction of the biofilms by the erosion processes. In the Ems-Dollard estuary, the sediments were covered by a prominent layer of microphytobenthos. The algae present were mainly diatoms and the pigment signals were discernible in the water column during the flood and ebb tides. It was clearly shown that the pigment signatures found in the upper $200\,\mu\mathrm{m}$ of sediments before erosion (i.e. specifically the markers chlorophyll c1 and carotene; Fig. 10b) appeared in the water column with the flood tide and re-appeared in the ebb waters. Interestingly, the chlorophyll breakdown product chlorophyllide, produced as a result of chlorophyllase activity, was found in greater amounts in the resuspended sediments and on the post-erosion surface than in the original intact sediments (Fig. 10). This may indicate that some algae were disrupted in the process of erosion and that cell lysis had begun. From the pigment signatures in the surface (Fig. 8a–c) and the LTSEM studies of the sediments before and after erosion, it can be estimated that a layer of up to 2 mm was sloughed off upon failure of the algal mat. This failure was not a uniform process over the mud-

flat, but rather it could be observed that the algae were peeled off as a layer, when a weak, possibly damaged, area responded to tidal action.

The MS system performed well in erosion trials and has previously been tested in conjunction with a number of erosion devices. It was found that for laboratory simulations of entrainment processes, at bottom shear stresses of less than $1\,\mathrm{N\,m^{-2}}$, the microcosm has the most suitable calibration characteristics. These include a bottom stress time series which closely resembles those of natural unidirectional flows (Gust & Müller 1997), a spatially homogenous bottom stress, a fine flow structure which has a variance similar to that of natural flows, simple and stable operation and reproducible performance. This preliminary study has shown that in combination with Cryolander techniques, pigment fingerprinting and LTSEM examination of the sediments, the MS system can be used for studying the fine-structure of the erosion process and the nature of pigment redistribution in natural and simulated erosion events. The differentiation between an eroded and an undistrubed sediment was successfully achieved using pigment distribution supported by detailed LTSEM examination of the sediment structures. By examining the re-distribution of algal cells and associated pigments by hydrodynamic stress, it has been shown that pigments may be potential markers for sediment erosion. Such analyses can be useful in studies on particulate matter transport with their associated pollutants and on the stabilization of sediments by algae. Changes in sediment microphytobenthic pigment signatures are detected in the water before particle erosion is initiated and thus serve as indicators of the initial erosion events in both the laboratory and field. Discrimination of the pigment ratios between fluid and sediment phases and their role in examining the EDTC cycle and of tidal flow components now becomes accessible in further studies.

We are very grateful to Ben De Winder, Fleur Van Duyl from the NIOO and the crew of the RV *Navicula* for all their help and interest during work in the Ems-Dollard. Also the help and support from Lucas Stal and the Netherlands BOA project is gratefully acknowledged. Thanks also to Dr K. Black for sedimentological analysis. This research was carried out under the auspices of the EU funded project PROMAT (EVSV-C94–0411) and a University of St Andrews studentship to T. Tolhurst.

This is LOIS publication number 406 of the LOIS Community Research Programme, carried out under a Special Topic Award from the Natural Environment Research Council.

References

AMOS, C. L. 1995. Siliciclastic tidal flats. *In*: PERILLO, G. M. E. (ed.), *Geomorphology and Sedimentology of Estuaries*, Elsevier, 273–301.

BLACK, K. S. 1997. Biophysical factors contributing to erosion resistance in natural cohesive sediments. *In*: BURT, N., PARKER, R. & WATTS, J. (eds) *Cohesive Sediments*, 4th Nearshore and Estuarine Sediment Transport Conference, 11–15th July 1994, Wallingford, England. Wiley and Sons, 231–244.

BURT, N., PARKER, R. & WATTS, J. 1997. *Cohesive Sediments*, 4th Nearshore and Estuarine Sediment Transport Conference, 11–15th July 1994, Wallingford, England. Wiley and Sons.

CARIOU-LE GALL, V. & BLANCHARD, G. 1995. Monthly HPLC measurements of pigment concentration from an intertidal muddy sediment of Marenns-Oleron Bay, France. *Marine Ecology Progress Series*, **121**, 171–179.

DELO, E. A. 1988. *Estuarine muds manual*. Report SR 164. Hydraulics Research Ltd, Wallingford, UK.

DÉFARGE, C., TRICHET, J., JAUNET, A., ROBERT, M., TRIBBLE, J. & SANSONE, F. J. 1996. Texture of microbial sediments revealed by cryo-scanning electron microscopy. *Journal of Sedimentary Research*, **66**, 935–947.

GIESKES, W. & KRAAY, G. W. 1983. Dominance of Cryptophyceae during the phytoplankton spring bloom in the central north sea detected by HPLC analyses of pigments. *Marine Biology*, **75**, 179–185.

GUST, G. 1990. Method of generating precisely-defined wall shearing stresses. US Patent No. 4, 973, 165.

— & MÜLLER, V. 1997. Interfacial hydrodynamics and entrainment functions of currently used erosion devices. *In*: BURT, N., PARKER, R. & WATTS, J. (eds) *Cohesive Sediments*, 4th Nearshore and Estuarine Sediment Transport Conference, 11–15th July, 1994, Wallingford, England. Wiley and Sons, 149–174.

HUMANN, K. 1995. *Der Einfluß des Mikrophytobenthos auf die Sedimentstabilität und die Schwebstoffbildung aus Sedimenten in Elbe-Ästuar*. PhD Thesis, Hamburg University.

HÜTTEL, M. & GUST, G. 1992. Impact of bioroughness on intertidal solute exchange in permeable sediments. *Marine Ecology Progress Series*, **89**, 253–267.

JEFFREE, C. E. & READ, N. D. 1991. Ambient- and low-temperature scanning electron microscopy. *In*: HALL, J. L. & HAWES, C. (eds) *Electron Microscopy of Plant Cells*. Academic Press, 313–413.

KÜHL, M., LASSEN, C. & JORGENSEN, B. B. 1994. Optical measurements of microbial mats: light measurements with fibre-optic microprobes. *In*: STAL, L. J. & CAUMETTE, P. (eds) *Microbial Mats*, NATO ASI series, **35**, 149–166.

MACINTYRE, H. L., GEIDER, R. J. & MILLER, D. C. 1996. Microphytobenthos: The ecological role of the "secret garden" of unvegetated, shallow-water marine habitats. I. Distribution, abundance and primary production. *Estuaries*, **19**, 186–201.

MEHTA, A. J. & PARTHENIADES, E. 1982. Resuspension of deposited cohesive sediment beds. *Eighteenth Conference Coastal Engineering*, 1569–1588.

PATERSON, D. M. 1995. Biogenic structure of early sediment fabric visualised by low-temperature scanning electron microscopy. *Journal Geological Society, London*, **152**, 131–140.

——1997. Biological mediation of sediment erodibility: ecology and physical dynamics. *In*: BURT, N., PARKER, R. & WATTS, J. (eds) *Cohesive Sediments*, 4th Nearshore and Estuarine Sediment Transport Conference, 11–15th July, 1994, Wallingford, England. Wiley and Sons, 215–229.

——, YALLOP, M. L. & GEORGE, C. 1994. Spatial variability in sediment erodabilty on the island of Texel. *In*: KRUMBEIN, W. E., PATERSON, D. M. & STAL, L. J. (eds) *Biostabilisation of Sediments*. BIS Verlag, Oldenburg.

——, YATES, M. G., WILTSHIRE, K. H., MCGRORTY, S. MILES, A. EASTWOOD, J. E. A., BLACKBURN, J. & DAVIDSON, I. Microbiological mediation of spectral reflectance from cohesive sediments. *Journal of Limnology and Oceanography* (submitted).

SALOMONS, W., SCHWEDHELM, E., SCHOER, J. & KNAUTH, H. D. 1987. Natural tracers to determine the origin of sediments and suspended matter from the Elbe estuary. *In*: AWAYS, J. & KUSUDA, T. (eds) *Coastal and Estuarine Pollution*. IAWPRC, London, 119–132.

SCHWEDHELM, E., SALOMONS, W., SCHOER, J. & KNAUTH, H. D. 1988. *Provenance of the Sediments and the Suspended Matter of the Elbe Estuary*. GKSS report 88/E/20.

SUTHERLAND, T. 1996. *Biostabilisation of Estuarine Subtidal Sediments* D.Phil. Thesis, Dalhousie University, Canada.

TAYLOR, I. & PATERSON, D. M. Microspatial variation in physical and biological sediment parameters. *Estuarine, Coastal and Shelf Science* (in press).

UNDERWOOD, G. J. C. & PATERSON, D. M. 1993. Recovery of intertidal benthic diatoms after biocide treatment and associated sediment dynamics. *Journal of the Marine Biological Association, UK*, **73**, 24–45.

——, —— & PARKES, R. J. 1995. The measurement of microbial carbohydrate exopolymers from intertidal sediments. *Limnology and Oceanography*, **40**, 1243–1253.

VAN DEN HOEK, C., MANN, D. G. & JAHN, H. M. 1995. *Algae: An Introduction to Phycology*. Cambridge, London.

VILLERIUS, L., WILTSHIRE, K. GIESKES, W. & PATERSON, D. M. 1996. The use of a binary reversed phase, non-endcapped C30 method for the separation of algal pigments. *JUPAC Symposium Abstract*, Germany.

WILTSHIRE, K. H. 1992. *Untersuchungen zum Einfluß des Mikrophytobenthos auf den Nährstoffaustausch zwischen Sediment und Wasser in der Tide-Elbe*. PhD. Thesis, University of Hamburg.

——, BLACKBURN, J. & PATERSON, D. 1997. The Cryolander: a new method for the *in situ* sampling of intertidal surface sediments minimising distortion of sediment structure. *Journal of Sedimentary Research*, **67**, 977–981.

——, GEISLER, C. D., SCHROEDER, F., & KNAUTH, H. D. 1994. Pigments in suspended matter from the Elbe estuary and the German Bight. Their use as marker compounds for the characterisation of suspended matter and in the interpretation of heavy metal loadings. *Archive. Fur Hydrobiologie, Special Issue. Advances in Limnology*, **47**, 53–63.

—— & SCHROEDER, F. 1994. Pigment patterns in suspended matter from the tidal river Elbe, northern Germany. *Netherlands Journal of Aquatic Ecology*, **23**, 255–265.

WRIGHT, S. W. & JEFFREY, S. W. 1987 Fucoxanthin pigment markers of marine phytoplankton analysed by HPLC and HPTLC. *Marine Ecology Progress Series*, **38**, 259–266.

YALLOP, M. L. DE WINDER, B., PATERSON, D. M. & STAL, L. J. 1994. Comparative structure primary production and biogenic stabilization of cohesive and non-cohesive marine sediments inhabited by microphytobenthos. *Estuarine Coastal and Shelf Science*, **39**, 565–582

The macrofaunal communities of the Skeffling muds (Humber estuary), with special reference to bioturbation

J. T. DAVEY[1] & V. A. PARTRIDGE[2]

[1] *Natural Environment Research Council, Plymouth Marine Laboratory, 1 Prospect Place, The Hoe, Plymouth PL1 3DH, UK*
[2] *Acadia Centre for Estuarine Research, Acadia University, Wolfville, Nova Scotia BOP 1XO, Canada*

Abstract: The macrofaunal communities are described for the four transect stations of the April 1995 LISP-UK (Littoral Investigation of Sediment Properties) project. Cores of different sizes were taken to sample major bioturbating macrofauna (500 μm sieve) and smaller annelids (125 μm sieve). Three species, the small clam *Macoma balthica* and the polychaetes *Nereis diversicolor* and *Nephtys hombergii*, are discussed in detail because they have the greatest impact on sediment properties through disturbance by feeding, the construction and irrigation of burrow structures and sediment movement. *Macoma* was the only species present at all four stations, but whilst their population densities were similar, their calculated potential feeding areas varied by a factor of between 2 and 5. This affects the rate at which they disturb and re-cycle sediment by feeding. *Nereis* burrow walls at the two most shoreward stations were estimated to provide an additional sediment/water interface equivalent to 0.2–0.3 of the unburrowed area. *Nephtys* at the two most seaward stations may produce slow homogenization of surface sediments to a few centimetres depth. All macrofaunal populations were well below annual maxima that would be reached later in the year.

At the outer end of the Humber estuary on its north side is a wide embayment called the Humber Bight containing extensive intertidal mudflats. A transect line of over 3 km length, running out from a point about midway across this bay near the village of Skeffling, was chosen by the originators of the LISP-UK project for an intensive interdisciplinary study of the properties of an intertidal cohesive sediment. More background to the LISP-UK project and to the precise details of the transect and its location are provided in this volume by Black and Paterson.

The faunas of the Humber estuary shores are not unknown, though much of the information is not in easily accessible form (Ratcliffe 1979; Rees et al. 1982; Key 1983; Morris 1994) Comprehensive surveys are lacking, probably because of the sheer size of this estuary, the largest in Britain. However, while there are no surprises in terms of the species recorded here, it was never our purpose to add significantly to an understanding of the general ecology of the estuary.

As contributors to this Project, our role was to sample the benthic macrofauna at the four stations during the April 1995 Field Campaign of LISP-UK to provide a picture of the composition of these invertebrate communities for correlation with all the other measurements and investigations of the sediments being made at that time. By recording as much detail as possible on the numbers, size classes and spatial distributions of dominant organisms such as *Macoma*

balthica, *Nereis diversicolor* and *Nephtys hombergii*, we intended to build a picture of their likely impact in terms of bioturbation, bioirrigation, etc., for comparison with all the other data being collected. We therefore report here the picture of the communities that emerged from our sampling of the four transect stations, and we offer an interpretive account of the impact on the sediments that these populations would have had at this particular time by drawing on the known capabilities of the animals to disturb the sediments in which they live.

Methods

The Transect stations A, B, C and D run in a downshore direction from below the saltmarsh zone at the NRA Pumping Station on the dyke at Skeffling. Station A was immediately beyond the limit of the saltmarsh, station B *c.* 0.5 km further out and stations C and D were at *c.* 2 and 3 km from A. They are all more precisely described by Black & Paterson (this volume). Our samples were taken on April 4th (A), 6th (C), 9th (B) and 19th (D).

Macrofauna were sampled with a 10 cm diameter corer. Four replicate cores (only three at station D) were taken at three 'sites', designated I, II and III, at each station, each separated by a distance of *c.* 2 m. Within these sites the replicates were taken within an area of a square metre or

DAVEY, J. T. & PARTRIDGE, V. A. 1998. The macrofaunal communities of the Skeffling muds (Humber estuary), with special reference to bioturbation. *In*: BLACK, K. S., PATERSON, D. M. & CRAMP, A. (eds) *Sedimentary Processes in the Intertidal Zone*. Geological Society, London, Special Publications, **139**, 115–124.

less. Three of the four replicates (all three at station D) were taken with core rings pushed down on top of each other and a thin metal plate used to section off the surface to 4 cm, 5–8 cm, 9–12 cm and 13–20 cm depth bands. The fourth core at stations A, B and C, taken to 20 cm, was not sectioned. All four cores were used to enumerate and describe the densities of the recovered macrofauna, while depth distributions were determined from the three sectioned cores. Cores were placed in labelled polythene bags, sieved the same or next day at 500 μm, and the retained material preserved in 4% buffered sea-water formalin. Later the material was transferred to 70% industrial methylated spirits (IMS), stained with rose bengal and the animals picked out and identified under a low-power dissecting microscope.

The polychaetes *Nereis diversicolor* and *Nephtys hombergii* and the bivalve *Macoma balthica* were individually measured for, respectively, first setiger width, maximum body width and maximum shell length. All measurements were made to 0.1 mm using an ocular micrometer. The size classes of *Nephtys hombergii* were converted to biomass using the equation in Warwick & Price (1975) for the month of April.

The surface areas of burrow walls of *Nereis diversicolor* were calculated using the formula derived by Davey (1994). The worms are divided into three size classes, those less than 1.0 mm first setiger width, those between 1.0 and 1.9 mm and those of 2.0 mm or more, and the burrow wall surface areas generalized as 1, 10 and 25 cm^2 for the individuals from each size class, respectively. The total surface area of the burrows for the worms measured in a given sample is then related to the surface area of the sediment cores from which the worms were recovered. The result is a dimensionless ratio of burrow wall surface area to sediment surface area.

The potential feeding areas of *Macoma balthica* were calculated using the formula derived by Brey (1991). He calculated a potential feeding area for *Macoma* in each 0.1 mm size class, thereby enabling the size frequency distribution of the animals in any sample to be converted to a total potential feeding area which relates to the surface area of the sediment cores from which the bivalves were recovered. As with the *Nereis* burrow walls, this is again a dimensionless ratio.

Smaller sediment cores were taken for those species we call 'mesofauna' which fall between the traditional definitions of 'macrofauna' and 'meiofauna', and which are often under-sampled. Three cores, 6.5 cm in diameter by 8 cm deep, were taken at each of three 'sites' on stations A, B and C (but not D). At the first two 'sites' these

were sectioned into the 0–2 cm and 3–8 cm depth bands. Replicates from the third 'site' were retained intact. All cores were fixed in 4% buffered sea-water formalin. After being sieved at 125 μm, animals were separated from sediments by flotation in Ludox™, a solution of colloidal silica in sodium hydroxide diluted with tap water to a specific gravity of 1.15. They were stored in 70% IMS, stained in rose-bengal and enumerated and identified under a low-power microscope.

To investigate spatial patterns in the distribution of *Macoma balthica*, a set of 29 cores, 15 cm in diameter and 5 cm deep, were taken at station A on April 5th and at station B on April 9th. Core rings were pressed into the sediment in a cross-shaped array of two rows of 15 contiguous replicates perpendicular to and parallel to the shoreline, intersecting at the centre. The cores were sieved within 24 h at 1 mm for the recovery of specimens of *Macoma balthica*. These were fixed in 4% formalin in sea-water and their shell lengths measured to 0.1 mm with a digital caliper. Individuals under 10 mm were measured under a low-power binocular microscope. Badly fractured shells were not measured but were included in the counts.

Data were analysed with S-Plus Version 3.3 Release 1 for Windows (MathSoft, Inc., Seattle, Washington, USA) and PRIMER Version 4.0 (Plymouth Marine Laboratory, Plymouth, UK).

Results

The complete data set resulting from all the samples taken has been supplied to the British Oceanographic Data Centre (BODC) and can be freely inspected.

Table 1 lists the species composition of the communities at stations A–D. The bivalve *Macoma balthica* was the dominant organism in the community at all four stations, with the polychaetes *Nereis diversicolor* present in significant numbers at the two upper-shore stations and *Nephtys hombergii* likewise at the two lower-shore stations. Apart from *Retusa obtusata* at stations B and C and the polychaete *Eteone longa* at station B, other species were always below a density of 127 m^{-2}, the equivalent of an average of one specimen in every replicate core.

The mesofauna were all small annelids (Table 1) and were not abundant. They were dominated at stations A and B by the oligochaete *Tubificoides benedi* and at station C by the small polychaete *Streblospio shrubsolii*. Mesofaunal samples were not taken at station D, but it was clear from the macrofauna samples that the

Table 1. *Macrofauna and mesofauna recovered from cores taken at stations A to D*

Family	Species	Station			
		A	B	C	D
Macrofauna					
Polychaeta	*Nereis diversicolor*	0–5; **340**	0–6; **360**	0–4; **160**	0–1
	Nephtys hombergii	0	0	0–13; **840**	2–11; **920**
	Eteone longa	0–2	0–4; **160**	0	0
Mollusca	*Macoma balthica*	1–30; **2250**	14–34; **2600**	5–27; **2000**	7–26; **2500**
	Cerastoderma edule	0	0–1	0–2	0
	Retusa obtusata	0–2	0–6; **300**	0–11; **700**	0–2
	Hydrobia ulvae	0–1	0–2	0–3	0
Amphipoda	*Corophium volutator*	0–1	0–1	0	0
Mesofauna					
Oligochaeta	*Tubificoides benedi*	21–115; **17 350**	21–46; **9300**	0–3	0
Polychaeta	*Manayunkia aestuarina*	2–7; **1500**	0–1	0–1	0
	Streblospio shrubsolii	3–17; **2500**	1–10	3–46; **5500**	p
	Pygospio elegans	0–1	0–3	0–2	≈**6000***
	Tharyx marioni	0	0	0–1	p

For each species at each station the range of counts from replicate cores is given followed by an average density estimate per metre squared (emboldened). This estimate is not given for species present at an average of 1 or fewer per replicate core.
* Density estimate for *Pygospio elegans* based on recoveries from macrofauna cores. Other mesofauna from station D not counted but indicated as present ('p') from unquantified recoveries in macorfauna cores.

small tube building spionid *Pygospio elegans* was moderately abundant. The tubes (tough sandy structures, many empty) were abundant and care was taken to break them all open and to count recovered worms. Some specimens could have left their tubes when sampled and then been lost through the 500 μm sieve, but their abundance was at least estimated.

The results are now considered in respect of the three commonest macrofauna species and of the most numerous mesofaunal species.

Macoma balthica

The bivalve was the dominant animal at all four stations with densities of between 2000 and 2600 m^{-2} (Table 1), which are similar and not statistically significantly different between sta-

tions. The spatial-array cores, however, gave estimates of 1700 m^{-2} at station A and 2900 m^{-2} at station B (Table 2), which are statistically significantly different from each other (Wilcoxon rank-sum $Z = -5.50$, p-value < 0.0001). Since the 29 cores sum to just over 0.5 m^2 at each station, they provide a potentially more accurate estimate than the macrofauna cores, which sum to only 0.09 m^2 at each station.

The size frequency distributions were markedly different between stations. The shell lengths of the animals suggested three possible size classes breaking around 5 and 10 mm, with by far the majority of the bivalves representative of the smallest class of <5 mm. More of the remaining animals were over 10 mm than under. Figure 1(a) shows the overall size frequency structure at a resolution of 1 mm size classes, based on all 822 *Macoma balthica* measured

Table 2. *Density and shell length of* Macoma balthica *from the spatial-array samples*

	Shell length (mm)		Density (indiv. m^{-2})	
	Station A	Station B	Station A	Station B
Range	1.5–13.9	1.4–18.2	623–2830	1754–3226
Median	2.5	2.8	1641	2999
Mean ± Std. Dev.	2.7 ± 1.2	4.6 ± 3.8	1729 ± 641	2886 ± 477
Count	878	1469		

Density is given as number of individuals per metre squared.

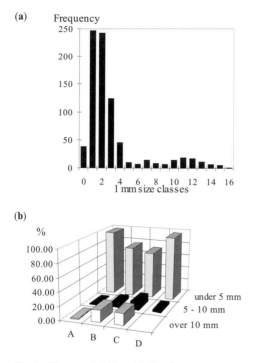

Fig. 1. *Macoma balthica*. (**a**) Size frequency distribution into 1 mm size classes of all 822 specimens recovered from all macrofauna cores taken at stations A, B, C and D. (**b**) Percentage size frequency in three 5-mm size classes for each station.

from the 45 depth-profile cores taken from the four stations; while Fig. 1(b) illustrates the gross differences in the size frequency distributions between the four stations based on the three 5-mm size classes. These were statistically significantly different amongst the four stations ($\chi^2 = 104.6$, d.f. = 6, p-value < 0.0001). At stations A and D over 90% of the *Macoma* were under 5 mm, with most of the two larger size classes confined to stations B and C. The size distributions of the spatial-array data indicated similar patterns. At station A, 98% of the individuals were <5 mm, while at station B, 77% of the individuals were <5 mm, a difference which is also statistically significant ($\chi^2 = 192$, d.f. = 2, p-value < 0.0001).

The spatial-array samples were taken to determine patch size of *Macoma* populations. Figures 2(a) and (b) display the densities of *Macoma* calculated from the spatial-array samples at stations A and B, respectively. However, no spatial patterns (patches, clusters or gradients) of statistical significance were detected on the scale sampled, nor were there any statistically significant differences in mean density or

size distribution within stations by direction (parallel vs perpendicular to shore).

Table 3 details the depth distribution of *Macoma* as recovered from the three sectioned cores from each station. Over 90% of all *Macoma*, of all sizes, were recovered from the top 4 cm depth band. Seventeen of 20 specimens found deeper than 8 cm were under 5 mm shell length and may have been carried to these depths by the coring action. It is not likely that such small *Macoma* would choose to live so deep (Zwarts & Wanink 1989; Zwarts *et al.* 1994). Of the individuals larger than 5 mm, only 22 out of 105 were found below 4 cm and only three of these were below 8 cm.

The impact of the feeding activity of *Macoma balthica* has been measured by calculating the potential feeding area as explained in the preceding section. These estimated feeding areas, expressed as the dimensionless ratio of m²/m², result in the figures shown in Table 4. At stations B and C, a near doubling of the calculated potential feeding area arises from 25–30% of the *Macoma* being in the two larger size classes, compared with only 5–10% at stations A and D (Fig. 1b). Potential feeding areas calculated from the (larger) numbers of *Macoma balthica* recovered from the spatial array samples suggest a greater difference between stations A and B of 1.65 and 5.2, respectively. The differential between the two sites is then threefold rather than twofold.

One of us (JTD) has unpublished data on *Macoma balthica* sampled on other dates at Skeffling close to station A on the LISP Transect, between July 1994 and August 1996. From these data the potential feeding area was found to vary seasonally between 1.7 and 5.2.

Nereis diversicolor

This species was present in similar numbers from stations A and B, about half as many at station C, and was effectively absent from station D. First setiger widths of <1.0 mm equate to settling stages and young *Nereis*; 1.0–2.0 mm to adults around a year old following their first winter, and larger specimens to yet older individuals (Davey 1994). Almost none of the *Nereis* recovered was larger than 2.0 mm first setiger width, and the differences between stations were simply that the smaller worms were absent from station C whilst a fair spread of size classes was represented at stations A and B.

Since *Nereis* burrow walls are extensions of the sediment surface and hence an interface for chemical exchange processes (Davey & Watson

(a)

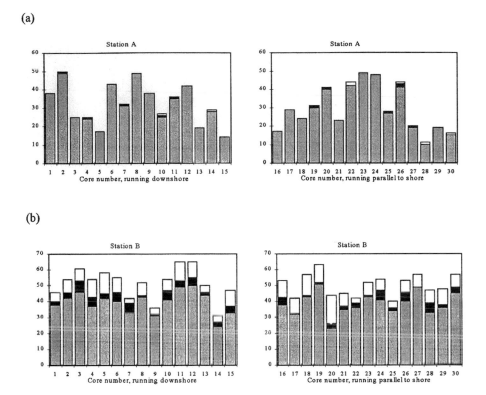

(b)

Fig. 2. The total numbers of *Macoma balthica* recovered from each spatial array core (*y*-axis): at
(a) station A and (b) station B. Shading indicates the numbers of *Macoma balthica* from each of three size classes
within each 15 cm diameter core taken: under 5 mm, grey; 5.0–9.9 mm, black; 10 mm and over, white. Cores 1–15
at each station ran downshore and cores 16–30 ran parallel to the shore, intersecting so that Core 8 was the same
as Core 23.

Table 3. *The depth distribution of* Macoma *by size class and station*

Depth	A			B			C			D			All			All	All as %
	<5	<10	>10	<5	<10	>10	<5	<10	>10	<5	<10	>10	<5	<10	>10		
0–4 cm	159	1	1	129	8	27	88	21	19	161	6	0	537	36	47	620	91.7%
5–8 cm	7	2	0	4	2	4	2	2	9	4	0	0	17	6	13	36	5.3%
9–12 cm	6	0	1	1	1	1	2	0	0	1	0	0	10	1	2	13	1.9%
13–20 cm	3	0	0	1	0	0	1	0	0	2	0	0	7	0	0	7	1.1%
Total	175	3	2	135	11	32	93	23	28	168	6	0	571	43	62	676	

Size classes are <5, >5 to <10 and >10 mm.
Data from 36 cores representing the nine sectioned replicates at each station.

Table 4. *The calculated potential feeding areas of* Macoma balthica *at each station*

	Station A	Station B	Station C	Station D
'Potential feeding area' in m²/m²	2.1 1.65	4.3 5.2	3.5	2.0

The second figure for stations A and B is the estimate from the (larger) spatial-array sampling.

Table 5. *Calculated increases in sediment surface area due to* Nereis diversicolor *burrows*

Sample date	Pyewipe	Brough	Paull	Skeffling		
				LISP Stn A	LISP Stn B	LISP Stn C
July 1994	–	**1.9**	1.2; 1.3	3.2; 1.4	n/s	n/s
Feb. 1995	0.9; 1.0	–	0.2; 0.3	0.2; 0.3	n/s	n/s
April 1995	–	–	–	**0.3**	**0.3**	**0.2**
Oct. 1995	1.8; 1.8	–	0.2; 0.2	0.4; 1.0	n/s	n/s
April 1996	–	**1.2**	**0.3**	–	n/s	n/s
Aug. 1996	–	**2.2**	**1.1**	**4.2**	n/s	n/s

Data is for transect stations A, B and C (this study) and (unpublished) on other dates at station A and three other Humber sites, Pyewipe, Brough and Paull.
Data in bold as per LISP transect data of April 1995 (at least 3×10 cm diameter cores).
Other data derived from paired cores of 20 cm diameter.
'–' no or too few (not more than 1 individual per core) *Nereis* in samples taken; n/s, no sample.

1995), the calculation of their surface area, as explained in the previous section, is useful. The increase was $c. 0.3$ at stations A and B and $c. 0.2$ at station C. For stations A and B, this may be visualized as 3000 cm^2 of burrow surface per 1 m^2 of mudflat surface.

As for *Macoma* above, one of us (JTD) has unpublished data from other dates for station A, as well as for three other sites in the Humber where *Nereis* occurs, namely Pyewipe, Paull and Brough. Table 5 summarizes all these data on burrow surface areas for comparison.

About 40% of the *Nereis* from stations A and B were in each of the first two depth intervals with the remaining 20% deeper than 8 cm. At station C only ten *Nereis* were recovered, but these were larger and occurred deeper than at stations A and B.

Nephtys hombergii

This species was recorded at stations C and D, with smaller worms at station C. The population density at both sites was $c. 900$ m^{-2}. Distribution with depth was more varied at station C, where 70% of the worms were in the top 4 cm of the

sediment column, but two specimens were found below 8 cm, and two below 12 cm. These were large specimens unlikely to have been displaced by coring. At station D nearly 90% of the worms were in the top 4 cm and only one specimen (out of 65) was below 8 cm.

The physical reality of the depth distribution is better appreciated from the biomass of the worms. At station C, 70% of the worms were in the top 4 cm but accounted for only 10% of the biomass since the 30% of worms below this horizon were all large. At station D, where the worms were nearly all in the top 4 cm, those buried deeper accounted for only about 20% of the biomass. Table 6 summarizes these data.

The mesofauna

These small annelids were not especially abundant except for *Tubificoides benedi* at station A. Even here the oligochaete was patchy, with between 21 to 115 per core (averaging $c. 17\,350$ m^{-2}) compared with 21 to 46 at station B. At station C the mesofauna were further impoverished and represented almost exclusively by the spionid *Streblospio shrubsolii* at a moderate

Table 6. *The distribution of* Nephtys hombergii *with depth in the sediment*

Depth	Station C				Station D			
	0–4 cm	5–8 cm	9–12 cm	13–20 cm	0–4 cm	5–8 cm	9–12 cm	13–20 cm
Number	42	14	2	2	58	6	1	0
Percent	70	24	3	3	89	9	2	0
Biomass, mg	32	185	64	33	170	35	4	0
Percent	10	60	20	10	81	17	2	0

Data shown as original counts (numbers) and as calculated biomass in mg.

density of $c. 5500\,m^{-2}$. At station D the tube-building spionid *Pygospio elegans* was estimated at $6000\,m^{-2}$ from the macrofauna samples. Numbers of their tubes would have been higher, given that many were empty.

Discussion

Scope for bioturbation by Macoma balthica

The size distribution of *Macoma* in this study, with the upper intertidal dominated by smaller, younger individuals and larger, older individuals further downshore, is consistent with patterns described elsewhere (e.g. Reading 1979).

While there was heterogeneity in the abundances of *Macoma* in the spatial-array samples, particularly at station A (Figs 2a and b), no statistically significant delineations of patch size were found. A study by Günther (1996) suggested a patch size $c. 4.5\,cm$ or less for settling *Macoma* larvae (much smaller than the juveniles found here), and aggregations at scales of 45 cm and 480 cm across, but lacked statistical justification. If patch sizes are as Günther suggested, then our 15 cm diameter cores were too large to detect patches of 4.5 cm and too small to detect aggregates of 480 cm diameter. Aggregates 45 cm across would also only be detected in our data if there were stark differences between 'patches' and 'non-patches'. While our data suggest, to the eye, greater variability at station A and greater uniformity at station B, we have to assume that this arose by chance rather than from biological or even physical, sedimentological interactions. There were, for instance, no tidal channels intersecting our sampling sites, which were deliberately chosen for physical uniformity. However, our spatial array data serve to demonstrate the value of recording what animals were present in any area of a sediment subjected to other, non-biological measurements. Such records are infrequently made and reliance on generalized estimates of community structure and species abundances may obscure real correlations between animal activity and sediment properties on small scales.

The impact of *Macoma balthica* has been given in terms of the potential feeding area (*sensu* Brey 1991). This assumes that the species is primarily a deposit-feeder. There is much in the literature now to suggest that *Macoma* not only can suspension-feed but may obtain the bulk of its food by this route (e.g. Hummel 1985). However, such observations and conclusions have stemmed from laboratory (vs field) studies. Because laboratory conditions differ from the

natural habitat, such results must be interpreted cautiously. Laboratory experimental studies usually involve individuals over 10 mm, a size class represented by less than 8% in our samples. On the eastern seaboard of the USA *Macoma balthica* attains a much larger size than is seen in Europe and at least one American study, which suggested that suspension-feeding was the animal's preferred mode (Lin & Hines 1994), involved animals of 29–36 mm shell length. Sediments used in laboratory studies tend to err towards sandier conditions than those in which *Macoma* frequently live, probably because very muddy sediments are difficult to maintain satisfactorily under laboratory conditions. In Lin and Hines' (1994) study, the animals, which originated from a sub-tidal sediment that was 90% mud, were held experimentally in mixtures of fine to coarse sands. Under such conditions it is not surprising that the animals did little deposit-feeding. Zwarts *et al.* (1994) observed that, under experimental conditions, several bivalve species including *Macoma balthica* stopped feeding after the first day. If the sediment was then disturbed or new sediment added, deposit-feeding was invariably stimulated to start again. These differences must be kept in mind when interpreting our *Macoma* data in relation to the conditions and situation of the Skeffling transect. Station A was at a very high tidal level, not covered by every high tide. Even station B would be subject to considerable periods of tidal emersion. The star-shaped feeding marks indicative of deposit-feeding by *Macoma* were abundant at these stations in April 1995. The *Macoma* collected from all four stations were predominantly very small (85% were under 5 mm). Small *Macoma* at stations A and B were most likely to be deposit-feeding and, given the size-class structure, the total amount of suspension-feeding by *Macoma* populations across all four stations was probably small.

We would be cautious before using Brey's term 'over-exploitation' to describe high values for potential feeding areas. That calculated feeding areas are multiples of the net sediment surface area seems to us to mean only that the animals in a given area are recycling the same sediments after a certain amount of time spent deposit-feeding. Moreover, the nutritional value of the sediment is continuously renewed through bacterial and algal growth, and by the import of material via the water column during tidal immersion. *Macoma* itself contributes to the process because its exhalant siphon vents below the surface. Reise (1983) found this feature to be associated with micro-oxic zones in the sediments inhabited by the bivalves, with consequences for localized concentrations of nutrients. The purely physical hydrodynamic effects of the tide and associated currents on the surface layer are also probably involved in the regenerative processes that affect the nutritional value of the sediment to any benthic deposit-feeder. Finally, Hummel (1985) pointed out that even when deposit-feeding, *Macoma* must 'inhale' considerable volumes of water drawn from close to the sediment surface. This water may contain particles originating from the water column. If we may be pardoned the pun, this fact muddies the waters when defining 'deposit' and 'suspension' feeding modes as if they were totally separate phenomena.

In addition to causing erosion by excavating feeding-pits and removing sediment-stabilizing diatoms, *Macoma* contribute to sediment dynamics through other aspects of their feeding activity. In deposit-feeding, *Macoma* reject as pseudofaeces *c.* eight times as much sediment as they ingest and eventually defecate as ovoid mucus-bound pellets (Black 1980). Pseudofaeces have a high water content and are easily broken down (Risk & Moffat 1977), while fecal pellets may persist for 1–2 weeks (Black 1980). Fecal pellets have settling velocities equivalent to smaller-sized sand grains and are transported easily by currents, thus contributing to the removal of surface material and adding to the turbidity of the overlying water (Risk & Moffat 1977).

Estimates of the amount of sediment so processed by *Macoma* vary, depending on population density and size distribution and on the amount of deposit- vs suspension-feeding, which, as stated earlier, is dependent on sediment type. For high densities ($3500\,\mathrm{m}^{-2}$) of clams of unreported size (though probably large because they were taken from a North American site in summer), Risk & Moffat (1977) estimated that $28\,\mathrm{cm/year/m}^2$ of surface sediment would be lost, assuming export of all fecal pellets and no input of fresh sediment. Black (1980) estimated that a population of unspecified density could turn over the top 2 mm of sediment ten times per year, which we suppose to mean the equivalent of 2 cm per year, if there were no net transport, i.e. that the fecal pellets would remain and would be broken down by wave action and colonized by bacteria.

We therefore expect that the *Macoma* at Skeffling in April 1995 were capable of measurable impacts on the surficial sediments resulting from deposit-feeding activity. We should expect to see such effects mediated both biologically and physically in terms of algal population dynamics and sediment shear strength.

Some of the results of other contributors to the LISP Transect study arguably support this interpretation. Taylor (Gatty Marine Laboratory, pers. comm.) noted a drop in algal (diatom) populations from station A to station B which would be consistent with the population difference in *Macoma* and could be attributed to the consequential difference in grazing pressure. This is strengthened by findings of Kamermans (1994) that more diatoms are found in the stomachs of *Macoma balthica* and other bivalves in April and May, periods of maximum feeding and growth, than during the rest of the year.

Bioirrigation by Nereis diversicolor

The increase in sediment surface area due to *Nereis diversicolor* burrows was relatively small at *c.* 0.2–0.3. But in summer at the equivalent of station A we have seen values as high as 4.2, and elsewhere in the Humber the factor is up to *c.* 2 (data not yet published) (Table 5). Factors of three have been routinely recorded throughout the year in the Tamar Estuary at Plymouth (Davey 1993). Moreover, active irrigation of burrows with overlying water further enhances chemical exchange fluxes across burrow surfaces. In experimental tests Davey *et al.* (1990) showed that transport of some metal species was enhanced by *Nereis* burrow irrigation over controls and that these metal species, which included iron, manganese, copper and zinc, were primarily transported in solution rather than associated with particulates eroded from burrow walls. In further studies involving nutrient fluxes, Davey & Watson (1995) calculated that Tamar Estuary populations of *Nereis*, with burrow surface areas representing 2–3-fold increases, could account for fluxes to the water column of between 10 and 20 times the measured inputs of soluble ammonium derived from riverine and sewage sources.

Sediment mixing impact of Nephtys hombergii

Nephtys hombergii populations were quite high at around $900\,\mathrm{m}^{-2}$ at stations C and D, although the size-class distribution was towards the smaller worms. Clearly the larger worms penetrate to greater depths, but the bulk of all burrowing by this species is done relatively superficially, involving perhaps the top 5 cm of the sediment column. Personal observations by the senior author using X-radiography (recorded in Contract Reports to the British Department of the

Environment) showed that the burrows are predominantly horizontal affairs, in contrast with the largely vertical burrows of *Nereis diversicolor*.

Moreover, *Nephtys* burrows tend to be transient, infilling with sediments of higher water content than that of the surrounding material. In terms of sediment mixing, the effect is small and mediated only slowly over time, months rather than days. The infilled passageways probably also contain the animals' ejecta, which may well enhance microbial communities in the sediments; *Nephtys hombergii* is a closer analogue of earthworms in terrestrial soils than is *Nereis diversicolor*.

The impact of mesofaunal sized annelids

Bioturbation by mesofaunal annelids is less well understood. Their numbers were fairly low and one species dominated at each station. The oligochaete, *Tubificoides benedi*, which feeds at a few centimetres depth and deposits its faeces at the surface (JTD, personal observation), was abundant but patchy at station A, but this abundance was down by 50% at station B and the worms were absent from stations C and D. At station C, the spionid *Streblospio shrubsolii* dominated. This species builds a tube and extends long tentacles over the sediment surface to glean food particles from either the surface or the water column, depending upon hydrodynamic conditions (Taghon *et al.* 1980). Both this spionid and the tubificid probably make a significant contribution to sediment conditions in terms of fecal pellets. The long, rod-like spionid pellets are fragile and easily break down, but oligochaete pellets are much smaller and more oval, and may remain longer, especially at station A, as a component of the surface sediment. Fecal pellets are colonized by bacteria but may take many weeks to be broken down.

Pygospio elegans at station D may be contributing to sediment stability through the binding effect of their semi-permanent tube structures. Brey (1991) calculated potential feeding areas of *c.* 1.8 for populations at $40\,000\,\text{m}^{-2}$. The population at station D was very patchy but might approach $10\,000\,\text{m}^{-2}$. With tubes 10–30 mm long, there would be *c.* 1 cm of tube per cm^2 of mudflat surface at station D. Allowing for patchiness, this could promote stabilization in the top few centimetres of the sediment.

Conclusions

The macrofaunal communities occurring at the four Humber estuary LISP sites in April 1995 have been described. Although April is not a peak month for high densities of bioturbating infauna, the major species recorded on the transect may reasonably be expected to have impacts on various physical parameters of the sediments and their properties. These have been described and discussed.

The senior author thanks G. Daborn of the Acadia Centre for Estuarine Research at Acadia University for assigning V. Partridge to work with me on the LISP Transect. I would not have managed without her. The junior author thanks G. Daborn for the opportunity to participate in this research and for assistance in the lab, K. Dyer of the University of Plymouth, and especially C. Vincent of the University of East Anglia for assistance in the field and with the sieving at station D, and M. Carr of the Plymouth Marine Laboratory for statistical consultation and assistance with PRIMER.

Both authors thank D. Plummer of NERC-LOIS for logistics and supplies in the lab at the University of Hull, and K. Black and D. Paterson of St Andrews University for logistics and support throughout the entire project. Support for V. Partridge was obtained through National Sciences and Engineering Research Council (Canada) grant A9679 to G. R. Daborn.

This is LOIS publication number 404 of the LOIS Community Research Programme, carried out under a Special Topic Award from the Natural Environment Research Council.

References

BLACK, K. S. & PATERSON, D. M. LISP-UK: an introduction and overview. *This volume.*

BLACK, L. F, 1980. The biodeposition cycle of a surface deposit-feeding bivalve, *Macoma balthica* (L.). *In*: KENNEDY, V. S. (ed.) *Estuarine Perspectives.* Academic Press, New York, 389–402.

BREY, T 1991. Interactions in soft bottom benthic communities: quantitative aspects of behaviour in the surface deposit-feeders *Pygospio elegans* (Polychaeta) and *Macoma balthica* (Bivalvia). *Helgolander Meeresuntersuchungen,* 45, 301–316.

DAVEY, J. T. 1993. Macrofaunal community bioturbation along an estuarine gradient. *Netherlands Journal of Aquatic Ecology,* 27, 147–153

—— 1994. The architecture of the burrow of *Nereis diversicolor* and its quantification in relation to sediment–water exchange. *Journal of Experimental Marine Biology and Ecology,* 179, 115–129.

—— & WATSON, P. G. 1995. The activity of *Nereis diversicolor* (Polychaeta) and its impact on nutrient fluxes in estuarine waters. *Ophelia,* 41, 57–70.

——, WATSON, P. G., BRUCE, R. H. & FRICKERS, P. E. 1990. An instrument for the monitoring and collection of vented burrow fluids of benthic infauna in sediment microcosms and its application to the polychaetes *Hediste diversicolor* and *Arenicola marina. Journal of Experimental Marine Biology and Ecology,* 139, 135–149.

GÜNTHER, C.-P. 1996. Small-scale patterns of recently settled *Macoma balthica* in the Wadden Sea. *Senckenbergiana maritima*, **26**, 117–125.

HUMMEL, H. 1985. Food intake of *Macoma balthica* (Mollusca) in relation to seasonal changes in its potential food on a tidal flat in the Dutch Wadden Sea. *Netherlands Journal of Sea Research*, **19**, 84–92.

KAMERMANS, P. 1994. Similarity in food source and timing of feeding in deposit- and suspension-feeding bivalves. *Marine Ecology: Progress Series*, **104**, 63–75.

KEY, R. S. 1983. The ecology of the infauna of Spurn Bight mudflats: an area proposed for reclamation. PhD Thesis, University of Hull, UK.

LIN, J. & HINES, A. H. 1994. Effects of suspended food availability on the feeding mode and burial depth of the Baltic clam, *Macoma balthica*. *Oikos*, **69**, 28–36.

MORRIS, E. 1994. Humber Estuary intertidal report 1993 – North Shore. Internal Report to the NRA (Anglian Region).

RATCLIFFE, P. J. 1979. An ecological study of the invertebrates of the Humber Estuary. PhD Thesis, University of Hull, UK.

READING, C. J. 1979. Changes in the downshore distribution of *Macoma balthica* (L.) in relation to shell length. *Estuarine Coastal and Marine Science*, **8**, 1–13.

REES, H. L., BARNETT, B. E. & URQUHART, C. 1982. Biological Surveillance. *In*: GAMESON, A. L. H. (ed.) *The Quality of the Humber Estuary: a Review of the Results of Monitoring 1961–1981*. Report of the Humber Estuary Committee, published by the Yorkshire Water Authority, Chapter 5.

REISE, K. 1983. Biotic enrichment of intertidal sediments by experimental aggregates of the deposit-feeding bivalve *Macoma balthica*. *Marine Ecology: Progress Series*, **12**, 229–236.

RISK, M. J. & MOFFAT, J. S. 1977. Sedimentological significance of fecal pellets of *Macoma balthica* in the Minas Basin, Bay of Fundy. *Journal of Sedimentary Petrology*, **47**, 1425–1436.

TAGHON, G. L., NOWELL, A. R. M. & JUMARS, P. J. 1980. Induction of suspension feeding in spionid polychaetes by high particulate fluxes. *Science*, **210**, 562–564.

WARWICK, R. M. & PRICE, R. 1975. Macrofauna production in an estuarine mud-flat. *Journal of the Marine Biological Association of the United Kingdom*, **55**, 1–18.

ZWARTS, L., BLOMERT, A.-M., SPAAK, P. & DE VRIES, B. 1994. Feeding radius, burying depth and siphon size of *Macoma balthica* and *Scrobicularia plana*. *Journal of Experimental Marine Biology and Ecology*, **183** 193–212.

—— & WANINK, J. 1989. Siphon size and burying depth in deposit- and suspension-feeding benthic bivalves. *Marine Biology*, **100**, 227–240.

In situ measurements of exopolymer production by intertidal epipelic diatom-dominated biofilms in the Humber estuary

GRAHAM J. C. UNDERWOOD & DAVID J. SMITH

Department of Biological Sciences, University of Essex, Colchester, Essex CO3 3SQ, UK

Abstract: Epipelic diatoms are a major component of the microphytobenthos inhabiting fine cohesive sediments. Epipelic diatoms produce carbohydrate-rich exopolymers (EPS) during locomotion. By binding adjacent sediment particles and through the production of a smooth surface layer, EPS can result in biostabilization of intertidal sediments. *In situ* EPS production rates were measured during spring and neap tide periods as part of the LISP investigation carried out in the Humber Estuary, UK, in Spring 1995. There was a significant relationship between the biomass of diatoms (chl. *a*) and the concentrations of colloidal carbohydrate on the Skeffling mudflats, and the production of colloidal carbohydrate was closely linked to rates of primary production (*c.* 10% of photoassimilates present as colloidal-S carbohydrate). However, the production of EPS (the polymeric component of colloidal carbohydrate) was not tightly correlated with the rate of primary production, and ranged between 0.1–1.0% of net benthic primary production. Measurements of incorporation and utilization of ^{14}C labelled carbohydrate fractions indicated that diatoms utilized intracellular carbohydrate stores in EPS production, and that EPS production was higher during darkness and just before tidal cover.

During the last ten years there has been increasing attention paid by both biologists and sedimentologists to the processes of biostabilization in intertidal sediments (Daborn *et al.* 1993; Paterson 1994). The appreciation that biological processes have an impact on the properties of sediments has led to the development of techniques and equipment which are capable of measuring the biological influence on sediment stability (Paterson 1989; Amos *et al.* 1992; Daborn *et al.* 1993). Parallel to these developments has been the search for biological variables that are good measures of biostabilization potential (Paterson 1994).

On intertidal, cohesive sediment mudflats the dominant microphytobenthic organisms are epipelic diatoms. Epipelic diatoms are capable of movement which is attributed to the expulsion of extracellular polymeric carbohydrate-rich mucilage (EPS or exopolymer) from a slit called the raphe in their cell wall (Edgar & Pickett-Heaps 1984). The EPS produced by diatoms binds together sediment particles and can form smooth surface layers (Paterson 1989, Paterson *et al.* 1990; Underwood *et al.* 1995). These processes increase the critical shear strength of the sediment leading to biostabilization (Paterson 1994). A number of studies have shown that the concentrations of colloidal (loosely attached) carbohydrates in sediments is closely related to the biomass of diatoms (Underwood *et al.* 1995; Underwood & Smith in press and refs therein). Colloidal carbohydrate extractions contain both small sugar moieties and polysaccharides. Our current understanding

suggests that it is the EPS present in colloidal carbohydrate fractions, rather than the simple sugars, which are responsible for biostabilization by epipelic diatoms (Decho 1994).

Therefore, an important aspect in understanding biostabilization by epipelic diatoms is the production of EPS, but currently there is very little information available concerning rates and patterns of EPS production by epipelic diatoms. Epipelic diatoms in many intertidal habitats possess endogenous migratory rhythms which bring the cells to the sediment surface during daytime emersion (Happey-Wood & Jones 1988). Such rhythms imply movement, hence EPS production at depth in sediments in the absence of light. Therefore, simply transferring the concepts derived from studies of EPS production by phytoplankton (maximum EPS production with high light intensities under nutrient limited conditions, Fogg 1983) is likely to misrepresent the processes governing epipelic diatom EPS production in sediments. Given that epipelic diatoms can survive long periods of darkness and retain their motility also suggests that EPS production is not directly linked to photosynthesis (Cooksey & Cooksey 1986; Smith & Underwood, unpublished observation).

In this paper we present values for EPS production rates obtained during the LISP-UK experimental period in the Humber estuary. Making direct measurements of sediment carbohydrate fractions, labelling photoassimilates using $H^{14}CO_3^-$ and measuring hourly rates of benthic primary production allowed estimates of the amount of photoassimilates used in EPS

UNDERWOOD, G. J. C. & SMITH, D. J. 1998. *In situ* measurements of exopolymer production by intertidal epipelic diatom-dominated biofilms in the Humber estuary. *In*: BLACK, K. S., PATERSON, D. M. & CRAMP, A. (eds) *Sedimentary Processes in the Intertidal Zone*. Geological Society, London, Special Publications, **139**, 125–134.

production and typical daily rates of EPS production to be calculated.

Methods

Sampling took place over both a spring and neap tidal cycle (4th and 11th April 1995, respectively) at Site A and A/B of the LISP-UK transect, respectively. The change of sites was necessary due to desiccation of surface sediments at site A during the period of neap tides which severely reduced epipelic algal populations. The experiments described below were conducted *in situ* on 4th April 1995 with samples placed on dry ice, or where appropriate, fixed in 1% v/v gluteraldehyde, and analysed in the laboratory. The full data for a similar set of experiments, carried out on 11th April 1995, are available via the LISP-UK data set.

A number of different methods were used to determine *in situ* patterns of primary production and colloidal carbohydrate, and EPS concentration and production. Concentrations of different carbohydrate fractions were measured directly in sediments at hourly intervals. Direct measurements of concentrations provided an indication of net changes occurring within a particular carbohydrate pool; they gave no indication of the possible fluxes of material within that particular pool (e.g. equal rates of production and utilization of EPS in sediment would not result in any concentration change). Rates of production and fluxes of photoassimilated carbon were followed using ^{14}C as a radiotracer. In 'time course' experiments, ^{14}C-labelled bicarbonate was only made available to the biofilm for a 1 h dark incubation and a 1 h illumination period before the start of an experiment. After this initial incorporation period, remaining ^{14}C-labelled bicarbonate was removed and the movement of incorporated-^{14}C through different carbohydrate fractions (colloidal-S, EPS) with time was measured. Separate hourly rates of primary production and EPS production ('hourly production') and measurement of the percentage incorporation of total ^{14}C fixed into EPS were also measured repeatedly over the tidal period. Hourly incorporation values indicated the amount of carbon entering the specified carbohydrate fractions from the photoassimilation that has occurred during the previous hour of illumination. These values are therefore different from those reported from the time-course experiment, which show the amount of ^{14}C moving between fractions in the time following assimilation during photosynthesis.

Time course experiment

At the start of the experimental period, two sets of colour-coded minicores (area 3.147 cm², length $c.$ 7 cm) were placed into the sediment with $c.$ 2 cm projecting out of the sediment. One set of cores was used to measure sediment carbohydrate concentrations and the second set was used to determine the incorporation of

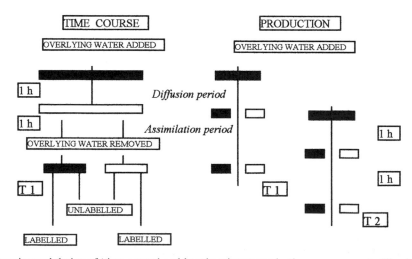

Fig. 1. Experimental design of 'time course' and hourly primary production measurements. Illuminated and non-illuminated periods are indicated by white and black fills, respectively. A single incorporation period was used in the time course experiment, with all cores illuminated for 1 hr before half were darkened. A 'dark' control was used in the production measurements (i.e. no period of illumination) and the procedure for primary production measurements was repeated every hour during tidal exposure.

[14]C-bicarbonate. In both cases sediment chlorophyll *a* concentrations were determined. Each set of cores were subdivided into two treatments, half received ambient light and half were placed in darkness (Fig. 1).

Radioactive $NaH^{14}CO_3^-$, with an activity of 20.35 kBq 3 ml^{-1} of ambient sea water, was added to labelled cores at the start of the experimental period. Care was taken to ensure surface biofilms were not disturbed. Unlabelled cores had the same volume of unmodified sea water added to them. All cores were then kept in the dark (by means of tin foil cups) for a period of 1 h to allow diffusion and equilibration of $NaH^{14}CO_3$ into the biofilm. Foil cups were then removed and all cores were subjected to ambient light conditions, for a further 1 h, to allow photoassimilation of the ^{14}C-bicarbonate by the microalgal population. Following this period of incorporation, overlying water was removed from all cores and covers replaced on the dark-treated cores.

At each sampling time, five cores from each treatment were removed and the top c. 3 mm of sediment placed into small vials. Vials containing unlabelled sediment were immediately placed on dry ice to limit biological activity. Gluteraldehyde (at a final concentration of 1% v/v) was added to the radiolabelled cores to stop any metabolic activity and further incorporation of the isotope. Gluteraldehyde was not added to the unlabelled cores as it interferes with the phenol-sulphuric acid assay (Underwood *et al.* 1995) The remaining cores were sampled at hourly intervals for a total of 4 h during the spring tide.

'Hourly' primary production measurements

To measure hourly rates of primary production, a similar protocol as above was used but the addition of $^{14}NaH^{14}CO_3$ labelled sea water was staggered by 1 h intervals over the course of the experiment (Fig. 1). A set of dark-treated cores was not exposed to ambient light during the second hour of incubation and was used as dark controls for the calculation of primary production rates.

Fractionation of carbohydrates

After collection, vials containing sediments were transported on dry ice back to the laboratory and lyophilized. Sediment samples were weighed and used to determine chlorophyll *a* concentrations and the quantity of, and ^{14}C incorporation

into, colloidal carbohydrate (colloidal-S) and EPS. Organic bound ^{14}C, remaining in the sediment after extraction of the water soluble carbohydrates, was determined to give total incorporation by summation of this residual and the colloidal-S fraction (see below). Chlorophyll *a* analyses (corrected for phaeoforbide content by acidification) was carried out on a 30 mg sub-sample using overnight extraction with cold (4°C) methanol (Yallop *et al.* 1994). To the remaining sediment samples, 6 ml of saline (salinity 25) was added and the suspension was thoroughly mixed to ensure equal distribution throughout the centrifuge tubes. The samples were then placed in a water bath at 20°C for 15 min, to extract the water soluble carbohydrates (see Underwood *et al.* 1995). Samples were centrifuged at 3620 g for 15 min, and 1 ml of the resulting supernatant removed and designated the colloidal-S fraction. A further 3 ml of supernatant was placed in centrifuge tubes with 7 ml of industrial methylated spirits (IMS) giving a final concentration of 70% IMS and left at 4°C for 24 h to precipitate the polymeric EPS fraction (see Underwood *et al.* 1995). The carbohydrate content of the sediment samples after extraction of the water soluble fraction (residual) was determined to give total carbohydrate content (by summation of the colloidal-S and residual fractions). The phenol-sulphuric acid assay (Dubois *et al.* 1956) was used to determine the concentration of carbohydrate present (as glucose equivalents) in the different extracts from the unlabelled cores.

To determine the radioactivity of the EPS and colloidal-S fractions, ^{14}C-bicarbonate that was not photoassimilated had to be removed from the samples by acidification with 5% HCl. Following a 24 h period in a well-vented area, 1 ml of the colloidal-S and EPS solution was added to 17 ml of scintillation fluid (Optiphase safe). To determine the activity incorporated into the residual fraction, the pellet remaining after colloidal-S extraction was acidified and oxidised at 900°C in a Biological Oxidizer (Harvey OX600). The CO_2-trapping scintillation fluid Oxosol was used to capture $^{14}CO_2$ produced from oxidized organic compounds. All counts were made on a scintillation counter (Packard Tricarb 460C) with internal quench correction.

Statistical analysis

Multiple comparisons were made by ANOVA followed by post-hoc analysis (Tukey test) to establish the significantly different groups. All manipulation and analysis of data for percentage of total photoassimilates incorporated into different carbohydrate fractions was carried out on arcsin-transformed data, with the back-transformed means and standard errors being presented. Statistical analyses on all other data (where appropriate) were log transformed [$\log_{10}(n+1)$, Zar 1984] to remove heteroscedasticity from the data sets.

Results

Species composition

Investigation of the species composition (Miles 1996; Underwood & Smith unpublished observations) found that the dominant autotrophs at both stations were epipelic diatoms, predominantly small species of *Navicula*, with *c.* 10–15% euglenoids at Site A.

Changes in sediment carbohydrate concentrations

There was a significant relationship between the concentrations of chlorophyll *a* and colloidal-S carbohydrate in sediments receiving ambient light. Humber sediment data (from spring tide, site A, and neap tide, site A/B) gave a β regression parameter (slope) of 1.108, while sediments which had been artificially darkened showed a lower β regression parameter ($\beta = 0.545$), and a number of the values fell outside the 95% prediction limits of Underwood & Smith's (in press) model (Fig. 2).

During the experimental period, there was no significant difference in sediment chlorophyll *a* concentration between illuminated and darkened sediments or with time, with a mean concentration of $7.5 \pm 0.34\,\mu g$ chl. *a* cm^{-2} (mean $\pm$ SE, $n = 49$). Concentrations of colloidal-S carbohydrate significantly decreased in both illuminated and darkened sediments ($F_{4,50} = 5.79$, $p < 0.01$) (Fig. 3a). These decreases were not due to decline in microphytobenthic biomass in the surface sediments, as the ratio of colloidal-S carbohydrate: chl. *a* (algal biomass) showed the same pattern of change as the areal concentrations of colloidal-S carbohydrate.

Sediment EPS concentrations were approximately an order of magnitude lower than colloidal-S concentrations. Though EPS is a fraction of the colloidal-S measured, EPS concentrations did not follow the same pattern of change as found for colloidal-S carbohydrates.

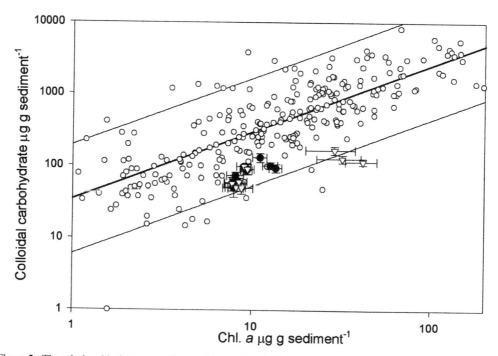

Figure 2. The relationship between sediment chl. *a* and colloidal-S carbohydrate concentration from illuminated (●) and darkened (▽) Humber sediments (each point mean ± SE, $n = 5$) compared to the model (○) of Underwood & Smith (in press).

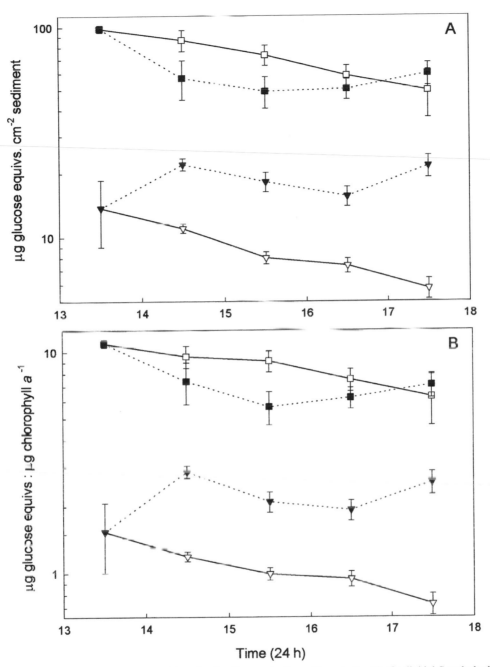

Fig. 3. Changes in the concentration (**a**) and ratio of concentration : chlorophyll *a* (**b**) of colloidal-S carbohydrate (□ & ■) and EPS (▽ & ▼) in illuminated and darkened sediments, respectively, over a 4 h spring tide emersion period on 04/04/1995. Each point mean ± SE, *n* = 5.

Concentrations of EPS showed a significant ($F_{1,29} = 16.69$, $p < 0.001$) decline in illuminated sediment, but in darkened sediments, EPS concentrations increased from 17.1 ± 2.7 to $21.3 \pm 2.5\,\mu\mathrm{g\,cm^{-2}}$ over the experimental period (4 h) (Fig. 3a). This increase in EPS concentrations in darkened sediments was not due to an accumulation of diatom biomass in the surface layers, and the EPS : chl. *a* ratio also increased (Fig. 3b).

Incorporation of ^{14}C into colloidal-S and
EPS ('time course')

The time-course experiment was designed to follow the incorporation of ^{14}C into colloidal-S and EPS fractions in the period of time following assimilation by photosynthesis. After the 1 h dark diffusion – 1 h photoassimilation period, overlying water containing unincorporated $H^{14}CO_3^-$ was removed, thereby preventing further incorporation of radiolabel throughout the remainder of the experiment. Total counts of incorporated ^{14}C were highest in the 13:30 hrs samples for both illuminated and darkened sediments, and decreased with time ($F_{4,50} = 5.44$, $p < 0.001$, data not shown), indicating that there was no significant incorporation of label after the initial hour in the time-course experiment. This is an important check and allows increases in ^{14}C in particular fractions at different times to be interpreted as due to movement of photoassimilated carbon (fixed during the first hour) into that fraction.

The amount of ^{14}C present in the colloidal-S carbohydrate fraction (normalized to biomass)

decreased with time ($F_{4,50} = 5.65$, $p < 0.001$), with no significant differences between treatments (Fig. 4). The highest activity in colloidal-S was in the hour immediately after assimilation, after which ^{14}C activity rapidly decreased. There was approximately an order of magnitude less ^{14}C incorporated into EPS than in the colloidal-S carbohydrate. However, there was a significant increase in the amount of ^{14}C present in EPS with time in both treatments ($F_{4,50} = 4.55$, $p < 0.01$), the greatest increase being in the last hour of the emersion period (16:30–17:30 hrs) (Fig. 4). There were no significant differences between treatments. The percentage of assimilated ^{14}C present in EPS sampled from the 'time-course' experiment in the hours after assimilation during the spring tide and also during the neap tide time-course experiments ranged between 0.17–0.54 % (Table 1).

Hourly measurements of primary production

The rate of benthic primary production (obtained from separate hourly measurements of ^{14}C incorporation) were significantly correlated with light

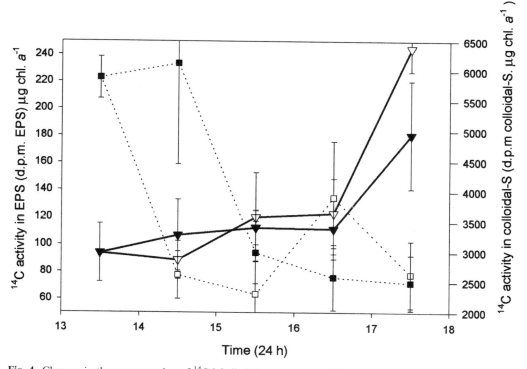

Fig. 4. Changes in the concentration of ^{14}C labelled [decays per min (DPM) per μg chl. a] colloidal-S carbohydrate ($\square$ & $\blacksquare$) and EPS ($\triangledown$ & $\blacktriangledown$) in illuminated and darkened sediments respectively, over a 4 h spring tide emersion period on 04/04/1995. Each point mean $\pm$ SE, $n = 5$. Incorporation of $H^{14}CO_3^-$ by biofilms was restricted to between 12:30–13:30 hrs.

Table 1. *Percentage of ^{14}C incorporated into EPS in sediments subjected to illuminated and dark treatments over emersion during spring tide exposure and before and after immersion during neap tide exposure. Values are mean ± SE (from arcsin-transformed data)*

Tidal phase	Time (24 h)	n	Percentage of total fixed carbon	
			Light EPS	Dark EPS
Spring tide	13:30	10	0.19 ± 0.04	0.19 ± 0.04
	14:30	5	0.2 ± 0.03	0.17 ± 0.02
	15:30	5	0.18 ± 0.06	0.25 ± 0.06
	16:30	5	0.2 ± 0.06	0.27 ± 0.07
	17:30	5	0.54 ± 0.21	0.34 ± 0.11
Neap tide	12:00	5	0.36 ± 0.02	0.36 ± 0.02
	13:30	5	0.27 ± 0.01	0.37 ± 0.03
	18:00	10	0.35 ± 0.03	0.32 ± 0.01
	19:00	10	0.25 ± 0.03	0.38 ± 0.02

intensity ($r^2 = 0.93$, $p < 0.01$) and decreased significantly over the course of the experiment (from 82.7 mg C m^{-2} h^{-1} to 4.7 mg C m^{-2} h^{-1}) (Fig. 5). Measurement of the activity of ^{14}C in colloidal-S and EPS carbohydrate fractions from the cores used to determine the rate of primary production allowed the percentage incorporation of photoassimilates into those fractions to be calculated. The percent incorporation of carbon into colloidal-S carbohy-

drate varied between 6.5–10.6% of net primary production, but there were no significant differences with time. However, the percentage incorporation of ^{14}C into EPS was negatively correlated with primary production ($r = -0.68$, $p < 0.001$) and increased significantly with time ($F_{2,24} = 9.06$, $p < 0.001$) from 0.14% to 0.98% of the total carbon fixed, with the maximum percentage incorporation measured in the hour before tidal immersion (16:30–17:30 hrs).

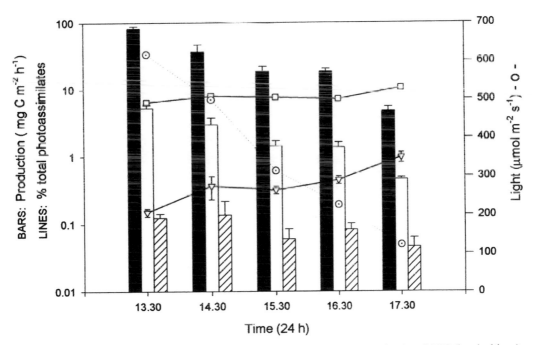

Fig. 5. Benthic primary production (solid bars), colloidal-S carbohydrate (open bars) and EPS (hatched bars) production and the percentage incorporation of photoassimilates into colloidal (□) and EPS (▽) over a 4 h spring tide emersion period on 04/04/1995. Each bar/point, mean + SE, $n = 5$. Light intensity (PAR) (○) derived from Met. Office data.

Table 2. *Benthic chl. a concentrations, rate of primary production and EPS production measured during the two hours prior to a neap tide immersion on 11/04/95 (mean ± SE, n = 5)*

Time (24 h)	PAR (μmol m^{-2} s^{-1})	chl. a (μg cm^{-2})	Primary prodn (mg C m^{-2} h^{-1})	% incorp. into EPS	EPS prodn (mg C m^{-2} h^{-1})
11:00–12:00	1390	9.37 ± 0.82	12.67 ± 0.56	0.43 ± 0.03	0.05 ± 0.002
12:00–13:00	1480	11.02 ± 1.03	21.93 ± 2.15	0.31 ± 0.05	0.07 ± 0.007

During the neap tide exposure period, primary production measures were only obtained during the 2 h period prior to mid-afternoon immersion. Primary production and chl. a values were lower than during the spring tide period (Table 2). The percent incorporation of ^{14}C into colloidal-S and EPS were similar (0.31–0.43%) (Table 2).

Multiplying the rate of primary production by the percentage incorporation data allowed hourly rates of colloidal-S and EPS production to be calculated. During the spring tide exposure the rate of production of colloidal-S was positively correlated with the rate of primary production ($r^2 = 0.77$, $p < 0.001$), and decreased by an order of magnitude (from 5.25 ± 0.58 to 0.46 ± 0.03 mg C m^{-2}h^{-1}, mean ± SE, $n = 5$) as primary production decreased. The production rate of EPS halved over the tidal period, from 0.12 ± 0.02 to 0.05 ± 0.02 mg C m^{-2} h^{-1} ($F_{4,20} = 10.56$, $p < 0.01$), the decrease in hourly primary production being partly compensated for by the increased percentage assimilation into EPS by the microphytobenthos.

Discussion

Much of the previous literature on biostabilization is concerned with sediment colloidal carbohydrate concentrations, and the concentration of colloidal carbohydrates in cohesive sediment habitats has been found to be closely related to the biomass (chl. a) of epipelic diatoms in a number of different estuaries (Underwood & Paterson 1993; Underwood 1997; Underwood & Smith in press). The relationship between colloidal carbohydrate and chl. a obtained from the Skeffling site in the Humber estuary was found to fit the model of Underwood & Smith (in press), suggesting that the Humber sites can be considered typical in their colloidal carbohydrate : chl a relationships. The model of Underwood & Smith (in press) is based on large data sets obtained over long periods of time, with measurements generally taken from around the time of low tide within each sampling trip. Thus the model can be seen as representing an average low tide situation. The data derived from our LISP experiments showed that over shorter time periods (hours during emersion), the relationships between diatom biomass (chl. a), colloidal carbohydrate and EPS concentrations are not as straight forward as the model suggests, particularly when sediments were manipulated.

Data obtained from artificially darkened sediments tended to deviate from the model, with lower colloidal carbohydrate concentrations than expected. Both the sediment concentration data and direct hourly measurements of colloidal carbohydrate production showed that production of colloidal carbohydrate was closely linked to the rate of primary production (between 6–10% of total primary production). The data from the time-course experiment showed that the flux of carbon through the colloidal-S pool was also rapid, with a large proportion of the ^{14}C-colloidal-S produced during a 1 h period of assimilation disappearing in the subsequent hour. Colloidal carbohydrate extracts contain both polymeric and non-polymeric carbohydrate material (Underwood et al. 1995) and it is known that algae produce low molecular weight carbohydrate exudates during photosynthesis (Fogg 1983). Sediment colloidal carbohydrate extracts contain this material. The close coupling between sediment concentrations of colloidal carbohydrate and rates of benthic primary production (Figs 3 and 5) and the data from the time course (Fig. 4) indicates a rapid turnover of such material within the sediment, with little accumulation over hourly time scales. Low molecular weight carbohydrate compounds are readily utilizable by bacteria (Sundh 1992) and are probably rapidly mineralized. Thus, darkening sediments would be expected to result in lowered colloidal carbohydrate concentrations as the supply of new colloidal material declined, and existing low molecular weight carbohydrates were mineralized.

In contrast to the pattern observed for colloidal carbohydrates, it appears that there is no direct relationship between the rate of primary production and rate of EPS production. Concentrations of EPS increased significantly in darkened sediments compared to illuminated sediments (Fig. 3) and the percentage incorporation of photoassimilates into EPS significantly increased as primary production decreased (Fig. 5). However, the pulse experiment, following the flux of ^{14}C through the EPS pool showed little change in the amount of ^{14}C present in EPS in both darkened and illuminated sediments until the last hour before immersion, when the amount of label in EPS significantly increased (Fig. 3, Table 1). As there was no new source of ^{14}C available to the cells at this time, the labelled material must have been assimilated during the 1 h assimilation period and retained in the cells for later utilization. Because diatoms appear to be able to utilize previously fixed carbon in EPS production, rates of production based on hourly measures of label incorporation (Fig. 5) may underestimate actual EPS production, because a proportion of previously fixed (and therefore unlabelled) carbon will also be being utilized in the current EPS production. This may explain why concentrations of EPS were shown to increase under darkened conditions, though the proportion of labelled EPS present did not differ from illuminated sediments.

Conclusions

The data described in this paper are, to our knowledge, the first measurements of sediment standing stocks (concentrations) of colloidal-S and EPS combined with measurements of fluxes of material into colloidal-S and EPS (the time-course experiment) and with hourly rates of benthic primary production. The substantial decrease in light intensity during the period of spring tide emersion (from 617 to 71 μmols m^{-2} s^{-1}) generated an additional variable into the data set, and allowed the effects of different rates of primary production to be observed.

The standing stock of EPS in sediments was shown to be variable over a tidal exposure period, but over longer time periods appears to be relatively constant with regard to biomass (Underwood & Smith in press). This would suggest that over a particular period of time, production of EPS is equal to loss. The data presented here gives evidence for the loss of EPS and colloidal-S from the sediment during the emersion period. This loss may be in the form of bacterial utilization, as a result of unselective deposit feeders which are known to feed on epipelic diatoms (e.g. N. diversicolor and C. volutator, Smith et al. 1996) or as wash away during tidal cover. Data obtained during the neap tide immersion period (not shown) indicated a significant ($p < 0.05$) loss (c. 40%) of colloidal-S during a 4.5 h period of tidal cover. This is similar to values reported by Grant et al. (1986) of a 45–46% loss of colloidal carbohydrate during tidal cover of intertidal sands.

Another important factor to consider is that changes in EPS concentrations may be as a result of EPS production by heterotrophs (e.g. meiofauna), whereas EPS concentrations as calculated from the ^{14}C-based production data are dependent on autotrophic organisms only.

Our data suggests that diatom biofilms do not only produce EPS during illuminated periods of emersion. While sediment colloidal-S carbohydrate concentrations appeared to be closely linked to rates of primary production, EPS production is more influenced by diatom motility, linked to endogenous migratory rhythms. While the biomass of diatoms present in a sediment is undoubtedly a factor in the degree of biostabilization, increases in sediment stability during emersion may be due to dewatering effects rather than to net increases in diatom-derived EPS. The polymeric carbohydrate material (EPS) produced by diatoms has been considered the responsible agent for biostabilization (Paterson 1994; Underwood et al. 1995). However, it is possible that utilization of the non-polymeric component of the colloidal carbohydrate fraction by bacteria may result in bacterial EPS production. In laboratory studies bacterial EPS has been shown to stabilize sands (Dade et al. 1990), but as yet no studies have been published for cohesive sediment. This is another potential linkage between biological components in sediments that needs to be resolved.

This work was undertaken as part of LISP-UK, NERC LOIS-RACS(C) Special Topic 122 and we thank Drs K. Black and D. M. Paterson for financial support and facilities during the field work. This work was part funded by NERC grant GR3/8907 and, D.J.S. was supported by a NERC Ph.D. studentship GT4/94/338/P. This is LOIS publication number 405 of the LOIS Community Research Programme, carried out under a Special Topic Award from the Natural Environment Research Council. We acknowledge the technical assistance of Mr P. Szyszko and Mr R. G. Perkins

References

AMOS, C. L., GRANT, J., DABORN, G. R. & BLACK, K. 1992. Sea Carousel–a benthic annular flume. Estuarine Coastal and Shelf Science, 34, 557–577.

COOKSEY, K. E. & COOKSEY, B. 1986. Adhesion of fouling diatoms to surfaces: some biochemistry. In: EVANS, L. V. & HOAGLAND, K. D. (eds) Algal Biofouling. Studies in Environmental Science, Elsevier, Amsterdam, 28.

DABORN, G. R., AMOS, C. L., BRYLINSKI, H. C. et al. 1993. An ecological 'cascade' effect: migratory birds affect stability of intertidal sediments. Limnology and Oceanography, 38, 225–231.

DADE, B. W., DAVIS, J. D., NICHOLS, P. D., NOWELL, A. R. M., THISTLE, D., TREXLER, M. B. & WHITE, D. C. 1990. Effects of bacterial exopolymer adhesion on the entrainment of sand. *Geomicrobiology Journal*, **8**, 1–16.

DECHO, A. W. 1994. Molecular-scale events influencing the macroscale cohesiveness of exopolymers. *In*: KRUMBEIN, W. E., PATERSON, D. M. & STAL, L. J. (eds) *Biostabilization of Sediments*, Oldenburg: Bibliotheks und Informationssystem der Universität Oldenburg (BIS) Verlag, 135–148,

DUBOIS, M., GILLES, K. A., HAMILTON, J. K., REBER, P. A., & SMITH, F. 1956. Colorimetric method for determination of sugars and related substances. *Analytical Chemistry*, **28**, 350–356.

EDGAR, L. A. & PICKETT-HEAPS, J. D. 1984. Diatom locomotion. *Progresses in Phycological Research*, **3**, 47–88.

FOGG, G. E. 1983. The ecological significance of extracellular products of phytoplankton photosynthesis. *Botanica Marina*, **26**, 3–14.

GRANT, J., BATHMANN, U. V. & MILLS, E. L. 1986. The interaction between benthic diatom films and sediment transport. *Estuarine, Coastal and Shelf Science*, **23**, 225–223.

HAPPEY-WOOD, C. M. & JONES, P. 1988. Rhythms of vertical migration and motility in intertidal benthic diatoms with particular reference to *Pleurosigma angulatum*. *Diatom Research*, **3**, 83–93.

MILES, A. L. 1996. In LISP – Littoral Investigation of Sediment Properties, LOIS RACS(C) Special Topic 122. Preliminary Results 1996. Unpublished report. University of St Andrews. BLACK, K. & PATERSON, D. M. (eds), 132–136.

PATERSON, D. M. 1989. Short-term changes in the erodibility of intertidal cohesive sediments related to the migratory behaviour of epipelic diatoms. *Limnology and Oceanography*, **34**, 223–234.

—— 1994. Microbial mediation of sediment structure and behaviour. *In*: STAL, L. J. & CAUMETTE, P. (eds) NATO ASI Series Vol. G35. *Microbial Mats*. Springer Verlag, Berlin, 97–109.

——, CRAWFORD, R. M. & LITTLE, C. 1990. Subaerial exposure and changes in stability of intertidal estuarine sediments. *Estuarine, Coastal and Shelf Science*, **30**, 541–556.

SMITH, D. J., HUGHES, R. G. & COX, E. J. 1996. Predation of epipelic diatoms by the amphipod *Corophium volutator* and the polychaete *Nereis diversicolor*. *Marine Ecology Progress Series*, **145**, 53–61.

SUNDH, J. 1992. Biochemical composition of dissolved organic carbon derived from phytoplankton and used by heterotrophic bacteria. *Applied and Environmental Microbiology*, **58**, 2938–2947.

UNDERWOOD, G. J. C. 1997. Microalgal colonisation in a saltmarsh restoration scheme. *Estuarine, Coastal and Shelf Science*, **44**, 471–481.

—— & PATERSON, D. M. 1993. Seasonal changes in diatom biomass, sediment stability and biogenic stabilization in the Severn Estuary. *Journal of the Marine Biological Association of the UK*, **73**, 871–887.

——, —— & PARKES, R. J. 1995. The measurement of microbial carbohydrate exopolymers from intertidal sediments. *Limnology and Oceanography*, **40**, 1243–1253.

—— & SMITH, D. J. (in press). Predicting epipelic diatom exopolymer concentrations in intertidal sediments from chl. *a Microbial Ecology*.

YALLOP, M. L., WINDER, B. DE., PATERSON, D. M. & STAL, L. J. 1994. Comparative structure, primary production and biogenic stabilisation of cohesive and non-cohesive sediments inhabited by microphytobenthos. *Estuarine, Coastal and Shelf Science*, **39**, 565–582.

ZAR, J. H. 1984. *Biostatistical analysis*. 2nd edn, Prentice Hall Inc., New Jersey.

Ecological interaction and sediment transport on an intertidal mudflat I. Evidence for a biologically mediated sediment–water interface

G. RUDDY[1]*, C. M. TURLEY[2] & T. E. R. JONES[1]

[1] University of Plymouth, Drakes Circus, Plymouth PL4 8AA, UK
[2] Plymouth Marine Laboratory, Citadel Hill, Plymouth PL1 2PB, UK

Abstract: Using biological, chemical and physical data, evidence of biologically mediated cohesive sediment dynamics is presented for an intertidal mudflat in the Humber Estuary, UK. The data suggest that in excess of 98% of sediment fluxes to the sediment bed on the mudflat are subject to resuspension, forming a bedload that is important in generating the shear stress required to erode the sediment bed. Benthic micro-algae photosynthesize and are grazed by macro-heterotrophs within this $300-3000\ \mu$m deep dynamic surface layer. The data suggest that the algal growth within this layer is limited by nitrogen fluxes, resulting in 'excess' carbon fixation by photosynthesis. A significant positive relationship is apparent between 'excess' carbon fixation rates and the sediment critical erosion stress. This indicates that nitrogen limitation and sediment stability were directly proportional to each other on the mudflat. Grazing of the algae by *Macoma balthica* (a burrowing bivalve) profoundly affects the carbon and nitrogen cycles in the dynamic surface layer, and hence also 'excess' carbon fixation. We propose that a highly interdependent community of benthic algae, bacteria and macro-heterotrophs, acts to regulate sediment dynamics via small-scale nitrogen cycling and the algal exudation of 'excess' carbon as sediment-binding polymers.

Intertidal mudflat environments represent an early phase of terrestrial progradation and comprise much of the intertidal zone in estuaries and sheltered coastlines along the eastern edge of the UK. The dynamics of these habitats are poorly understood, but widely recognized as important for long-term flood defence, as sources and sinks for particulate and dissolved, natural and anthropogenic compounds and as important biologically and ecologically productive and sensitive areas. From a theoretical point of view, they offer an analogue for understanding many important long-term (geological) and large-scale (land–sea exchange) processes as well as for understanding how living systems and the environment interact.

It has been recognized that biology plays a crucial role in regulating fluxes to and from intertidal environments (e.g. Krumbein *et al.* 1994). These fluxes include both the biogeochemical fluxes of dissolved substances such as nitrate (Nixon 1981), metals (Griffin *et al.* 1989) and sulphides (Swider & Mackin 1989) and the fluxes of particulate substances, such as particulate organic carbon (POC, Hines & Jones 1985). Many of the cycles of these substances interact (Berner 1980; Rizzo 1990; Froclich *et al.* 1979; Ruddy 1997*a*). Processes such as bioturbation (Sharma *et al.* 1987) and bioirrigation (Aller 1982) have an important modifying effect on the balance of reactions occurring in the sediment (Aller & Yingst 1985) and therefore also fluxes to and from the sediment. The feeding activities of bioturbators and bioirrigators, such as the burrowing bivalve *Macoma balthica*, modify physical sediment properties (Widdows *et al.* 1996) and depend at least in part on a diet of *in situ* and resuspended benthic micro-organisms (Kamermans 1994). The microbial algae (e.g. epipelic diatoms), living in great abundance in the uppermost layers of intertidal sediments, have also been shown to affect the physical stability of the sediment surface (Paterson 1989; Underwood & Paterson 1993). The potential mediation of sediment stability by biology has profound implications for the understanding of the biogeochemistry of intertidal mudflat systems. This is because the accretion rate may determine the benthic biology and chemistry (Boudreau 1994) by changing the flux of growth materials (e.g. nutrients) into the sediment, and likewise the biology may affect the sediment accretion rate.

Many of the biogeochemical reservoirs that determine growth conditions in the sediment (e.g. nitrate concentrations) turnover on the scale of days and hours (Ruddy *et al.* 1997*b*), with large gross but small net fluxes. The longer term, deeper processes of the mudflat (e.g. long-term carbon storage) result directly from the burial of these highly dynamic uppermost layers and feed back on short-term processes occurring at the sediment–water interface (e.g. via nutrient fluxes). The sediment–water system is therefore highly interdependent; a change in one variable will affect many others. This highlights the need

---

*Current address: Plymouth Marine Laboratory, Citadel Hill, Plymouth PL1 2PB, UK.

RUDDY, G., TURLEY, C. M. & JONES, T. E. R. 1998. Ecological interaction and sediment transport on an intertidal mudflat I. *In*: BLACK, K. S., PATERSON, D. M. & CRAMP, A. (eds) *Sedimentary Processes in the Intertidal Zone*. Geological Society, London, Special Publications, **139**, 135–148.

for an integrated approach to interpreting and/ or predicting any particular variable in the intertidal environment. The difficulty in understanding this environment is one of finding an appropriate spatial and temporal level of sampling from which to view the interactions of the whole system.

One potentially important scale is that associated with the microscale algal production of extracellular polymeric substances (EPS). These substances are composed of carbohydrates (Decho 1990, 1994) and bind sediment grains together, increasing sediment cohesion (Paterson 1989). In structuring microbial interactions (Wachendorfer *et al.* 1994; Gerdes *et al.* 1994), EPS may play a major role in sediment biogeochemistry. Benthic diatom EPS is thought to be formed by the excretion of glucan (an intracellular carbohydrate storage product) (Hoagland 1993) and results in diatom motility (Edgar & Pickett-Heaps 1984). Other organisms are also known to produce forms of EPS (Decho 1990). What remains unclear is how an algal cell partitions the carbon fixed by photosynthesis between (a) biomass growth or intracellular carbohydrate storage, and (b) intracellular carbohydrate respiration or exudation of the carbohydrate as EPS.

Nutrient limitation has been recognized as important in this respect (Lehmann & Wober 1976; Stal 1994). Nitrogen, in particular, has been observed to be limiting in a number of different intertidal sediments (Sundback 1994; Flothmann & Werner 1992; Nilsson *et al.* 1991; Hoppner & Wonnenberger 1985) and may therefore be important in determining benthic carbohydrate exudation and sediment stability. The aim of this paper is to establish whether nitrogen limitation and carbohydrate production are linked. We aim to determine whether EPS production results in the modification of sediment stability, and how this is effected by bioturbating macro-fauna. Results from the LISP-UK (Littoral Investigation of Sediment Properties-UK) project are used to characterize the dynamics of the surface sediment layer. Two time-scales are examined and combined. Daily and hourly time series measurements are used in conjunction with time-averaged measurements to demonstrate the existence of a biologically mediated sediment–water interface.

Methods

Study site

The 2.4 km LISP transect extended orthogonally from the Pump Station at Skeffling onto the Skeffling intertidal mudflats in the mouth of

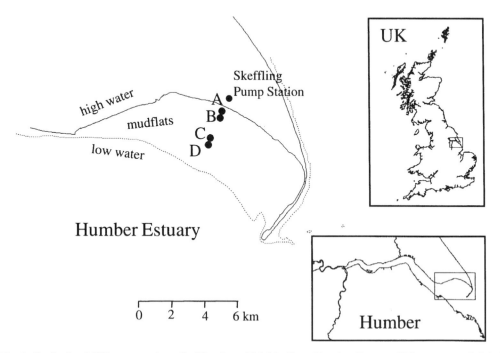

Fig. 1. Study site. LISP transect sites, Skeffling Intertidal Mudflats, Humber Estuary, UK, were sampled 4–21 April 1995 for a variety of sediment and water properties.

the Humber estuary, UK (Fig. 1). Four sampling sites were established, of which the two closest to the shore (site A = 53°38.5′N 0°4.25′E, elevation 5.3 m above Chart Datum (mCD), 200 m from mean high water mark, and site B = 53°38.4′N 0°4.10′E, elevation 4.9 mCD, 550 m from mean high water mark) are discussed here. The muds comprise a 4 m deep sequence of clays, silts and fine sands [site A modal particle size = 17.5 μm, site B = 45.4 μm (Cox *et al.* 1996)] overlying till material. A distinct shore-normal metre-scale ridge-runnel topography was observed on the mudflats, as were centimetre-scale mud ripples. Intensive sampling for a wide range of variables occurred at the sites along the transect from 4–21 April 1995.

Bacterial exo-enzyme activities

The activity of leucine-aminopeptidase (an enzyme that cleaves peptides from proteins) was measured daily, one hour after low tide, at sites A and B, and hourly over two spring tidal exposure periods at sites A and B, using the fluorogenically labelled substrate method of Köster *et al.* (1991) and based on three replicate

experiments for each sample. Surface mud samples, 1 cm deep, were collected using adapted 24 well Corning microtitre plates, providing 24 replicate cores of 3.5 cm^3 each. Subsamples were diluted and mixed 1:1 with 0.2 μm filtered water collected at the sites. Rates of enzymatic activity per dry weight sediment were measured within two hours by the addition of maximal concentrations of enzyme-specific substrate. Maximal concentrations were established during preliminary kinetic studies. The accumulation of fluorogen was measured at 3–4 time steps during short-term incubations (<1 hour total) at *in situ* temperatures (ranging 2.6–17.9°C). The V_{max} rate was then taken as the linear regression slope of fluorogen accumulation over time. An example of the results can be seen in Fig. 2.

Critical erosion stress

Specially designed perspex annular coring miniflumes (miniflume diameter 12.8 cm with an annular channel width of 6.8 cm) enabled erosion experiments of undisturbed sediment surfaces. Analysis occurred within six hours of sampling. Co-sampled water from nearby hollows on the

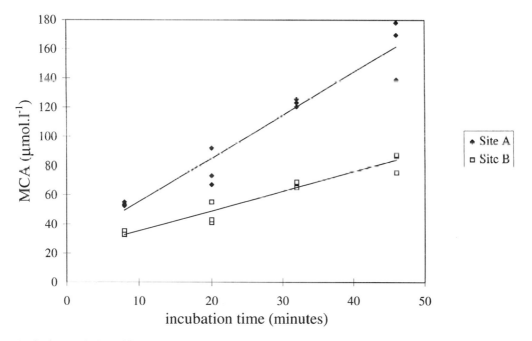

Fig. 2. Accumulation of fluorogen MCA (4-methylcoumarinyl-7-amide) during typical short-term aminopeptidase enzyme assay of surficial sediment sample (three replicates shown for LISP Sites A and B on 13 April 1995). The fluorogen is liberated by the hydrolysis of MCA-labelled-leucine added to sediment samples at V_{max} concentrations, and the linear regression slope taken as the V_{max} enzyme activity.

(a)

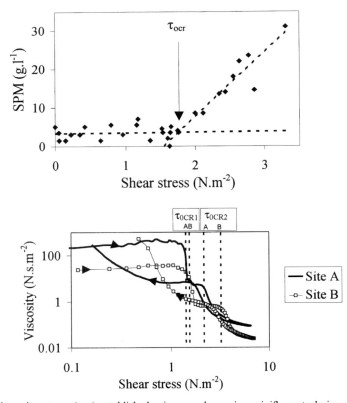

(b)

Fig. 3. (**a**) Critical erosion stress (τ_{0cr}) established using annular coring miniflume technique. Sediment surface is cored directly into miniflume and inserted into constant torque rheometer with overlying water. Lid velocity forces water movement and generates well-characterized shear stress at the sediment–water interface. Suspended particulate matter (SPM) is sampled and critical erosion stress is taken as intersection (τ_{0cr}) of pre- and post-erosion linear regression lines of shear stress against SPM. (Site A sediment on 7 April 1995 shown.) (**b**) Sediment structure breakdown using concentric cylinder geometry in rheometer. In this technique, the sample maintains contact between the wall of a static cup and the wall of an inserted rotating cylinder. A known gap between the cup and cylinder, and a measured rotation velocity for given torque, allows the measurement of fluid viscosity with changes in shear stress. Shear stress is increased incrementally and structure breakdown points are identified by sudden decreases in fluid viscosity. Two distinct critical breakdown points (τ_{0CR1} and τ_{0CR2}) are observed in the sediments of both sites A and B (samples on 7 April 1995 shown). The shear stress is subsequently decreased incrementally (hence arrows) to observe the degree of structure re-establishment.

mudflat was placed carefully over the sampled sediment bed, and the miniflume placed in a Carrimed rheometer. Flow in the miniflume has been well-characterized (Graham *et al.* 1992; James *et al.* 1996) and the rheometer enabled constant torque, variable velocity, shear stress control and flow viscosity observations within the miniflumes. Suspended particulate matter (SPM) concentrations within the flume were established by subsampling (500 μl) using a fine pipette inserted into the flow. SPM concentrations were established by drying and weighing the subsamples. An example of the results is shown in Fig. 3a.

Sediment rheological properties

The rheometer was also used to determine the dynamic viscosity, elasticity and fluidity of sediment samples. These properties were measured using variable oscillation frequency at a specified gap height between parallel plates (Walters 1977). Samples were taken from the microtitre plates used for exo-enzyme sampling. In addition, the dynamic viscosity of sediment slurries from sites A and B was measured in concentric cylinder geometry in response to changing shear stress (Hughes *et al.* 1996). Both techniques pinpoint structure breakdown in viscous fluids (e.g. mud) at precisely known shear stresses. An example of the results of a concentric cylinder experiment is shown in Fig. 3b.

Results and discussion

An overview of sediment dynamics on the upper shore

Given the average sediment density, sediment porosity and tidal coverage (Table 1a), the net sediment flux to the bed giving rise to the long-term sedimentation rate can be calculated. This flux represents the net sedimentation rate and is shown in Table 1a. The gross sediment flux to the bed can also be estimated given the measured *in situ* settling velocities of flocs, the tidal coverage and the concentration of suspended particulate matter, since turbulent dispersion in the water column was small (Christie and Dyer 1996).

The gross sediment flux to the bed calculated in this manner (Table 1a) is two orders of magnitude higher than the net flux to the bed, but compares well with the sediment flux generated by the maximum rates of erosion (shown in Table 1a integrated over tidal coverage). These calculations imply that in excess of 98% of the gross sediment flux to the bed is subject to resuspension.

Erosion was observed at a given point on the mudflat for about the first and last 30 min of tidal coverage (Law 1996). Using the gross sediment flux to the bed (Table 1a) for deposition and the observed maximum sediment flux from the bed (Table 1a) for erosion, a maximum depth of sediment deposited and eroded can be estimated (Table 1b). The estimates in Tables 1a and b suggest that a maximum of a few hundred to a few thousand microns of sediment exchanges with suspended sediment, leaving behind only 1–2% of the gross sediment flux to the bed to generate the long-term sedimentation rate.

The resuspension of deposited material depends on whether the shear stress of the moving water on the bed (τ_0) exceeds the critical erosion threshold of the bed (τ_{0cr}). In the miniflume experiments (e.g. Fig. 3a), sediment was observed to erode in a two stage process. Initially, as τ_0 increased, strips of sediment were torn from the bed to form 'flocs' in suspension. As τ_0 increased further the 'flocs' broke down into their constituent 'flocules' with a sudden increase in the viscosity of the eroding water, at which point the suspended particulate matter became measurable by the pipetting method and τ_{0cr} (average shown in Table 1c) could be identified.

Critical shear points similar to τ_{0cr} were observed in the concentric cylinder analyses (particularly shear point τ_{0CR1} in Table 1c and Fig. 3b). The concentric cylinder technique measures the internal cohesive sediment structure breakdown (Hughes *et al.* 1996) rather than the bed breakdown measured by miniflumes. The two critical shear points observed using this technique (τ_{0CR1} and τ_{0CR2} in Table 1c and Fig. 3b) suggest that internal cohesive structure of the sediment first broke down irreversibly and was followed, at higher shear stresses, by a further reversible breakdown. The initial breakdown may be associated with the physical and irreversible destruction of EPS, whereas the second shear point may reflect reversible abiotic grain–grain interactions.

The shear stresses (τ_0) that occur during tidal coverage and cause structure breakdown, result from the shear rate of the fluid (with units of s^{-1}) and the dynamic viscosity of the fluid (with units of $N\,s\,m^{-1}$). At the viscosity of water and the measured and estimated shear rates during tidal inundation (Law 1996; Black & Jago 1996), flow shear stress and bed shear stress are very low (Table 1d) despite current velocities in the region of $0.2\,m\,s^{-1}$ (Law 1996). This implies that SPM is required to augment the eroding fluid viscosity and hence may be required for bed shear stress (τ_0) to exceed (τ_{0cr}). Given the measured sediment dynamic viscosity (Table 1d), sediment density (Table 1a), sediment porosity (Table 1a) and the critical erosion threshold (Table 1c), the suspended load required to give the necessary eroding fluid viscosity can be estimated (Table 1d). These estimates ($0.3–0.6\,kg\,m^{-3}$) are very close to the SPM concentrations found in the water ($0.5–1\,kg\,m^{-3}$). This indicates that sediment erosion was likely to occur during tidal inundation as a result of increased fluid viscosity in addition to high fluid shear rates.

The degree to which the $300–3000\,\mu m$ deep dynamic surface layer exchanges between the mudflat and the estuary (i.e. the large-scale sediment dispersion coefficient) depends on the amount of bedload transport (where resuspended sediment remains close to the bed) across the mudflat. At a current velocity of $0.2\,m\,s^{-1}$ (Law 1996), a floc fall distance of $0.5\,m$ during tidal coverage (assuming a $1\,m$ deep tide) and settling velocities as in Table 1a, the minimum time in suspension of a resuspended particle is $c.1700\,s$, during which time the particle would have moved more than $300\,m$ before redeposition. A 98% resuspension flux would therefore produce a dispersion coefficient of the order of $17\,km^2\,d^{-1}$. However, grain

Table 1. *Sediment dynamics at LISP sites A and B. Mean values over the LISP experimental period are used where available*

(a) Observed and calculated sediment fluxes

	Site A	Site B	Units	Reference
Long-term sedimentation rate	3.12		$mm\,yr^{-1}$	Widdows *et al.* (1996)
Sediment porosity	0.530	0.480	volume ratio	Ruddy *et al.* (1996)
Sediment density	1095.1	1211.6	$kg\,m^{-3}$	Wiltshire *et al.* (1996)
Tidal coverage	0.167	0.25	d^{-1}	Widdows *et al.* (1996)
∴ Net sediment flux to bed*	6.48×10^{-7}	4.79×10^{-7}	$kg\,m^{-2}\,s^{-1}$	
Suspended particulate matter	0.5–1		$kg\,m^{-3}$	Christie & Dyer (1996)
In situ floc settling velocity	0.3		$mm\,s^{-1}$	Fennessey & Dyer (1996)
∴ Gross sediment flux to bed†	3.75×10^{-5}	5.62×10^{-5}	$kg\,m^{-2}\,s^{-1}$	
Observed max sediment flux from bed	1.64×10^{-5}	2.41×10^{-5}	$kg\,m^{-2}\,s^{-1}$	Widdows *et al.* (1966)
∴ % Resuspension‡	98.27	99.15		

* = (grain density @ quartz ($2330\,kg\,m^{-3}$) × (1-porosity) × sedimentation rate)/tidal coverage.
† = SPM × settling velocity × tidal coverage.
‡ = 100 − (100 × net sediment flux/gross sediment flux).

(b) Estimated erosion and deposition depths

	Site A	Site B	Units	Reference
Eroding tidal coverage	3 600	3 600	s	Law (1966)
Depositing tidal coverage	14 429	21 600	s	from Table 1(a)
∴ Max sediment erosion depth*	322	2 864	$\mu m\,tide^{-1}$	
∴ Max sediment deposition depth†	988	1 506	$\mu m\,tide^{-1}$	

* = (eroding tidal coverage × max sediment flux from bed)/tides per day/(water density-sediment density).
† = (depositing tidal coverage × gross sediment flux to bed)/tides per day/(water density-sediment density).

(c) Summary of sediment cohesion variables

	Site A	Site B	Units	Reference
Miniflume;				
critical erosion threshold (τ_{0cr})	2.06	1.28	$N\,m^{-2}$	Ruddy *et al.* (1966)
Concentric cylinders;				
critical shear point 1 (τ_{0CR1})	1.423	1.540	$N\,m^{-2}$	See Fig. 4
critical shear point 2 (τ_{0CR2})	2.022	2.963	$N\,m^{-2}$	See Fig. 4

(d) Shear stress estimates

	Site A	Site B	Units	Reference
Water viscosity	0.001035		$N\,s\,m^{-2}$	
Flow shear stress*	0.00105–0.003275		$N\,m^{-2}$	from Law (1996)
Estimated bed shear stress by water†	0.022		$N\,m^{-2}$	from Black & Jago (1996)
Sediment dynamic viscosity	90.64	113.57	$N\,s\,m^{-2}$	Ruddy *et al.* (1966)
∴ Critical suspended load‡	0.622	0.309	$kg\,m^{-3}$	from sediment porosity, Table 1(a) and τ_{0cr}, Table 1(c)

* = water viscosity × flow shear rate.
† = water viscosity × bed shear rate estimated from velocity profiles.
‡ = suspended load required to give necessary flow shear stress to equal critical erosion stress at the observed shear rates, sediment porosity and dynamic viscosity.

sorting along the transect (Cox *et al.* 1996), bedforms and other small-scale sediment heterogeneity suggest smaller scale transport, via bedload rather than pure suspension. Indeed, calculations from the temporal and spatial variability of sediment rheology and enzyme activities suggest an *in situ* dispersion coefficient of only $10 \, \text{m}^2 \, \text{d}^{-1}$ at Site A during spring tides (Ruddy *et al.* 1997*b*). This suggests that 98% of the dynamic sediment layer may remain for some time, albeit redistributed, in a similar area of the mudflat.

An overview of ecological dynamics on the upper shore

Photosynthesis occurs within the dynamic sediment layer. Light penetration into the sediment extends to 1200 μm at Site A and 2000 μm at Site B (Miles 1996), supporting significant, but variable, chlorophyll *a* concentrations and photosynthesis rates predominantly in the uppermost 200 μm (Miles 1996; Wiltshire *et al.* 1996; Underwood *et al.* 1996; Herman 1996).

In terms of the carbon concentrations of this layer (Table 2a), algal biomass [estimated at 50 times the chlorophyll *a* concentration (see Jonge 1980)] makes up only a small proportion of the total POC (Table 2a). The total carbohydrate carbon concentrations (colloidal plus bulk, Table 2a) are significantly larger than algal biomass. Carbohydrate is mainly present as the bulk carbohydrates thought to reflect the accumulated products of colloidal carbohydrate polymerization and degradation (Decho 1990). The presence of high carbohydrate concentrations suggests that either a high degree of algal carbohydrate exudation occurs in the sediment or that the bulk carbohydrates are significantly less labile than other carbon compounds.

The algal growth conditions in the dynamic surface layer can be assessed from a mass balance point of view, since for balanced growth, carbon fixation rates must be matched by the total nitrogen fluxes times the algal biomass C : N ratio. Phosphorus and silica, which show non-conservative behaviour in the Humber estuary (R. Howland pers. comm.), may also influence growth conditions, but are beyond the scope of this paper. A shortfall in the nitrogen flux relative to photosynthesis results in unbalanced growth and intracellular carbohydrate accumulation (Lehmann & Wober 1976). The intracellular carbohydrate can be regarded as 'excess' fixed carbon. Given the measured photosynthesis rates (Table 2b) and assuming that the biomass approaches Redfield C : N ratio

(Redfield 1958), nitrogen demands can be calculated (Table 2b). This demand must be met by new and recycled nitrogen fluxes for balanced growth to occur. New nitrogen is supplied to the dynamic layer by a diffusion flux originating from the degradation of allochthonous particulate organic matter (POM) in the sediment and a diffusion flux of nitrate from the overlying water. The particulate organic nitrogen (PON) degradation flux to the dynamic layer can be estimated from the measured C : N ratio of the sediment and the measured POC degradation rates (Table 2b). The resultant PON degradation flux is small (2–$3 \, \text{mmol} \, \text{N} \, \text{m}^{-2} \, \text{d}^{-1}$) relative to demand ($22$–$51 \, \text{mmol} \, \text{N} \, \text{m}^{-2} \, \text{d}^{-1}$) and compares reasonably well with the flux that would be expected from the long term sedimentation rate (Table 1a), POC concentrations (Table 2a) and the complete stripping of nitrogen from POM during burial (*c.* $5 \, \text{N} \, \text{mmol} \, \text{N} \, \text{m}^{-2} \, \text{d}^{-1}$, Table 2b). Net dissolved inorganic nitrogen (DIN) diffusion fluxes to the sediment (2–$3 \, \text{mmol} \, \text{N} \, \text{m}^{-2} \, \text{d}^{-1}$, Table 2b) were measured for these sediments in mesocosm experiments (Watson & Frickers 1995) and are recalculated to allow for tidal coverage (Table 1a). Denitrification, a loss of nitrogen from the sediment, was relatively small (Table 2b).

Together, these new nitrogen fluxes account for only 5.2 and 33.9% of the daily demand at Sites A and B, respectively (Table 2b). For balanced growth under steady state conditions, the recycled nitrogen fluxes (from algal respiration and mortality) must account for the remaining nitrogen demand. In order to supply the remaining nitrogen, average algal loss rates through respiration and mortality of 94.8 and 66.1% d^{-1} are required at sites A and B, respectively. The activity of the bacterial exo-enzyme leucine-aminopeptidase gives another estimate of respiration and mortality losses via the bacterial hydrolysis of proteins (Meyer-Reil 1991). The activity of this enzyme therefore integrates the degradation of allochthonous PON (Table 2b) with the respiration and mortality of biomass (i.e. the recycled nitrogen flux). Assuming that protein degradation is the rate-limiting step in nitrogen recycling and that the proteins have Redfield C : N ratios, then the recycled nitrogen flux (Table 2c) can be estimated. This is done by removing the PON degradation flux (Table 2c) from the total leucine-aminopeptidase (Ruddy *et al.* 1996) divided by the Redfield C : N ratio.

The magnitude of the recycled nitrogen fluxes compared to new nitrogen fluxes (Table 2c) suggests that the benthic community on the mudflat was heavily dependant on nitrogen recycling. Furthermore, the total nitrogen fluxes

Table 2. *Ecological dynamics at LISP sites A and B. Mean values over the LISP experimental period are used where available*

(a) Carbon concentrations in surficial sediment

	Site A		Site B		Reference
	mmol C l^{-1}	% dwt C	mmol C l^{-1}	% dwt C	
Total POC	3833	(4.2)	3353	(3.7)	Herman (1966)
					Wiltshire *et al.* (1996)
Algal biomass	108	(0.12)	64	(0.07)	Miles (1966)
					Wiltshire *et al.* (1966)
					Herman (1996)
					Underwood *et al.* (1996)
Colloidal carbohydrate	36	(0.04)	16	(0.016)	Herman (1996)
					Taylor & Paterson (1996)
Bulk carbohydrate	1643	(1.8)	971	(0.96)	Herman (1996)
					Taylor & Paterson (1996)

(b) Algal growth at the sediment surface

	Site A	Site B	Units	Reference
Observed photosynthesis	4.082	1.943	gC m^{-2} d^{-1}	Miles (1996)
∴ Nitrogen demand*	51.34	21.87	mmolN m^{-2} d^{-1}	assuming Redfield C : N
PON degradation†	2.11	3.02	mmolN m^{-2} d^{-1}	Clifton & Smallman (1996)
				Wiltshire *et al.* (1996)
Maximum PON degradation‡	4.71	5.22	mmolN m^{-2} d^{-1}	Tables 1(a) and 2(a)
				Wiltshire *et al.* (1996)
Net DIN flux from water §	1.67	3.5	mmolN m^{-2} d^{-1}	Watson & Frickers (1995)
dentrification		0.073	mmolN m^{-2} d^{-1}	Barnes (1995)
∴ New nitrogen flux¶	3.71	6.45	mmolN m^{-2} d^{-1}	

* = photosynthesis/Redfield C : N.
† = SO$_4$ reduction rate × 2/sediment C : N.
‡ = sedimentation rate × POC concentration/sediment C : N.
§ = measured DIN flux × tidal coverage.
¶ = PON degradation + net DIN flux from water−denitrification.

(c) Nitrogen recycling and 'excess' carbon fixation

	Site A	Site B	Units	Reference
New nitrogen flux	3.71	6.45	mmolN m^{-2} d^{-1}	from Table 2(b)
Recycled nitrogen flux	16.57	11.82	mmolN m^{-2} d^{-1}	Ruddy *et al.* (1996)
∴ Total nitrogen flux*	20.56	18.34	mmolN m^{-2} d^{-1}	
∴ 'Excess' carbon fixation†	60.0	16.1	% of photosynthesis in Table 2(b)	
Total algal losses‡	38.0	91.6	% d^{-1}	

* = new nitrogen flux + recycled nitrogen flux.
† = (photosynthesis − (new nitrogen flux) + recycled nitrogen flux) × Redfield C : N)/photosynthesis.
‡ = recycled N flux × algal biomass/Redfield C : N.

(d) Grazing of algae by M. balthica

	Site A	Site B	Units	Reference
M. balthica density	2600	2500	m^{-2}	Davey & Partridge (1996)
M. balthica size	5	10	mm	Davey & Partridge (1996)
M. balthica dietary requirement	0.213	0.658	gC m^{-2} d^{-1}	Bubnova (1974)
Algal new growth*	0.302	0.579	gC m^{-2} d^{-1}	
∴ Algal mortality due to grazing†	16.3	75.6	% d^{-1}	

* = new N flux × Redfield C : N.
† = *M. balthica* dietary requirement/algal biomass. Volume to area conversions use observed sediment porosity and appropriate sample depth.

are less than nitrogen demand, indicating that on average unbalanced growth (and hence 'excess' carbon fixation) occurred at site A, while site B was more in balance over the LISP period (Table 2c). Total algal losses by respiration and mortality can be estimated from algal biomass and the recycled nitrogen flux. The implied respiration and mortality rates are 38.0 and 91.6% d^{-1} at sites A and B, respectively.

Clearly, the degree to which photosynthesis is nitrogen limited depends strongly on the rate of photosynthesis. On a cloudy day, or a day with high tidal coverage, incident light levels may be very low, hence photosynthesis rates are also low and total nitrogen concentrations may remain high. The respiration, mortality, dissolved nitro-

gen diffusion gradients and PON degradation that produce the total nitrogen fluxes are less sensitive to light, and therefore may generate a more constant nitrogen supply than algal nitrogen demand. Hence, algal growth on the LISP transect may alternate between light limitation (e.g. during tidal inundation) and nitrogen limitation (e.g. after a day's growth).

Total nitrogen fluxes are effected by macro-heterotroph grazing rates and may account for the high total algal losses shown in Table 2c. The dominant macro-heterotroph on the mudflat during the LISP experiment is thought to have been *M. balthica* (Davey & Partridge 1996; Widdows *et al.* 1996). The dimensions and population densities of this burrowing

Table 3. *Summary of algal carbon cycling at LISP sites A and B*

	Site A	Site B	Units	Reference
Total algal carbon fixation	100	100	%	of Miles (1996) see Table 2(b)
Algal new growth	7.1	26.3	% of C fixed	from Table 2(b)
Algal grazing by *M. balthica*	5.1	34.0	% of C fixed	from Table 2(d)
∴ Net algal growth	2.0	−7.7	% of C fixed	
Replacing total algal losses	38.0	91.6	% of C fixed	from Table 2(c)
'Excess' carbon fixation	60.0	16.1	% of C fixed	from Table 2(c)

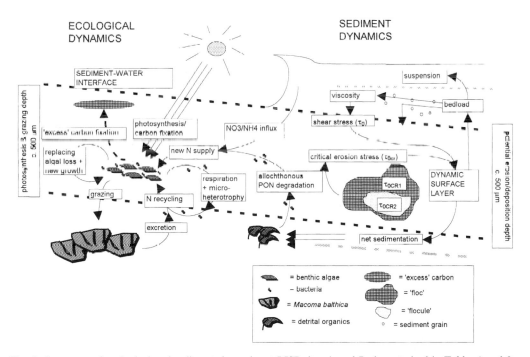

Fig. 4. Summary of ecological and sediment dynamics at LISP sites A and B characterized in Tables 1 and 2. Photosynthesis and grazing depth, and potential erosion/deposition depth are both of the order of a few hundred microns thick, suggesting that ecological and sediment dynamics are occurring at a similar physical scale.

bivalve (Table 2d) have been shown to profoundly affect sediment stability on the transect and in mesocosm experiments (Widdows *et al.* this volume). The steady state dietary requirements of *M. balthica*, as a function of size, can be assessed using an empirical formulation by Bubnova (1974). The estimated dietary flux of this organism (Table 2d) can be seen to account for virtually all of the algal new growth (Table 2d) and also much of the total algal losses (Table 2c). *M. balthica* has been shown to be

unable to survive on a diet of bacteria alone (Harvey & Luoma 1984), but is known to eat carbohydrates (Bubnova 1974), in which case the nitrogen for *M. balthica* growth must be obtained from another dietary source. We assume that, directly or indirectly, *M. balthica* dietary requirements are met by benthic and/or resuspended benthic algae (Kamermans 1994). If this is the case, then algal growth may not only have been limited by nitrogen and light, but also by grazing, and, furthermore, that grazing by

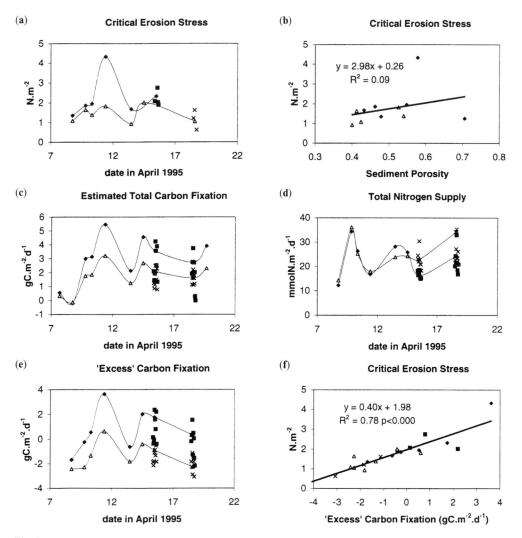

Fig. 5. Integrated sediment and ecological dynamics. (**a**) Temporal variation in critical erosion stress, (**b**) critical erosion stress vs sediment water content (porosity), (**c**) temporal variation in estimated total photosynthetic carbon fixation (see text), (**d**) temporal variation in total nitrogen supply to surficial sediment layer (see text), (**e**) temporal variation in 'excess' carbon fixation (i.e. nitrogen limited photosynthesis – see text), and (**f**) relationship between critical erosion stress and 'excess' carbon fixation. Legend: LISP site A (◆) and LISP site B (△) sampled daily 1 hour after low tide, LISP site A (■) and LISP site B (×) sampled hourly during spring tide exposure on 15 and 18 April 1995.

M. balthica $(0.21–0.66 \, \mathrm{gC \, m^{-2} \, d^{-1}})$ and algal new growth $(0.3–0.6 \, \mathrm{gC \, m^{-2} \, d^{-1}})$ were roughly balanced (Table 2d). This implies that the new nitrogen flux which determines new algal growth was directly proportional to grazing. The new nitrogen flux is composed of a DIN flux, enhanced by bioirrigation, and a PON flux, associated with bioturbation. This supports the 'gardening' hypothesis (Hylleberg 1975). Given a feeding efficiency of 0.615 (Bubnova 1974), the sediment porosity (Table 1a) and an algal biomass based upon the chlorophyll *a* concentrations (Table 2a), the depth of sediment reworked to give the dietary requirement would be 79 and $369 \, \mu\mathrm{m \, d^{-1}}$ at sites A and B, respectively. This compares reasonably well with the depth of the dynamic layer at the two sites $(322–2864 \, \mu\mathrm{m};$ Table 1b).

The carbon cycle summary shown in Table 3 confirms the unbalanced growth conditions and 'excess' carbon fixation at site A. It is apparent that the more balanced growth conditions at site B were associated with grazing of the dynamic layer, maintaining a low algal biomass (and therefore photosynthesis rate; Tables 2a and b) in relatively nitrogen replete conditions.

The fluxes calculated in Tables 1–3 are summarized in the scheme shown in Fig. 4. The results demonstrate that benthic carbon and nitrogen cycling between algae, *M. balthica* and bacteria occurred on a physical scale similar to the sediment dynamics $(<1 \, \mathrm{mm})$ and at rates that resulted in the rapid turnover of reservoirs (hourly and daily). The fact that the biological and physical processes occur at similar scales is important because it suggests that the sediment and ecological dynamics discussed in this paper may be directly linked to each other.

Integrated sediment and biological dynamics based on time-series observations

The daily and hourly measured sediment critical erosion stresses at sites A and B (Fig. 5a), sampled only from ridges in the ridge-runnel system, (cf. Widdows *et al.* this volume) show a weak positive linear relationship with irradiance $(R^2 = 0.35,$ data not shown). Samples from site A tended to be more cohesive than site B. This might be expected as site A is higher on the shore and exposure/irradiance will tend to consolidate sediment by interstitial water evaporation. However, if there is a trend between sediment porosity (water content) and cohesion at all, it is increasing (Fig. 5b). Irradiance also controls algal photosynthesis rates. The rheological measurements (Table 1c, Fig. 3b) suggest that the sediment

structure breakdown ($\tau_{0\mathrm{cr}}$ and $\tau_{0\mathrm{CR1}}$) is dependent on an irreversibly destroyed sediment cohesion. This suggests that sediment cohesion may be associated with sediment carbohydrate concentrations, and therefore unbalanced growth and 'excess' carbon fixation.

At site A, the rate of carbon fixation was shown to be proportional to the light intensity (Underwood *et al.* 1996). Using the measured light intensity (Hull University weather station) and an empirical relationship between light and photosynthesis (Underwood *et al.* 1996), the daily and hourly *in situ* carbon fixation rate can be estimated over the LISP period. The relationship is adjusted on a per chlorophyll a basis to the average chlorophyll a concentrations observed at sites A and B [23.7 and $14.0 \, \mu\mathrm{g}$ chl g dry^{-1}, respectively (Wiltshire *et al.* 1996; Herman 1996; Miles 1996; Underwood *et al.* 1996)]. Although these estimates will be subject to much variability due to spatial heterogeneity of chlorophyll *a* (Miles 1996), the estimated rates for the LISP period (shown in Fig. 5c) compare well with those observed (Miles 1996) and used in the calculations above (Tables 2 and 3).

We have suggested that the rate of 'excess' carbon fixation resulting from the total carbon fixation (Fig. 5c) depends upon the total nitrogen supply (Table 2c). An estimated daily and hourly total nitrogen supply can be calculated from the measured daily and hourly leucine-aminopeptidase activities (as in Table 2c) by assuming that the new nitrogen fluxes (Table 2c), *M. balthica* dietary requirements, *M. balthica* population density and *M. balthica* excretion rates (Table 2d) remain constant. The resultant total nitrogen supply is shown in Fig. 5d. The 'excess' carbon fixation rate over the LISP period can then be calculated (Fig. 5e) as the difference between the total carbon fixation (in $\mathrm{mol \, m^{-2} \, d^{-1}}$) and total nitrogen supply (in $\mathrm{mol \, m^{-2} \, d^{-1}}$) times the C:N ratio of the growing algal biomass (Redfield).

The highly significant relationship in Fig. 5f connects 'excess' carbon fixation and critical erosion stress at the $100 \, \mu\mathrm{m}$ scale depicted in Fig. 4. The relationship indicates that biological nitrogen limitation and sediment stability at the sediment–water interface strongly co-vary. 'Excess' carbon fixation, occurring as a result of nitrogen limitation, has the effect of increasing sediment cohesion because the algae may exude the resultant carbohydrates during vertical (or lateral) migration. The correlation in Fig. 5f suggests that a constant proportion of the 'excess' carbon was exuded, hence EPS concentrations in surficial sediments reflected nitrogen limited growth conditions.

A dynamic physical and biological sediment–water interface

The fluxes shown in Fig. 4 simplify the dynamics of a mudflat system. In terms of sediment dynamics, the data suggest a highly dynamic surface layer, particularly lower on the transect, dispersing predominantly on a small scale via bedload transport. The bedload appears to be a necessary part of the erosion mechanism, since water viscosity by itself may not generate sufficient shear to overcome the cohesion of the sediment. Sediment cohesion may be associated with a biogenic 'floc' and an abiotic 'flocule' component. The excess density of the suspended flocs, calculated from their settling velocity (Table 1a), indicates an average floc porosity of 0.79, not dissimilar to the sediment porosity at the sediment–water interface. Hence, the SPM may originate from the sediment bed rather than the estuary. Concentrations of SPM above the mudflat are high (Table 1a) and this suggests that the mudflat may generate much of the SPM observed in the water during inundation.

Much of the POC in the dynamic layer may be autochthonous and therefore ultimately dependent on *in situ* photosynthesis. The fluxes in Tables 2 and 3 suggest a highly interdependent community of low biomass, rapidly growing benthic algae and recycling bacteria, grazed by high biomass, slow growing, bioirrigating macro-heterotrophs (Fig. 4). The interactions between these organisms occur in such a way that growth conditions and sediment stability may be co-regulated. This is because at least a proportion of the 'excess' carbon produced during nitrogen limited benthic photosynthesis has the effect of adjusting sediment cohesion. The correlation in Fig. 5f implies that the proportion of 'excess' carbon fixation that is exuded does not vary. Hence

(a) exuded 'excess' carbon production (i.e. EPS) can be accounted for in terms of nitrogen limitation;
(b) critical erosion stress can be accounted for in terms of exuded 'excess' carbon.

The role of *M. balthica* in sediment destabilization is also central to the sediment dynamics of the mudflat. However, this may not be simply due to sediment reworking, but also because the sediment reworking reduces algal populations and increases new nitrogen fluxes, leading to lower 'excess' carbon fixation rates and algal sediment stabilization.

The complex situation discussed in this paper is modelled in Ruddy *et al.* (this volume) with a view to testing the likelihood of such a biologically and physically dynamic system to self-stabilize, and its ability to account for the observations made during the LISP-UK project. Particular attention is given to establishing the selective advantage that the exudation of 'excess' carbon might confer on benthic algae.

Funding for this work was provided by NERC LOIS grant GST/02/787 and LOIS LISP grant GST/02/759. Co-workers in LISP-UK, particularly K. Black and D. Paterson, are gratefully acknowledged for data, discussions and organization.

This is LOIS publication number 226 of the LOIS Community Research Programme, carried out under a Special Topic Award from the Natural Environment Research Council.

References

ALLER, R. C. 1982. The effects of macrobenthos on chemical properties of marine sediment and overlying water. *In:* MCCALL, P. L. & TEVESZ, M. J. S. (eds) *Animal–Sediment Relations*, Plenum Press, New York. p. 53–102.

—— & YINGST, J. L. 1985. Effects of marine deposit-feeders *Heteromastus filiformis* (Polychaeta), *Macoma balthica* (Bivalvia) and *Tellina texana* (Bivalvia) on averaged sedimentary solute transport, reaction rates, and microbial distributions. *Journal of Marine Research*, **43**, 615–645.

BARNES, J. 1995. Denitrification and nitrous oxide flux. LOIS RACS(C) Second annual workshop, Burwalls, Bristol, September 1995.

BERNER, R. A. 1980. *Early Diagenesis; a Theoretical Approach*. Princeton University Press, USA.

BLACK, K. S. & JAGO, C. 1996. Hydrographic and sedimentological investigation in the Humber Estuary, LISP-UK. *In:* BLACK, K. S. & PATERSON, D. M. (eds) *LISP Preliminary Results*. Interim Report, SERG, University of St Andrews, UK.

BOUDREAU, B. P. 1994. Is burial velocity a master parameter for bioturbation? *Geochimica et Cosmochimica Acta*, **58**, 1243–1249.

BUBNOVA, N. P. 1974. Consumption and assimilation of carbohydrates from marine sediments by the detritus-feeding mollusks *Macoma balthica* (L) and *Portlandia arctica* (Gray). *Oceanology*, **12**, 743–747.

CHRISTIE, M. C. & DYER, K. R. 1996. Summary of LISP-UK velocity and concentration data obtained by POST. *In:* BLACK, K. S. & PATERSON, D. M. (eds) *LISP Preliminary Results*. Interim Report, SERG, University of St Andrews, UK.

CLIFTON, R. & SMALLMAN, D. 1996. Oxygen consumption rates, sulphate reduction rates, stable sulphate and radionuclide concentrations in the sediments of the four LISP sites – Results to date. *In:* BLACK, K. S. & PATERSON, D. M. (eds) *LISP Preliminary Results*. Interim Report, SERG, University of St Andrews, UK.

COX, J., GRANT, A., MAHER, B., PETHICK, J. & MIDDLETON, R. 1996. Coastal-estuary sediment transfers – a geochemical and mineralogical study of sources. *In:* BLACK, K. S. & PATERSON, D. M. (eds) *LISP Preliminary Results.* Interim Report, SERG, University of St Andrews, UK.

DAVEY, J. & PARTRIDGE, V. 1996. The macro-fauna of the Skeffling mudflats. *In:* BLACK, K. S. & PATERSON, D. M. (eds) *LISP Preliminary Results.* Interim Report, SERG, University of St Andrews, UK.

DECHO, A. W. 1990. Microbial exopolymer secretions in ocean environments: their role(s) in food webs and marine processes. *Oceanography and Marine Biology Annual Reviews,* **28,** 73 153.

——1994. Molecular-scale events influencing the macro-scale cohesiveness of exopolymers. *In:* KRUMBEIN, W. E., PATERSON, D. M. & STAL, L. J. (eds) *Biostabilization of Sediments.* Bibliotheks und Informationssystems der Carl von Ossietzky, Univsitat Oldenburg, 135–148.

EDGAR, L. A. & PICKETT-HEAPS, J. D. 1984. Diatom locomotion. *Progress in Phycolological Research,* **3,** 47–88.

FENNESSEY, M. J. & DYER, K. R. 1996. Floc spectra of suspended sediment obtained with INSSEV during tidal advance over the Skeffling mud-flats, Humber Estuary, April 1995. *In:* BLACK, K. S. & PATERSON, D. M. (eds) *LISP Preliminary Results.* Interim Report, SERG, University of St Andrews, UK.

FLOTHMANN, S. & WERNER, I. 1992. Experimental eutrophication on an intertidal sandflat: effects of microphytobenthos, meio- and macrofauna. *In:* COLUMBO, G. E. A. (ed.) *Marine Eutrophication and Population Dynamics.* Olsen & Olsen, Fredensborg, 93–100.

FROELICH, P., KLINKHAMMER, G., BENDER, M. *et al.* 1979. Early oxidation of organic matter in pelagic sediments of the eastern equatorial Atlantic: suboxic diagenesis. *Geochimica et Cosmochimica Acta,* **41,** 1075–1090.

GERDES, G., KRUMBEIN, W. E. & REINECK, H-E. 1994. Microbial mats as architects of sedimentary structures. *In:* KRUMBEIN, W. E., PATERSON, D. M. & STAL, L. J. (eds) *Biostabilization of Sediments.* Bibliotheks und Informationssystems der Carl von Ossietzky, Univsitat Oldenburg, 165–182.

GRAHAM, D. I., JAMES, P. W. & JONES, T. E. R. 1992. Measurement and prediction of surface shear stress in an annular flume. *Journal of Hydraulic Engineering,* **118,** 1270–1286.

GRIFFIN, T. M., RRABENHORST, M. C. & FANNING, D. S. 1989. Iron and trace metals in some tidal marsh soils of Chesapeake Bay. *Soil Science of America Journal,* **53,** 1010–1019.

HARVEY, R. W. & LUOMA, S. N. 1984. The role of bacterial exopolymer and suspended bacteria in the nutrition of the deposit-feeding clam *Macoma balthica. Journal of Marine Research,* **42,** 957–968.

HERMAN, W. M. 1996. The *in situ* determination of intertidal sediment erodibility in the Humber Estuary. *In:* BLACK, K. S. & PATERSON, D. M.

(eds) *LISP Preliminary Results.* Interim Report, SERG, University of St Andrews, UK.

HINES, M. E. & JONES, G. E. 1985. Microbial biogeochemistry and bioturbation in the sediments of Great Bay, New Hampshire. *Estuarine, Coastal and Shelf Science,* **20,** 729–742.

HOAGLAND, K.D, ROSOWSKI, J. R., GRETZ, M. R. & ROEMER, S. C. 1993. Diatom extracellular polymeric substances: function, fine structure, chemistry and physiology. *Journal of Phycology,* **29,** 537–566.

HOPPNER, T. & WONNENBERGER, K. 1985. Examination of the connection between the patchiness of benthic nutrient flux and epiphytobenthic patchiness on intertidal flats. *Netherlands Journal of Sea Research,* **19,** 227–285.

HUGHES, J. P., JONES, T. E. R. & DAVIS, J. M. 1996. End effects in the concentric cylinder geometry. *Proceedings of the 12th International Congress of Rheology,* 391.

HYLLEBERG, J. 1975. Selective feeding by *Abarenicola pacifica* with notes on *Abearenicola vagabunda* and a concept of gardening in lugworms. *Ophelia,* **14,** 113–137.

JAMES, P. W., JONES, T. E. R. & STEWART, D. M. 1996. Numerical and experimental studies of flume flow. *Applied Mathematical Modelling,* **20,** 225–231.

JONGE, V. N. DE 1980. Fluctuations in the organic carbon to chlorophyll a ratios for estuarine benthic diatom populations. *Marine Ecology Progress Series,* **2,** 345–353.

KAMERMANS, P. 1994. Similarity in food source and timing of feeding in deposit- and suspension-feeding bivalves. *Marine Ecology Progress Series,* **104,** 63–75.

KOSTER, M., JENSEN, P. & MEYER-REIL, L.-A. 1991. Hydrolytic activities of organisms and biogenic structures in deep-sea sediments. *In:* CHRÓST, R. J. (ed) *Microbial Enzymes in Aquatic Environments.* New York, Springer Verlag, 298.

KRUMBEIN, W. E., PATERSON, D. M. & STAL, L. J. 1994. *Biostabilization of Sediments.* Bibliotheks und Informationssystems der Carl von Ossietzky, Univsitat Oldenburg.

LAW, D. J. 1996. In situ laser back-scattering particle size analysis. *In:* BLACK, K. S. & PATERSON, D. M. (eds) *LISP Preliminary Results.* Interim Report, SERG, University of St Andrews, UK.

LEHMANN, W. & WOBER, G. 1976. Accumulation, mobilization and turnover of glycogen in the blue-green bacterium *Anacystis nidulans. Archives of Microbiology,* **111,** 93–97.

MEYER-REIL, L.-A. 1991. Ecological aspects of enzymatic activity in marine sediments. *In:* CHRÓST, R. J. (ed) *Microbial Enzymes in Aquatic Environments,* New York, Springer Verlag, 84.

MILES, A. 1996. LISP-UK April 1995. *In:* BLACK, K. S. & PATERSON, D. M. (eds) *LISP Preliminary Results.* Interim Report, SERG, University of St Andrews, UK.

NILSSON, P., JONSON, B., SWANBERG, L. I. & SUNDBACK, K. 1991. Response of shallow-water sediment system to an increased load of inorganic nutrients. *Marine Ecology Progress Series,* **71,** 275–290.

NIXON, S. W. 1981. Remineralization and nutrient dynamics in coastal marine ecosystems. *In:* NEILSON, B. J. & CRONIN, L. E. (eds) *Estuaries and Nutrients,* Humana Press, Clifton, New Jersey, 111–137.

PATERSON, D. M. 1989. Short-term changes in the erodibility of intertidal sediments related to the migratory behaviour of epipelic diatoms. *Limnology and Oceanography,* **34,** 223–234.

REDFIELD, A. C. 1958. The biological control of chemical factors in the environment. *American Scientist,* **46,** 205–221.

RIZZO, W. 1990. Nutrient exchanges between the water column and a subtidal benthic microalgal community. *Estuaries,* **13,** 219–226.

RUDDY, G., TURLEY, C. M. & JONES, T. E. R. (in preparation) Bacterial exo-enzyme activities and the geotechnical properties of intertidal sediments of the Humber, UK.

——, —— & ——1996. The influence of microbiology on cohesive sediment dynamics. *In:* BLACK, K. S. & PATERSON, D. M. (eds) *LISP Preliminary Results.* Interim Report, SERG, University of St Andrews, UK.

——1997*a*. An overview of carbon, sulphur and oxygen cycling in marine sediments. *In:* JICKELLS, T. & RAE, J. (eds) *Biogeochemistry of Intertidal Sediments.* Cambridge University Press, Cambridge, 99–118.

RUDDY, G., TURLEY, C. M., JONES, T. E. R., PATERSON, D. M. & TAYLOR, I. 1997*b*. The influence of microbiology on cohesive sediments. *LOIS Annual Report.* NERC, UK.

——, —— & ——1998. Ecological interaction and sediment transport on an intertidal mudflat II. *This volume.*

SHARMA, P., GARDNER, L., MOORE, W. & BOLLINGER, M. 1987. Sedimentation and bioturbation in a salt marsh as revealed by ^{210}Pb, ^{137}Cs and ^{7}Be studies. *Limnology and Oceanography,* **32,** 313–326.

STAL, L. J. 1994. Microbial mats: ecophysiological interactions related to biogenic sediment structures. *In:* KRUMBEIN, W. E., PATERSON, D. M. & STAL, L. J. (eds) *Biostabilization of Sediments.* Bibliotheks und Informationssystems der Carl von Ossietzky, Univsitat Oldenburg, 41–54.

SUNDBACK, K. 1994. The response of shallow-water sediment communities to environmental changes. *In:* KRUMBEIN, W. E., PATERSON, D. M. & STAL, L. J. (eds) *Biostabilization of Sediments.* Bibliotheks und Informationssystems der Carl von Ossietzky, Univsitat Oldenburg, 17–40.

SWIDER, K. T. & MAKIN, J. E. 1989. Transformations of sulfur compounds in marsh-flat sediments. *Geochimica et Cosmochimica Acta,* **53,** 2311–2323.

TAYLOR, I. & PATERSON, D. M. 1996. Carbohydrates on the LISP-UK transect. *In:* BLACK, K. S. & PATERSON, D. M. (eds) *LISP Preliminary Results.* Interim Report, SERG, University of St Andrews, UK.

UNDERWOOD, G. J. C., SMITH, D. & SZYSZKO, P. 1996. *In situ* production of microalgal exopolymers over spring and neap tide exposure periods. *In:* BLACK, K. S. & PATERSON, D. M. (eds) *LISP Preliminary Results.* Interim Report, SERG, University of St Andrews, UK.

—— & PATERSON, D. M. 1993. Recovery of intertidal benthic diatoms after biocide treatment and associated sediment dynamics. *Journal of the Marine Biological Association UK,* **73,** 25–45.

WACHENDORFER, V., KRUMBEIN, W. E. & SCHELLNHUBER, H.-J. 1994. Bacteriogenic porosity of marine sediments – a case of biomorphogenesis of sedimentary rocks. *In:* KRUMBEIN, W. E., PATERSON, D. M. & STAL, L. J. (eds) *Biostabilization of Sediments.* Bibliotheks und Informationssystems der Carl von Ossietzky, Univsitat Oldenburg, 203–220.

WALTERS, K. 1977. *Rheometry.* Chapman and Hall.

WATSON, P. & FRICKERS, P. E. 1995. Nutrient fluxes in the pore waters of the Skeffling mudflat sediments. *LISP Conference,* 14 December 1995, Cardiff.

WIDDOWS, J., BRINSLEY, M. & ELLIOT, M. 1996. Use of *in situ* benthic annular flume to investigate particle flux at the sediment–water interface in relation to changes in current velocity and macrofauna community structure. *In:* BLACK, K. S. & PATERSON, D. M. (eds) *LISP Preliminary Results.* Interim Report, SERG, University of St Andrews, UK.

——, —— & ——1998. Use of an *in situ* flume to quantify particle flux (biodeposition rates and sediment erosion) for an intertidal mudflat in relation to changes in current velocity and benthic macrofauna. *This volume.*

WILTSHIRE, K., BLACKBURN, J. & PATERSON, D. M. 1996. Pigments in sediment particulate matter. Report on preliminary LISP data. *In:* BLACK, K. S. & PATERSON, D. M. (eds) *LISP Preliminary Results.* Interim Report, SERG, University of St Andrews, UK.

Ecological interaction and sediment transport on an intertidal mudflat II. An experimental dynamic model of the sediment–water interface

G. RUDDY[1]*, C. M. TURLEY[2] & T. E. R. JONES[1]

[1] *University of Plymouth, Drakes Circus, Plymouth PL4 8AA, UK*
[2] *Plymouth Marine Laboratory, Citadel Hill, Plymouth PL1 2PB, UK*

Abstract: A one-dimensional model is presented which combines simplified biological, chemical and physical dynamics across the sediment water interface of intertidal mudflat sediments. Interactions between ecology, biogeochemistry and sediment dynamics are simulated during iteration through a short-term sequence of light and tides. The model shows that, under 'normal' intertidal conditions, a biolayer composed of unicellular algae can develop at the sediment–water interface. Rapid algal growth generates regularly recurring nitrogen limited conditions in the biolayer. In the model, the algal carbohydrate polymers produced and exuded during nitrogen limitation profoundly influence model sediment dynamics by adjusting sediment cohesion. Stable, but dynamic, sediment surfaces result in the model from a combination of carbohydrate exuding algae, bacterial remineralization of exuded carbohydrate and grazing of the algae by bioturbating macro-heterotrophs. Model predictions for sites on an intertidal mudflat in the Humber Estuary, UK show good agreement with the field observations for a range of different physical, chemical and biological variables. The results imply that sediment accretion may be more directly coupled to nitrogen supply than to sediment supply. The results are discussed in terms of an algal growth advantage to carbohydrate exudation.

In Ruddy *et al.* (this volume), data and mass balance calculations indicate that cohesive sediment stability and microbial nitrogen limitation were directly proportional to each other in the surficial layer of the sediment of the intertidal mudflats at Skeffling, Humber Estuary, UK during April 1995 (LISP-UK: Littoral Investigation of Sediment Properties-UK). Ruddy *et al.* suggest that, in the absence of the nitrogen required for growth, benthic photosynthesis by the abundant micro-algae (Miles 1996; Wiltshire *et al.* 1996; Underwood *et al.* 1996; Herman 1996) resulted in the production of carbohydrates. The carbohydrate therefore indicates unbalanced growth conditions (Lehmann & Wober 1976) in benthic algal populations. The observations suggest that a constant proportion of the resulting carbohydrate (or 'excess' carbon) was exuded, forming the extracellular polymeric substances (or EPS) observed in intertidal sediments (Underwood & Paterson 1993; various papers in Krumbein *et al.* 1994) and on the LISP-UK transect (Underwood *et al.* 1996; Taylor & Paterson 1996). EPS is thought to bind sediment grains together and adjust sediment cohesion (Gerdes *et al.* 1994; Chenu 1993; Paterson 1989; Grant & Gust 1987; Paterson 1994). Hence, under these conditions, sediment stability reflected benthic nitrogen limitation.

The validity of this hypothesis depends upon two considerations: firstly, that nitrogen limited growth conditions can occur at the sediment–water interface of intertidal sediments, and secondly, that there is an advantage to algal carbohydrate exudation as opposed to intracellular storage.

Recycled nitrogen fluxes (produced by the excretion and mortality of benthic organisms) appeared to form most of the total nitrogen supply in the photosynthetic micro-layer of the sediment during the LISP-UK experiment (between 65 and 80%; Ruddy *et al.* this volume). Net growth of the benthic algae accounts for seasonal algal growth and replaces net algal losses. This net growth depends upon sources of nitrogen external to the photosynthetic layer (referred to as new nitrogen) which make up the remaining proportion (between 35 and 20%) of the total nitrogen flux within the photosynthetic layer. Under steady state conditions, if algal growth exceeds algal respiration and mortality plus 35 to 20% from new nitrogen, then nitrogen limited growth conditions result in this layer. Hence, at an algal respiration rate of $0.36\,d^{-1}$ (see Table 2c), carbon fixation rates in excess of $0.45-0.55\,d^{-1}$ would result in nitrogen limitation. Measured carbon fixation rates in the surficial layer of intertidal sediments are of the order of $2.53-3.15\,d^{-1}$ (Miles 1996), $0.40-6.63\,d^{-1}$ (Pinckney & Zingmark 1993), $0.16-6.21\,d^{-1}$ (Yallop & Paterson 1994). Given in addition that algal

---

*Current address: Plymouth Marine Laboratory, Citadel Hill, Plymouth PL1 2PB, UK.

RUDDY, G., TURLEY, C. M. & JONES, T. E. R. 1998. Ecological interaction and sediment transport on an intertidal mudflat II. *In*: BLACK, K. S., PATERSON, D. M. & CRAMP, A. (eds) *Sedimentary Processes in the Intertidal Zone*. Geological Society, London, Special Publications, **139**, 149–166.

growth can be stimulated by the addition of
nitrogen to the surface of intertidal sediments
(Hopner & Wonnenberger 1985; Nilsson *et al.*
1991; Flothmann & Werner 1992; Sundback
1994), this strongly suggests that nitrogen limited
growth conditions can occur at the sediment–
water interface of intertidal sediments.

Algal nitrogen limitation is complicated by
the fact that benthic algae are grazed by macro-
heterotrophs (Hummell 1985) and migrate vertically (Pinckney & Zingmark 1991). Macro-
heterotrophic activity affects the balance of
new and recycled nitrogen fluxes by (a) promoting recycled nitrogen fluxes relative to carbon
fixation by increasing algal turnover during
grazing and filter-feeding (Kamermans 1994;
Ruddy *et al.* this volume), (b) bioirrigating the
sediment and increasing nutrient fluxes across
the sediment–water interface (e.g. Aller 1982;
Marinelli 1994; Clavero *et al.* 1994; Pelegri *et al.*
1994) and (c) destabilizing and mixing sediment
by bioturbation (Hines & Jones 1985; Widdows
et al. 1996, this volume). The vertical migration
of algae within the sediment column (Edgar &
Pickett-Heaps 1984; Hoagland 1993; Pinckney
1994) has the effect of balancing erosion losses
and light intensity (hence, carbon fixation rates)
against nitrogen supply. The cycles of other
growth nutrients (e.g. PO_4^{3-}, SiO_2, etc.) may also
be affected by similar processes (Pratska &
Jickells 1995; Malcolm & Sivyer 1997) but are
beyond the scope of this paper.

The model presented here explores benthic
nitrogen limitation and algal exudation in a
physically dynamic context. The results of the
simulations (see Results and Discussion) suggest that an advantage in the algal exudation
of carbohydrate depends on sediment cohesion
affecting sediment accretion, a process which
traps allochthonous particulate organic matter
(POM) within and below the benthic layer
where photosynthesis occurs. Because allochthonous POM contains nitrogen and the bacterial
remineralization of the POM generates pore
water diffusion gradients of nitrogen (Klump
& Martens 1989; references in Blackburn &
Sorensen 1988; Jorgensen 1989) sediment accretion will have the effect of generating new nitrogen fluxes to the benthos, and hence promote
net growth.

The model simulates the biology, chemistry
and physical dynamics of a one-dimensional
sediment–water column. The model 'tests' the
feasibility that the processes outlined above
and in Ruddy *et al.* (this volume) reproduce
'realistic' sediment behaviour at the four sites of
the LISP-UK transect. We use a whole system
model approach [in a form qualitatively out-

lined in Malcolm & Sivyer (1997) and Fig. 4,
Ruddy *et al.* this volume] to (a) account for
the observation that critical erosion stress and
benthic nitrogen limitation covary (Ruddy *et al.*
this volume) and (b) demonstrate a growth
advantage associated with the algal exudation
of carbohydrates.

Model structure

Background

Model constituents are shown in Table 1. The
parameters that are involved in the dynamics of
these constituents and the relationships between
them are listed in Tables 1 and 2(a–c). Conditions for the simulations define the characteristics of the biology (Table 2b) and the boundary
conditions (Table 2b) from which the concentrations of the constituents, the light intensity and
the hydrodynamics of the depth intervals of the
sediment–water column are calculated. The
resultant hydrodynamics and biological activity
give rise to particle and dissolved dispersion
and advection coefficients [Table 2a, equations
(13)–(15)]. Exchange processes [such as algal
growth, Table 2a, equation (4)] transfer materials between the constituents which are subject to
vertical dispersive and advective transport
(Table 1). The rate constants of the decomposition and redox reactions which control the
biogeochemical exchange processes are shown
in Table 2c. The lower boundary of the 10 cm
model sediment–water column remains closed,
while the upper boundary allows exchange with
flooding and ebbing water. Conditions are set,
either as constants (e.g. NO_3^- concentration in
flooding water, Table 2b), or functions of time
(e.g. tides and light, Table 2b, Fig. 1), and the
simulation iterates, calculating each constituent
at the prescribed timesteps (7.2 mins) and depth
intervals (1.125 mm). The model runs within
the ECoS shell (Harris & Gorley 1992) and
solves the general dispersion–advection equation shown in Table 2a [equation (1)].

Algal growth

In the model, algae are composed of carbon and
nitrogen in the Redfield ratio (Redfield 1958).
Growth [Table 2a, equation (4)] adds to algal
concentrations, reducing the NO_4^- and/or NH_4^+
concentrations, and increasing the dissolved
O_2 concentration. A respiration rate (Table 2c)
and a grazing rate [Table 2a, equation (22)]
reduce algal concentrations and regenerate NH_4^+
concentrations via decomposition and excretion

(Table 1 and see below). Algal carbon fixation is proportional to light intensity [Table 2a, equations (2) and (3)] and is calculated according to the equations of Cullen (1990) with a modification by Skidmore (in preparation). All carbon fixation constants (Table 2b) are taken from Cullen (1990), but we have simplified carbon fixation by assuming equal carbon fixation efficiency using NH_4^+ and NO_4^-. The light dispersion equation [Table 2a, equation (3)] works by dispersing light downwards against a notional light velocity acting upwards. For steady state light profiles, the dispersion coefficient shown in the equation results in light attenuation, from the upper boundary day–night cycle (Fig. 1 and Table 2b), by the material in the sediment–water column. Tidal inundation (Fig. 1) is assumed to block out light entirely. Algal growth occurs as long as the dissolved nitrogen concentration is greater than zero [Table 2a, equation (6)]. When nitrogen limitation occurs, oxygenic carbon fixation continues but forms carbohydrate concentrations, which are subject to decomposition and transport (Table 2c and Table 1). The internal conditions of the algae are assumed to be in steady state, hence all carbohydrate production results in exudation.

Algal migration

Benthic algae migrate vertically in response to tides and light (Pinckney & Zingmark 1991). Within the model, algal migration is treated as a velocity term (Tables 1 and 2b) and occurs at $0.2\,\mu m\,s^{-1}$ (Hopkins 1963) in response to (a) greater algal respiration than carbon fixation in the presence of light (i.e. light limitation during daytime sediment exposure) and (b) greater carbohydrate production rates than growth rates (i.e. nitrogen limitation). Light limited migration is assumed to occur in an upward direction, while nitrogen limited migration occurs downwards. Under nitrogen limited conditions, this couples carbohydrate production to migration.

Table 1. *Dynamic constituents and processes within the simulation model*

Constituent	Advection	Dispersion	Exchange processes	Direction
Algae	w_s and *migrtn*	D_s	Growth	+
			Respiration	−
			Grazing	−
Carbohydrate	w_s	D_s	Formation/exudation	+
			Decomposition	
Sediment	w_s	D_s	None	
Oxygen	n/a	D_w	Growth/exudation	+
			Respiration	−
			Decomposition	−
			Sulphide oxidation	−
			NH_4^+ oxidation	−
Nitrate	n/a	D_w	Growth	−
			Sulphide oxidation	−
			NH_4^+ oxidation	+
			NO_3^- reduction	−
Ammonium	n/a	D_w	Growth	−
			Respiration	+
			Excretion	|
			Decomposition	+*
			NH_4^+ oxidation	−
			NO_3^- reduction	+
POC	w_s	D_s	Excretion	+
			Decomposition	−
Sulphide	n/a	D_w	Sulphide oxidation	−
			Decomposition	+
Light	See text		None	

The physical dynamics of each constituent results from dispersion and advection. Additional changes in constituents are brought about by stoichiometric exchange processes (based on the Redfield ratio and constituent oxidation states). Table 2 contains a complete description of the dynamics controlling the behaviour of model constituents. (Direction: + = adds, − = removes. w_s = floc settling velocity, *migrtn* = vertical migration velocity of algae, D_s = solid dispersion coefficient, D_w = dissolved dispersion coefficient. * decomposition addition to NH_4^+ = (POC decomposition-POC excretion)/C:N. n/a = not applicable).

Table 2. *Model structure and conditions*
(a) Model equations

1. General dispersion–advection equation	$\dfrac{dC}{dt} = \dfrac{\partial(w_s \pm migrtn) \cdot C}{\partial z} + \dfrac{\partial\left((D_w \text{ or } D_s) \cdot \dfrac{\partial C}{\partial z}\right)}{\partial z} + R$	Solved within ECoS
2. Carbon fixation per chlorophyll	$P^B = I \cdot \phi_{max}^C \cdot a_p \cdot (1 + I \cdot \sigma \cdot \tau)^{-1}$	Cullen (1990); Skidmore (in prep.)
3. Light dispersion through depth	$\dfrac{dI}{dz} = \dfrac{\lambda}{(b \cdot CONC)} \dfrac{\partial I^2}{\partial^2 z}$	After R. Gorley (pers. comm.)
4. Algal growth	$G^B = B_p \cdot C^B \cdot E_N$	—
5. Carbon fixation rate	$C^B = P^B \cdot \dfrac{Chl}{C}$	—
6. Nutrient limitation	$E_N = step[nutrient]_N \geq [nutrient]_{int.N}$	—
7. Respiration rate	$R^B = k_R \cdot$ Respiration substrate	See Table 2(c)
8. Sediment–water velocity	$U = U_i \cdot \left(\dfrac{z}{depth}\right)^A$	In Ruddy *et al.* (in prep.)
9. Velocity attenuation factor	$A = \left(\dfrac{V}{vw}\right) - 1$	In Ruddy *et al.* (in prep.)
10. Sediment–water viscosity	$V = vzw \cdot [(1 + 2.5 \cdot (1 - \phi)) + (100 \cdot \eta \cdot (1 - \phi))]$	Adapted from Einstein (1906)
11. Porosity	$\phi = 1 - \dfrac{CONC}{\rho_s}$	—
12. Laminar shear	$S = V \cdot A \cdot U_i \cdot \left(\dfrac{z}{depth}\right)^{A-1}$	In Ruddy *et al.* (in prep.)
13. Dissolved dispersion coefficient	$D_w = 5.48 \cdot 10^{-9} \cdot \phi^2 + D_s$	Ullman & Aller (1982); Aller (1980)
14. Particle dispersion coefficient	$D_s = \dfrac{TS^2 + S^2}{V \cdot CONC} \cdot \dfrac{S}{CES} + DD$	In Ruddy *et al.* (in prep.)
15. Settling velocity	$w_s = \dfrac{(\rho_a - (1 - \phi) \cdot \rho_s) \cdot g \cdot size_a^2}{18 \cdot \mu}$	Adapted from Stokes' Law
16. Stickiness	$\eta = \dfrac{a \cdot [carbohydrate]}{CONC + a \cdot [carbohydrate]}$	In Ruddy *et al.* (in prep.)

17. Aggregated particle size — In Ruddy et al. (in prep.) — $size_a = (grainsize\ in\ microns)^{\gamma+1}$

18. Flow depth — $depth = WL - z_i$

19. Turbulent shear — In Ruddy et al. (in prep.) — $TS = \left(\dfrac{V \cdot U}{depth}\right) - S$

20. Critical erosion stress — Adapted from Sheilds parameter — $CES = 0.06 \cdot (\rho_c - (1 - \phi) \cdot \rho_s) \cdot g \cdot size_a$

21. Bioturbation coefficient — Adapted from Berner (1980) — $DD = 4.16 \cdot 10^{-7} \cdot \dfrac{macreq}{B_p}$

22. Grazing flux — Bubnova (1974) — $macreq = popuplation \cdot (1.069(0.008 \cdot length^{2.91})^{0.578})$

23. Aggregated particle density — Fennessey et al. (1994) — $\rho_a = \dfrac{8375 \cdot (size_a\ in\ microns)^{-1.084}}{10^6}$

(b) Model conditions

Parameters		Constituents	Initial value	Upper boundary value
		Algae	5×10^{-2} at sediment surface	1×10^{-12}
		Carbohydrate	$2.5 \times 10^{-6} \times SED/12$	0
		Sediment	$POS(z_i - z)^{0.25}\,\rho_s$	1
		Light	200	$\cos(2\pi t) \times 200$
		Oxygen	0.2×10^{-4}	0.2×10^{-4}
		Nitrate	1×10^{-4}	1×10^{-4}
		Ammonium	1×10^{-10}	1×10^{-10}
		POC	$(0.07 - (z_i - z_0) - (z - z_0)(SED)/12$	$0.1/12 \times SED$
		Suphide	0	0
All growth parameters	as Cullen (1990)			
λ	10^3			
b	0.05			
E_N	0			
Chl/C	0.0125 (Jonge 1980)			
g	9.81			
μ	1.31			
a	10^3			
grainsize	30×10^{-6}			
ρ_s	2250			
migrtn	0.2×10^{-6} (Hopkins 1963)			
slope	1.57 radians			
		U_i	0	$(4.166\pi \cdot \cos(4.166\pi t) \cdot (amp/2))/\cos(slope)$
		WL	4	$\sin(4.166\pi t) \cdot (amp/2) + 4$

Table 2. (c) *Model decomposition and redox chemistry*

Respiration substrate	Rate constant k_R (d^{-1})	Reference
POC (reacting with O_2, NO_3 or SO_4)	0.003	Toth & Lerman (1977)
Algae (reacting with O_2, NO_3 or SO_4)	0.36	based on Reinfelder *et al.* (1993), @10°C, D. Paterson (pers. comm.)
Carbohydrate (reacting with O_2, NO_3 or SO_4)	1.80	based on Taylor & Paterson (1996)
Sulphide (reacting with O_2)	6.62	based on $-\Delta G^\circ$ relative to Algal k_R (after Coleman 1985)
Sulphide (reacting with NO_3)	6.03	based on $-\Delta G^\circ$ relative to Algal k_R
NH_4 (reacting with O_2)	1.44	based on $-\Delta G^\circ$ relative to Algal k_R

(d) *Simulation Forcings*

	Site on LISP-UK Transect				Reference	Units
	A	B	C	D		
Elevation of bottom boundary (z_0)	5.30	5.00	4.30	4.00	Christie & Dyer (1996)	m above Chart Datum
Elevation of upper boundary (z_i)	5.40	5.10	4.40	4.10		m above Chart Datum
Initial sediment–water interface (z_i)	5.35	5.05	4.35	4.05		m above Chart Datum
M. balthica population	2600	2500	1200	2400	Davey & Partridge (1996)	individuals m^{-2}
Average *M. balthica* length	5	10	10	5	Davey & Partridge (1996)	mm

Symbol	Definition	Units	Symbol	Definition	Units
$[nutrient]_{lim\,N}$	concentration at which growth stops	kmol m^{-3}	$length$	average *M. balthica* shell length	m
$[nutrient]_N$	nitrogen concentration	kmol m^{-3}	μ	molecular viscosity	kg m^{-1} s^{-1}
A	velocity attenuation factor	dimensionless	$macreq$	*M. balthica* dietary requirement	molC m^{-2} d^{-1}
a	stickiness coefficient	dimensionless	$migrtn$	algal migration	m s^{-1}
AMP	tidal amplitude $[2\sin(t2\pi/21)] + 4$	m	P^B	carbon fixation	kmolC kmol Chl^{-1} s^{-1}
a_p	adsorption coefficient	m^2 kmol Chl^{-1}	POC	allochthonous particulate organic carbon	kmol m^{-3}
b	light attenuation by solids	dimensionless	$population$	*M. balthica* population density	indiv m^{-2}
Bp	algae	kmolC m^{-3}	R	summed exchange processes	kmol m^{-3} s^{-1}
C	concentration of constituent	kmol m^{-3}	R^B	aggregated particle density	kg m^{-3}
$carbohydrate$	carbohydrate concentration	kmol m^{-3}/kg m^{-3}	ρ_a	respiration	kmolC m^{-3} s^{-1}
C^B	carbon fixation	kmolC kmolC^{-1} s^{-1}	ρ_s	grain density	kg m^{-3}
CES	critical erosion stress	N m^{-2}	σ	adsorptional cross-section of PSU	m^2 kmol PSU^{-1}
Chl/C	algal chlorophyll to carbon ratio	dimensionless	S	laminar shear	N m^{-2}
$CONC$	concentration of solid material	kg m^{-3}	$size_a$	aggregated particle size	m
DD	bioturbation dispersion coefficient	m^2 s^{-1}	$slope$	transect slope	radians
$depth$	depth of flow above bottom boundary	m	$step$	function returning 1 when true and returning 0 when false	–
D_s	solid dispersion coefficient	m^2 s^{-1}	t	time	s
D_w	dissolved dispersion coefficient	m^2 s^{-1}	τ	turnover time of PSU	s
E_N	nutrient limitation factor	dimensionless	TS	turbulent shear	N m^{-2}
ϕ	porosity	dimensionless	U	velocity at depth z	m s^{-1}
ϕ_{max}	quantum carbon yield	kmolC kmol photons^{-1}	U_i	velocity at water surface	m s^{-1}
g	gravity	m s^{-2}	V	sediment–water dynamic viscosity	N s m^{-2}
G^B	algal growth	kmolC m^{-3} s^{-1}	vw	background water viscosity	N s m^{-2}
$grainsize$	average grain size	dimensionless	WL	water level	m
η	stickiness	m	w_s	settling velocity	m s^{-1}
I	irradiance in sediment–water	μmol m^{-2} s^{-1}	z	depth	m
k_R	rate constant [see Table 2(c)]	s^{-1}	z_0	bottom boundary depth	m
λ	notional light velocity	m s^{-1}	z_i	initial depth of sediment–water interface	m

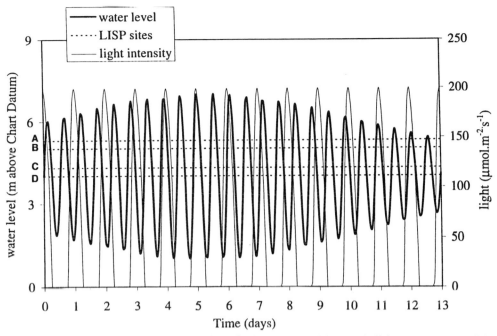

Fig. 1. Hypothetical light an tidal conditions through which the model (see Table 2) iterates. These conditions represent part of a spring-neap tidal cycle occurring at light intensities typical of the LISP-UK experiment.

Remineralization processes

Decomposition, respiration and remineralization reactions are simplified in the model to a series of bacterially mediated decay processes. Hence, the decomposition of exuded carbohydrate, algal biomass and POM (Table 2c) simulates both algal respiration and heterotrophic bacterial metabolism. This combined respiration results from the stoichiometric reaction of the respiration substrate (see Table 2c) with available oxidizing agents (Table 2c) at the rate constants given in Table 2c. The oxidizing agents are sequentially depleted (O_2, then NO_3^-, then SO_4^{2-}) during sediment diagenesis (Cho 1982; Richards et al. 1965; Canfield et al. 1993; Schlesinger 1991; Aller & Rude 1988). SO_4^{2-} concentrations are assumed to be present to excess and sulphide mineral accumulation assumed to be small and in steady state (Ruddy 1997). The NH_4^+ and sulphide that result from the remineralization of respiration substrates may then diffuse into more oxidizing conditions where reaction with NO_3^- and/or O_2 (Table 2c) simulates abiotic oxidation and bacterial chemotrophy. Rate constants for chemotrophic and abiotic oxidation reactions are subject to very large uncertainties (e.g. Morse et al. 1987), but may be approximated from the

free energy change of the reaction (Coleman 1985). Model rate constants (Table 2c) are estimated relative to algal decomposition, by assuming that dissolved substances are 100 times more reactive than equivalent solid substances and that the strength of the reducing agent in the reaction follows the scheme in Coleman (1985). This gives rate constants comparable to those measured. For instance, Morse et al. (1987) estimate sulphide oxidation rates of between 0.18 and 30 d^{-1}. The model gives 0.03 6.62 d^{-1} (Table 2c). The combination of these reactions approximates remineralization and respiration to first order decomposition processes in which bacterial growth and respiration are assumed to be equal. Remineralization of algae and POM regenerate NH_4^+ concentrations in the proportion of Redfield C:N (Redfield 1958). Nitrogen fixation and denitrification are assumed to be small and in steady state over the simulation period (Seitzinger 1988; Ruddy et al. this volume).

Grazing by macro-heterotrophs

The burrowing bivalve *Macoma balthica* is thought to have been the dominant macro-heterotroph on the mudflats during the

LISP-UK experiment (see Widdows *et al.* this volume; Davey & Partridge 1996, this volume). Measured population densities and sizes at the four sites of the LISP-UK transect (Table 2d) are used to estimate steady state dietary requirements for this organism [via Bubnova 1974, see Table 2a, equation (22)]. In the model, the *M. balthica* dietary requirement is met solely by grazing of algae (Hummell 1985) in the oxic surface layer of the sediment. *M. balthica* carbohydrate consumption (shown to be low; Harvey & Luoma 1984) and suspension-feeding (Kamermans 1994) are ignored since steady state *M. balthica* require nitrogen (Harvey & Luoma 1984) and the nutritional content of the overlying water may result predominantly from resuspended benthic algae (Kamermans 1994). Grazing of bacteria is also assumed to be small (Harvey & Luoma 1984) and in steady state. The dietary requirement is treated as constant over the 13 day simulation period due to very low *M. balthica* growth rates (McGreer 1983). Steady state *M. balthica* populations result in an excretion flux equal to dietary requirements [Table 2a, equation (22)]. Bioirrigation [Table 2a, equation (21); Aller 1980; Aller & Yingst 1985; Marinelli 1994] remains constant in all simulations in order that the direct effect of grazing on nitrogen cycling can be observed. By contrast, the bioturbation associated with grazing is inversely proportional to algal concentrations [Table 2a, equation (21)]; hence, when algal concentrations are low, sediment reworking increases to compensate. Because bioturbation was intense on the LISP-UK transect (Clifton & Smallman 1996), and *M. balthica* produces surface or near-surface excreted pseudo-faeces and faeces (Gilbert 1977; Reise 1983; Davey & Partridge this volume; Widdows *et al.* this volume), we have assumed that all *M. balthica* excretion occurs in the bioturbated oxic layer. Excretion results in regenerated NH_4^+ concentrations and a flux of particulate organic carbon (POC; see Table 1).

Shear stress

Physical dynamics are expressed in the form of continuous functions of velocity, viscosity, laminar and turbulent shear stress with depth [Table 2a, equations (8–12) and (19)]. The hydrodynamics are based upon the simplifying assumption that water velocity [Table 2a, equation (8)] is forced at the water surface by tidal flow (Table 2b) and is attenuated with depth in the sediment–water by viscosity [Table 2a, equations (9–10)]. This situation effectively defines

the hydrodynamics in Newtonian terms, since the viscosity of the moving fluid is proportional only to particle concentrations. For the calculation of tidal velocity profiles [Table 2a, equation (8)], the model water approximates to a frictionless fluid, hence velocity attenuation at the sediment–water interface only occurs as a result of particle dynamics. The water velocity at the upper boundary varies as a function of the water level, tides and tidal amplitude (Table 2b and Fig. 1), generating current velocities above the bed of between 0 and $0.3\,\mathrm{m\,s^{-1}}$ [observed velocities fall in the region of $0.2\,\mathrm{m\,s^{-1}}$ (Black & Jago 1996; Law 1996; Christie & Dyer 1996)]. Laminar shear stress in the flow [Table 2a, equation (12)] is calculated from the first differential of the emergent velocity profile and the viscosity of the fluid [Table 2a, equation (10)]. Turbulent shear stress accounts for the remainder of momentum [Table 2a, equation (19)] and effectively disperses constituent concentrations in the free flowing water above the emergent benthic boundary layer.

Solid and dissolved constituent transport

The total shear stress (laminar and turbulent) then gives rise to the dispersion coefficients for solid and dissolved constituents [Table 2a, equations (13) and (14)]. In the model, dissolved constituents disperse by molecular diffusion, bioirrigation and at the rate of particle dispersion [Table 2a, equation (13)]. Particles disperse by erosion and bioturbation [Table 2a, equation (14)]. Model erosion is strongly dependent on the laminar shear which dominates shear stress at the sediment–water interface due to strong velocity attenuation by viscosity [Table 2a, equation (10)]. A modified form of the Shield's entrainment function (that in effect adjusts particle size and fluid density to approximate the cohesive sediment to an equivalent non-cohesive bed) is used to define the critical erosion stress [Table 2a, equation (20)]. This critical erosion stress then slows down particle dispersion during erosion [Table 2a, equation (14)]. In the model, particles exist in a more or less flocculated state, their sizes calculated according to the proportion of algal carbohydrate to particles [or stickiness, Table 2a, equation (16)]. The stickiness defines the aggregated particle size [Table 2a, equation (17)], from which the critical erosion stress is estimated. Flocculated particles also have a settling velocity [Table 2a, equation (15)] based upon Stokes Law, which assumes that the particles are spherical and that their settling velocities are a function of their sizes and densities. Settling occurs through a sediment–water medium of variable porosity due to changes in particle concentration [Table 2a, equation (11)] and is thereby 'hindered' by high particle concentrations (e.g. in the sediment). Flocculated particle densities are calculated from floc size according to the empirical relationship of Fennessey *et al.* (1994). We assume that particle size and density are in a steady state with conditions, hence flocculation processes (e.g. particle collisions) impose no limitation on physical dynamics and transport.

Time courses and model behaviour

In the model, the oscillating exposure and inundation of the sediment by tides necessitates the removal and addition of constituent concentrations above the sediment bed during the periods when the water level (Table 2c) is greater than the sediment elevation but less than the elevation of the upper boundary (Table 2d) (i.e. the tide is in, but does not reach the upper boundary of the simulation). This is dealt with using functions which rapidly remove constituent concentrations and slow dispersion (with the exception of O_2) above the sediment during

tidal exposure. The same functions are used to re-introduce the constituent concentrations in overlying water when the flooding tide first arrives. With the exception of O_2, this allows sediment–water exchange, and the build-up of bedload concentrations etc., only during tidal inundation.

The model (Tables 1 and 2) is run through the 13 day sequence of light and tides shown in Fig. 1. The conditions remain constant (Table 2b) for each simulation, except where otherwise stated. Self-stabilizing behaviour of the model sediment or complete sediment destabilization emerge rapidly during iteration (see Fig. 2). Day 13 is chosen as the cut-off point for the simulations since this allows the estimation of short-term sediment accretion rates unaffected by the simulation boundaries. The cut-off point relates to a neap period in the model tidal cycle (Fig. 1) which occurs immediately after the first algal population maximum (Fig. 2a) and approximates to the long-term average. Hence, by day 13, algal growth rates settle to maintenance growth rates (Fig. 2d, see Table 2c) and most of total nitrogen flux within the biolayer is recycled rather than from external sources (i.e. new nitrogen). This situation reflects maximal algal populations in steady

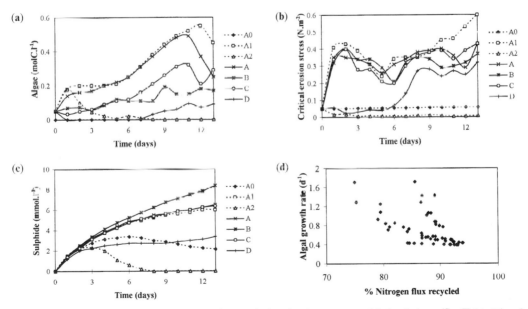

Fig. 2. Daily changes in selected model constituents during the short-term model simulations. (See Table 2d and Figs 3 and 4 for simulation conditions.) Algal concentration (**a**) and critical erosion stress (**b**) refer to the upper 1.125 mm of the eroding and depositing model sediment sampled daily at midday. The variation shows sediment stabilization from day 1 and peak algal concentrations between day 9 and 12 associated with neap tides and tide-light phasing (Fig. 1). Algal growth rate (**d**) stabilizes at maintenance growth in nitrogen limited conditions during the 13 day simulations (all simulations shown). Recycled and new nitrogen fluxes are discussed in the text. Sulphide concentrations (**c**) sampled daily immediately above bottom boundary of the model sediment at midday, show slightly longer term accumulation associated with sediment accretion/erosion.

state with the simulation conditions. Average diurnal changes in simulation A (for details see below) range + to −12.8% for algal carbon, + to −36.8% for critical erosion stress, and < + to −2% for sulphide. Average long-term (data not shown) spring-neap changes in simulation A range + to −28.2% for algae, + to −13.9% for critical erosion stress and + to −5.2% for sulphide.

Results and discussion

Biological influences on sediment dynamics

In Fig. 2a, the development of algae is evident at the sediment–water interface of simulations A, B, C, D and A^1. Conditions for these simulations are discussed below. Algal growth at the surface of the model sediment is sufficiently rapid (Fig. 2d) for nitrogen limited conditions to develop, carbohydrate exudation to occur and critical erosion stress (Fig. 2b) to increase above background levels (simulation A^0) within the first day's growth. Nitrogen supplies to algal growth are therefore rapidly dominated by recycled nitrogen fluxes (Fig. 2d). Net algal growth and nitrogen limited conditions occur

in simulations A, B, C and D despite macro-heterotrophic grazing rates of the algae that account for between 17.1 (simulation A) and 73.6% (simulation B) of algal growth per day (based on average simulation algal populations and *Macoma balthica* dietary requirements from Tables 2a and 2d). The rapid bacterial decomposition of the exuded carbohydrate in the model (1.8 d^{-1}; Table 2c) does not undermine the ability of algal exudation rates to affect sediment stability. Algal growth and migration rates (Table 2b) are also sufficient to keep pace with the burial and erosion of the sediment–water interface occurring during these simulations (Figs 3 and 4). The effect of light limitation can be observed in the stabilizing of algal population (Fig. 2a) and the reduction in critical erosion stress (Fig. 2b) from day 1 to 6, corresponding to increasing daytime spring tidal inundation (Fig. 1). In simulations A^2 and A^0 algal exudation does not occur, resulting in system destabilization (Figs 2 and 3).

Figure 3 shows the changes in the elevation of the sediment–water interface for simulations A, A^0, A^1 and A^2, run at LISP-UK site A conditions [see Table 2d; locations of the LISP-UK sites can been seen in Fig. 1, Ruddy *et al.*

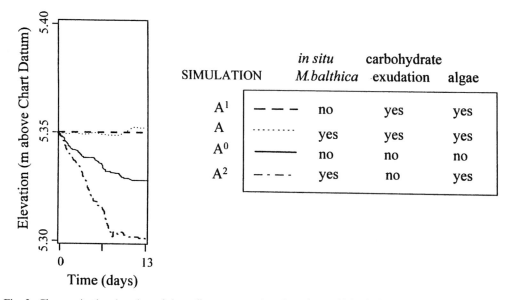

Fig. 3. Changes in the elevation of the sediment–water interface due to biological processes during model simulations of LISP-UK site A. The upper boundary of the simulation remains open while the lower boundary is closed. Iteration occurs through the sequence of tides and light shown in Fig. 1. In simulation A^0, with no biological influence, sediment erodes in response to tidal shearing forces. In simulation A^1, algal exudation results in rapid and complete stabilisation of the sediment–water interface. In simulation A^2, *M. balthica* rework surficial sediment during grazing, leading to rapid sediment erosion in the absence of algal exudation. In simulation A, the combined reworking of sediment by *M. balthica* and algal exudation in the surficial sediment produce a dynamic but stable sediment–water interface.

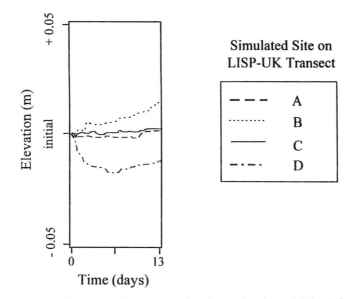

Fig. 4. Changes in the elevation of the sediment–water interface during the model simulation of sites A, B, C and D on the LISP-UK transect. (See fig. 1, Ruddy *et al.* this volume for site location.) Initial sediment–water interface elevation and *M. balthica* dimensions and numbers vary between simulations (see Table 2d). All simulations include algae, algal exudation, *M. balthica*. Varying degrees of erosion and deposition occur in response to biological and physical changes at the sediment–water interface. Sediment characteristics arising from each simulation are compared to held observations of the four sites in Table 3a and b.

(this volume)]. Simulation A^0 in Figs 2 and 3 is run without *M. balthica*, algae or algal exudation. Non-biological A^0 sediment erodes at an average of 1.92 mm d^{-1} (calculated from the elevation change of the sediment–water interface over the 13 day period). This rate of erosion compares well with the maximum observed at LISP-UK site A (Widdows *et al.* this volume), equivalent to 1.98 mm d^{-1} (Ruddy *et al.* this volume). Critical erosion stress at the sediment–water interface in simulation A^0 (Fig. 2b) shows a small increase over time as deeper, more consolidated layers of sediment are exposed. The critical erosion stress of between 0.05 and 0.06 N m^{-2} predicted by simulation A^0 (Table 3b, Fig. 2b) is almost an order of magnitude lower than in simulations where algal carbohydrate exudation occur (see simulations A, B, C, D and A^1 in Table 3b), but is very similar to the observed critical erosion stress of intertidal sediments after the addition of metabolic poisons (Black 1994). Erosion of the model sediment in simulation A^0 (Fig. 3) shows that the initial sediment elevation used to simulate LISP-UK site A conditions (Table 2d) is not in physical equilibrium with the model tidal scheme shown in Fig. 1. Hence, the sediment accretion, stabilization and destabilization evi-

dent in simulations A, A^1 and A^2 (Fig. 3) reflect biological processes.

Simulation A^1 in Figs 2 and 3 includes the effect of algae and algal exudation in the absence of *M. balthica*. This simulation shows high algal populations (Fig. 2a) and a high critical erosion stress (Fig. 2b) resulting from the high carbohydrate concentrations (Table 3b). The high chlorophyll *a* concentrations at day 13 (164 μg g dry^{-1}, Table 3b) indicates that surficial A^1 algae approach algal mat concentrations (e.g. 58–781 μg g dry^{-1}, Riege & Villbrant 1994). A non-dynamic A^1 sediment–water interface (Fig. 3) results at model tidal shear stresses. The inclusion of *M. balthica* (simulations A and A^2 in Figs 2 and 3) at the sizes and dimensions used to simulate LISP-UK site A (Table 2d) results in sediments of lower critical erosion stress (Fig. 2b). In the presence of algal carbohydrate exudation (simulation A), *M. balthica* sediment grazing results in little net erosion or accretion (Fig. 3) and has only a small effect on the surficial algal population (Fig. 2a) and sediment critical erosion stress (Fig. 2b). However, in the absence of algal exudation (simulation A^2), the same *M. balthica* dietary requirement results in catastrophic sediment destabilization (Fig. 3). This destabilization results from the lowering

Table 3. *Observed (a) and simulated (b) LISP-UK sediment properties*

(a)

Site	Algae (μg chl g dry^{-1})	Carbohydrate (mg gluc eq g dry^{-1})	CES* (N m^{-2})	POM (% dwt)	Recycled N flux† (mmol m^{-2} d^{-1})	New N flux† (mmol m^{-2} d^{-1})
A	23.7	43.98	0.7	7.98	16.57	2.11
B	14	23.5	0.34	3.75	11.82	3.02
C	na	na	0.33	6.63	na	na
D	na	na	0.31	6.45	na	na

(b)

Simulation	Algae (μg chl g dry^{-1})	Carbohydrate (mg gluc eq g dry^{-1})	CES (N m^{-2})	POC (% dwt)	Recycled N flux‡ (mmol m^{-2} d^{-1})	New N flux‡ (mmol m^{-2} d^{-1})
@ day 0 (unless mm)	12	0.84	0.05	3.7	0.82	1.33
A	38.45	26.28	0.43	6.95	15.02	2.13
B	21.87	22.50	0.37	9.18	14.81	2.42
C	33.27	22.11	0.43	6.54	10.88	1.73
D	14.66	10.53	0.32	5.78	4.55	1.29
A^0	nm	nm	0.057	3.60	nm	1.48
A^1	164.30	20.15	0.6	5.57	10.65	1.76
A^2§	2.53	nm	0.008	2.92	4.28	1.24

Observed sediment properties of the surficial sediment were sampled at different times during LISP-UK experiment, from Black & Paterson (1996). Emergent sediment properties from simulations were sampled from the upper 1.125 mm of the model sediment at midday on day 13. Simulations A, B, C, D are simulated LISP-UK sites, forced only by initial elevation and observed *M. balthica* numbers and dimensions (see Fig. 4, Table 2d). Simulations A^0, A^1 and A^2 represent the effect of algal exudation and *M. balthica* (see Fig. 3). (* critical erosion stress, † estimated in Table 2c, Ruddy *et al.* this volume, ‡ recycled and new N fluxes estimated by Equations 1 and 2 in text, § A^2 simulation sampled at dusk on day 5, due to rapid erosion, nm = not modelled, na = not available.)

of critical erosion stress (Fig. 2b), rapid erosion (Fig. 3) and loss of algae (Fig. 2a), and hence increasing grazing by *M. balthica* to meet dietary requirements as algal populations diminish [see Table 2a, equation (22)]. Facultative suspension-feeding by *M. balthica* (Hummell 1985) is thought to increase in proportion to water velocity (Levington 1991) and will therefore tend to counteract the positive feedback grazing described in the model. Given, however, that suspended matter is largely resuspended bed material (see Ruddy *et al.* this volume; Kamermans 1994), the destabilization of simulation A^2 will be unaffected since the shift from sediment grazing to suspension feeding occurs when erosion rates are already high.

The simulations in Fig. 3 indicate that the maintenance of algal populations at the sediment–water interface may be directly dependent on algal exudation, particularly in the presence of sediment grazing macro-heterotrophs. The effect of varying *M. balthica* dietary requirements and sediment bed elevation are shown in simulations A, B, C and D in Figs 2 and 4. These simulations are given conditions that reflect

LISP-UK sites A, B, C and D respectively. Simulations A, B, C and D include algae, algal exudation and *M. balthica*. The *M. balthica* grazing rates and initial sediment elevations used in the simulations are shown in Table 2d. Whilst simulations A, C and D have similar *M. balthica* dietary requirements, *M. balthica* dietary requirement in simulation B is three to four-fold higher (Tables 2a and 2d). The combined effect of *M. balthica* and sediment elevation can be seen in Fig. 2a and Table 3b. Highest algal concentrations are found in simulations A and C. Due to the high grazing flux in simulation B, algal populations remain low despite the high tidal elevation of the site (Table 2d). Lowest algal populations are found in simulation D (mid-water mark, Figure 1) and follow an initial period of erosion which ceases during the neap tide, allowing the re-establishment of the algal biolayer after days 6–8. This re-establishment occurs from catastrophic conditions similar to those of simulation A^2 (Figs 2a, 2b and 3) and demonstrates the effectiveness of nitrogen limited algal exudation in regulating sediment conditions.

Simulations A and C show little net erosion or accretion (Fig. 4) and higher critical erosion stress than simulations B and D (Fig. 2b, Table 3b). Simulation B, however, shows a sustained sediment accretion rate of $c.$ 1 mm d^{-1} (Fig. 4). This sediment accretion results from an initially destabilized sediment surface (relative to simulations A and C) due to the high $M.$ $balthica$ grazing rates (Fig. 2b). The resulting erosion flux from the sediment, however, contains carbohydrate concentrations, which, in conjunction with the low critical erosion stress (Table 3b), are sufficient to flocculate material in suspension and produce a settling flux that exceeds the initial erosion flux. At the lower grazing rates and higher critical erosion stresses of simulations A and C, sediment accretion is relatively reduced, since the erosion flux is lower. Because the POC concentrations in the suspended matter of the tidal water are higher than in the sediment (e.g. Eisma et $al.$ 1983; Eisma 1986; and model, Table 2b) POC concentrations in the surficial sediment of simulation B are increased by this process (Table 3b).

A growth advantage in algal exudation

A comparison of LISP-UK simulations and field observations for the surficial layer of the sediment is shown in Table 3. Generally good agreement is evident. The model indicates that between 25 and 55% of algal carbon fixation results in carbohydrate formation (estimated from Table 3b values using decomposition rates in Table 2c). Equivalent estimates from LISP-UK field observations range from 17 to 60% (Ruddy et $al.$ this volume). POC concentrations are somewhat higher in the simulations than observed in the field (shown as POM), particularly where sediment accretion is high (simulation B). This suggests that either the 10% POC dry weight used in the model for suspended particulate matter is high, or that exchange of material across the model sediment–water interface is more efficient in the model than on the LISP-UK transect. In Ruddy et $al.$ (this volume), measured critical erosion stresses were slightly higher than those measured using other techniques (see Black & Paterson 1996; other LISP-UK results, this volume; cf. Table 3 with Ruddy et $al.$, this volume). Critical erosion stress in the model [Table 2a, equation (20)] is a function of carbohydrate stickiness [Table 2a, equation (16)] which may have been underestimated. In addition, dynamic considerations (Ruddy et $al.$ this volume) suggest that much of the suspended particulate matter above the

LISP-UK transect may have originated from the sediment surface. This effect would tend to dilute POM concentrations in the suspended particulate matter observed over intertidal mudflats, reducing POM incorporation rates into the sediment.

Despite the potential underestimation of surficial sediment critical erosion stress and overestimation of POM incorporation rates, a similar trend between critical erosion stress and sediment carbohydrate is found in the simulations and on the LISP-UK transect (Fig. 5a). Furthermore, algal populations and carbohydrate concentrations compare well with observations from the four sites (Table 3a and b). This suggests that the dynamic processes of the model sediment (forced only by bed elevation and $M.$ $balthica$ sizes and numbers; Table 2d) can reproduce the surficial sediment of the LISP-UK sites (described in Ruddy et $al.$ this volume). Algae, carbohydrate concentrations and sediment stability in the model are connected via the nitrogen cycle [see Tables 1 and 2a, equations (5), (6), (16) and (20)]. The new and recycled nitrogen fluxes which constitute the nitrogen cycle are shown in Table 3b and also show good agreement with the observations (Table 3a). This implies that algae, carbohydrate concentrations and sediment stability on the LISP-UK transect were also mechanistically connected via nitrogen cycling, supporting the conclusions of Ruddy et $al.$ (this volume).

The model nitrogen fluxes are estimated from model results in Table 3b by assuming steady state grazing, steady state dissolved inorganic nitrogen diffusion fluxes and steady state algal growth conditions at midday on day 13. These fluxes are calculated by;

$$\text{new } N \text{ flux} = 1.125 \cdot 10^3 \frac{k_{POC} \cdot [POC]}{C : N_{POC}}$$

$$\text{recycled } N \text{ flux} = 1.125 \cdot 10^3$$

$$\cdot \frac{k_{algae} \cdot [algae] + macreq}{C : N_{algae}}$$

where k_{POC} = POC decomposition rate (Table 2c), $[POC]$ = POC concentration (mol C l^{-1}), $C : N_{POC}$ = C:N ratio of POM (Redfield), k_{algae} = algae respiration rate (Table 2c), $[algae]$ = algae concentration (mol C l^{-1}), $macreq$ = $M.$ $balthica$ dietary requirement [Table 2a, equation (22)], $C : N_{algae}$ = C:N ratio of algae (Redfield), and the factor converts mol N per model depth interval into mmol N per square metre.

In the model, the surficial new and recycled nitrogen fluxes regularly limit the growth of benthic algae (Fig. 2d), resulting in carbohydrate

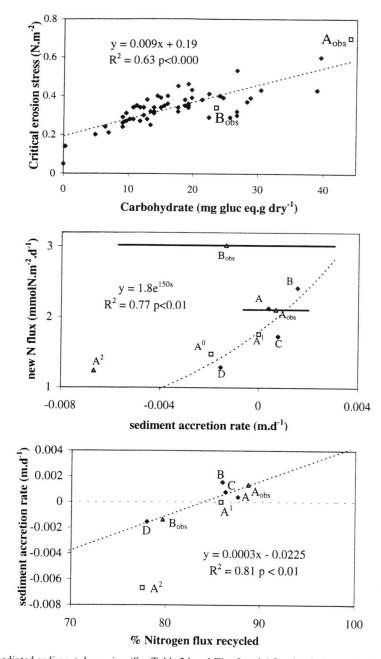

Fig. 5. Biomediated sediment dynamics. (See Table 2d and Figs 3 and 4 for simulation conditions. A_{obs} and B_{obs} refer to field observations of LISP-UK sites A and B shown in Table 3.) **(a)** Algal carbohydrate exudation vs critical erosion stress for model simulations. In the model carbohydrate concentrations (sampled in top 1.125 mm of sediment daily at midday in simulations A, B, C, D and A^1) are produced and exuded during nitrogen limited photosynthesis by the benthic algae. The carbohydrates stabilise the sediment. This results in a similar relationship to that in observed in the field. **(b)** Sediment accretion vs new nitrogen flux to the benthic layer. Sediment accretion supplies new nitrogen to benthic algae via the burial and bacterial remineralisation of organic matter. The regression line refers to carbohydrate-exuding simulations A, B, C, D and A^1. (Accretion rates are calculated from the net elevation change over 13 days for simulations A^0, A^1, A, B, C and D – see Figs 3 and 4; the net elevation change over 5 days for simulation A^2; the potential elevation changes for A_{obs} and B_{obs}, bars show uncertainty – see Table 1, Ruddy *et al.* this volume. New nitrogen fluxes are calculated by an equation in the text.) **(c)** Benthic nitrogen cycling vs sediment accretion rate. Sediment accretion estimated as in **(b)** occurs in proportion to benthic nitrogen recycling, see text. Regression line refers to carbohydrate-exuding simulations A, B, C, D and A^1. Non-carbohydrate-exuding simulations (A^0 and A^2) do not fall on trend.

production [Table 2a, equations (2)–(6)] and a dynamic sediment stabilization (Fig. 2b) that reflects benthic nitrogen limitation. Net algal growth under these circumstances depends on increasing the new nitrogen flux which, in turn, depends on increasing the POM concentration of the surficial sediment. The effect of sediment accretion on the new nitrogen flux is apparent in Fig. 5b. A rapid sediment accretion rate produces a high flux of POM across the sediment–water interface, high bacterial decomposition rates and a relatively large flux of new nitrogen to the benthic algae via bacterial remineralization. Therefore, in conjunction with sediment grazing (see above), the algal exudation of carbohydrates under nitrogen limited conditions increases new nitrogen fluxes, decreases nitrogen limitation and promotes net algal growth. Hence, an algal population benefits from increasing the sediment accretion rate.

Because high nitrogen fluxes reduce algal carbohydrate production, high nitrogen fluxes also reduce sediment accretion, thereby reducing new nitrogen fluxes. This raises the possibility that algal carbohydrate production under nitrogen limited conditions (or 'excess' carbon fixation) constitutes part of a negative feedback which links and regulates the sediment accretion, algal populations and algal growth conditions of intertidal sediments. The effect of this feedback on the short-term dynamics at the sediment–water interface can be seen in Fig. 5c. The proportion of total nitrogen flux (i.e. new and recycled) that recycles in the surficial sediment layer indicates the extent to which the total algal growth is dependent on nitrogen recycling relative to external nitrogen supplies. High percentages imply high degrees of recycling within the benthos (including heterotrophic organisms; see equations in text), while low percentages imply the potential for algal population growth. By day 13 in the model simulations the high degrees of recycling (Figs 2d and 5c, and Table 3b) indicate a relatively high biological nitrogen demand. Similar values were observed during the LISP-UK experiment (Table 3a). Figure 5c shows that model sediment accretion rates are approximately proportional to model biological nitrogen demand, indicating that sediment accretion may be decoupled from sediment supply by biological activities. The ability of the model to simulate the LISP-UK observations demonstrates that the nitrogen limited exudation of carbohydrates by algae in a dynamic context is a sufficiently robust self-regulating mechanism to withstand diurnal variation, intense grazing, sediment–water exchange processes, sediment burial and sediment erosion.

Conclusions

(1) At the growth, respiration and migration rates typical of benthic algae, a biolayer can develop at the sediment–water interface of intertidal sediments, in which primary production considerably exceeds detrital carbon production. Hence, recycled nitrogen fluxes in the biolayer tend to exceed new nitrogen fluxes.

(2) Within this layer, algae exist in a state of sustained unbalanced growth, where c. 50% of algal carbon fixation does not lead to growth due to limited nitrogen supply.

(3) Nitrogen limitation in the biolayer results from the rapid carbon fixation and growth rates of benthic algae, and occurs despite high light attenuation by sediment and macro-heterotrophic grazing of the algae.

(4) Because unbalanced growth conditions occur in the biolayer, we suggest that benthic algae use the resulting carbohydrate to search for better growth conditions by migration, and in doing so exude sediment-stabilizing carbohydrate polymers. Modelling indicates that the sediment system stabilizes when algal exudation results in increases in the cohesion of the sediment by about an order of magnitude relative to unstabilized sediment. This produces sediment stability consistent with field observations.

(5) Grazing of the biolayer by macro-heterotrophs such as *M. balthica* destabilizes the sediment surface. This occurs by (a) reworking the sediment surface and (b) reducing algal populations whilst also increasing nitrogen supplies. Modelling suggests that grazing can be expected to reduce sediment cohesion by about an order of magnitude for a given rate of algal exudation.

(6) Acting in conjunction, carbohydrate exuding algae, bacterial remineralization and grazing macro-heterotrophs produce a dynamic sediment–water interface which can sequester new material from tidal water by accretion and liberate material back to tidal water by erosion. Modelling these processes generates sediment dynamics and sediment properties consistent with observations.

(7) In the model, carbohydrate exudation is linked to nitrogen supply and biologically influenced sediment accretion occurs in proportion to benthic nitrogen requirements.

(8) Hence, algal exudate may not be a waste product. Modelling the dynamic factors that determine the exudation process suggests that there may be a fundamental growth advantage to exudation associated with the stabilization of physical conditions and the regulation of nitrogen supply.

(9) The model results demonstrate that the ecological and chemical dynamics of the sediment–water interface can potentially dominate sediment dynamics. Over short timescales this may result in the decoupling of sediment accretion from sediment supply. The model confirms the conclusion in Ruddy et al. (this volume) that nitrogen limitation may be an important factor in understanding intertidal dynamics.

Funding for this work was provided by NERC LOIS grant GST/02/787 and NERC LOIS grant GST/02/759. J. R. W. Harris and R. Gorley are gratefully acknowledged for help in implementing the model within ECoS. This manuscript benefitted from an anonymous review and comments by J. R. W. Harris.
This is LOIS publication number 227 of the LOIS Community Research Programme, carried out under a Special Topic Award from the Natural Environment Research Council.

References

ALLER, R. C. 1980. Diagenetic processes near the sediment–water interface of Long Island Sound 1. Decomposition and nutrient elements in geochemistry (S, N, P). In: SALTZMAN, B. (ed.) Estuarine Physics and Chemistry: Studies in Long Island Sound, Advances in Geophysics, Academic Press, New York, 22, 238–350.

—— 1982. The effects of macrobenthos on chemical properties of marine sediment and overlying water. In: McCALL, P. L. & TEVESZ, M. J. S. (eds) Animal–Sediment Relations, Plenum Press, New York, 53–102.

—— & YINGST, J. L. 1985. Effects of marine deposit-feeders Heteromastus filiformis (Polychaeta), Macoma balthica (Bivalvia) and Tellina texana (Bivalvia) on averaged sedimentary solute transport, reaction rates, and microbial distributions. Journal of Marine Research, 43, 615–645.

—— & RUDE, P. D. 1988. Complete oxidation of solid phase sulphides by manganese and bacteria in anoxic marine sediments. Geochimica et Cosmochimica Acta, 52, 751–765.

BERNER, R. A. 1980. Early Diagenesis; a Theoretical Approach. Princetown University Press.

BLACK, K. S. 1994. Bio-physical factors contributing to erosion resistance in natural cohesive sediments. Proceedings of the 4th Nearshore and Estuarine Cohesive Sediment Transport Conference, Paper 18.

—— & JAGO, C. 1996. Hydrographic and sedimentological investigation in the Humber Estuary, LISP-UK. In: BLACK, K. S. & PATERSON, D. M. (eds) LISP Preliminary Results. Interim Report, SERG, University of St Andrews, UK.

BLACK, K. S. & PATERSON, D. M. 1996. LISP Preliminary Results. Interim Report, SERG, University of St Andrews, UK.

BLACKBURN, T. H. & SORENSEN, J. 1988. Nitrogen Cycling in Coastal Marine Environments. SCOPE 33. John Wiley & Sons, Chichester.

BUBNOVA, N. P. 1974. Consumption and assimilation of carbohydrates from marine sediments by the detritus-feeding mollusks Macoma balthica (L) and Portlandia arctica (Gray). Oceanology, 12, 743–747.

CANFIELD, D. E. et al. 1993. Pathways of organic carbon oxidation in three continental margin sediments. Marine Geology, 113, 27–40.

CHENU, C. 1993. Clay- and sand-polysaccharide associations as models for the interface between micro-organisms and soil: water related properties and microstructure. Geoderma, 56, 143–156.

CHRISTIE, M. C. & DYER, K. R. 1996. Summary of LISP-UK velocity and concentration data obtained by POST. In: BLACK, K. S. & PATERSON, D. M. (eds) LISP Preliminary Results. Interim Report, SERG, University of St Andrews, UK.

CHO, C. M. 1982. Oxygen consumption and denitrification kinetics in soil. Soil Science of America Journal, 46, 756–762.

CLAVERO, V., NIELL, F. X. & FERNANDEZ, J. A. 1994. A laboratory study to quantify the influence of Nereis diversicolor O. F. Muller in the exchange of phosphate between sediment and water. Journal of Experimental Marine Biology and Ecology, 176, 257–267.

CLIFTON, R. & SMALLMAN, D. 1996. Oxygen consumption rates, sulphate reduction rates, stable sulphate and radionuclide concentrations in the sediments of the four LISP sites – Results to date. In: BLACK, K. S. & PATERSON, D. M. (eds) LISP Preliminary Results. Interim Report, SERG, University of St Andrews, UK.

COLEMAN, M. L. 1985. Geochemistry of diagenetic non-silicate minerals: kinetic considerations. Philosophical Transactions of the Royal Society London, A315, 39–56.

CULLEN, J. J. 1990. On models of growth and photosynthesis in phytoplankton. Deep Sea Research, 37, 667–683.

DAVEY, J. & PARTRIDGE, V. 1996. The macrofauna of the Skeffling mudflats. In: BLACK, K. S. & PATERSON, D. M. (eds) LISP Preliminary Results. Interim Report, SERG, University of St Andrews, UK.

—— & ——1998. The macrofaunal communities of the Skeffling muds (Humber Estuary) with special reference to bioturbation. This volume.

EDGAR, L. A. & PICKETT-HEAPS, J. D. 1984. Diatom locomotion. Progress in Phycological Research, 3, 47–88.

EINSTEIN, A. 1906. Annal. Physik. 4.19, 289.

EISMA, D. 1986. Flocculation and deflocculation of suspended matter in estuaries. Netherlands Journal of Sea Research, 20, 183–199.

——, BOON, J. J., GROENEWEGEN, R., ITTEKKOT, V. & MOOK, W. G. 1983. Observations on macroaggregates, particle size and organic composition of suspended matter in the Ems estuary. Mitteilungen Geologische Palaeontologischen Institut der Universitat Hamburg SCOPE/UNEP Sonderbereich, 55, 295–314.

FENNESSEY, M. J., DYER, K. R. & HUNTLEY, D. A. 1994. INSSEV: an instrument to measure the size and settling velocity of flocs *in situ*. *Marine Geology*, 117, 107–117.

FLOTHMANN, S. & WERNER, I. 1992. Experimental eutrophication on an intertidal sandflat: effects of microphytobenthos, meio- and macrofauna. *In*: COLUMBO, G. E. A. (ed.) *Marine Eutrophication and Population Dynamics*. Olsen & Olsen, Fredensborg, 93–100.

GERDES, G., KRUMBEIN, W. E. & REINECK, H.-E. 1994. Microbial mats as architects of sedimentary structures. *In*: KRUMBEIN, W. E., PATERSON, D. M. & STAL, L. J. (eds) *Biostabilization of Sediments*. Bibliotheks und Informationssystems der Carl von Ossietzky, Univsitat Oldenburg, 165–182.

GILBERT, M. A. 1977. The behaviour and functional morphology of deposit feeding in *Macoma balthica* (Linne, 1758), in New England. *Journal of Mollusc Studies*, 43, 18–27.

GRANT, J. & GUST, G. 1987. Prediction of coastal sediment stability from photopigment contents of mats of purple sulphur bacteria. *Nature*, 330, 244–246.

HARRIS, J. R. W. & GORLEY, R. 1992. ECoS Version 2. Plymouth Marine Laboratory, UK.

HARVEY, R. W. & LUOMA, S. N. 1984. The role of bacterial exopolymer and suspended bacteria in the nutrition of the deposit-feeding clam *Macoma balthica*. *Journal of Marine Research*, 42, 957–968.

HERMAN, W. M. 1996. The *in situ* determination of intertidal sediment erodibility in the Humber Estuary. *In*: BLACK, K. S. & PATERSON, D. M. (eds) LISP Preliminary Results. Interim Report, SERG, University of St Andrews, UK.

HINES, M. E. & JONES, G. E. 1985. Microbial biogeochemistry and bioturbation in the sediments of Great Bay, New Hampshire. *Estuarine, Coastal and Shelf Science*, 20, 729–742.

HOAGLAND, K. D., ROSOWSKI, J. R., GRETZ, M. R. & ROEMER, S. C. 1993. Diatom extracellular polymeric substances: function, fine structure, chemistry and physiology. *Journal of Phycology*, 29, 537–566.

HOPKINS, J. 1963. A study of the diatoms of the Ouse estuary, Sussex I. The movement of the mudflat diatoms in response to some chemical and physical changes. *Journal of the Marine Biological Association, UK*, 43, 653–663.

HOPNER, T. & WONNENBERGER, K. 1985. Examination of the connection between the patchiness of benthic nutrient flux and epiphytobenthic patchiness on intertidal flats. *Netherlands Journal of Sea Research*, 19, 227–285.

HUMMELL, H. 1985. Food intake of *Macoma balthica* (Mollusca) in relation to seasonal changes in its potential food on a tidal flat in the Dutch Wadden Sea. *Netherlands Journal of Sea Research*, 19, 52–76.

JONGE, V. N. DE 1980. Fluctuations in the organic carbon to chlorophyll a ratios for estuarine benthic diatom populations. *Marine Ecology Progress Series*, 2, 345–353.

JORGENSEN, K. 1989. Annual pattern of denitrification and nitrate ammonification in estuarine sediment. *Applied Environmental Microbiology*, 55, 1841–1847.

KAMERMANS, P. 1994. Similarity in food source and timing of feeding in deposit- and suspension-feeding bivalves. *Marine Ecology Progress Series*, 104, 63–75.

KLUMP, J. V. & MARTENS, C. S. 1989. The seasonality of nutrient regeneration in an organic rich coastal sediment: kinetic modelling of changing pore-water nutrient and sulphate distributions. *Limnology and Oceanography*, 34, 559–577.

KRUMBEIN, W. E., PATERSON, D. M. & STAL, L. J. (eds) 1994. *Biostabilization of Sediments*. Bibliotheks und Informationssystems der Carl von Ossietzky, Univsitat Oldenburg.

LAW, D. J. 1996. In situ laser back-scattering particle size analysis. *In*: BLACK, K. S. & PATERSON, D. M. (eds) LISP Preliminary Results. Interim Report, SERG, University of St Andrews, UK.

LEHMANN, W. & WOBER, G. 1976. Accumulation, mobilisation and turnover of glycogen in the blue-green bacterium *Anacystis nidulans*. *Archives of Microbiology*, 111, 93–97.

LEVINGTON, J. S. 1991. Variable feeding behaviour in three species of *Macoma* (Bivalvia: Tellinacea) as a response to water flow and sediment transport. *Marine Biology*, 110, 375–383.

MALCOLM, S. J. & SIVYER, D. B. 1997. Nutrient recycling in intertidal sediments *In*: JICKELLS, T. & Rae, J. (eds) *Biogeochemistry of Intertidal Sediments*. Cambridge University Press, Cambridge, 84–98.

MARINELLI, R. L. 1994. Effects of burrow ventilation on the activity of a terebellid polychaete and silicate removal from pore waters. *Limnology and Oceanography*, 39, 303–317.

MCGREER, E. R. 1983. Growth and reproduction of *Macoma balthica* (L.) on a mud flat in the Fraser River estuary, British Columbia *Canadian Journal of Zoology*, 61, 887–894.

MILES, A. 1996. LISP-UK April 1995. *In*: BLACK, K. S. & PATERSON, D. M. (eds) *LISP Preliminary Results*. Interim Report, SERG, University of St Andrews, UK.

MORSE, J., MILLERO, F., CORNWELL, J. & RICKARD, D. 1987. The chemistry of the hydrogen sulphide and iron sulphide systems in natural waters. *Earth Science Review*, 24, 1–42.

NILSSON, P., JONSON, B., SWANBERG, L. I. & SUNDBACK, K. 1991. Response of shallow-water sediment system to an increased load of inorganic nutrients. *Marine Ecology Progress Series*, 71, 275–290.

PATERSON, D. M. 1989. Short-term changes in the erodibility of intertidal sediments related to the migratory behaviour of epipelic diatoms. *Limnology and Oceanography*, 34, 223–234.

——1994. Biological mediation of sediment erodibility: ecology and physical dynamics. *Proceedings of the 4th Nearshore and Estuarine Cohesive Sediment Transport Conference*, Paper 17.

PELEGRI, S. P., NIELSEN, L. P. & BLACKBURN, T. H. 1994. Denitrification in estuarine sediment stimulated by the irrigation activity of amphipod *Corophium volutator*. *Marine Ecology Progress Series*, 105, 285–290.

PINCKNEY, J. L. 1994. Development of an irradiance-based eco-physiological model for intertidal benthic microalgal production. *In:* KRUMBEIN, W. E., PATERSON, D. M. & STAL, L. J. (eds) *Biostabilization of Sediments.* Bibliotheks und Informationssystems der Carl von Ossietzky, Univsitat Oldenburg, 55–84.

—— & ZINGMARK, R. 1991. Effects of tidal stage and sun angles on intertidal benthic microalgal productivity. *Marine Ecology Progress Series,* **76**, 81–89.

—— & ——1993. Biomass and production of benthic microalgal communities in five typical estuarine habitats. *Estuaries,* **16**, 881–891.

PRATSKA, K. E. & JICKELLS, T. D. 1995. Sediment/water exchange of phosphorus at two intertidal sites on the Great Ouse estuary, S.E. England. *Netherlands Journal of Aquatic Ecology,* **29**, 245–255.

REDFIELD, A. C. 1958. The biological control of chemical factors in the environment. *American Scientist,* **46**, 205–221.

REISE, K. 1983. Biotic enrichment of intertidal sediments by experimental aggregates of the deposit-feeding bivalve *Macoma balthica. Marine Ecology Progress Series,* **12**, 229–236.

REINFELDER, J. R., FISHER, N. S., FOWLER, S. W. & TEYSSIE, J-L. 1993. Release rates of trace elements and protein from decomposing planktonic debris 2. Copepod carcasses and sediment trap particulate matter. *Journal of Marine Research,* **51**, 423–442.

RICHARDS, F. A., CLINE, J. D., BROENKOW, W. W. & ATKINSON, L. P. 1965. Some consequences of the decomposition of organic matter in Lake Nitinat, an anoxic fjord. *Limnology and Oceanography Supplement,* **10**, R185–R201.

RIEGE, H. & VILLBRANT, M. 1994. Microbially mediated processes in tide influenced deposits and their importance in stabilisation and diagenesis of sediments; Nordeney survey. *In:* KRUMBEIN, W. E., PATERSON, D. M. & STAL, L. J. (eds) *Biostabilization of Sediments.* Bibliotheks und Informationssystems der Carl von Ossietzky, Univsitat Oldenburg, 339–360.

RUDDY, G. 1997. An overview of carbon, sulphur and oxygen cycling in marine sediments. *In:* JICKELLS, T. & RAE, J. (eds) *Biogeochemistry of Intertidal Sediments.* Cambridge University Press, Cambridge, 99–118.

——, TURLEY, C. M. & JONES, T. E. R. 1998. Ecological interaction and sediment transport on an intertidal mudflat I. *This volume.*

SCHLESINGER, W. H. 1991. *Biogeochemistry: An Analysis of Global Change.* Academic Press, New York, 243–253.

SEITZINGER, S. P. 1988. Denitrification in freshwater and coastal marine ecosystems: ecological and geochemical significance. *Limnology and Oceanography,* **33**, 702–724.

SKIDMORE, S. in prep. A size structured phytoplankton model.

SUNDBACK, K. 1994. The response of shallow-water sediment communities to environmental changes. *In:* KRUMBEIN, W. E., PATERSON, D. M. & STAL, L. J. (eds) *Biostabilization of Sediments.* Bibliotheks und Informationssystems der Carl von Ossietzky, Univsitat Oldenburg, 17–40.

TAYLOR, I. & PATERSON, D. M. 1996. Carbohydrates on the LISP-UK transect. *In:* BLACK, K. S. & PATERSON, D. M. (eds) *LISP Preliminary Results.* Interim Report, SERG, University of St Andrews, UK.

TOTH, D. J. & LERMAN, A. 1977. Organic matter reactivity and sedimentation rates in the ocean. *American Journal of Science,* **266**, 265–285.

ULLMAN, W. L. & ALLER, R. C. 1982. Diffusion coefficients in nearshore sediments. *Limnology and Oceanography,* **27**, 552–556.

UNDERWOOD, G. J. C. & PATERSON, D. M. 1993. Recovery of intertidal benthic diatoms after biocide treatment and associated sediment dynamics. *Journal of the Marine Biological Association, UK,* **73**, 25–45.

——, SMITH, D. & SZYSZKO, P. 1996. *In situ* production of microalgal exopolymers over spring and neap tide exposure periods. *In:* BLACK, K. S. & PATERSON, D. M. (eds) *LISP Preliminary Results.* Interim Report, SERG, University of St Andrews, UK.

WIDDOWS, J., BRINSLEY, M. & ELLIOT, M. 1996. Use of *in situ* benthic annular flume to investigate particle flux at the sediment–water interface in relation to changes in current velocity and macrofauna community structure. *In:* BLACK, K. S. & PATERSON, D. M. (eds) *LISP Preliminary Results.* Interim Report, SERG, University of St Andrews, UK.

——, —— & —— 1998. Use of an *in situ* flume to quantify particle flux (biodeposition rates and sediment erosion) for an intertidal mudflat in relation to changes in current velocity and benthic macrofauna. *This volume.*

WILTSHIRE, K., BLACKBURN, J. & PATERSON, D. M. 1996. Pigments in sediment particulate matter. Report on preliminary LISP data. *In:* BLACK, K. S. & PATERSON, D. M. (eds) *LISP Preliminary Results.* Interim Report, SERG, University of St Andrews.

YALLOP, M. L. & PATERSON, D. M. 1994. Microbially mediated processes in tide influenced deposits and their importance in stabilisation and diagenesis of sediments; survey of Severn Estuary. *In:* KRUMBEIN, W. E., PATERSON, D. M. & STAL, L. J. (eds) *Biostabilization of Sediments.* Bibliotheks und Informationssystems der Carl von Ossietzky, Univsitat Oldenburg, 279–326.

Measurements and preliminary modelling of current velocity over an intertidal mudflat, Humber estuary, UK

R. G. WOOD[1], K. S. BLACK[2] & C. F. JAGO[3]

[1] Plymouth Marine Laboratory, Prospect Place, West Hoe, Plymouth PL1 3DH, UK
[2] Gatty Marine Laboratory, St Andrews University, St Andrews, Fife KY16 8LB, UK
[3] School of Ocean Sciences, University of Wales Bangor,
Menai Bridge, Anglesey LL59 5EY, UK

Abstract: This paper presents tidal current velocity data from Station D on the LISP transect, Humber estuary, UK, collected during April 1995. Ten impeller-type current meters, aligned along the major flood-ebb tidal axis, were deployed in a vertical array at the site. Five of these measured flood speeds and five measured ebb speeds. First, depth-averaged flow is considered. Observed depth-averaged velocities are compared to results from three sets of modelled velocities: one set in the Hawke channel taken from a 2D model of the Humber estuary, one from a 1D hydrodynamic model of a flooding/drying transect, and one from a uniform elevation, volume-conservation model of a flooding/drying transect. The uniform elevation model is simpler, faster and gives a smoother response than the hydrodynamic model at this scale; and the observed velocities are closest in magnitude and direction to results from this model. The nature of the vertical velocity profile is then considered for both Spring and Neap tidal cycles. It is suggested that the vertical advection of horizontal velocities (due to the large ratio of water level change to water depth) has a significant effect on the velocity profile during the ebb, modifying the expected deviation in profile due to the flow acceleration.

Tidal flat environments have increasingly become the focus for research since the early classic studies of a number of Dutch workers (Hantzschel 1939; van Straaten 1961; van Straaten & Kuenen 1957). In view of their importance to the ecology of birdlife, coastal conservation issues, and sediment transport and sediment budgets within estuaries, man has sought to understand the complicated dynamics of these environments. This understanding forms the cornerstone of effective environmental management, and is a tool which can be usefully used both to assess change and to ensure that such environments are not misused or stressed unnecessarily. A holistic approach to tidal mudflat dynamics will combine real-time observations of the important processes with numerical modelling. Not only will this provide realistic and reliable physical data sets, but it may allow a future predictive capacity with respect to water and sediment movement in these environments. This paper reports some observations of current velocity made at Station D of the UK LISP transect (see Black & Paterson this volume) during April, 1995, in conjunction with some preliminary modelling efforts utilizing several different approaches.

Although perhaps not as intensively studied over the last few decades as intertidal sandflats (Amos 1995), a resurgence of interest has resulted in a number of important recent studies of tidal mudflats. The Canadian LISP study (Daborn 1991) provided some information on water circulation patterns and suspended sediment transport processes across the massive Bay of Fundy mudflats. Measurements were made from moored instruments and a series of semi-permanent barges. A number of similar studies have been conducted on the extensive mudflats bordering China (Shi & Chen 1996) and Korea (Wells et al. 1990). The recent publications edited by Wartel (1991), Krumbein et al. (1994) and Burt et al. (1997) also contain several papers of relevance to muddy intertidal zones. However, there is only one study to the authors' knowledge of a detailed appraisal of the flow structure across a proper cohesive mudflat. This is the study of Ke et al. (1994) in the Wash, UK. Analogous studies have been conducted almost entirely over sandy tidal flats (e.g. Evans & Collins 1975; Carling 1978, 1981; Collins et al. 1981; van Smirren & Collins 1982). This situation is probably due to the inhospitable and inaccessible nature of most mudflat environments.

However, others have measured near-bed flow structure in the sea e.g. Dyer (1970), Channon & Hamilton (1971) and Harvey & Vincent (1977). These studies often showed logarithmic profiles close to the seabed, although several factors should be considered carefully before matching

WOOD, R. G., BLACK, K. S. & JAGO, C. F. 1998. Measurements and preliminary modelling of current velocity over an intertidal mudflat, Humber estuary, UK. In: BLACK, K. S., PATERSON, D. M. & CRAMP, A. (eds) Sedimentary Processes in the Intertidal Zone. Geological Society, London, Special Publications, 139, 167–175.

observed profiles to a logarithmic form. Firstly, the errors involved in fitting a small number of vertically-spaced current measurements to a logarithmic profile, and their consequences for estimates of bed roughness and bottom shear stress, have been discussed by Wilkinson (1984). Even with six current meters, Wilkinson found errors in shear stress of ±35% and errors in roughness length of ±77%, using 95% confidence limits. These errors will be markedly larger when current meters at only five heights are used. Secondly, the time over which velocity measurements are averaged appears important (Heathershaw & Simpson 1978; Gross & Nowell 1983). These studies found that velocity data had to be averaged over at least ten minutes to minimize errors due to random variations, and produce appropriate tidally-varying velocity profiles and accelerations. Thirdly, a logarithmic form is only expected from dimensional scaling arguments for steady, uniform flow. Many effects will cause the velocity profile to deviate from a logarithmic form. Changes in velocity profiles due to acceleration in a spatially uniform flow have been examined by Soulsby & Dyer (1981). These had the effect of reducing (during acceleration) or increasing (during deceleration) upper velocities compared to the profile for steady flow. Variations due to spatially-varying bed roughness were examined by Chriss & Caldwell (1982), leading to segments of log profiles corresponding to the different roughnesses appearing at varying heights downstream.

Modifications due to bedforms were considered by Dyer (1970), giving increasing bed stress as the flow approaches the crest of a bedform, and decreasing bed stress (possibly with areas of zero bed stress caused by flow separation) on the lee side of the bedform. The effect of these processes on the velocity profiles is discussed in Dyer (1986). However, all of these studies consider water which is deep compared to the tidal elevation amplitude, so the sites are permanently inundated. The observations in this paper are from a location which is flooded for only half the tidal cycle, and where the surface elevation is driven by a large tidal signal propagating in a nearby deep, permanently flooded channel (Hawke Channel). Very few observations of flow in such areas have been published, and the little research to date indicates that logarithmic velocity profiles are present through a portion of the tide only (e.g. Collins *et al.* 1981).

Similarly, modelling of the flow specifically over mud-flats has rarely been reported. Intertidal areas have in the past been considered only within large models of entire estuaries or embayments, such as Flather (1994) and Cheng *et al.* (1993). However, it is reasonable to expect that simplifications can be made when constructing a localized model of a small area of mudflat. The mudflat considered here, like many others, is extensive and generally uniform in the longshore direction, but has a short cross-shore extent. The main driving force for the flow is expected to be the tidal variation in sea-level in the nearest main estuary channel. Thus, it is natural to try a modelling approach where longshore variations are ignored (except to determine the timing and magnitude of the offshore elevation level). A suitable local model for flow over mudflats will be a useful tool for examining sediment transport processes in intertidal areas.

Methodology

Study area

Measurements of current velocity were collected at Station D of the intertidal LISP transect on the north shore of the Humber estuary (see Black & Paterson this volume). The transect runs approximately North–South from Skeffling village. Station D comprises cohesive silts and clays and is located roughly 2100 m offshore at approximately the mid-shore level (drying height of 3.56 m CD). The sediment surface is characterized by a low amplitude ridge-runnel type topography and the region is traversed by several narrow and deep drainage channels.

Measurement program

A velocity gradient unit (VGU) was used to collect current speed data on the ebb and flood tides (Fig. 1). The unit was aligned with the dominant flood-ebb direction [30° (flood), 210° (ebb)] which was determined by previous hydrographic surveys (Black, unpublished data). Ten current meters were deployed in a vertical array. Flood tidal speeds were recorded at heights 13 cm, 28 cm, 48 cm, 88 cm and 153 cm above the bed. Ebb speeds were recorded at heights 7 cm, 22 cm, 42 cm, 82 cm and 147 cm above the bed. The instrument spacing was designed to resolve the expected logarithmic behaviour of the velocity profile. Every ten minutes the number of impeller turns occurring in one minute was counted and logged electronically. On recovery, the data were calibrated against 17 point measurements from a current meter deployed off

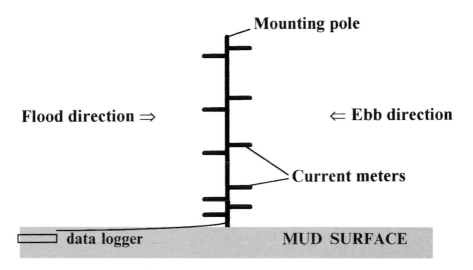

Fig 1. Schematic of the velocity gradient unit (VGU). Ott (impeller type) current meters are mounted logarithmically spaced on a post. The rig is aligned with the flood-ebb axis so five current meters face into the flood tide direction and five face into the ebb tide direction. Instrument owned by CFJ (University of Wales, Bangor).

a boat. These measurements gave speed and direction simultaneous with the VGU data at a number of water depths. They were made above Station D during flood tides on 5th and 6th April, and at Station C (while the VGU rig was operating there) during a flood tide on 4th April and an ebb tide on 7th April. In the subsequent analyses, we use VGU data from a Neap tidal cycle on 6th April 1995 and a Spring tidal cycle on 15th April 1995.

Numerical models for depth-averaged flow

Land-based and sea-based surveys have provided measurements of bed height relative to Chart Datum along the LISP transect (see Black & Paterson this volume). There is also Admiralty bathymetric chart of this area (Chart No. 1188). These charts, and visual observations, show that the mudflat has a smooth 'background' height profile which is approximately uniform in the alongshore direction. Narrow, deep drainage channels cut across the mudflat between certain height levels. Two of these channels intersect the LISP transect and appear as discrete dips on the bathymetric profile. The line of steepest descent across the mudflat is taken to be 210° clockwise from due North. This is approximately perpendicular to both the shoreline and to the direction of the

Hawke channel. The LISP transect runs north–south, so bed levels on the model transect were calculated assuming uniformity of the 'background' profile in the alongshore direction. Dips due to drainage channels were ignored. Starting from the shoreline, there is a thin band of saltmarsh, a step down onto mudflat, which then extends for c. 4 km offshore, with shallow bottom slopes, and muddy cohesive sediment, grading into sandier deposits; then there is a steep descent into the deep Hawke channel which connects directly to the estuary mouth. Using $\sqrt{gh}$ to estimate gravity wave speed, the tidal signal will propagate about twice as fast along the deep channel as it will along the mudflat. So, at D, the main driving force is expected to be elevation in the nearest part of the channel rather than elevations upstream along the mudflat.

All the models discussed are depth-averaged. The first model (M1) is a 1D onshore–offshore hydrodynamic model, aligned with the current meter orientation. Assuming the velocities were driven mainly by surface elevation in the Hawke channel, a depth-averaged model was constructed using a transect profile from a combination of the land-based and sea-based bathymetric surveys. The *x*-direction in the model ran offshore at an angle of 210°, ending in the main estuary 5 km from the shore. Offshore velocities were positive. All variables were taken as constant in the longshore direction. Equations were as follows:

$$\frac{\partial u}{\partial t} + u\frac{\partial u}{\partial x} = -g\frac{\partial \eta}{\partial x} - \frac{C_D|u|u}{H+\eta}$$

$$\frac{\partial \eta}{\partial t} + \frac{\partial}{\partial x}(u(H+\eta)) = 0$$

where u = depth-averaged velocity in x-direction, bed level = $-H(x)$, sea surface elevation = η, friction coefficient = C_D. Several values of C_D were tried; the results were not sensitive to this value. The runs shown used $C_D = 0.0025$, which is appropriate for tidally dominated mudflat environments (Ke *et al.* 1994). When the water column height in a cell dropped below 5 cm, the cell was considered dry, and outflow from it was no longer allowed. The model had a grid cell length of 50 m, and a time-step of 2.8 s. Elevation at the seaward end was taken as equal to the gauged Immingham tide levels, but leading Immingham times by 20 min (as observed by Christie & Dyer 1996). It is assumed that elevation in the main channel is not appreciably affected by flow over the mudflats.

Due to the appearance of some spurious oscillatory flow within the 1D model due to the flooding and drying of model cells, it was apparent that a simple volume-conserving model would be more suitable for obtaining depth-averaged speeds. A model of this type was constructed within Microsoft Excel. This is the second model (M2). For each ten-minute time interval, it simply calculated the volume flux required at D to raise the water level across the whole mudflat to the Immingham level. This was then divided by the average water depth at D over this time interval to give the depth-averaged speed. As in model M1, speeds are taken as normal to the shoreline and the depth profile used has been derived from the LISP transect depths assuming longshore uniformity of mudflat height.

A third model (M3) is a 2D vertically averaged model of the whole Humber estuary, from Trent Falls to seaward of Spurn Head, with a grid cell size of *c*. 550 m by 600 m. This was forced by nine tidal harmonic components at the seaward boundary. The model was not run for the particular dates observed, but results from a similar spring tidal cycle in another year were used for the comparisons. This model (Wood, DoE interim report) uses a simple flooding/drying scheme, and quadratic bottom friction. The Skeffling transect was resolved by six points within this model.

Results and discussion

Observed and modelled elevation

Figure 2 shows results from all three models and also minimum elevations as deduced from the

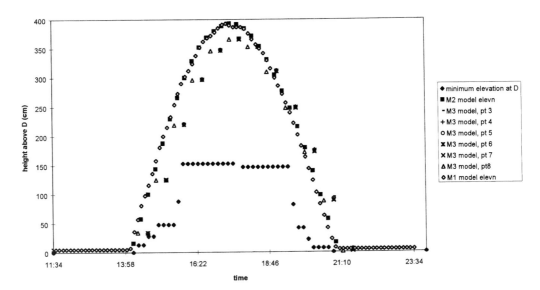

Fig 2. Comparison of observed and modelled elevation on 15th April. Measured elevation deduced from the highest submerged current meter (to a maximum of 1.53 m).

data. The observed minimum elevations at D correspond to the height of the highest current meter which can be identified as covered with water at that time. Sub-aerially exposed current meters tended to give very large readings. These values are necessarily underestimates of the actual elevation, because unless a current meter was well-covered with water, it would tend to be exposed intermittently by wind waves. Note that water elevation can only be determined to a maximum depth of 1.53 m from the current meter data (the height of the top-most current meter). For model M1, elevation propagated very rapidly onshore at all times. For model M3, points 3 to 8 are positioned approximately along the Skeffling transect, with point 3 being the most inshore, and point 8 lying in the main estuary channel. These show that the predicted cross-shore elevation gradient is small.

Further and better field data of tidal elevation are necessary before we are able to check model elevation predictions with confidence. Notwithstanding this, one should note that actual tide height in the estuary can vary by as much as 0.35 m from predicted height due to atmospheric conditions (Black, unpublished data). The models developed here are not sufficiently sophisticated to resolve these changes or, for example, water level changes due to tide surges. In practise, therefore, it may be easier to determine water depth at Station D from real-time tide data (from Immingham) and knowledge of the bed height.

Observed and modelled depth-averaged flow

Modelled and observed depth-averaged speeds are compared in Fig. 3. The similarity between the results of the models M1 and M2 should be noted. This shows that for this scale of situation the simpler, uniform cross-shore elevation approach of M2 gives better results than the more complex wave propagation model M1, because it is less prone to numerical errors. The speed and simplicity of M2 also makes it suitable for use in experimental intertidal sediment transport models (Wood, in preparation).

The models M1 and M2 give velocities which lag surface elevation by $c.90°$, which is consistent with the phase lag observed in the flow data. Peak flow speeds at Station D are $c.0.5 \, ms^{-1}$, which is of the same magnitude as measured peak flow speeds. As noted by Christie & Dyer (this volume) and Black & Paterson (1996), cross-shore flows of this order on the mudflat are responsible for entraining even relatively firm muds (bulk density $> 1400 \, kg \, m^{-3}$) into suspension.

The plotted M3 model speed is taken from the nearest model point to Station D. The speeds at this point are about half the magnitude of those observed, and they are not aligned with the cross-shore directions. The M3 velocities for all the points 3 to 8 have greater longshore than cross-shore components, hence aligning more with the Hawke channel than the observed velocities.

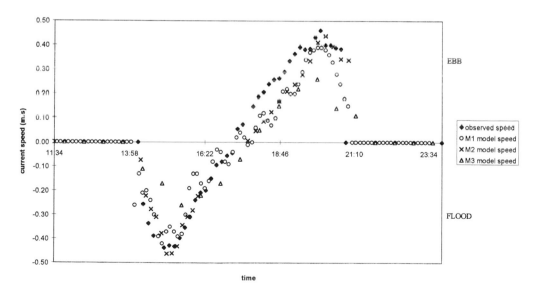

Fig 3. Comparison of modelled and observed depth-averaged speeds on 15th April. Ebb speeds are positive, flood speeds are negative.

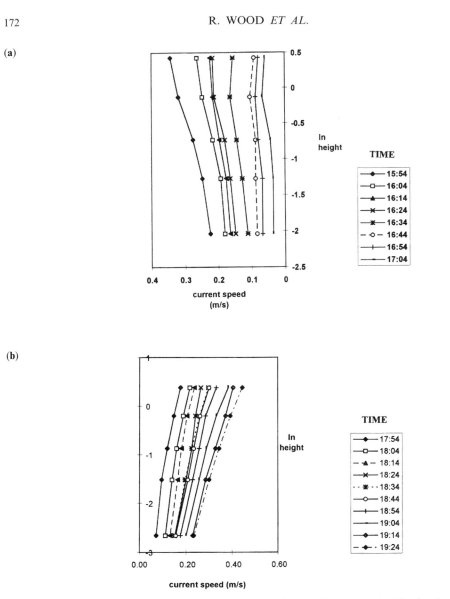

Fig 4. Graphs of modulus of current speed against natural log height above the bed for flood and ebb tides on 15th April (Spring tides). Note flood speeds (**a**) are decelerating, ebb speeds (**b**) are accelerating. One line plotted for each observation time.

The 1D model M2 was modified to allow non-linear transport of longshore velocity in the onshore direction. This was forced with Hawke channel longshore velocities imposed at the seaward end. However, this did not give appreciable increase in current speeds as far inshore as D. The observed speeds show closest agreement both in magnitude and direction with the M2 modelled speeds. As noted previously, ideally one should average speeds over at least ten minutes to minimize random errors (Heather-shaw & Simpson 1978; Gross & Nowell 1983).

The lack of directional information from the current meter's rig also makes interpretation of the data difficult. Data from both the boat observations (as used for calibration) and from Christie & Dyer (this volume) show that although the flood direction is predominantly onshore (between 20° and 60°), the ebb is initially alongshore, veering towards offshore as the ebb progresses. Such circulation patterns are not uncommon across intertidal regions (e.g. Perillo *et al.* 1993). It is likely that during peak flood and peak ebb conditions, the cross-shore flows will

(a)

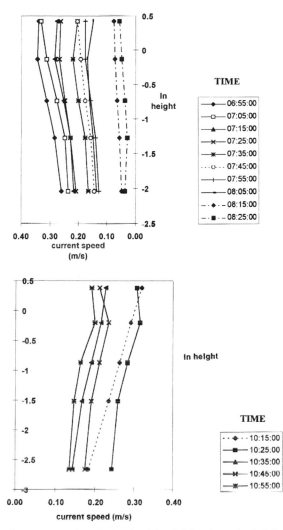

(b)

Fig 5. Graphs of modulus of current speed against natural log height above the bed for flood and ebb tides on 6th April (Neap tides). Note flood speeds (**a**) are decelerating, ebb speeds (**b**) are accelerating. One line plotted for each observation time.

dominate, as elevation changes in the Hawke channel propagate rapidly onshore, but near high tide times, local effects may steer the flow alongshore. During the initial ebb, the observed speeds exceed the M1 and M2 model speeds. They correspond to predominantly alongshore flows (having a component in the offshore direction) which are driven by processes not included in the M1, M2 models.

Vertical profiles of speed

Speed against natural log height profiles are shown in Figs 4 and 5. Because we are only examining speeds when all five current meters are covered, the flood profiles are representative of decelerating flow; and the ebb profiles all correspond to accelerating flow. Comparing flood and ebb velocities, for the same depth-averaged speed, there is greater top-to-bottom shear during the ebb than during the flood. For the decelerating flood, at points higher up the water column, speeds are higher than expected for a log profile. This is in agreement with Soulsby & Dyer (1981), who examined deviations from a logarithmic profile caused by weak acceleration in horizontally uniform flow over a flat bed. However, for the accelerating ebb, the speeds still increase with height beyond what is expected from a log profile. The effect is far larger for the Spring tide (Fig. 4) than the Neap tide (Fig. 5). Indeed for much of the Neap tide data (including that for days not shown here), the top-most current meter often registered lower speeds than the one below it (although below this the profile looks reasonable).

As the water advances and retreats over the mudflat, five primary factors may be expected to affect the velocity profile. These are (i) local acceleration of the flow, (ii) the changing water column height and associated vertical velocities, (iii) the boundary layer being advected either onto or away from the mudflat surface, (iv) horizontal spatial variation of the flow due to the onshore rise in bed level and volume conservation of the flow, and (v) topographic steering of the flow due to meandering channels in the mudflat surface. Soulsby & Dyer (1981) derived a correction to the log profile which increased in magnitude with height above the bed. Dimensional arguments were used to obtain the analytical form of the modified profile, and this profile must be consistent with the equation of motion for the flow, namely

$$\frac{\partial u(z)}{\partial t} = -g\frac{\partial \eta}{\partial x} + \frac{\partial}{\partial z}\left(\frac{\tau}{\rho}\right)$$

where the direction x is aligned with the flow direction. However, for tidally-varying flow over a mudflat, the full Lagrangian time derivative must be included, giving

$$\frac{\partial u(z)}{\partial t} + u\frac{\partial u}{\partial x} + w\frac{\partial u}{\partial z} = -g\frac{\partial \eta}{\partial x} + \frac{\partial}{\partial z}\left(\frac{\tau}{\rho}\right)$$

We will compare sizes of the first three terms at a point which is on the mudflat but not close to the waters edge, taking x to be directed onshore. Letting U be a scaling factor for u where the water depth is h, L_H be the horizontal length over which bed height rises by vertical distance h, and T be the tidal period, the first term has magnitude U/T, and the second has magnitude U^2/L_H. An order of magnitude for $w(\partial u/\partial z)$ can be estimated using $w = (\partial \eta/\partial t)$ at the sea surface, and $w = 0$ at the bed. The scale for u is determined by $hu \approx (\partial \eta/\partial t)L_H$ and the vertical length scale is h. So, the third term has magnitude U^2/L_H. The inertial (second and third) terms will dominate over the acceleration (first) term when $(L_H/U) < T$. So, the horizontal and vertical terms will be at least as important as local acceleration over the submerged part of the mudflat. Now, we will consider the signs of the three terms during those parts of a tidal cycle for which the scalings apply. In the latter half of the

flood, velocity is directed onshore, water level is rising, velocities are decreasing shorewards, and locally velocity is slowing. This gives $\partial u/\partial t$ negative, $u(\partial u/\partial x)$ negative and $w(\partial u/\partial z)$ positive. In the first half of the ebb, velocity is directed offshore, water level is falling, speed is increasing generally and locally offshore. This again gives $\partial u/\partial t$ negative, $u(\partial u/\partial x)$ negative and $w(\partial u/\partial z)$ positive. The vertical inertial term opposes the local acceleration term. A more detailed examination of the interaction of these terms may explain the observed difference in velocity profile behaviour.

Conclusions

A measurement program and modelling exercise were undertaken of the tidal current flow at Station D of the LISP study. For the time and location modelled, the flow magnitude and direction can be well represented by a local 1D model of flooding and drying over the mudflat. A simple cubature model, with elevation everywhere equal to that imposed at the seaward boundary performs better than a more complex model which allows wave propagation of elevation onshore. The model agrees best with data while the observed flows are directed on or offshore, but poorly during the initial ebb phase, while observed flows are longshore.

Vertical profiles of velocity are observed to deviate from log profiles such that speeds are higher than expected as height above the bed increases, both for the decelerating flood and accelerating ebb parts of the tide. The flow over mudflat areas is not uniform. It varies in the onshore direction and has a significant vertical component. Consideration of these factors indicates that the full Lagrangian time derivative is necessary for understanding flow behaviour. It is important to realize that a good fit may be obtained with a log profile even if the flow is following a modified profile, however spurious slope and intercept parameters can arise if the modifications are not taken into account. The water column dynamics are therefore modified in very shallow tidal flat environments and analysis of field data requires careful consideration.

This is LOIS publication number 320 of the LOIS Community Research Programme carried out under a Special Topic Award from the Natural Environment Research Council. The study was part of the interdisciplinary LISP-UK study. Thanks to all of the LISP team who helped with the logistics and sampling for the experimental work and to members of the St. Andrews Sedi-ment Ecology Research Group (SERG) for their help.

References

AMOS, C. L. 1974. Intertidal flat sedimentation of the Wash – E. England. Unpublished PhD Thesis, University of London.

AMOS, C. L. 1995. Siliciclastic Tidal Flats. *In*: PERILLO, G. M. E. (ed.) *Geomorphology and Sedimentology of Estuaries, Developments in Sedimentology*, **53**, Elsevier, 273–306.

BLACK, K. S. & PATERSON, D. M. 1986. LISP-UK: an holistic approach to the interdisciplinary study of tidal flat sedimentation. *Terra Nova*, **8**, 304–307.

BLACK, K. S. & PATERSON, D. M. 1998. Introduction to LISP-UK. *This volume*.

BURT, N., PARKER, W. R. & WATTS, J. (eds) 1997. *Cohesive Sediments*. 4th Nearshore and Estuarine Sediment Transport Conference, 11–15 July 1994, Wallingford, England. Wiley and Sons.

CARLING, P. A. 1978. The influence of creek systems on intertidal flat sedimentation. Unpublished PhD Thesis, University of Wales, UK.

CARLING, P. A. 1981. Sediment transport by tidal currents and waves: observation from a sandy intertidal zone (Burry Inlet, S. Wales). *Special Publication International Association of Sedimentologists*, **5**, 65–80.

CHANNON, R. D. & HAMILTON, D. 1971. Sea bottom velocity profiles on the continental shelf southwest of England. *Nature*, **231**, 383–385.

CHENG, R. T., CASULLI, V. & GARTNER, J. W. 1993. Tidal, residual and intertidal mudflat (TRIM) model and its applications to San Francisco Bay, California. *Estuarine Coastal Shelf Science*, **36**, 235–280.

CHRISS, T. M. & CALDWELL, D. R. 1982. Evidence for the influence of form drag on bottom boundary layer flow. *J. Geophysical Research*, **89**, 6403–6414

CHRISTIE, M. & DYER, K. R. 1996. Velocity and concentration data obtained by POST 14/4/95 – 20/4/95. In LISP–Littoral Investigation of Sediment Properties, Preliminary Results, compiled by K. Black and D. Paterson, St Andrews University.

CHRISTIE, M. & DYER, K. R. 1998. Measurements of the turbid tidal edge over the skeffling mudflats. *This volume*.

COLLINS, M. B., AMOS, C. L. & EVANS, G. 1981. Observation of some sediment transport processes over intertidal flat, the Wash, UK. *Special Publication International Association of Sedimentologists*, **5**, 81–89.

DABORN, G. R. (ed.) 1991. Littoral Invesitgation of Sediment Properties, Minas Basin 1989, Final Report, ACER, Acadia University, ACER Publication 17.

DYER, K. R. 1970. Current velocity profiles in a tidal channel. *Geophysical Journal Royal Astronomical Society*, **22**, 153–161.

DYER, K. R. 1986. *Coastal and Estuarine Sediment Dynamics*. John Wiley & Sons.

EVANS, G. & COLLINS, M. B. 1975. The transportation and deposition of suspended sediment over the intertidal flats of the Wash. *In*:

HAILS, J. & CARR, A. (eds) *Nearshore Sediment Dynamics and Sedimentation*, Wiley, London, 273–304.

FLATHER, R. A. 1994. A storm-surge prediction model for the northern Bay of Bengal with application to the cyclone disaster in April 1991. *J. Physical Oceanography*, **24**, 172–190.

GROSS, T. F. & NOWELL, A. R. M. 1983. Mean flow and turbulence scaling in a tidal boundary layer. *Continental Shelf Research*, **2**, 109–126.

HANTZSCHEL, W. 1939. Tidal Flat deposits (wattenschlick). *In*: TRASK, P. D. (ed.) *Recent Marine Sediments*. Dover Publications Inc., 195–206.

HARVEY, J. G. & VINCENT, C. E. 1977. Observation of shear in near-bed currents in the southern North Sea. *Estuarine and Coastal Marine Science*, **5**, 715–731.

HEATHERSHAW, A. D. & SIMPSON, J. H. 1978. The sampling variability of the Reynolds stress and its relation to boundary shear stress and drag coefficient measurements. *Estuarine and Coastal Marine Science*, **6**, 263–274.

KE, X., COLLINS, M. B. & POULOS, S. E. 1994. Velocity structure and sea bed roughness associated with intertidal (sand and mud) flats and saltmarshes of the Wash, U.K. *J. Coastal Research*, **10**, 702–715.

KRUMBEIN, W. E., PATERSON, D. M. & STAL, L. J. (eds) 1994. *Biostabilisation of Sediments*. BIS-Verlag, Oldenburg.

PERILLO, G. M. E., DRAPEAU, G., PICCOLO, M. C. & CHAOUQ, N. 1993. Tidal circulation pattern on a tidal flat, Minas Basin, Canada. *Marine Geology*, **112**, 219–236

SHI, Z. & CHEN, J. Y. 1996. Morphodynamics and sediment dynamics on intertidal mudflats in China (1961–1994). *Continental Shelf Research*, **16**, 1909–1926.

SOULSBY, R. L. & DYER, K. R. 1981. The form of the near-bed velocity profile in a tidally accelerating flow. *J. Geophysical Research*, **86**, 8067–8074.

VAN SMIRREN, J. R. & COLLINS, M. B. 1982. Short-term changes in sedimentological and hydrographical characteristics over a sandy intertidal zone, the Wash, UK. *Geomarine Letters*, **2**, 55–60.

VAN STRAATEN, L. M. J. U. 1961. Sedimentation in tidal flat areas. *J. Alberta Society Petroleum Geologists*, **9**, 203–226.

VAN STRAATEN, L. M. J. U. & KUENEN, P. D. 1957. Accumulation of fine-grained sediment in the Dutch Wadden Sea. *Geologie en Mijnbouw*, **19**, 329–354.

WARTEL, S. (ed.) 1991. Characterisation of mud sediments. *Geomarine Letters*, **11** (Special Issue).

WELLS, J. T., ADAMS, C. E., PARK, Y.-A. & FRANKENBURG, E. W. 1990. Morphology, sedimentology and tidal processes on high-tide-range mudflats, west coast of South Korea. *Marine Geology*, **95**, 111–130.

WILKINSON, R. H. 1984. A method for evaluating statistical errors associated with logarithmic velocity profiles. *Geomarine Letters*, **3**, 49–52.

Considerations on wave-induced fluid mud streaming at open coasts

HUGO N. RODRIGUEZ & ASHISH J. MEHTA

*Coastal and Oceanographic Engineering Department,
University of Florida, Gainesville, FL 32611, USA*

Abstract: Wave-induced streaming of fluid mud at open coasts under damped, non-breaking waves is examined as a likely mechanism to explain nearshore bottom evolution in such an environment. For a two-layered, water-fluid mud domain in which mud is considered to be a viscous continuum, an expression for the streaming velocity is obtained. Preliminary data on alongshore streaming of fluid mud in a wave basin show an order of magnitude agreement with theory. Previous observations on the rates of mud movement along the coasts of Surinam, Guyana and Louisiana are shown to yield alongshore velocities that are commensurate with those obtained by considering streaming to be the prevalent cause of mud transport. These velocities are considerably lower than those which would occur due to breaking waves. Off the southwestern coast of India, shoreward streaming of mud under monsoonal waves results in the formation of shore-fast mudbanks. It is argued that among transport mechanisms which govern the dynamics of microtidal muddy coasts, streaming may be an important means by which fluid mud influences the formation, migration and dissipation mudbanks in areas where wave breaking is significantly attenuated by viscous damping.

Soft bottom mud, whose viscosity can be two to four orders of magnitude greater than that of water, characteristically causes the dissipation of significant fractions of the incoming wave energy at open coasts. In some cases, in excess of 90% of the offshore wave energy is dissipated with the result that waves practically disappear before they reach the shore. In this event, wave breaking, which can suspend and advect significant quantities of mud and thereby influence bottom profile evolution, tends to be weak and confined to a narrow littoral zone (Wells 1983; Mathew *et al.* 1995). Yet field observations suggest that even in that environment mud is transported, both cross-shore and alongshore, at significant rates (Wells 1983; Eisma *et al.* 1991; Mathew & Baba 1995). A question which naturally arises is: by what mechanism does this transport occur? Here we will explore mass transport under non-breaking waves along open coasts as a potential mechanism, a problem previously visited in the laboratory flume setting by, among others, Sakakiyama & Bijker (1989).

Mass transport in the wave direction over a hard bottom is a second order hydrodynamic effect arising from the co-variance of wave elevation and wave-induced velocity over the wave period (Dean & Dalrymple 1991). This effect manifests as an asymmetric motion of the fluid particle orbit such that the orbital loop is 'unclosed', due to a net forward motion of particles. The vertical distribution of the mass transport velocity over the water column is determined by the wave height and period, water depth and dissipation in the bottom boundary layer (Phillips 1966). In turn, the depth-mean

mass transport or streaming velocity, U_m, can be shown to be dependent on wave energy and speed (Dean & Dalrymple 1991). When hard bottom is replaced by fluid mud, the rate of transfer of momentum from water to mud and associated energy dissipation are considerably enhanced, and in the limiting case nearshore wave breaking ceases because the wave amplitude essentially vanishes. The problem examined here is whether the magnitude of U_m within fluid mud is commensurate with the rate of mud transport observed at microtidal coasts having highly dissipative mudbanks. In what follows, we will focus on laboratory and field assessments of a formula for the streaming velocity in a layer of fluid mud continuum beneath the water column subject to monochromatic progressive waves. Details of the analytic development of this formula are given elsewhere (Rodriguez 1997), and are briefly noted next.

Mud streaming

By way of liquefaction, waves can generate fluid mud, whose density is characteristically in the range of $1030-1300 \, kg \, m^3$ (Wells 1983). Mud within this range can be retained in this 'fluid-supported' state as long as wave-induced agitation continues; however, once wave action ceases, a particle-supported matrix with a measurable resistance to shear is rapidly re-established (Mehta 1996).

Focusing attention on wave-generated fluid mud, under non-breaking waves viscous dissipation of wave energy causes the wave-induced radiation stress, which is proportional to the wave

RODRIGUEZ, H. N. & MEHTA, A. J. 1998. Considerations on wave-induced fluid mud streaming at open coasts. *In*: BLACK, K. S., PATERSON, D. M. & CRAMP, A. (eds) *Sedimentary Processes in the Intertidal Zone*. Geological Society, London, Special Publications, **139**, 177–186.

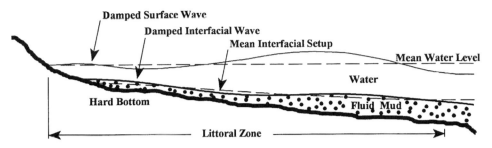

Fig. 1. Fluid mud interface setup under a non-breaking wave train.

energy, to decrease with distance along the wave direction (Dean & Dalrymple 1991). It can be shown that, because the wave–mean interfacial gradient in the wave direction is proportional to the negative of the corresponding gradient in the radiation stress, a decrease in the radiation stress with distance shoreward must imply a corresponding rise in the wave–mean interface, i.e. an interfacial setup (Longuet-Higgins 1972). Over dissipative mudbanks that are wide in the cross-shore direction and have gradually varying slopes, wave damping with distance can dominate the opposing effect of shoaling, thus leading to an interfacial setup shown qualitatively in Fig. 1. Here, the surface wave, and also the interfacial wave which lags the former, are shown to practically vanish by the time they reach the shoreline. Under this scenario the change in the mean water surface is typically small in comparison with the interfacial setup, because the former is scaled by the ratio of fluid mud density in excess of the water density divided by water density (Rodriguez 1997) .

As shown in Fig. 2, when the shoreward flux in momentum is not opposed by a shore-supported hydrostatic head, the setup will be equivalent to a mass transport with velocity U_{m} which, for obliquely incident waves (in the s-direction, subtending an angle α with the normal to the shoreline) will have cross-shore and alongshore

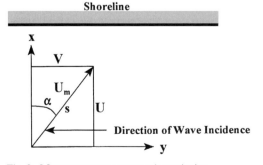

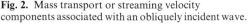

Fig. 2. Mass transport or streaming velocity components associated with an obliquely incident wave.

components, U and V, in the x- and y-directions, respectively (Longuet-Higgins 1972). Whereas U would cause mud to be transported toward shore, V would advect fluid mud alongshore. In turn, local gradients in the wave energy in the alongshore direction would mean corresponding gradients in V, which can result in localized accretion or erosion of the mud beach profile.

To calculate U and V, considering steady state, streaming is driven by the wave–mean pressure gradient due to setup. In a two-layered system the upper (water) layer may be assumed to be inviscid in comparison with the high viscosity of the lower (mud) layer. Within the fluid mud density range, mud is a non-Newtonian fluid in which the viscosity varies with the rate of shear (Williams & Williams 1989). Here, considering the need for analytic simplicity in dealing with dynamics within a 'mesoscale' coastal domain, we will assume fluid mud to possess a suitably representative mean viscosity. Then, from a balance between the net hydrostatic pressure force and viscous bottom stress, $\tau_0(s)$, the mean water velocity, U_{w}, and U_{m}, both as functions of distance, s, are easily obtained as

$$U_{\mathrm{w}}(s) = \frac{\tau_0(s)h_{\mathrm{m}}}{2\mu_{\mathrm{m}}} \qquad (1)$$

$$U_{\mathrm{m}}(s) = \frac{\tau_0(s)h_{\mathrm{m}}}{3\mu_{\mathrm{m}}} \qquad (2)$$

where h_{m} is the thickness of the fluid mud layer and μ_{m} is its viscosity. The water layer above fluid mud moves faster by a factor of 1.5 because the upper layer is characteristically less encumbered by bottom drag than the lower layer.

Once $U_{\mathrm{m}}(s)$ is obtained, following the convention of Fig. 2 the corresponding velocity components can be obtained from: $U(s) = U_{\mathrm{m}}(s)\sin\alpha$ and $V(s) = U_{\mathrm{m}}(s)\cos\alpha$. To use equation (2) for that purpose, it remains to determine τ_0, which can be evaluated from a steady-state force balance for the two-layered element of length Δs shown in Fig. 3. In this plot, $H(s)$ is the wave height which decreases with distance and $\bar{\eta}_m(s)$ is the interfacial setup. The corresponding surface setup, which is much smaller, $\bar{\eta}_w(s)$, is not shown. The result of force balance is

$$\tau_0(s) = [(h_w + \bar{\eta}_w - \bar{\eta}_m)\rho_w + (h_m + \bar{\eta}_m)\rho_m]g\frac{\partial\bar{\eta}_w}{\partial s}$$

$$+ [(h_m + \bar{\eta}_m + h_w + \bar{\eta}_w)\rho_m$$

$$+ (h_w + \bar{\eta}_w - \bar{\eta}_m)\rho_m]g\frac{\partial\bar{\eta}_m}{\partial s} \quad (3)$$

where h_w is water layer thickness, ρ_w is water density, ρ_m is mud density and g is acceleration due to gravity. In equation (3), τ_0 depends on distance, because the surface and interfacial setups and their gradients vary with s.

Eliminating τ_0 between equation (2) and (3), the following dimensionless expression for the streaming velocity results after discarding terms of order higher than two, because they are characteristically small in relation to those retained:

$$U_m^*(s^*)$$

$$= \frac{1}{3}\left(\frac{\rho_w H_0^2}{\mu_m T}\right)\left\{\frac{h_m^*\rho_m^*(2 - \rho_m^*)}{h_w^*(\rho_m^* - 1)}\overline{\eta_m^*\frac{\partial\overline{\eta_w^*}}{\partial s^*}}\right.$$

$$- \frac{h_m^*\rho_m^*(2 - \rho_m^*) + h_w^*(\rho_m^* - 1) + \rho_m^*h_w^*h_m^*}{h_w^*(\rho_m^* - 1)}$$

$$\times \overline{\eta_m^*\frac{\partial\overline{\eta_m^*}}{\partial s^*}} - [(h_m^* + h_w^*)\rho_m^* - h_w^*]\overline{\eta_m^*\frac{\partial\overline{\eta_w^*}}{\partial s^*}}\right\} \quad (4)$$

in which $U_m^*(s^*)$ is the dimensionless value of $U_m(s)$, H_0 is a characteristic offshore wave height and T is the wave period. Quantities superscripted by an asterisk are dimensionless values. To obtain them, normalization was carried out as follows: distance, s, by the characteristic wave length gT^2, depths and setups by H_0; U_m by the characteristic wave velocity H_0/T; and ρ_m by ρ_w, so that ρ_m^* is the specific gravity of fluid mud. Overbars denote wave–mean second order correlations of surface and interfacial oscillations, which vary with $s^* = s/gT^2$. The scaling term, $\rho_w H_0^2/\mu_m T$, is a characteristic streaming Reynolds number (Re), which must be small for mud flow to be nonturbulent.

It follows from equation (4) that U_m varies with distance, wave height, wave period, water depth, mud thickness, mud specific gravity and viscosity. To simplify the treatment, we will explore the behaviour of $\tilde{U}_m$, i.e. the mean value of U_m obtained by integrating it over the width of the littoral zone. The corresponding x- and y-velocity components will be $\tilde{U}$ and $\tilde{V}$.

Experimental evidence

Experiments were conducted at room temperature in a laboratory wave basin shown in plan form in Fig. 4, using tap water having a nominal density of 1000 kg m^{-3}. A brief description of the chemistry of this water source is provided by Parchure (1984). The flume consisted of a paddle-type wavemaker at one end, a mud bottom

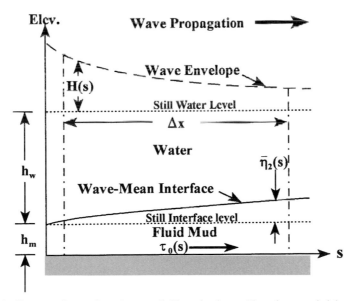

Fig. 3. Schematic diagram of wave-forced water–fluid mud column. Note the wave height envelope and the interfacial setup (the corresponding change in the mean level is not shown).

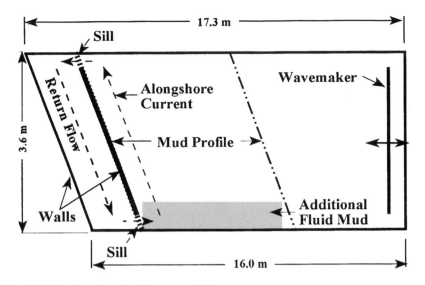

Fig. 4. Wave basin in plan view (not drawn to scale).

profile, and a flow return channel for alongshore streaming generated by obliquely approaching waves. The angle of wave incidence, α, was selected to be 20° in order to generate flows of measurable strength. Basin walls were covered with a layer of horse-hair to minimize any wave reflection.

The mud profile, with a mean slope of 1:40, was composed of a thixotropic mixture of a kaolinite and an attapulgite clays in equal proportion by weight. Feng (1992) has provided the mineralogical makeup of these two Floridian clays. The composite median (dispersed) particle size was c. 1.5 μm. Vertically the mud profile was composed of a dense, practically non-erodible lower layer of the clay mixture having a nominal density of 1400 kg m^{-3}, overlain by c. 2.5 cm thick fluid mud layer with a density of 1150 kg m^{-3} and a representative mean viscosity of 0.98 Pa s.

At the beginning of each test, fluid mud was carefully placed over the denser sediment, since the waves generated in the basin were found to be too small to generate the desired thickness of fluid mud, *in situ*, over the experimental time scales. The mean water depth over the profile was maintained at 0.1 m. Additional fluid mud forming a 1–2 cm thick layer was placed along the updrift end of the beach to serve as a sediment source. The wave height near the offshore toe of the profile was varied from 1.6 to 4.4 cm and the wave period from 1.2 to 3.9 s. The cross-shore mean alongshore flow over the 80 cm estimated width of the littoral zone was measured by

video-imaging coloured, 2.5 cm diameter and 1 cm thick, Styrofoam disc tracers. Since the tracers essentially measured the water layer velocity, the corresponding fluid mud velocity was obtained by dividing the measured value by 1.5, in accordance with equations (1) and (2). The density of the flowing mud was monitored by collecting fluid samples using a syringe pump in the vicinity of the downstream sill separating the main basin from the return channel. The crest of this sill, 5 cm below the still water level, as well as another on the updrift side, was kept flush with the mud profile, which was configured near the sills in such a way as to provide flow access between the main basin and the return flow channel.

For each setting of wave height and period, the wavemaker was actuated to generate five to six waves, as it was found that due to the laterally confining dimensions of the basin as well as some wave refraction, tests run over longer durations tended to generate horizontal circulation cells that interfered with the measurement of alongshore flow. In the analysis procedure, wave shoaling and breaking were accounted for, but refraction was ignored. For calculating a representative alongshore velocity over the littoral zone, the velocities of three tracers within the littoral zone were averaged from images corresponding to motion recorded during the last three waves.

For testing equation (4) it was essential to create a mud bottom profile over which waves would vanish before reaching the shoreline. In general, this condition can be met if the profile length is long in comparison with the wave length (Lee & Mehta 1997). In the basin used, the comparatively short wave travel distance resulted in wave damping and some breaking, so that the alongshore velocity was due to streaming as well as wave breaking. By considering these two effects to be linearly additive, the velocity generated by breaking was subtracted from the measured velocity for each run to determine the corresponding streaming velocity. For that purpose, the breaking wave-induced alongshore velocity was calculated from an expression developed by Longuet-Higgins (1972). In this expression, two significant quantities are the breaker height and the bottom resistance coefficient. Since the waves over the mud profile were characteristically non-sinusoidal with sharp crests and shallow troughs, the breaker height was determined from the measured wave height near the toe of the bottom profile by using the non-linear stream function analysis of Dean (1974). The bottom resistance coefficient was obtained by running a separate series of tests using the same ranges of wave height and period, but without fluid mud, and calibrating the expression for longshore velocity due to breaking. This calculation was thus based on the assumption that in the breaker zone, fluid mud did not significantly alter bottom resistance.

Equation (4) requires a knowledge of the surface and interfacial wave profiles over the littoral zone for calculating the three correlation terms (with overbars). It can be shown from the wave-mud modelling work of Jiang & Mehta (1996) that:

$$\overline{\eta_w^* \frac{\partial \eta_w^*}{\partial s^*}} = -\frac{gT^2}{8} k_i e^{-2k_i s};$$

$$\overline{\eta_m^* \frac{\partial \eta_m^*}{\partial s^*}} = -\frac{gT^2}{2} \frac{b^2}{H_0^2} k_i e^{-2k_i s};$$

$$\overline{\eta_m^* \frac{\partial \eta_w^*}{\partial s^*}} = -\frac{gT^2}{4} \frac{b}{H_0} k_i e^{-2k_i s} \qquad (5)$$

in which b is the interfacial wave amplitude and k_i is the wave damping coefficient. These two quantities depend on the same input parameters as those required for solving equation (4). To calculate b and k_i, the second order analytic solutions of Jiang & Mehta (1996) for wave propagation over the water–mud column were used.

For the nine test runs carried out, a comparison between the measured and calculated streaming velocities is given in Fig. 5, in which the theoretically calculated value of $\bar{V} - \tilde{U}_m \cos(20°) = 0.342 \tilde{U}_m$ is included. The observed data smearing can be attributed ultimately to the small size of the basin, in which only low velocities of the order of a centimetre per second or less could be generated, and these were subject to measurement error due to flow gyres, which could not be entirely avoided. Furthermore, wave breaking and associated alongshore transport led to some contamination of data. Despite these experimental limitations however, it is

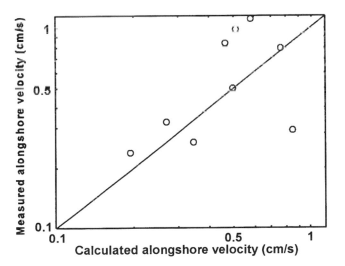

Fig. 5. Comparison between measured alongshore velocity due to streaming and corresponding values obtained from equation (4).

seen that the calculated and measured values are generally of the same order of magnitude. It was also found during the tests that the alongshore flow carried fluid mud of about the same density as that initially placed.

Muddy coasts

To examine the applicability of equation (4) in the prototype environment, we selected three open coasts where expansive and dissipative mudbanks occur: the northeastern shore of South America, the southern shore of Louisiana and the southwestern coast of India. At these locations, spatially organized patterns of deposited mud have developed as a result of characteristic variations in mud supply and wave climate.

The rhythmic mudbanks along the nearly 1500 km long contiguous coastlines of Surinam and Guyana are formed by trade-wind induced steady wave action from the northeast, in combination with a temporally pulsating supply of mud from the Amazon River (Fig. 6). The cross-shore amplitudes of the resulting mudbanks range from 10 to 30 km, and in the alongshore directions they are between 10 and 50 km wide (Augustinus 1987; Froidefond *et al.* 1988; Augustinus *et al.* 1989; Eisma *et al.* 1991). These banks, which absorb on the order of 90% or more of the incoming wave energy, migrate westward at a rate that varies between 0.5 and 2.5 km a^{-1} in

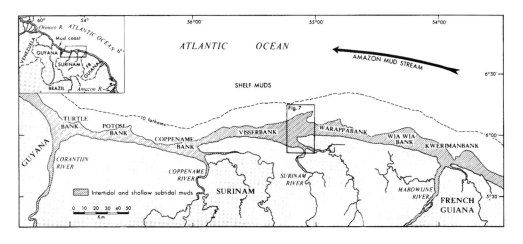

Fig. 6. Northeastern South America showing coastal mudbanks (after Wells 1983).

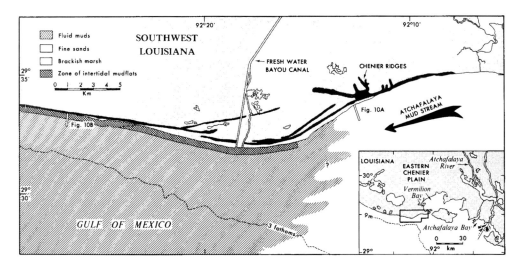

Fig. 7. Louisiana chenier plain showning fluid mud derived from Atchafalaya Bay to the east (after Wells 1983).

Surinam, and between 0.4 and 2.0 km a^{-1} in Guyana. This migration is believed to be largely due to obliquely incident waves, since the Guyana Current is too far offshore to act as the main transporting agent. The reason for the lower rates of transport in Guyana is a change in the shoreline orientation with respect to the wave direction, from 45° relative to the normal to the shoreline in Surinam to 25° in Guyana (inset of Fig. 6). Thus the less oblique waves in Guyana are less effective in transporting mud than in Surinam.

The undulant, wave-dominated mudbanks bordering the chenier plain in Louisiana west of the mouth of the Atchafalaya River result from a comparatively steady supply of mud from this river and seasonally-varying wave forcing in the Gulf of Mexico (Fig. 7). Cross-shore amplitudes of these undulations are considerably smaller than those in Surinam and Guyana, ranging between 0.5 and 3 km (Wells 1983; Kemp 1986). The nearshore mud has fluid-like consistency, with a characteristic westward drift of the order of 0.5–3 km a^{-1}. This mud also absorbs significant fractions of the incoming wave energy, although waves are not damped out as much as in Surinam.

The monsoonal mudbanks of Kerala in India tend to be shaped like semi-elliptical disks in plan form, and occur intermittently along a nearly straight sandy shoreline, giving it a

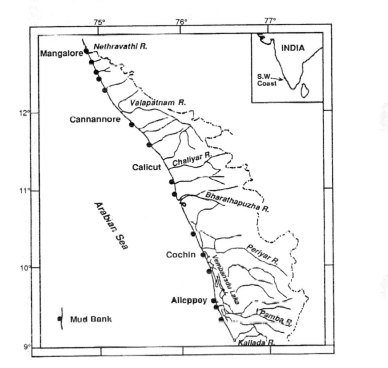

Fig. 8. Locations of monsoonal mudbanks along the southwest coast of India (after Mathew *et al.* 1995).

Table 1. *Relevant physical parameters for selected muddy coasts*

Parameter	Surinam/Guyana	Louisiana	India
Tidal range (m)	1.0–3.0	0.5–0.8	0.6–0.7
Wave height (m)	0.5–1.5	0.1–1.0	0.1–2.0*
Wave period (s)	5–10	5–6	7–9
Submerged bottom slope	1:1600–1:3000	1:1000	1:500–1:1000
Fluid mud thickness (m)	0.5–2.0	0.2–1.5	1.0–2.0
Fluid mud density (kg m^{-3})	1030–1250	1150–1300	1080–1300
Particle size (μm)	0.5–1	3–5	0.5–3
Mudbank cross-shore length (km)	10–30	0.5–3	0.5–3
Mudbank alongshore length (km)	10–50	1–5	2–8

* The higher value is for monsoonal waves.

crenulate appearance (Fig. 8). Cross-shore disk amplitudes range between 0.5 and 3 km. As Mathew & Baba (1995) have shown, shoreward transport of mud at the onset of the monsoon is influenced by wave refraction due to offshore bathymetry, and this leads to shore-fast mud-bank formation at known locations where wave energy is concentrated. As a result, monsoonal wave breaking activity shows a distinct variation ranging from practically nil in the mudbank areas to plunging breakers along the intervening sandy beaches. The shoreward fluid mud transport velocity at the onset of a monsoon in May–June each year is of the order of 0.3–0.9 km day^{-1}. Toward the end of the monsoon in August the associated decrease in wave energy leads to a gravity slide of fluid mud toward a deeper water mud sink, where it remains until the next monsoon.

Relevant characteristic parameters for the selected locations are summarized in Table 1. The tidal ranges indicate that these areas are microtidal (<2 m) except during spring tide in Surinam/Guyana, which is mesotidal. However, the mean tidal range there is 1.8 m. Also given are wave height and period, submerged bottom slope, thickness of the fluid-like mud layer, its density, dispersed particle size, cross-shore length (amplitude) of mudbank and its along-shore extent. The characteristic velocity of mud transport is alongshore in Surinam/Guyana and Louisiana, and cross-shore in India.

Field velocities

Because of the great complexity of the flow field in the prototype environment, the analytic idealizations considered for calculating fluid mud streaming result in an inherently crude formula for predicting actual velocities. Further-more, measurements of streaming rates in Surinam, Guyana and Louisiana are based on net movements of the mudbanks, which inte-grate the effects of flow intensity changes, flow reversals, sediment deposition and resuspension. The data for cross-shore streaming in India are more direct because the distance over which fluid mud travels from offshore to nearshore is approximately known, and because during this travel fluid mud is believed to remain largely intact, without undergoing significant cycles of deposition and resuspension. In any event, representative values of the relevant physical parameters required to solve equation (4) are selected in Table 2, in which cross-shore mudbank amplitudes are chosen to represent littoral zone widths. Representative mean mud viscosity for Surinam and Guyana was obtained by calibrating the model of Jiang & Mehta (1996) using wave damping data reported by Wells (1983). Mud viscosity for Louisiana was determined similarly from previously obtained prototype data on wave damping in the Gulf of Mexico (Lee & Mehta 1997). For India, rheo-metric measurements on bottom mud carried

Table 2. *Selected values of relevant parameters for calculation of mud streaming velocity*

Location	Wave height (m)	Wave period (s)	Littoral zone (km)	Water depth (m)	Mud thickness (m)	Mud specific gravity*	Mud viscosity (Pa s)
Surinam/Guyana	1.0	9	11.5	3.0	1.0	1.08	1.3
Louisiana	0.6	5	1.5	1.0	0.5	1.17	1.6
India	2.0	7	0.5	6.0	1.5	1.07	0.5

*To obtain the corresponding density, multiply by the selected salt water density of 1027 kg m^{-3}.

Table 3. *Calculated streaming velocities and measured characteristic velocity ranges*

Location	Cross-shore velocity, $\tilde{U}$ (km day^{-1})	Angle of wave incidence, α (deg)	Alongshore velocity, $\tilde{V}$ (km a^{-1})	Measured velocity range	Streaming Reynolds number, Re	Alongshore velocity due to breaking*
Surinam	–	45	1.7	0.5–2.5 (km a^{-1})	88	9500
Guyana	–	25	1.0	0.4–2.0 (km a^{-1})	88	5700
Louisiana	–	15	2.3	0.5–3.0 (km a^{-1})	46	9150
India	0.3†	–	–	1.2–2.4 (km day^{-1})	1170	–

*Calculated by using the formula of Longuet-Higgins (1972). Wave shoaling was determined by the method of Dean (1974). Wave refraction was ignored.
† Equivalent to 109.5 km a^{-1}.

out by Faas (1995) were used to calculate the viscosity.

Calculated streaming velocities are compared with mud transport rates in Table 3, in which the wave approach angles are based on dominant wave conditions in the littoral zone. The streaming Reynolds number, Re, is seen to range from 46 to 88 for Surinam/Guyana and Louisiana, indicating a viscous regime, as required for using equation (4). Observe that at these sites the calculated velocity is within the bounds of measurement. For mud transport in India the Re value is considerably higher (1170), but not high enough to violate the viscid flow assumption in equation (4) (Kamphuis 1975). The measured and computed velocities in India agree reasonably well. In general, however, because there is considerable uncertainty in the values of all input parameters for equation (4), the agreement between measurements and predictions may be fortuitous. Yet we note that this high degree of correspondence suggests that the physical premise upon which equation (4) is based seemingly captures the dominant causative factor of mud streaming, i.e. incident waves. It should also be noted that if the alongshore current generated by breaking waves over a hard bottom was assumed to be responsible for mud transport, the rate of motion would considerably larger, as shown in Table 3. These numbers only have a qualitative significance, because wave refraction was ignored in their calculation. Refraction would reduce the alongshore current values; however, they would still remain considerably larger than those due to streaming.

The cross-shore transport rate from India ($0.3 \, \text{km day}^{-1}$) is obtained directly from equation (4), because $\bar{U} = U_m$. Note that the rate (equivalent to $109.5 \, \text{km a}^{-1}$) is both measured and predicted to be considerably higher than that at the other three locations, notwithstanding the difference in the direction of transport. Observe however from Table 2 that the input parameters for India seemingly do not differ significantly from those at the other locations to cause streaming of fluid mud in India to differ significantly from streaming elsewhere, irrespective of the direction of transport. To examine this apparent disparity, in Table 4 we have reported, for all the sites, calculated values of a characteristic interfacial wave amplitude, b_0, i.e. its value corresponding to the input offshore wave height H_0, the wave damping coefficient, k_i, and the three correlation terms in equation (4). The wave damping coefficients are in general commensurate with those obtained in prototype muddy environments (Lee & Mehta 1997). However, the values of these and the other parameters do not explain the high velocity in India. It can also be shown that multiplying the three correlation terms with their corresponding coefficients in equation (4) would not change this observation. It follows that the main difference is due to scaling by Re, which as noted is considerably higher for the conditions in India than elsewhere (Table 3). This high value is due to the combination of high waves and low mud viscosity, both germane to rapid mud transport.

Concluding comments

The results suggest that the mass transport mechanism for mud motion, in areas where wave damping precludes a significant contribution by wave breaking, can be encapsulated by a treatment which considers mud to be a viscous continuum driven by non-breaking waves. This approach may have further merit in examining some of the intriguing features of muddy coasts, including the way in which they develop rhythmic patterns. As noted, modes by which such features are dependent on the variabilities in mud supply and wave climate. However, other causative factors may also be present, such as the self-organizing mechanistic modes that generate rhythmic beach cusps (Werner & Fink 1993). It may thus be feasible to invoke the continuum hypothesis for the simulation of undulant mudbank patterns.

The predictive technique would improve if depth variation with distance was accounted for; however, in that case the solution to the governing equations will in general have to be

Table 4. *Magnitudes of and correlation terms in equation (4) and characteristic parameters in equation (5)*

Location	Characteristic interfacial amplitude, b_0 (m)	Wave damping coefficient, k_i ($1 \, \text{m}^{-1}$)	$\overline{\eta_w^* \dfrac{\partial \eta_w^*}{\partial s^*}}$	$\overline{\eta_m^* \dfrac{\partial \eta_w^*}{\partial s^*}}$	$\overline{\eta_m^* \dfrac{\partial \eta_m^*}{\partial s^*}}$
Surinam/Guyana	0.22	0.00039	-5.4×10^{-6}	-2.4×10^{-6}	-1.1×10^{-6}
Louisiana	0.17	0.00250	-4.2×10^{-5}	-2.4×10^{-5}	-1.4×10^{-5}
India	0.32	0.00010	-1.2×10^{-5}	-3.8×10^{-6}	-1.2×10^{-6}

numerical, rather than analytical. To achieve a proper validation of theory, laboratory experiments will have to be conducted in facilities that are larger than the one used. To that end, the main criteria that must be met include complete or near-complete absorption of wave energy by mud, and generation of measurable mud flows.

Further prototype data collection efforts must seek to obtain temporal and spatial rates of mud streaming, as distinct from mean rates of translation of mudbanks. The coast of Kerala seems to provide such an opportunity because there, in the absence of significant supplies of riverine sediment, it should be feasible to establish a mesoscale mud mass balance as an essential step in determining accurate mud transport rates.

References

AUGUSTINUS, P. G. E. F. 1987. The geomorphologic development of the coast of Guyana between the Corentyne River and the Essequibo River. In: GARDINER, V. (ed.) International Geomorphology 1986 Part I. Wiley, London, 1281–1292.

——, HAZELHOFF, L. & KROON, A. 1989. The chenier coast of Suriname: modern and geological development. Marine Geology, 90, 269–281.

DEAN, R. G. 1974. Evaluation and development of water wave theories for engineering application, CERC Special Report No.1, Vols 1 and 2, U.S. Army Corps of Engineers, Fort Belvoir, VA.

—— & DALRYMPLE, R. A. 1991. Water Wave Mechanics for Engineers and Scientists. World Scientific Publishing, Singapore.

EISMA, D., AUGUSTINUS, P. G. E. F. & ALEXANDER, C. 1991. Recent and subrecent changes in the dispersal of Amazon mud. Netherlands Journal of Sea Research, 28, 181–192.

FAAS, R. W. 1995. Mudbanks of the southwest coast of India III: role of non-Newtonian flow properties in the generation and maintenance of mudbanks. Journal of Coastal Research, 11, 911–917.

FENG, J. 1992. Laboratory experiments on cohesive soil bed fluidization by water waves, UFL/COEL-92/005, Coastal and Oceanographic Engineering Department, University of Florida, Gainesville, Florida.

FROIDEFOND, J. M., PUJOS, M. & ANDRE, X. 1988. Migration of mud banks and changing coastline in French Guiana. Marine Geology, 84, 19–30.

JIANG, F. & MEHTA, A. J. 1996. Mudbanks of the southwest coast of India: wave attenuation. Journal of Coastal Research, 12, 890–897.

KAMPHUIS, J. W. 1975. Friction factor under oscillatory waves. Journal of the Waterways, Harbors and Coastal Engineering Division of ASCE, 101, 135–144.

KEMP, G. P. 1986. Mud Deposition at the Shoreface: Wave and Sediment Dynamics on the Chenier Plain of Louisiana. PhD Thesis, Louisiana State University, Baton Rouge, LA.

LEE, S.-C. & MEHTA, A. J. 1997. Problems in characterizing dynamics of mud shore profiles. Journal of Hydraulic Engineering, 123, 351–361.

LONGUET-HIGGINS, M. S. 1972. Recent progress in the study of longshore currents. In: MEYER, R. E. (ed.) Waves on Beaches and Resulting Sediment Transport. Academic Press, New York, 203–248.

MATHEW, J. & BABA, M. 1995. Mudbanks of the southwest coast of India II: wave mud interactions. Journal of Coastal Research, 11, 179–187.

——, BABA, M. & KURIAN, N. P. 1995. Mudbanks of the southwest coast of India I: wave characteristics. Journal of Coastal Research, 11, 168–178.

MEHTA, A. J. 1996. Interaction between fluid mud and water waves. In: SINGH, V. P. & HAGER, W. H. (eds) Environmental Hydraulics. Ch. 5, Kluwer, Dordrecht, The Netherlands, 153–187.

PARCHURE, T. M. 1984. Erosional Behavior of Deposited Cohesive Sediments. PhD Thesis, University of Florida, Gainesville, Florida.

PHILLIPS, O. M. 1966. The Dynamics of the Upper Ocean. University Press, Cambridge, UK.

RODRIGUEZ, H. N. 1997. A mechanism for non-breaking wave-induced transport of fluid mud at open coasts, UFL/COEL-97/004, Coastal and Oceanographic Engineering Department, University of Florida, Gainesville, Florida.

SAKAKIYAMA, T. & BIJKER, E. W. 1989. Mass transport velocity in mud layer due to progressive waves. Journal of Waterway, Port, Coastal and Ocean Engineering, 115, 614–633.

WELLS, J. T. 1983. Dynamics of coastal fluid muds in low-, moderate-, and high-tide-range environments. Canadian Journal of Fisheries and Aquatic Sciences, 40, 130–142.

WERNER, B. T. & FINK, T. M. 1993. Beach cusps as self-organizing patterns. Science, 260, 968–970.

WILLIAMS, D. J. A. & WILLIAMS, P. R. 1989. Rheology of concentrated cohesive sediments. Journal of Coastal Research, 5, 165–173.

The impact of fluid shear and the suspended sediment concentration on the mud floc size variation in the Dollard estuary, The Netherlands

W. T. B. VAN DER LEE

Institute for Marine and Atmospheric Research Utrecht (IMAU), Department of Physical Geography, Utrecht University, P.O. Box 80.115, 3508 TC Utrecht, The Netherlands

Abstract: Observations of floc sizes in the Dollard estuary in a tidal channel and above a tidal flat were used to obtain more insight into the contributions of fluid shear and suspended sediment concentration to flocculation. The suspended sediment concentration dominated the floc sizes in the tidal channel. There was no visible effect of fluid shear disrupting the larger flocs. The fluid shear dominated the floc sizes above the tidal flat. Measured fluid shear in both environments was, however, comparable. The close proximity of the bed above the tidal flat, with high fluid shear along this boundary, may have caused floc breakup and resuspension of the mud. This near-bed floc breakup probably decreased floc sizes over the whole water column above the tidal flat.

Mud particles tend to clog together and form flocs that have a much larger settling velocity than the constituent particles. A downward vertical flux of sediment in the water is only possible when the settling velocity of the sediment particles is larger than the upward transport by turbulence. Flocculation therefore enables sedimentation. There would be little accumulation of fine-grained material, if the suspended fine sediment particles did not aggregate (Partheniades 1984; Van Leussen 1994). Floc sizes and settling velocities are determined by many physical factors like differential settling, fluid shear and the suspended sediment concentration (SSC). They are also determined by physico-chemical or biological factors like the presence of sticky biopolymers on the flocs, surface charge, salinity, etc. The presented research focuses on the relative contributions of, in particular, fluid shear and SSC to floc size and settling velocity in the Dollard estuary within a tidal cycle. Floc size variations in two environments, tidal channel and tidal flat, were studied to obtain more insight into the contribution of fluid shear and SSC to the flocculation/breakup process.

Theory

Flocculation is determined by the number of floc collisions (collision frequency) and the efficiency of these collisions in aggregation (collision efficiency). The collision frequency is determined by:

(1) Differential settling, i.e. falling flocs scavenging smaller flocs on their way down. This is particularly important in deeper water.
(2) Fluid shear or turbulence intensity. Increased turbulence causes an increased

collision frequency and thereby flocculation. However, it is also considered to be the most important limiting factor of floc size (Dyer 1989; Eisma 1986; Luettich *et al.* 1993; Van Leussen 1994). Larger flocs are more fragile and will break more easily due to turbulent shear (Dyer 1989).

(3) The number of flocs in suspension or the SSC. The more flocs there are in suspension, the higher the collision frequency. Several field studies in estuaries have shown that the median floc settling velocity increases with SSC raised to a power (Burt 1984; Dyer 1989; Pejrup 1988; Van Leussen & Cornelisse 1993*a*).

Both turbulence and SSC show the largest variation on the time scale of a tidal cycle. This paper focuses on the floc size variation within the tidal cycle as a function of both mentioned parameters. The collision efficiency is determined by physico–chemical or biological factors (biopolymers, surface charge, salinity) which mainly vary on larger time scales than the tidal cycle (e.g. seasonal variation in biopolymer concentrations). The collision efficiency is therefore assumed to be constant throughout the tidal cycle.

Dyer (1989) described the effects of fluid shear and SSC on floc size in a conceptual model (Fig. 1). An increase of SSC increases floc sizes, while an increase of shear stress only initially increases floc size due to an increased collision frequency of the suspended particles. Further increase of shear stress, however, causes flocs to break and decreases floc diameter.

A measure of turbulence intensity in the water column is the root mean square velocity gradient G, defined as the square root of the energy

VAN DER LEE, W. T. B. 1998. The impact of fluid shear and the suspended sediment concentration on the mud floc size variation in the Dollard estuary, The Netherlands. *In*: BLACK, K. S., PATERSON, D. M. & CRAMP, A. (eds) *Sedimentary Processes in the Intertidal Zone*. Geological Society, London, Special Publications, **139**, 187–198.

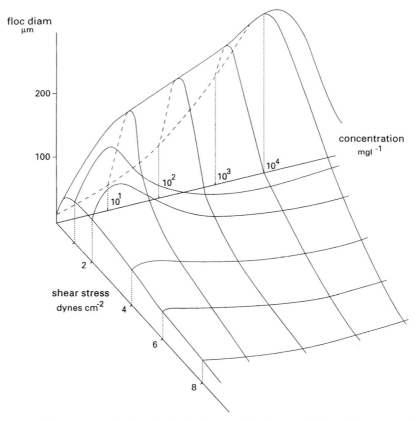

floc diam
μm

200

100

concentration
mgl $^{-1}$

10^4

10^3

10^2

10^1

2

shear stress
dynes cm^{-2} 4

6

8

Fig. 1. Conceptual diagram showing the relationship between floc diameter, SSC and shear stress (Dyer 1989).

dissipation ε divided by the kinematic viscosity ν of the fluid (Van Leussen 1994):

$$G = \sqrt{\frac{\varepsilon}{\nu}} \qquad (1)$$

It is reasonable to assume that the turbulent energy dissipation ε equals the turbulent energy production P (Van Leussen 1994):

$$\varepsilon = P = \frac{\tau}{\rho} \frac{\mathrm{d}U}{\mathrm{d}z} \qquad (2)$$

In the case of a logarithmic velocity profile:

$$\frac{\mathrm{d}U}{\mathrm{d}z} = \frac{u_*}{\kappa z} \qquad (3)$$

and assuming that the maximum shear τ at the bed decreases linearly to zero at the surface:

$$\frac{\tau(z)}{\rho} = u_*^2 \left[1 - \frac{z}{h} \right] \qquad (4)$$

then:

$$G(z) = \sqrt{\frac{u_*^2 \left[1 - \dfrac{z}{h} \right]}{\nu \kappa z}} \qquad (5)$$

where:

$G(z) =$ root mean square velocity gradient or turbulence intensity at level z;
$z =$ level above the bed;
$\varepsilon =$ turbulent energy dissipation;
$P =$ turbulent energy production;
$\nu =$ kinematic viscosity;
$\tau(z) =$ shear stress at level z;
$\rho =$ water density;
$U =$ current velocity;
$u_* =$ friction velocity;
$\kappa =$ Von Karman constant (≈ 0.4);
$h =$ water depth.

For the determination of $G(z)$, u_* needs to be determined from velocity measurements. In the case of a logarithmic velocity profile:

$$U(z) = \frac{u_*}{\kappa} \ln\left(\frac{z}{0.033k_s}\right) \qquad (6)$$

where:

k_s = bed roughness.

Field experiment

The research was carried out in the Dollard, which is the upper reach of the Ems–Dollard estuary (Fig. 2). This meso-tidal estuary may be classified as well mixed, even at high discharges (Van Leussen 1994). The tidal prism is $c.\,115 \times 10^6\,\mathrm{m}^3$ and the tidal excursion is $c.\,12\,\mathrm{km}$ (De Jonge 1992). In total, 85% of the Dollard consists of tidal flats along the main tidal channel 'Het Groote Gat'. The surface of the flats is quite smooth and uniform. The largest

regular bed forms are small wave ripples and dewatering channels are present on the lower parts of the flats.

On 11th and 19th October 1995 floc sizes and settling velocities were measured in the tidal channel 'Het Groote Gat' in the Dollard estuary (Fig. 2). Measurements took place throughout the tidal cycle with an underwater video camera, the Video *In Situ* (VIS) (Van Leussen & Cornelisse 1993*b*). The VIS was deployed from a research vessel floating with the current, in a quasi-Lagrangian approach. The VIS consists of an *in situ* settling tube in which the falling flocs are filmed by a videocamera (Fig. 3). During a VIS operation the measurement section in the settling tube was 2.9 m below the water surface. The VIS floated some 30 m away from the research vessel, and was connected to the research vessel by power and video cables. Floating with the current minimized the effect of turbulence around the VIS, which could

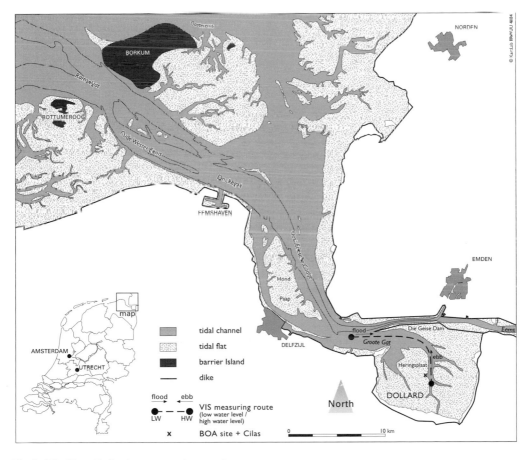

Fig. 2. The Ems–Dollard estuary and research area.

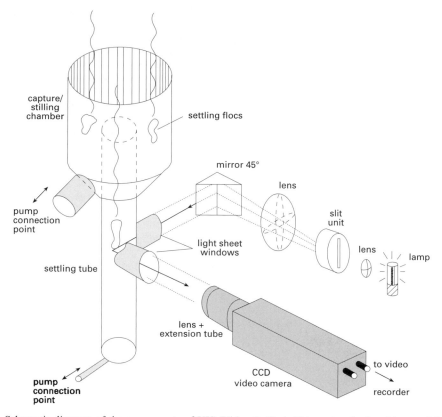

Fig. 3. Schematic diagram of the components of VIS (Video *In Situ*). This system is placed in a stainless steel underwater housing (Van Leussen & Cornelisse 1993*b*).

cause floc break-up. It also minimized the effect of horizontal advection on the measurement. Changes in suspended sediment concentration or floc sizes were therefore the result of local erosion/sedimentation or flocculation/break-up and not due to horizontal advection. Besides floc size measurements with the VIS, velocity and concentration profiles were also measured. Velocities were measured with an OTT-type propeller current meter and concentrations were measured by a pump sampling system and consecutive filtration over glass fibre filters. The velocity profile measurements required the ship to anchor. After each anchoring, the position of the original water column in which the preceding VIS measurement took place was calculated from the current velocity data. The ship sailed to this position before starting the next VIS measurement. A typical series of a VIS measurement, a measurement of the velocity and concentration profile and sailing to the original water column took *c*. 1 h and 15 min. This measurement series was continued throughout the tidal cycle. The tidal excursion of the VIS is shown in Fig. 2.

Simultaneously with the VIS measurements, floc sizes were measured by an *in situ* laser particle sizer (CILAS 925) on the adjacent tidal flat, the Heringsplaat. The Cilas consists of a 75 cm long tube with a diameter of 25 cm. The tube contains a laserdiode and a detector array, with a sensor unit with a measurement section of 30 mm on top of the tube. The Cilas was placed on the tidal flat in a frame with the sensor unit at 30 cm above the bed. At the same site there was also a platform (the 'BOA-site', Fig. 2) from which current velocities, SSC, wave heights, water levels and meteo data were measured. The output of the Cilas particle sizer is a particle size distribution of spherical particles. Since mud flocs are generally not spherical, this leads to inaccuracies in the measured size distributions. The values produced by the CILAS therefore needed to be considered as uncalibrated results. An attempt to intercalibrate the Cilas against the VIS in the tidal channel failed because there was too little overlap in instrument resolution. The VIS only distinguished flocs from 80 μm and larger; smaller flocs could be confused with noise pixels and were discarded from the analysis. The Cilas distinguished only flocs smaller than c. 290 μm. Trends of increasing or decreasing floc sizes were, however, perceived by both instruments. Therefore, only qualitative variations in particle size measured by the Cilas were used in the analysis of the data and not the absolute sizes.

Data analyses

Some collected field data needed some more data processing. The video recorded images from the VIS were digitized and processed to calculate floc diameters.

Fluid shear or turbulence intensity G experienced by the mud flocs needed to be calculated from the friction velocity u_* with equation (5). In the case of a stationary, uniform current and very accurate measurements of velocity at well-defined levels above the bed, the friction velocity u_* and bed roughness k_s can be derived from a logarithmic fit on the velocity data [equation (6)]. In an estuary, however, the current is not uniform and not stationary, which limits the logarithmic velocity profile to the near-bed region. In practice, the measured velocities and especially the measured levels above the bed in the Dollard were not accurate enough to calculate both u_* and k_s from the data. This was mainly caused by the movement of the research vessel on the waves in the channel and the low current velocities on the tidal flat. Bed roughness in the channel varied between 7×10^{-7} m and 5.3 m which is totally unrealistic. The median bed roughness k_s however was 0.03 m which is a more realistic value. For realistic calculations of u_* and G, a bed roughness k_s had to be estimated and u_* was calculated from the current velocity at one level above the bed assuming a near bed logarithmic velocity profile and zero velocity at $z = z_0 = 0.033 k_s$.

The bed roughness can also be expressed as a drag coefficient C_d where:

$$C_d = \left(\frac{\kappa}{\ln\left(\frac{z}{0.033 k_s}\right)} \right)^2 \qquad (7)$$

Drag coefficients were deduced from measurements in several estuaries by different authors. Lewis & Lewis (1987) found drag coefficients ranging from 0.0019 to 0.0131 on an ebb tide and C_d lying between 0.002 and 0.0053 on the flood in the Tees estuary. A drag coefficient of $C_d = 0.003$ at $z = 1$ m seems to be a reasonable estimate for estuarine studies according to Van

Leussen (1994) and Sternberg (1968). This corresponds to a k_s of 0.02 m, which agrees quite well with the median k_s of 0.03m found from the logarithmic fits. Therefore, $k_s = 0.02$ m was used for the calculation of current related friction velocities in the channel as well as on the tidal flat. While the uncertainties in estimating k_s are large, the impact of a 100% increase in k_s results in only 16% increase in G in the channel and a 26% increase in G above the tidal flat. The percentages differ because the velocity was measured at 1.1 m above the bed in the channel and at 0.079 m above the bed on the tidal flat.

On the tidal flat, waves also needed to be taken into account. Outside the wave boundary layer, the velocity profile under waves is different from a velocity profile without waves. This can be expressed by using an apparent roughness k_a due to waves instead of a k_s in equation (6). Based on analysis of experimental data from flumes with rippled beds, Van Rijn (1993) found.

$$\frac{k_a}{k_s} = e^{\gamma(\hat{U}_\delta/U)} \qquad (8)$$

where:

k_a – apparent roughness due to waves;
k_s = current related bed roughness;
$\hat{U}_\delta$ = peak orbital velocity near bed;
U = mean current velocity;
$\gamma = 0.8 + \phi - 0.3\phi^2$;
ϕ – angle between current and wave direction (in radians between 0 and π).

$\hat{U}_\delta$ and U were measured with an electromagnetic current meter that sampled at a 2 Hz frequency at 0.079 m above the bed on the tidal flat.

Results

The field data from the channel on 11th and 19th October 1995 showed similar results for both days. This proves that the findings are not only valid for one day. Only the data from 11th October 1995 will be presented here, since it is representative for both days.

Tidal channel data: results of the Video In Situ system

The results of the floc size measurements in the tidal channel are shown in Fig. 4(a–c). Figure 4(a) shows the tidal elevation and the bed level referenced to Dutch ordnance datum (N.A.P.). The bed level varies along the track of the VIS. The measurements started at low water at a deeper part of the estuary towards

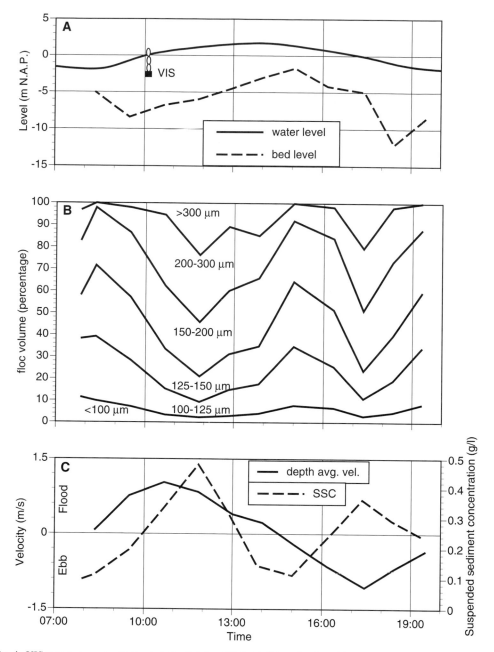

Fig. 4. VIS measurements, Dollard, 11th October 1995. (**a**) Water level and bed level against time. (**b**) Floc size distribution against time. (**c**) Depth averaged velocity and suspended sediment concentration in the VIS against time.

Delfzijl (Fig. 2). Then the VIS floated into the estuary until high water slack where it reached shallower water. After high water the VIS floated back to approximately its original position at low tide in deeper water again.

Figure 4(b) is an area chart that shows the measured floc size distributions. (Note that descending lines between the size classes mean increasing floc sizes and vice-versa.) Figure 4(c) presents the depth-averaged velocity and the

suspended sediment concentration in the settling tube of the VIS during the measurements.
Measured floc sizes ranged from 80 μm (detection limit) to 660 μm. Peaks in floc size appeared
at about one hour after maximum flood velocity and at maximum ebb velocity. At these
moments c. 20% volume percentage of the flocs
was larger than 300 μm. The peaks in floc sizes
correlate well with the peaks in SSC, correspond-

ing to the conceptual model of Dyer (1989).
There is no evidence of shear stresses disrupting
the larger flocs. While this does not mean that
floc break-up does not occur, it implies that SSC
dominates the flocculation process.

In Fig. 5(a, b) the floc size distribution and the
velocity and concentration profiles are plotted.
At the start of the measurements, after slack
water, increasing current velocities resuspended

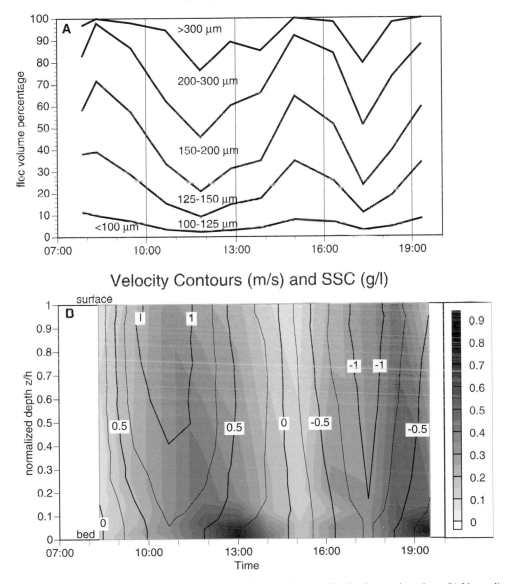

Fig. 5. VIS measurements, Dollard, 11th October 1995. (**a**) Floc size distribution against time. (**b**) Normalized
velocity profiles (contours) and SSC profiles (grey-scales) against time.

mud into the water column. This mud was quickly mixed through the water column, so no vertical concentration gradient developed. As the SSC increased, the floc size also increased.

This may be caused by either flocculation of smaller flocs or resuspension of larger flocs or both. This mixing process continued towards maximum flood velocity. When the flood current

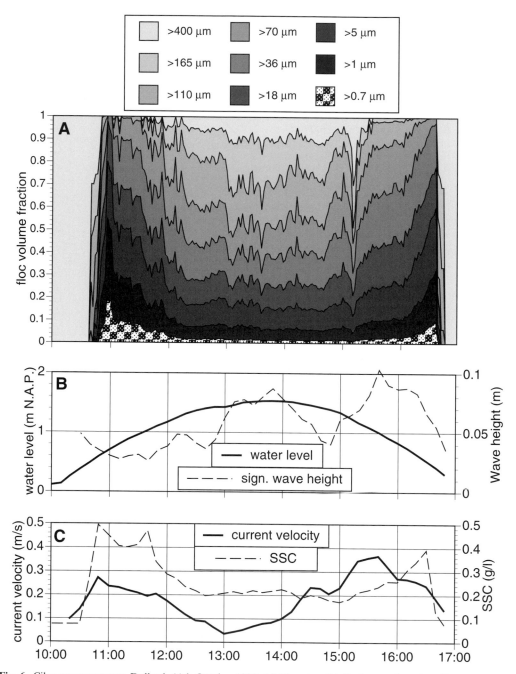

Fig. 6. Cilas measurements, Dollard, 11th October 1995. (**a**) Floc size distribution against time. Source: M. Ebben, National Institute for Coastal and Marine Management of the Ministry of Public Works and Transport. (**b**) Water level and significant wave height against time. (**c**) Current velocity and SSC against time.

velocity started to decrease, a vertical concentration gradient immediately developed. The current was no longer capable of keeping the larger flocs in suspension and therefore settling started. The maximum floc sizes appeared about one hour after maximum flood velocity, when the larger flocs were already settling and the SSC at the surface was decreasing. The SSC at the level of the VIS peaked however at this moment [Fig. 4(b, c)]. Differential settling may, however, also have enhanced floc size at this time. With further decreasing current velocities, the larger flocs kept settling, a lutocline developed and the floc sizes at the level of the VIS decreased again because the larger flocs had already passed towards the bed. At high water slack the settling sediment near the bed was deposited on the bed and the vertical concentration gradient disappeared. After high water slack a similar process occurred but now due to the ebb current. During ebb the maximum floc sizes appeared simultaneously with the maximum ebb current velocity [Fig. 4(b, c)], when the SSC in the VIS also reached its maximum value.

Tidal flat data: results of the Cilas laser particle sizer

Floc sizes on the tidal flat were measured with the Cilas laser particle sizer. As already stated above, the floc sizes measured by the Cilas are uncalibrated. Note that the Cilas was deployed on a fixed location so horizontal advection may have influenced the measurements. The floc size distribution, the water level and wave height, and the current velocity and SSC are presented in Fig. 6(a c), respectively. (Note that Fig. 6(a) is an area chart where descending lines between the size classes mean increasing floc sizes and vice-versa.) Only the high water period is shown since during low water the flat is emerged.

About half an hour after immersion, the flocs were relatively small and the flood velocity and SSC reached their maximum value. The second peak in SSC at about 11:45 h coincided with the concentration peak in the channel (Fig. 4c) and may be due to advection of sediment from the channel but may also be a coincidental event. Towards high water the current velocity and SSC decreased, but the floc sizes increased. During ebb the current increased to its maximum velocity of $0.36\,\mathrm{m\,s^{-1}}$ going along with a little increase in SSC. The peak of SSC however occurred just before emersion when the water was very shallow again. The floc sizes decreased again towards the end of the ebb tide.

Discussion

In contrast with the measurements in the tidal channel with a positive correlation between SSC and floc size, there is a negative correlation between SSC and floc size above the tidal flat. Large turbulence intensity due to currents and waves seems to inhibit the development of large flocs during flood and ebb tide. Larger flocs occurred only around high water slack, with low current velocities, larger water depth and, therefore, low relative wave height. This may have been caused by a decrease in turbulence intensity, but also by differential settling. The latter is however less likely because of the shallow water (max. 1.5 m) above the tidal flat. In the tidal channel, floc sizes are determined by the SSC, whereas above the tidal flat, floc sizes seem to be dominated by the shear stresses.

In Fig. 7(a) the current velocity in the channel and the turbulence intensity G at the level of the VIS are plotted. In the channel, obviously G depends on the current velocity. G ranged from $0.9\,\mathrm{s^{-1}}$ at slack tide to $11.2\,\mathrm{s^{-1}}$ at 17:25 h during maximum ebb current when the water was quite shallow (c. 5 m depth) and the VIS was relatively close to, but still 1.9 m above, the bed. In Fig. 7(b) current velocity, wave height and G above the tidal flat are plotted. A distinction was made for G due to the current and G due to current and waves combined. G was calculated at the level of the Cilas at 30 cm above the bed. Since there were only small waves, the waves do not contribute very much to the turbulence intensity. Only at 13:50 h a peak in wave-generated shear appears but this is probably due to a measurement error in the orbital velocities because the peak does not appear in the wave height data. Above the tidal flat G ranged from 1 to $14.8\,\mathrm{s^{-1}}$. This is about the same range as measured in the tidal channel. The ranges of SSC are also comparable in both the tidal channel and above the tidal flat. The Cilas data Fig. 6(a) however suggest that the decrease in floc size at maximum current velocity is caused by floc break-up due to large shear (G). Since G above the tidal flat is not significantly larger than G in the tidal channel another explanation needs to be found. There are three hypotheses for the differences in floc size behaviour between the tidal flat and the tidal channel:

(1) *Advection*. Horizontal advection of flocs may cause changes in floc size distribution. On the flood tide the water comes from the tidal channel. Since the course of floc sizes in the tidal channel do not correlate with the course of floc sizes above the tidal flat, it is

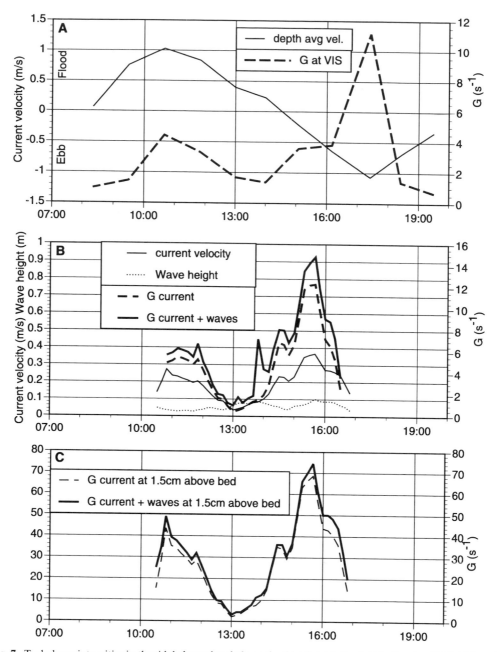

Fig. 7. Turbulence intensities in the tidal channel and above the tidal flat, Dollard, 11th October 1995. (**a**) Depth averaged velocity and turbulence intensity in the tidal channel. (**b**) Current velocity, wave height and turbulence intensities at 30 cm above the tidal flat. (**c**) Turbulence intensities at 1.5 cm above the tidal flat.

not likely that the floc size variation above the tidal flat can be explained by advection.

(2) *Instrument induced turbulence*. The Cilas instrument is quite large in a fairly large frame. Therefore, the instrument itself may

have generated turbulence and may have been capable of floc break-up during higher current intensity. The sensor unit is, however, quite small and most of the time there were no frame elements upstream of the sensor unit (depending on the current direction). This makes floc break-up due to instrument induced turbulence less likely but not impossible.

(3) *Near-bed shear*. Near the bed, the turbulence intensity G can be very large. As an example, the turbulence intensity at 1.5 cm above the tidal flat is plotted in Fig. 7(c). G ranges from $3\,s^{-1}$ at slack tide to $74\,s^{-1}$ at maximum ebb velocity. This very high near-bed shear is probably capable of floc break-up. Mehta and Partheniades (1975) stated that the strong shear and lift forces near the bed control the size distribution of the flocs in suspension. Van Leussen (1994) distinguished a number of turbulent zones in the water column. The flocs are continuously moving through these zones in a continuous process of flocculation and break-up resulting in the ultimate floc size. In the tidal channel the near bed shear is also very high, however the water is much deeper and therefore the frequency by which flocs move through the near-bed region is lower. This might explain why shear seems to dominate floc sizes above the tidal flat and SSC seems to dominate floc sizes in the tidal channel.

The floc sizes measured with the Cilas may have been influenced by instrument induced turbulence as well as near-bed shear. Although floc break-up due to instrument induced turbulence is less likely than break-up due to near bed shear, it is not possible to determine from the Cilas measurements how important the contribution of near-bed shear is to the floc size distribution. The impact of near-bed shear on the floc sizes throughout the water column on the tidal flat is most probably higher than in the channel because of the close proximity of the bed.

It seems that SSC dominates the floc size as long as turbulence and the floc size itself are below a certain limit. The channel measurements show that SSC dominates floc sizes when $G < 14\,s^{-1}$. Very large flocs may, however, be so fragile that they will break under this fluid shear intensity. Near the bed the shear is so high that it may also cause break-up of smaller flocs. This is very important for the sedimentation of mud in estuaries because flocculation could produce large flocs that settle to the region near the bed. These flocs may break and be resuspended in the water column, which inhibits deposition. This may cause large SSC near the bed as can be seen in Fig. 5(b). Only at slack tide, when the near bed shear is much lower, does actual sedimentation occur.

Conclusions

In October 1995 strong variations of floc sizes in the Dollard occurred within the tidal cycle. In the channel these variations correlated directly with the SSC and indirectly with the current velocity. Increasing current velocities caused increasing SSC, increasing floc sizes and good vertical mixing. Decreasing current velocities coincided with settling of larger flocs and the development of a vertical concentration gradient. It is possible that the high shear near the bed disrupted the large flocs and inhibited sedimentation. Deposition of mud to the bed was only observed with further decreasing current velocities.

Above the tidal flat the fluid shear instead of SSC seemed to dominate the floc sizes. Only at high water slack, did fluid shear not inhibit floc growth. The measured fluid shear and SSC above the tidal flat were, however, comparable to SSC and fluid shear in the tidal channel. The close proximity of the bed above the tidal flat, with high fluid shear along this boundary, may have caused floc breakup and resuspension of the broken flocs during ebb and flood tides, which explains the smaller flocs above the tidal flat during high current velocities. This is in contrast with the tidal channel where the water is deeper and the frequency by which flocs approach the bed is much lower, which explains why SSC is able to dominate floc sizes in the tidal channel.

The investigations were supported by the Netherlands Geosciences Foundation (GOA/NWO) and by the European Community grant MAS3-CT95-022-INTRMUD. The author would like to thank the National Institute for Coastal and Marine Management for the use of the Video *in Situ* and M. Ebben of the same institute and A. van Beuzekom for the use and processing of Cilas data. Also 'Rijkswaterstaat, Meetdienst Noord' is thanked for the use of the RV Regulus and RV Dr Ir. Johan van Veen. The author is grateful to the crew of both vessels and especially M. Hansen for their hospitality and contributions to the measurements, to R. Visser, D. Timmer, J. Croqué and T. Provily for their help with data collection and processing, to R. van der Ham for his advice in calculating turbulence intensities and to P. Hoekstra, J. Terwindt, W. ten Brinke and an anonymous reviewer for their comments on the manuscript.

References

Burt, T. N. 1984. Field settling velocities of estuary muds. *In*: Mehta, A. J. (ed.) *Estuarine Cohesive Sediment Dynamics. Lecture Notes on Coastal and Estuarine Studies*, **14**, Springer Verlag, Berlin, 126–150.

DE JONGE, V. 1992. *Physical processes and dynamics of microphytobenthos in the Ems estuary (The Netherlands)*. PhD Thesis, University of Groningen, The Netherlands.

DYER, K. R. 1989. Sediment processes in estuaries: future research requirements. *Journal of Geophysical Research*, **94**, 14 327–14 339.

EISMA, D. 1986. Flocculation and de-flocculation of suspended matter in estuaries. *Netherlands Journal of Sea Research*, **20**, 183–199.

LEWIS, R. E. & LEWIS, J. O. 1987. Shear stress variations in an estuary. *Estuarine, Coastal and Shelf Science*, **25**, 621–635.

LUETTICH, R. A., JR, WELLS, J. T. & SEOK-YUN, K. 1993. *In situ* variability of large aggregates: preliminary results on the effects of shear. *In*: MEHTA, A. J. (ed.) *Nearshore and Estuarine Cohesive Sediment Transport. Coastal and Estuarine Studies*, **42**, 447–466.

MEHTA, A. J. & PARTHENIADES, E. 1975. An investigation of the depositional properties of flocculated fine sediments. *Journal of Hydraulic Research*, **13**, 361–381.

PARTHENIADES, E. 1984. A fundamental framework for cohesive sediment dynamics. *In*: MEHTA, A. J. (ed.) *Estuarine Cohesive Sediment Dynamics. Lecture Notes on Coastal and Estuarine Studies*, **14**, Springer Verlag, Berlin, 219–250.

PEJRUP, M. 1988. Flocculated suspended sediment in a micro-tidal environment. *Sedimentary Geology*, **57**, 249–256.

STERNBERG, R. W. 1968. Friction factors in tidal channels with differing bed roughness. *Marine Geology*, **6**, 243–260.

VAN LEUSSEN, W. & CORNELISSE, J. M. 1993*a*. The role of large aggregates in estuarine fine-grained sediment dynamics. *In*: MEHTA, A. J. (ed.) *Nearshore and Estuarine Cohesive Sediment Transport. Coastal and Estuarine Studies*, **42**, 75–91.

—— & ——1993*b*. The determination of the sizes and settling velocities of estuarine flocs by an underwater video system. *Netherlands Journal of Sea Research*, **31**, 231–241

——1994. *Estuarine macroflocs and their role in fine-grained sediment transport*. PhD Thesis, Utrecht University, The Netherlands.

VAN RIJN, L. C. 1993. *Principles of Sediment Transport in Rivers, Estuaries and Coastal Seas*. Aqua Publications, Amsterdam, The Netherlands.

Comparison of flocculated and dispersed suspended sediment in the Dollard estuary

OLE MIKKELSEN & MORTEN PEJRUP

Institute of Geography, University of Copenhagen, Øster Voldgade 10, DK-1350 Copenhagen K, Denmark

Abstract: The purpose of this paper is to give a Lagrangian description of the changes in field settling diameter over a tidal period, while carrying out a tidal excursion with a research vessel. Settling tube analyses were carried out in the Dollard estuary, North-East Netherlands, by use of the Braystoke SK110 settling tube. From each tube settling velocity and grain size grading curves for the suspended material were computed. Subsequently, the sediment was dispersed from the filters and analysed in a laser diffraction analyser, a Malvern Mastersizer/E. The resulting grain size distribution of the primary particles was plotted together with the *in situ* distribution as bar diagrams. In this way it was possible to graphically determine the smallest equivalent floc size occurring in each sample as the intersect between the two distributions. Plotting this size against SSC, a linear relationship appeared. the greater the SSC, the smaller the smallest floc. It is suggested that this relates to high current velocities, at the same time causing both high values of SSC and high internal shear rates causing floc breakage. Plotting the settling velocities of the smallest floc against SSC yields an exponential relationship. Examples of the use of these relationships are presented. Flocs in the Dollard were larger than flocs sampled in the Danish Wadden Sea in earlier experiments. For comparative purposes, settling tube analyses were also carried out over the tidal flat.

It is well known that flocculation depends on several parameters, e.g. suspended sediment concentration, shear stress, salinity, organic coatings on the surface of the particles and mineralogy. As flocs grow, their diameter increases, but at the same time floc density decreases (Fennessy *et al.* 1997). However, the net result is that field settling velocities increase. An exponential relationship between suspended sediment concentration (SSC) and the median settling velocity (W_{50}) has been demonstrated by several authors (e.g. Dyer *et al.* 1996; Pejrup 1988; Puls *et al.* 1988; Burt 1986; Owen 1971). This relationship takes the form $W_{50} = a \cdot SSC^b$, where a and b are empirically-determined constants. Almost all investigations on this subject have been carried out from anchored vessels, giving an Eulerian description of the tidal variation of SSC, W_{50} and median settling diameter (D_{50}). In some of these investigations, the variation in SSC is found to explain up to 80% of the variation in W_{50} (Pejrup 1988; Pejrup & Edelvang 1996).

However, on any anchor station it must be acknowledged that measurements reflect both the immediate and local conditions, and the fact that material has been advected to the sampling point from locations with differing conditions. Therefore, changes in SSC are not necessarily just caused by changes in the local hydrodynamics. It may be that sediment is transported to the anchor station from a location where SSC is always higher or lower than at the anchor station, and where the hydrodynamical conditions are quite different from the conditions at the anchor station. This is very likely to influence the measured W_{50} and its relation to SSC.

The only way in which it is possible to separate the resultant effect of the local conditions from advective components is to carry out sampling in the Lagrangian mode. Andrade *et al.* (1991), Van Leussen & Cornelisse (1993) and Van Leussen (1997) have presented studies that make use of the Lagrangian sampling mode. This has, to the knowledge of the authors of this paper, not been used very often in estuaries when compared to the Eulerian mode. This probably relates to two factors: unawareness of the potential for the Lagrangian mode to differentiate the advective component from the resultant effect of the immediate local conditions and the fact that sampling in the Lagrangian mode can be more demanding with respect to manpower and/or equipment. For example, on an anchor station one only has to pay attention to the sampling protocol, and sampling can be carried out from even a small inflatable or a pontoon. If sampling is carried out in the Lagrangian mode in a tidal channel, one most often needs a research vessel and a crew constant on guard as the vessel drifts with the current. Furthermore, over the tidal flats it can be difficult to carry out Lagrangian sampling with a research vessel due to the limited water depth.

In this study, the same water body was followed during a tidal excursion to give a

MIKKELSEN, O. & PEJRUP, M. 1998. Comparison of flocculated and dispersed suspended sediment in the Dollard estuary. *In*: BLACK, K. S., PATERSON, D. M. & CRAMP, A. (eds) *Sedimentary Processes in the Intertidal Zone*. Geological Society, London, Special Publications, **139**, 199–209.

Lagrangian description of the tidal variation of SSC, W_{50} and D_{50} in order to minimize the advective component of the variation of SSC.

Study area

The Dollard is a well-mixed, meso-tidal, coastal plain estuary situated in the NE part of the Netherlands, near the German border. It comprises the SE part of the Ems–Dollard estuary (Fig. 1). The Ems discharges in the northern part of the estuary, but is partly separated from the Dollard itself by a wall, the Geisedamm. The total area of the Dollard basin is $c.\,112\,km^2$, of which the intertidal flats comprise $76\,km^2$, tidal channels and gullies $22\,km^2$ and marsh areas $14\,km^2$ (Dankers et al. 1984).The tidal range at Delfzijl is $2.79\,m$ while at Emden it is $3.03\,m$, increasing towards the SE of the Dollard (de Jonge 1988). The tidal prism is $c.\,145 \times 10^6\,m^3$ (Dankers et al. 1984) and the mean depth is $1.2\,m$ (de Jonge 1988). The mean depth at high water can thus be calculated to be $c.\,2\,m$.

Fieldwork and methods

On 29 May 1996, 16 settling tube analyses with the Braystoke SK110 settling tube (a derivative of the Owen Tube) were carried out at eight locations in the tidal channel Groote Gat (Fig. 1). Samples were taken, almost simultaneously, both near the surface and near the bottom. Sampling took place on board the Rijkswaterstaat vessel RV Regulus, while it carried out a tidal excursion from HW to HW (Fig. 2). On 30th May 1996, three settling tube analyses were carried out from the BOA Research Bridge, a fixed platform, situated adjacent to Groote Gat (Figs 1 and 2). A description of the Braystoke SK110 is given by Pejrup (1988) and Edelvang et al. (1992).

Ten subsamples of 200 ml each were withdrawn from each settling tube at logarithmic time intervals and filtered through preweighed $0.45\,\mu m$ Millipore CEM filters. The filters were dried at $65°C$ for $1\frac{1}{2}$ hrs, and the weight of sediment on each filter was determined with an accuracy of $0.2\,mg$. Preweighed blanks followed

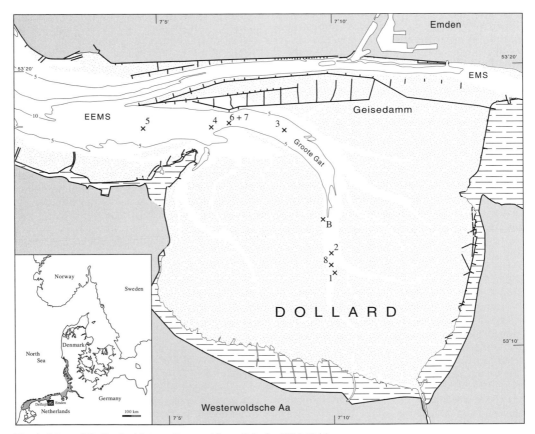

Fig. 1. Map of Dollard with sampling positions. B is the BOA Bridge.

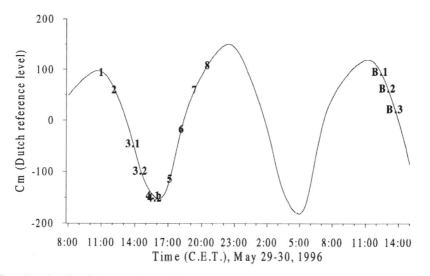

Fig. 2. Sampling time in relation to time on day and tidal stage.

the same procedure to determine whether or not the filters themselves gained or lost weight. A more detailed description of the sampling procedure is given by Pejrup & Edelvang (1996).

For each settling tube sample, the ten sub-sample filtered sediment weights were used to determine the *in situ* settling velocity and the equivalent size distribution of the suspended sediment, according to the method developed by Subcommittee on Sedimentation (1953). These are plotted as log/probability plots in Fig. 3.

Finally, the ten filters from each settling tube were dispersed in a solution of 0.002 M $Na_4P_2O_7$ and sonified for three minutes. The dispersed sediment was then analysed in a laser diffraction analyser, the Malvern Mastersizer/E, equipped with a 100 mm lens, capable of analysing grain sizes in the range 0.5–180 μm. The resulting grain size distributions were plotted as log/probability plots together with the *in situ* equivalent grain size distribution (Fig. 3). The standard deviation of the median diameter computed by the Malvern Mastersizer/E was determined by analysing one sample 31 times within 1 hour. The standard deviation of the median diameter of this one sample ($D_{50} = 9.08$ μm) was determined to be 0.2 μm. This shows the good reproducibility of the Malvern laser.

Results and discussion

A total of 19 settling tubes was sampled on 29–30th May. Of these, 17 were found to be useful for further analysis. All results are shown in Table 1.

Salinity

The mean salinity in the water body followed in Groote Gat was 18.6 whereas over the tidal flat it was 18.9. It is noteworthy that the salinity drops to 16.9 near the surface at position 5. When Figs 1 and 2 are compared, it is apparent that the vessel moved West against the flood-current between positions 4 and 5. The drop in salinity then relates to dilution with freshwater from the Ems, flowing in with the flood-current. It appears that it was not possible to follow exactly the same waterbody during the cruise.

Temperature

In Groote Gat, the mean temperature of the water on the 29th was 13.6°C, whereas over the tidal flat it was 16.0°C on the 30th. The difference relates to the fact that on the 29th it was cloudy, while on the 30th it was bright sunshine. Thus, the flats had been heated during exposure at LW. Therefore it was to be expected that settling velocities over the tidal flats could be slightly higher than in the tidal channel, due to the change in viscosity with temperature. However, this was not confirmed, as it was not possible to calculate W_{50} from any of the three settling tubes sampled over the tidal flat.

Flocculation

In Fig. 3 both the *in situ* and dispersed distributions are shown as log/probability plots.

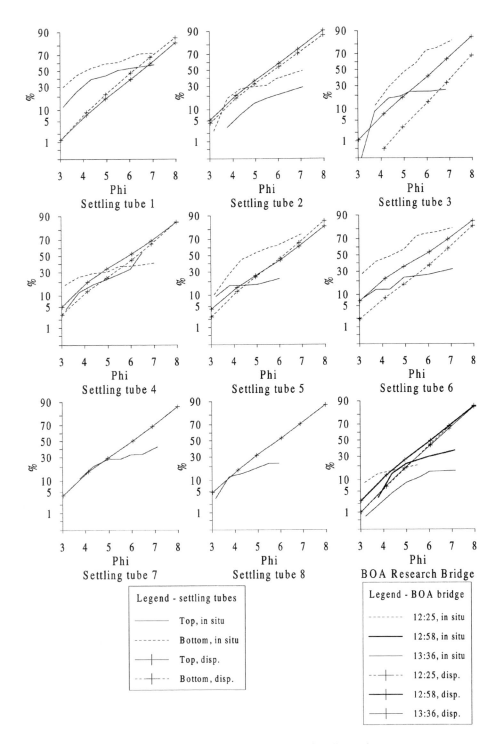

Fig. 3. Log/probability plots of *in situ* and dispersed distributions for all samples.

Table 1. *Results for all settling tubes sampled on 29–30 May 1996. D is sampling depth, Dt is total water depth, D_{50} is the median settling diameter, $D_{50}D$ is the median diameter after dispersion and sonification, W_{50} is the median settling velocity. Numbers in italics have been extrapolated from Fig. 3, the number of asterisks indicates the number of decades over which extrapolation has taken place*

Tube No.	Time	D (m)	Dt (m)	T (°C)	Sal. (0/00)	SSC (mg/l)	D_{50} (μm)	$D_{50}D$ (μm)	D_{50} (phi)	$D_{50}D$ (phi)	W_{50} (mm/s)
1	1100	1	4	12.9	18.7	29.1	22.9	10.9	5.5	6.5	0.4
	1104	3	4	12.6	18.7	26.0	58.7	13.9	4.1	6.2	2.5
2	1205	1	3.5	13.6	18.6	10.6	–	20.2	–	5.6	–
	1209	3	3.5	13.2	18.4	19.2	*6.8*	17.4	*7.2*	5.8	*0.06*
3	1350	2	5.7	13.3	18.8	26.5	*0.04****	11.9	*14.5****	6.4	–
	1425	4	5.0	14.9	18.7	145.4	28.2	5.8	5.2	7.4	0.6
4	1540	0.5	9.2	15.5	18.5	12.3	12.1	16.8	6.4	5.9	0.1
	1553	8	9.2	13.5	18.9	20.4	*0.9**	13	*10.1**	6.3	–
5	1710	0.5	7.8	13.3	16.9	12.4	–	12.4	–	6.3	–
	1712	6.5	7.8	13.2	19	19.9	38.4	13.6	4.7	6.2	1.1
6	1816	0.5	7.8	13.4	18.2	10.8	*2.9***	17.2	*8.4***	5.9	–
	1814	7	7.8	13.4	18.8	105.5	45.8	10.5	4.5	6.6	1.6
7	1924	0.5	6.8	14	18.8	13.2	*5.1***	15.2	*7.6***	6	–
	1926	6	6.8	13.7	19	–	–	–	–	–	–
8	2033	0.5	4.8	13.7	18.4	13.1	–	16.7	–	5.9	–
	2035	4	4.8	13.5	18.9	211.4	–	8.8	–	6.8	–
B.1	1225	0.4	0.8	15.5	19.2	13.0	*0.03****	13.2	*15.0****	6.2	–
B.2	1258	0.4	–	15.2	18.9	10.5	*3.6***	14.7	*8.1***	6.1	–
B.3	1336	0.2	0.4	17.2	18.6	21.6	–	12.6	–	6.3	–

The near bed *in situ* distributions are always coarser than the surface *in situ* distributions. Furthermore, it is seen that the coarse fractions are reduced substantially after sonification. For example, in settling tube 1, before sonification, up to 55% of the sample was coarser than 4.5Φ (44 μm), whereas after sonification, this fraction was reduced to 14%. In general, the median diameter (D_{50}) was strongly reduced after sonification. Before sonification, D_{50} was in the range 5.5Φ–4.1Φ (22 μm–58 μm), whereas after, it dropped to 6.5Φ–6.2Φ (11 μm–14 μm). Together, these observations are a strong indication of flocculation. It can be seen from Fig. 3 that the dispersed grain size distribution for all samples takes a Gaussian form. It can also be seen, that no difference in D_{50} between the tidal flat and the channel exists after sonification.

Converting the log/probability plots in Fig. 3 to bar diagrams with 0.5Φ intervals (Fig. 4) reveals a clearer picture of which fractions are broken by sonification. In the following it is assumed that the smallest equivalent floc size can be determined as the Φ-value where the dispersed distribution intersects the *in situ* distribution in the bar diagrams.

It is of course different diameters that are compared; settling diameter vs spherical diameter. However, as the flocs get smaller their density increases and gets close to particle density (Dyer *et al.* 1996; Fennessy *et al.* 1994).

Therefore, at the intersect the two different diameters may be considered comparable. However, a very high content of organics in the sediment will cause problems.

In situ *floc sizes*. From Fig. 4 it appears that in settling tube 1, the flocs are coarser than 4.5Φ at the bottom as well as near the surface, as this fraction is significantly reduced after sonification. Near the surface, the fractions 4.5–5Φ (32–44 μm) and 5–6.5Φ (11–22 μm) increased, suggesting that mainly these fractions make up the flocs. Near the bottom, flocculation takes part especially in the fraction 5–5.5Φ (22–32 μm). In tube 3 (bottom) the flocs were coarser than 6Φ (16 μm), made up of particles mainly smaller than 6Φ. In tube 5 (bottom) the flocs were coarser than 4.5Φ (44 μm), consisting mainly of particles smaller than 5.5Φ (22 μm). Finally, in tube 6 (bottom) the flocs were coarser than 5.5Φ, made up of particles finer than this size.

From these findings it can be concluded, that in the Dollard estuary, the flocculated sediment has settling diameters larger than 6Φ (16 μm) in the investigated tidal period and that a rather large percentage of the flocs have settling diameters coarser than 3Φ (125 μm).

Research in the Danish Wadden Sea over the last decade has revealed that the flocs in this area have settling diameters in the range 4.5–6Φ (16–44 μm) (Pejrup 1988, 1991; Edelvang &

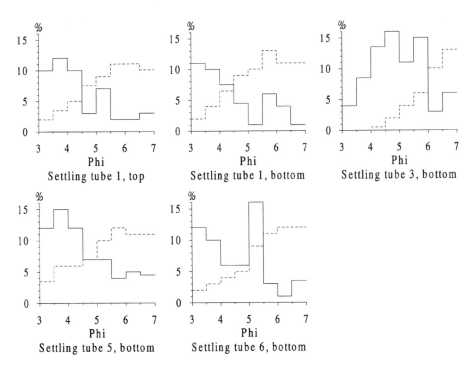

Fig. 4. Bar diagrams of *in situ* and dispersed distributions for five settling tubes.

Larsen 1995; Møller 1996). In these four papers, all *in situ* distributions have been obtained with the Braystoke SK110. The dispersed distributions described by Møller (1996), were found by dispersing the sediment from the ten filters of each settling tube and subsequently analysing it in the Malvern Mastersizer/E, as in this study. Edelvang & Larsen (1995) and Pejrup (1991) re-analysed the dispersed sediment in the Braystoke SK110. Pejrup (1988) carried out two simultaneous samples with two settling tubes. One sample was analysed immediately *in situ*, while the other was taken to the laboratory, sonified for 15 min and analysed in the Braystoke SK110, yielding the dispersed distribution. As these four papers, using three different analysis techniques, all find that the smallest floc in the Danish Wadden Sea is *c.* 6Φ (16 μm), this gives further support to assume that the Malvern Mastersizer/E yields a dispersed distribution that is comparable with the *in situ* distribution.

It appears that in the Dollard the flocs become larger than in the Danish Wadden Sea. The reasons for this are not obvious, but perhaps the flocs in the Dollard are less fragile than flocs in the Danish Wadden Sea or it could be that turbulence in the Dollard is less violent than in

the Danish Wadden Sea. This would cause flocs to grow to a larger size before breaking up due to shear stress along their surfaces.

Flocs with a high content of organic material may have a higher shear strength than flocs with a lower content, all other things being equal. The importance of the organic content of the suspended matter for the flocculation process have been adressed by several authors. Kranck (1984) showed that a mixture of inorganic and organic sediment attain higher settling velocities than suspensions of all organic or all inorganic, and Eisma *et al.* (1991) and Eisma (1986) showed that the surface characteristics of suspended particles are very much controlled by organic material adhered to the particles or contained in the flocs. The fresh water discharge to the Danish Wadden Sea is much smaller than the fresh water discharge to the Dollard. It is possible that the content of organic material in the Dollard waters is greater than in the Danish Wadden Sea, due to the combined discharge of polluted water from the drainage channel Westerwoldsche Aa in the SE corner of the Dollard (de Jonge 1988) and the river Ems to the NE. If flocculation is partly due to heavy adsorption of organic material on the surface of the particles, the flocs tend to be more

Table 2. *Relation between SSC, the smallest equivalent floc (Φ_{min}) to occur at a given value of SSC and the settling velocity (Ws_{min}) associated with Φ_{min}*

Settling tube	1, top	1, bottom	5, bottom	6, bottom	3, bottom
SSC (mg/l)	29	25.9	19.9	105.4	145.4
Φ_{min}	4.5	4.5	4.5	5.5	6
Ws_{min} (mm/s)	1.43	1.43	1.45	0.36	0.20

resistant to shear than flocs created by salt flocculation. It thus seems reasonably to assume that the flocs in the Dollard are less fragile than the flocs in the Danish Wadden Sea, due to a higher content of 'glue', i.e. organic material.

The tidal range in the Dollard is about twice that in the Danish Wadden Sea. Therefore, it does not seem reasonable to assume that the Dollard is less turbulent than the Danish Wadden Sea.

Correlation between SSC and W_{50}. A good correlation between SSC and field settling velocity was not found in this study. In fact, a poor correlation was found ($R^2 = 0.01$). This could relate to the different sampling modes used; the Lagrangian mode used in the tidal channel of this study vs the Eulerian mode used in most previous studies. However, as it was only possible to calculate the median settling velocities from 6 out of the 19 collected settling tubes, it is also possible that the poor correlation relates to the limited data set.

Relation between the smallest floc size and SSC. Table 2 reveals that the smallest equivalent floc size (determined from Fig. 3) decreases as SSC increases.

There is a good, linear correlation between SSC and the smallest floc size. The correlation equation takes the form

$$\Phi_{min} = 4.19 + 0.0124 \cdot SSC\,(mg/l)$$
$$(R^2 = 0.99) \quad (1)$$

where Φ_{min} denotes the smallest equivalent floc occuring at a given SSC. This relationship appears from Fig. 5.

This phenomenon probably relates to high current velocities, at the same time causing both high values of SSC by local resuspension and floc breakage due to high internal shear rates in the water. This is somewhat supported by current velocity profiles that were measured almost simultaneously with the sampling of the settling tubes. In Fig. 6 the current velocity measured *c.* 30 cm above the bed (u_{30}), Φ_{min} at the bottom, and the depth-averaged current velocity and depth-averaged suspended sediment concentration are plotted. From the figure it appears that there is a relationship between Φ_{min} and u_{30}. Starting at *c.* 11:00 hours u_{30} is low and Φ_{min} is relatively large. From 11:00 to 14:45 hours there is a general increase in u_{30} and a corresponding decrease in Φ_{min}. From 14:45 to 17:30 hours u_{30} weakens and Φ_{min} increases. Finally, after 17:30 hours u_{30} begins to increase and Φ_{min} decreases once again.

There is a good linear correlation between Φ_{min} and $(u_{30})^2$ (Fig. 7):

$$\Phi_{min} = 8.42 \cdot (u_{30})^2 + 3.98 \quad (R^2 = 0.80) \quad (2)$$

Because the squared current velocity is proportional to the internal shear stress in a turbulent flow this supports the idea that the smallest floc size found *in situ* (Φ_{min}) is related to the current velocity, causing high internal shear rates resulting in floc breakage.

Settling velocity of the smallest floc. As it seems possible, in this study, to determine the smallest equivalent floc size from SSC, it is also possible to determine the lowest settling velocity for the flocculated sediment to occur, the only variable being SSC. This gives one the possibility to give a rough estimate of (1) how large a percentage (by weight) of the suspended sediment that exists in the water as part of flocs and (2) to determine the time needed for the flocculated part of the sediment to deposit.

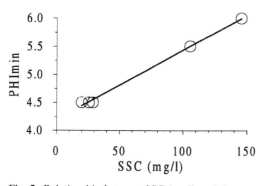

Fig. 5. Relationship between SSC (mg/l) and the smallest floc, Φ_{min}.

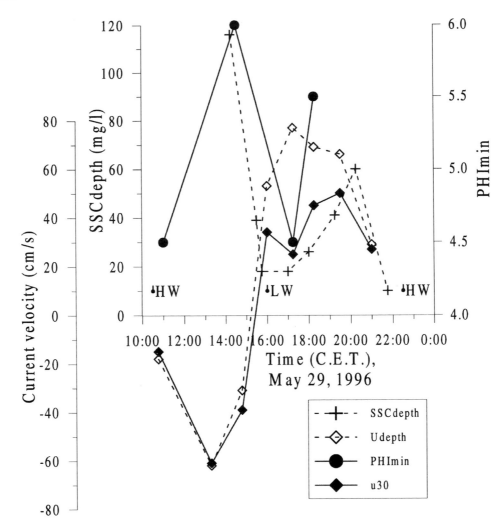

Fig. 6. Plots of $\Phi_{\min}$ at the bottom (PHImin), current velocity 30 cm off the bed (u_{30}), depth-averaged suspended sediment concentration (SSCdepth) and depth-averaged current velocity (Udepth).

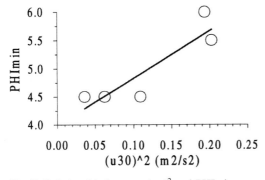

Fig. 7. Relationship between $(u_{30})^2$ and PHImin.

Correlating the settling velocities for the smallest equivalent flocs from Table 2 with SSC yields an exponential relationship:

$$Ws_{\min}\,(\text{mm/s}) = 2.152 \cdot 0.984^{\text{SSC}}$$

$$(R^2 = 0.99) \quad (3)$$

where $Ws_{\min}$ denotes the settling velocity for the smallest equivalent floc.

When $Ws_{\min}$ from Table 2 is compared with the W_{50} from the settling tubes (Table 1), the relationship between W_{50} and $Ws_{\min}$ appears (Table 3).

Table 3. *The relation between* Ws_{min} *and* W_{50}. *In parentheses the time (in minutes) to settle to the bottom at a water depth of 2 m (mean depth in Dollard at HW) is indicated*

Settling tube	1, top	1, bottom	3, bottom	5, bottom	6, bottom
W_{80} (mm/s)	–	–	0.07 (477)	–	0.06 (556)
W_{70} (mm/s)	–	–	0.24 (139)	–	0.46 (72)
W_{60} (mm/s)	–	0.62 (54)	0.36 (93)	–	0.73 (46)
W_{50} (mm/s)	0.39 (86)	2.53 (13)	0.62 (54)	1.10 (30)	1.57 (21)
W_{40} (mm/s)	1.59 (21)	–	–	2.30 (15)	–
Ws_{min} (mm/s)	1.43 (23)	1.43 (23)	0.20 (167)	1.45 (23)	0.36 (93)
Ws_{min}/W_{50}	3.67	0.56	0.32	1.32	0.23

From Table 3 it can be seen, that in two settling tubes (1, top and 5, bottom) all flocs will have settled out before half of the suspended sediment (in percentage by weight) has settled, as Ws_{min} is larger than W_{50}, i.e. in these cases the flocs constitute less than half of the suspended sediment and Ws_{min}/W_{50} are therefore larger than 1.

Furthermore, settling velocities and settling time for a water depth of 2 m (the mean depth in the Dollard at HW), has been calculated for the 40, 60, 70 and 80% fractiles in Table 3. When compared with Ws_{min}, these settling velocities have potential as a rough estimate of the amount of sediment (in percentage by weight) that exist in the water as part of flocs.

For example, in settling tube 1, bottom, Ws_{min} is 1.43 mm s^{-1}, W_{50} is 2.53 mm s^{-1} and W_{60} is 0.62 mm s^{-1}. It is seen, that Ws_{min} is lying between W_{50} and W_{60}. This means that half of the suspended sediment (in percentage by weight) will have settled out before the smallest floc. On the other hand, the smallest floc (and thus all flocs) will have settled out before 60% of the suspended sediment (in percentage by weight) has settled out. Therefore, the flocculated part of the sediment must make up between 50 and 60% (by weight) of the suspended sediment.

Then, from Table 3 one finds that in settling tubes 3 and 6 the flocculated sediment constitutes between 70 and 80% (by weight) of the suspended sediment and in tube 1, top and 5 between 40 and 50% (by weight).

However, because single grains exist in the fractions with flocs, these estimates certainly are a maximum value. This is illustrated in Table 4, where the amount of flocs has been calculated

from Figs 3 and 4. In Fig. 4 the flocculated part of the sample can easily be found as the difference between the *in situ* distribution and the dispersed distribution. To this, should be added the amount of flocs coarser than 3Φ (125 μm), read from Fig. 3 as the difference between the *in situ* and dispersed distributions at 3Φ. It then appears that the flocculated sediment constitute 32–56% by weight of the suspended sediment.

Furthermore, it is seen from Table 4 that there is a systematic difference between the two methods, the graphical solution undoubtedly being more precise than the Ws_{min}-method. In general, however, the graphical solution yields a result that is 80% of the lowest fractile in Table 4, rendering the latter method useful by applying the 80% as an empirical constant to the settling velocity grading curve.

No clear relation between SSC and settling velocity was found in this study. It could be due to the limited number of observations, or it could be due to the fact that sampling took place in the Lagrangian mode, rather than the Eulerian. Further investigations have to be carried out to clarify this. For the same reasons, the relation found between the smallest floc size and SSC needs to be investigated further. Relating multiple observed sediment characteristics (e.g. W_{50}, Ws_{min} and Φ_{min}) to a single variable, SSC, may be too simplistic. However, the technique may be of use for remote sensing studies of estuaries and coastal waters.

Conclusions

No relationship between SSC and W_{50} was found. This may be related to the Lagrangian

Table 4. *The amount of flocculated sediment calculated in two different ways. See text for explanations*

Settling tube	1, top	1, bottom	3, bottom	5, bottom	6, bottom
Ws_{min}	40–50%	50–60%	70–80%	40–50%	70–80%
Fig. 3/4	32%	43%	56%	32%	50%

sampling mode or to the limited number of observations.

Median settling diameters of the suspended sediment are always coarser near the bottom than at the surface. The dispersed distributions show no significant differences in median diameters.

There was no difference in the median diameter of the dispersed sediment from the channel and the flat. However, no difference in median settling velocity was found between the tidal channel and the adjacent tidal flat, as it was not possible to compute any field settling velocities.

Flocs in the Dollard have a settling diameter of at least 6Φ ($16\,\mu m$), and up to $c.\,20\%$ of the flocs attains a size of at least 3Φ ($125\,\mu m$). Thus, flocs in the Dollard become larger than in the Danish Wadden Sea, where flocs with a settling diameter larger than 3Φ have not been observed. This may be a result of a larger content of organic material in the Dollard flocs.

An inverse relationship between SSC and the smallest equivalent floc (Φ_{min}) has been demonstrated. This relationship is presented in equation (1) and takes the form $\Phi_{min} = 4.19 + 0.0124 \cdot SSC$. The settling velocity associated with the smallest equivalent floc can be calculated from equation (3), Ws_{min} (mm/s) $= 2.152 \cdot 0.984^{SSC}$ ($R^2 = 0.99$).

Together with the settling velocity grading curve these relations have been used in two ways; to determine the amount of sediment that exists in the water as flocs and to determine the time needed for the flocculated part of the sediment to deposit. In this way, it could be calculated that in the Dollard the flocculated part of the sediment made up 32–56% of the total suspended sediment and that these flocs would all have settled out in 23–167 min.

The field work was carried out as part of an EU MASTIII-project, INTRMUD (contract no. MAS3-CT95-0022). We are indebted to Willem van der Lee and Bart Kornman (Institute of Geography, University of Utrecht) for organizing the logistics and making the current measurements available to us, the crew on RV Regulus for good seamanship during the cruise and Thorbjørn Andersen (Institute of Geography, University of Copenhagen) for taking part in the field work.

References

ANDRADE, F., REIS, M. & DUARTE, P. 1991. The dynamics of the tide excursion in the Mira Estuary (Vila Nova de Milfontes, Portugal). A Lagrangian approach. *In*: ELLIOT, M. & DUCROTOY, J.-P. (eds) *Estuaries and Coasts: Spatial and Temporal Intercomparisons*. Proceedings of ECSA19 Symposium, University of Caen. Olsen & Olsen, Frederiksborg, 49–55.

BURT, T. L. 1986. Field settling velocity of estuary muds. *In*: MEHTA, A. J. (ed.) *Lecture Notes on Coastal and Estuarine Studies*, **14**, Springer-Verlag, Berlin, 126–150.

DANKERS, N., BINSBERGEN, M., ZEGERS, K., LAANE, R., & RUTGERS VAN DER LOEFF, M. 1984. Transportation of water, particulate and dissolved organic and inorganic matter between a salt marsh and the Ems–Dollard Estuary, The Netherlands. *Estuarine, Coastal and Shelf Science*, **19**, 143–165.

DE JONGE, V. N. 1988. The abiotic environment. *In*: BARETTA, J. & RUARDIJ, P. (eds) *Tidal Flat Estuaries. Simulation and Analysis of the Ems Estuary. Ecological Studies*, **71**, Springer–Verlag, 14–27.

DYER, K.R, CORNELISSE, J., DEARNALEY, M. P., FENNESSY, M. J., JONES, S. E., KAPPENBERG, J., McCAVE, I. N., PEJRUP, M., PULS, W., VAN LEUSSEN, W. & WOLFSTEIN, K. 1996. A comparison of in situ techniques for estuarine floc settling velocity measurements. *Journal of Sea Research*, **36**, 15–29.

EDELVANG, K., LARSEN, M. & PEJRUP, M. 1992. Tidal variation in field settling velocities of suspended sediment in a tidal channel. *Geografisk Tidsskrift*, **92**, 116–121.

—— & ——1995. The flocculation of fine-grained sediments in Ho Bugt, the Danish Wadden Sea. *Folia Geographica Danica*. Tom XXII.

EISMA, D. 1986. Flocculation and de-flocculation of suspended matter in estuaries. *Netherlands Journal of Sea Research*, **20**, 183–199.

——, BERNARD, P., CADEÉ, G. C., ITTEKKOT, V., KALF, J., LAANE, R., MARTIN, J. M., MOOK, W. G., VAN PUT, A. & SCHUMACHER, T. 1991. Suspended-matter particle size in some West-European estuaries; Part II: a review on floc formation and break-up. *Netherlands Journal of Sea Research*, **28**, 215–220.

FENNESSY, M. J., DYER, K. R. & HUNTLEY, D. A. 1994. INSSEV: An instrument to measure the size and settling velocity of flocs *in situ*. *Marine Geology*, **117**, 107–117.

——, ——, & BALE, A. J. 1997. Estimation of settling flux spectra in estuaries using INSSEV. *In*: BURT, N., PARKER, R. & WATTS, J. (eds) *Cohesive Sediments*. Proceedings of the 4th Nearshore & Estuarine Cohesive Sediment Transport Conference (INTERCOH '94) Wallingford. John Wiley & Sons, 87–104.

KRANCK, K. 1984. The role of flocculation in the filtering of particulate matter in estuaries. *In*: KENNEDY, V. (ed.) *The estuary as a Filter*. Academic Press, New York, 159–175.

MØLLER, A. L. 1996. Flokkulering af finkornet sediment. En kvalitativ analyse af flokkuleringsprocessen i to niveauer i Lister Dybs tidevandsområde (in Danish). Unpublished student report. Institute of Geography, University of Copenhagen.

OWEN, M. W. 1971. The effect of turbulence on the settling velocities of silt flocs. Proceedings of the 14. Congress of IAHR, Paris. Paper D4, 1–6.

PEJRUP, M. 1988. Flocculated suspended sediment in a micro-tidal environment. *Sedimentary Geology*, **57**, 249–256.

——1991. The influence of flocculation on cohesive sediment transport in a microtidal estuary. *In*: SMITH, D. G., REINSON, G. E., ZAITLIN, B. A. & RAHMANI, R. A. (eds) *Canadian Society of Petroleum Geologists*. Memoir **16**, 283–290.

—— & EDELVANG, K. 1996. Measurements of in situ settling velocities in the Elbe estuary. *Journal of Sea Research*, **36**, 109–113.

PULS, W., KUEHL, H. & HEYMANN, K. 1988. Settling velocity of mud flocs: Results of field measurements in the Elbe and the Weser Estuary. *In*: DRONKERS, J. & VAN LEUSSEN, W. (eds) *Physical Processes in Estuaries*. Springer-Verlag, Berlin, 404–427.

SUBCOMMITTEE ON SEDIMENTATION 1953. *Accuracy of sediment size analysis made by the bottom withdrawal tube medthod. A study of methods used in measurement and analysis of sediment loads in streams*, Report No. 10. St Anthony Falls Hydraulic Laboratory, Minneapolis, Minnesota.

VAN LEUSSEN, W. 1997. The Kolmogorov microscale as a limiting value for the floc sizes of suspended fine-grained sediments in estuaries. *In*: BURT, N., PARKER, R. & WATTS, J. (eds) *Cohesive Sediments*. Proceedings of the 4th Nearshore & Estuarine Cohesive Sediment Transport Conference (INTERCOH '94) Wallingford. John Wiley & Sons, 45–62.

—— & CORNELISSE, J. M. 1993. The determination of the sizes and settling velocities of estaurine flocs by an underwater video system. *Netherlands Journal of Sea Research*, **31**, 231–241.

Seasonal variability of subtidal and intertidal sediment distributions in a muddy, macrotidal estuary: the Humber–Ouse, UK

R. J. UNCLES, J. A. STEPHENS & C. HARRIS

NERC, Centre for Coastal and Marine Sciences, Plymouth Marine Laboratory, Prospect Place, Plymouth PL1 3DH, UK

Abstract: Surveys of subtidal and intertidal sediment distributions were undertaken in the upper Humber and Ouse during autumn (fall) and winter. Within the Ouse, the great majority of sediment samples comprised a mixture of predominantly silt and clay ($<63 \mu$m) and very fine sand (>63 and $<125 \mu$m). A pronounced seasonal transport was observed both in subtidal lag sediments and intertidal bank sediments. The strongest difference between autumn and winter distributions of subtidal bed sediments resulted from the down-estuary movement of very fine sand from the upper reaches of the Ouse during winter. This feature was also evident in the intertidal sediments. Intertidal banks in the upper reaches of the Ouse utilized very fine sand to grow during summer and autumn, and were eroded back to stronger silt and clay substrates over the winter period. The down-channel redistribution of sand-sized sediment was a response to increased freshwater inflows over winter. This movement is approximately balanced in summer and autumn, during low freshwater inflows, by an up-channel sediment transport due to tidal velocity asymmetry and its associated flood dominance.

The aims of this study were to investigate the influences of season on the variations of near-surface (uppermost 0.1 m) sediment types in the upper reaches of the Humber–Ouse system (Fig. 1). The data will provide an essential, if somewhat qualitative, framework for subsequent modelling studies of bed-load sediment transport in the area. Although information exists on the near-surface sedimentary regime in the Humber, down-channel of the Apex (BGS, 1990), none appears to have been published for the Ouse.

The Humber was a river-carved valley during the last (Devensian) glaciation when the North Sea basin was covered with ice. The Devensian ended *c.* 12 000 a BP and the retreating ice then deposited large quantities of glacial till over the region (e.g. Pethick 1988). Sea level rose in response to the retreating ice sheets and reached a level similar to its present level *c.* 6000 a BP. Sediments (which included reworked till) were transported into the Humber during the sea-level rise and then deposited in the Humber's former river channels. Finer sediments were deposited over the shallower subtidal regions and on intertidal areas to form mudflats and mudbanks.

Up-channel, tidally-driven transport of marine-derived sediment continued from the Humber into the Ouse and Trent (Fig. 1). In these estuaries, however, the opposing influence of fluvial discharges eventually limited the incursion of marine-derived sediment. Sedimentation, further up-channel, was then the result of deposition from fluvial discharges derived from the terrestrial catchment area.

In terms of the classification of 'primary' estuaries (according to Perillo 1995) the Humber–Ouse is a macrotidal, coastal plain estuary derived from the drowning and subsequent sediment infilling of former, low relief river valleys and their river flood plains during the Flandrian transgression of the last 10 000 a. The Ouse is tidal to Naburn Weir, which is located *c.* 62 km up-channel from the Apex (Figs 1 and 2). The Apex, located at the confluence of the Ouse, Trent and Humber, is *c.* 60 km up-channel from the mouth of the Humber and North Sea.

Methods

Surveys of subtidal and intertidal sediment distributions were undertaken in the upper Humber and Ouse during early autumn and winter. Measurements during February 1996 supplied an indication of winter distributions and measurements during September 1995 and October 1996 supplied an indication of autumn conditions. Pot and Van Veen grab samples (Buller & McManus 1979) were collected from an inflatable boat that travelled the 70 km distance between the weir at Naburn to Whitton Channel in the upper Humber (UW in Figs 1 and 2).

Grain sizes were determined by using a flow of water to pass a subsample of the homogenized, wet sediment through a stack of shaking sieves which possessed decreasing mesh sizes towards its base. The silt and clay fraction was determined from the dried weight of that part of the

UNCLES, R. J., STEPHENS, J. A. & HARRIS, C. 1998. Seasonal variability of subtidal and intertidal sediment distributions in a muddy, macrotidal estuary. *In*: BLACK, K. S., PATERSON, D. M. & CRAMP, A. (eds) *Sedimentary Processes in the Intertidal Zone.* Geological Society, London, Special Publications, **139**, 211–219.

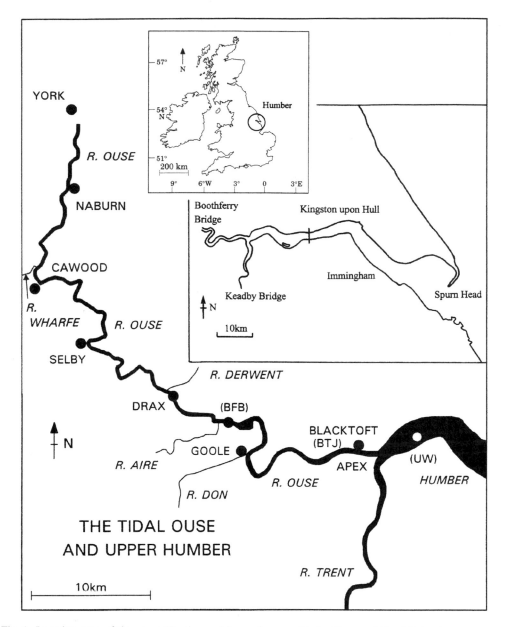

Fig. 1. Location map of the upper Humber and its confluence with the Ouse and Trent Estuaries superimposed on a map of the Humber Estuary and its position on the UK coastline. Upper Whitton light vessel in the upper Humber is abbreviated (UW); Blacktoft Jetty in the Ouse is abbreviated (BTJ) and Boothferry Bridge in the Ouse is abbreviated (BFB).

sample which passed through the finest, 63 μm sieve at the base of the stack. Coarser fractions were retained on sieves which had mesh sizes of 63, 125, 250, 500, 1000 and 2000 μm. Drying and weighing the retained fractions enabled the relative proportions of silt and clay (<63 μm), very fine sand (63–125 μm), fine sand (125–250 μm), medium sand (250–500 μm), coarse sand (500–1000 μm), very coarse sand (1000–2000 μm) and gravels (>2000 μm) to be determined.

The water content of the intertidal sediment was determined by weighing a subsample of the homogenized sediment before and after oven-drying at 85°C.

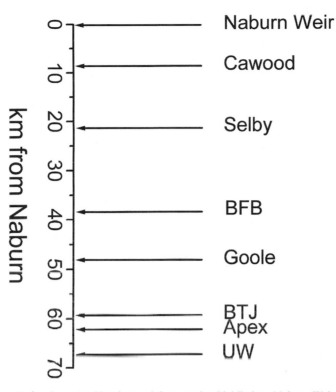

Fig. 2. Distance scale for the upper Humber and Ouse to the tidal limit at Naburn Weir.

Results

The great majority of subtidal and intertidal sediment samples within the Ouse comprised a mixture of predominantly silt and clay and very fine sand. A pronounced seasonal transport was observed both in subtidal and intertidal sediments.

Bed sediments

During the winter period of February 1996 the proportions of medium sand and coarser fractions were negligible except near the Apex, where sediment was c. 50% medium sand (Fig. 3, top panel). The proportion of fine sand was generally <10% except at the most down-channel site in the upper Humber, where it was c. 50%. The silt and clay fraction was >70% near the head, within c. 30 km of Naburn Weir, and constituted a sticky, cohesive bed. Silt and clay was also generally dominant from 45 km down-channel of Naburn to the Apex and constituted a hard, mud bed with smaller amounts of very fine sand. Very fine sand was dominant between 30–45 km from Naburn, within and immediately up-channel of the turbidity maximum (TM) region of highest suspended loads. The TM was located c. 40–50 km from Naburn at spring tides during winter. In this area the silt and clay fraction of the bed was generally <20%, but with a patch c. 55%, and very fine sand dominated the sediment.

During the autumn period of September 1995 the proportions of medium sand and coarser fractions were negligible except next to the weir at Naburn, where the bed comprised gravel, and at the most down-channel station in the upper Humber, which again had a gravel bed (Fig. 3, bottom panel). The proportion of fine sand was generally <10% except in the vicinity of the Apex, where it was c. 60%. The silt and clay fraction generally was >70% near the head, within 10 km of Naburn and constituted a sticky, cohesive bed. Silt and clay was again generally dominant down-channel of 45 km from Naburn Weir to the Apex and constituted a hard mud bed with small amounts of very fine sand. Within the TM region of highest suspended loads, between c. 15–35 km from Naburn at spring tides during autumn, the silt and clay fraction of the bed generally was c. 25% but with patches c. 35% and, as during winter, very fine sand dominated the bed sediment.

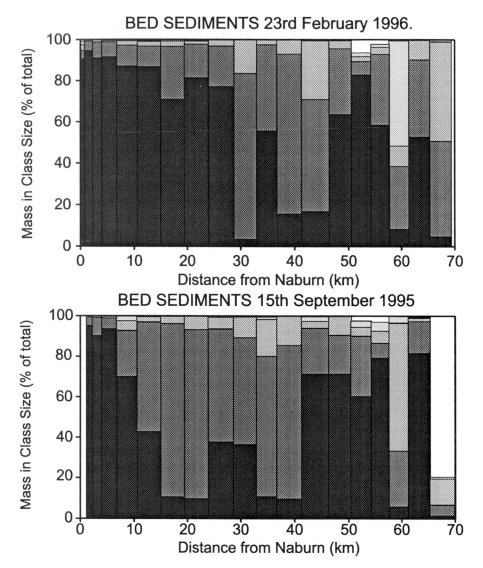

Fig. 3. Subtidal bed-sediment distributions in the upper Humber and Ouse. The sediment mass in a particular size class is expressed as a percentage of the total sediment mass in a sample and plotted against distance from Naburn Weir (km). The size classes (silt and clay, very fine sand, fine sand and medium sand) are represented by a grey scale with darkest grey illustrating the silt and clay component. A white background indicates no data (whole column blank) or coarser fractions. Top panel: winter distributions; bottom panel: autumn distributions.

Intertidal sediments

During the winter period of February 1996 the proportions of medium and coarser sand were negligible in the intertidal areas throughout the upper Humber and Ouse (Fig. 4, top panel). The proportion of fine sand was generally < 10% except in the upper Humber and Apex, where it was *c.* 25–40%. There was a general trend for the silt and clay component to decrease from >80% near Naburn ,to <15% in the upper Humber. Approximately 50% of the variance in this component could be explained by its location. The silt and clay proportion was very low down-channel of 45 km and the sediment there was mainly very fine sand with an amount of fine sand that increased progressing further down-channel. Up-channel of 45 km the silt and

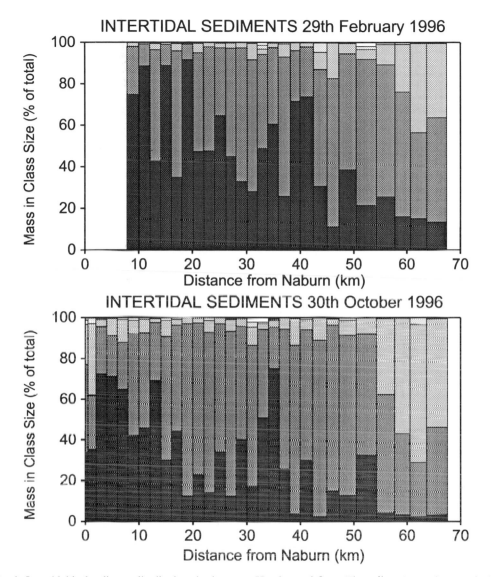

Fig. 4. Intertidal bed-sediment distributions in the upper Humber and Ouse. The sediment mass in a particular size class is expressed as a percentage of the total sediment mass in a sample and plotted against distance from Naburn Weir (km). The size classes (silt and clay, very fine sand, fine sand and medium sand) are represented by a grey scale with darkest grey illustrating the silt and clay component. A white background indicates no data (whole column blank) or coarser fractions. Top panel: winter distributions; bottom panel: autumn distributions.

clay fraction generally increased, and the very fine sand fraction generally decreased, although there was considerable variability in their relative proportions. The ratio of very fine sand to silt and clay proportions generally increased down-channel from ≪1 at 10 km from Naburn to >3 down-channel of 55 km. About 40% of the variance in this ratio could be explained by location.

During the autumn period of October 1996 the proportions of medium and coarser sand were again negligible in the intertidal areas throughout the upper Humber and Ouse (Fig. 4, bottom panel). The proportion of fine sand was also generally <10%, except in the immediate vicinity of Naburn Weir, where the intertidal sediment was soil-like and the proportion was c. 30%, and in the upper Humber and Apex, where it was *c.* 50%. There was a general trend for the silt and clay component to decrease from >70% near Naburn to <10% in the upper Humber. Approximately 40% of the variance in this component could be explained by location. Very fine sand generally dominated between 15–55 km from Naburn and in particular within the TM area, located between *c.* 15–35 km during autumn. Down-channel of 55 km the sediments were mainly very fine sand and fine sand, with increasing amounts of fine sand progressing further down-channel. The ratio of very fine sand to silt and clay proportions generally increased down-channel from <1 at 10 km from Naburn to >10 down-channel of 55 km. About 40% of the variance in this ratio, with one outlier removed, could be explained by location. Therefore, relative to the silt and clay proportion, there was significantly more very fine sand present during the autumn period. Overall, the

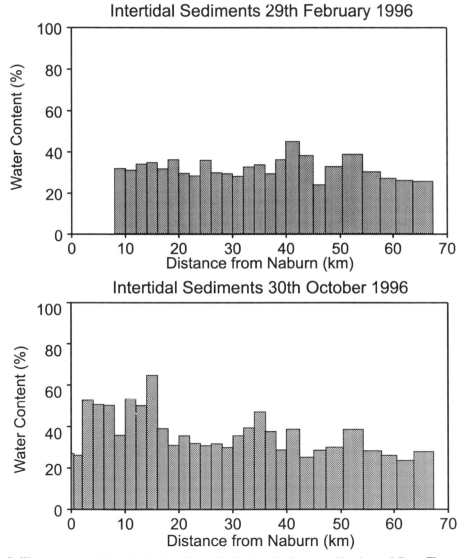

Fig. 5. Water contents of intertidal bed-sediment distributions in the upper Humber and Ouse. The water content in a particular sample is expressed as a percentage of the total mass of a sample and plotted against distance from Naburn Weir (km). A white background indicates no data (whole column blank). Top panel: winter distributions; bottom panel: autumn distributions.

ratio of proportions was 6 ± 9 during autumn as opposed to 1.5 ± 1.6 during winter.

During February 1996 the water contents of the intertidal sediments varied from 25 to 45% with a mean and standard deviation of $33\% \pm 6\%$ (Fig. 5, top panel). There was a weak but significant positive correlation between the water content and the percentage of intertidal sediment comprising silt and clay. Approximately 30% of the variance in water content could be explained in terms of silt and clay percentage. This implies that water content was significantly affected by the sediment grain size and that substrates possessing a higher proportion of fines held more water.

During October 1996 the water contents of the intertidal sediments varied from 25 to 55%, with a mean and standard deviation of $37\% \pm 10\%$ (Fig. 5, bottom panel). There was a significant positive correlation between the water content and the percentage of intertidal sediment comprising silt and clay. About 70% of the variance in water content could be explained in terms of the silt and clay percentage. This again implies that water content was largely dependent on the grain size within the sediment and that substrates possessing a higher proportion of fines held more water.

Generally, higher water contents for a given silt and clay proportion occurred during autumn, when the silt and clay proportions, relative to the very fine sand proportions, were comparatively smaller.

Discussion

The major difference between autumn and winter distributions of subtidal bed sediment was caused by the down-estuary movement of very fine sand during the winter period. The up-channel margin of very fine sand moved down-estuary from 10 to 30 km from Naburn and exposed an underlying, scoured bed of highly cohesive mud. This feature was also evident in the intertidal sediments. The intertidal areas up-channel of 30 km comprised significantly less very fine sand during winter and more silt and clay.

The down-channel transport of very fine sand between the autumn and winter periods was also apparent in the lower Ouse. During winter, greater fractions of very fine subtidal sand occurred down-channel of 40 km and in the upper Humber. This pattern was reflected in an increased very fine sand component of the associated intertidal areas. Similar down-channel shifts between autumn and winter were also

evident in the small proportions of subtidal fine sand and medium sand. A corresponding shift was also evident for fine sand on the intertidal areas, although medium sand and coarser components were negligible there, during both winter and autumn.

These data therefore indicate that a strong, down-channel redistribution of the sand-sized subtidal sediment occurred between autumn and winter in response to increased freshwater inflows during winter. A similar seasonal pattern was also reflected in the intertidal sediments. This suggests that the up-channel, intertidal banks utilized very fine sand to grow during summer and autumn, and that they were eroded back to stronger, silt and clay substrates over the winter period. For a given silt and clay proportion, water contents of the intertidal sediments were somewhat greater during autumn. This suggests that an improved drainage of the recently uncovered areas occurred during winter, which may have been associated with the generally greater steepness of eroded banks.

In mesotidal estuaries, the up-channel transport of sand as bed-load is limited by the decreasing tidal currents and the increasing ratio of ebb-directed to flood directed current speeds close to the tidal limit (e.g. Postma 1961, Nichols & Poor 1967). In macrotidal estuaries, such as the Ouse, the flood-ebb asymmetry of the tidal velocities is pronounced (e.g. Uncles 1981) and is such that flood currents may be capable of transporting sand-sized sediment almost to the tidal limit (Dyer 1986; McDowell & O'Connor 1977). During autumn, the very fine sand proportion of subtidal lag sediment reached a maximum of 85% at 18 km from the Ouse's tidal limit at Naburn. Proportions then decreased almost linearly approaching Naburn. During winter, the very fine sand fraction maximized at 80% some 30 km from Naburn and then decreased precipitously to <20% at 25 km from Naburn. This strongly suggests that tidal velocity asymmetry played a major role in the transport of very fine sand. Increasing ebb currents and reduced flood currents, in the presence of high winter freshwater inflows, shifted the up-channel margin of very fine sand towards the Apex.

An up-channel transport of sand has also been observed in the macrotidal Cobequid Bay–Salmon River Estuary (Dalrymple et al. 1990) where marine sand is accumulating at a faster rate than local sea-level rise can accommodate. There is a down-channel increase in grain size, which is interpreted as an inability of the weak fluvial inflow to transport sediments as bedload, so that transport of the lag sediment is affected only by the flood-dominant tidal currents. In the

Gironde Estuary, grain size along the axis of the estuary initially decreases down-channel from the head, reaches a minimum and then increases toward the mouth (Allen 1991). This minimum is thought to represent the down-channel limit of fluvial sand, which is envisaged to be trapped in the upper estuary by the flood-dominant tidal currents. The eventual down-channel increase in grain size corresponds to that observed in the Cobequid Bay–Salmon River Estuary.

In the Ouse, the very fine sand proportion exhibits a mid-estuarine maximum with distance from Naburn, whereas proportions of coarser fractions tend to increase continuously down-channel. This suggests that the majority of sand-sized lag sediment is derived from the Humber, seawards of the Apex, and is transported and then deposited up-estuary by tidal action during low freshwater inflow, summer and autumn conditions. Much, if not all, of this sediment is then transported back down-channel, and into the lower Ouse and upper Humber during high freshwater inflow, winter conditions. Fine and very fine sand are the dominant sediment types within the Humber (BGS 1990) thereby providing a source of material for this seasonal cycling of lag sediment within the Ouse. Gravelly sediment is found in only a few areas of the Humber and is probably derived from exposures of glacial till on the channel bed.

A similar conclusion, of predominantly seaward provenance for the sediment supply of the Humber Estuary as a whole, was reached by Pethick (1988). He considered that the majority of Humber lag sediment was derived from the North Sea, rather than from rivers. Over the last 6000 yrs of relatively slowly varying sea level, this input has deposited sediment within the Humber to thicknesses of between 2 and 20 m. O'Connor (1987) calculated that $c.\ 2.2 \times 10^6\ m^3\ a^{-1}$ of sediment is transported into the estuary from the North Sea, compared with $0.3 \times 10^6\ m^3\ a^{-1}$ from the rivers.

Our measurements would suggest that an approximate balance is reached between the up-channel transport of lag sediment by tidal-velocity asymmetry during low freshwater inflow, summer and autumn periods, and down-channel scouring of lag sediment during the high inflow winter periods. Unfortunately, these data cannot confirm this 'budget' because they do not determine the thicknesses of lag sediment involved in the transport, but only the grain sizes of the sediment. For this reason, hydrodynamic and sediment transport modelling studies will be invaluable as a guide to the quantities of sediment that are involved in the seasonal cycling.

Conclusions

Subtidal and intertidal sediments within the Ouse comprised a mixture of predominantly silt and clay, and very fine sand. A strong seasonal transport occurred both in subtidal and intertidal sediments.

Over the winter period, the up-channel margin of very fine sand moved from 10 to 30 km from the tidal limit and left a scoured, highly cohesive mud bed. This feature was also evident in the intertidal sediments and areas up-channel of 30 km comprised significantly less very fine sand during winter, and more silt and clay.

Marked seasonality was also evident in the lower Ouse. Greater subtidal fractions of very fine sand occurred down-channel of 40 km within the Ouse and in the upper Humber during winter. There was an associated increase in the very fine sand component of the intertidal areas down-channel of 50 km.

Similar seasonality was also evident in the much smaller proportions of fine and medium sand that constituted the subtidal bed sediment. The down-channel migration over winter was reflected in the fine sand component of the intertidal areas, although the medium sand and coarser fractions were negligible.

The water content of the recently exposed intertidal sediments was $33\% \pm 6\%$ by mass during winter and $37\% \pm 10\%$ during autumn. Greater water contents were associated with greater proportions of silt and clay.

The down-channel redistribution of sand-sized sediment over winter was a response to increased freshwater inflows. Sand moved back into the upper reaches during low inflow periods and the intertidal banks there utilized very fine sand to grow during summer and autumn. With the onset of high winter inflows, banks were eroded back to stronger silt and clay substrates.

We are grateful to Peter Sarjeant and Tim Rhodes (Master and Survey Officer, respectively, *RV Sea Vigil*, UK Environment Agency) and Norman Bowley (Technician and Coxswain, PML) for their invaluable assistance and support during this work. This is LOIS publication number 223 of the LOIS Community Research Programme, carried out under a Special Topic Award from the Natural Environment Research Council. Email for correspondence: RJU@PML.AC.UK.

References

ALLEN, G. P. 1991. Relationship between grain size parameter distribution and current patterns in the Gironde Estuary (France). *Journal of Sedimentary Petrology*, **41**, 74–88.

BGS 1990. Spurn: Sheet 53°N–00° including part of Humber–Trent Sheet 53°N–02°W, British Geological Survey, 1:250 000 Series, Sea bed sediments. BGS, Keyworth, Nottingham, UK.

BULLER, A. T. & McMANUS, J. 1979. Sediment sampling and analysis. *In*: DYER, K. R. (ed.) *Estuarine Hydrography and Sedimentation*. Cambridge University Press, Cambridge, UK, 87–130.

DALRYMPLE, R. W., KNIGHT, R. J., ZAITLIN, B. A. & MIDDLETON, G. V. 1990. Dynamics and facies model of a macrotidal sand-bar complex, Cobequid Bay-Salmon River Estuary (Bay of Fundy). *Sedimentology*, **37**, 577–612.

DYER, K. R. 1986. *Coastal and Estuarine Sediment Dynamics*. John Wiley and Sons, Chichester, UK.

McDOWELL, D. M. & O'CONNOR, B. A. 1977. *Hydraulic Behaviour of Estuaries*. McMillan Press, London, UK.

NICHOLS, M. & POOR, G. 1967. Sediment transport in a coastal plain estuary. *Journal of the Water,*

Harbor and Coastal Engineering Division of the ASCE, **93**, 83–95.

O'CONNOR, B. A. 1987. Short and long-term changes in estuary capacity. *Journal of the Geological Society of London*, **144**, 187–195.

PERILLO, G. M. E. 1995. Definitions and geomorphologic classifications of estuaries. *In*: PERILLO, G. M. E. (ed.) *Geomorphology and Sedimentology of Estuaries* (*Developments in Sedimentology*, 53), Elsevier, Amsterdam, 17–46.

PETHICK, J. S. 1988. The physical characteristics of the Humber. *In*: JONES, N. V. (ed.) *A Dynamic Estuary: Man, Nature and the Humber*. Hull University Press, Hull, UK, 31–45.

POSTMA, H. 1961. Transport and accumulation of suspended matter in the Dutch Wadden Sea. *Netherlands Journal of Sea Research*, **1**, 148–190.

UNCLES, R. J. 1981. A note on tidal asymmetry in the Severn Estuary. *Estuarine, Coastal and Shelf Science*, **13**, 419–432.

Spatial variability of tidal flats in response to wave exposure: examples from Strangford Lough, Co. Down, Northern Ireland

N. M. RYAN & J. A. G. COOPER

*School of Environmental Studies, University of Ulster,
Coleraine BT52 1SA, Northern Ireland*

Abstract: Strangford Lough is a shallow marine embayment, whose present form resulted from the late Glacial and Holocene marine erosion of a drumlinized coastal lowland platform. Constriction at the Lough mouth means that most waves are generated by wind blowing over restricted fetches. Tidal flats in the northern parts of Strangford Lough show variable morphology and sediment composition. Tidal flats on the up-wind margin are mud-dominated and located in an intact drowned drumlin landscape. Those on the downwind margins are sandy and exist in partly or wholly eroded former drumlin topography. Our preliminary results indicate strong control by wave exposure (mediated by fetch distance) over tidal flat sediments and morphology which has led to the formation of a series of spatially variable tidal flats within a single depositional basin.

At the time scale of the Holocene, exposure to wave action appears to exert a major influence on tidal flat morphology in this sediment-limited setting though its long-term control of topographical change (seen here as variable extent of drumlin erosion) and the consequent and subsequent role of this topography in determining exposure to contemporary wave action.

Siliciclastic tidal flats are widely distributed depositional landforms best developed in meso to macrotidal areas (Amos 1995). Their temporal evolution has been intensively studied and conceptual sedimentary models have been formulated that typically involve the seaward advance of successively higher water facies to produce a characteristic stratigraphic sequence (Evans 1965, Wang *et al.* 1990). Shorter term spring-neap tidal and seasonal variability has similarly been documented (Van Straaten 1961; Kirby *et al.* 1993).

Spatial variability within individual tidal flats is commonly ascribed to variation in inundation, and in particular to the associated faunal and floral control on morphology (Evans 1965). Tidal current velocity is also known to exert control on tidal flat morphology (Amos 1995). The role of waves, while generally acknowledged as important has received comparatively little attention. Boyd *et al.* (1992) note that tidal flats are best developed in areas sheltered from waves and where sediment is derived mainly from marine sources. Masselink & Short (1993) in a discussion of meso to macrotidal beaches present a model which illustrates the variation in the nature of waves and wave energy dissipation across tidal flats and relates shore-normal facies variability to a change from breaking wave dominance at the low tide level to shoaling waves in the intermediate zone and breaking waves at high tide.

In general, however, little attention has been paid to the role of wave energy in tidal flat morphology on a broad spatial and temporal scale, and in particular its role in controlling

morphological and facies variability between different tidal flats. In this paper we consider three tidal flat areas within Strangford Lough, Northern Ireland and assess the variation in morphology and grain size between each of these systems in terms of the effect of different levels of exposure to wave energy over the period of their formation.

Most tidal flats are located in relatively low energy, high sediment supply environments (Van Straaten 1961; Evans 1965; Carling 1982), where sediments are not extensively reworked on longer than tidal time scales. Pethick (1984) identified four potential sources of tidal flat sediment: marine; coastal; fluvial; and *in situ* erosion of pre-existing sediments. In Strangford Lough there is no evidence to suggest an external sediment supply (DoE (NI) 1991). The coast outside the Lough is rocky and inflowing rivers supply negligible quantities of sediment. Consequently, the sediment of Holocene age within the Lough appears to be derived internally from the erosion and re-distribution of pre-existing glacial and marine deposits. This appears similar to the situation described by Guilcher & Berthois (1957) in Brittany estuaries.

Temporal changes in sediment texture and morphology of the Strangford Lough tidal flats have been noted previously (Lynn 1936), although no quantitative assessment of temporal changes has yet been conducted outside a section of Ardmillan Bay. Here, Kirby *et al.* (1993) established a probable seasonal trend of erosion and accretion. Ongoing work by the authors aims to assess the nature of and controls on

RYAN, N. M. & COOPER, J. A. G. 1998. Spatial variability of tidal flats in response to wave exposure: examples from Strangford Lough, Co. Down, Northern Ireland. *In*: BLACK, K. S., PATERSON, D. M. & CRAMP, A. (eds) *Sedimentary Processes in the Intertidal Zone*. Geological Society, London, Special Publications, **139**, 221–230.

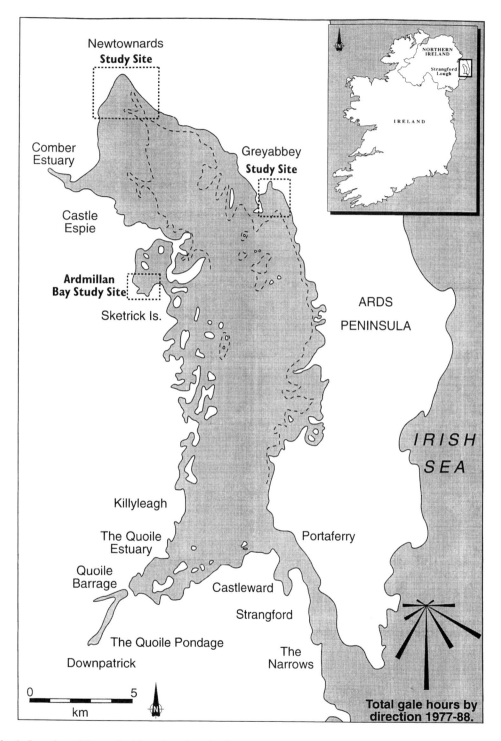

Fig. 1. Location of Strangford Lough and study sites.

these changes and ultimately to produce a conceptual model that can describe the dynamics and sedimentary regimes of tidal flats in sediment-limited environments.

Environmental setting

Strangford Lough is a semi-enclosed, shallow marine embayment situated on the east coast of Northern Ireland (Fig. 1). The present landscape of Strangford Lough has been most affected by a drumlinization phase closely followed by a sea level highstand of $c. +20$ m Ordnance Datum (O.D.) in late glacial times during which a widespread red marine clay was deposited as a drape over the drumlin topography. This has recently been dated at $c. 13.1$ ka BP at Rough Island near Newtownards (Fig. 1) (McCabe 1997). Sea level dropped below the present by 12 000 BP (Morrison & Stephens 1965; Carter 1982) and continued to fall to a minimum thought to be $c. -30$ m O.D. (Carter 1982). During the Holocene, sea level rose rapidly and overstepping of peat deposits in Belfast Lough and Strangford Lough indicates that sea level crossed the present low tide mark between 7000 and 8000 BP (Carter 1982). Thus the present tidal flats in Strangford Lough have formed through the combined effects of waves and tidal currents during this period. Evidence for a higher postglacial sea level in County Down (Morrison & Stephens 1965) is regarded as equivocal (Carter 1982) although topographic evidence does suggest a high post glacial sea level. This has not firmly been distinguished from potential supratidal deposits of present or lower sea level.

The present Lough has an elongated, indented shoreline, a tidal range of 2.0–3.5 m dominated by the M2 (semi diurnal) period and a tidal prism of $c. 350$ million m^3 (DoE (NI) 1993). The freshwater input is negligible ($c. 10$ m^{3}s^{-1}). The Lough is separated from the Irish Sea by the Ards Peninsula, its only connection with the open sea is through 'The Narrows', a 8 km long channel with a minimum width of 0.5 km. This feature prevents the entry of swell waves and means that waves within the Lough are generated internally by local winds, the prevailing wind direction for which is SSW.

Remnants of a drumlin field are preserved as islands within and around the Lough. In many areas, especially along the east coast these drumlin islands have been eroded to produce scattered lags of cobbles and boulders locally known as 'pladdies' (DoE (NI) 1993). The sediment present in the Lough appears to be derived from the redistribution of this glacial material. Tidal flats cover an area of 50 km^2 (DoE(NI) 1993) and are distributed mainly in the upper reaches of the Lough (Fig. 1).

Three tidal flats were chosen for detailed study on the basis of their position within the Lough and orientation with respect to the prevailing wind direction. Newtownards is situated at the northern end of the Lough and has the longest potential fetch. Tidal flats at Newtownards comprise relatively thick sandy deposits with low relief pladdies present in the lower intertidal zone. Greyabbey Bay is positioned on the east coast which receives strong wave attack. Pladdies are present throughout the intertidal zone and are draped by only a thin (on average no more than a few cm) layer of sand. Tidal flats at Newtownards and Greyabbey Bay are sand dominated (67–98% by weight of total sediment). Drumlins encircle Ardmillan Bay on the west coast of Strangford Lough and produce a wave-sheltered environment. Intertidal sediments within Ardmillan Bay are predominantly muddy.

Methods of study

A series of profile lines was established in each study area (Figs 2–4) in order to assess tidal flat morphology and to determine a baseline for monitoring temporal change at two month intervals. Topographic profiles related to O.D. Belfast were measured using an Electronic Distance Meter (EDM) on these fixed transects. In Ardmillan Bay (Fig. 4) difficulty of pedestrian access across the mudflats led to the establishment of a grid of accretion pins (2 m long steel rods) as a basis for morphological measurement using a hovercraft. Here, initial levelling of the steel rods by EDM was followed by sequential measurement of sediment level at the base of the pins at two-month intervals. At Newtownards and Greyabbey, sampling of the upper 2 cm of sediment was undertaken at intervals along the profile lines between high and low water levels. Grain size analysis of the sand fraction was subsequently carried out using an automated settling column after removal of the mud (<63 micron) fraction.

Significant wave heights were hindcast using wind data obtained from Belfast Climate Office for the Killough station 2 km south of the Lough entrance. Effective fetch distances were calculated from topographic maps and a computer program by Black and Healy (1981) was used to determine wave parameters using the JONSWAP Spectrum following the Shore Protection Manual (US Army Corps of Engineers 1977).

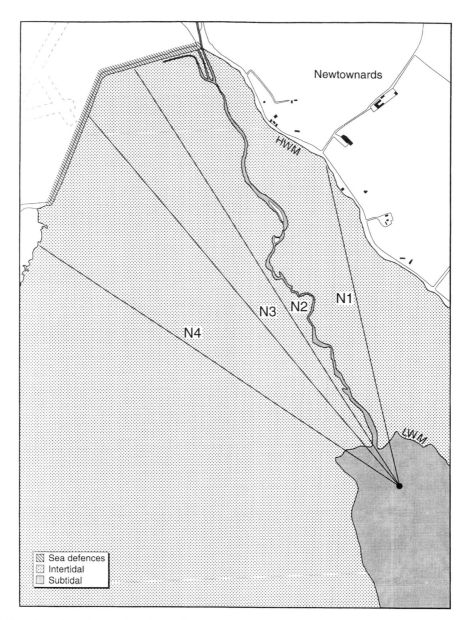

Fig. 2. Location of profile lines, Newtownards.

Results

Wave parameters

Winds in the Strangford area are dominantly from S, SSW and W directions. Newtownards is exposed to the highest potential effective wave fetch (12.4 km) when winds are from the SSE which is a common wind approach direction

both for gales and lower wind speeds (Fig. 1). Maximum effective fetch at Greyabbey (10.9 km) is associated with winds from the south while maximum effective fetch at the entrance to Ardmillan Bay (7.4 km) is associated with winds from the SE. None of these effective fetch distances take account of potential refraction and are based purely on the longitudinal distance over which the wind is blowing mediated in the

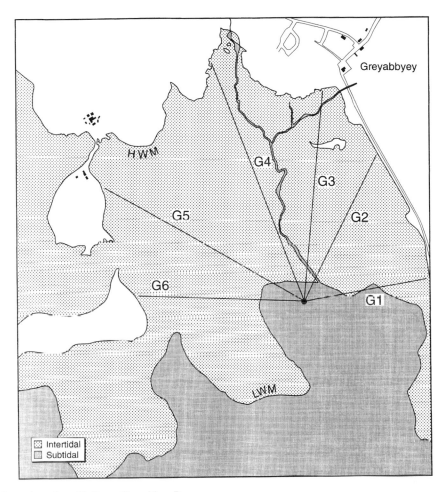

Fig. 3. Location of profile lines, Greyabbey Bay.

case of narrow sections of the lough by its width (US army Corps of Engineers 1977). All are calculated for the high tide fetch.

Hindcasting of significant wave heights for each of the most common wind directions and for the maximum fetch at each site (Table 1) showed that waves at Ardmillan Bay are consistently lower than at the two other sites. Only during strong winds ($27.5\,\mathrm{ms}^{-1}$) blowing from the SE are significant wave heights over 1 m recorded. The maximum fetch here was calculated to the entrance of the bay and will not describe energy conditions within the bay. The refraction and attenuation of waves as they enter the bay means wave energy is probably greatly reduced within Ardmillan Bay.

Newtownards has the longest potential fetch area and is most likely to be exposed to maximum wave energy during SSE winds. Here, wave

heights over 1 m are generated by winds blowing at $16.5\,\mathrm{ms}^{-1}$ while winds at $27.5\,\mathrm{ms}^{-1}$ generate waves with over 1.5 m significant height. The orientation of the upper Lough means that small variations in wave approach direction can produce marked fluctuation in fetch distance and hence wave height at Newtownards.

The most common wind direction in Strangford Lough is southerly (especially for storm events) and this coincides with the maximum fetch at the Greyabbey site. Here the hindcast significant wave heights are only slightly smaller than those at Newtownards (Table 1).

Geomorphology

The tidal flats at Newtownards extend over a shore-normal distance of 2500 m at their maximum extent (Fig. 5) with an average gradient of

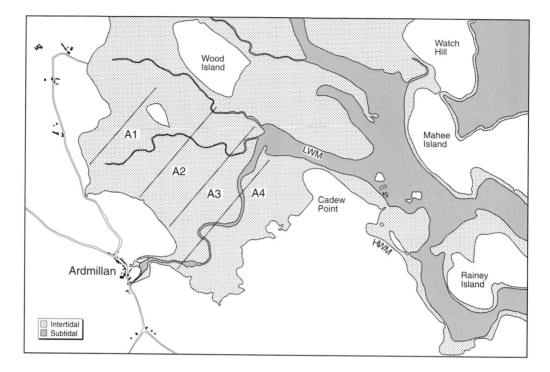

Fig. 4. Ardmillan Bay study site and profile lines.

about 1:700. Three breaks in slope are evident
across the intertidal area on the axial profile
shown in Fig. 5 and define low gradient upper
and lower tidal flat sectors with an intermediate
steep gradient zone.

Surface sediments on the tidal flat at Newtownards are almost entirely sandy and a plot
of mean sand grain size vs elevation for one samp-

Table 1. *Significant wave height for maximum fetch*

Location	Wind speed (m/s)	Significant wave height	
		SMB (m)	Jonswap (m)
Newtownards	6.5	0.40	0.37
	16.5	1.13	0.94
	27.5	1.87	1.56
Greyabbey	6.5	0.38	0.34
	16.5	1.08	0.88
	27.5	1.81	1.47
Ardmillan	6.5	0.33	0.28
	16.5	0.95	0.72
	27.5	1.61	1.22

ling period (June 1996) indicates a linear trend
of decreasing grain size in a shoreward direction (Fig. 6) but at no stage does the sediment
grade into mud.

At Greyabbey the tidal flats are bounded to
the north by largely intact drumlin islands but
are open to the Lough on their southern margin.
The tidal flats are up to 1200 m in shore-normal
extent and display an overall gradient of about
1:340 (Fig. 5). The site is irregular in shape as a
result of the incomplete erosion of the underlying glacial topography, but nonetheless an
apparent break in slope separates a more gently
sloping upper intertidal flat from a steeper lower
zone. The surface of this intertidal flat is
composed largely of an erosional surface cut in
underlying glacial sediments (diamict and late
glacial red marine clay). Contemporary intertidal sediment is commonly limited to a thin
veneer on the eroded surface of these underlying
deposits and shows no consistent grain size trend
with variation in elevation (Fig. 7).

The geomorphology of Ardmillan Bay contrasts markedly with both Newtownards and
Greyabbey Bay. The surrounding topography
at Ardmillan Bay comprises essentially intact
drumlins with up to 30 m relief. These surround

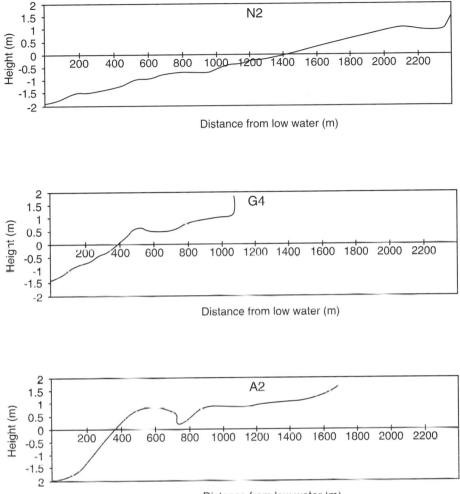

Fig. 5. Shore-normal tidal flat profiles at Newtownards, Greyabbey Bay and Ardmillan Bay. All profiles related to OD Belfast and reduced to same scale.

the bay and a narrow tidal channel permits tidal exchange with the main body of the Lough. Human alteration of the sedimentary regime has occurred over the past two centuries as drumlin islands have been connected by causeways. This has altered tidal currents within the bays that connect with Ardmillan, however, the main tidal connection between the study area and the open Lough has been maintained.

The intertidal sediment at Ardmillan is predominant soft mud that maintains a gentle gradient from high tide to about mid-tide level (Fig. 5). Seaward of this the gradient increases markedly as the tidal flat slopes steeply into a well-defined tidal channel.

Discussion

The tidal flats at Newtownards comprise a sandflat with little relief. At Greyabbey, sandy sediment forms a thin veneer over a wave cut platform of glacial sediments. At Ardmillan, the intertidal zone is dominated by thick mud deposits intersected by distinct tidal channels, located between remnant drumlin islands. This variation in the nature of the intertidal flats in Strangford Lough may be at least in part ascribed to the degree of wave energy exposure and sediment availability in a Lough that was formerly (during the Late Glacial sea level highstand) fairly ubiquitous in character.

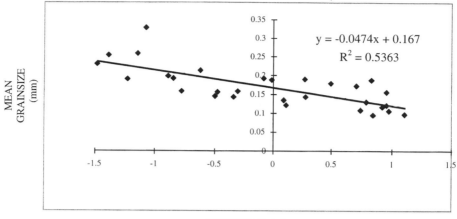

Fig 6. Variation in mean sediment grain size with elevation, Newtownards. Note the reduction in mean grain size with elevation.

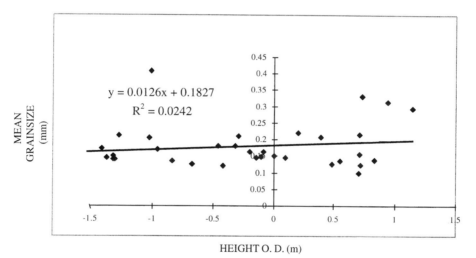

Fig 7. Variation in mean sediment grain size with elevation, Greyabbey Bay. No consistent trend is apparent.

At Newtownards in the northern part of the Lough, large waves are generated across the most extensive fetch in the Lough. These have been able to completely erode the topographic highs on former glacial landforms which are now only exposed at the lower intertidal zone as coarse lags. Due to the presence of a sediment source (eroded from the underlying glacial material) this area has been a net depositional zone for sandy sediments, and grain size variation on its sandy surface provides evidence of maturity and equilibrium with contemporary cross-shore hydrodynamic variations.

At Greyabbey Bay, although wave energy appears to be only slightly lower than Newtownards the morphological contrast between the sites is marked. At Greyabbey the drumlin topography is partly preserved and the presence of only an intertidal erosional platform with a thin depositional veneer suggests that the site is still undergoing erosion and equilibration with contemporary sea level and wave conditions. This is further suggested by the lack of consistent sediment grain size variation across the shore. Although the wave regimes at both Newtownards and Greyabbey appear similar from this simple analysis of maximum fetch it is likely that further analysis of the complete wind–wave spectrum will elucidate further differences between the sites in terms of duration of winds and of storm magnitude from various directions.

The western (upwind) margin of the Lough at Ardmillan Bay contains numerous drumlins which have not been significantly eroded as a result of shelter from large waves. Here, the protection afforded by this topography has led to intertidal mud sedimentation. This is apparently promoted by low wave energy on relatively narrow intertidal zones in the inter-island depressions. The topography of the intertidal flats here is consistent with other mud-dominated tidal flats elsewhere (Pethick 1984) and comprises a low gradient upper zone and steep lower zone sloping to the tidal channel.

Although preliminary, our results indicate an apparent link between wave energy and tidal flat morphology within Strangford Lough on a time-averaged scale. The tidal flats at Newtownards are exposed to maximum wave fetch that coincides with a high frequency wind direction. The lack of drumlin remnants other than boulder lags is indicative of prolonged planation at this site. These flats are the widest and exhibit the gentlest shore-normal topographic gradient within Strangford Lough. The link between sediment mean grain size and elevation on this tidal flat is indicative of a depositional system in equilibrium with dissipating wave energy.

The flats at Greyabbey are also exposed to wave energy but the preservation of drumlin landforms around the margins of the bay suggests lower rates of long-term erosion than at Newtownards. The tidal flats here comprise a thin veneer of sand dispersed across an eroded drumlin surface. It is suggested that as a result of the lower wave energy this tidal flat has not evolved to the same level of maturity as that at Newtownards. It is primarily an erosional surface which is steep and which may be expected to either evolve into a wide flat over time or to maintain this profile in response to lower prevailing wave energy.

The largely intact drumlin topography at Ardmillan is indicative of low rates of long-term erosion and is consistent with the position on the upwind margin and minimal wave fetch. This relict topography coupled with prevailing low wave energy levels has proved favourable for the accumulation of muddy tidal flats. In the Strangford system as a whole we therefore envisage an essentially closed sedimentary system that derives its sediment from erosion of pre-existing glacial lithologies. The extent to which the pre-existing topography is eroded is related to wave energy levels mediated by wave fetch. The resulting topographic variation in the contemporary Lough, coupled with the persisting variation in contemporary wave energy has resulted in marked variation between tidal flats in different parts of the Lough. We thus conclude that in areas of limited sediment supply and where topographic control of wave conditions is important, tidal flat morphology may be spatially variable. While potentially difficult to interpret if preserved in the geological record such an observation may assist in basin-wide reconstruction of former tidal and estuarine environments.

The variation in wave exposure appears to be the prime control on tidal flat variation within Strangford lough and has produced intertidal flats of markedly different morphology and character within a relatively small area. While we cannot yet distinguish the relative roles of storm or fairweather conditions in this process it appears that at the time averaged scale of the past 7000 years, variations both in erosional and depositional wave action have produced several spatially variable types of tidal flat within Strangford Lough as a result of differential erosion and depositional rates on a broadly homogenous drumlinized surface.

This paper has focused on the spatial variability that has resulted from the long term sum of wave action during storm and fairweather conditions. Whereas it has been established that seasonal patterns of sedimentation do exist at one of these sites (Ardmillan Bay, Kirby et al. 1991) apparently in response to winter storms, we have not attempted to address the temporal variability of these tidal flats here, although it might be anticipated that the marked spatial differences that exist both in form and wave exposure, may induce different temporal behavioural patterns throughout the Lough.

Conclusions

Evidence from three sites within Strangford Lough shows marked spatial variation in the character of the intertidal flats in response to exposure to wave action.

The Ardmillan flats on the upwind margin of the basin are located in a largely intact drowned drumlin landscape where planation by waves has been negligible and the resultant sheltered aspect has promoted deposition of mud-dominated tidal flats where tidal currents are the dominant sedimentary agent.

The Greyabbey flats are associated with an intermediate fetch on the downwind margin of the basin. They consist essentially of an erosional platform in semi-consolidated glacial deposits with a thin sedimentary veneer that is dominantly sandy. Under natural conditions progressive erosion of the high tide shoreline may in time lead to the development of a depositional tidal flat system, but the steep contemporary gradient associated with this tidal flat and lack of clear gradients in grain size characteristics is indicative of a relatively immature state.

The Newtownards flats which are exposed to the maximum wave fetch are dominated by sand and are largely depositional in nature. Eroded drumlin remnants are present locally, particularly on the lower tidal flats where the sedimentary cover is thin, but essentially the former drumlin landscape has been planed by wave erosion during the formation of the tidal flat. Preliminary results indicate that a link exists between elevation and sediment grain size on these low gradient tidal flats which appears indicative of a dynamic equilibrium status.

The influence of differential wave action (controlled by effective fetch length and coastal aspect) on a drumlin topography of apparently relatively uniform nature in Strangford Lough has led to the formation of a closely spaced series of intertidal flat deposits of markedly different character within a single depositional basin. These observations suggest an important role for wave action in determining the spatial variation of intertidal flats, particularly in sediment-limited settings.

This research is part of a Co-operative Award in Science and Technology, postgraduate studentship, part-funded by Environment and Heritage service, DoE (NI) and Department of Education (NI) and the School of environmental studies, University of Ulster. The authors are grateful to Robert Stewart, Peter Devlin and Sam Smith and numerous colleagues in the Coastal Studies Research Group for assistance in the field and to Mark Millar for drafting the diagrams.

References

AMOS, C. L. 1995. Siliciclastic tidal flats. In: PERILLO, G. M. E. (ed.) Geomorphology and Sedimentology of Estuaries. Developments in Sedimentology, 53. Elsevier.

BLACK, K. P. & HEALY, T. R. 1981. Computer programs for wave analysis, wind wave generation, wave reflection diagrams and fast fourier analysis. Occasional report number 6, Department of Earth Sciences, University of Walkato.

BOYD, R., DALRYMPLE, R. & ZAITLIN, B. A. 1992. Classification of clastic coastal depositional environments. Sedimentary Geology, 80, 139–150.

CARLING, P. A. 1982. Temporal and spatial variation in intertidal sedimentation rates. Sedimentology, 29, 17–23.

CARTER, R. W. G. 1982. Sea level changes in Northern Ireland. Proceedings of the Geologist's Association, 93, 7–23.

DoE(NI) 1991. Strangford Lough. A consultation paper. HMSO, Belfast.

——1993. Strangford Lough, proposed Marine Nature Reserve. Guide to Designation. HMSO, Belfast.

EVANS, G. 1965. Intertidal flat sediments and their environments of deposition in the Wash. Quarterly Journal of the Geological Society, 121, 209–245.

GUILCHER, A. & BERTHOIS, L. 1957. Cinq années d'observations sedimentologiques dans quatre estuaires-temoins de l'oeust de la Bretagne. Revue Geomorphologie Dynamique, 5, 67–86.

KIRBY, R., BLEAKLY, R. J., WEATHERUP, C., RAVEN, P. J. & DONALDSON, N. D. 1993. Effect of episodic events on tidal mud flat stability, Ardmillan Bay, Strangford Lough, Northern Ireland. In: Nearshore and Estuarine Marine Cohesive Sediment Transport, 42, 378–392.

LYNN, M. J. 1936. The scarcity of Zostera Marina (slitch, eel-grass, or grass-wrack) in Strangford Lough. The Irish Naturalists' Journal, vi, 107–117.

MASSELINK, G. & SHORT, A. D. 1993. The effect of tide range on beach morphodynamics and morphology: a conceptual model. Journal of Coastal Research, 9, 785–800.

MCCABE, A. M. 1997. Geological constraints on geophyisical models of relative sea-level change during deglaciation of the western Irish Sea Basin. Journal of the Geological Society, 154, 601–604.

MORRISON, M. E. S. & STEPHENS, N. 1965. A submerged late-Quaternary deposit at Roddans Port on the north-east coast of Ireland. Philosophical Transactions of the Royal Irish Academy, Series B.249, No. 758, 221–255.

PETHICK, J. 1984. An Introduction to Coastal Geomorphology. Edward Arnold, London.

US ARMY CORPS OF ENGINEERS 1977. Shore Protection Manual, Vol. 1. Fort Belvoir, Virginia 22060.

VAN STRAATEN, L. M. J. U. 1961. Sedimentation in tidal flat areas. Journal of the Alberta Society of Petroleum Geologists, 9, 203–226.

WANG, Y., COLLINS, M. B. & ZHU, D. 1990. A comparative study of open coast tidal flats: the Wash (U. K.), Bohai Bay and west Hunghai Sea (Mainland China). In: Proceedings International Symposium on Coastal Zone of China 1988. China Ocean Press, Beijing, 120–134.

Temporal variation in sediment erodibility and suspended sediment dynamics in the Dollard estuary

BART A. KORNMAN[1,2] & ERIC M. G. T. DE DECKERE[3]

[1] Institute for Marine and Atmospheric Research Utrecht, Utrecht University, Department of Physical Geography, P.O. Box 80.115, 3508 TC Utrecht, The Netherlands
[2] Present adress: National Institute for Coastal and Marine Management/RIKZ, P.O. Box 8039, 4330 EA Middelburg, The Netherlands
[3] Netherlands Institute of Ecology, Centre for Estuarine and Coastal Ecology, P.O. Box 140, 4400 AC Yerseke, The Netherlands

Abstract: The influence of biological activity on sediment erodibility was studied in the Dollard estuary, The Netherlands. The sediment erodibility was measured with an *in situ* flume on an intertidal flat. The hydrodynamics and suspended sediment concentrations above the flat were monitored from a measuring-bridge and in the tidal channel from a platform, using conventional instrumentation. The data from the flume, bridge and platform show that erosion resistance varied considerably from March until August 1996. A diatom bloom at the beginning of April appears to have resulted in an increase in resistance. Currents and waves were no longer able to resuspend sediment from the flat. This resulted in very low mean suspended sediment concentrations. The increase in erosion resistance did not only occur at the research site but on all flats in the Dollard. At the beginning of June, sediment erodibility increased and consequently the suspended sediment concentrations increased. This coincided with the disappearance of diatoms in May and with an increasing density of the amphipod *Corophium volutator* on the flat in June.

Presently, it is commonly recognized that biological processes may result in the stabilization or destabilization of cohesionless and cohesive sediments in subtidal and intertidal environments (Neumann *et al.* 1970; Young & Southard 1978; Montague 1984; Paterson 1989; Black 1997). Heinzelmann & Wallisch (1991) state that benthic settlement can have a decisive influence on sediment erosion and sediment transport. Black (1997) postulates that the presence of micro-organisms is essential for the mere and continued existence of the mudflat, because in absence of the binding influence of micro-organisms these sediments may be washed away by even moderate tidal currents.

The biological activity may influence sediment erodibility in various ways. The net effect depends on the species composition and the density of the benthos present in the sediment, as shown in detail by Heinzelmann & Wallisch (1991) and Paterson (1997). Because species and density change throughout the year a temporal variation in sediment erodibility can be expected. Little is known about the seasonal effect of the biological activity on the sediment erodibility on an intertidal flat. Are there distinct periods where the activity increases or decreases the erodibility? How long are these periods? In what time span does a certain species significantly change the erodibility?

The aim of the present research was to study the influence of the biological activity on sediment erodibility in an intertidal setting. The investigation focused on the temporal variation in erodibility and its effect on sediment resuspension from the flat.

The benthic community at the present field site is characterized by sediment-dwelling diatoms as the primary producers (De Jonge 1992) and benthic fauna species grazing on these diatoms.

Diatoms enhance the erosion resistance of the sediment by the secretion of biopolymers. They secrete these biopolymers to move in the surface millimetres of the sediment, to attach to surfaces of grain particles and as a protective layer against changing environmental conditions (Decho 1990). The secretions are denoted by the term Extracellular Polymeric Substances (EPS) and consist mainly of polysaccharides (Holland *et al.* 1974; Grant *et al.* 1986a; Paterson 1988). The EPS can be subdivided into a water extractable fraction which dissolves quite easily into the water and into an EDTA extractable fraction. The latter fraction causes grain to grain and floc to floc adhesion (Dade *et al.* 1990). Detailed information on the chemical characteristics of the EPS is given by Harris & Mitchell (1973) and Decho (1990). During a diatom bloom, diatom mats can develop on the sediment surface (Vos *et al.* 1988). The

KORNMAN, B. A. & DE DECKERE, E. M. G. T. 1998. Temporal variation in sediment erodibility and suspended sediment dynamics in the Dollard estuary. *In*: BLACK, K. S., PATERSON, D. M. & CRAMP, A. (eds) *Sedimentary Processes in the Intertidal Zone*. Geological Society, London, Special Publications, **139**, 231–241.

mats protect the sediment against current and wave action. The diatom population can be reduced by grazing by the benthic fauna, like *Corophium volutator*, which can be present in large amounts at the field site (Admiraal *et al.* 1983; Dekker 1996).

The research area

The research was carried out in the Dollard, which is the upper reach of the Ems–Dollard estuary (Fig. 1). This estuary is located in the northeastern part of the Dutch Wadden Sea on the border between The Netherlands and Germany. The area of the Ems–Dollard estuary is *c.* 500 km^2 and has a tidal prism of 1×10^9 m^3 at the tidal inlet. The main fresh water input issues from the river Ems (80% of the total input). The average discharge is *c.* 80 m^3 s^{-1}; the variation throughout the year is large and can range from

as low as 25 m^3 s^{-1} in summer to as high as 390 m^3 s^{-1} in the winter (De Jonge 1992). The estuary is classified as well mixed, even at high discharge levels.

The total area of the Dollard is 100 km^2 and 85% of this area is composed of intertidal flats. The tidal prism of the Dollard is 115×10^6 m^3 and the tidal range is 3 m (De Jonge 1992). The maximum depth-averaged velocity in the tidal channel is *c.* 1 ms^{-1}. Above the flat, at the field site on the Heringsplaat (see Fig. 1), the highest current velocities occur during ebb. The maximum depth-averaged velocity above the flat is *c.* 0.3 ms^{-1}. The wave climate is dominated by locally-generated waves. Due to the fetch of a few kilometres and the relatively shallow water depth (1.5 m) the maximum significant wave height above the flat is *c.* 0.5 m. At the field site sediment varies from sandy mud to muddy sand (80 to 20 % <53 m). The bed surface of the flat is quite planar. Dewatering gullies are present on the lower parts of the flat.

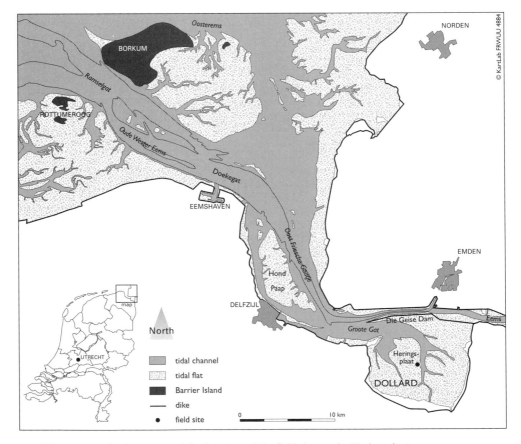

Fig. 1. The Ems–Dollard estuary and the location of the field site on the Heringsplaat.

Instruments and methods

Three types of measurements were carried out: (1) erodibility measurements, (2) hydrodynamic and concentration measurements, and (3) biological measurements.

Erodibility measurements

The *In Situ* Erosion Flume (ISEF) (Houwing & Van Rijn 1995) was used to measure the sediment erodibility. The ISEF is a vertical standing annular flume (Fig. 2). Shear stress on the bed is exerted by a variable unidirectional flow. The open section of the flume is 0.9 m long and 0.2 m wide. The total volume of water in the flume is c. 100 l.

During an experiment, the bed is subjected to increasing bottom shear stresses and the change in suspended sediment concentration (SSC) is monitored. The shear stress is increased in discrete steps but only after the SSC has become constant; sediment is then no longer eroded and the bed shear stress then equals the bed shear strength (Parchure & Mehta 1985).

The flow velocity in the flume is measured with an Electro Magnetic Flow meter (EMF) at 0.025 m above the bed. The SSC is monitored with a turbidity sensor. Both instruments measure at a frequency of 1 Hz. A water sample (0.5 l) is taken from the flume before the start of the experiment and with each applied shear stress when the turbidity has become constant. The concentration is determined by filtering two sub-samples through glassfibre-filter. The volume of a sub-sample was 0.2 l.

Bed shear stress is calculated from the measured velocity with the following equation (Houwing & Van Rijn 1995):

$$\tau_b = \rho \kappa^2 (\alpha U)^2$$

$$\times \left[\ln \left(\frac{d}{0.033 k_s + 0.11 \nu (\tau_b/\rho)^{-0.5}} \right) \right]^{-2}$$

where τ_b = bed shear stress (Nm^{-2}); ρ = water density (1020 kg m^{-3}); κ = constant of von Karman (0.4); α = calibration coefficient (0.9); U = velocity measured in flume (ms^{-1}); d = height of EMF above bed (0.025 m); k_s – Nikuradse roughness height (m); ν = kinematic viscosity (m^2 s^{-1}).

The value of the calibration coefficient α was determined by Houwing & Van Rijn (1995). The only unknown coefficient is the Nikuradse roughness height. Based on Van Rijn (1993) the roughness height is set to three times the particle diameter at which 90% of the grain particles is smaller ($3 \times D_{90}$). This gives for the present field site $k_s = 3 \times 10^{-4}$ (m). It is assumed that the hydraulic roughness of the bed is determined by the grains. The influence of the bed forms on the roughness is not taken into account.

The ISEF was deployed from a boat and was placed on the bed as soon as the flat emerged. The selected surface of the bed where the flume was placed was as uniform and smooth as possible. This was done to avoid the generation

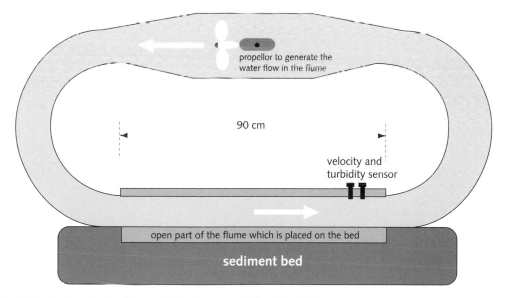

propellor to generate the
water flow in the flume

90 cm

velocity and
turbidity sensor

open part of the flume which is placed on the bed

sediment bed

Fig. 2. The *In Situ* Erosion Flume, ISEF (Houwing & Van Rijn 1995).

of turbulence due to bed disturbances in the flow. The flume was filled with water from the tidal channel. The temperature and salinity of the water were measured. On average it took 90 min to place and fill the flume and start the experiment. The experiment ended just before the location became immersed.

Sediment samples were recovered next to the flume, parallel to the open section of the flume. They were stored in a freezer and analysed in the laboratory for density, water content, grain size by sieving and pipet-withdrawl method, chlorophyll-*a* content and colloidal carbohydrate content (EPS); for analysis methods of the latter two, see Biological measurements. For each analysis the upper 2 mm of the bed was sampled in triplicate, with a core of diameter 3.6 cm. The erodibility measurements were carried out every month, from March until August 1996. The location of the individual flume measurements is shown in Fig. 3.

Hydrodynamic and concentration measurements

At the field site, a measuring bridge, 6 m high and 25 m long (Fig. 4), was situated on the flat,

220 m from the low water line (see Fig. 3). Current velocities, water level, waves, suspended sediment concentration and meteorological data were measured from the platform. Velocities were measured with six EMF-meters, waves and water level with two capacitance wires and suspended sediment concentrations with three turbidity sensors. The instruments measured continuously from April until August with a 2 Hz sampling frequency.

From a platform in the tidal channel (see Fig. 3), suspended sediment concentration and flow velocity was also continuously measured in the watercolumn. Three EMF-meters and turbidity sensors were used.

Biological measurements

The biological activity was monitored in two plots, each 100 m², close to the measuring bridge (see Fig. 3). Monthly sampling of chlorophyll-*a*, EPS and macrobenthos was done. The upper 5 mm of the sediment was sampled to measure chlorophyll-*a* and EPS. Five cores with diameters of 23 mm were taken, sliced and immediately put into a freezer in the field. The sediment was freeze-dried in the laboratory and 0.2 mg of the sediment was used for the EPS

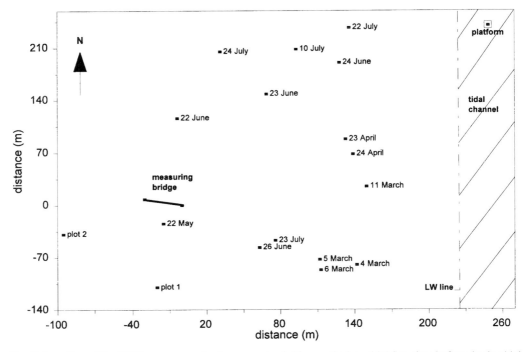

Fig. 3. Location of the ISEF measurements, the measuring bridge on the intertidal flat, the platform in the tidal channel and the biological monitoring plots, at the field site. Markers with date are the locations of the ISEF experimentations, plot 1 and plot 2 are the biological monitoring plots. Distances are measured from the bridge.

Fig. 4. The measuring bridge, photo is taken from the south. The instruments are attached to the pole in the middle of the bridge.

analysis and 0.1 mg for chlorophyll analysis. The chlorophyll-*a* concentration was determined by spectrophotometry (Lorenzen 1967). One ml of distilled water was added to the sediment for the EPS analysis. The samples were incubated for one hour at 30°C and subsequently centrifuged at 4000 rpm. 1.5 ml of 100 mM EDTA was added to the remaining pellet and this was incubated for one night at room temperature and again centrifuged at 4000 rpm. 200 μl of the supernatant after the extraction with EDTA was mixed with 200 μl phenol solution (5%) and 1 ml concentrated sulphuric acid. The absorbance was measured after 15 min at 488 nm.

The macrobenthos samples were taken in triplicate, with a core of diameter 12 cm. The above 30 cm of the sediment was sampled. The samples were fixed with borax-buffered formaldehyde and sieved in the lab with a 0.5 mm sieve. The residue is counted under a binocular microscope to determine the number of macrobenthos present.

Results

Erodibility measurements

From the flume measurements the critical erosion shear stress or erosion threshold was determined.

Although sediment erodibility is characterized by erosion threshold and erosion rate (Amos *et al.* 1992), erodibility is here expressed in erosion threshold. The results are given in Fig. 5. The erodibility clearly varies on a temporal scale. At the beginning of March an average value of $0.2\,\mathrm{Nm^{-2}}$ for the erosion threshold was determined. Around 23 April the threshold had risen to an average of $0.3\,\mathrm{Nm^{-2}}$. On 22 May a value of $0.6\,\mathrm{Nm^{-2}}$ was determined. Measurements carried out from 21 to 23 May at the same field site with an other erosion device, namely the SedErode, resulted in comparable values of the critical erosion stress (Mitchener & Feates 1996). At the end of June the threshold value had reduced to $0.1\,\mathrm{Nm^{-2}}$ and this value was also found in July.

The differences in threshold between April–May and June–July could not be explained by differences in water content, density or grain size of the upper 2 mm of the sediment. Visual observations at the field site in April showed that the amount of diatoms on the flat had increased. The chlorophyll-*a* contents substantiate this observation (Fig. 6a); there is a distinct peak in the content in April compared to the other months. The colloidal carbohydrate contents show a similar trend (Fig. 6b). The data show that low chlorophyll and carbohydrate

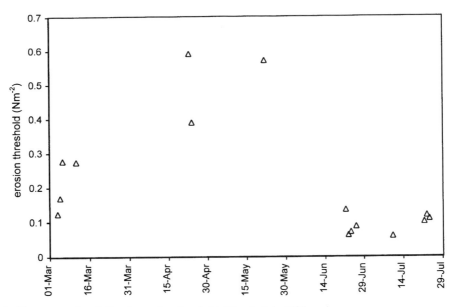

Fig. 5. The temporal variation in erosion threshold, March–July 1996.

contents coincide with lower thresholds and high contents with higher thresholds. However, the measurement on 22 May does not observe this relationship.

Hydrodynamic and concentration measurements

The bed shear stress of the tidal current above the flat was calculated by fitting a logarithmic velocity profile to near-bed velocity data (Wilkinson 1983). The results showed that the maximum shear stress was c. 0.3 Nm^{-2}.

The suspended sediment concentration (SSC) and significant wave height measured above the flat is shown in Fig. 7(a, b). A temporal variation in the SSC is clearly recognizable. At the beginning of April, the SSC gradually decreased from 0.12 g l^{-1} to 0.02 g l^{-1}. Although SSC was not measured in the second half of May, due to malfunction of the turbidity sensors, visual observations showed that SSC remained low until the end of May. At the beginning of June, the SSC gradually increased again. The same temporal variation in suspended sediment concentration was measured in the tidal channel (Fig. 8).

Figure 7(a, b) shows that peak values in the mean concentration correlate well with increased wave activity. In April and May, resuspension of sediment from the flat by waves was very small.

This is in contrast with June and July when wave action resulted in considerable resuspension.

Biological measurements

The chlorophyll-*a* concentrations in the two plots show a similar trend to the data from the ISEF samples (see Fig. 6a). There was a strong increase of chlorophyll-*a* in April due to a diatom bloom. The concentrations in the plots in April are lower than the ISEF samples because the upper 5 mm of the sediment was taken, as for the ISEF samples the upper 2 mm of the sediment was taken. The EDTA extractable EPS concentrations also peaked in April and decreased during the next months (see Fig. 6b).

Discussion

From the data presented it is clear that sediment erodibility varied from March until August 1996 as the result of biological activity. The erosion threshold was considerably higher in April and May, compared to the other months. This was not only shown by the *in situ* flume measurements, but also by the fact that resuspension of sediment from the flat by wave action was very small in April and May. This was in contrast to June and July, when erosion thresholds were five times lower and waves resuspended sediment in large amounts.

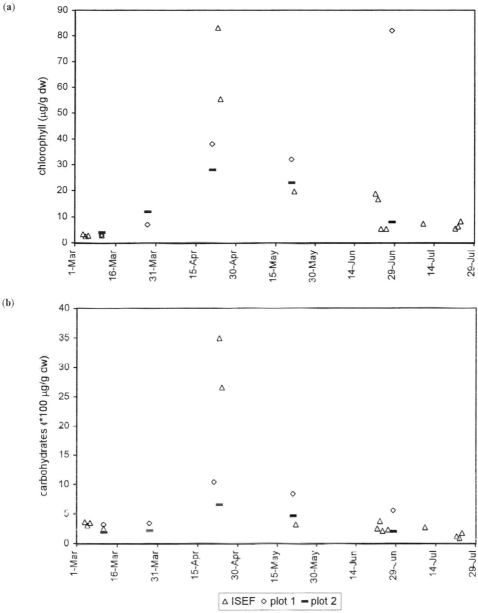

Fig. 6. (a) Chlorophyll-*a* content of the sediment samples recovered during the ISEF experimentations and from the biological plots. (b) Colloidal carbohydrate content of ISEF sediment samples and biological plot samples, March–July 1996.

The temporal variation in mean suspended sediment concentration (SSC), measured above the flat and in the tidal channel is the result of the temporal variation in erodibility. The trend in SSC can only be explained by the following process: the bed shear strength (τ_e) is higher than the bed shear stress (τ_b) of the tidal current and

sediment is no longer resuspended. Sediment can deposit because during a tidal cycle the shear stress becomes smaller than the shear stress for deposition (τ_d) (Fig. 9). When a part of the deposited sediment is not resuspended during the next tidal cycle the SSC will decrease and eventually become zero. The value of the erosion

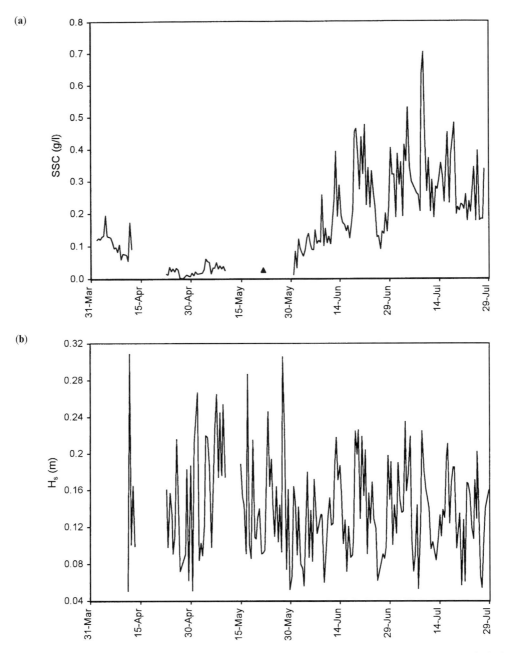

Fig. 7. (a) Mean suspended sediment concentration (SSC) above the flat, measured at 5 cm above the bed. Triangle denotes the suspended sediment concentration measured by Mitchener & Feates (1996). (b) The significant wave height (H_s) above the flat, April–July 1996.

threshold in April and May ($c. 0.5 \, \mathrm{Nm^{-2}}$) and the value of the maximum bed shear stress of the current above the flat ($c. 0.3 \, \mathrm{Nm^{-2}}$) agree with this explanation. It is likely that enhanced trapping of deposited sediment took place in April, due to the presence of large amounts of

polysaccharides in the sediment (Grant *et al.* 1986*b*; Underwood & Paterson 1993).

The temporal variation in the SSC implies that the increase in erosion threshold did not only occur on the flat at the field site but on all the flats in the Dollard estuary. If the increase in

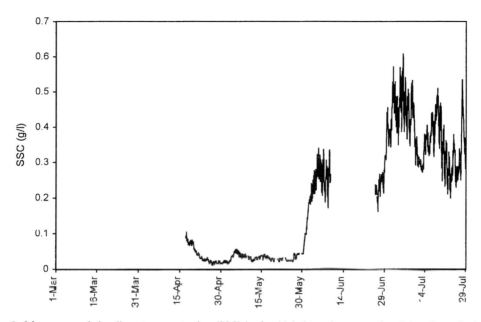

Fig. 8. Mean suspended sediment concentration (SSC) in the tidal channel, measured at 1.4 m above the bed, March–July 1996.

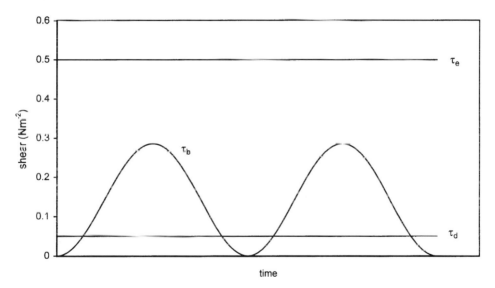

Fig. 9. Relation between bed shear strength (τ_e), bed shear stress (τ_b) and shear stress for deposition (τ_d) for the explanation of the decrease in suspended sediment concentration.

threshold had only occurred at the field site the SSC would certainly not have decreased as much as observed. Resuspension from the other flats would have continued as the total area of the Dollard consists of 85% of intertidal flats. These data may indicate that the SSC in the Dollard is predominantly determined by erosion of sediment from the intertidal flats.

The temporal changes in erodibility were the result of biological activity: a diatom bloom, which started in the end of March, resulted in an increase in carbohydrate content of the sediment. This caused adhesion of the particles and an increase in threshold (Underwood & Paterson 1993; Black 1997). Sediment could not be resuspended from the bed and the undisturbed top-layer of the bed was able to consolidate. When in May the diatoms gradually disappeared and the carbohydrate content and thus the adhesion decreased also, the bed had a high erosion threshold because of this consolidation. At the beginning of June the erosion threshold decreased because the consolidation of the sediment bed diminished. This was probably caused by bioturbation and grazing by *Corophium volutator* (Admiraal *et al.* 1983; Gerdol & Hughes 1994). *Corophium* densities increased from May 20 until June 28 from a few hundred to more than 50 000 numbers per square metre (unpublished data). Amos *et al.* (1992) believe that, in the absence of *Corophium volutator*, benthic biological activity is important in the consolidation process of the topmost millimetres of the sediment bed.

The data have shown on which temporal scale biological activity can influence sediment stability. Strong increases and decreases in erosion threshold can take place within a period of two weeks. An increase in erosion threshold can last for nearly two months. Whether the observed influence of biological activity on sediment erodibility in 1996 is typical for the Dollard is still a question to be answered.

Conclusions

In situ flume, suspended sediment concentration and hydrodynamic measurements show that a temporal variation in sediment erodibility occured in the Dollard estuary, from March until August 1996. This variation was the result of the biological activity on the intertidal flats. Sediment stability at the beginning of April increased with the increase of carbohydrates. Sediment was no longer resuspended from the intertidal flats and a strong decrease in suspended sediment concentration in the estuary took place. The bed did not erode and the undisturbed top-layer of the bed consolidated. In May, when the diatoms disappeared and the carbohydrate content (adhesion) decreased, the top-layer of the bed had a high erosion threshold due to consolidation. At the beginning of June, the consolidation was diminished by bioturbation and grazing by *Corophium volutator*. Consequently, the erosion threshold decreased and sediment was resuspended from the flats again.

The data show that an increase and decrease in erosion threshold can take place within two weeks. The biologically induced (adhesion and consolidation) increase in erosion threshold lasted for nearly two months. The used research procedure of monthly measurement of sediment erodibility and the continuous measurement of suspended sediment concentrations and hydrodynamics has proven to give valuable data about the biological influence on erodibility. However, the data show that erodibility measurements have to be carried out every two weeks because of the rapid changes in erodibility.

The investigation was supported by the Netherlands Geosciences Foundation (GOA) with financial aid from the Netherlands Organization for Scientific research (NWO) and by the European Community grant MAS3-CT95–0022-INTRMUD. 'RWS Directie Noord-Nederland' and 'Meetdienst Noord' of The Ministry of Transport, Public Works and Water Management are thanked for their assistance. Mr M. Lolcama and Ms P. Jeurissen are acknowledged for their help with the flume measurements. NIOO publication no. 2392.

References

ADMIRAAL, W., BOUWMAN, L. A., HOEKSTRA, L. & ROMEYN, K. 1983. Qualitative and quantitative interactions between microphytobenthos and herbivorous meiofauna on a brackish intertidal mudflat. *International Revue der gesamten Hydrobiologie*, **68**, 175–191.

AMOS, C. L., DABORN, G. R., CHRISTIAN, H. A., ATKINSON, A. & ROBERTSON, A. 1992. *In situ* erosion measurements on fine-grained sediments from the Bay of Fundy. *Marine Geology*, **108**, 175–196.

BLACK, K. S. 1997. Microbiological factors contributing to erosion resistance in natural cohesive sediments. *In*: BURT, N., PARKER, R. & WATTS, J. (eds) *Cohesive Sediments*, 231–244.

DADE, W. B., DAVIS, J. D., NICHOLS, P. D., NOWELL, A. R. M., THISTLE, D., TREXLER, M. B. & WHITE, D. C. 1990. Effects of bacterial exopolymer adhesion on the entrainment of sand. *Geomicrobiology Journal*, **8**, 1–16.

DE JONGE, V. N. 1992. Physical processes and dynamics of microphytobenthos in the Ems estuary. PhD Thesis, University of Groningen, The Netherlands.

DECHO, A. W. 1990. Microbial exopolymer secretions in ocean environments: their role(s) in food webs and marine processes. *Oceanography and Marine Biology, Annual Review*, **28**, 73–153.

DEKKER, R. 1996. Het macrozoobenthos op twaalf raaien in de Waddenzee en de Eems–Dollard in 1995 (in Dutch). NIOZ-rapport 1996-1.

GERDOL, V. & HUGHES, R. G. 1994. Effect of *Corophium volutator* on the abundance of benthic diatoms, bacteria and sediment stability in two estuaries in southeastern England. *Marine Ecology Progress Series*, **114**, 109–115.

GRANT, J., BATHMANN, U. V. & MILLS, E. L. 1986*a*. The interaction between benthic diatom films and sediment transport. *Estuarine, Coastal and Shelf Science*, **23**, 225–238.

——, MILLS, E. L. & HOPPER, C. M. 1986*b*. A chlorophyll budget of the sediment–water interface and the effect of stabilising biofilms on particle fluxes. *Ophelia*, **26**, 206–219.

HARRIS, R. H. & MITCHELL, R. 1973. The role of polymers in microbial aggregation. *Ann. Rev. Microbiol.* **27**, 27–50.

HEINZELMANN, C. H. & WALLISCH, S. 1991. Benthic settlement and bed erosion. A review. *Journal of Hydraulic Research*, **29**, 355–371.

HOLLAND, A. F., ZINGMARK, R. G. & DEAN, J. M. 1974. Quantitative evidence concerning the stabilization of sediments by marine benthic diatoms. *Marine Biology*, **17**, 191–196.

HOUWING, E. J. & VAN RIJN, L. C. 1995. *In-situ* determination of the critical bed shear stress for erosion of cohesive sediments. *Proceedings of the 24th International Conference on Coastal Engineering*, Kobe, Japan, 2058–2069.

LORENZEN, C. J. 1967. Determination of chlorophyll and phaeopigments: spectrophotometric equations. *Limnology and Oceanography*, **12**, 343–346.

MITCHENER, H. J. & FEATES, N. G. 1996. *Field measurements of erosional behaviour and settling velocities of intertidal sediments at the Dollard, Netherlands 21–23 May 1996*. Report TR 16, HR Wallingford.

MONTAGUE, C. L. 1984. Influence of biota on erodibility of sediments. *In*: MEHTA, A. J. (ed.) *Estuarine Cohesive Sediment Dynamics*. Springer-Verlag, 251–269.

NEUMANN, A. C., GEBELEIN, C. D. & SCOFFIN, G. P. 1970. The composition, structure and erodibility of subtidal mats, Abaco, Bahama's. *Journal of Sedimentary Petrology*, **40**, 274–297.

PARCHURE, T. M. & MEHTA, A. J. 1985. Erosion of soft cohesive sediment deposits. Journal of Hydraulic Engineering, **111**, 1308–1326.

PATERSON, D. M. 1988. The influence of epipelic diatoms on the erodibility of an artificial sediment. *10th Diatom Symposium*, 345–355.

——1989. Short-term changes in the erodibility of intertidal cohesive sediments related to the migratory behaviour of epipelic diatoms. *Limnology and Oceanography*, **34**, 223–234.

——1997. Biological mediation of sediment erodibility: ecology and physical dynamics. *In*: BURT, N., PARKER, R. & WATTS, J. (eds) *Cohesive Sediments*, 215–230.

UNDERWOOD, G. J. C. & PATERSON, D. M. 1993. Recovery of intertidal benthic diatoms after biocide treatment and associated sediment dynamics. *Journal of the Marine Biological Association of the United Kingdom*, **73**, 25–45.

VAN RIJN, L. C. 1993. Principles of sediment transport in rivers, estuaries and coastal seas. *Aqua Publications*, Amsterdam, The Netherlands.

VOS, P. C., DE BOER, P. L. & MISDORP, R. 1988. Sediment stabilization by benthic diatoms in intertidal sandy shoals; Qualitative and quantitative observations. *In*: DE BOER, P. L. *et al.* (eds) *Tide-Influenced Sedimentary Environments and Facies*, 511–526.

WILKINSON, R. H. 1983. A method for evaluating statistical errors associated with logarithmic velocity profiles. *Geo-Marine Letters*, **3**, 49–52.

YOUNG, R. N. & SOUTHARD, J. B. 1978. Erosion of fine-grained marine sediments: seafloor and laboratory experiments. *Geological Society of American Bulletin*, **89**, 663–672.

100 years of environmental change in a coastal wetland, Augusta Bay, southeast Sicily: evidence from geochemical and palaeoecological studies

ANDREW B. CUNDY[1], PHILIP E. F. COLLINS[1], SIMON D. TURNER[1] ,
IAN W. CROUDACE[2] & DAVID HORNE[3]

[1] Department of Geography and Earth Sciences, Brunel University, Uxbridge UB8 3PH, UK
[2] Southampton Oceanography Centre, European Way, Southampton SO14 3ZH, UK
[3] Department of Zoology, University of Cambridge, Downing Street,
Cambridge CB2 3EJ, UK

Abstract: Recent (post-1950 AD), industrial development in southeast Sicily has resulted in extensive modification of the coastline (port construction) and a potential for persistent, chronic pollution (oil refinery and petrochemical developments). High resolution radiometric dating (^{210}Pb and ^{137}Cs) and palaeoenvironmental analysis of a short saltmarsh core from the Mulinello estuary (Augusta Bay) provides a record of change over the period 1880–1995 AD. Palynological data indicate expansion of halophytic vegetation across the study area between c. 1880 and 1945 AD. An increase in sediment accumulation occurred between 1945–1965 AD, with an associated rapid change in saltmarsh vegetation occurring at the beginning of this period. Palynological and geochemical data indicate that this increase in sediment accretion is probably due to an enhanced input of catchment-area derived material. This ante-dates the main period of industrial activity in the area, and probably reflects fluvial/catchment processes rather than local anthropogenic changes. Port and industrial developments, in comparison, have had a less significant impact on marsh vegetation and sediment supply, despite large scale disturbance at the rear of the marsh. Trace element analyses show little input of industrial effluent to the Mulinello despite its location in a heavily-industrialized area. This, combined with preliminary diatom studies, indicates that the Mulinello receives most of its sediment from inland and local sources. The rapidity of local environmental change revealed in this sequence illustrates the dynamic nature of wetlands in microtidal settings and emphasizes their potential sensitivity to both local and regional disturbance. This study also demonstrates the use of combining palaeoecological with geochemical analyses to reconstruct environmental change in fluvial and estuarine wetland settings.

Intensive coastal urbanization and industrialization often have a major impact on natural coastal dynamics. Coastal wetlands, lying between terrestrial and marine systems, are often dramatically affected, undergoing changes in sedimentary processes and vegetation assemblages and acting as a sink for pollutant inputs. These are of concern on both local and global scales due to the considerable economic importance of wetlands and the significant role they play in conserving global biodiversity (Williams 1990; R.C.B. 1996). Due to their often high rates of sediment accretion and stabilized, vegetated nature, these wetlands may be highly efficient recorders of environmental change. As a result, analysis of coastal wetland sediment sequences has been used extensively to reconstruct coastal changes over Holocene (e.g. Dominik & Stanley 1993; Robinson 1993; Carter & Woodroffe 1994; Daoust et al. 1996) and more recent timescales (post Industrial Revolution) (e.g. McCaffrey & Thomson 1980; French et al. 1994; Cundy &

Croudace 1995, 1996). For the latter, the use of high resolution radiometric dating techniques (such as ^{210}Pb and ^{137}Cs dating) provides the opportunity to link short-term, direct observation studies of coastal dynamics with records of longer-term development as these methods provide both chronological control and information on short-term variability in sediment accretion/erosion. The age range of these dating techniques (up to 120 a for ^{210}Pb) covers the period of most recent anthropogenic disturbance in many regions but may also include earlier periods when more 'natural' conditions may have prevailed.

The impact of anthropogenic activities on wetland processes is often difficult to distinguish from natural system dynamics, particularly in wetland areas subject to rapid changes in sedimentation as a result of seasonal fluvial activity and long-term soil erosion, e.g. the central Mediterranean. Determining anthropogenic impact in these environments using sedimentary

CUNDY, A. B., COLLINS, P. E. F., TURNER, S. D. et al. 1998. Recent environmental change, southeast Sicily. In: BLACK, K. S., PATERSON, D. M. & CRAMP, A. (eds) Sedimentary Processes in the Intertidal Zone. Geological Society, London, Special Publications, **139**, 243–254.

records requires a multi-proxy approach combining precise dating with a range of palaeo-environmental indicators such as geochemical and pollen analyses. Individually, these analyses may be prone to misinterpretation. For example, in fluvial and estuarine settings, there is a potential for variations to occur in the ratio between autochthonous and allocthonous pollen and diatom inputs (e.g. Vos & De Wolf 1993), and assemblages may be influenced by sorting and differential preservation (e.g. West *et al.* 1993).

This study thus uses a combination of palaeo-ecological and geochemical data to assess the

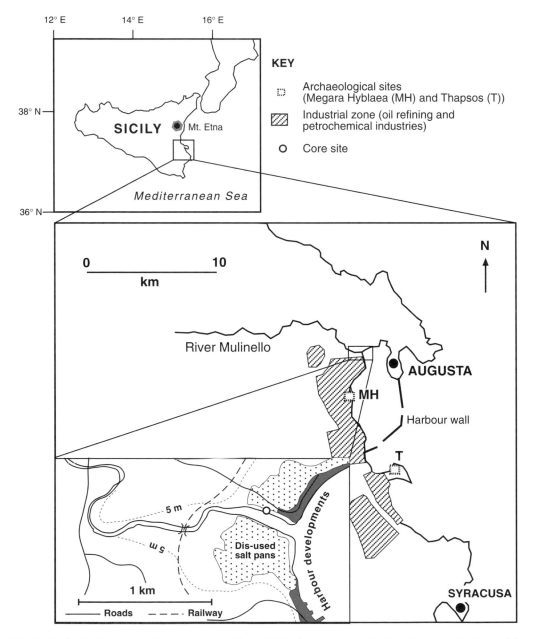

Fig. 1. The Mulinello estuary, Augusta Bay, southeast Sicily showing core collection site and major industrial and urban developments.

impact of rapid coastal development in Augusta Bay, southeast Sicily. The island of Sicily (Fig. 1) has experienced considerable anthropogenic impact for several thousand years. Since 1950 AD, the exploitation of oil reserves to the south of Sicily and the island's central location for the import of crude oil from the Middle East and North Africa has acted as a stimulus for intensive industrialization, particularly in the coastal zone between Augusta and Syracusa. By the late 1960s, the Augusta–Syracusa industrial zone contained oil refineries and petrochemical industries, and by 1969 Augusta was Sicily's major port (Chester et al. 1985). Rapid changes in land-use, sedimentary processes, local vegetation and pollutant input are likely to be associated with this development. Magazzu et al. (1995) note a high state of degradation of water quality in Augusta Bay, with occasional eutrophication from urban and industrial run-off, while Castagna et al. (1985) measured high heavy metal concentrations in marine organisms from the west–southwest part of the Bay.

Study site

The wetland sampled is a microtidal saltmarsh situated at Porto Magarese (Augusta), on the north bank of the Mulinello River, southeast Sicily [15°15'E 37°15'N; Fig. 1]. Mean tidal range in this area (based on tide gauge records at Catania) is less than 30 cm (0.3 m springs, 0.1 m neaps, Hydrographer of the Navy 1996).

While the northeast coast of Sicily and the Etna area is apparently undergoing uplift at a rate of 1–2 mm a^{-1} (Firth et al. 1996; Stewart et al. 1997), slightly submerged Roman remains at Thapsos and other coastal sites (Basile et al. 1986) indicate that the southeast Sicily coastal zone is stable or only slowly subsiding. The nearest tide gauge record of longer-term (>20 a) sea level change is from Catania (Tsimplis & Spencer 1997), an area tectonically distinct from the Augusta–Syracusa coastal zone and so unlikely to give a representative record of sea level trends at the study site. While the southeast Sicily area is considered to be a region of high seismic risk, available data indicate that significant seismic activity ceased after 1850 (Mulargia et al. 1985; although a small (magnitude 5.5) earthquake occurred in 1990), hence the wetland sequences examined are unlikely to have been affected by rapid changes in relative sea level caused by earthquake activity. A tsunami related to the 1908 Straits of Messina earthquake may have affected the Porto Magarese area (Platania

1909), although the data presented here show no clear evidence of this. Over the time period of interest in this study, relative sea level is likely to have shown only minor change.

Cores collected from the study site revealed a 70 cm sequence of organic clays and silts overlying water saturated sands. The area of marsh sampled consisted of a narrow strip (10–20 m wide) between the port access road and the Mulinello channel. Surface vegetation was dominated by Sueda maritima (L.) Dumort and Atriplex portulacoides (L.). Much of the Mulinello estuary has been managed for salt production. Air photographs (1942) show that almost the entire low-lying area around the channel consisted of saltings or salinas (Fig. 1). The marsh area sampled, however, showed little evidence for direct disturbance by this activity. The marsh was 100 m inland from the commercial port at Augusta, which has been built on reclaimed land. A limestone rubble embankment for the access road, up to 150 m wide, has been constructed across part of the marsh. Immediately next to the sample site, this embankment was c. 2 m high.

Methods

A 30 cm core was retrieved from the Sueda maritima dominated interior of the marsh (4.5 m from the Mulinello channel), using a hand-driven 9 cm diameter PVC tube. On return to the laboratory the core was sliced in half, photographed, X-radiographed and described before being sampled for geochemical, palaeoecological and radiometric analysis.

Sediment accumulation rates were determined using the ^{210}Pb and ^{137}Cs dating methods. The natural radionuclide ^{210}Pb has been extensively used in the dating of recent sediments. Dating is based on determination of the vertical distribution of unsupported ^{210}Pb (^{210}Pb$_{excess}$), or ^{210}Pb arising from atmospheric fallout, which then allows ages to be ascribed to sedimentary layers based on the known decay rate of ^{210}Pb (see Appleby & Oldfield 1992 for synthesis of the ^{210}Pb method). ^{210}Pb activity was determined by a proxy method through alpha spectrometric measurement of its grand daughter nuclide ^{210}Po. The method employed was based on Flynn (1968), using double acid leaching of the sediment with ^{209}Po as an isotopic tracer and autodeposition of the Po isotopes in the leachate on to silver discs. Detection limits were 1 Bq kg^{-1}. The ^{210}Pb$_{excess}$ activity was estimated by subtraction of the value of constant ^{210}Pb activity at depth (22 Bq kg^{-1}). Sediments were dated in this study using the CRS (Constant Rate of Supply) model of ^{210}Pb dating (Goldberg 1963), allowing construction of an age-depth curve for sediments between the surface and 20 cm depth (estimated dates for core sections deeper than this are based on extrapolation of the age-depth curve), (Fig. 2).

^{137}Cs is an artificially produced radionuclide, present in the study area due to atmospheric fallout from nuclear weapons testing and reactor accidents. Marked maxima in the deposition of ^{137}Cs occurred in 1958, 1963 (from nuclear weapons testing) and 1986 (from the Chernobyl accident). In favourable conditions, these periods of peak fallout provide subsurface activity maxima in accumulating sediments and can be used to derive rates of sediment accumulation (e.g. Ritchie & McHenry 1990; Cundy

& Croudace 1996). ^{137}Cs activities were determined by gamma spectrometry with a Canberra 30% P-type HPGe detector. Errors were typically in the order of 4% (1σ), detection limits were 0.5 Bq kg^{-1}.

Pollen samples were collected to reflect sedimentological variations within the core and prepared for analysis following standard techniques (Moore *et al.* 1991) with *Lycopodium* tablets added to estimate pollen concentrations. Pollen nomenclature follows Moore *et al.* (1991) with modifications following Bennett *et al.* (1994). Pollen counts are relatively low (typically *c.* 100 identified grains), reflecting the minerogenic nature of the sediments, but it is felt that this is sufficient to reflect the major changes in pollen assemblages outlined below. Detailed relative pollen frequencies based on total pollen,

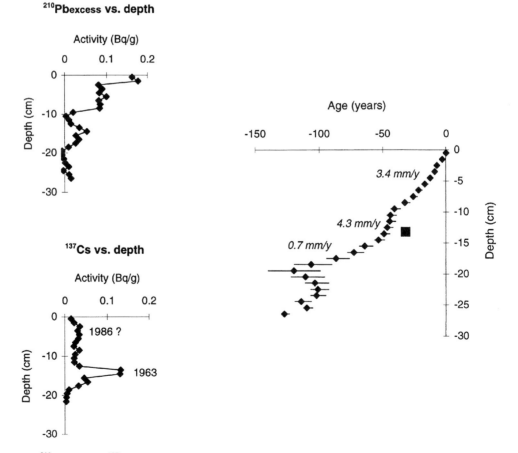

Fig. 2. ^{210}Pb$_{excess}$ and ^{137}Cs vs depth for River Mulinello saltmarsh, Augusta Bay. Age–depth curve derived using ^{210}Pb data (CRS model) is also shown. Sediment accretion rates are shown in italics, and ^{137}Cs date is shown by the filled square.

including unidentifiable deteriorated pollen grains together with estimated total concentrations, are presented here and are plotted against date, as determined by ^{210}Pb dating (Fig. 2).

For diatom analysis, samples were pretreated with H_2O_2 prior to mounting on slides and examination. Diatom nomenclature follows Sims (1996). Provisional count data are presented in Table 1.

Geochemical analyses were carried out at 1 cm depth increments. Samples were pelletized for trace element determinations and fused for major

Table 1. *Diatom assemblage data from selected depth horizons, River Mulinello saltmarsh core*

	0 cm	1 cm	3 cm	5 cm	6 cm	7 cm	8 cm	12 cm
No diatoms present						yes		
Rare diatom fragments		yes		yes			yes	yes
Abundant diatom fragments	yes		yes		yes			
Fresh								
cf. *Achnanthes biorettii* Germain	6							
Caloneis bacillum (Grunow) Cleve	1							
Cocconeis placentula Ehrenberg	3							
Gomphonema angustatum (Kützing) Rabenhorst	2							
Martyana martyi (Heribaud) F. E. Round					2			
cf. *Navicula angusta* Grunow	13							
Naviclua cryptotenella Lange-Bertalot	2		1					
Navicula leptostriata Jorgensen			1					
cf. *Navicula subrotundata* Hustedt	2							
cf. *Nitzschia perminuta* (Grunow in Van Heurck) M. Peragallo	6						1.5	
Synedra rumpens Kutzing					1			
Synedra ulna (Nitzsch) Ehrenberg		0 5						
Fresh–brackish								
Achnanthes delicatula (Kützing) Grunow in Cleve et Grunow					1			
Brackish–fresh								
Nitzschia epithemoides Grunow in Cleve et Grunow					1			
Tryblionella debilis Arnott in O'Meara	6							
Brackish								
Rhopalodia musculus (Kützing) O. Müller	4							
Marine–brackish								
Amphora coffaeformis (Agardh) Kützing	7				7			
Marine								
Amphora holsatica Hustedt	9				5			
Cocconeis scutellum Ehernberg	8				1		0.5	
Diploneis didyma (Ehrenberg) Cleave	1		2		1		1	
cf. *Nitzschia bilobata* W. Smith	2							
Unassigned								
Achnanthes sp.	2				1			
Amphora sp.	3	1						
Caloneis/Stauroneis sp.							1	
Cymbella sp.					1			
Epithemia sp.					1			
Fragilaria/Synedra sp. (agg.)	5				2			
Gomphonema sp.	3							
Naviculoid (agg.)	91				66		2	
Nitzschia sp. (agg.)	20		0.5		2			
Pleurosigma sp.					1			
Surirella sp.	0.5							
Tabellaria sp.	0.5							
Total	196	1.5	4.5	0	93	0	6	0

element determinations, and analysed using a Philips PW1400 sequential X-ray fluorescence spectrometer system (Cundy & Croudace 1995).

Results

Core stratigraphy

Sediments at the site studied are dominantly fine-grained throughout the cored depth (0–30 cm), and show clear vertical zonation, consisting of four horizons:

- Horizon A (core base to −14 cm). Brown/grey silty clay with distinct red/brown mottling.
- Horizon B (−14 cm to −4.5 cm). Dark brown silty clay with black organic-rich layers. A black, organic-rich layer at −7.5 cm contained numerous plastic beads (3 mm diameter).
- Horizon C (−4.5 to −2.5 cm). Brown/grey silty clay with distinct red/brown mottling and incorporated fine roots.
- Horizon D (−2.5 to 0 cm). Humic peat with roots, surface litter, and gastropod shells (*Hydrobia* sp.).

Radiometric dating

^{210}Pb. In addition to providing high resolution chronological control ^{210}Pb dating reveals considerable variability in sediment accretion over the hundred year time period studied (Fig. 2). For sediments below 19 cm age estimations are inconclusive and cannot be used to determine rates of sediment accumulation due to the low $^{210}Pb_{excess}$ activity, which limits the accuracy of ^{210}Pb dating at ages greater than c. 120 a. Between c. 1880 and 1940 (c. 19–15 cm) sediment accreted at a mean rate of 0.7 mm a^{-1}, which increased to a mean rate of 4.3 mm a^{-1} over the period c. 1945–1965 (c. 15–9 cm). The errors in the age-depth curve occurring over this period of increased sedimentation indicate that the rate of deposition may have been even more rapid, however, the discrete 1963 ^{137}Cs peak (see below) indicates that sedimentation was not instantaneous (due to, for example, dumping of dredged spoil on the marsh surface) and more likely indicates a more widespread change in marsh deposition rates. Post-1965 (above c. 9 cm depth), mean sediment accretion at the site decreased to 3.4 mm a^{-1}, and has shown little variation since, even though this has been a period of extensive port and industrial development in the area (Mountjoy 1970).

^{137}Cs. The site examined shows a distinct maximum in ^{137}Cs activity at 13–15 cm depth (Fig. 2) most likely corresponding to the 1963 period of peak fallout from atmospheric weapons testing. The remote position of Sicily in relation to the track of the 'plume' from the Chernobyl accident, the absence of detectable ^{134}Cs and the rapid drop in activity to zero below this peak, indicate a weapons testing, rather than a Chernobyl, source. Ascribing this activity peak to 1963 gives an average sediment accumulation rate of 4–5 mm a^{-1}. There is some discrepancy between this rate and the age-depth curve obtained using ^{210}Pb dating. ^{137}Cs may give a slightly greater rate of sediment accumulation due to downward mixing following deposition, although the magnitude of this downward mixing is likely to be small due to the 'sharp' nature of the subsurface maximum ascribed to 1963 and the stabilized, vegetated nature of the salt marsh and consequent lack of post-depositional disturbance. The remainder of the discrepancy may be due to variation in sediment source and composition influencing the flux of $^{210}Pb_{excess}$ to the marsh and the supported ^{210}Pb activity (both may slightly affect ages given by the CRS model). The CRS model assumes ^{210}Pb input to the marsh is dominantly from atmospheric fallout, rather than from ^{210}Pb-labelled sediment particles. This is a reasonable assumption for this microtidal setting and for the shape of the $^{210}Pb_{excess}$ curve (other models require a near log-linear decrease in $^{210}Pb_{excess}$ vs depth). The calculated $^{210}Pb_{excess}$ flux for this marsh is 0.02 Bq cm^{-2} a^{-1}, slightly higher than estimates for typical atmospheric input of ^{210}Pb to northern continental landmasses (0.014 Bq cm^{-2}a^{-1}, Appleby & Oldfield 1992). This means that a fraction of the annual $^{210}Pb_{excess}$ supply is derived from labelled particles, probably causing the slight difference between CRS model derived ages and the ^{137}Cs-derived age. Despite this slight discrepancy, the age–depth curve in Fig. 2 clearly shows considerable variation in the sediment accumulation rate, with increased sediment accumulation over the period 1945–1965.

Pollen analysis

Three local pollen assemblage zones (LPAZ: A1–3) are defined (Fig. 3) which reflect both progressive development of the local wetland environment over time and sudden change.

LPAZ:A1 Base of core to 13.5 cm depth (1865(?) to 1945 AD). There is a progressive increase in the relative frequency of Chenopodiaceae with a

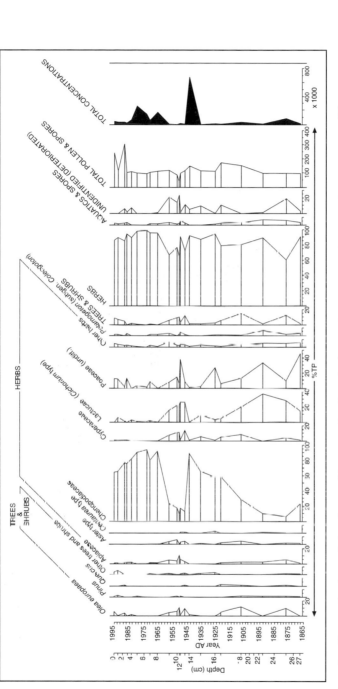

Fig. 3. Relative pollen diagram showing variations in assemblages over time from the Augusta Bay core. Sample ages are determined by the ^{210}Pb CRS model for 0–19 cm depth. Sample ages below 19 cm depth are extrapolated.

reciprocal fall in Lactucae and, to some extent Poaceae. *Olea europaea* occurs at various frequencies, as do *Aster* type, Apiaceae, *Quercus* and *Potomogeton* (subgenus *Coleogoton*). This suggests expansion of saltmarsh vegetation across the coring site resulting in both increased local pollen input and also the swamping of allocthonous pollen types derived from less saline wetland and also terrestrial areas. Complete dominance of the local surface by halophytic vegetation was accomplished by the top of the zone. This surface may have been relatively stable for a short interval, resulting in a sudden increase in the absolute number of pollen grains present. Alternatively, the vegetation provided a more favourable setting for pollen deposition by gravitational fallout and incorporation in faecal pellets (Chmura & Eisma 1995).

LPAZ:A2 13.5cm to 8.5cm depth (1945 to 1965 AD). The transition from A1 to A2 is extremely abrupt, marked by a fall in Chenopodiaceae from 93% to 13% over 1 cm, or possibly less than 3 a (the temporal resolution of the pollen record at this depth). Associated with this fall in halophytes is the rise of terrestrial, mainly catchment-derived, taxa. The low absolute concentrations for most of this zone suggests that the local saltmarsh was not directly replaced by, for example, Lactucae. Rather, an increased supply of sediment-laden fresh water suppressed pollen production by either killing or damaging the saltmarsh vegetation.

LPAZ:A3 8.5 cm to surface (1965 to 1995 AD). Chenopodiaceae again dominates. The rapid rise from 23% to 95% over 1 cm reflects recovery by local halophytes in 7 a or less. The reduction in allocthonous elements and the rise in absolute concentrations suggests a more stable surface with higher local pollen input. There is a marked fall in pollen concentration in the upper 4 cm of the core (post-1980), associated with a decline in the relative frequency of Chenopodiaceae. This may reflect direct physical disturbance of the marsh surface immediately adjacent to the coring site or a reduction in the extent of halophytic vegetation locally, for example following construction of the port's access road. This latter event would have buried a significant proportion of the saltmarsh surface beneath rubble and tarmac, and may have acted as a barrier for pollen travelling from other parts of the marsh to the coring site.

The pollen record implies a sequence of environmental changes in the coring locality. Initially, sediments incorporated pollen largely

from the catchment. The low frequencies of wind-dispersed types, such as *Pinus*, may indicate that most were supplied via the Mulinello river. Progressively, colonization by halophytic vegetation occurred so that, by 1945 AD, the site was dominated by saltmarsh which had stabilized the surface to some extent. A sudden environmental change then occurred, probably resulting in significant reduction in the extent and vigour of the local saltmarsh community. The most likely cause is inundation by sediment laden fresh water from the adjacent channel of the Mulinello. The cause of this is unclear, though channel migration is unlikely given the presence of managed salinas along the channel margins. Multiple flooding events are indicated both by the delay before the halophytic vegetation expanded (*c.* 17 a) and perhaps by variations in the pollen assemblages representing this interval, though this variability may be an artefact of taphonomic processes, including sorting and selective preservation in a fluvial deposit (cf. Burrin & Scaife 1984; West *et al.* 1993; Collins 1994; Chmura & Eisma 1995), and of sample size. The rate of post-flooding saltmarsh recovery reconstructed from the core is similar to that documented from other sites (e.g. Allison 1996).

Geochemistry: reconstruction of pollution histories and changes in sediment provenance

Variations in geochemical composition within the core are mainly a result of changes in sediment provenance, variation in sedimentary dynamics within the channel/estuarine system and anthropogenic (contaminant) inputs. Near-surface sediments, deposited during the post-1965 industrial expansion within Augusta Bay, show little evidence of contamination by industrial and port effluents. In fact, heavy metals characteristic of industrial (particularly refinery/ petrochemical) effluent (Cu, Ni, Zn, V) show dramatically increased fluxes over the period *c.* 1945–1965, prior to major industrialization, and a decreasing flux post-1965 (Fig. 4). (Fluxes, or rate of input, rather than concentrations, are referred to throughout this section as elevated concentrations of trace metals may be caused by a decrease in sediment accumulation rate rather than an increase in contamination, while an increase in wt.% for major elements may reflect a reduced input of other sedimentary components (organic matter, shell material) rather than increasing input.) The presence of this flux increase prior to the period of most rapid industrialization, and the strong correlation of these

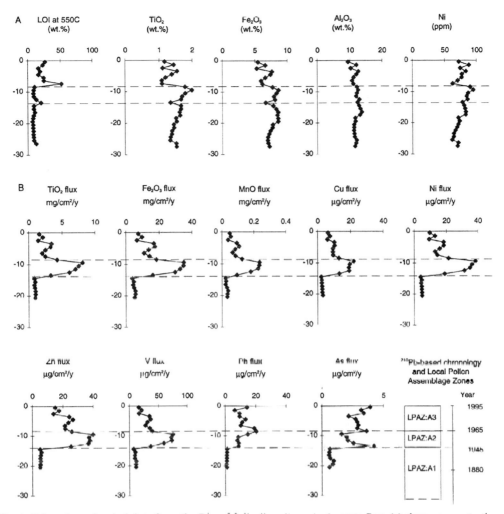

Fig. 4. Selected geochemical data from the River Mulinello saltmarsh, Augusta Bay. (a) shows concentration data for LOI, TiO₂, Fe₂O₃, Al₂O₃ and Ni (b) shows fluxes of TiO₂, Fe₂O₃, MnO, Cu, Ni, Zn, V, Pb and As. On each graph, error bars are smaller than the diamond marker symbol. Fluxes are calculated using the equation Flux = ρ × concentration × sediment accumulation rate (based on ^{210}Pb dating). Depth boundaries of local pollen assemblage zones are shown by dotted lines.

elements with TiO_2, Fe_2O_3 and MnO (which are dominantly detrital, rather than anthropogenically-produced) indicates the increased fluxes are a consequence of a change in sedimentary dynamics, rather than pollution input. The drainage basin of the River Mulinello is characterized by Pliocene/Pleistocene basic igneous and volcanic sequences, and Miocene to Quaternary limestone sequences (Lentini 1987). The surrounding coastal area mainly consists of carbonate sequences of similar age (Lentini 1987). While catchment rocks were not directly geochemically characterized in this study, the volcanic rocks present in the upper catchment

are dominantly Na-alkaline in composition (Cristofolini & Romano 1982) and present a likely primary source for material enriched in Ti, Fe and trace elements. Recent lavas contain Ti concentrations of 1.5–1.8% (wt.% TiO_2) and Fe up to 10% (wt% Fe_2O_3 and FeO) (Armienti et al. 1989). Enhanced erosion of these materials, or reworking of alluvial deposits containing eroded volcanic material, may have caused the observed flux increases in Ti, Fe, Cu, Ni, Zn and V. This interpretation agrees well with changes in wetland development proposed on the basis of palynological data: although calculated fluxes are highly dependant on the model of

^{210}Pb dating used, the distinct increase in input of Ti, Fe and trace elements, and the corresponding rapid relative decrease in LOI (loss on ignition) over the period 1945–1965 (Fig. 4) is consistent with input of catchment-derived material by multiple flooding events (pollen zone LPAZ:A2). (NB. A reduction in mean grain size between −13.5 and −8.5 cm could also cause the observed increase in concentration of Ti, Mn, Fe etc. due to fine sediment association. This is not consistent, however, with the decrease in ^{210}Pb$_{excess}$ and lack of enrichment in Pb over the same depth interval.)

The subsequent (post-1965) decrease in fluxes and increase in LOI indicate a relative decrease in fluvial input of sediments and an increased importance of *in situ* saltmarsh vegetation growth and burial of incompletely decomposed plant matter under saturated conditions (corresponding to pollen zone LPAZ:A3). Pb and As fluxes are more variable over this zone and do not reflect the variations in detrital input suggested above: total Pb flux increases from $1\,\mu g\,cm^{-2}\,a^{-1}$–$20\,\mu g\,cm^{-2}\,a^{-1}$ over the period 1950–1970, with a slight decrease to $14\,\mu g\,cm^{-2}\,a^{-1}$ at present (Fig. 4), and As flux, while showing a more variable distribution, increases from $0.5\,\mu g\,cm^{-2}\,a^{-1}$ (pre-1945) to $4\,\mu g\,cm^{-2}\,a^{-1}$ at present. The increased Pb flux is probably a consequence of increasing road traffic following industrialization and port construction, fluxes being comparable to those observed near to urbanized/industrialized coastal areas elsewhere (e.g. Bricker 1993; Cundy *et al.* 1997). The source of As is not clear, although the lack of enrichment in other heavy metals suggests it may be derived from agricultural processes (e.g. pesticide use) rather than urban run-off or petrochemical sources (the decrease in As flux between 13 and 8 cm depth is likely to be a consequence of dilution by catchment-derived material). An artificial, rather than detrital, source for As is likely as Ti/Fe/Mn/Cu/Zn/Ni fluxes all decrease over the period of As flux increase. Despite the slight recent increase in Pb and As flux, the sediments of the Mulinello marshes show little contamination by industrial effluent, and there is apparently little input of contaminated sediment from refinery and petrochemical developments along the coastal zone to the south.

Diatom analysis

Diatom valves were generally very poorly preserved in samples from the Augusta core and, consequently, counts could not be made for the whole core depth. Two samples (6 cm depth

and surface) did yield identifiable valves, though both were dominated by unidentifiable fragments of pennate diatoms. The fragmentary nature of the majority of the diatom remains possibly reflects mechanical stresses produced during ingestion by grazing molluscs and other invertebrates.

The two assemblages were mainly composed of the central portions of naviculoid types which cannot be used to accurately reconstruct palaeo-environmental conditions. The remainder of the assemblages represent a variety of habitats, ranging from freshwater epiphytes (e.g. *Synedra ulna*) to taxa more tolerant of saline conditions, such as *Diploneis didyma*.

As might be expected for sediments from an estuarine setting, this mixed representation of habitat types indicates a range of sources. All of the species identified are benthic, living either on macrophytes or the sediment. Of some note is the apparent absence of marine planktonic species which implies that, unlike coastal wetlands influenced by larger tidal ranges (Vos & De Wolf 1993) the assemblages are not significantly affected by marine inputs. The greater representation of freshwater species at the surface compared to 6 cm depth may be a reflection of an increased input from the Mulinello river, although this may be an artefact of sample size and selective preservation.

Discussion

The present study indicates that the coastal marsh site investigated has undergone considerable variation in sediment supply and vegetation over the last 100 a. High-resolution radiometric dating indicates an increase in sediment input over the period 1945–1965, which, on the basis of palynological and geochemical data, is probably due to an increased input of catchment-area derived material. Palynological evidence indicates that the onset of this period of increased allocthonous supply produced a rapid vegetational response, local pollen production being suppressed perhaps due to the degradation or death of local vegetation. This change in sediment provenance ante-dates the main period of industrial activity in the area, and is likely to be a consequence of changing fluvial/catchment processes rather than local anthropogenic activity. The reason for this increased input of catchment-derived material is not clear from present data. Precipitation records for Catania (35 km N of Augusta) show major rainfall maxima in December 1944 and January 1946 [559 mm and 592 mm, compared with a typical January mean rainfall of *c.* 90 mm (1892–1930 and 1941–1950 mean)

(Clayton 1934; US Department of Commerce 1959)]. The magnitude of these precipitation events recorded at Catania would almost certainly have affected the Mulinello catchment, possibly resulting in regional flooding, increased soil erosion and flushing of existing channel sediment. Continued supply of sediment to the Augusta site following these events may reflect reworking of sediment delivered to the valley floor during the initial storm episodes. Anthropogenic activity may also have played a significant role; the post-Second World War period was one of considerable agricultural development in the region, possibly causing enhanced erosion/run-off in a catchment prone to erosion (Ferro *et al.* 1991). The impact of port and industrial developments on vegetation and sediment accumulation at the core site has apparently been quite minor in comparison with the changes in sediment supply discussed above, despite large-scale disturbance at the rear of the marsh. Numerous plastic beads (possibly debris generated by local construction events) at −7.5 cm (*c.* 1971) and a decline in pollen concentration in the upper 4 cm of the core (post-1980) may reflect local anthropogenic activity (such as road construction at the rear of the marsh), although little change in vegetation community type, sediment source or rate of sediment supply is evident. Trace element analyses imply little inwash of industrial effluent to the Mulinello over the period following industrial development of the Augusta–Syracusa coastal zone (post-1960). In combination with preliminary diatom analyses, which show an apparent absence of marine planktonic species, this implies that most sedimentary material in the area sampled is derived from inland and local sources.

Conclusions

This study demonstrates the benefits of a combined palaeoecological and geochemical approach in reconstructing recent environmental change in fluvial and estuarine settings, which overcomes many of the interpretational difficulties associated with using a single palaeoenvironmental indicator. As illustrated by the Augusta sequence, regional/local processes may cause rapid changes in sediment accumulation rate and sediment source, considerably affecting geochemical and palynological records. Without accurate, high-resolution dating of individual sediment layers (in this case by use of ^{210}Pb) and an understanding of variation in sediment accretion rates and provenance derived from a

number of palaeoenvironmental indicators, such changes may be erroneously interpreted as being a result of regional climatic or vegetational change. The rapidity of environmental change identified from the short Augusta core illustrates the often dynamic nature of coastal wetlands in microtidal settings and shows their sensitivity to both local and regional disturbance. A full appreciation of this sensitivity is essential when assessing potential response to future human-induced environmental change.

The authors are grateful to J. Firth for pollen preparation, F. Barbano for information on the 1908 tsunami, M. Neri for logistical help during core retrieval and P. Boella for technical assistance at Southampton. Two anonymous reviewers are thanked for helpful comments on an earlier draft of this paper.

References

ALLISON, S. K. 1996. Recruitment and establishment of salt-marsh plants following disturbance by flooding. *American Midland Naturalist*, **136**, 232–247.

APPLEBY, P. G. & OLDFIELD, F. 1992. Applications of ^{210}Pb to sedimentation studies *In:* IVANOVICH, M. & HARMON, R. S. (eds) *Uranium Series Disequilibrium. Applications to Earth, Marine and Environmental Sciences.* 2nd edn, Oxford Science, Oxford.

ARMIENTI, P., INNOCENTI, F., PETRINI, R., POMPILIO, M. & VILLARI, L. 1989. Petrology and Sr-Nd isotope geochemistry of recent lavas from Mt Etna: bearing on the volcano feeding system. *Journal of Volcanology and Geothermal Research*, **39**, 315–327.

BASILE B., DI STEFANO, G. & LENA, G. 1986. Landings, ports, coastal settlements and coastlines in southeastern Sicily from Prehistory to Late Antiquity. *British Archaeological Reports International Series*, **404**, 15–33.

BENNETT, K. D., WHITTINGTON, G. & EDWARDS, K. J. 1994. Recent plant nomenclatural changes and pollen morphology in the British Isles. *Quaternary Newsletter*, **73**, 1–6.

BURRIN, P. J. & SCAIFE, R. G. 1984. Aspects of Holocene valley sedimentation and floodplain development in southern England. *Proceedings of the Geologists' Association*, **95**, 81–96.

BRICKER, S. B. 1993. The history of Cu, Pb, and Zn inputs to Narragansett Bay, Rhode Island as recorded by salt-marsh sediments. *Estuaries*, **16**, 589–607.

CARTER, R. W. G. & WOODROFFE, C. D. (eds) 1994. *Coastal Evolution: Late Quaternary Shoreline Morphodynamics.* Cambridge University Press, Cambridge.

CASTAGNA, A., SINATRA, F., CASTAGNA, G., STOLI, A. & ZAFARANA, S. 1985. Trace element evaluations in marine organisms. *Marine Pollution Bulletin*, **16**, 416–419.

CHESTER, D. K., DUNCAN, A. M., GUEST, J. E. & KILBURN, C. R. J. 1985. *Mount Etna, the Anatomy of a Volcano*. Chapman and Hall, London.

CHMURA, G. L. & EISMA, D. 1995. A palynological study of surface and suspended sediments on a tidal flat: implications for pollen transport and deposition in coastal waters. *Marine Geology*, **128**, 183–200.

CLAYTON, H. H. 1934. World weather records 1921–1930. Smithsonian Miscellaneous Collections, **90**, Smithsonian Institution, Washington.

COLLINS, P. E. F. 1994. *Floodplain environmental change since the Last Glacial Maximum in the lower Kennet valley, south-central England*. PhD Dissertation, University of Reading, UK.

CRISTOFOLINI, R. & ROMANO, R. 1982. Petrological features of Etnean volcanic rocks. *Memoir of the Italian Geological Society*, **23**, 99–116.

CUNDY, A. B. & CROUDACE, I. W. 1995. Sedimentary and geochemical variations in a salt marsh/mud flat environment from the mesotidal Hamble estuary, southern England. *Marine Chemistry*, **51**, 115–132.

—— & ——1996. Sediment accretion and recent sea-level rise in the Solent, southern England: inferences from radiometric and geochemical studies. *Estuarine, Coastal and Shelf Science*, **43**, 449–467.

——, ——, THOMSON, J. & LEWIS, J. T. 1997. Reliability of salt marshes of "geochemical recorders" of pollution input: a case study from contrasting estuaries in southern England. *Environmental Science and Technology*, **31**, 1093–1011.

DAOUST, R. J., MOORE, T. R., CHMURA, G. L. & MAGENHEIMER, J. F. 1996. Chemical evidence of environmental changes and anthropogenic influences in a Bay-of-Fundy salt-marsh. *Journal of Coastal Research*, **12**, 520–533.

DOMINIK, J. & STANLEY, D. J. 1993. Boron, beryllium and sulfur in Holocene seidments and peats of the Nile delta, Egypt: their use as indicators of salinity and climate. *Chemical Geology*, **104**, 203–216.

FERRO, V., GIORDANO, G. & IOVINO, M. 1991. Isoerosivity and erosion risk map for Sicily. *Hydrological Sciences Journal-Journal des Sciences Hydrologiques*, **36**, 549–564.

FIRTH, C., STEWART, I., MCGUIRE, W. J., KERSHAW, S. & VITA-FINZI, C. 1996. Coastal elevation changes in eastern Sicily: implications for volcano instability at Mount Etna. *In*: MCGUIRE, W. J., JONES, A. P. & NEUBERG, J. (eds) *Volcano Instability on the Earth and Other Planets*. Geological Society Special Publication 110.

FLYNN, W. W. 1968. Determination of low levels of polonium-210 in environmental materials. *Analytica Chimica Acta*, **43**, 221–227.

FRENCH, P. W., ALLEN, J. R. L. & APPLEBY, P. G. 1994. 210-Lead dating of a modern period saltmarsh deposit from the Severn estuary (southwest Britain), and its implications. *Marine Geology*, **118**, 327–334.

GOLDBERG, E. D. 1963. Geochronology with 210Pb in radioactive dating. *IAEA*, Vienna, 121–131.

HYDROGRAPHER OF THE NAVY 1996. Admiralty Tide Tables. Vol. 1 European Waters, HMSO, London.

LENTINI, F. 1987. Carta Geologica della Sicilia sud-orientale, 1:100000. Ente Minerario Siciliano.

MAGAZZU, G., ROMEO, G., AZZARO, F. & DECEMBRINI, F. 1995. Chemical pollution from urban and industrial sewages in Augusta Bay (Sicily). *Water Science and Technology*, **32**, 221–229.

MCCAFFREY, R. J. & THOMSON, J. 1980. A record of the accumulation of sediment and trace metals in a Connecticut salt marsh. *Advances in Geophysics*, **22**, 165–236.

MOORE, P. D., WEBB, J. A. & COLLINSON, M. E. 1991. *Pollen Analysis*. Blackwell Scientific Publications, Oxford.

MOUNTJOY, A. B. 1970. Planning and industrial developments in eastern Sicily. *Geography*, **55**, 441–444.

MULARGIA, F., BROCCIO, F., ACHILLI, V. & BALDI, P. 1985. Evaluation of a seismic quiescence pattern in southeastern Sicily. *Tectonophysics*, **116**, 335–364.

PLATANIA, G. 1909. Il maremoto dello Stretto di Messina del 28 dicembre 1908, *Bulletin of the Geological Society of Italy*, **13**, 369–458.

R. C. B. 1996. The convention on wetlands (Ramsar, Iran, 1971). Ramsar Convention Bureau, http://www.iprolink.ch/iucnlib/themes/ramsar/brochure-e.htm.

RITCHIE, J. C. & MCHENRY, J. R. 1990. Application of radioactive fallout cesium-137 for measuring soil erosion and sediment accumulation rates and patterns: a review. *Journal of Environmental Quality*, **19**, 215–233.

ROBINSON, M. 1993. Microfossil analyses and radiocarbon dating of depositional sequences related to Holocene sea-level change in the Forth Valley, Scotland. *Transactions of the Royal Society of Edinburgh, Earth Sciences*, **84**, 1–60.

SIMS, P. A. (ed.) 1996. *An Atlas of British Diatoms*. Biopress, Bristol.

STEWART, I. S., CUNDY, A. B., KERSHAW, S. & FIRTH, C. 1997. Holocene coastal uplift and palaeoseismicity of north-eastern Sicily. *Journal of Geodynamics*, **24**, 37–50.

TSIMPLIS, M. N. & SPENCER, N. E. 1997. Collection and analysis of monthly mean sea level data in the Mediterranean and Black Sea. *Journal of Coastal Research*, **13**, 534–544.

US DEPARTMENT OF COMMERCE 1959. World Weather records 1941–1950, US Department of Commerce Weather Bureau, Washington.

VOS, P. C. & DE WOLF, H. 1993. Diatoms as a tool for reconstructing sedimentary environments in coastal wetlands; methodological aspects. *Hydrobiologica*, **269/270**, 285–296.

WEST, R. G., ANDREW, R. & PETIT, M. 1993. Taphonomy of plant remains on floodplains of tundra rivers, present and Pleistocene. *New Phytologist*, **123**, 203–221.

WILLIAMS, M. 1990. Understanding wetlands. *In*: WILLIAMS, M. (ed.) *Wetlands: a Threatened Landscape*. Blackwell, Oxford, 1–41.

Observations of the morphodynamic behaviour of an intertidal mudflat at different timescales

RICHARD J. S. WHITEHOUSE & HELEN J. MITCHENER

Marine Sediments Group, HR Wallingford, Howbery Park, Wallingford, Oxon OX10 8BA, UK

Abstract: This paper concerns the morphological (bed level) behaviour of the intertidal mudflat at Portishead on the Severn Estuary and discusses how the prevailing hydraulic and cohesive sediment processes contribute to observed changes in the bed level. The characteristics of the mudflat behaviour during a fortnightly cycle is presented, based upon a continuous high resolution time series of the bed level measured at one location during 31 tidal immersions. During spring tides the sediment supply to the mudflat is increased and the tidal-mean bed elevation is at least 10 mm higher following the peak of spring tides than on the previous or following neaps. On a tide by tide basis the bed level varies by 10–20 mm and the preservation of fresh mud deposits on the intertidal area is controlled by the hydraulic conditions prevailing during the shallow water phase of the tide (less than 0.5 m depth) and the processes operating during the dry part of the tide. Hence, the bed level is controlled by the phasing of the tidal range (ambient sediment supply) with local water depth and wave activity. In comparison, on the annual timescale the bed level variation on the middle and upper mudflat is of the order of 100 mm and seasonal changes in storminess, subaerial environment and biostabilization appear to play a significant role.

Quantitative methods of predicting the surface elevation of sub-tidal and intertidal areas in muddy estuaries and coasts are required to enable effective management strategies and engineering design. The management of subtidal deposits usually concerns the navigability of an estuary and the need for dredging whilst the intertidal deposits and saltmarshes provide valuable natural protection against coastal flooding (Brampton 1992; Leggett & Dixon 1994).

Recently, Moeller *et al.* (1996) have quantified the typical level of protection against waves that these areas can provide.

Mudflats are three-dimensional systems in which there are transfers of water and sediment both in the alongshore direction, and also between the mudflat and the subtidal nearshore zone and between the mudflat and the adjacent saltmarsh (Fig. 1). Some idea of the importance of these links is described below. Kendrick &

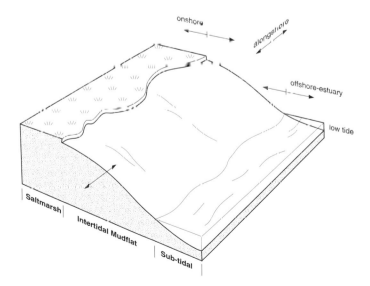

Fig. 1. The context of the mudflat in the estuarine or coastal system.

WHITEHOUSE, R. J. S. & MITCHENER, H. J. 1998. Observations of the morphodynamic behaviour of an intertidal mudflat at different timescales. *In*: BLACK, K. S., PATERSON, D. M. & CRAMP, A. (eds) *Sedimentary Processes in the Intertidal Zone*. Geological Society, London, Special Publications, **139**, 255–271.

Derbyshire (1976) observed that the reduction (to virtually nothing) in the volume of maintenance dredging in one reach of the tidal Thames between 1963 and 1966 resulted in higher silt concentrations being carried in the flood tidal flow. Survey data showed a corresponding increase in the mean bed level for the reach and presumably (Kendrick 1984) more material was available for deposition in regions of low tidal velocity, i.e. bankside areas. The exchanges between mudflat and saltmarsh are controlled by tidal cycles and storm events (Leggett & Dixon 1994). The trapping of suspended sediments by saltmarsh has been monitored by French et al. (1993). Sediment eroded from the marsh by wave action during storms can be stored on the intertidal flats (Pethick 1992) until it is recycled back onto the marsh surface by tidal action.

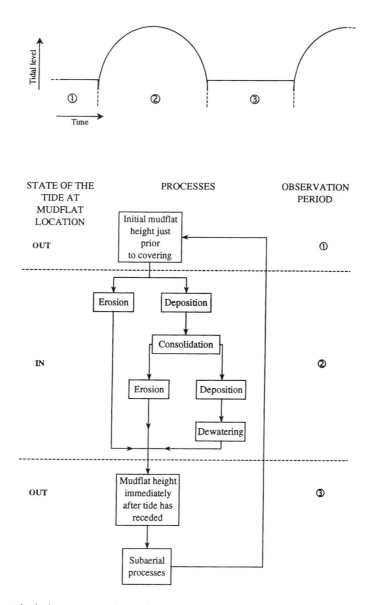

Fig. 2. Sedimentological processes acting on intertidal mudflat sediments and observation periods for morphology with respect to tidal level.

Changes in the surface elevation of the mudflat occur as the result of sedimentological processes such as deposition, consolidation, fluidization, re-entrainment or erosion, mediated by the influence of sediment mixtures, chemistry and biology on the sediment stability and transport. Most of these sedimentological processes can be described to an acceptable level, at least in comparison with laboratory data (Teisson *et al.* 1993), and there is growing literature on the influence of mixtures (e.g. Mitchener *et al.* 1996; Torfs *et al.* 1996) and biogeochemical factors (e.g. Krumbein *et al.* 1994). The influence of subaerial factors must be considered in the intertidal context and hence the modelling of intertidal sediments is far more complex and is not yet at an advanced stage. As a precursor to making bed level predictions it is necessary to understand the natural behaviour of coastal and estuarine mudflats.

Most observations of mudflat morphology have been made when they are uncovered by water (observation periods 1 and 3 in Fig. 2) but can, nonetheless, indicate how the morphology and bed elevation varies in response to different tidal forcing and wave activity (Ockenden & Atkins 1993; Freeman 1994). These observations have been made using conventional surveying techniques or by taking spot measurements against erosion/accretion pins (SERG: Severn Estuary Research Group 1992; Ockenden & Atkins 1993). In addition, some measurements of the hydrodynamics, sediment dynamics and associated within-tide bed level variations using an ultrasonic bed level probe have been made on mudflats in the Severn (West Usk) and Mersey (Diserens *et al.* 1991) and at Portishead on the Severn (unpublished HR data).

Recently, continuous measurements of the within tide variation in bed level have been made at Portishead during 31 tides covering a period of neap–spring–neap tides between 27 January and 12 February 1995 (Whitehouse & Williamson 1996). These data correspond to observation period 2 of Fig. 2 and have been used to assess the relative contributions to bed level change from tidal and wave activity both over the period of a fortnight and on the scale of individual tides. A survey of the mudflat elevation (periods 1 or 3, Fig. 2) has been made by the University of Bristol between March 1990 and February 1991 at monthly intervals, with supporting measurements of the stability and biological properties of the sediment. This has resulted in a year long dataset for the bed level behaviour at Portishead (SERG 1992). The new field data from 1995 has been placed within the

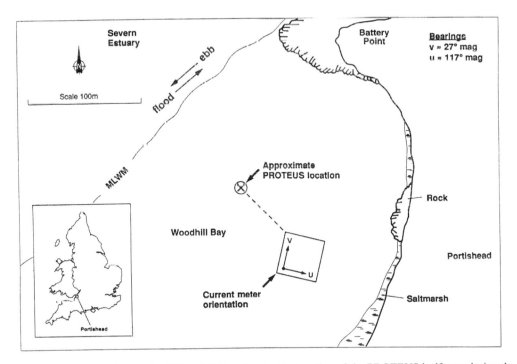

Fig. 3. Map of the northern end of Woodhill Bay showing the location of the PROTEUS bedframe during the winter 1995 measurements.

context of the previous observations to investigate how the bed level at this site changes over long and short timescales.

Description of site

The Portishead mudflat is situated in Woodhill Bay on the southern shore of the macro-tidal Severn Estuary (Fig. 3). The geometry of the coastal embayment means that the tidal velocities at the measurement location are generally low, the embayment provides shelter from the strong tidal currents in the main estuary channel. Woodhill Bay comprises both saltmarsh and mudflat regimes and near Battery Point the mudflat is backed by rocks and pebbles. At the time of the 1995 deployment the study area contained very soft mud, particularly within well defined runnels running down the beach (Fig. 4). The geology, tidal and wind/wave regime and sediment transport in the estuary are comprehensively described

for the whole estuary following the extensive work for the Severn Barrage (ICE 1982).

Measurement equipment and typical data

The new data were collected with the PROTEUS system (Atkins & Ockenden 1993) deployed in January 1995 on the mudflat to monitor the hydrodynamics, cohesive sediment processes and bed levels at one location (Fig. 3). The measurement system consists of a 'goalpost' framework to which is attached an array of sensors and waterproof housings for signal filtering, data logging and power supply. The following equipment was deployed within 0.5 m of the bed (see Fig. 4): two Valeport Series 800 model annular ECMs (170 mm diameter heads), two Chelsea turbidity sensors (infra-red backscatter), one Druck pressure transducer (model PDCR 930), and one ultrasonic bed level detector (ARX sludge blanket detector; frequency 1.1 MHz, beam width 10°, accuracy

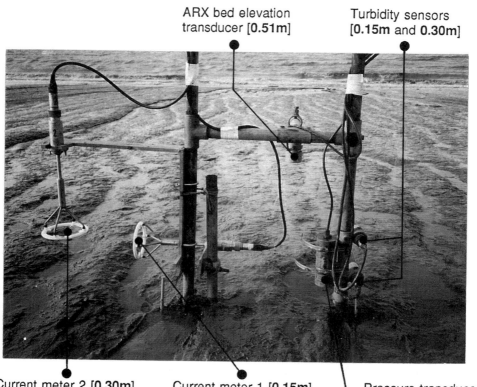

ARX bed elevation transducer [0.51m]

Turbidity sensors [0.15m and 0.30m]

Current meter 2 [0.30m], orientated to measure u-v velocity components

Current meter 1 [0.15m], orientated to measure u-w velocity components

Pressure transducer [0.15m]

Fig. 4. The PROTEUS bedframe deployed on the intertidal flat at Portishead in winter 1995.

Tide data from Avonmouth Signal Station for the period of the Proteus deployments at Portishead site (Jan/Feb 1995)
(H represents times at which the ARX instrument was underwater (ARX position was 0.505m above local surface, ~2.5m ODN)

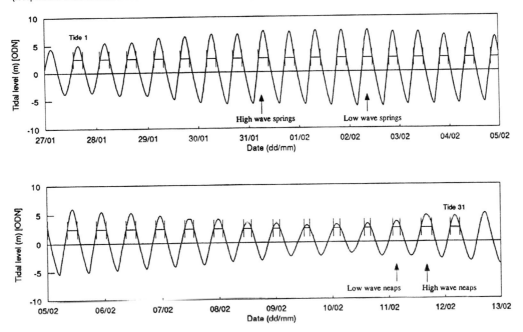

Fig. 5. Tidal elevation during the winter 1995 measurements, the 'H' symbols denote periods of submergence at the measurement site (data supplied by the Avonmouth Signal Station).

±1 mm). However, a fault in the electronic circuitry in the logging system meant that the data from the pressure transducer was unreliable and hence was not used.

The tidal level at Avonmouth varied between −6.5 m and +7 m ODN (Fig. 5) and PROTEUS was located at 2 m above ODN allowing for 3.5–4.5 hrs submergence per tide, as indicated by the 'H' symbols on Fig. 5.

The bed level measurements were obtained every 5 min when the local water depth exceeded 0.5 m and data was obtained over the full 15 days of the deployment (Fig. 6a). The rest of the data was logged at 5 Hz and burst-averaged (over 10 min) to produce time series of the cross-shore and long-shore velocity components at 0.30 m above the bed and sediment concentrations at heights of 0.15 m and 0.30 m. The wave activity was determined from the ECM velocity data, giving the wave orbital velocity amplitude and associated zero-down crossing period. Typical hydraulic conditions are summarized in Table 1. Details of the data collection and analysis are reported by Whitehouse & Williamson (1996). The calculation method for the bed shear stress due to waves and currents is contained in the same report, after the method of Soulsby (1995), assuming a bed roughness

length z_0 appropriate for mud (0.2×10^{-3} m). Typical results are discussed below for two contrasting tides followed by a summary of the relative roles of tides and waves at this site.

Current-dominated conditions
(spring tide, tide 12, 2/2/95)

During this tide the local water level varied between 0 m and 6 m, and the horizontal mean current speed varied from $c.\,0.1\,\mathrm{ms}^{-1}$ to $0.25\,\mathrm{ms}^{-1}$ (Fig. 7). The wave activity was low, bottom orbital velocity amplitude less than $0.1\,\mathrm{ms}^{-1}$, and the wave–current shear stresses were generally below $0.2\,\mathrm{N\,m}^{-2}$ but twice this during the early part of the flood tide.

Four sedimentological 'events' were observed in the bed level time series (Fig. 7d), labelled A to D. Event 'A' was characterized by a drop in level of $c.\,5\,\mathrm{mm}$ during the shallow water phase of the tide when the wave–current shear stresses were at their highest. Event 'B', almost 10 mm increase, coincided with decreases in the suspended sediment concentration time series at both elevations (Fig. 7c). Although there is some uncertainty about the zero offsets for these two records the trends are considered reliable;

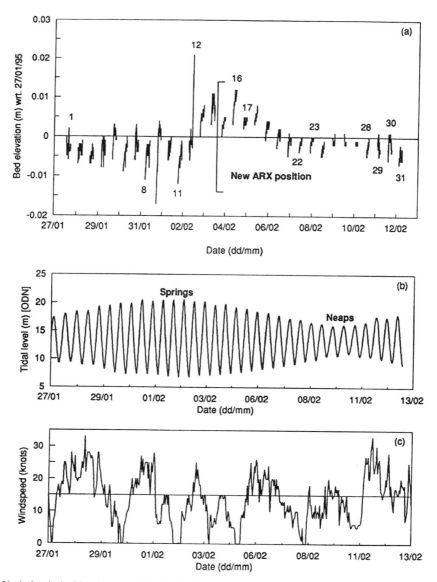

Fig. 6. Variation in bed level measured at the PROTEUS bedframe, plus wind speed and tidal level provided by the Avonmouth Signal Station.

previous observations have shown the water column at these elevations to be well mixed. Event 'C' occurred after the high water slack period displaying a gradual reduction in the bed level of c. 4 mm. This reduction in bed level appears to be related either to the consolidation of low density deposits or to their resuspension. The large difference in sensor response at around 09:30 during the ebbing tide is the reason why both traces have been included in Fig. 7c despite the uncertainty in the offset values. As the mean flow reverses to a southerly direction (Fig. 7b)

there is a sudden increase in the sediment concentration at 0.3 m which does not appear to be related to local erosion as a similar response is not observed at 0.15 m. Thus it appears that the upper sensor has sampled an advective event transporting sediment across the mudflat.

Event 'D' comprises a substantial increase in bed level of 20 mm during the last half hour of the receding tide, including a rise of greater than 10 mm over a period of only 10 min, i.e. a sudden deposition event. The magnitude of the observed fall in the suspended sediment concentration

Table 1. *Summary of the influence of waves and tides on the hydraulic conditions, suspended sediment concentration and bed behaviour at Portishead (winter 1995 data)*

Tide number	8	12	29	30
Definition	HWS	LWS	LWN	HWN
Tidal range at Avonmouth (m)	13	13	7	7
Maximum local water depth (m)	5	6	2	2
Wind speed (knots)	20–25	0–10	22–30	15
Maximum horizontal current speed (F)	0.30	0.25	0.17	0.2
$(m s^{-1})$ (E)	0.10	0.25	0.05	0.3
Maximum wave orbital velocity (F)	0.30	0.10	0.05	0.3
$(m s^{-1})$ (E)	0.15	0.05	0.05	0.6
Period of wave orbital motion (s) (variation through tide)	3.0–4.0	3.5–2.5	3.5–2.0	2.5–4.0
Wave velocity ÷ current velocity	8.0	<0.5	<0.5	1.0–3.0
Mean SSC @ 0.15 m $(kg m^{-3})$	1.60	1.42	0.26	0.75
Maximum SSC @ 0.15 m $(kg m^{-3})$	3.10	2.76	0.40	1.73
Mean bed level for tide, z (mm)	−5	0	−2	−1
Root-mean-square (rms) bed level change in tide, z_{rms} (mm)	2	7	2	2
Change in bed level through tide, last z − first z (mm)	10	22	−2	0

HWS is high wave activity plus spring tide; LWS is low wave activity plus spring tide; LWN is low wave activity plus neap tide; HWN is high wave activity plus neap tide; (F) means flood tide; (E) means ebb tide.

record does not appear to account for the accretion observed and it is suggested that this deposit was produced by the advection of a thin, mobile mud sheet on the now northerly flowing current. These mobile mud sheets have been observed previously at this site, but not measured, by Ockenden & Atkins (1993).

Wave-dominated conditions
(neap tide, tide 30, 11/2/95)

During this tide the local water depth ranged from 0 m to just over 2.5 m (Fig. 8). The mean horizontal current velocity (U_{30}) dropped from 0.2 ms^{-1} to c. 0.05 ms^{-1} over the flood period, and then increased to in excess of 0.3 ms^{-1} over the ebb tide. The cross-shore velocity was directed offshore and remained relatively small apart from a significant increase over the last hour of the tide to −0.2 ms^{-1}. After slack high water the long-shore velocity switched from flowing towards Battery Point to down the coast.

The wave-related parameters during this tide were typical of those observed on mudflats (e.g. Christie *et al.* 1995) where the wave orbital velocity at a point on the mudflat is often highest in the shallow water at the start and end of the tide. The root-mean-square wave–current shear stress was dominated by the wave activity, 1–2 N m^{-2} on the flood, 0.5 N m^{-2} at slack water and rising from 1 to 3 N m^{-2} during the ebb (Fig. 8c). After some erosion initially, the bed level data (Fig. 8a) showed a short period of increase (by c. 3 mm) at the start of the tide, presumably due to the deposition of sediment

carried on the advancing tide. This coincided with a drop in the sediment concentration measured at 0.15 m. The bed level remained at this higher level during the greater part of the tide. Over the ebb tide there was a gradual drop in the bed level, c. 5 mm, presumably due to local erosion or resuspension of material as there is an associated rise in the suspended sediment concentration. There was no net change in bed level during this tide.

The relative role of waves and tides

The correlation between suspended sediment concentration and combined shear stress (Fig. 9) indicates the different response of the sediment concentration to the wave–current forcing between spring and neap tides. The spring tide data illustrate the ease with which the soft mud supplied to the intertidal area is resuspended, whereas the neap tide data probably reflects the erosion behaviour of more consolidated sediment. The threshold shear stress between the two types of behaviour is c. 0.3 N m^{-2}. Direct measurements of the critical erosion shear stress at this site by Williamson & Ockenden (1996) indicate values for τ_{cr} of between 0.06 N m^{-2} and 0.17 N m^{-2} over a range of different mud types. Based upon sediment concentration measurements at 0.37 m above the bed, Ockenden & Atkins (1993) concluded that sediment was eroded from the bed when the shear stress exceeded 0.20 N m^{-2}.

The same four tides used for Fig. 9 were chosen to examine the influence of waves during

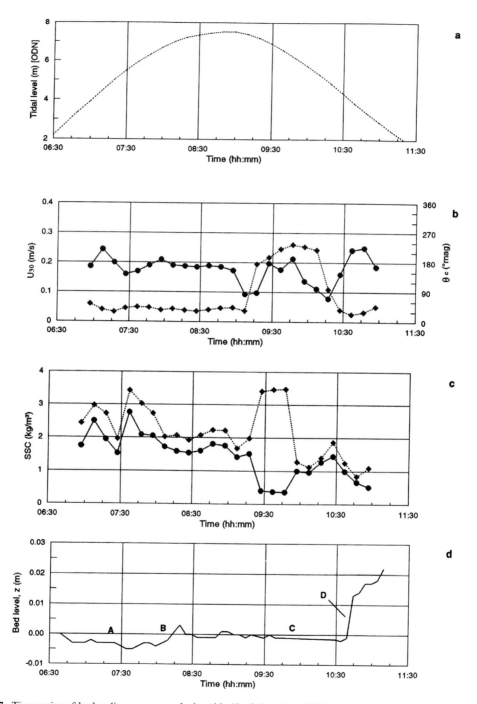

Fig. 7. Time series of hydraulic parameters during tide 12 of the winter 1995 measurements (spring tide, 2/2/95): (**a**) tidal level, (**b**) total current speed at 0.3 m (solid line) and direction (stippled line), (**c**) suspended sediment concentration at 0.15 m (solid line) and at 0.30 m (stippled line), and (**d**) bed level (see text for explanation).

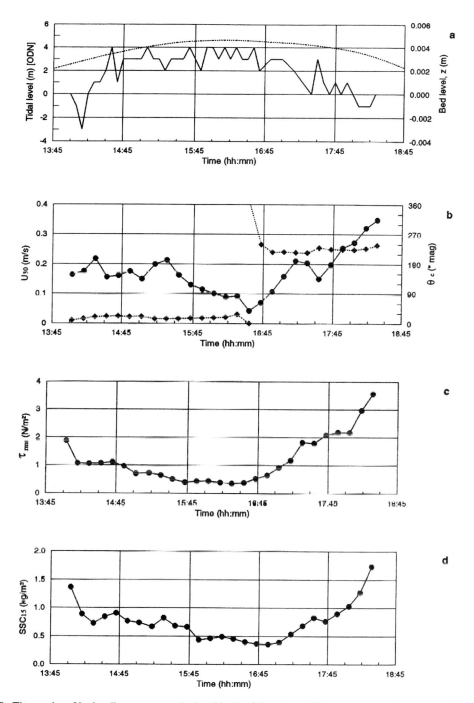

Fig. 8. Time series of hydraulic parameters during tide 30 of the winter 1995 measurements (neap tide, 11/2/95): (a) tidal level (stippled line) and bed level (solid line), (b) total current speed at 0.3 m (solid line) and direction (stippled line), (c) bed shear stress due to combined wave and current action τ_{rms}, and (d) suspended sediment concentration at 0.15 m.

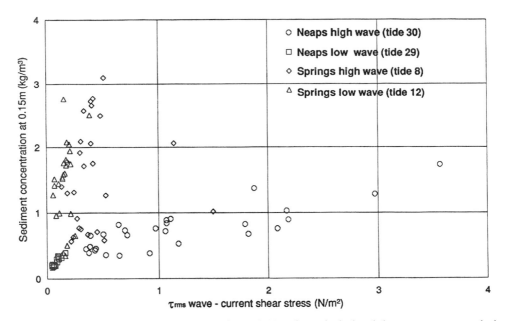

Fig. 9. Relationship between sediment concentration at 0.15 m above the bed and the root-mean-square bed shear stress due to combined waves and currents.

spring (s) and neap (n) tide conditions corresponding to periods of high wave activity [i.e. tides 8(s) and 30(n)] and low wave activity [i.e. tides 12(s) and 29(n), see Fig. 6a]. Using the data from these tides, firstly we compare the relative effects of spring and neap tidal conditions on sediment concentrations and bed level behaviour, and secondly the effect of waves. The numbers in brackets refer to the numbering of the tides and various parameters for these tides are summarized in Table 1.

On the spring tide with low wave activity (12) the mean sediment concentration at 0.15 m is five times larger than on the corresponding neap tide (29). The bed level behaviour, as indicated by the rms (root-mean-square) bed level variation, is almost four times larger on the low wave spring tide (12) than on the corresponding neap tide (29). For the tides with higher wave activity, the mean concentrations on spring tides (8) are twice those on neaps (30) and yet the rms bed level variations under conditions of higher wave activity are the same.

To illustrate the wave effects we compare the neap tides (29) and (30) for low and high wave activity, respectively. The data shows that the mean sediment concentrations are increased three-fold by the action of waves. The rms bed level variation in bed level is the same for tides (29) and (30), but as has been discussed above, the response of the sediment concentration during

these tides suggests that the processes causing the bed change may be different in each case: consolidation of sediments (29) as opposed to erosion of sediment (30). In contrast, during spring tides the increase in the mean concentration with increased wave action (8) is only about 10% larger than was observed during the tide with lower wave stirring (12). Spring tide (12) with low wave stirring generates a three times larger value for the rms bed level change and a two-fold higher increase in the bed level through the tide than for tide (8) with more wave activity. This indicates that waves act as a controlling mechanism on bed levels during the shallow phases of the tide. During spring tides the bed level observed before the tide recedes below 0.5 m depth, is higher than at the start of the tide whereas the net tidal difference is much less on neap tides.

It is noticeable (Fig. 6a) that the bed level at the start of tide (13) is 20 mm lower than was recorded at the end of the previous tide, either because the sediment was washed off the mudflat during the receding limb of tide (12) (depth less than 0.5 m) or because it was resuspended by increased wave activity at the start of tide (13) before the water depth reached 0.5 m. As a result of previous investigations at this site, Ockenden & Atkins (1993) postulated that the sediment bed is softened and fluidized during the incoming tide and washed off as the tide recedes in the form of a highly concentrated mobile sheet.

Bed level change at various timescales

The variation in bed level data at this site is examined at three scales; firstly, at the scale of individual tides [within tide observations by Whitehouse & Williamson (1996); between tide observations by Ockenden & Atkins (1993) and Freeman (1994)], secondly at the fortnightly scale [15 day dataset from Whitehouse & Williamson (1996)], and thirdly on an annual basis (data from SERG 1992).

The bed level behaviour measured through 31 tides at this site is shown in Fig. 6a along with the tidal elevation and windspeed data for Avonmouth (supplied by the Avonmouth Signal Station). The bed level data are plotted with respect to the first measured value in tide (1) on 27 January 1995. Unfortunately, the ARX sensor was moved slightly (deliberately) between tides (14) and (15) resulting in an apparent drop in the bed level of 5 mm (measured manually). As a result, the relation between the levels obtained at the beginning and the end of the deployment are somewhat uncertain and the data for tide (15) onwards are plotted with respect to the first measurement in tide (15). Therefore, whilst the actual net bed level variation between tides (1) and (31) cannot be assessed with certainty, the data provide a valuable insight into the bed level behaviour at the tidal and fortnightly timescales. The bed level data for the tidal, fortnightly and annual timescales are presented in the following three sections of the paper.

Tidal timescale

Earlier observations at this site using the PROTEUS bed-frame in March 1994 showed that during consecutive spring tides (local depth 6 m) the bed level within the tide increased by 4 mm when the wave action was negligible. On the following tide with more wave action the net bed level change was more or less zero. Interestingly, the bed level increased by c. 4 mm in the shallow water period between the tides (depth less than 0.5 m) when the processes could not be monitored by the equipment. Similar behaviour was observed in the 1995 deployment (Fig. 6a).

Table 2 summarizes previous observations of the between-tide changes in elevation at this site (observation periods 1 and 3, Fig. 2). The data show directly that the magnitude of bed level change between tides is c. 10–20 mm, this also indicates a tendency for deposition during calm weather and erosion by wave action.

Further investigation of the bed level change on a tidal scale was carried out by calculating the tidal-mean bed level, rms bed level variation within the tide, and the difference between the last and first bed level measurement for all tides (Fig. 10). This shows mainly net deposition during recording periods. As the mean bed level does not rise continuously this implies that a net reduction in bed level must occur in shallow water or dry periods, as observed in the bed level record (Fig. 10a). The bed level 'activity' (Figs 10c, d) is highest during peak spring tides.

Fortnightly timescale

The tidal-mean bed level varied by c. 10 mm through the neap–spring–neap cycle, being highest in the period immediately following the maximum spring tides (Fig. 10b). The mean bed level for the first 11 tides, spanning the period up to the peak of the spring tide, was −3 mm. Subsequently, the mean level increased markedly by

Table 2. *Previous observations of bed level change on a tide by tide basis (observations by HR and University of Birmingham reported by Ockenden & Atkins 1993)*

Date	Observations
29–30 July 1991	Calm conditions Spring tide (range = 11 m) 10 mm deposition
17 October 1991	Windy conditions (20–25 knots, SW–WNW) Neap tide (range = 4 m) 15–20 mm erosion
6–7 November 1991	Windy conditions (25 knots, WSW–NW) Spring tide (range = 11.5 m) No bed change against pegs (50 mm erosion on plate)
6–7 February 1992	Calm conditions (ripples, 5–10 knots, S–W) Spring tide (range = 11.5 m) 10 mm erosion

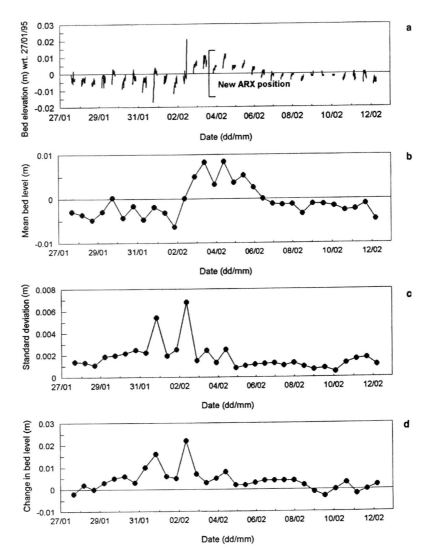

Fig. 10. Time series of bed level related quantities in winter 1995 deployment: (**a**) original time series (as Fig. 6), (**b**) tidal-mean bed level, (**c**) root-mean-square of the bed level variation around the tidal mean value, and (**d**) the difference between bed levels at the end and beginning of tidal covering. The lines joining the derived points in (**b**), (**c**) and (**d**) are added to help follow the trends in these quantities.

at least 15 mm between tides (11) and (14) coinciding with the gradual reduction in tidal range during a period of relatively calm weather, windspeed generally less than 15 knots. During tides (16) to (22) the bed elevation decreased once again as the tidal range progressively changed to neaps, coinciding with a period of increased windspeed. At the end of the deployment there was a period of erosion associated with increased windspeed and increasing tidal range. The net increase in bed level over the 15 day period of the survey was at least 3 mm.

Annual timescale

The annual variation in bed elevation measured at this site in 1990/91 is plotted in Fig. 11 (data from SERG 1992). The data obtained on the middle mudflat are at the most comparable cross-shore position to the 1995 experiment. The annual variation in level is c. 100 mm typified by the increased level during the late summer months. The increase in bed level (SERG 1992) is related to the period of relatively calm weather that occurred between July and November, and

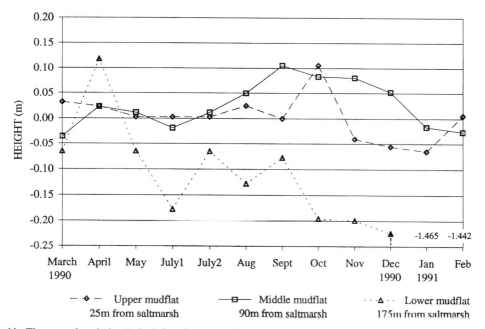

Fig. 11. The annual variation in bed elevation at Portishead observed between March 1990 and February 1991 (data from SERG 1992).

may also be attributed to an increase in the biostabilization and strengthening of the sediment between July and September. The importance of bed strengthening due to subaerial exposure in the summer months has been documented by Amos *et al.* (1988). The variability in level on the upper mudflat was also *c.* 100 mm whilst the lower mudflat was characterized by a progressive erosion throughout the survey period.

Discussion

The detailed bed behaviour depends strongly on the phasing of periods of high and low wave activity within the spring neap cycle and in particular the phasing of wave activity with times of tidal immersion and emersion. The spring–neap variation produces a modulation both in the length of time the measurement location is covered by water and the sediment load in the water column (water depth and concentration of sediment), and it moderates the influence of the wave action. The bed level at the end of a particular tidal record is generally, but not always, higher than the level at the start of the next tide unless wave erosion at the end of the tide is significant.

The bed level varies in response to the prevailing tidal conditions and the largest amount of deposition occurred during spring tides when the increased tidal stirring enhances the flux of sediment onto the mudflats. As a result of the increased sediment supply during spring tides the bed level variation within and between tides is larger generally than on neap tides. This spring–neap modulation in suspended solids in the estuary has been observed previously during a three month survey by Parker (1997) who also observed a trend of decreasing tidally-averaged suspended solids through the months of July to early September. During spring tides with low wave activity rapid increases in bed level of more than 10 mm can occur; these do not appear be related to the local sediment dynamics parameters. Instead, it is likely that these changes in bed level are due to the advection and deposition of a soft, mobile mud sheet into the measurement area as previously suggested by Ockenden & Atkins (1993) and Freeman (1994). This phenomenon has also been suggested by other researchers (e.g. Wit 1995). Providing the waves are sufficiently small fresh spring tide deposits can remain on the intertidal zone during calm weather. However, under the influence of wave action these deposits can be easily eroded during the final shallow water phases of the depositing tide or the initial stages of the following tide.

During neap tides when there is less sediment supplied to the mudflat surface wave action can produce erosion of the consolidated underlying material. If the material remains on the mudflat, consolidation will lead to an increase in the strength of the bed and, especially with the hardening caused by exposure to strong sunlight, an increase in its resistance to erosion. Amos *et al.* (1988) have observed the importance of subaerial exposure on mudflat sediments in the Bay of Fundy. They reported a dramatic increase in bed strength over a 6 day period in August which was attributed to the coincidence of a period of high relative exposure (i.e. sunlight striking the mudflat for the whole exposure period) and high evaporation.

Depositional events, leading to a higher bed level, were also observed over some slack water conditions. Close inspection of the shear stress and concentration results indicate that deposition occurred when the combined shear stress dropped below a value of *c.* 0.5 to $1.0 \, \text{N m}^{-2}$. Once the available sediment has been deposited there is an 'inactive' period at around slack high water and any decrease in the local bed level during this time is probably attributable to consolidation of the new deposit. The importance of consolidation during slack water periods has also been suggested by Christie *et al.* (1995).

The tidal-mean bed level varied through the fortnight of the winter 1995 experiment. During the spring tides in the middle of the 15 day deployment the bed level was typically 10 mm higher than was associated with the neap tide periods at the beginning and end of the deployment. There was also a net increase in the bed level of at least 3 mm over the 31 tides. The slight adjustment to the position of the bed level sensor during this experiment resulted in an artificially imposed drop in bed level of 5 mm and hence the net increase could have been as much as 8 mm.

Hence the data illustrate an important controlling factor for the bed level, namely that the tidal and fortnightly trends in bed level are strongly controlled by the phasing of tidal elevation and the spring–neap cycle (tidal range) with periods of low or high wave activity. This possibly implies a random response of the bed in the long term, at least at this site, as the occurrence of spring or neap tides and wave activity is not correlated.

By comparing the tidal and fortnightly data for bed change with the annual data it becomes apparent that the annual variation in the level of the sediment surface arises from the integration of the tide by tide behaviour, with the additional influences of seasonal variations in storminess and climate, and biological activity within the sediment. The increase in bed levels (Fig. 11) for the upper and middle flat from July onwards through the summer has been attributed (SERG 1992) to the reduced occurrence of storm waves which allows sediment to accumulate on the flat. With maximum sediment temperatures occurring on 2 July the enhanced biological activity results in increased algal biomass and sediment stabilization, as evidenced by measurements of colloidal carbohydrate levels in the sediment, and as directly measured with CSM (Cohesive Strength Meter; SERG 1992). The months of October through to December 1990 experienced stronger winds from SW and W which generated higher wave activity at the site and hence erosion (SERG 1992). Owing to the present lack of detailed information on the phasing of waves and tides we cannot refine this analysis but the independent observations in Table 2 for July 1991 (deposition) and October/December 1991 (erosion) are broadly consistent with the observations in Fig. 11. Although it is only speculation given the available evidence, the data for November to January may reflect the transfer of eroded sediment from the upper flat to the middle flat. This could possibly explain why the bed elevation remains high at the middle site in November and December.

Parker's (1997) observation of a gradual decrease in the tidally-averaged suspended solids concentration during the late summer, from July through to September, appears to suggest a link between the subtidal sediments and the increased sediment storage observed on the middle and upper mudflat at Portishead, and presumably on the other flats that flank the estuary.

Measurements reported from two other mudflat environments demonstrate the importance of seasonal influences on bed levels. These data are from the meso-tidal Deben Estuary in Suffolk (1971; Frostick & McCave 1979) and Ardmillan Bay in Northern Ireland (1989/90; Kirby *et al.* 1993).

Frostick & McCave (1979) reported a clear seasonal variation in accretion and erosion obtained from the monitoring over a calendar year of erosion pins set into the mud. Pronounced accretion of sediment on the flats occurred between April and September and erosion occurred during the winter months. As an example, at three of their ten sites they measured accretion of 33, 85 and 55 mm between April and September, and the corresponding total winter erosion was 35, 79 and 49 mm. The authors concluded that accretion and erosion were roughly equal over the period of a year. The accretion occurred because of the reduced wave action in the summer but it was maintained and aided by the simultaneous growth of algae on the sediment which enhanced its resistance to erosion and the trapping efficiency of the sediment surface. Without the algal growth the authors considered that although there would still be some seasonal variation in bed levels it would be unlikely that such a large volume of sediment could be retained on the flats. The source of the large volume of sediment deposited on the flats during the summer months was postulated to be the flanks of the subtidal estuary channel.

Kirby *et al.* (1993) also found a significant seasonal variation in bed levels from an extensive survey of erosion pin transects over a period of 22 months. The seasonal cycle at this site exhibited a summer rise in elevation to a peak between August and October followed by erosion due to waves in the winter months. The evidence suggested that the accreted sediment was derived from a seasonal reworking and redistribution of sediment within the bay. The data also showed some shorter-term variation in mudflat elevation due to episodic events related to tidal reworking and storm waves.

In summary, the typical variation in bed level due to seasonal effects is 50 mm in the Deben and 30–50 mm in Ardmillan Bay, approximately half the annual range measured at Portishead. The magnitude and exact timing of the summer increase in bed levels at Portishead, and elsewhere in the Severn (SERG 1992), in the Deben and in Ardmillan Bay will be controlled by the local geographical and environmental/climatic conditions.

Conclusions

(1) There are three different sedimentological processes which cause bed level change on the intertidal mudflats:

   (1.1) Deposition and erosion as a vertical exchange process between the sediment surface and the overlying water column. These processes produce direct correlation of sediment concentration and bed level change at a point, but cause only gradual bed level changes.

   (1.2) Advection of high density fluid mud sheets onto the intertidal mudflats during spring tide conditions, producing large depositional events. Resuspension of these deposits also takes place on a tide by tide basis.

   (1.3) Bed level changes due to consolidation of the bed (dewatering of the sediments).

(2) The annual variation in surface elevation of the middle mudflat at Portishead is typically 100 mm. This is mainly associated with an increased bed level in the late summer which appears to be related to an increased sediment stability over the summer months arising from the reduced incidence of storm waves as well as biological and subaerial influences. This general behaviour has been observed at other sites although the magnitude and timing of the seasonal variation will depend upon the geography and environment of an individual site.

(3) Spring–neap variation at Portishead: the tidal-mean bed level in the period immediately following maximum spring tides appeared to be *c.* 10 mm higher than the level recorded during the preceding and following periods of neap tides. The net increase in bed level over 15 days was at least 3 mm.

(4) Tidal-timescale variation at Portishead: erosion or deposition between tides occurs depending upon the phasing of tidal range (sediment supply), tidal level, wind/wave conditions. Typically the change observed is ±10–20 mm. The largest accretion event (over 20 mm) occurred during a spring tide associated with calm weather. During neap tides associated with calm weather the bed level change is negligible.

(5) It appears that a large contribution to the bed level change is made during the periods at the beginning and end of the tide when the water depth is very shallow (<0.5 m). Therefore the coincidence of these shallow water periods with low or high wave activity appears to exert a strong controlling influence on the bed level.

(6) The within-tide variation in bed level can exceed that due to the mean variation over spring and neap tides, and is of the same order of magnitude as the between tide variation.

(7) The net long-term variation in the bed level is controlled by seasonal variations in the local wave-dominated erosion processes plus the deposition and consolidation of locally eroded and advected sediment, coupled with the additional influence of biological and subaerial factors.

(8) Predictive morphological models of intertidal mudflats must take account of the behaviour both of fluid mud and the more consolidated sediments, including the processes of deposition and consolidation, and re-entrainment or erosion. The processes of bed consolidation (dewatering) must be

included as these operate continuously regardless of the hydraulic conditions (Teisson 1997). The thickness and density of freshly deposited sediment remaining on the intertidal zone once the tide has receded determines the degree of self-consolidation and strengthening that can take place before the next tidal immersion, as well as the susceptibility of underlying layers to erosion by waves. The phasing of periods of emersion with the daylight hours controls the subaerial hardening and biological activity (sediment stabilization or destabilization) which can take place and these factors vary seasonally (e.g. Amos *et al.* 1988; SERG 1992; Teisson 1997).

The funding for parts of this work was provided by the UK Ministry of Agriculture, Fisheries and Food (Flood and Coastal Defence Division) and the Environment Agency, and for other parts by the Commission of the European Communities Directorate General for Science, Research and Development as part of the INTRMUD collaborative research programme, under Contract Number MAS3-CT95-0022. The 1995 data collection exercise was funded by the Department of the Environment (Construction Sponsorship Directorate) and by MAST contract MAS2-CT92-0027.

We are indebted to Messrs R. Atkins and R. W. Adams who deployed the field equipment and to Dr D. Paterson for providing details of earlier work at the site (SERG 1992). We are also grateful to colleagues in the INTRMUD project with whom we have had valuable discussions on some of the topics included in this paper and for the constructive comments made by two anonymous referees.

References

AMOS, C. L., VAN WAGONER, N. A. & DABORN, G. R. 1988. The influence of subaerial exposure on the bulk properties of fine-grained intertidal sediment from Minas Basin, Bay of Fundy. *Coastal, Estuarine and Shelf Science*, **27**, 1–13.

ATKINS, R. & OCKENDEN, M. C. 1993. *Near-Bed Cohesive Sediment Processes. Development of a Self-Contained System for Long-Term Field Measurements.* HR Wallingford Report SR 341, September 1993.

BRAMPTON, A. H. 1992. Engineering significance of British saltmarshes. *In*: ALLEN, J. R. L. & PYE, K. (eds) *Saltmarshes: Morphodynamics, Conservation and Engineering Significance*, Cambridge University Press, UK, 115–122.

CHRISTIE, M. C., DYER, K. R., FENNESSY, M. & HUNTLEY, D. A. 1995. POST – a system for in-situ sediment erosion measurements. *In*: STIVE, M. J. F., DE VRIEND, H. J., FREDSØE, J., HAMM, L., SOULSBY, R. L., TEISSON, C. & WINTERWERP, J. C. (eds), *Advances in Coastal Morphodynamics:*

An overview of the G-8 Coastal Morphodynamics Project, Delft Hydraulics, Delft, Netherlands, 6-57–6-60.

DISERENS, A. P., DELO, E. A. & OCKENDEN, M. C. 1991. *Estuarine Sediments – Near Bed Processes. Field measurement of near bed cohesive sediment processes.* HR Wallingford Report SR 262, April 1991.

FREEMAN, D. P. 1994. *Cohesive Sediment Transport on an Estuarine Intertidal Zone.* PhD Thesis, University of Birmingham, Faculty of Engineering, January 1994.

FRENCH, J. R., CLIFFORD, N. J. & SPENCER, T. 1993. High frequency flow and suspended sediment measurements in a tidal wetland channel. *In*: CLIFFORD, N. J., FRENCH, J. R. & HARDISTY, J. (eds) *Turbulence: Perspectives on Flow and Sediment Transport*, John Wiley & Sons, 249–278.

FROSTICK, L. E. & McCAVE, I. N. 1979. Seasonal shifts of sediment within an estuary mediated by algal growth. *Estuarine and Coastal Marine Science*, **9**, 569–576.

ICE 1982. *Severn Barrage*. Proceedings of a symposium organised by the Institution of Civil Engineers, London, 8–9 October 1981. Thomas Telford.

KENDRICK, M. P. 1984. Impact of engineering structures on tidal flow and sediment distribution in the Thames. *Quarterly Journal of Engineering Geology*, **17**, 207–218.

KENDRICK, M. P. & DERBYSHIRE, B. V. 1976. *Factors Influencing Estuary Sediment Distribution*. Proceedings 15th Coastal Engineering Conference, 11–17 July 1976, Honolulu, 2072–2091.

KIRBY, R., BLEAKLEY, R. J., WEATHERUP, S. T. C., RAVEN, P. J. & DONALDSON, N. D. 1993. Effect of episodic events on tidal mud flat stability, Ardmillan Bay, Strangford Lough, Northern Ireland. *In*: *Nearshore and Estuarine Marine Cohesive Sediment Transport*, **42**, 378–392.

KRUMBEIN, W. E., PATERSON, D. M. & STAL, L. J. (eds) 1994. *Biostabilization of Sediments.* Oldenburg: Bibliotheks und Informationssytem de Carl von Ossietzky Universität Oldenburg (BIS).

LEGGETT, D. J. & DIXON, M. 1994. Management of the Essex saltmarshes for flood defence. *In*: FALCONER, R. A. & GOODWIN, P. (eds) *Wetland Management*, Thomas Telford, 232–245.

MOELLER, I., SPENCER, T. & FRENCH, J. R. 1996. Wind wave attenuation over saltmarsh surfaces: preliminary results from Norfolk, England. *Journal of Coastal Research*, **12**, 1009–1016.

MITCHENER, H., TORFS, H. & WHITEHOUSE, R. 1996. Erosion of mud/sand mixtures. *Coastal Engineering*, **29**, 1–25.

OCKENDEN, M. C. & ATKINS, R. 1993. *Field measurements of wave effects at Portishead, Severn Estuary.* HR Wallingford Report SR 342, March 1993.

PARKER, W. R. 1997. On the characterisation of cohesive sediment for transport modelling. *In*: BURT, N., PARKER, R. & WATTS, J. (eds) *Cohesive Sediments*, John Wiley & Sons, 3–14.

PETHICK, J. 1992. Saltmarsh geomorphology. *In*: ALLEN, J. R. L. & PYE, K. (eds) *Saltmarshes: Morphodynamics, Conservation and Engineering Significance*, Cambridge University Press, UK, 41–62.

SERG 1992. *Algal stabilisation of estuarine sediments.* Report ETSU TID 4088 – P1 and P2 to the Energy Technology Support Unit by the Severn Estuary Research Group (SERG), University of Bristol.

SOULSBY, R. L. 1995. Bed shear-stresses due to combined waves and currents. *In*: STIVE, M. J. F., DE VRIEND, H. J., FREDSØE, J., HAMM, L., SOULSBY, R. L., TEISSON, C. & WINTERWERP, J. C. (eds) *Advances in Coastal Morphodynamics: An overview of the G-8 Coastal Morphodynamics Project*, Delft Hydraulics, Delft, Netherlands, 420–423.

TEISSON, C. 1997. A review of cohesive sediment transport models. *In*: BURT, N., PARKER, R. & WATTS, J. (eds) *Cohesive Sediments*, John Wiley & Sons, 367–381.

——, OCKENDEN, M. C., LE HIR, P., KRANENBURG, C. & HAMM, L. 1993. Cohesive sediment transport processes. *Coastal Engineering*, **21**, 129–162.

TORFS, H., MITCHENER, H., HUYSENTRUYT, H. & TOORMAN, E. 1996. Settling and consolidation of mud/sand mixtures. *Coastal Engineering*, **29**, 27–45.

WHITEHOUSE, R. J. S. & WILLIAMSON, H. J. 1996. *The relative importance of tide and wave influences on bed level change at an intertidal cohesive mudflat site.* HR Wallingford Report SR 445, February 1996.

WILLIAMSON, H. J. & OCKENDEN, M. C. 1996. ISIS: an instrument for measuring erosion shear stress *in situ. Estuarine, Coastal and Shelf Science*, **42**, 1–18.

WIT, P. J. DE 1995. *Liquefaction of Cohesive Sediments caused by Waves.* Published in 'Communications on Hydraulic and Geotechnical Engineering', Report No. 95-2, ISSN-01690-6548. Faculty of Civil Engineering, Delft University of Technology, The Netherlands.

Mapping intertidal sediment distributions using the RoxAnn System, Dornoch Firth, NE Scotland

J. HULL & R. NUNNY

Ambios Environmental Consultants Ltd, The Ferns, Kilkenny Ave, Taunton, Somerset TA2 7PJ, UK

Abstract: The RoxAnn system (manufactured by Marine Micro Systems Ltd) is a remote sensing technique available for mapping sediment distributions. The acoustic returns from a standard boat-mounted echo sounder are electronically processed and the output stream logged together with accurate position data from a Differential Global Positioning System (or similar high accuracy positioning systems). The RoxAnn output comprises depth and indices of bed roughness (E1) and bed hardness (E2). The combination of these indices require to be translated into traditionally used parameters (such as visual appearance and sediment particle size) to provide useful mapping data. The most reliable means of achieving this is through a ground-truthing exercise, where grab samples and video footage are collected at sites of known RoxAnn values. Two problems are encountered in this process: firstly RoxAnn acoustic signatures often do not uniquely represent a specific bed type as described in traditional terms, secondly positioning errors can lead to poor calibration of the RoxAnn signatures in the ground truthing process. The first problem is difficult to correct, and can only be mitigated against through good survey design and execution. The second problem can be addressed in the data processing, and procedures for this are discussed. The RoxAnn data collected from the Dornoch Firth, used in conjunction with qualitative analysis of colour aerial photographs of the upper intertidal areas, provided a detailed classification of substrate types, including a classification of sands which allowed detailed insight into active processes of transport.

Mapping distributions of sediment characteristics is a long-practised art, providing data basic to any appreciation of sedimentary processes, and often yielding much detailed information about the nature of the processes themselves. Remote sensing technologies available today enable us to move away from a process of guesswork around a matrix of spot samples into the realm of Spatially Continuous Mapping using spot sampling for ground truthing.

Satellite imagery, aerial photography, swath bathymetry, side-scan sonar and RoxAnn-type systems are regularly in use to provide effectively Spatially Continuous Data on seabed characteristics. Each remote-sensing system maps its own suite of optical or acoustic parameters, and each varies in efficiency according to the conditions of the local environment and the objectives of the survey.

This paper is concerned with the practical aspects of the use of the RoxAnn system, an acoustic methodology (Chivers *et al.* 1990; Collins & Voulgaris 1993), through reference to a study undertaken in 1996 of an estuary in the north-east of Scotland, the Dornoch Firth.

This study was undertaken for Scottish National Heritage for conservation purposes. The aim of the study was to produce a biotope map of the intertidal and subtidal areas within the Firth. Biotopes, in the marine context, may be defined as 'the physical habitat together with its associated community of species'. The physical habitat can be broadly defined as a function of:

(1) Depth: intertidal drying heights (times) and subtidal water depths.
(2) Salinity.
(3) Water column energies: tidal currents, river-driven currents, wave energy.
(4) Substratum: rock outcrops and sediments.

A RoxAnn survey was employed to provide information about depth, water column energies (through resultant sediment characteristics, namely compaction and bed forms) and substratum.

The Dornoch Firth (Fig. 1) has 44 km of tidal watercourse, although the survey was restricted to the downstream 25–30 km. The width of the waterbody varies from 1 to 5 km. It is an area of strong tides, with a 4 m tidal range, and much of the Firth is dry at low water springs and has large areas only shallowly inundated at high water springs. The water is turbid, due both to sediment suspension and peat discolouration of the fresh waters feeding the Firth.

Field methods

Mapping of the estuary posed logistical problems: it is large, some 25% of the area is always inundated with turbid water and the extensive

HULL, J. & NUNNY, R. 1998. Mapping intertidal sediment distributions using the RoxAnn system, Dornoch Firth, NE Scotland. *In*: BLACK, K. S., PATERSON, D. M. & CRAMP, A. (eds) *Sedimentary Processes in the Intertidal Zone*. Geological Society, London, Special Publications, **139**, 273–282.

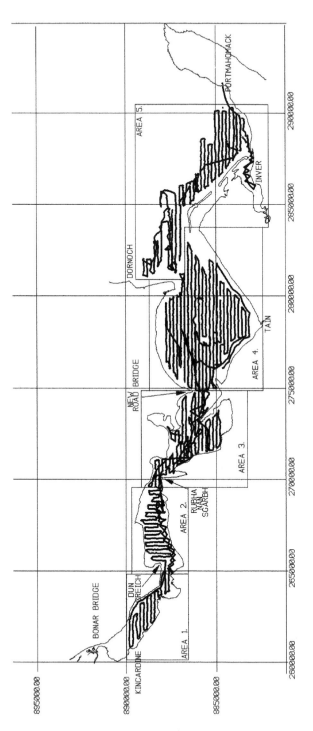

Fig. 1. The Dornoch Firth, showing survey areas and RoxAnn trackplot. The National Grid is shown.

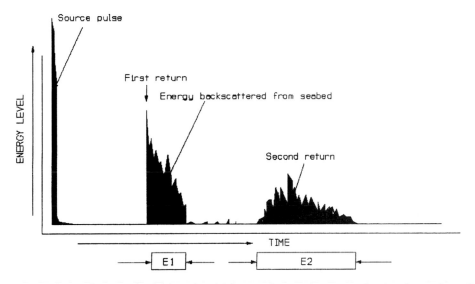

Fig. 2. Graph of acoustic energy level (*y*) vs time (*x*) for an echo sounder output, showing the portions of the acoustic return quantified by the RoxAnn system.

upper flats are only shallowly inundated for short periods of time. The approach adopted was to:

(1) use the RoxAnn system mounted in a very shallow draft vessel (capable of operating in 1m of water), to survey the bulk of the Firth and
(2) fly a 'qualitative' set of aerial photographs of the intertidal areas to provide a complementary data source, in particular providing information about the extremely shallow areas where a boat could not reach.

This approach provided photographic data of the uppermost intertidal levels, photo and acoustic data of the middle intertidal levels, and acoustic data of the subtidal channel floor areas.

Position fixing was by public broadcast Differential GPS throughout the exercise, giving an accuracy of ±8 m.

Ground truthing was achieved by visiting 80 intertidal sites, and collecting grab samples and underwater video footage from a further 64 intertidal and subtidal sites. Particle-size analyses (dry sieving at 0.5ϕ intervals) were undertaken of sediment samples taken from the grab.

RoxAnn is an echo-sounder signal processing system (Nunny 1995). In this particular survey a 200 kHz echo-sounder was used, this being highly sensitive to signals returning from the seabed sediment/water interface. With the RoxAnn system the following aspects of the returning acoustic signal (Fig. 2) are examined in an analogue fashion, and digitally recorded:

(1) the time to first return, giving water depth;
(2) the length of the tail associated with the first return, giving a seabed roughness index, annotated E1;
(3) the volume of the second return (first multiple), giving an index of the strength of the returning signal, and hence the seabed hardness, annotated E2.

These three pieces of data, together with the time and the DGPS position, were logged at 2 s intervals. Survey lines were run at 200 m spacing (Fig. 1).

Data analysis

The successful utilization of RoxAnn data in seabed mapping requires care in two critical areas:

(1) *Positioning-errors in ground-truthing.* The need for a high level of positioning accuracy during data collection and the taking into account of the effects of positioning errors when relating the acoustic data to the ground-truth observations.

Table 1. *Potential positioning errors*

Acoustic data position DGPS error	Grab/video position DGPS error	Grab/video vessel location error	Potential compound error (sum of individual errors)
±8 m	±8 m	±10 m	26 m

COMPOUNDING OF POSITIONING ERRORS

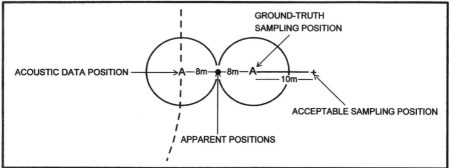

Fig. 3. Illustration of maximum potential compound error involved in relating ground-truth observations to the RoxAnn trackplot.

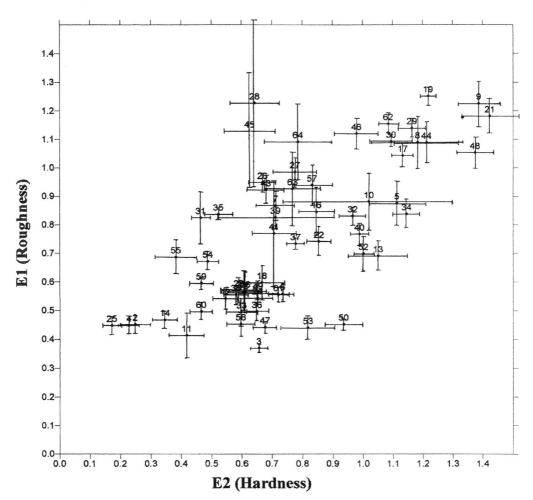

Fig. 4. Scatter plot of the means of RoxAnn E1 and E2 values in the vicinity of each ground-truth sampling site. One standard deviation error-bars are also plotted.

(2) *Uniqueness of acoustic signal.* The recognition that RoxAnn does not uniquely categorize sediments in terms of traditionally used parameters, e.g. particle-size characteristics.

These are now dealt with in further detail.

Positioning-errors in ground-truthing

Attempts to calibrate RoxAnn prior to a survey by successively running the instrument over several areas of apparently known and uniform sediment types have met with little success (Broffey 1996). The alternative approach

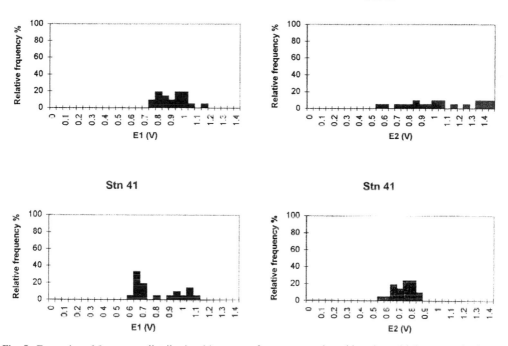

Fig. 5. Examples of frequency distribution histograms for two ground-truthing sites with large standard deviations. In processing, Station 10 was rejected as an unsuitable calibration site, and the mean E1 value at Station 41 was adjusted to equal one of the modal values.

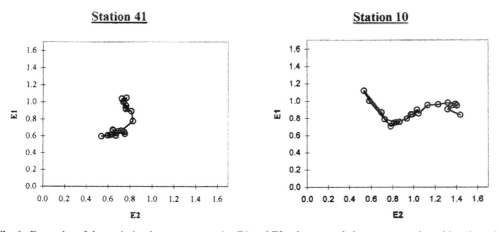

Fig. 6. Examples of the variation between successive E1 and E2 values recorded at two ground-truthing sites with large standard deviations (see Fig. 5).

involves producing an *xy* scatterplot of the E1 and E2 values associated with each of a large number of grab/video ground-truthing sites visited during the survey, and then producing sub-divisions of the graph area based upon the observed groupings of the various types of substratum.

The inter-relation of acoustic and ground-truth data in this fashion relies heavily upon accurate position fixing. Compound errors may build during sampling (Table 1, Fig. 3).

Thus, when a position is located on the acoustic trackplot, and ground truth data collected from that location, the actual truthing position may be up to 20–30 m away from the originally identified point. To take account of this potential variability, the RoxAnn values along the vessel's course for an equivalent distance either side of the selected location should ideally be examined. This procedure gives insight into the potential effect of positioning errors in the data calibration process, and the heterogeneity of the sediment body at each ground-truthing site.

During the Dornoch survey acoustic variability at each sampling site was quantified by determining the mean and standard deviation of the twenty data points ($\approx$30 m) centred on the theoretical sample location (Fig. 4), by producing a histogram showing the frequency distribution of these twenty E1 and E2 values (Fig. 5), and by plotting the succession of the twenty individual E1 and E2 values as an *xy* graph (Fig. 6). These three types of plot provided a more informed basis from which to embark upon the calibration process than simply the raw E1 and E2 values from the theoretical sampling location.

A scatter plot of the mean E1 (*y*-axis) and E2 (*x*-axis) values from each ground-truthing station was produced, coded according to particle-size content (%mud, %sand, %gravel, modal grain size of sand population), and/or visual description in the case of rock, boulder or coarse 'lag' deposits. These plots were contoured or block-categorized accordingly, using a contouring package with a kriging routine for the former.

Each point on this calibration scatter-plot was then examined individually. Where the standard deviations of the E1/E2 values were small, and where the histogram frequency distribution showed a 'normal' situation, confidence was given to the individual point, and particle-size content isolines and/or block categories consistent with these data points accepted. Where, however, standard deviations were large, the mean values of E1/E2 could not be used with confidence in the calibration process. Two situations become apparent when examining the

histograms for calibration points with large standard deviations:

(1) A wide scatter of RoxAnn values existed, suggesting a highly variable seabed on a small scale. Data points of this nature were not considered suitable for calibration purposes, and were abandoned.

(2) The data indicated the presence of two (or more) seabed reflector types within the sampled area, i.e. the presence of two (or more) modal values for E1/E2. In this instance it was considered realistic to adopt the E1/E2 modal value that best fitted the calibration pattern established using data points with an associated high level of confidence (low standard deviations).

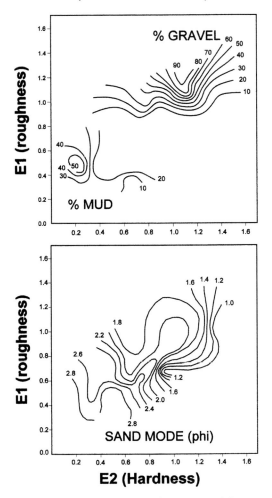

Fig. 7. RoxAnn E1E2 scatter plots contoured for %gravel and %mud values (upper) and sand grain population mode in phi units (lower) for data from sedimentary ground-truthing sites in the Dornoch Firth.

Through an iterative process, the original calibration scatter plots and fitted seabed-type distributions were reworked, removing or modifying rogue points and generally allowing a simpler pattern to emerge (Fig. 7). Finally, the E1/E2 scatter plot was 'boxed' into seabed-type classification based on a combination of particle-size and visual appearance (Fig. 8).

Uniqueness of acoustic signal

A problem basic to all Spatially Continuous Mapping is a traditional reliance upon particle-size and visual appearance in classification of seabed types, whereas remote sensing methods map other parameters. In the case of RoxAnn, aspects of the acoustic reflectivity of the seabed are being mapped, viz the local variability in backscatter (E1, equating to physical roughness) and sound-absorptive properties (E2, equating

to physical hardness). Although grain-size and bed morphology play a role in determining roughness and hardness of the seabed, other factors such as sediment compactness (history of disturbance) play an equal role. Thus it frequently happens that sediments with a similar RoxAnn signature have very different visual appearance and particle-size content. There are three steps which can be practically applied to mitigate this problem.

(1) The collection of a large number of ground truth samples, with several samples from each acoustic type, thus giving scope for identification of differences.

(2) The initially production of calibration diagrams for areas of similar water energies, e.g. upper estuary, lower estuary, sea coast. If these prove to be compatible they may be amalgamated at a later stage, but it is commonly found that parts of the calibrations will vary between such areas.

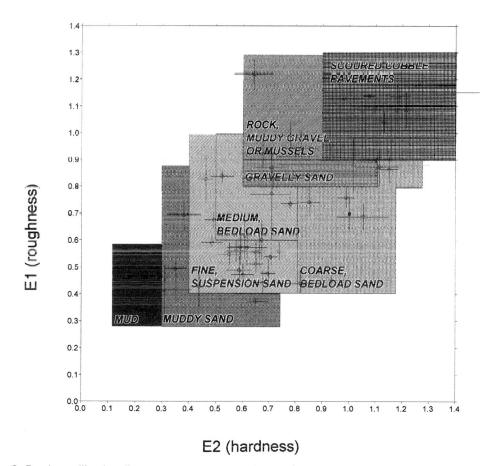

Fig. 8. RoxAnn calibration diagram showing estuary-bed categories mapped in the Dornoch Firth.

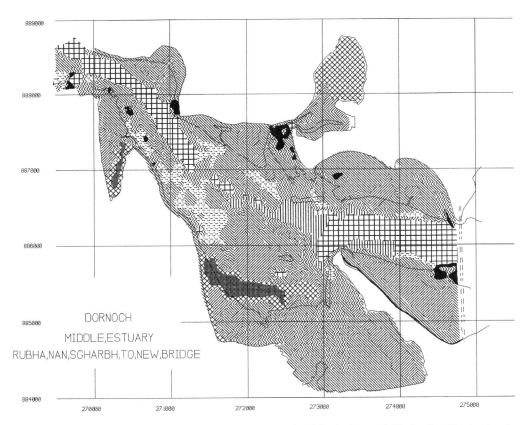

Fig. 9. Example of substrate map produced for Area 3 (see Fig. 1) in the Dornoch Firth. Classification key is provided in Table 2.

(3) Acceptance that it may be necessary to revisit sites to further ground truth areas of acoustic signal where ambiguity of classification may exist.

In the Dornoch Firth two situations of acoustic signature 'overlay' were encountered. The first posed little problem as the sediment areas were clearly geographically separate: areas of very soft (mobile) medium/fine sands on the sea beaches outside the estuary had signatures similar to sandy muds within the estuary. The other situation involved three substrate types with similar acoustic signatures (Fig. 8) and sometimes overlapping geographical extents:

(1) Channel floor mussel/gravel areas.
(2) Upper intertidal rock/brown algae areas.
(3) Fans of fine-gravels located in upper mud-flat areas where small rivers discharge into the estuary, thought to be introduced during winter spates.

Fortunately area (1) could be differentiated from areas (2) and (3) on the basis of bathymetry,

and areas (2) and (3) were differentiable with reference to the aerial photographs.

On completion of the calibration process, the RoxAnn E1 and E2 data from all the surveyed tracks were contoured (using a contouring package with a Kriging routine) to produce maps of blocks of the estuary, and these maps then combined according to the E1 and E2 groupings identified in Fig. 8, to produce a map of sediment distributions.

Results

From the RoxAnn data, complemented in the upper intertidal areas by colour aerial photographs, it was possible to produce a quite detailed substratum classification system and map of the Firth. The classification system related quite clearly to water energies and sedimentary processes, as identified in the Table 2. An example map of a portion of the estuary is shown in Fig. 9, illustrating the level of detailed mapping possible using this system.

Table 2. *Estuary bed classification system derived for the Dornoch Firth based on aerial photography and RoxAnn survey information*

Aerial photo data	RoxAnn data
Stable sediments. Characterized by a dark coloration relating to fines/organic content and importantly a surface biological film. Generally smooth texture but often algal patches where cobbles or other holdfasts available. Commonly exhibits range of drainage rill patterns. Muds, muddy sands and sands.	**Mud.** >30% sediment finer than 63 μm
	Muddy sand. 10-30% mud, 70-90% sand.
	Sand. >90% sand (2mm – 63 μm) *Suspension sands* (mean <200 μm) *Fallout zones* Low energy stable sand areas
Mobile sands without bedforms. Characterized by light colour. Commonly contain small-scale rippled surfaces below the resolution of the camera.	*Recirculation zones* High tidal energy sand shoals
Mobile sands with bedforms. Waveforms indicating regular (tidal) transport of sediments.	*Medium sands* (mean 200-500 μm)
Irregularly mobile sands with bedforms. Light coloured but less well-defined bedforms with dark trough floors of stable sediment/biological film.	
(not visible)	*Coarse (bedload) sands* (mean >500 μm, channel floor sands)
As **Stable sediments** above.	**Gravelly sand**. 10-40% gravel, 60-90% sand. (Channel floor deposits, intertidal fluvial fans and gravel spreads).
Rock. Structure visible.	**Rock.**
(not visible)	**Scoured cobble pavements.** (Channel floor areas)
(not visible)	**Mussel beds**

Conclusions

The RoxAnn seabed mapping system was originally marketed principally as a tool for the marine fishing industry working in coastal and offshore waters. Studies such as this work in the Dornoch Firth show that the system can be used to provide detailed maps of substrate characteristics in shallowly inundated (intertidal) areas. To enable translation of the acoustic parameters measured into traditionally recognized descriptions of the seabed careful ground-truthing is required, which relies upon very accurate position fixing and the application of a rigorous approach to the calibration process. Through reference to the characteristics of grain-size populations, the map data can reveal much about sand transport processes active within the mapped area.

References

BROFFEY, M. 1996. *A Study of Coastal Processes and Material Transportation at Kingsdown, Kent.* Dept of Ocean Sciences, University of Plymouth, Year 3 Dissertation.

CHIVERS, R. C, EMERSON, N. & BURNS, D. 1990. New acoustic processing for underway surveying. *The Hydrographic Journal*, April 1990.

COLLINS, M. B. & VOULGARIS, G. 1993. *Empirical Field and Laboratory Evaluation of a Real-Time Acoustic Seabed Surveying System.* Proceedings of the Institute of Acoustics, **15**(2).

NUNNY, R. S. 1995. *The Potential for Small-Boat Mounted Acoustic Seabed Mapping Systems in Tropical Marine Habitats.* University College of Belize Marine Research Centre Technical Report Series 1.

Relating erosion shear stress to tidal flat surface colour

R. RIETHMÜLLER, J. H. M. HAKVOORT, M. HEINEKE, K. HEYMANN,
H. KÜHL & G. WITTE

*Institute of Hydrophysics, GKSS Research Centre Geesthacht, Max-Planck-Strasse,
D-21502 Geesthacht, Germany*

Abstract: The relationships between erosion shear stress and bio-geochemical parameters, and between the optical reflectance spectra and bio-geochemical parameters of different tidal flats were investigated in the North Frisian part of the Wadden Sea. Erosion shear stress shows clear dependencies both on fine-grain fraction $<63\,\mu$m and on the benthic diatom chlorophyll *a* concentration present in the uppermost 1 mm sediment layer. The strongest dependence of erosion shear stress on the benthic diatom chlorophyll *a* surface concentration was found for muddy areas. This dependence vanishes for sandy surface sediments. The reflectance spectra show two main classes. The first class contains information on the fine-grain fraction $<63\,\mu$m of areas not covered by phytobenthos. The second class corresponds to the phytobenthos which can be subdivided into benthic diatoms and other macrophytes. A significant correlation was found between reflectance spectra and the amount of the fine-grain fraction $<63\,\mu$m present and also between reflectance spectra and the benthic diatom chlorophyll *a* concentration. Thus, erosion shear stress can be related to tidal flat surface colour yielding a basis to map the erodibility of tidal flats using optical remote sensing.

Change in seabed morphology is regarded as one of the most critical issues for the development of coastal areas. Movements of seabed structures, changes in the average water depth, steady loss of bed material or changes in its composition have significant consequences for coastal protection measures and ecosystem properties. Recent studies in the East Frisian (Flemming & Nyandwi 1994) and North Frisian Wadden Sea (Higelke 1996; Bayerl *et al.* 1996; Reise *et al.* 1996) indicated a depletion of fine-grained surface sediments together with a net loss of sediments and tidal flat areas over the past few decades. A continuation of these processes may degrade the Wadden Sea's ability to act as a large-scale wave breaker and also affect the benthic species compositions and abundances as well as the benthic primary productivity. Monitoring and forecasting morphological evolution on a broad range of scales have been formulated as an issue of concern for the Wadden Sea (Kellermann *et al.* 1994), but efficient and reliable methods have still to be developed. Here, optical remote sensing can be a useful tool.

Morphological characteristics, benthic biological activity and sediment stabilization processes are closely interrelated: the average water depth and the dry area during low water are determinant parameters for the wave climate and for the benthic biological activity; at the same time, benthic organisms both stabilize and destabilize the sediment surfaces. The erodibility of sediments in the absence of biogenic influences depends on the grain-size distribution as the predominant controlling parameter (Yalin 1977). Williamson & Ockenden (1996) showed consistency between data from muddy and sandy sites when the erosion shear stress is considered as a function of dry density. The microphytobenthos increases the resistance of sediment surfaces to tidal currents and waves (Holland *et al.* 1974; Coles 1979; Grant *et al.* 1986). Particularly, benthic diatoms form a tough network of Extracellular Polymeric Substances (EPS) which stabilizes the sediment by trapping the particles (Führböter 1983; de Jonge & van den Berg 1987; Paterson *et al.* 1994; Yallop *et al.* 1994). Additionally, the EPS reduce the current induced shear stress by smoothing the surface. Yet, clear relationships between chlorophyll *a* concentration as a measure of microbial biomass and erosion shear stress are still lacking. The sometimes inconclusive and contradictory results indicate a multifunctional dependence of erosion shear stress and show the need for large data sets sufficient to disentangle the contributions of the main determinant factors. An overview on this issue is given by Paterson (1994).

In our investigations presented here we statistically combined two sets of field measurements, (1) the erosion shear stress with bio-geochemical parameters and (2) the optical reflectance with bio-geochemical parameters of tidal flat surfaces. To minimize bias in the data the measurements covered a representative range of sediment types and phytobenthic assemblages. The initial part of our investigations

RIETHMÜLLER, R. *ET AL.* 1998. Relating erosion shear stress to tidal flat surface colour. *In:* BLACK, K. S., PATERSON, D. M. & CRAMP, A. (eds) *Sedimentary Processes in the Intertidal Zone*. Geological Society, London, Special Publications, **139**, 283–293.

deals with ranking the importance of the biological, chemical and physical factors which may influence the erosion shear stress of undisturbed tidal flat sediments. The aim was to derive quantitative relationships between erosion shear stress on the one hand, and the fine-grain fractions and chlorophyll *a* concentrations as the main determinant factors on the other. The second part deals with the relationship between optical reflectance spectra of sediment surfaces on the one hand, and the fine-grain fractions and chlorophyll *a* concentrations of microphytobenthos on the other. If significant relationships exist between the erosion shear stress, microphytobenthos concentration, sediment fine-grain fraction and the optical signals, it should be feasible to derive a map of the erosion sensitivity of the tidal flats using optical remote sensing. The possibility of determining the amount of the grain-size fractions $<63\,\mu m$ present in surface sediments using optical remote sensing has been already demonstrated (Kleeberg 1990, Yates *et al.* 1993) using information from the Thematic Mapper sensor onboard of the LANDSAT satellites. In our investigations an additional relationship has to be found between reflectance spectra and chlorophyll *a* concentrations of microphytobenthos.

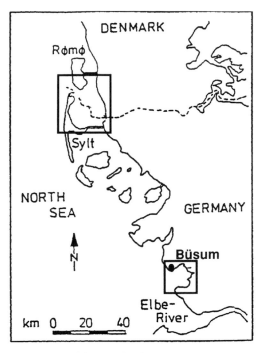

Fig. 1. Map of the North Frisian Wadden Sea showing the experimental sites of the Sylt–Rømø Bight and the Meldorfer Bight.

Material and methods

Study sites

For the present study two intertidal flats in the German Bight, the Sylt–Rømø Bight and the Meldorfer Bight near Büsum were selected (Fig. 1). The choice of these sites was based on former research which showed that together they covered the complete range of sediment types from mud to sand (Austen 1994; Gast *et al.* 1984). Also the representative assemblages of the microphytobenthos (Asmus & Bauerfeind 1994) and significant stands of macrophytobenthic species were covered (Reise & Lackschewitz 1996; Asmus *et al.* 1996). The microphytobenthos was dominated by diatoms.

For the erosion measurements presented here the Sylt–Rømø bight was sampled at spring and late summer between the years 1992 to 1995. The *in situ* optical studies were performed during the spring and late summer of 1996 at both sites.

Erosion measurements

For the erosion measurements, sediment cores were sampled on the tidal flats using 10 cm diameter perspex tubes. Sampling time was always about one hour after the sampling position was free of water. The samples were immediately transported to a nearby laboratory and carefully filled with sea water to a height of 30 cm.

The EROMES device (Kühl & Puls 1990; Schünemann & Kühl 1993; Cornelisse *et al.* 1994; Witte & Kühl 1996) was used to determine the erosion shear stress. Turbulence induced by this system simulates the conditions of turbulent flow and waves with randomly varying bursts of velocity and shear stress which are typical at the bed of rivers, estuaries and the Wadden Sea (Raudkivi 1976). If the random distribution of the current shear stress overlaps the random distribution of the shear stresses at which bed particles move, they will be eroded during the peaks in the velocity bursts. Turbulence in the sample tube, and hence the erosion, is induced by a propeller above the sediment surface. Special mounting baffles prevent rotation of the water column and vertical balancing currents. The applied average shear stress is a function of the propeller speed and was calibrated by means of quartz sands of specified grain size with known critical shear stress up to values of $3.0\,\mathrm{N\,m^{-2}}$. For the field samples, the

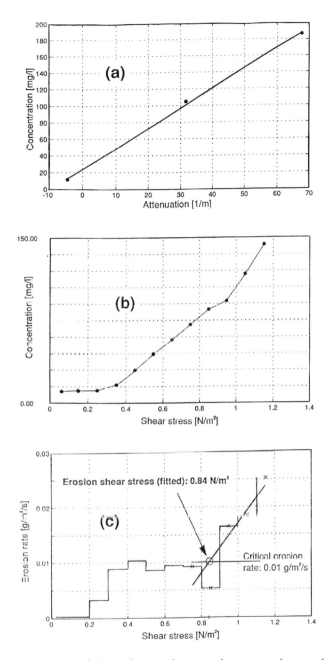

Fig. 2. Experimental curves of one of the erosion experiments to demonstrate the procedure to determine the erosion shear stress: (**a**) Calibration curve relating the attenuation coefficient of the transmission readings to the suspended sediment concentration in the perspex tube. (**b**) Suspended sediment concentration versus the applied shear stress. (**c**) Erosion rate vs applied shear stress. To determine the erosion shear stress a linear function is fitted to the data in the region around the second significant increase of the erosion rate (denoted by the crosses). For further details see text.

shear stress was increased by $0.1\,N\,m^{-2}$ every 5 min in general. This ensured an almost constant erosion rate at the end of each shear stress interval (quasi-static erosion state). The generated turbulence keeps the eroded matter stored in suspension. Suspended sediment concentration is continuously determined by measuring the light attenuation due to the eroded particles in a by-pass loop. In the course of each experiment, the attenuation is calibrated by repeated determination of the suspended sediment concentration. Sandy samples with a fine-grain fraction $<63\,\mu m$ of less than 5% were not considered for further analysis because most of the grains are to heavy to be kept in suspension by the generated turbulence.

Erosion shear stress is determined by significant increase of the erosion rate. In Fig. 2, the evaluation procedure is illustrated for a sample of muddy sediment. The three diagrams show the individual concentration calibration curve (a) and as a function of the applied shear stress the suspended sediment concentration (b) and the erosion rate (c). The latter is calculated by the time derivative of the measured quasi-static suspended matter concentration for each shear stress interval. The determination of the erosion shear stress requires a detailed study of the erosion rate progress during the experiment because in most cases there are two distinct shear stress values where the erosion rate increases significantly. The smooth increase to a first erosion rate level indicates erosion of non-consolidated material deposited on the surface during low tide. The amount of this resuspended material is controlled by the wave and current conditions right before sampling (de Jonge & van Beusekom 1995). The second, higher increase in the erosion rate indicates the onset of erosion of the consolidated bed. A linear function is fitted to the erosion rates in this region. The erosion shear stress is computed from the intersection of the fit function with a critical erosion rate level of $0.01\,mg\,l^{-1}\,s^{-1}$. It is important to note that the material eroded from the core's surface below this level contributes only a little to the reflectance signal. The optically most significant case represents a horizontally homogeneous erosion. This would correspond to a thickness of some $10\,\mu m$. With typical light penetration depths of $300\,\mu m$ at 650 nm (Kühl & Jørgensen 1994) this very upper layer contributes to less than 10% of the reflected light signal. In most cases this material consists of fluffy flocs loosely bound to the sediment surface and therefore is assumed to contribute even less to the reflected light signal. The EROMES results fit favourably into the ISIS data (Williamson &

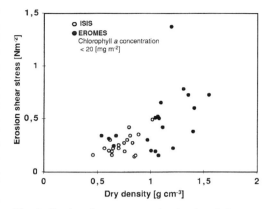

Fig. 3. Erosion shear stress vs dry density of the sediment surface. The EROMES data are limited to diatom chlorophyll *a* concentrations <20 mg m^{-2} in the surface to minimize biogenic influence. ISIS data are adapted from Williamson & Ockenden (1996).

Ockenden 1996) for the considered abiotic cohesive sediments which are simply characterized by their dry density (Fig. 3).

Optical measurements

Reflectance spectra with a 4 nm wavelength resolution were simultaneously measured in the optical window 420–780 nm at different detection angles simultaneously using a modified CCD-based Portable Multi-Channel Spectrometer (Spectral Signatures, Dublin, Ireland). The modification was necessary on the fibre optic connectors to the spectrometer to stabilize the optical pathway. Light collected by optical fibres is fed into the spectrometer and dispersed across the horizontal array of the CCD. The input fibres are stacked vertically at the entrance to the spectrometer, thus producing high resolution reflectance spectra along the vertical array of the CCD. Dark currents (i.e. the instrument's background) also are measured simultaneously and subtracted from the measured light signal. For the present work five optical fibres were employed. They had a 20° angle of view and were mounted into a frame at a height of 2 m height above the sediment surface. One fibre was directed downwards towards a reference reflectance panel, thus collecting the incident light spectrum L_d. The other four were directed towards the tidal flat surface, thus measuring the reflected light spectrum L_u. One of these L_u fibres collected light arriving perpendicular from the sediment surface and the other three collected light from an angle of 30° zenith and variable azimuth angle with 90° interval. The detected sediment surface was some $0.7 \, m^2$. Typical signal integration times used for the present work were of the order of this work was five mins. The reflectance spectra were calculated by L_u / L_d.

Bio-geochemical measurements

For the bio-geochemical measurements the uppermost 1 mm layer of the sediment surface was sampled. In the case of the optical studies this comprised the whole detected area immediately after the measurements. For comparison with the erosion measurements, additional cores with diameters of 5 cm were taken close to the erosion cores. The samples were well mixed and sub-samples were taken to measure the pigment-pigments concentration of the microphytobenthos, the amount of the fine-grain fraction $<63 \, \mu m$ present, the water content, the hydrocarbon content, and the amount of the total and particulate organic matter present. Pigment concentrations were measured using the acetone extraction and reverse-phase column HPLC technique of Wright et al. (1991). The fine-grain fraction of most samples was determined by wet sieving with mesh-size $63 \, \mu m$ (DIN 4188 1977) in most cases. In all other cases it was derived from the wet density which has a close relationship to the fine-grain fraction. The water content of the sediment was determined by drying to constant weight for 24 hrs drying at a temperature of 105°C. For the determination of hydrocarbons the phenol-sulphuric acid method of Liu et al. (1972) was used. The total organic matter fraction was measured by loss of ignition (DIN 18128 1990) after the samples had been oven-dried at a temperature of were put into a oven at 550°C for 1 hr. The particulate organic carbon was measured by means of the infrared absorption of the combustion gases after the converting process at high temperature.

Results

Erosion measurements

In order to disentangle the influences of the different parameters on the erosion shear stress, a stepwise analysis of the erosion data was applied. In the analysis, a total of 73 samples with a complete set of erosion and bio-geochemical parameters was considered. First, the complete data set was subjected to a factor analysis. This

Table 1. *Factor analysis of the measured bio-geochemical parameters measured in the uppermost 1 mm surface and the erosion shear stress*

	Factor 1	Loads 2
Dry density	0.97	0.08
Water content	−0.96	0.06
Porosity	−0.91	0.05
Carbohydrates	−0.90	0.01
POC	−0.89	−0.12
Fine-grain fraction $<63 \, \mu m$	−0.88	−0.14
Wet density	0.88	0.14
Chlorophyll a	0.02	0.87
Erosion shear stress	0.07	0.85

calculation resulted in two factors (see Table 1) which divide the measured parameters into two distinctive groups: the first factor corresponds to all parameters describing the physical characteristics, the hydrocarbon content, and the amount of the total and particulate organic matter present. In the second factor, exclusively chlorophyll a concentration and erosion shear stress with a significant correlation coefficient are present. However, a distinct dependence of the erosion shear stress on chlorophyll a concentration was not found. In general, erosion shear stresses do not exceed values of $1.0 \, N/m^2$ for chlorophyll a concentrations $<50 \, mg \, m^{-2}$ and are significantly above $1.0 \, N \, m^{-2}$ for chlorophyll a concentrations $>60 \, mg \, m^{-2}$ (Fig. 4). The scattering of the data suggests additional influence of other parameters.

Much clearer dependencies of erosion shear stress on chlorophyll a concentration emerge

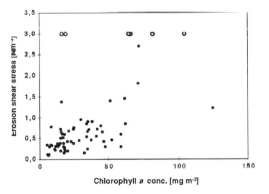

Fig. 4. Erosion shear stress versus diatom chlorophyll a concentration in the surface of purely diatom covered sites for all data. Open circles represent the cases where the erosion shear stress was beyond the specifications of the present EROMES device (limit is $3.0 \, N \, m^{-2}$).

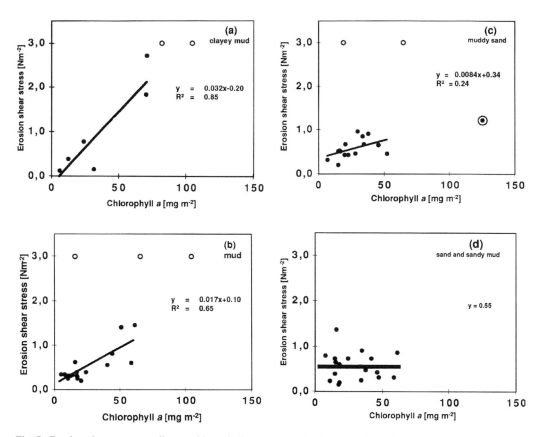

Fig. 5. Erosion shear stress vs diatom chlorophyll *a* concentration in the surface of purely diatom covered sites, data subdivided into four sediment classes by fine-grain fraction <63 μm: (**a**) clayed mud (fine-grain fraction >85%); (**b**) mud (fine-grain fraction 50–85%); (**c**) muddy sand (fine-grain fraction 25–50%); (**d**) sand and sandy mud (fine-grain fraction 10–25%). The lines in (**a**)–(**c**) are fitted linear functions; in (**d**) a constant value was fitted to the data. Open circles represent the cases where the erosion shear stress was beyond the specifications of the present EROMES device (limit is $3.0 \, \mathrm{N \, m^{-2}}$).

only after the data were subdivided by fine-grain fraction <63 μm into four sediment classes: sand and sandy mud (fine-grain fraction 10–25%), muddy sand (fine-grain fraction 25–50%), mud (fine-grain fraction 50–85%), and clayey mud (fine-grain fraction >85%) (see Fig. 5) (classification after Figge *et al.* 1980). In mud and clayey mud, erosion shear stress increases strongly with chlorophyll *a* concentration. With decreasing fine-grain fraction present this dependence becomes weaker. For sand and sandy mud, no correlation was found.

To study exclusive dependencies on physical parameters, all samples with a chlorophyll *a* concentration below $20 \, \mathrm{mg \, m^{-2}}$ were examined separately. They show a slight decrease of erosion shear stress from 0.6 to $0.3 \, \mathrm{N \, m^{-2}}$ with increasing amounts of fine-grain fraction <63 μm from 10% to 85% present (Fig. 6).

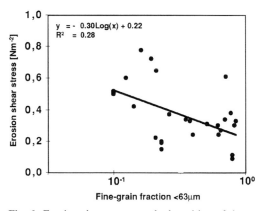

Fig. 6. Erosion shear stress vs the logarithm of the fine-grain fraction < 63 μm of the sediment surfaces. Included are only data with diatom chlorophyll *a* concentrations $<20 \, \mathrm{mg \, m^{-2}}$ in the surface to minimize biogenic influence. The line is the fitted linear function.

A nearly identical result was also found for undisturbed natural sediments from various different sites within the United Kingdom (Mitchener & Torfs 1996).

Optical measurements

The measured reflectance spectra of the different surface types have very distinctive signatures (Fig. 7). Two main classes of spectra can be distinguished. The first class of spectra corresponds to uncovered areas and contains information on the fine-grain fraction $<63\,\mu m$ of the sediment surface (class I spectra). These spectra are characterized by a gradual increase in reflectance with increasing wavelength. Sandy areas can be distinguished from muddy sediment types by having a steeper slope, due to the fact that sandy sediments have a higher reflectance in the near-infrared region. Irrespective of sediment type, however, all spectra showed a drop in the reflectance around 670 nm due to the light absorption by chlorophyll a which seems to be always is present on these tidal flats. The second class of reflectance spectra corresponds to the phytobenthos (class II spectra): diatoms, brown algae, seagrass and green macroalgae. These spectra are characterized by a high reflectance in the near-infrared region (around 750 nm) and a low reflectance in the red region (670 nm).

Using these unique spectral signatures of surface types it is possible to separate uncovered sediment from phytobenthic types based on the ratio of the logarithmic reflectances $\log R(750)/$ $\log R(670)$. The numbers in brackets are the wavelengths in nm. A ratio greater than 0.92 for a given spectrum is considered to be a signal originating from almost uncovered sediment, whereas a ratio less than 0.92 means that the dominant surface reflectance originates from plant material. In the case of diatom coverage this corresponds to a concentration of chlorophyll a greater than $20\,mg\,m^{-2}$. Furthermore, diatoms can be separated from other plants by the existence of a local maximum of R around 590 nm and $R(640) > R(630)$.

From the class I spectra the amount of the fine-grain fraction present in the upper 1 mm of sediment can be derived using the ratio $\log R(750)/\log R(420)$ (Fig. 8). Effects due to absorption by accessory plant pigments are minimal at both wavelengths. Values indicated by dots were measured under a dark overcast sky and hence are excluded from the regression. For the class II diatom reflectance spectra, the ratio $\log R(750)/\log R(670)$ decreases almost linearly with the concentration of chlorophyll a in the upper 1 mm of sediment (Fig. 9). The only exception from this relationship was found for a sandy area in a small basin within the Sylt–Rømø Bight with considerable amounts of large sand grains. These values were also excluded from the regression.

Discussion

Our investigations show that the erosion shear stress of tidal flats depends mainly on two

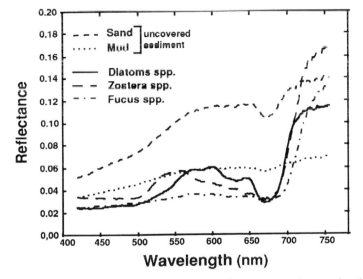

Fig. 7. Typical reflectance spectra of two almost uncovered sediment types and some phytobenthic species.

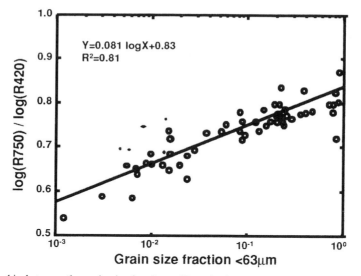

Fig. 8. Relationship between the grain-size fraction $<63\,\mu m$ in the sediment surface and the ratio of the logarithms of the reflectance at 420 nm and 750 nm. Only sediments with a diatom chlorophyll a concentration of $<20\,mg\,m^{-2}$ in the surface were used.

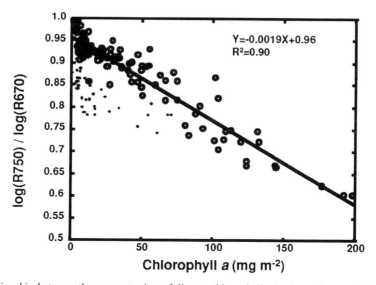

Fig. 9. Relationship between the concentration of diatom chlorophyll a in the surface and the ratio of the logarithms of the reflectances at 670 nm and 750 nm. The points indicate measurements from stations in a sandy area having a large grain size and low organic matter content. They were not included in the fit.

factors: the chlorophyll a concentration of diatoms and the amount of the fine-grain fraction $<63\,\mu m$ present on the sediment surface. At low biogenic influences, erosion shear stress is of the order of $0.5\,N\,m^{-2}$ and gradually decreases with increasing fine-grain fraction present. Increasing surface concentration of diatoms leads to significantly higher erosion shear stresses. The efficiency of diatoms in stabilizing the sediment surface is higher in muddy than sandy sediments. As a consequence, the grain-size dependence of erosion shear stress is reversed and becomes more pronounced with increasing diatom presence. Taxonomic data may help to identify whether this effect can be assigned to different diatoms species dominant in different sediment types. In addition, the grain-size dependent physical environment (porosity, water content) may influence the diatoms capabilities to trap individual sediment particles by EPS.

Both fine-grain fraction $<63\,\mu m$ and diatom chlorophyll a concentration at the tidal flat surface have a significant relationship with the reflectance spectra. Therefore a basis has been established to enable erosion shear stress mapping using optical remote sensing. To relate erosion shear stress to the optical signal for diatom covered areas, the dependencies of erosion shear stress on diatom chlorophyll a concentration were approximated by linear function fits for clayey mud, mud and muddy sand. For sand and sandy mud, the mean value of $0.55\,N\,m^{-2}$ was assumed as a constant. Excluded from the fit are the cases where the erosion shear stresses exceed the specifications of the present EROMES device. For chlorophyll a concentrations below $20\,mg\,m^{-2}$ these are regarded as outliers for statistical reasons although we can only speculate about their particular causes. The high pigment concentration data point in Fig. 5(c) has also been excluded from the fit, since it would dominate the result. The functional relationship between erosion shear stress and the logarithm of the fine grain fraction for low biogenic influence was also assumed to be a linear function (Fig. 6).

The resulting functions with their associated parameters are shown in Figs 5 and 6. They have to be considered as first approximations for a number of reasons. Too few measurements have been obtained from sites with high pigment concentrations, so the definition range of the functions has to be restricted to diatom chlorophyll a concentrations below $60\,mg\,m^{-2}$. In some cases (Figs 5(c), 5(d), and 6) the statistical significance of the fits is weak due to the scatter of the data. This scatter probably reflects the small-scale patchiness of the surface. Furthermore, since the EROMES device does not allow any measurements on erosion shear stress above $3.0\,N\,m^{-2}$, it remains open whether a linear relationship is still valid at higher pigment concentrations.

To improve the statistical significance of the above functional relations more erosion data will be gathered. An extension of the EROMES device to measure shear stresses above $3.0\,N\,m^{-2}$ is in preparation. Particularly, the diatom chlorophyll a range above $60\,mg\,m^{-2}$ will be explored for all sediment types. To achieve a more regularly distributed sampling in the chlorophyll a concentration/fine-grain fraction parameter space the selection of the sampling positions will be guided by foregoing optical remote sensing using the transfer functions (1)–(5). The dependencies for low biogenic influence will be more thoroughly investigated during winter time campaigns.

Combining the relationships of the erosion and optical measurements to chlorophyll a concentration and fine-grain fraction in the surface layer, respectively, yields the following transfer functions of tidal flat reflectance $R(\lambda)$ with λ being the wavelength in nm to erosion shear stress τ_{ero}:

Class I: low biogenic influence (chlorophyll a concentration $<20\,mg\,m^{-2}$)

$$\tau_{ero}[N\,m^{-2}] = -3.7 \times \log R(750) \times \log R(420) + 3.3 \qquad (1)$$

Class II: diatom dominated influence (diatom chlorophyll a concentration $20\,mg\,m^{-2}$–$60\,mg\,m^{-2}$)

fine grain-fraction $<63\,\mu m$ present

$>85\%$

$$\tau_{ero}[N\,m^{-2}] = -17.0 \times \log R(750) \times \log R(670) + 16.0 \qquad (2)$$

$50–85\%$

$$\tau_{ero}[N\,m^{-2}] = -8.9 \times \log R(750) \times \log R(670) + 8.7 \qquad (3)$$

$25–50\%$

$$\tau_{ero}[N\,m^{-2}] = -4.4 \times \log R(750) \times \log R(670) + 4.6 \qquad (4)$$

$10–25\%$

$$\tau_{ero}[N\,m^{-2}] = 0.55 \qquad (5)$$

The values of the parameters have to be considered as first approximations due to the arguments given in the previous paragraph for the erosion results. The error in these formulas is dominated by the erosion measurements; therefore, the R^2 values of the fits in Figs 5 and 6 are also valid for the transfer functions (1)–(5). It is expected that further erosion measurements will lead to significant refinements of the results.

To derive values of erosion shear stress from the reflectance spectra measured on a surface covered with diatoms the fine-grain fraction has to be known since a choice must be made for which algorithm should be applied. It remains to be investigated to what extent ground-truth measurements are needed or mapping from periods with a minimal diatom coverage can be used.

Also the fine-grain fraction classification from reflectance spectra needs further attention. The reflectance signal is a linear function of the logarithmic fine-grain fraction and the above defined sediment types cover a third of the measured range shown in Fig. 8. The statistical significance found for the correlation between the reflectance spectra and fine-grain fraction may not yet be sufficient to discriminate the sediment types. It has to be investigated whether factors can be found which may help to improve the discrimination power.

The present research initiated a statistically robust library of reflectance spectra of the most frequently uncovered sediment types and phytobenthic species. Also the dependence of the spectral reflectance on the angular distribution of the incident light is included. This effect is of the order of 5 mg m^{-2} chlorophyll *a*. It is known that diatoms can migrate vertically (Harper 1977; Paterson 1986; Hay *et al.* 1993). This may spoil the relationship between the observed optical signal and the erosion shear stress. At the locations of our present study this effect was not observed during long-time measurements of several hours. The footprint of airborne or spaceborne imaging spectroscopy may include a mixture of plant species and sediment types resulting in a composed reflectance spectrum. Procedures to calculate the contributions of the different plant species to the total bottom coverage will be developed in the near future.

Fine-grain fraction and diatom chlorophyll *a* concentration cannot be measured at the same time by optical methods. To map erosion shear stress using optical remote sensing techniques the fine-grain fractions and the chlorophyll *a* concentrations have to be measured at different times. It is best to map the fine-grain fraction shortly after the period of spring storms is over and before the first diatom bloom. Under the assumption that from this moment the horizontal distribution of surface sediments remains constant until the next winter, this distribution can be used to select the appropriate algorithm to derive erosion shear stress from the reflectance spectra.

I. Austen, B. Diercks, M. Henle, M. Janik, B. Peters and Ch. Stein are acknowledged for their help in sampling and analysis. We want to thank the 'Biologische Anstalt Helgoland' in ListlSylt and the 'Forschungs- und Technologiezentrum Büsum' of the University of Kiel and their staff for hosting us and giving technical support during the field campaigns.

References

Asmus, R. M. & Bauerfeind, E. 1994. The microphytobenthos of Königshafen − spatial and seasonal distribution on a sandy tidal flat. *Helgoländer Meeresuntersuchungen*, **48**, 257–276.

——, Jensen, M. H., Murphy, D. & Doerffer, R. 1996. Primärproduktion von Mikrophytobenthos, Phytoplankton und jhrlicher Biomasseertrag des Makrophytobenthos. *In*: Reise, K. *et al.* (eds) *SWAP Sylter Wattenmeer Austauschprozesse Projektsynthese*, Tönning, 299–318.

Austen, I. 1994. The surficial sediments of Königshafen-variations over the past 50 years. *Helgoländer Meeresuntersuchungen*, **48**, 163–171.

Bayerl, K.-A., Austen, I., Köster, R., Pejrup, M. & Witte, G. 1996. Dynamik der Sedimente im Lister Tidebecken. *In*: Reise, K. *et al.* (eds) *SWAP Sylter Wattenmeer Austauschprozesse Projektsynthese*, Tönning, 102–132.

Coles, S. M. 1979. Benthic microalgal populations on intertidal sediments and their role as precursors to salt marsh development. *In*: Jeffries, R. L. & Davy, A. J. (eds) *Ecological Processes in Coastal Environments*. Blackwell, Oxford, 25–42.

Cornelisse, J. M., Mulder, H. P. J., Williamson, H., Witte, G. & Houwing, E. J. 1994. In the development of instruments for in situ erosion measurements. *In*: Burt, N., Parker, R. & Watts, J. (eds) *Cohesive Sediments*. John Wiley & Sons, Chichester, UK, 175–186.

de Jonge, V. N. & van Beusekom, J. E. E. 1995. Wind and tide induced resuspension of sediment and microphytobenthos from tidal flats in the Ems estuary. *Limnology and Oceanography*, **40**, 766–778.

—— & van den Berg, J. 1987. Experiments on the resuspension of estuarine sediments containing benthic diatoms. *Estuarine, Coastal and Shelf Science*, **24**, 725–740.

DIN 4188, Teil 1, 1977. Siebböden; Drahtsiebböden für Analysensiebe. *Deutsche Normen*, October.

DIN 18128, 1990. Baugrund, Versuche und Versuchsgeräte; Bestimmung des Glühverlusts. *Deutsche Normen*, November.

Figge, K., Köster, R., Thiel, H. R. & Wieland, P. 1980. Schlickuntersuchungen im Wattenmeer der deutschen Bucht (Zwischenbericht über ein Forschungsprojekt des KFKI). *Die Küste*, **35**, 187–204.

Flemming, B. W. & Nyandwi, N. 1994. Land reclamation as a cause of fine-grained sediment depletion in backbarrier tidal flats (southern North Sea). *Netherland Journal of Aquatic Ecology*, **28**(3–4), 229–307.

Führböter, A. 1983. Über Mirkobiologische Einflüsse auf den Erosionsbeginn bei Sandwatten. *Wasser und Boden*, **3**, 106–116.

Gast, R., Köster, R. & Runte, K. H. 1984. Die Wattsedimente der Nördlichen und Mittleren Meldorfer Bucht. Untersuchung zur Frage der Sedimentverteilung und der Schlicksedimentation. *Die Küste*, **40**, 165–257.

Grant, J., Bathman, U. V. & Mills, E. L. 1986. The interaction between benthic diatom films and sediment transport. *Estuarine, Coastal and Shelf Science*, **23**, 225–238.

Harper, M. A. 1977. Movements. *In*: Werner, D. (eds) *The Biology of Diatoms*. Botanical Monographs, **13**, Blackwell Science, Oxford, 224–249.

HAY, S. I., MAITLAND, T. C. & PATERSON, D. M. 1993. The speed of diatom migration through natural and artificial substrata. *Diatom Research*, **8**, 371–384.

HIGELKE, B. 1996. Morphodynamik des Lister Tidebeckens. *In*: REISE, K. *et al.* (eds) *SWAP Sylter Wattenmeer Austauschprozesse Projektsynthese*, Tönning, 81–101.

HOLLAND, A. F. ZINGMARK, R. G. & DEAN, J. M. 1974. Quantitative evidence concerning the stabilization of sediments by marine benthic diatoms. *Marine Biology*, **27**, 191–196.

KELLERMANN, A., LAURSEN, K. RIFTHMÜLLER, R., SANDBECK, P., UYTERLINDE, R. & VAN DE WETERING, B. 1994. Concepts for a trilateral integrated monitoring program in the Wadden Sea. *In*: FREDERIKSEN, M. & DAHL, K. (eds) *Birds and their Ecology in the Wadden Sea. Esbjerg 1993; Proceedings of the 8th International Scientific Wadden Sea Symposium*. Marine Biological Laboratory, Helsingör, Denmark, *Ophelia Suppley*, **6**, 57–68 (September 94).

KLEEBERG, U. 1990. Kartierung der Sedimentverteilung im Wattenmeer durch integrierte Auswertung von Satellitendaten und Daten aus der Wattenmeerdatenbank der GKSS. Diplom Thesis, Universität Trier, Germany.

KÜHL, H. & PULS, W. 1990. Offenlegungsschrift DE 3826044 A1. Deutsches Patentamt.

KÜHL, M. & JØRGENSEN, B. B. 1994. The light field of microbenthic communities: radiance distribution and microscale optics of sandy coastal sediments. *Limnol. Oceanogr.*, **39**(6), 1368–1398

LIU, D., WONG, P. T. S. & DUTKA, B. J. 1972. Determination of carbohydrate in lake sediment by a modified phenol-sulphuric acid method. *Water Research*, **7**, 741–746.

MITCHENER, H. J. & TORFS, H. 1996. Erosion of mud/sand mixtures. *Coastal Engineering*, **29**, 1–25.

PATERSON, D. M. 1986. The migratory behaviour of diatom assemblages in a laboratory tidal microecosystem examined by low temperature scanning electron microscopy. *Diatom Research*, **1**, 227–239.

—— 1994. Biological mediation of sediment erodibility: ecology and physical dynamics. *Proc. Intercoh 1994*, Oxford.

——, YALLOP, M. L. & GEORGE, C. 1994. Spatial variability in the sediment erodibility on the Island of Texel. *In*: KRUMMBEIN, W. *et al.* (eds) *Biostabilization of Sediments*, Oldenburg. 107–120.

RAUDKIVI, A. J. 1976. *Loose Boundary Hydraulics*. Pergamon Press, Oxford.

REISE, K. & LACKSCHEWITZ, D. 1996. Benthos des Wattenmeeres zwischen Sylt und Rømø. *In*: REISE, K. *et al.* (eds) *SWAP Sylter Wattenmeer Austauschprozesse Projektsynthese*, Tönning, 47–54.

REISE, K., KÖSTER, P., MÜLLER, A. *ET AL.* 1996. Austauschprozesse im Sylt–Rømø Wattenmeer–Zusammenschau und Ausblick. *In*: REISE, K. *et al.* (eds.) *SWAP Sylter Wattenmeer Austauschprozesse Projektsynthese*, Tönning, 423–446.

SCHÜNEMANN, M. & KÜHL, H. 1993. Experimental investigations of the erosional behaviour of naturally formed mud from the Elbe-estuary and the adjacent Wadden Sea. *In*: METHA, A. J. (ed.) *Coastal and Estuarine Studies*, **42**, 314–330.

WILLIAMSON, H. J. & OCKENDEN, M. C. 1996. ISIS. an instrument for measuring erosion shear stress *in situ*. *Estuarine, Coastal and Shelf Science*, **42**, 1–18.

WITTE, G. & KÜHL, H. 1996. Facilities for sedimentation and erosion measurements. *Archieves for Hydrobiology Special Issues Advanced Limnology*, **47**, 121–125.

WRIGHT, S. W., MANTOURA, R. F. C., JEFFREY, S. W., LLEWELLYN, C. A., BJØRNLAND, T., REPETA, D. & WELSCHMEYER, N. 1991. Improved HPLC method for the analysis of chlorophylls and carotinoids from marine phytoplankton. *Marine Ecology Progress Series*, **77**, 183–196.

YALIN, M. S. 1977. *Mechanics of Sediment Transport*. Pergamon Press, Oxford.

YALLOP, M., DE WINDER, B., PATERSON, D. M. & STAL, L. J. 1994. Comparative structure, primary production and biogenic stabilization of cohesive and non-cohesive marine sediments inhabited by microphytobenthos. *Estuarine, Coastal and Shelf Sciences*, **39**, 183–196, 565–582.

YATES, M. G., JONES, A. R. MCGRORTY, S. & GOSS-CUSTARD, J. D. 1993. The use of satellite imagery to determine the distribution of intertidal surface sediments of the Wash, England. *Estuarine, Coastal and Shelf Science*, **36**, 333–344.

The erosion threshold of biotic sediments: a comparison of methods

T. F. SUTHERLAND[1], C. L. AMOS[2] & J. GRANT[1]

[1] *Department of Oceanography, Dalhousie University, Halifax,*
Nova Scotia B3H 4J1, Canada
[2] *Geological Survey of Canada – Atlantic, Bedford Institute of Oceanography,*
P.O. Box 1006, Dartmouth, Nova Scotia B2Y 4A2, Canada

Abstract: Laboratory and field studies were carried out to determine the effect of biofilms on sediment erodibility. In the laboratory setting, a diatom culture of *Nitzschia curvilineata* was incubated on sediment and eroded in a recirculating flume at successive stages of growth. Several methods for determining erosion thresholds were employed: (1) the visual determination of particle and bed threshold, (2) an extrapolation method and (3) a digitization method. A comparison of the derived erosion thresholds by these three methods is discussed. In the field setting, an *in situ* flume (Sea Carousel) was deployed at stations along a transect in a microtidal temperate estuary (Upper South Cove, Nova Scotia, Canada). The extrapolation method was used to determine the erosion thresholds of seabed constituents, such as chlorophyll, phaeopigment and sediment. The differences observed between the erosion threshold of chlorophyll, phaeopigment, and sediment lead to ambiguities in the definition of the erosion threshold of a seabed.

Several descriptions of the onset of cohesive sediment movement, transport and resuspension exist in the literature leading to ambiguities in the definition of erosion threshold. The precision by which the erosion threshold is determined is limited because of the numerous and incompatible definitions (Miller *et al.* 1977). For example, the erosion threshold of sediment has been defined in terms of critical shear velocity when: (1) ten or more inorganic grains move at the same time (Heizelmann & Wallisch 1991); (2) both organic material and inorganic grains move (Madsen *et al.* 1993); (3) erosion at four distinct stages occurs (Grant *et al.* 1986; Yallop *et al.* 1994); and (4) resuspended sediment leads to a substantial reduction ($>$30%) in light transmission (Paterson 1989). In general, 'particle threshold' is defined as the friction velocity or bed shear stress required to move or erode single particles, while 'bed threshold' is defined as the point at which a bed of particles begins to move (Lavelle & Mofjeld, 1987).

Further subjectivity in the definition of erosion threshold arises due to the variations in the methodologies used to measure sediment motion and the sediment type examined across investigations. For example, the non-standard design of existing flumes results in variations in the area of the seabed exposed to erosive flows and the duration of the observation period. The determination of the erosion threshold of particles is sensitive to these two parameters (Lavelle & Mofjeld 1987). Critical erosion values have been reported in terms of: (1) the revolution speed of a stirring mechanism (Holland *et al.* 1974); (2) the angular velocity of concentric cylinders (de Jonge & van den Bergs 1987); (3) a spatial and time-averaged bed shear stress (Amos *et al.* 1992*b*) and shear velocity (Grant *et al.* 1986; Madsen *et al.* 1993); (4) the current speed at a given height above the bed (Manzenrieder 1983); and (5) the pressure of a vertical jet (Paterson 1989).

The application of a single definition or description of sediment movement has been inconsistently applied to a wide variety of sediment types including sand to organic rich mud. Stabilization coefficients (Holland *et al.* 1974; Grant & Gust 1987; Paterson 1994), defined as the ratio of the erosion threshold of biotic sediment to that of abiotic sediment (control), have been used to compare erosion values of investigations of a wide range of sediment or biofilm types (Paterson & Daborn 1991). In this paper, definitions such as, particle threshold, bed threshold and discharge threshold of SPM, were used to determine the initiation of sediment movement. The objective of this paper is to compare these various methods derived throughout the growth period of a diatom biofilm incubated on sediment.

Methods

Critical shear velocity values (U_{*crit}) reported in this paper are based on measurements made during a laboratory and field study carried out to determine the effect of biofilms on sediment erodibility (Sutherland 1996). Several approaches were used to determine U_{*crit} values of the various stages of sediment erosion during

SUTHERLAND, T. F., AMOS, C. L. & GRANT, J. 1998. The erosion threshold of biotic sediments: a comparison of methods. *In*: BLACK, K. S., PATERSON, D. M. & CRAMP, A. (eds) *Sedimentary Processes in the Intertidal Zone.* Geological Society, London, Special Publications, **139**, 295 307.

the laboratory study. A comparison of U_{*crit} values determined for the various biofilm-sediment constituents (chlorophyll, phaeopigment and sediment) was carried out on natural sediment during the field study.

Laboratory study

Erosion measurements were carried out in a recirculating flume 1.5 m long, 0.2 m wide and 0.15 m high with a working section located 0.9 m downstream of the inlet. A Dantec 55R46 stress sensor was placed in the working area of the flume floor and calibrated to the rpm of the propeller motor that drove the flow in the flume. Shear velocity values (U_*) were converted from shear stress values (τ) using the formula, τ (N m^{-2}) $= \rho$ (kg m^{-3}) $\cdot U^2$ (m s^{-1}), where $\rho = 1028$ (kg m^{-3}), the density of seawater.

Determination of erosion threshold. Three approaches were used to determine U_{*crit} values during the growth period of a culture of diatoms incubated on artificial sediment (Table 1).

Particle or bed threshold (video observations). The surface of the prepared cores were videotaped (SuperVHS) to discriminate between the U_{*crit} values for (1) the detachment of a single particle, (2) the detachment of ten particles simultaneously, (3) the onset of ripple migration and (4) the detachment of various sized, flake-shaped aggregates. The time stamp on the video gave the exact time for each threshold, which was then related to U_* from the corresponding rpm of the motor.

Resuspension threshold (extrapolation method). Shields (1936) determined U_{*crit} by extrapolating back to the point of zero discharge of suspended particulate matter (SPM) on a plot of SPM against shear velocity. However, the exact procedure of extrapolation was not clear and therefore cannot be reproduced (Lavelle & Mofjeld 1987). In this study, U_{*crit} values were derived by plotting SPM against log U_* and extrapolating, using a regression line, to the point of zero concentration of SPM. U_{*crit} was determined as the *x*-intercept of a regression analysis of SPM against log U_*. This analysis also produced an erosion threshold for the surface material of the sediment-laden biofilm.

Biofilm threshold (digitization method). Erosion of the biofilm revealed a white diatomite sediment beneath. The digitization of the exposed area of the underlying white diatomite after the release of the golden-brown diatom-mat aggregates was performed from frozen videoframes using the software package OPTIMUS. U_{*crit} was determined as the U_* value at which the smallest visible area of underlying sediment was exposed upon aggregate erosion. Since erosion took place by the erosion of biofilm sheets of up to 2.5 mm in thickness, this analysis produced a depth-integrated U_{*crit} of the biofilm (Sutherland *et al.* 1997*b*).

Preparation of sediment biofilms. Sediment cores were first prepared by creating a mixture of 200 ml of Celatom diatomite and 200 ml of 0.45 μm filtered seawater, which was settled in core barrels (inner diameter: 11.4 cm) designed to be inserted into the base of a recirculating

Table 1. *A description of methods used to determine* U$_{*crit}$

Stage of erosion	Method	Depth of erosion
Observation method		
(1) Motion of a particle	Video observations	Biofilm or sediment surface
(2) Simultaneous movement of 10 or more particles		
(3) Onset of ripple migration		
(4) Erosion of aggregates		Biofilm surface or subsurface
Extrapolation method		
Resuspension of SPM from seabed	Extrapolation of SPM curve against U_* to the point of zero concentration	Biofilm or sediment surface
Digitization method		
Release of diatom biofilm and subsequent exposure of underlying sediment	Digitization of exposed sediment	Biofilm–sediment interface (biofilm base)

flume. A stock culture of *Nitzschia curvilineata* was obtained from the Provasoli–Guillard Centre for Culture of Marine Phytoplankton (CCMP555) and maintained in F/2 medium (Guillard 1972) at 18°C on a light:dark cycle of 16:8 hrs. Two hundred ml of this diatom culture, in exponential phase of growth, were inoculated on to each of 17 sediment cores.

Fourteen diatom-sediment cores were prepared for erosion trials, while three cores were reserved for a time-series record of chlorophyll concentration and carbohydrate concentration as the biofilm developed. Each day, the wide-diameter ends of two pipettes were used to core the sediment for analysis of chlorophyll and carbohydrate concentrations. These analyses are outlined in Sutherland *et al.* (1997b). The thickness of the biofilm was systematically measured under a dissecting microscope. A 5-ml syringe core was collected on days 2, 4, 6, 9, 12, 15 and 18, frozen in liquid nitrogen, and stored overnight at −20°C, and then split lengthwise using a razor blade. The base of the biofilm was evident as a sharp boundary between the golden-brown biofilm and the underlying white sediment.

Two hundred ml of 0.45 filtered seawater were placed in each of two sediment-laden core barrels. One of these cores served as a control for the erosion trials, while the other core was subsampled daily for chlorophyll, in order to determined the potential for aerial contamination throughout the 18-day incubation period.

Erosion experiment. One abiotic core was eroded on the first day of the experiment series. Two diatom-sediment cores were chosen at random every few days and eroded in the recirculating flume. A selected core sample was inserted into the working section of the flume from below and raised until the upper rim of the core barrel was flush with the flume floor. The flume was slowly filled with 89 l of 2 μm filtered seawater. The core contents were raised with a scissor jack until the sediment surface was flush with the barrel rim and flume floor. A Sony Handycam 8 mm video-recorder was mounted above the sediment core to record bed erosion.

The flow in the flume was increased stepwise at 500 rpm intervals of the propeller motor every ten minutes in a stepwise manner. Water samples were collected at time zero and every speed increment thereafter by siphoning 100 ml of flume seawater at the height of the OBS. This volume was filtered to determine SPM concentrations. One hundred ml of 2 μm filtered seawater were then added to the flume to maintain a constant volume. The weight of the SPM was determined gravimetrically after drying pre-weighed Whatman glass-fibre filters (GF/C) at 55°C and desiccating the filters for two hours. An isotonic solution of ammonium formate was used to rinse the filters to remove any salts. Water samples were collected for only one of the two cores that were eroded at each stage of growth and used for the calibration of the OBS. However, due to the intermittency of the OBS signal at higher flow velocities, erosion measurements by the extrapolation method were calculated from a single erosion trial. The erosion measurements by means of the digitization method occasionally included duplicates. A description of these erosion measurements is outlined below.

Field study

An *in situ* flume, the Sea Carousel, was deployed at six stations along a transect in Upper South Cove, Nova Scotia, Canada. A description of the flume is outlined in Amos *et al.* (1992a), while a description of the deployment procedures is outlined in Sutherland *et al.* (1997a). Each deployment consisted of a step-wise increase in the current speed, similar to that of the laboratory experiments. Water samples were collected at each speed increment and analysed for SPM, chlorophyll and phaeopigment. The extrapolation method was used to determine U_{*crit} of natural sediment.

The sediment in the inner half of Upper South Cove showed little variation in physical properties, such as sediment grain size (20 μm) and porosity (up to 87%), and is characterized by unconsolidated muds of 20–30% silt-clay by weight (Grant *et al.* 1995). The sediment located outside Upper South Cove, was very well-sorted with a mean grain size of *c.* 200 μm.

Results and discussion

U_{*crit} determination by the observation method

If we define the particle threshold as the point at which single particles are released from the bed by an applied flow, then the duration of the observation period and the area of erosion of a designated experiment must influence the outcome. The limit of detection is controlled by the bed area to water volume and the duration over which the erosion process proceeds. At intermediate Reynolds numbers, a high variation of stresses exists temporally and spatially in the turbulent boundary layer, due to turbulent eddies that can, on occasion, penetrate the viscous sublayer (Lavelle & Mofjeld 1987). The correlation of sediment resuspension and turbulent bursts has been established in the literature (Sutherland 1967). Given an extended observation period or working area, the probability of particle movement would increase. Such occasional movements may be considered to be irrelevant, but could amount to significant quantities of sediment transport over time. Instantaneous bursting could potentially occur below the time-averaged bed threshold value. Therefore, the determination of erosion threshold using the onset of a given number of particles is strongly influenced by the bursting phenomenon. This influence on bed threshold or net transport becomes less important as the number of grains in motion increases.

The fewer number of the particles required to be in motion by definition of bed erosion, the lower the bed threshold will be. For example, during exponential growth of the diatom, *Nitzschia curvilineata*, on sediment in the laboratory (Fig. 1), the U_{*crit} value for particle motion was always less than the erosion threshold for the simultaneous movement of ten particles (Fig. 2a). In addition, as individual particles became incorporated into the biofilm matrix, during the

stationary phase of growth, the chances of detecting ten particles moving simultaneously at the onset of erosion diminished. Instead, fewer numbers of larger flake-sized aggregates were released. The U_{*crit} values deterined for particle motion (diameter <1 mm) are shown in Fig. 2a, while the U_{*crit} values determined for the aggregate motion (>1 mm) are shown in Fig. 2b. Therefore, particle or bed threshold is a function of the eroding particle or aggregate size selected, which corresponds to the developmental stage or age of the biofilm. A steady increase in the size of the particles or aggregates eroded was observed during the growth period of *N. curvilineata* (Fig. 2b). The formation of a biofilm-sediment microfabric through the growth and migration of diatoms and associated pervasion of extracellular polymeric substances (EPS) in the sediment may have been responsible for the observed increase in eroded aggregate size.

Problems arise when applying observational definitions of erosion thresholds to sediments of different grain sizes or to biofilms of different developmental stages. Neill (1968) reported that the erosion thresholds of larger particles would be lower than those of smaller particles because the former category will be detected sooner. Although the erosion of individual particles

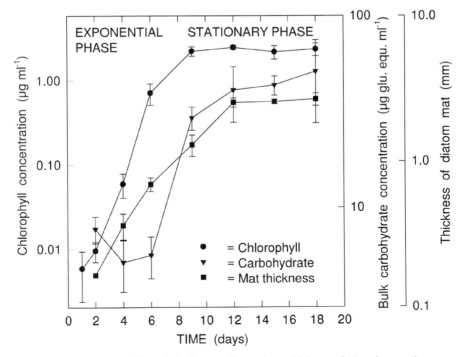

Fig. 1. The mean growth curve, bulk carbohydrate profile, and mat thickness of *Nitzschia curvilineata* grown on replicate sediment cores. Error bar = 1 standard deviation, $n = 3$.

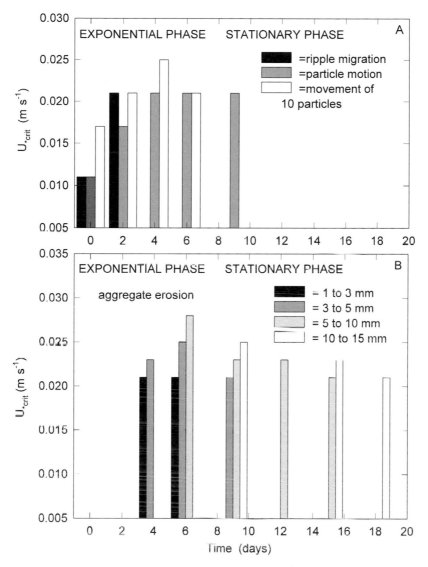

Fig. 2. U_{*crit} values for (1) particle motion, (2) simultaneous motion of ten particles, and (3) ripple migration of the *Nitzschia curvilineata* mat at successive stages of growth (**a**). U_{*crit} values for aggregate erosion determined using the observation method (**b**). An abiotic control core was eroded on day zero.

from the biofilm cores in stationary phase was not visible, erosion was evident from a flattening of the sediment core surface and the detection of SPM by the OBS. In addition, the U_{*crit} values of the control core may be too high, since the detection of the movement of the individual grains of the diatomite (mean diameter = 20 μm) would be difficult. Larger aggregates, visible to the naked eye, were eroded at higher shear velocities within the erosion trials of days six and nine (Fig. 2).

The movement of aggregates (diameter >1 mm) occurred only after four days of diatom growth (Fig. 2b). During the exponential phase of growth, the size of the aggregates eroded increased with increasing U_{*crit} within each erosion trial. The erosion of smaller-sized aggregates (diameter = 1–3 mm) during the exponential growth phase was gradually replaced with the erosion of larger-sized aggregates (diameter = 10–15 mm) during the stationary growth phase. The saturation of sediment with EPS with age of biofilm resulted in an increase in size of eroding particles or aggregates. This shift in eroded particle size was probably due to changes in the 'stickiness' of the sediment microfabric with age of biofilm. A change in the behaviour of sediment erosion throughout the development of the biofilm shows us that a single erosion criterion used to describe sediment erosion would not be valid using the above method.

U$_{*crit}$ determination by the extrapolation method

Regression analysis was used to define the best fit line of SPM to U_*. The x-intercept (U_*) of this regression line was used to determine U_{*crit}. High correlation coefficients were observed for SPM vs U_* regressions for data collected from Sea Carousel deployments along a transect in Upper South Cove, Nova Scotia (Fig. 3). This method is an analytical approach that is reproduceable, statistically valid and adopts the entire data set to define the erosion threshold.

The erosion threshold of the seabed was found to be ambiguous as the onset of suspension of chlorophyll, phaeopigment and SPM, determined by the extrapolation method, differed. An example of differences between the U_{*crit} values of chlorophyll, phaeopigment, and SPM is shown in Fig. 4. The U_{*crit} values for chlorophyll (0.0185 m s^{-1}) are less than those for phaeopigment (0.0256 m s^{-1}), which are less than those for SPM (0.0312 m s^{-1}). Smaller differences in the U_{*crit} values of chlorophyll, phaeopigment and SPM were observed throughout Upper South Cove (Fig. 5). Since the sediments of Upper South Cove are largely made up of fecal pellets and mud aggregates colonized with diatoms, a discriminatory suspension between these three sediment biofilm constituents would not be expected. The gel muds in Upper South Cove may be the result of a growth structure as opposed to a sedimentary structure (Sutherland *et al.* 1997a). These findings lead one to ask the question, what defines the surface of the seabed?

The variation in erosion threshold between chlorophyll, phaeopigment and SPM in Upper South Cove was the result of a distinct layering of these components within the sediment or differential sorting of the biofilm components. During erosion experiments of estuarine sediment, de Jonge and van den Bergs (1987) observed that the size spectrum of suspended material was not in proportion to that of the seabed, with the finer sediment being suspended at lower velocities.

Also, a differential suspension of diatom cells was observed, depending on whether the diatoms were associated with the mud fraction or with the sand fraction. These observations are in agreement with those of this study in that the chlorophyll was associated with finer particles and was suspended before sand grains larger than 200 μm. In addition, there appears to be two distinct gradients to the suspended chlorophyll time-series curve. The first slope may reflect the suspension of a recently deposited planktonic chlorophyll or fluff layer which was not part of the seabed, or the suspension of benthic chlorophyll associated with a mud fraction that was more easily eroded in relation to the sand fraction. The second increase or linear portion of the chlorophyll curve may reflect the suspension of a chlorophyll layer more closely associated with the consolidating bed and limited to the top 2 mm of sediment.

The 'linearity' of the SPM vs log U_* regression would depend on the extent of binding, microfabric formation and lamination within the near-surface sediment column. In certain cases in the field study, the SPM curve appeared to be made up of two linear parts divided by an inflection point, representing two distinct layers in the sediment with differing erosion rates (Fig. 3a). Mitchener & Torfs (1996) found that the erosion resistance and erosion rate were affected by density variations of layered seabeds. Therefore, the extrapolation method of determining U_{*crit} must be used with caution in sediment exhibiting strong vertical gradients in strength.

In some cases when the extrapolation method was applied, the first data point for SPM fell below the regression intercept determined as the erosion threshold. Emphasis was not placed on the initial suspended data point due to a low signal to noise ratio that occurs at very low concentrations. Noise may be in the form of: (1) resuspension due to instantaneous turbulent bursting; (2) patchiness of large-diameter suspended aggregates; (3) the erosion of aggregates attached to non-seabed material (seagrass fragments); and (4) a recently deposited fluff layer not associated with the seabed. Since the SPM signal was measured through the collection of water samples, the source of the 'noise' required validation through observation.

U$_{*crit}$ determination by the digitization method

This method measures the exposure of sediment underlying the diatom mat or the release of the

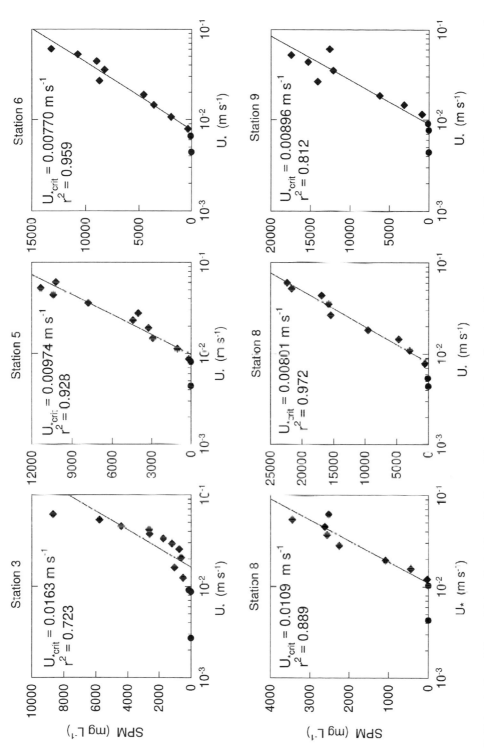

Fig. 3. Determination of U_{*crit} of data collected from Sea Carousel deployments at six stations located along a transect in Upper South Cove. U_{*crit} was taken as the x-intercept of the regression between suspended particulate matter (SPM) and U_* (extrapolation method). Diamond symbols represent data points used in the regression.

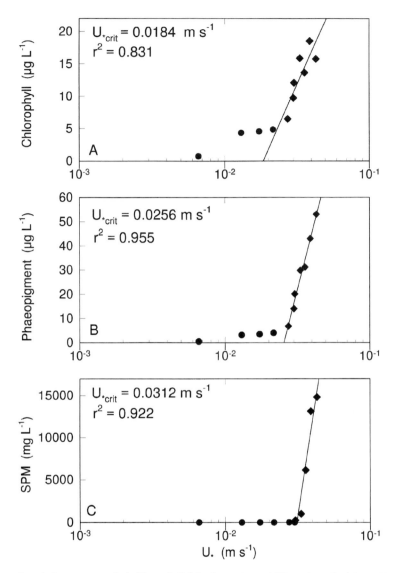

Fig. 4. Regressions between suspended chlorophyll (**a**), phaeopigment (**b**), and particulate matter (**c**) and U_* showing large differences between the respective U_{*crit} values. These data were collected in Lunenburg Bay, near Upper South Cove.

diatom mat at the base level or mat-sediment interface, as observation showed that failure occurred at this plane of weakness. The video recordings of the eroded cores containing less than two days of growth could not be digitized, because the diatom mat (non-eroded area) could not be discerned from the eroded area of the core; therefore, the results for the digitization method are limited to the period between days 4 and 18 of the diatom mat growth.

The erosion threshold for each erosion trial was taken as the point when 0.5% of the core area of the white underlying sediment was exposed (the smallest observed area exposed after the erosion of a diatom mat aggregate). This threshold is a depth-integrated threshold (representing the erosion of the entire thickness of the biofilm), since this method relies on the exposure of the underlying abiotic sediment. A general increase in U_{*crit} was observed for the duration of the stationary

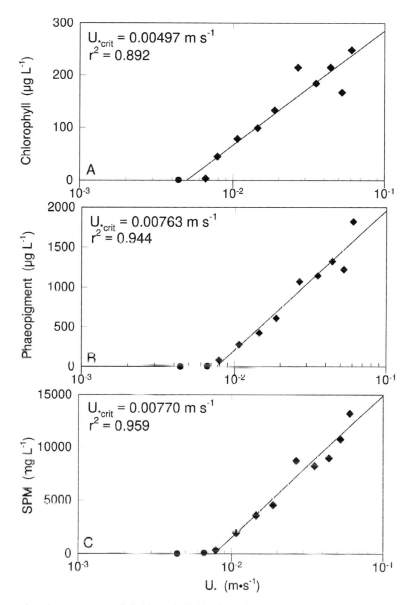

Fig. 5. Regressions between suspended chlorophyll (**a**), phaeopigment (**b**), and particulate matter (**c**) and U_* at station 6 showing small differences between the respective U_{*crit} values.

growth phase (Fig. 6). The erosion threshold of the core on the last day of the experiment was greater than the highest U_* value generated by the flume and as a result is represented by a dashed line. An increase in both the depth-integrated U_{*crit} determined by the digitization method and the sediment bulk carbohydrate concentration between days 6 to 15 are evident, suggesting a link through adhesion (Figs 1 and 6).

Surface erosion thresholds and depth-integrated erosion thresholds

The erosion thresholds for the base of the biofilm (digitization method) were generally higher (up to 3 times greater) than those determined for the surface of the biofilm (observation and extrapolation method), indicating that the biofilm created a stratified layer of increasing strength

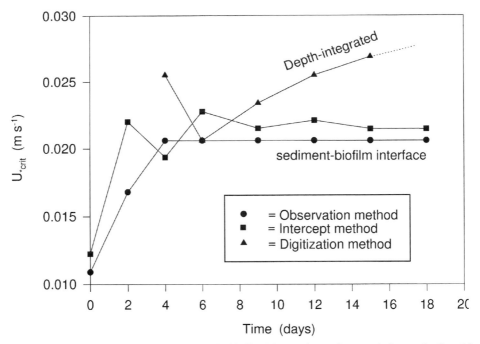

Fig. 6. U_{*crit} values determined for the surface of the biofilm (observation and extrapolation method) and for the thickness of the biofilm (digitization method) at successive stages of growth of *Nitzschia curvilineata*.

with depth. The critical threshold for either the movement of particles (Fig. 2a) or aggregates (Fig. 2b) was constant ($U_{*crit} = 0.021 \ m \ s^{-1}$) indicating little change in surface stabilization with time. Figure 6 shows that the largest changes in erosion threshold occurred at the base of the biofilm, while the smallest changes in erosion thresholds occurred at the surface of the biofilm.

The impact of a diatom biofilm on surface U_{*crit}

A concurrent laboratory biostabilization study suggested that the physiological state of the diatom biofilm influenced the nature and degree of sediment stability (Sutherland *et al.* 1997b). A time-series of chlorophyll and bulk carbohydrate concentrations and diatom mat thickness are shown in Fig. 1. Stationary phase of growth was reached on day 9 following a period of exponential growth of the biofilm. Bulk carbohydrate concentration was observed to increase at the end of exponential phase or the onset of stationary phase. The diatom mat reached a maximum thickness of 2.5 mm on day 12 of the experimental period. Both the U_{*crit} values for particle motion and the sediment chlorophyll concentrations increased between day 0 and 6.

The mean U_{*crit} value obtained for particle motion between days 2 and 9 was $0.019 \ m \ s^{-1}$, which was 1.8 times greater than the U_{*crit} value obtained for the abiotic control core. The mean U_{*crit} value obtained for the simultaneous movement of ten particles was $0.022 \ m \ s^{-1}$, which was 1.3 times greater than that of the control core (Fig. 2a). The U_{*crit} value obtained on day 2 was 1.8 times greater than the U_{*crit} value obtained for the abiotic control core. The U_{*crit} values remained fairly constant between days 2 and 18 of growth. The mean U_{*crit} value obtained from the biotic cores (days 2 to 18) was 1.76 times greater than the control.

Ripple migration during erosion ceased after two days of diatom growth, reflecting the transition from a non-cohesive tractive load, to a cohesive bed eroding directly into suspension. The movement of particles as bedload ceased at the onset of the stationary phase. The initial increase in erosion threshold and cessation of ripple migration, relative to the control, indicated that the diatom, *Nitzschia curvilineata*, strongly influenced the erosion characteristics of the sediment (Fig. 2).

Experiments carried out on abiotic sediments are clearly not representative of natural erosion thresholds. The age of the diatom biofilm appeared to affect the size and shape of the aggregates eroded, since larger sizes and flake-shaped aggregates were eroded at later stages of growth (Figs 2a and 2b). The microfabric of the sediment may be influenced by (1) the amount of biofilm coverage around sediment particles and associated changes in porosity, (2) the extent of diatom migration and reworking of sediment, (3) the increase in the thickness of the biofilm, (4) the extent of bubble formation and 'flaking' of sediment (Sutherland *et al.* 1997*b*), (5) the increase in the production of bulk carbohydrates, or (6) the potential changes in the carbohydrate composition or 'stickiness'. The composition of extrapolymeric substances is influenced by nutrient status and growth phase (Decho 1990). The changes in monosaccharide composition observed during growth of a *Navicula* culture were attributed to an increase in hydrogen bridges and the potential for the formation of ion bridges with multi-valent cations (Stal *et al.* 1994).

Changes in the number, size and shape of the eroded particles or aggregates with age of the culture discounts the use of a single particle erosion criterion. The erosion threshold or onset of particle/aggregate motion determined through the observation method generally remained constant at *c.* 0.02 m s^{-1} throughout the exponential growth phase of the biofilm. This time-invariant threshold may be due to (1) a vertically accreting diatom matrix that maintained constant physical properties or (2) the sensitivity of the method involved. For example, the accretion of surface mucilage matrices (open card-house structure) overlying the sediment layer may maintain constant density properties and promote consistent behaviour in particle/aggregate movement or erosion. Paterson (1988) observed the development of a surface matrix layer made up solely of diatoms and mucilage that extended 22 μm above a diatom inhabited-artificial substrate. Furthermore, the observation method is sensitive to the early stages of erosion or the incipient movement of the topmost biofilm material which will be influenced largely by the developing properties of the accreting surface of the biofilm.

The erosion threshold values of the biotic sediment cores, determined by the extrapolation method, were higher than their respective values for the abiotic control cores, reconfirming that the diatom, *Nitzschia curvilineata*, influenced the erosion characteristics of subtidal sediment (Fig. 6). However, the increases in erosion threshold determined by the observation and the extrapolation methods took place over a short initial period and did not follow the increases in chlorophyll and carbohydrate concentrations that took place over a longer time period.

The impact of a diatom biofilm on the depth-integrated U$_{*crit}$ of the biofilm-sediment layer

Stratification of the thickening biofilm layer could occur due to (1) the maintenance of a diatom-mucilage matrix layer (Paterson 1988) at the biofilm surface, (2) the extent of diatom migration, (3) a porosity gradient, (4) changes in the hydration state of the mucilage with depth and (5) bubble formation. The development of a permanent diatom-mucilage, sediment-free layer at the topmost layer of the biofilm in a submerged setting would maintain constant properties such as, bulk density, water content, microstructure, and thus, maintain constant erosion threshold values with time. A density gradient may be formed due to the concentration and migration of diatoms nearer to the illuminated surface of the biofilm. An enlarged pore structure of a recently-deposited sediment was observed to be related to the migration of diatoms within this layer (Hay *et al.* 1993). The increase in erosion threshold observed in this study at the base of the biofilm with time may be due to changes in composition or 'stickiness' of the aging mucilage.

Stabilization coefficient

Since a standard approach to the determination of erosion thresholds does not exist, it is difficult to put the results reported in this paper into context with those of other laboratory and field studies. Stability coefficients have been used to compare the effect of different diatoms (Holland *et al.* 1974) or different biofilm types (Paterson 1994) on the erodibility of sediment. Paterson (1994) defined a stabilization coefficient as the percent ratio of a U_{*crit} value of a biofilm to a U_{*crit} value of an abiotic sediment (control). Stabilization coefficients were determined for the surface of the biofilm and for the base of the biofilm (Table 2). These coefficients cover a much narrower range (123–258%) compared to those across various investigations (25–770%) reported by Paterson (1994).

In order to make comparisons between investigations, it is important to distinguish between the stage of erosion examined and the depth at which this erosion occurred within the sediment. For example, the erosion thresholds determined for the topmost layer of the sediment were not an indication of the maximum erosion thresholds determined below the sediment surface. The change in erosion thresholds determined

Table 2. *Stabilization coefficients for growth stages of the diatom,* Nitzschia curvilineata, *incubated on sediment. Stabilization coefficients are expressed as the percent increase in* U_{*crit} *values relative to that of the abiotic control*

Criterion for erosion		Method		
		Observation	Extrapolation	Digitization
Particle motion	min	154%		
	max	189%		
Simultaneous movement of ten particles	min	123%		
	max	152%		
Erosion of aggregates	min	189%		
	max	214%		
Onset of ripple migration		189%		
Resuspension	min		158%	
	max		185%	
Biofilm base	min			189%
	max			>258%

for the base of the biofilm, along with a constant value of erosion thresholds of the surface of the biofilm with time support this observation (Fig. 6). The determination of $U_{*crit}(z)$ as a function of depth (z) in the sediment would minimize the amount of variation across investigations.

Summary

The entrainment of particles is a critical event as it is used widely in transport formulas and numerical models for the prediction of seabed stability (Paterson 1994; Lavelle & Mofjeld 1987). Numerous observational definitions of seabed erosion threshold exist in the literature leading to inconsistencies between investigations and, therefore to, a wide scatter in quantitative results. In addition, investigations have focused predominantly on the erosion thresholds of well-sorted, non-cohesive, abiotic sediment that behave differently than naturally occurring bio-mediated sediment mixtures. If the observation method is used to determine erosion thresholds, the area of the eroding seabed, the duration of the observation period, and the number and size of particles must be standardized in order to derive consistent results. The variation in eroded aggregate size that occurs at successive stages of biofilm production may cause biases in the detection of the movement of larger aggregates and introduce subjectivity in the determination of U_{*crit} through visual observation.

If the extrapolation method is used to determine erosion thresholds, attention should be drawn to (1) the subdivision of the SPM curve into a series of distinct gradients which represent differing sediment layers and (2) 'noise' arising from the erosion of epiphytic material not associated with the seabed. Also, sediment erodibility experiments which do not differentiate the nature of material suspended (i.e. simple gravimetric determination of total suspended load) can lead to errors. If the digitization is used to determine depth-integrated erosion thresholds, these measurements should not be compared to erosion thresholds of surface material. The type of method used for erosion threshold determination varies between investigations and applications. In addition, the term 'sediment erodibility' should include both concepts of erosion thresholds and erosion rate, due to (1) the discrepancies between definitions of erosion thresholds and (2) the greater range of erosion rates relative to erosion thresholds (Sutherland *et al.* 1997a, b). The larger range in erosion rate relative to erosion threshold supports Lavelle & Mofjeld's (1987) suggestion that more emphasis should be placed on erosion rate when describing sediment transport.

We would like to thank Brian Schofield and Paul MacPherson for building the core inserts for the flume and Curtis Roegner for assisting in the erosion experiments. A Hi-8 tape recorder and Optimus software package was provided by Ron O'Dor and Danny Jackson. Financial support for this study was provided by a NSERC PG4, a Dalhousie Graduate Fellowship, and an NSERC operating grant to Jon Grant.

References

AMOS, C. L., GRANT, J., DABORN, G. R. & BLACK, K. 1992a. Sea Carousel – a benthic, annular flume. *Estuarine, Coastal and Shelf Science*, **34**, 557–577.

——, DABORN, G. R., CHRISTIAN, H. A., ATKINSON, A. & ROBERTSON, A. 1992b. *In situ* erosion measurements on fine-grained sediments from the Bay of Fundy. *Marine Geology*, **108**, 175–196.

DECHO, A. W. 1990. Microbial exopolymer secretions in ocean environments: their role(s) in food webs and marine processes. *Oceanography and Marine Biology Annual Review*, **28**, 73–153.

GRANT, J. & GUST, G. 1987. Prediction of coastal sediment stability from photopigment content of mats of purple sulphur bacteria. *Nature*, **330**(6145), 244–246.

——, BATHMANN, U. V. & MILLS, E. L. 1986. The interaction between benthic diatom films and sediment transport *Estuarine, Coastal & Shelf Science*, **23**, 225–238.

——, HATCHER, A., SCOTT, D. B., POCKLINGTON, P., SCHAFER, C. T. & WINTERS, G. V. 1995. A multi disciplinary approach to evaluating impacts of shellfish aquaculture on benthic communities. *Estuaries*, **18**(1A), 124–144.

GUILLARD, R. R. L. 1972. Culture of marine phytoplankton for feeding marine invertebrates. *In*: SMITH, W. L. & CHANLEY, M. H. (eds) *Conference on Culture of Marine Invertebrate Animals*. Plenum Press, New York, 29–60.

HAY, S. I., MAITLAND, T. C. & PATERSON, D. M. 1993. The speed of diatom migration through natural and artificial substrata. *Diatom Research*, **8**(2), 371–384.

HEIZELMANN, C. H. & WALLISCH, S. 1991. Benthic settlement and bed erosion. A review. *Journal of Hydraulic Research*, **29**, 355–371.

HOLLAND, A. F., ZINGMARK, R. G. &, DEAN J. M. 1974. Quantitative evidence concerning the stabilization of sediments by marine benthic diatoms. *Marine Biology*, **27**, 191–196.

DE JONGE, V. N. & VAN DEN BERGS, J. 1987. Experiments on the resuspension of estuarine sediment containing benthic diatoms. *Estuarine Coastal Shelf Science*, **24**, 725–740.

LAVELLE, J. W. & MOFJELD, H. O. 1987. Do critical stresses for incipient motion and erosion really exist? *Journal of Hydraulic Engineering*, **113**(3), 370–393.

MADSEN, K. N., NILSSON, P. & SUNDBACK, K. 1993. The influence of benthic microalgae on the stability of a subtidal sediment. *Journal of Experimental Marine Biology and Ecology*, **170**, 159–177.

MANZENRIEDER, H. 1983. Retardation of initial erosion under biological effects in sandy tidal flats. *In*: PATERSON, D. M. 1994. Microbial mediation of sediment structure and behaviour. *In*: STAL, L. J.

& CAUMETTE, P. (eds) *Microbial Mats: Structure, Development, and Environmental Significance*, NATO ASI Series, Vol. G35, 97–109.

MILLER, M. C., MCCAVE, I. N. & KOMAR, P. D. 1977. Threshold of sediment motion under unidirectional currents. *Sedimentology*, **24**, 507–527.

MITCHENER, H. & TORFS, H. 1996. Erosion of mud/sand mixtures. *Coastal Engineering*, **29**, 1–25.

NEILL, C. R. 1968. Note on initial movement of coarse uniform bed-material. *Journal of Hydraulic Research*, **6**(2), 173–176.

PATERSON, D. M. 1988. The influence of epipelic diatoms on the erodibility of an artificial sediment. *In*: SIMOLA, H. (ed.) *Proceedings of the 10th International Symposium on Living and Fossil Diatoms*. Joensuu, Koenigstein, 345–355.

——1989. Short-term changes in the erodibility of intertidal cohesive sediments related to the migratory behaviour of epipelic diatoms. *Limnology and Oceanography*, **34**(1), 223–234.

——1994. Microbiological mediation of sediment structure and behaviour. *In*: STAL, L. J. & CAUMETTE, P. (eds) *Microbial Mats*, NATO ASI Series, Vol. G35.

—— & DABORN, G. R. 1991. Sediment stabilization by biological action: significance for coastal engineering. *Developments in Coastal Engineering*, University of Bristol, 111–119.

SHIELDS, A. 1936. Application of similarity principles and turbulence research to bed-load movement. *In*: LAVELLE, J. W. & MOFJELD, H. O. 1985. *Journal of Hydraulic Engineering*, **113**(3), 370–393.

STAL, L. J., VILLBRANDT, M. & DE WINDER, B. 1994. Ecophysiology. EPS in benthic phototrophic microorganisms. *In*: KRUMBIEN, W. E., PATERSON, D. M. & STAL, L. J. (eds) *Biostabilization of Sediments*. Verlag, Oldenburg, 337–399.

SUTHERLAND, T. F. 1967. Proposed mechanism for sediment entrainment by turbulent flows. *Journal of Geophysical Research*, **72**(24), 6183–6194.

——1996. Biostabilization of subtidal estuarine sediments. PhD Thesis, Dalhousie University, Halifax, Nova Scotia, 184pp.

——, AMOS, C. L. & GRANT, J. 1998a. The effect of buoyant biofilms on sediment erodibility in a microtidal temperate estuary. *Limnology and Oceanography*, **43**

——, —— & ——1998b. The effect of carbohydrate production of the diatom, *Nitzschia curvilineata*, on the erodibility of sediment. *Limnology and Oceanography*, **43**, 65–72.

YALLOP, M. L., DE WINDER, B., PATERSON, D. M. & STAL, L. J. 1994. Comparative structure, primary production and biogenic stabilization of cohesive and non-cohesive marine sediments inhabited by microphytobenthos. *Estuarine Coastal Shelf Science*, **39**, 565–582.

Biological control of avalanching and slope stability in the intertidal zone

MASROOR A. SHAIKH, AZRA MEADOWS & PETER S. MEADOWS

Biosedimentology Unit, Division of Environmental and Evolutionary Biology, IBLS, Graham Kerr Building, University of Glasgow, Glasgow G12 8QQ, UK

Abstract: Sediment structure and stability are important features of soils and sedimentary environments, and are of great importance for the maintenance of estuarine, and intertidal banks and channels. Avalanching and slope stability are critical factors controlling the shape of intertidal dunes. The role of biological activity in these processes, either in the form of vegetation and roots, animal burrows, algal mats or microbial glues, is now a forefront area of research. The objective of our research has been to quantify the effects of biological activity on the avalanching of intertidal sediments. Natural microbial and meiofaunal communities and particularly burrowing infauna such as *Corophium volutator* and *Nereis diversicolor* dramatically increase angles of avalanche and factors of safety. They do not significantly alter angles of repose. Factors of safety, duration of avalanches, and percentage increase in sediment volume, all increase with increasing angles of avalanche. Video analysis of the avalanching process shows that different slope failure mechanisms are associated with the different types of biological activity, and probably reflect specific chemical and mechanical stabilizing effects produced by the different types of biological activity. These latter include tubes, extracellular polymeric materials, and a small element of compaction. These mechanisms include rotational failure, block and wedge failure and translational failure. The significance of our results for the stability of slopes under field conditions is discussed, and it is concluded that field seeding experiments in the intertidal zone with the species that we have used would be very productive.

Intertidal sedimentary environments in the coastal zone are of considerable interest, from both a scientific and also an economic point of view. They exhibit a wide range of biodiversity, and are used by man for recreational purposes, as well as a source of minerals and biological resources. The long term stability of these environments is therefore of major importance, particularly in view of projected changes in sea level in the 21st century. There has therefore been growing interest in their protection by engineering, and environmental analyses and management. For example, geomembranes are now in routine use as a means of stabilizing slopes and biological seeding is being considered as an environmentally friendly method of coastal zone protection (Gray & Leiser 1982). Slope stability in the intertidal zone is an important feature of a range of high energy and low energy sedimentary environments. It is therefore surprising that it has received so little attention (Forster & Nicolson 1981*a, b*; Meadows *et al.* 1994) in view of the considerable literature on slope stability in terrestrial and riverine environments (Bagnold 1941, 1966; Allen 1968, 1970; Perla & Martinelli 1976; Bache & MacAskill 1984; Brunsden & David 1984; Brunsden & Prior 1984; Nash 1987; Chandler 1991; Bromhead 1992; Van Rhee &

Bezuijen 1992, Mitchener & Damgaard 1997) and in marine subtidal environments (Warme *et al.* 1971; Coleman & Garriso 1977; Hecker 1982; Busch & Keller 1982; Mehta & Rao 1985; Piper *et al.* 1985; Baraza *et al.* 1992; Cochonat *et al.* 1993; Lee *et al.* 1993; Baltzer *et al.* 1994; Baraza & Ercilla 1994; Duperret *et al.* 1995).

It has been well known for a number of years that biological and microbiological activity affects sediment stability (Dapples 1942; Scoffin 1970; Rhoads *et al.* 1978; Rhoads & Boyer 1982; Meadows & Meadows 1991). Many infaunal invertebrates that burrow alter the shear strength and permeability of sediments and alter their erodability (Ginsburg & Lowenstam 1958; Luckenbach 1986; Meadows & Tait 1989; Meadows *et al.* 1990; Jones & Jago 1993; Gerdol & Hughes 1994; Meadows & Meadows 1994; Pender *et al.* 1994). Similar effects have been shown by single species and mixed species micro-organisms (Holland *et al.* 1974; Forster & Nicolson 1981*a, b*; Meadows & Tufail 1986; Paterson 1987, 1989; Dade *et al.* 1990; Paterson & Daborn, 1991; Madsen *et al.* 1993; Underwood & Paterson 1993; Meadows *et al.* 1994). All of these investigations have been conducted on flat surfaces either in the sea or in the laboratory. There have been only a few investigations into

SHAIKH, M. A., MEADOWS, A. & MEADOWS, P. S. 1998. Biological control of avalanching and slope stability in the intertidal zone. *In*: BLACK, K. S., PATERSON, D. M. & CRAMP, A. (eds) *Sedimentary Processes in the Intertidal Zone*. Geological Society, London, Special Publications, **139**, 309–329.

the effects of biological activity on the avalanching slopes (Meadows *et al.* 1994; Muir Wood *et al.* 1994).

In this paper we assess the role of two species of intertidal infaunal invertebrates, *Nereis diversicolor* and *Corophium volutator*, and of naturally occurring intertidal microbial and meiofaunal populations on slope stability of intertidal sediments as assessed by angles of avalanche and angles of repose. We also consider factors of safety of slopes and the duration of the avalanching process.

Materials and methods

Collection and treatment of sediment and animals

Sediment was collected from the mid-tide level at Ardmore Bay Clyde Estuary, Scotland (Latitude: 55°58′32″N Longitude: 4°41′29″W Nat. Grid: NS 321 792). *Corophium volutator* (Cv) was collected from the high-tide area of the same bay. *Nereis diversicolor* (Nd) was collected from the mid-tide area at Langbank, in the Clyde Estuary (Latitude: 55°55′39″N Longitude: 4°33′49″W Nat. Grid: NS 398 735). Sediment and organisms were used for experiments within 6 hrs of collection.

In the laboratory, the sediment was prepared by wet sieving through a 710 μm sieve to remove invertebrate infauna and large particles thus leaving only microorganisms and meiofauna in the sediment. This wet sieving was done twice. Microscopic examination of the twice-sieved sediment showed that it contained large numbers of microorganisms on the surfaces of the sediment particles (bacteria, diatoms, blue green algae) and some meiofauna between the particles (large ciliates, nematodes, ostracods, harpacticoids). This sediment was then maintained in sea water until used for the experiments – which were conducted within 12 hrs of collection of the sediment. *Corophium volutator* (Cv) and *Nereis diversicolor* (Nd) were removed from the sediment by using a 710 μm sieve, which was then backwashed gently into sea water. The animals were maintained in this sea water until used in the experiment.

Sediment particle size was obtained by dry sieving three replicate samples using British standard test sieves of sizes 500 μm (1ϕ), 355 μm (1.5ϕ), 250 μm (2ϕ), 180 μm (2.5ϕ), 125 μm (3ϕ), 90 μm (3.5ϕ), 63 μm (4ϕ) and pan. This gave a mean particle size (ϕ) = 2.177 ± 0.0242, standard deviation = 0.5691 ± 0.0049, skewness = 0.2134 ± 0.0319 and kurtosis = −0.6864 ± 0.1173. The sediment consisted almost entirely of quartz particles.

Equipment design for avalanching

Glass containers (internal size 15 cm × 7.5 cm, depth 40 cm) in which the sediment was to be avalanched were constructed by bonding 4 mm thick glass sheets with silicone sealant transparent gel. The glass containers were then graduated by sticking a self adhesive transparent scale on the outer walls.

A clinometer for avalanching the sediments was constructed (Fig. 1). It consisted of a lever arm, one end of which rested on a wooden sliding block and the other end of which rested on an Archimedes screw. The glass container was held on the lever arm by a wooden block and retained by a tight length of cord (Fig. 1; 3, 5).

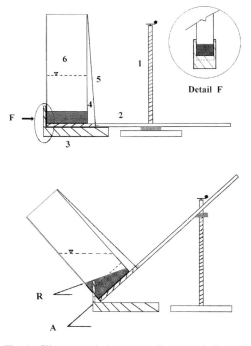

Fig. 1. Clinometer design. **Top**: clinometer before an avalanche. 1, Archimedes screw; 2, lever arm; 3, U frame and sliding block; 4, container holder; 5, cord; 6, glass container with sediment and water. Detail F = magnified side view of equipment as seen from F. **Bottom**: clinometer after an avalanche. A = angle of avalanche. R = angle of repose.

Conduct of experiments

Experiments 1 and 2. Twenty four glass containers were set up, 12 for experiment 1 (*Nereis diversicolor*) and 12 for experiment 2 (*Corophium volutator*) (Fig. 2). In each experiment these were divided into six containers with animals (Nd, Cv) and six control containers without animals (CNd, CCv). Two replicate containers of the six

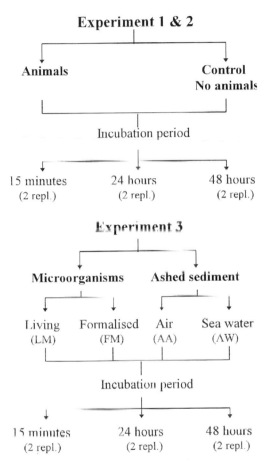

Fig. 2. Top: design of experiments 1 and 2. Animals: sediment containing *Nereis diversicolor* (Nd) in experiment 1 and *Corophium volutator* (Cv) in experiment 2. Control: sediment containing no *Nereis diversicolor* (CNd) in experiment 1 and sediment containing no *Corophium volutator* (CCv) in experiment 2. Two replicate containers for each time; 15 mins, 24 hrs and 48 hrs. **Bottom**: design of experiment 3. Natural sediment from the field containing living microorganisms and meiofauna in sea water (LM) and the same treated with formalin (FM). Ashed sediment: sediment from the field ashed in a furnace at 480°C. Ashed sediments in air (AA) and in GF/F filtered sea water (AW). Two replicate containers for each time; 15 mins, 24 hrs and 48 hrs.

were left to stand for 15 min before avalanching, two for 24 hrs before avalanching, and two for 48 hrs before avalanching. The numbers of animals used in the experiments were as follows. In experiment 1 each of the *Nereis diversicolor* containers contained 33 animals. This is equivalent to 2933 animals m^{-2}. In experiment 2 each of the *Corophium volutator* containers contained 100 animals. This is equivalent to 8888 animals m^{-2}. The animal densities were chosen to be equivalent to average densities on the intertidal zone in the Clyde Estuary. Animals were counted at the beginning and end of each experiment. There was no mortality of animals during the experiments and animals displayed normal burrowing behaviour. Both species feed on detrital material in and on the sediment.

Experiment 3. Twenty four glass containers were set up. These were divided into four groups each containing six containers (Fig. 2). The first group of six containers contained natural sediment in sea water, the second group contained previously formalized sediment, the third group contained ashed sediment in GF/F (0.7 μm) filtered sea water (AW), and the fourth group contained ashed sediment in air (AA). The containers in ashed sediment treatments were sterilized by 70% alcohol before use. Two replicate containers were set up for all treatments as in experiments 1 and 2.

The sediment in the first group therefore contained living microorganisms and meiofauna (LM), the sediment in the second group contained dead microorganisms and meiofauna killed by formalin (FM), and the third and fourth groups contained no microorganisms, no meiofauna, and no organic matter of any sort. Sediment was ashed at 480°C for 4 hrs for the third and fourth group. In each of the four groups two replicate containers were left to stand for 15 mins before avalanching, two were left to stand for 24 hrs before avalanching, and two were left to stand for 48 hrs before avalanching. Great care was taken to ensure that the ashed sediment in the containers in group 4 were kept completely dry. This was done by covering the container with a porous bag containing silica gel.

Avalanching procedure

At the end of the designated time, the sediment surface in each of the containers was examined and the depth of the sediment was recorded. The container was then carefully transferred to the clinometer (Fig. 1). The clinometer was then gently raised at a rate of 0.5 to 0.8 degrees per second until avalanching occurred. This was done by turning the Archimedes screw on which the lever arm rested. The first angle of avalanche (A_1) and the first angle of repose (R_1) were then recorded using an inclinometer that read to an accuracy of $0.1°$. The duration of the first avalanche in seconds (T_1) and the depth (mm) of the sediment after the avalanche were also recorded. The sediment in the container was then avalanched a second time, and the second angle of avalanche (A_2), second angle of repose (R_2), depths of sediment and the duration of second avalanche (T_2) were recorded. The second angles of avalanche and angles of repose were measured in the same way as the first angles of avalanche and repose. A corrected value A_2' for the second angle of avalanche was calculated using the following relationship $A_2' = (A_2 - A_1) + R_1$. This is the accepted procedure for calculating the true second angle of avalanche (see Meadows *et al.* 1994). From here on, the second angle of avalanche refers to the true corrected second angle of avalanche (A_2').

The factor of safety, angle of dilatation and percentage increase in sediment volume after an avalanche were calculated as follows: factor of safety = (tan A_1)/(tan R_1), angle of dilatation = $(A_1) - (R_1)$, and percentage increase in volume of sediment = {[(volume of sediment after first avalanche) − (volume of sediment before first avalanche)]/(volume of sediment before first avalanche)} × 100.

Results

The results are divided into the following sections. We firstly describe the effects of biological, and microbiological/meiofaunal activity on the first angle of avalanche (A_1) and the first angle of repose (R_1), and on the second angle of avalanche (A_2') and second angle of repose (R_2). This is followed by a section on the factor of safety and the angle of dilatation. We then describe the effects of biological and microbiological and meiofaunal activity on the duration of avalanching and resultant increase in volume of the sediment during the avalanching process.

First angle of avalanche (A_1) and first angle of repose (R_1)

The results of experiment 1 (effects of *Nereis diversicolor*), experiment 2 (effects of *Corophium volutator*), and experiment 3 (effects of microorganisms and meiofauna) are shown in Table 1 and their statistical analyses are shown in Tables 2–5.

Experiments 1 and 2. Both *Nereis diversicolor* (experiment 1; Table 2) and *Corophium volutator* (experiment 2; Table 3) increased the angles of avalanche when compared with control sediments. This effect increased as the experiment progressed, being most marked at 48 hrs. *Nereis diversicolor* had a greater effect than *Corophium*

Table 1. *Data from experiment 1, 2 and 3. First angle of avalanche (A_1) and first angle of repose (R_1). Mean ± SD of two replicate readings*

Treatment	A_1 (degrees)			R_1 (degrees)		
	15 mins	24 hrs	48 hrs	15 mins	24 hrs	48 hrs
Experiment 1. *Nereis diversicolor*						
Nd	42.90 ± 0.707	60.75 ± 1.061	63.80 ± 0.849	34.55 ± 0.354	37.45 ± 3.606	41.75 ± 1.061
CNd	40.25 ± 0.354	45.60 ± 0.566	50.35 ± 1.909	32.25 ± 0.354	35.25 ± 0.354	36.40 ± 0.283
Experiment 2. *Corophium volutator*						
Cv	44.80 ± 2.263	51.55 ± 0.919	56.85 ± 0.919	31.70 ± 0.707	32.95 ± 0.778	32.45 ± 0.495
CCv	40.65 ± 0.778	47.55 ± 1.909	49.45 ± 0.778	31.95 ± 0.212	32.90 ± 2.687	34.05 ± 1.626
Experiment 3. Microorganisms and meiofauna						
LM	39.55 ± 1.344	44.20 ± 1.414	48.85 ± 1.344	32.00 ± 1.697	34.00 ± 0.707	34.75 ± 1.344
FM	38.95 ± 0.212	38.15 ± 0.495	37.70 ± 0.283	32.95 ± 0.071	31.65 ± 0.495	30.10 ± 0.424
AA	35.70 ± 1.838	37.00 ± 0.283	36.20 ± 1.273	33.15 ± 0.495	33.95 ± 0.212	33.10 ± 0.566
AW	41.95 ± 0.212	43.90 ± 1.273	44.60 ± 0.849	32.00 ± 1.131	29.15 ± 0.919	30.85 ± 2.330

Nd = sediment containing *Nereis diversicolor*, CNd = control sediment containing no *Nereis diversicolor*, Cv = sediment containing *Corophium volutator*, CCv = control sediment containing no *Corophium volutator*, LM = sediment containing living microorganisms and meiofauna, FM = sediment containing dead (formalized) microorganisms and meiofauna, AA = ashed sediment in air, and AW = ashed sediment in GF/F filtered sea water.

Table 2. *Experiment 1. Statistical analyses of the effects of animal activity* (Nereis diversicolor) *on the first angle of avalanche* (A_1) *and the first angle of repose* (R_1)

Factors		A_1		R_1	
		F ratio	Probability	F ratio	Probability
(a) Nd/CNd	15 mins	22.47	0.042*	42.32	0.023*
	24 hrs	317.7	0.003**	0.740	0.481 ns
	48 hrs	82.89	0.012*	47.51	0.020*
(b) 15 mins/24 hrs/48hrs	Nd	326.1	$P < 0.0001$***	5.520	0.099 ns
	CNd	37.46	0.008**	83.47	0.002**

The table gives the F ratios and probability values obtained from one-way analyses of variance. (a) Three 1×2 analyses comparing sediment containing *Nereis diversicolor* (Nd) and the control sediment containing no *Nereis diversicolor* (CNd). (b) Two 1×3 analyses comparing 15 mins, 24 hrs and 48 hrs. Probability: $0.05 > P > 0.01$*; $0.01 > P > 0.001$**; $P < 0.001$***; ns = not significant.

Table 3. *Experiment 2. Statistical analyses of the effects of animal activity* (Corophium volutator) *on the first angle of avalanche* (A_1) *and the first angle of repose* (R_1)

Factors		A_1		R_1	
		F ratio	Probability	F ratio	Probability
(a) Cv/CCv	15 mins	6.020	0.134 ns	0.320	0.679 ns
	24 hrs	7.130	0.116 ns	0.000	0.982 ns
	48 hrs	75.53	0.013*	1.770	0.315 ns
(b) 15 mins/24 hrs/48 hrs	Cv	32.14	0.009**	1.760	0.312 ns
	CCv	26.50	0.012*	0.670	0.575 ns

The table gives the F ratios and probability values obtained from one-way analyses of variance. (a) Three 1×2 analyses comparing sediment containing *Corophium volutator* (Cv) and the control sediment containing no *Corophium volutator* (CCv). (b) Two 1×3 analyses comparing 15 mins, 24 hrs and 48 hrs.

Table 4. *Experiment 3. Statistical analyses of the effects of living microorganisms and metofauna (LM) and formalized microorganisms and metofauna (FM), and of ashed sediment dry (AA) and wet (AW) on the first angle of avalanche* (A_1) *and the first angle of repose* (R_1)

Factors		A_1		R_1	
		F ratio	Probability	F ratio	Probability
(a) Treatment					
15 mins					
LM/FM/AA/AW	1×4	10.06	0.025*	0.680	0.609 ns
LM/FM/AW	1×3	7.980	0.063 ns	0.430	0.683 ns
24 hrs					
LM/FM/AA/AW	1×4	28.82	0.004**	25.94	0.004**
LM/FM/AW	1×3	18.05	0.021*	22.20	0.016*
48 hrs					
LM/FM/AA/AW	1×4	66.72	0.001**	4.660	0.086 ns
LM/FM/AW	1×3	72.93	0.003**	5.030	0.110 ns
(b) 15 mins/24 hrs/48 hrs	LM	23.13	0.015*	2.340	0.244 ns
	FM	6.500	0.081 ns	28.41	0.011*
	AA	0.510	0.646 ns	2.240	0.254 ns
	AW	4.740	0.118 ns	1.630	0.332 ns

The table gives the F ratios and probability values obtained from one-way analyses of variance. (a) Three 1×4 analyses between the four sediment treatments: LM, FM, AA, AW and three 1×3 analyses between the three sediment treatments: FM, LM, AW. (b) Four 1×3 analyses between the 15 mins, 24 hrs and 48 hrs.

volutator. In detail, there were significant differences between the animal and control sediments at 15 mins, 24 hrs and 48 hrs for *Nereis diversicolor* (experiment 1), but this difference was only significant at 48 hrs for *Corophium volutator* (experiment 2). The effects of the two species on angles of repose were much less marked and only significant at 15 mins and 48 hrs for *Nereis diversicolor* (experiment 1).

Experiment 3. Sediment containing living microorganisms and meiofauna (LM) had a greater angle of avalanche than control sediment containing dead (formalized) microorganisms and meiofauna (FM) (Table 4). Ashed sediment in sea water (AW) had a higher angle of avalanche than both ashed sediment in air (AA) and sediment containing dead (formalized) microorganisms and meiofauna (FM). There were statistically significant differences in the angles of avalanche between the treatments at 15 mins, 24 hrs and 48 hrs. The angle of avalanche in the sediment containing living microorganisms and meiofauna (LM) increased as the experiment progressed, being most marked at 48 hrs. This increase with time in angle of avalanche did not occur in the sediments containing the dead (formalized) microorganisms (FM), or in the ashed sediment whether in sea water (AW) or in air (AA). The effects of treatments on angles of repose were usually not significant.

Comparison of 48 hrs data in experiments 1, 2 and 3. The 48 hrs data from experiments 1, 2 and 3 were compared in detail by a series of one way analyses of variance on the angle of avalanche and the angle of repose. The F ratios from these comparisons are shown in Table 5 in which the top right-hand triangle represents the F ratios for the angle of avalanche comparisons and the bottom left-hand triangle represents the F ratios for the angle of repose comparisons.

Twenty four out of the 28 angle of avalanche comparisons were significant, while only 13 out of the 28 angle of repose comparisons were significant.

A detailed inspection of the statistical comparisons in Table 5 together with the 48 hrs data of experiments 1, 2 and 3 in Table 1 reveal a number of important points. The highest angles of avalanche were obtained with *Nereis diversicolor* (experiment 1: 63.80°) followed by *Corophium volutator* (experiment 2: 56.85°). The angles of avalanche of the control sediments containing no animals (CNd) (experiment 1: 50.35°), the control sediment containing no animals (CCv) (experiment 2: 49.45°) and the sediment containing living microorganisms and meiofauna (experiment 3: 48.85°) were all lower than both those of the sediment containing *Nereis diversicolor* (experiment 1 Nd) and *Corophium volutator* (experiment 2 Cv) but were not significantly different from each other. In fact, these three treatments are experimentally equivalent because they all contained living microorganisms and meiofauna. The ashed sediment in water (AW) had an angle of avalanche significantly lower than the above three sediments (44.60°) as did the formalised sediment containing dead (formalized) microorganisms and meiofauna (37.70°). The lowest angle of avalanche was shown by the ashed sediment in air (36.20°).

There were fewer significant differences between the angles of repose. However, we wish to draw attention to a significantly higher angle of repose of the sediment containing *Nereis diversicolor* (experiment 1: 41.75°) compared with all the other angles of repose in experiments 1, 2 and 3. The lowest angle of repose was shown by the formalized sediment (30.10°) which was significantly lower than five out of the seven other angles of repose. The angle of repose of the formalized sediment (FM) was not significantly different from the angle of repose of the

Table 5. *Experiments 1, 2 and 3 (48 hrs). Pairs of treatments were compared in turn by 1 × 2 one way analyses of variance. The table gives F ratios from these analyses. Upper right triangle: first angle of avalanche (A_1). Lower left triangle: first angle of repose (R_1)*

Treatment	Nd	CNd	Cv	CCv	LM	FM	AA	AW
Nd		82.89*	61.73*	310.8**	177.0**	1703.0**	651.08**	512.0**
CNd	47.51*		18.83*	0.380 ns	0.830 ns	85.92*	76.06*	15.15*
Cv	126.3**	96.02*		75.53*	48.30*	792.9**	345.98**	191.8**
CCv	31.45*	4.050 ns	1.770 ns		0.300 ns	403.1**	157.81**	35.51*
LM	33.45*	2.890 ns	5.160 ns	0.220 ns		131.9**	93.44*	14.31*
FM	208.0**	305.3**	25.99*	11.05 ns	21.70*		2.65 ns	119.0**
AA	103.6*	54.45*	1.500 ns	0.610 ns	2.560 ns	36.00*		60.31*
AW	36.17*	11.15 ns	0.900 ns	2.530 ns	4.200 ns	0.200 ns	1.76 ns	

Nd, CNd, Cv, CCv, LM, FM, AA and AW as in Table 1.

ashed sediment in water (AW), however it was significantly lower than the angle of repose of ashed sediment in air (AA).

Second angle of avalanche (A_2') and second angle of repose (R_2)

The results of experiments 1, 2 and 3 are shown in Table 6 and their statistical analyses are shown in Tables 7–10.

Second angle of avalanche (A_2'). The 48 hrs data for the second angle (A_2') of avalanche in Table 6 column 4 were compared by a series of 1×2 one way analyses of variance between the treatments in the three experiments (Table 7 top right-hand triangle). Fourteen out of the 28 comparisons were significant. The equivalent number of significant comparisons for the first angle of avalanche was much higher at 24 out of 28 (see Table 5).

There are two important differences in experiments 1 and 2 between the first angle of avalanche (A_1) and the second angle of avalanche (A_2') at 48 hrs. Firstly, in experiment 1 there was no difference between the second angle of avalanche (A_2') of the sediment containing animals and the control sediment containing no animals (Table 6, Table 7 Nd/CNd: 45.60°/ 45.20°, F ratio = 0.19 not significant). This difference was significant for the first angle of avalanche (A_1). Secondly, in experiment 2 the second angle of avalanche (A_2') of the sediment containing animals was significantly lower than the control sediment containing no animals (Table 6, Table 7 Cv/CCv: 37.75°/40.20°, F ratio = 36.94*). It had been significantly higher for the first angle of avalanche (A_1).

The second angle of avalanche (A_2') of the sediment containing living microorganisms and meiofauna in experiment 3 (LM) was not significantly different from the second angle of

Table 6. *Data from experiment 1, 2 and 3. True second corrected angle of avalanche ($A_2' = (A_2 - A_1) + R_1$) and second angle of repose (R_2) Mean $\pm$ SD of two replicate readings*

Experiment	A_2' (degrees)			R_2 (degrees)		
	15 mins	24 hrs	48 hrs	15 mins	24 hrs	48 hrs
Experiment 1. *Nereis diversicolor*						
Nd	42.65 ± 0.778	42.25 ± 4.313	45.60 ± 0.283	34.65 ± 2.051	40.75 ± 2.192	40.90 ± 4.384
CNd	40.25 ± 0.354	42.80 ± 0.283	45.20 ± 1.273	34.50 ± 0.707	34.90 ± 0.141	36.30 ± 0.707
Experiment 2. *Corophium volutator*						
Cv	38.65 ± 0.212	40.35 ± 1.485	37.75 ± 0.495	31.80 ± 0.000	35.15 ± 0.495	34.85 + 0.495
CCv	39.25 ± 0.212	38.35 + 2.475	40.20 ± 0.283	34.75 + 2.192	34.85 ± 0.919	34.60 ± 0.849
Experiment 3. *Microorganisms and meiofauna*						
LM	40.15 ± 1.485	40.70 ± 0.849	41.20 ± 1.556	34.60 ± 0.566	35.25 ± 0.354	36.00 ± 0.849
FM	40.20 ± 0.283	37.10 ± 0.283	35.70 ± 0.849	33.10 ± 0.141	29.85 + 1.344	30.20 ± 0.283
AA	37.25 ± 2.051	37.15 + 0.071	37.35 ± 0.778	33.35 ± 0.212	33.20 ± 1.273	33.50 ± 0.990
AW	35.40 ± 1.556	32.35 ± 1.626	35.00 ± 2.404	32.80 ± 0.707	31.55 + 0.778	32.15 ± 1.344

Nd, CNd, Cv, CCv, LM, FM, AA and AW as in Table 1.

Table 7. *Experiments 1, 2 and 3 (48 hrs). Pairs of treatments compared in turns by 1×2 one way analyses of variance. The table gives F ratios from these analyses. Upper right triangle: true second corrected angle of avalanche (A_2'). Lower left triangle: second angle of repose (R_2).*

Treatment	Nd	CNd	Cv	CCv	LM	FM	AA	AW
Nd		0.190 ns	379.2**	364.5**	15.49 ns	245.0**	198.7**	38.35*
CNd	2.150 ns		59.52*	29.41*	7.920 ns	77.14*	55.39*	28.12*
Cv	3.760 ns	5.640 ns		36.94*	8.930 ns	8.710 ns	0.38 ns	2.510 ns
CCv	3.980 ns	4.740 ns	0.130 ns		0.800 ns	50.62*	23.72*	9.230 ns
LM	2.410 ns	0.150 ns	2.740 ns	2.720 ns		19.27*	9.80 ns	9.380 ns
FM	11.86 ns	128.3**	133.1**	48.40*	84.10*		4.11 ns	0.150 ns
AA	5.420 ns	10.59 ns	2.980 ns	1.420 ns	7.350 ns	20.55*		1.730 ns
AW	7.280 ns	14.94 ns	7.110 ns	4.750 ns	11.74 ns	4.030 ns	1.31 ns	

Nd, CNd, Cv, CCv, LM, FM, AA and AW as in Table 1.

avalanche in the control sediment of experiment 1 (CNd) or the control sediment of experiment 2 (CCv) (Table 7 *F* ratios = 7.92 and 0.80). However there was a statistically significant difference between the two control sediments of experiments 1 and 2 (Table 7 CNd/CCv: *F* ratio = 29.41*). As already noted, the three sediments CNd, CCv, and LM are experimentally equivalent, containing only living microorganisms and meiofauna.

The second angle of avalanche (A'_2) for the formalized sediment (FM) in experiment 3 was significantly lower than the second angle of avalanche of all the sediments in experiment 1 and 2 except for the Cv sediment. It was also significantly lower than the second angle of avalanche of the LM sediment containing living microorganisms and meiofauna in experiment 3. These results are broadly similar to the FM comparisons for the first angle of avalanche.

Second angle of repose (R_2). The 48 hrs data for the second angle of repose (R_2) in Table 6 column 7 were compared by a series of 1×2 one

Table 8. *48 hrs data from experiments 1, 2 and 3. Comparison of first angle of avalanche* (A_1) *and true corrected second angle of avalanche* (A'_2) *by Student's paired t-test*

Experiment	Treatment	Repl.	$(A'_2/A_1) \times 100$	t	P
1. *Nereis diversicolor*	Nd	1	70.50	22.75	0.028*
		2	72.50		
	CNd	1	94.10	2.290	0.260 ns
		2	85.70		
2. *Corophium volutator*	Cv	1	67.80	19.10	0.033*
		2	65.00		
	CCv	1	80.80	26.43	0.024 *
		2	81.80		
3. Microorganisms	LM	1	83.70	51.00	0.012*
		2	84.90		
	FM	1	95.80	5.000	0.130 ns
		2	93.60		
	AA	1	107.4	−0.360	0.780 ns
		2	99.20		
	AW	1	73.70	−1.860	0.310 ns
		2	83.40		

Nd, CNd, Cv, CCv, LM, FM, AA and AW as in Table 1.

Table 9. *48 hrs data from experiments 1, 2 and 3. Comparison of first angle of repose* (R_1) *and second angle of repose* (R_2) *by Student's paired t-test*

Experiment	Treatment	Repl.	$(R_2/R_1) \times 100$	t	P
1. *Nereis diversicolor*	Nd	1	92.20	0.360	0.780 ns
		2	103.5		
	CNd	1	97.80	0.140	0.910 ns
		2	101.7		
2. *Corophium volutator*	Cv	1	107.3	Replicate values are	
		2	107.5	identical	
	CCv	1	96.60	−0.310	0.810 ns
		2	107.0		
3. Microorganisms	LM	1	104.7	−3.570	0.170 ns
and meiofauna		2	102.5		
	FM	1	98.70	−0.200	0.870 ns
		2	102.0		
	AA	1	104.6	−0.360	0.780 ns
		2	97.90		
	AW	1	106.8	−1.860	0.310 ns
		2	101.8		

Nd, CNd, Cv, CCv, LM, FM, AA and AW as in Table 1.

way analyses of variance between the treatments in the three experiment (Table 7 bottom left-hand triangle). Five out of the 28 comparisons of the second angle of repose were significant. The equivalent number of significant comparisons for the first angle of repose (R_1) was much higher at 13 out of 28 (see Table 5).

As in the first angle of repose (R_1), the sediment containing formalized dead microorganisms and meiofauna (FM) in experiment 3 had a lower second angle of repose (R_2) than all the other sediments. However, the second angle of repose (R_2) of the sediment containing *Nereis diversicolor* in experiment 1 (Nd) was not significantly different from any of the other second angles of repose (Table 7 column 2). This is in marked contrast to the results of the first angles of repose (R_1), in which the first angle of repose of *Nereis diversicolor* was significantly greater than all the other first angles of repose (Table 5 column 2).

Statistical comparison of first and second angles of avalanche and repose

The second angle of avalanche (A_2') increased much more slowly than the first angle of avalanche (A_1) during the experiment, while the second angle of repose (R_2) was broadly the same as the first angle of repose (R_1). For example, in experiment 1 at 48 hrs, the first angle of avalanche (A_1) was 63.80° and the second angle of avalanche (A_2') was 45.60° for Nd, and the same angles for CNd were 50.35° and 45.20°. In contrast the equivalent angles of repose were 41.75° and 40.90°, and 36.40° and 36.30° respectively (Tables 1 and 6).

The differences between the first and second angles of avalanche, and the first and second angles of repose in 48 hrs were quantified by

expressing them as $[(A_2'/A_1) \times 100\%]$ and as $[(R_2/R_1) \times 100\%]$. The statistical significance between these first and second angles were assessed by Student's paired t-test. The differences and their statistical significance are shown in Tables 8 and 9. The percentages comparing the first and second angles of avalanche $[(A_2'/A_1) \times 100\%]$ shown in Table 8 column 4 are all less than 100%, except for one replicate treatment in the ashed sediment in air (AA) of experiment 3 (107.4%). The paired t-tests shown in Table 8 column 5 show that the second angle of avalanche (A_2') in three out of the four treatments in experiments 1 and 2 (Nd, Cv, CCv) were significantly different from the first angle of avalanche (A_1). However, only one of the treatments in experiment 3, the sediment containing living microorganisms and meiofauna (LM), had a significantly lower second angle of avalanche (A_2') than the first angle of avalanche (A_1).

The 48 hrs ratios for the first angles of avalanche (A_1) and second angles of avalanche (A_2') between treatments in the three experiments were compared by a series of 1×2 one way analyses of variance. The F ratios from these 28 analyses are shown in the top right hand triangle of Table 10. Fourteen out of the 28 comparisons are significant. In experiments 1 and 2 the sediment containing animals had significantly lower percentages $[(A_2'/A_1) \times 100\%]$ than the control sediment containing no animals. (Experiment 1: 70.50%, 72.50%/94.10%, 85.70% F ratio = 18.16*; Experiment 2: 67.80%, 65.00%/80.80%, 81.80% F ratio = 100.5*) (see Tables 8 and 10). In contrast there were no significant differences between the sediment containing animals in experiments 1 and 2, and between the control sediments in experiments 1 and 2 and the sediment containing living microorganisms and meio-fauna (LM) in experiment 3 (Table 10

Table 10. *48 hrs data from experiments 1, 2 and 3. Pairs of treatments compared in turns by 1 × 2 one way analyses of variance. The table gives F ratios from these analyses. Upper right triangle: ratio of true second corrected angle of avalanche to the first angle of avalanche (A_2'/A_1). Lower left triangle: ratio of second angle of repose to the first angle of repose (R_2/R_1)*

Treatment	Nd	CNd	Cv	CCv	LM	FM	AA	AW
Nd		18.16*	8.790 ns	76.83*	120.5**	243.6**	56.78*	2.030 ns
CNd	0.100 ns		28.18*	4.130 ns	1.740 ns	1.220 ns	5.210 ns	3.130 ns
Cv	2.860 ns	0.140 ns		100.5*	138.1**	252.7**	72.54*	5.790 ns
CCv	2.860 ns	0.140 ns	1.160 ns		14.75 ns	123.0**	28.37*	0.320 ns
LM	1.000 ns	1.000 ns	11.84 ns	11.84 ns		68.89*	21.03*	1.380 ns
FM	0.060 ns	0.060 ns	0.070 ns	0.070 ns	2.690 ns		4.100 ns	10.55 ns
AA	0.270 ns	0.270 ns	3.370 ns	3.370 ns	0.440 ns	0.060 ns		15.19 ns
AW	2.060 ns	2.060 ns	0.190 ns	0.707 ns	0.070 ns	1.740 ns	0.530 ns	

Nd, CNd, Cv, CCv, LM, FM, AA and AW as in Table 1.

top right-hand triangle: *F* ratio; 8.79, 4.13, 1.74, 14.75 all not significant). These latter three sediments (CNd, CCv, LM) are exactly equivalent because they all contain living microorganisms and meiofauna. The percentages for the formalized sediment (FM) containing dead microorganisms and meiofauna in experiment 3 (Table 8 95.80%, 93.60%) were significantly higher than the percentages of three out of the four treatments in experiments 1 and 2 (Nd, Cv, CCv).

The 48 hrs ratios for the first and second angles of repose between treatments in the three experiments were compared by a series of 1×2 one way analyses of variance. The *F* ratios from these 28 analyses are shown in the bottom left-hand triangle of Table 10. None of these were significant.

The percentages comparing the first and second angles of repose $[(R_2/R_1) \times 100\%]$ shown in

Table 9 column 4 are all close to 100%. The paired *t*-tests shown in Table 9 column 5 are all non-significant showing that there is no difference between the first and second angles of repose.

Factor of safety and angles of dilatation

The factor of safety and angles of dilatation calculated from the first angles of avalanche (A_1) and the first angles of repose (R_1) with statistical analyses are shown for experiments 1 and 2 in Tables 11a and 11b and for experiment 3 in Tables 12a and 12b.

Experiments 1 and 2. Factors of safety and angles of dilatation increased with time in both experiments. These increases were all statistically

Table 11(a). *Data from experiments 1 and 2. Angle of dilatation (*$A_1 - R_1$*) and factor of safety (tan (*A_1*)/tan (*R_1*)). Mean ± SD of two replicate readings*

Treatment	Angle of dilatation			Factor of safety		
	15 mins	24 hrs	48 hrs	15 mins	24 hrs	48 hrs
Experiment 1. *Nereis diversicolor*						
Nd	8.350 ± 1.061	23.30 ± 2.546	22.05 ± 1.909	1.350 ± 0.057	2.340 ± 0.204	2.290 ± 0.164
CNd	8.000 ± 0.707	10.35 ± 0.212	13.95 ± 2.192	1.340 ± 0.035	1.460 ± 0.009	1.650 ± 0.116
Experiment 2. *Corophium volutator*						
Cv	13.10 ± 2.970	18.60 ± 1.697	24.40 ± 1.414	1.610 ± 0.172	1.950 ± 0.122	2.410 ± 0.130
CCv	8.700 ± 0.990	14.65 ± 0.778	15.40 ± 0.849	1.380 ± 0.049	1.690 ± 0.061	1.730 ± 0.059

Nd, CNd, Cv and CCv, as in Table 1.

Table 11(b). *Statistical analyses of the effects of animals* Nereis diversicolor *(experiment 1) and* Corophium volutator *(experiment 2) on angle of dilatation and factor of safety. The table gives the F ratios and probability values obtained from one-way analyses of variance. (a) Three 1 × 2 analyses comparing sediment containing animals and the control sediment containing no animals. (b) Two 1 × 3 analyses comparing 15 mins, 24 hrs and 48 hrs*

Factors			Angle of dilatation		Factor of safety	
			F ratio	Probability	*F* ratio	Probability
Experiment 1. *Nereis diversicolor*						
(a) Nd/CNd		15 mins	0.060	0.824 ns	0.010	0.948 ns
		24 hrs	51.40	0.019*	38.45	0.025*
		48 hrs	17.53	0.053 ns	20.11	0.046*
(b) 15 mins/24 hrs/48 hrs		Nd	37.13	0.008**	26.13	0.013*
		CNd	12.72	0.034*	9.830	0.048*
Experiment 2. *Corophium volutator*						
(a) Cv/CCv		15 mins	3.950	0.185 ns	3.470	0.204 ns
		24 hrs	8.950	0.096 ns	6.920	0.119 ns
		48 hrs	56.56	0.016*	45.33	0.021*
(b) 15 mins/24 hrs/48 hrs		Cv	13.98	0.030*	15.72	0.026*
		CCv	35.08	0.008**	23.53	0.015*

Nd, CNd, Cv and CCv as in Table 1.

Table 12(a). *Experiment 3. Angle of dilatation* $(A_1 - R_1)$ *and factor of safety* $(tan\ (A_1)/tan\ (R_1))$. *Mean $\pm$ SD of two replicate readings*

Treatment	Angle of dilatation			Factor of safety		
	15 mins	24 hrs	48 hrs	15 mins	24 hrs	48 hrs
LM	7.550 ± 3.041	10.20 ± 2.121	14.10 ± 0.000	1.320 ± 0.149	1.440 ± 0.109	1.650 ± 0.004
FM	6.000 ± 0.283	6.500 ± 0.000	7.600 ± 0.141	1.250 ± 0.013	1.270 ± 0.002	1.330 ± 0.008
AA	2.550 ± 2.333	3.050 ± 0.495	3.100 ± 0.707	1.100 ± 0.096	1.120 ± 0.021	1.120 ± 0.028
AW	9.950 ± 0.919	14.75 ± 2.192	13.75 ± 3.182	1.440 ± 0.052	1.730 ± 0.142	1.660 ± 0.202

LM, FM, AA and AW as in Table 1.

Table 12(b). *Statistical analyses of the effects of living microorganisms and meiofauna, and of ashed sediment on angle of dilatation and factor of safety in experiment 3. The table gives the F ratios and probability values obtained from one-way analyses of variance. (a) Nine one-way analyses of variance. One 1 $\times$ 4 analyses comparing the four sediment treatments: LM, FM, AA, AW, one 1 $\times$ 2 analyses comparing the two sediment treatments: LM, FM and one 1 $\times$ 2 analyses comparing the two sediment treatments: AA, AW on each of the time 15 mins, 24 hrs and 48 hrs. (b) Four 1 $\times$ 3 analyses comparing the 15 mins, 24 hrs and 48 hrs, one on each of the four treatments: LM, FM, AA, AW*

Factors		Angle of dilatation		Factor of safety	
		F ratio	Probability	F ratio	Probability
(a) Treatment					
15 mins					
LM/FM/AA/AW	1×4	4.930	0.079 ns	4.730	0.084 ns
FM/LM	1×2	0.520	0.547 ns	0.530	0.542 ns
AA/AW	1×2	17.41	0.053 ns	19.22	0.048*
24 hrs					
AA/AW/FM/LM	1×4	21.11	0.006**	16.66	0.010*
FM/LM	1×2	6.080	0.132 ns	4.750	0.161 ns
AA/AW	1×2	54.21	0.018*	35.97	0.027*
48 hrs					
AA/AW/FM/LM	1×4	20.97	0.007**	13.02	0.016*
FM/LM	1×2	4225	< 0.0001***	2233.09	< 0.0001***
AA/AW	1×2	21.35	0.044*	13.78	0.066 ns
(b) 15 mins/24 hrs/48 hrs	LM	4.740	0.118 ns	4.830	0.115 ns
	FM	40.20	0.007**	48.53	0.005**
	AA	0.090	0.917 ns	0.080	0.927 ns
	AW	2.440	0.235 ns	2.150	0.264 ns

LM, FM, AA and AW as in Table 1.

significant (Table 11b rows 4, 5, 9, 10). Inspection of the data in Table 11a shows that the effect had become stabilized by 24 hrs for the Nd sediment, while the Cv sediments had its highest values at 48 hrs. In experiment 1, the factors of safety were higher for the sediments containing animals than for the control sediments at 24 hrs and 48 hrs (Table 11b column 5 rows 2, 3). The differences between the angles of dilatation of the sediment containing animals and of the control sediments containing no animals were only significant at 24 hrs (Table 11b column 3 row 2). In experiment 2 the factors of safety and angle of dilatation were significantly higher for the sediments containing animals than for the control sediments only at 48 hrs (Table 11b row 8).

Experiment 3. In general, factors of safety and angles of dilatation increased with time, as they did in experiments 1 and 2, however the effect was only significant for the formalized sediment containing dead microorganisms and meiofauna (FM) (Table 12b rows 10–13). There were significant differences between the sediment treatments which were most obvious at 48 hrs (Table 12b rows 7, 8). In particular, the factor of safety and angles of dilatation of the sediment containing living microorganisms and meiofauna (LM) were higher than those of formalized sediment containing dead microorganisms and meiofauna (FM) (Table 12a rows 1, 2: 1.65/ 1.33, 14.10/7.60). The factor of safety and angles of dilatation of the ashed sediment avalanched in water (AW) were also higher than those of ashed sediment avalanched in air (AA) (Table 12a rows 3, 4: 1.66/1.12, 13.75/3.10).

Figure 3, which includes the data for all the experiments, shows that there is a strong linear relationship between the factor of safety and the angle of avalanche, but not between the factor of safety and angle of repose. These two contrasting effects are to be expected. The higher angles of avalanche, which have higher factors of safety, are caused by extracellular polymeric

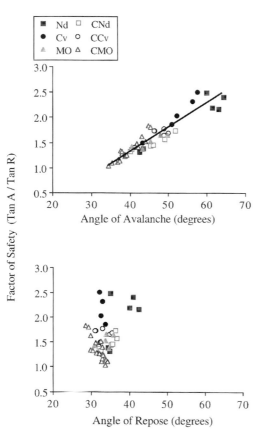

Fig. 3. Data from experiment 1 (*Nereis diversicolor*), experiment 2 (*Corophium volutator*) & experiment 3 (microorganisms). **Top**: relation between angle of avalanche and factor of safety ($y = 0.0200x + 0.4460$, $F_{1,45} = 112.7$, $P < 0.001$***). **Bottom**: relation between angle of repose and factor of safety. Nd = *Nereis diversicolor*; CNd = control containing no *Nereis diversicolor*; Cv = *Corophium volutator*; CCv = control containing no *Corophium volutator*; LM = living microorganisms and meiofauna; CMO = control containing either killed or no microorganisms and meiofauna ($y = 0.00738x + 1.100$, $F_{1,45} = 0.5900$, $P = 0.440$ ns).

materials produced by the animals and micro-organisms. The extracellular polymeric materials bind the sediment together. The avalanching process destroys this binding. As a result the angles of repose do not alter a great deal and have no significant relationship with the factor of safety. The relationship between the factor of safety and the angle of avalanche was further analysed by considering the following sets of data separately: experiment 1 (Nd + CNd), experiment 2 (Cv + CCv), experiment 3 (LM + FM) and experiment 3 (AA + AW). These separate sets of data are shown in Fig. 4 and were analysed by four regression analyses (see legend of Fig. 4). The slopes of the four separate regression lines were compared by F ratios (Snedecor & Cochran 1980). These F ratios are presented in Table 13. There were significant differences between the slopes of all the lines except for the A/C comparison. The ashed sediment in air and water (Fig. 4d: AA + AW) had a highest slope (0.0697). The data from experiment 2 (Fig. 4b: Cv + CCv) had a lower slope (0.0607). The lowest slopes were shown by the sediments containing the micro-organisms and meiofauna in experiment 3 and the sediments in experiment 1 (Fig. 4c: LM + FM, Fig. 4a: Nd + CNd) (0.0331, 0.0467).

Duration of avalanche

Table 14 shows the duration in seconds of the first and second avalanches at 15 mins, 24 hrs and 48 hrs in experiments 1, 2 and 3. There are large differences in duration of avalanches particularly at 48 hrs. The 48 hrs data for the duration of the first avalanche (T_1) were analysed by one way analyses of variance (not presented here), and the following statements are based on the statistically significant analyses. The avalanches with the longest duration occurred with sediments containing animals in experiments 1 and 2 (130 and 42 s). Intermediate durations were shown by the controls in experiments 1 and 2, and the LM and FM treatments in experiment 3 (23–37 s). The AA treatment had an extremely short duration of between 1 and 2 s. When the data for the duration of the first avalanche (T_1) of all three experiments were plotted against the first angle of avalanche for the duration of the first avalanche (A_1) there was a highly significant positive relationship (Fig. 5).

At 48 hrs the duration of the second avalanche (T_2) was broadly similar to the duration of the first avalanche (T_1) in spite of the duration of the second avalanche (T_2) being higher than the

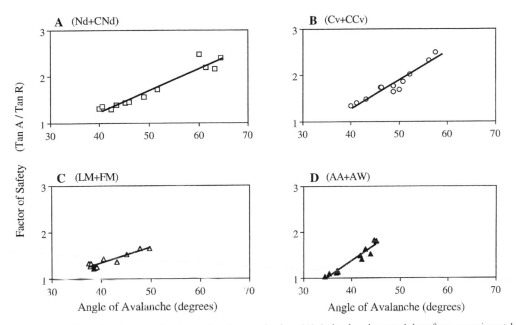

Fig. 4. Regression of angle of avalanche against factor of safety. (**A**) Animal and control data from experiment 1 (*Nereis diversicolor*) ($y = 0.0467x - 0.6280$, $F_{1,10} = 128.6$, $P < 0.001***$). (**B**) Animal and control data from experiment 2 (*Corophium volutator*) ($y = 0.0607x - 1.150$, $F_{1,10} = 96.55$, $P < 0.001***$).
(**C**) Living microorganisms and meiofauna and formalized microorganisms and meiofauna data from experiment 3 (microorganisms and meiofauna) ($y = 0.0331x + 0.012$, $F_{1,10} = 59.08$, $P < 0.001***$).
(**D**) Ashed sediment in air and ashed sediment in GF/F filtered sea water data from experiment 3 ($y = 0.0697x - 1.420$, $F_{1,10} = 129.2$, $P < 0.001***$).

Table 13. *Comparisons of regression equations. Factor of safety (Y-axis) against angle of avalanche (X-axis). Regression equations given in Fig. 7 legend. Pairs of regression equations of categories A, B, C and D were compared in turns. Table gives* F_{slope} *and level of significance.* $A = (Nd + CNd)$; *experiment 1.* $B = (Cv + CCv)$; *experiment 2.* $C = (LM + FM)$; *experiment 3.* $D = (AA + AW)$; *experiment 3*

	A	B	C	D
A		14.99**	4.566 ns	15.96**
B			12.96*	5.441*
C				27.22***
D				

duration of the first avalanche (T_1) in experiments 1 and 2. However in experiment 3, the duration of the second avalanche (T_2) was lower than the duration of the first avalanche (T_1).

Percentage increase in sediment volume

All the sediments increased in volume during the first avalanche (Table 15). The increase in volumes range from a maximum of c. 31% (experiment 1: Nd 48 hrs) to a minimum of less

than 1% (experiment 3: AA 15 mins). In both experiments 1 and 2 the sediment containing animals showed a greater increase in volume than the control sediment not containing animals (48 hrs: Nd/CNd; 30.74%/7.21%, Cv/CCv; 12.95%/7.2%). In experiment 3 the increases in volume shown by the LM, FM and AW sediments at 48 hrs were 5%–8% and the AA sediment was c. 3%. It is interesting that the CNd, CCv and LM sediments, all of which are exactly equivalent containing living microorganisms and meiofauna, had increases in sediment volume of 7.21%, 7.26% and 7.39%. When the

Table 14. *Data from experiments 1, 2 & 3. Duration of first avalanche* (T_1) *and duration of second avalanche* (T_2). *Mean ± SD of two replicate readings*

Treatment	T_1 (s)			T_2 (s)		
	15 mins	24 hrs	48 hrs	15 mins	24 hrs	48 hrs
Experiment 1. *Nereis diversicolor*						
Nd	69.38 ± 10.08	134.55 ± 13.58	130.0 ± 22.13	27.50 ± 4.950	138.2 ± 31.40	153.0 ± 41.22
CNd	22.33 ± 4.914	27.25 ± 4.384	35.60 ± 24.96	17.63 ± 2.652	36.45 ± 15.84	44.85 ± 0.283
Experiment 3. *Corophium volutator*						
Cv	23.60 ± 3.606	40.95 ± 11.80	42.60 ± 10.82	26.78 ± 14.74	141.4 ± 69.79	76.50 ± 73.33
CCv	21.80 ± 2.758	23.30 ± 11.24	23.13 ± 7.036	21.23 ± 1.237	56.63 ± 23.23	23.10 ± 3.889
Experiment 3. Microorganisms and meiofauna						
LM	34.35 ± 15.98	83.50 ± 55.65	37.05 ± 5.940	31.25 ± 6.930	49.55 ± 13.86	28.25 ± 0.141
FM	74.70 ± 66.82	76.43 ± 68.84	35.20 ± 5.586	20.30 ± 11.53	25.18 ± 1.662	24.10 ± 2.051
AA	1.000 ± 0.707	1.330 ± 0.177	1.550 ± 0.778	1.330 ± 0.318	1.850 ± 0.424	1.230 ± 0.035
AW	25.50 ± 0.919	31.70 ± 3.748	53.35 ± 28.14	17.53 ± 4.490	31.15 ± 3.960	27.35 ± 10.11

Nd, CNd, Cv, CCv, LM, FM, AA and AW as in Table 1.

percentage increases in volume for all the experiments were plotted against angle of avalanche, the data showed a highly significant positive relationship (Fig. 6).

Discussion

Sediment stability is one of the most important features of the coastal zone, particularly in those parts that are exposed by the tides to produce intertidal sandy and muddy beaches. As a result, there has been a wide range of studies on the physical and biological aspects of sedimentary

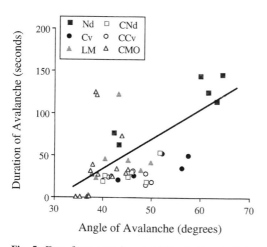

Fig. 5. Data from experiment 1 (*Nereis diversicolor*), experiment 2 (*Corophium volutator*) & experiment 3 (microorganisms and meiofauna). Relation between angle of avalanche and duration of avalanche ($y = 3.600x - 112.0$, $F_{1,45} = 11.49$, $P = 0.001$**).

stability. In this paper we have explored the effects of biological activity on intertidal sandy sediments with special reference to slope stability. Our test procedure has consisted of inducing sediments to avalanche, measuring the angles at which they avalanche, and measuring the subsequent angle of repose once the avalanching process has terminated.

We have shown that biological activity in the form of burrows produced by two species of intertidal infaunal invertebrates (*Nereis diversicolor*, *Corophium volutator*) and microbiological and meiofaunal activity produced by natural communities of microorganisms and meiofauna have dramatic effects on the angles at which slopes avalanche, and also on the avalanching process itself. The greatest increase in angles of avalanche occurred with *Nereis diversicolor* where angles in excess of 60° were regularly recorded (Table 1). These were followed closely by angles recorded for *Corophium volutator* of about 56°. Natural populations of microorganisms and meiofauna also had a significant effect, where angles of avalanche of 48°–50° were recorded (CNd, CCv, LM). These angles should be compared with control values of 44° for ashed sediment in water and 37° for formalized sediment containing dead microorganisms and meiofauna (FM). This biological, microbiological and meiofaunal stabilization is clearly of great significance where waves and water currents impinge on the intertidal zone and where steep sided run-off channels form on estuarine sediment banks.

The enhanced slope stability produced by biological activity is caused by three mechanisms, two of which depend on the production of

Table 15. *Data from experiments 1, 2 & 3. Percentage increase in volume of sediment after the first avalanche. Mean ± SD of two replicate readings*

Treatment	Percentage increase in volume		
	15 mins	24 hrs	48 hrs
Experiment 1.	*Nereis diversicolor*		
Nd	5.980 ± 0.269	14.64 ± 10.387	30.74 ± 5.586
CNd	5.320 ± 1.676	4.030 ± 2.256	7.210 ± 1.492
Experiment 3.	*Corophium volutator*		
Cv	12.19 ± 0.078	10.91 ± 2.404	12.95 ± 0.870
CCv	5.370 ± 0.693	8.070 ± 0.721	7.260 ± 3.083
Experiment 3.	Microorganisms and meiofauna		
LM	4.640 ± 5.381	3.990 ± 2.256	7.390 ± 5.530
FM	0.780 ± 1.103	3.970 ± 1.711	5.170 ± 1.082
AA	0.230 ± 2.312	1.870 ± 0.636	3.170 ± 1.068
AW	2.910 ± 0.573	6.110 ± 4.547	7.840 ± 0.898

Nd, CNd, Cv, CCv, LM, FM, AA and AW as in Table 1.

extracellular polymeric material and one of which depends on a small element of compaction. The two mechanisms depending on extracellular polymeric material are as follows. The animals construct vertical (*Nereis diversicolor*) or U shaped (*Corophium volutator*) burrows whose walls are bound together by extracellular polymeric material produced by the animals. These tubes act as a vertical and horizontal reinforcement of the sediment fabric (Meadows & Tait 1989; Meadows *et al.* 1990). The microorganisms also produce extracellular polymeric material.

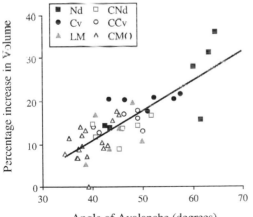

Fig. 6. Data from experiment 1 (*Nereis diversicolor*), experiment 2 (*Corophium volutator*) & experiment 3 (microorganisms and meiofauna). Relation between angle of avalanche and percentage increase in volume (arcsine) of sediment after an avalanche ($y = 0.685x - 16.41$, $F_{1,45} = 76.55$, $P < 0.001$***).

However the microorganisms are significantly smaller than the majority of the individual sediment particles. Sedimentary microorganisms range in size from $c. 0.5 \mu m$ to $5 \mu m$ (bacteria) and from $20 \mu m$ to $60 \mu m$ (diatoms). In our sediment, particles range in size from $63 \mu m$ to $710 \mu m$. This means that the extracellular polymeric material produced by the microorganisms will glue the sediment particles together to produce a three-dimensional fabric (Tufail 1987; Meadows *et al.* 1994). Each sedimentary particle is likely to be bound to one or more of the particles surrounding it although no tubes are produced. In contrast to the large amount of information that is available about extracellular polymeric material produced by microorganisms, very little is known about similar production by meiofauna (Platt & Warwick 1980; Chandler & Fleeger 1984; Riechelt 1991), so it is difficult for us to assess its significance. However, we are of the view that microbial extracellular material is likely to be of more importance in our experiments than meiofaunal extracellular material is. In either case, our results certainly suggest that animal tubes whose walls are bound by extracellular polymeric material are more effective in stabilizing slopes than microbial or meiofaunal extracellular polymeric material which may glue particles together.

The third mechanism of biological stabilization depends on sediment compaction. We noticed a small degree of compaction after 24 and 48 hrs in the Nd and Cv containers containing animals (experiments 1 and 2) and the LM containers (experiment 3) when compared with the control containers. The compaction observed was 6–8% of the control containers. This means that biologically induced sediment compaction may be a significant factor in stabilizing slopes in addition to the production of extracellular polymeric material.

Parallels between engineering and biological stabilization

Our results are not only important for a sedimentological and geomorphological understanding of slope stability in the intertidal zone, but are also likely to have major implications in an environmental engineering context. This has recently been recognized by Muir Wood *et al.* (1990, 1994), Meadows *et al.* (1994) and Pender *et al.* (1994) in studies on microbiological effects on slope stability and on biological strengthening of sediments. In this context we wish to draw attention to parallels between engineering methods and biological stabilization (Fig. 7). Engineers use vibration and compaction to pack and thus stabilize a sediment, infaunal invertebrates

can have parallel effects by reworking and mixing the sediment. Engineers reinforce sediments using geomembranes, piling and retaining structures (Craig 1992; McCarthy 1993). These are paralleled by biological activity in the form of biomembranes often formed by microorganisms and algal mats, armouring by large animals such as mussels, reinforcement by the roots of plants and reinforcement by burrows and tubes produced by infaunal animals. Engineering chemical methods of stabilization included the use of lime, cement, bitumen and bentonite. The biological equivalent is the production of extracellular polymeric material and other organic matter which bind particles together. In general, biological stabilization tends to be more environmentally friendly, but often acts on a smaller scale than conventional engineering methodology.

Factors of safety

Factors of safety are widely used in soil engineering to assess the stability of slopes. Their

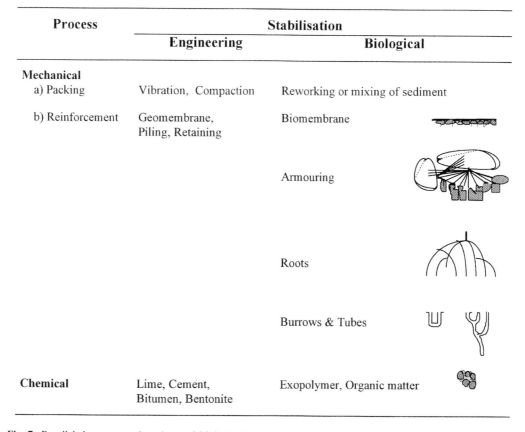

Process	Stabilisation	
	Engineering	**Biological**
Mechanical		
a) Packing	Vibration, Compaction	Reworking or mixing of sediment
b) Reinforcement	Geomembrane, Piling, Retaining	Biomembrane
		Armouring
		Roots
		Burrows & Tubes
Chemical	Lime, Cement, Bitumen, Bentonite	Exopolymer, Organic matter

Fig. 7. Parallels between engineering and biological stabilization.

calculation for static non-avalanching slopes are often complex (Lee *et al.* 1983; Bromhead 1992). We have assessed the stability of slopes in our experiments by a factor of safety which we have defined as tan (angle of avalanche)/tan (angle of repose), following similar approaches referred to by Lambe & Whitman (1979, p. 193), Lee *et al.* (1983, p. 292, 303) and Craig (1992, p. 377) and used by Muir Wood *et al.* (1994). The highest factors of safety were exhibited by sediments containing *Nereis diversicolor* and *Corophium volutator* (Table 11a; 2.29, 2.41). Sediments containing living microorganisms and meiofauna (LM) (Table 11a CNd, CCv; Table 12a LM) had lower values of 1.65, 1.73 and 1.65. These were higher than the factor of safety of the sediments containing dead (formalized) microorganisms and meiofauna (FM) (1.33). The lowest factor of safety was shown by ashed sediment avalanched in air (AA) (1.12). In our experiments, therefore, the two animal species have a major effect on slope stability as measured by the factor of safety, with microorganisms also being important, but to a lesser degree.

Slope failure mechanisms

Visual observations of the avalanching process together with video analyses show that different slope failure mechanisms (Lee *et al.* 1983 pp. 284–487; Bromhead 1992; Craig 1992; McCarthy 1993 p. 494) were associated with the different types of biological activity. These probably reflect specific mechanical and chemical stabilization effects produced by the tubes of the animals, together with extracellular polymeric material produced by these animals and by microorganisms and meiofauna (Fig. 8) In particular, the processes taking place during avalanching in the sediment containing *Nereis diversicolor* are very similar to rotational failure of slopes. In rotational failure, the slip surface is curved forming a bowl shape trench after failure. The failed mass characteristically slumps to the toe area of the original slope. Rotational failure is associated with slopes of homogenous material possessing cohesion. The processes taking place during avalanching in the sediment containing *Corophium volutator* are very similar to the block and wedge failure. In block and wedge failure an intact mass of sediment avalanches, subsequent to cracks developing over the surface of the sediment. The mechanisms taking place during the avalanching in the sediment containing living and dead microorganisms and meiofauna are very similar to translational failure. Translational failure is generally associated with slopes of layered material. It involves sliding of a thin layer of sediment over a stratum of significantly different strength. During failure the sliding surface remains roughly parallel to the slope, and the sliding mass either remains intact or breaks up into large slabs.

Implications for slope stabilization under field conditions

It would be interesting to know whether the slope failure mechanisms that have been observed in laboratory experiments can be detected on slopes in the field where abundant populations of *Corophium volutator* and *Nereis diversicolor* and abundant microbial and meiofaunal growth occur. Our highest angle of avalanche was 62° (*Nereis diversicolor*) which is an increase of 62% over that for the formalized control sediment. Our highest factor of safety was 2.40 (*Corophium volutator*) which is an increase of 80% over that for the formalized control sediment. Slopes in excess of 55° certainly occur on the banks of run-off channels in estuarine cohesive sediments where both *Corophium volutator* and *Nereis diversicolor* are abundant. Our results suggest that these high slope angles are maintained by biological and microbiological and meiofaunal activity. The high values of the factor of safety that we have observed suggest that the slopes are relatively stable. This appears to be so as many run off channels are semi-permanent features of the geomorphology of estuarine ecosystems. It would be extremely interesting to know the angles of avalanche and factors of safety of some of these naturally occurring slopes in the intertidal zone.

Conclusions

Our experiments have shown that two species of infaunal invertebrates and populations of microorganisms and meiofauna that live in intertidal sandy sediments stabilize sediment slopes by increasing the angles of avalanche and increasing factors of safety. The most dramatic effects are produced by the two invertebrates. Furthermore, slopes that avalanche at higher angles take longer to avalanche and also increase in sediment volume to a greater degree, possibly due to sediment reworking by the infauna. Angles of repose after avalanching are not affected by biological activity.

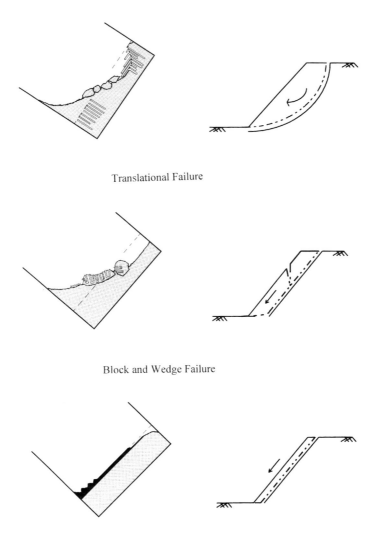

Translational Failure

Block and Wedge Failure

Rotational Failure

Fig. 8. Slope failure mechanisms. **Top**: left, shape of the slope after an avalanche in sediment containing animals in experiment 1 (*Nereis diversicolor*); right, illustration of rotational failure (Craig 1992; McCarthy 1993). **Middle**: left, shape of the slope after an avalanche in sediment containing animals in experiment 2 (*Corophium volutator*); right, illustration of block and wedge failure (McCarthy 1993). **Bottom**: left, shape of the slope after an avalanche in sediment containing living microorganisms and meiofauna in experiments 1, 2 and 3; right, illustration of translational failure (Craig 1992; McCarthy 1993).

The mechanisms of failure of slopes as they avalanche due to the presence of biological activity, parallel well-known mechanisms of slope failure that are described by civil engineers and geologists when considering slope stability. Biological activity as produced by the organisms that we have investigated probably stabilize slopes by mechanical and chemical methods. Tubes of invertebrates will act as piles, and their

walls are bound together by extracellular polymeric materials produced by the animals. Binding by microorganisms and meiofauna is likely to be caused mainly by the secretion of extracellular polymeric materials.

The significant biological effects that we have described extend our knowledge of the influences of living organisms on slope stability to the intertidal zone, where slope protection is likely to be of increasing concern as coastal zones become endangered by rising sea levels during the 21st century. It may be possible to consider the use of environmentally-friendly methods of stabilizing the intertidal zone by seeding with organisms such as those used in the present study. The two invertebrates and the natural populations of microorganisms and meiofauna used by us are robust organisms which are common in intertidal sediments. It would be very worthwhile to conduct field seeding experiments with them.

M. A. Shaikh wishes to thank the Ministry of Education, Government of Pakistan (EG/2436 1993) and the Committee of Vice-Chancellors and Principals of the Universities of the United Kingdom (CVCP) (ORS/C20/4 1996) for their financial support.

References

ALLEN, J. R. L. 1968. The diffusion of grains in the lee of ripples, dunes and Gilbert-type deltas. *Journal of Sedimentary Petrology*, **38**, 621–633.

—— 1970. The avalanching of granular solids of dune and similar slopes. *Journal of Geology*, **78**, 326–351.

BACHE, D. H. & MACASKILL, I. A. 1984. *Vegetation in Civil and Landscape Engineering*. Granada, London.

BAGNOLD, R. A. 1941. *The Physics of Blown Sand and Desert Dunes*. Methuen & Co., London.

—— 1966. The shearing and dilatation of dry sand and the 'singing' mechanism. *Proceedings of The Royal Society of London*, **295A**, 219–232.

BALTZER, A., COCHONAT, P. & PIPER, D. J. M. 1994. *In situ* geotechnical characterisation of sediments of the Nova Scotian slope, Eastern Canadian continental-margin. *Marine Geology*, **120**, 291–308.

BARAZA, J., ERCILLA, G. & LEE, H. J. 1992. Geotechnical properties and preliminary assessment of sediment stability on the continental-slope of the north-western Alboran sea. *Geo-Marine letters*, **12**, 150–156.

—— & —— 1994. Geotechnical properties of near-surface sediments from the north-western Alboran sea slope (SW Mediterranean) – Influence of texture and sedimentary processes. *Marine Georesources & Geotechnology*, **12**, 181–200.

BROMHEAD, E. N. 1992. *The Stability of Slopes*. Chapman and Hall, UK.

BRUNSDEN, D. & DAVID, B. P. 1984. *Slope Instability*. John Wiley & Sons Ltd, UK.

—— & PRIOR, D. B. (ed.) 1984. *Slope Instability*. John Wiley, Chichester.

BUSCH, W. H. & KELLER, G. H. 1982. Consolidation characteristics of sediments from the Peru–Chile continental-margin and implications for past sediment instability. *Marine Geology*, **45**, 17–39.

CHANDLER, G. T. & FLEEGER, J. W. 1984. Tube-building by a marine meiobenthic harpacticoid copepod. *Marine Biology*, **82**, 15–19.

CHANDLER, R. J. (ed.) 1991. *Slope Stability Engineering: Development & Applications*. Thomas Telford Ltd, London.

COCHONAT, P., BOURILLET, J. F., SAVOYE, B. & DODD, L. 1993. Geotechnical characteristics and instability of submarine slope sediments, the Nice slope (N–W Mediterranean Sea). *Marine Georesources and Geotechnology*, **11**, 131–151.

COLEMAN, J. M. & GARRISO, L. E. 1977. Geological aspects of marine slope stability, Northwestern Gulf of Mexico. *Marine Geotechnology*, **2**, 9–45.

CRAIG, R. F. 1992. *Soil Mechanics* (5th edn). Chapman & Hall, London, UK.

DADE, W. B., DAVIS, J. D., NICHOLS, P. D., NOWELL, A. R. M., THISTLE, D., TREXLER, M. B. & WHITE, D. C. 1990. Effects of bacterial exopolymer adhesion on the entrainment of sand. *Geomicrobiology Journal*, **8**, 1–16.

DAPPLES, E. C. 1942. The effects of microorganisms upon near shore marine sediments. *Journal of Sedimentary Petrology*, **12**, 118–126.

DUPERRET, A., BOURGOIS, J., LAGABRIELLE, Y. & SUESS, E. 1995. Slope instabilities at an active continental margin: Large-scale polyphase submarine slides along the northern Peruvian margin, between 5° and 6°S. *Marine Geology*, **122**, 303–328.

FORSTER, S. M. & NICOLSON, T. II. 1981a. Aggregation of sand from a maritime embryo sand dune by microorganisms and higher plants. *Soil Biology Biochemistry*, **13** 199–203.

—— 1981b. Microbial aggregation of sand in a maritime dune succession. *Soil Biology Biochemistry*, **13**, 205–208.

GERDOL, V. & HUGHES, R. G. 1994. Effect of *Corophium volutator* on the abundance of benthic diatoms, bacteria and sediment stability in two estuaries in South-eastern England. *Marine Ecology Progress Series*, **114**, 109–115.

GINSBURG, R. N. & LOWENSTAM, H. A. 1958. The influence of marine bottom communities on the depositional environment of sediments. *Journal of Geology*, **66**, 310–318.

GRAY, D. H. & LEISER, A. T. 1982. *Biotechnical Slope Protection and Erosion Control*. Van Nostrand Reinhold, New York.

HECKER, B. 1982. Possible benthic fauna and slope instability relationships. *In:* SAXOV, S. & MIEUWENHUIS, J. K. (eds) *Marine Slides and other Mass Movements*. Plenum Press, New York, 335–345.

HOLLAND, A. F., ZINGMARK, R. G. & DEAN, J. M. 1974. Quantitative evidence concerning the stabilisation of sediments by marine benthic diatoms. *Marine Biology*, **27** 191–196.

JONES, S. E. & JAGO. 1993. *In situ* assessment of modification of sediment properties by burrowing invertebrates. *Marine Biology*, **115**, 133–142.

LAMBE, W. T. & WHITMAN, R. V. 1979. *Soil Mechanics*. SI Version. John Wiley & Sons, New York.

LEE, I. K., WHITE, W. & INGLES, O. G. 1983. *Geotechnical Engineering*. Pitman Publishing Inc. Massachusetts, USA.

LEE, H. J., CHUN, S. S., YOON, S. H. & KIM, S. R. 1993. Slope stability and geotechnical properties of sediment of the Southern margin of Ulleung basin, East Sea (Sea of Japan). *Marine Geology*, **110**, 31–45.

LUCKENBACH, M. W. 1986. Sediment stability around animal tubes: the roles of hydrodynamic processes and biotic activity. *Limnology and Oceanography*, **3**, 779–787.

MADSEN, K. N., NILSSON, P. & SUNDBACK, K. 1993. The influence of benthic microalgae on the stability of a subtidal sediment. *Journal of Experimental Marine Biology and Ecology*, **170**, 159–177.

MCCARTHY, D. F. 1993. *Essentials of Soil Mechanics and Foundations* (4th edn). Prentice Hall Carer & Technology, New York.

MEADOWS, P. S. & TUFAIL, A. 1986. Bioturbation, microbial activity and sediment properties in an estuarine ecosystem. *Proceeding of The Royal Society of Edinburgh*, **90B**, 129–142.

—— & TAIT, J. 1989. Modification of sediment permeability and shear strength by two burrowing invertebrates. *Marine Biology*, **101**, 75–82.

——, —— & HUSSAIN, S. A. 1990. Effects of estuarine infauna on sediment stability and particle sedimentation. *Hydrobiologia*, **190**, 263–266.

—— & MEADOWS, A. 1991. The geotechnical and geochemical implications of bioturbation in marine sedimentary ecosystems. *In:* MEADOWS, P. S. & MEADOWS, A. (eds) *The Environmental Impact of Burrowing Animals and Animal Burrows*. Zoological Society of London Symposia. Clarendon Press, Oxford, **63**, 157–181.

—— & ——1994. Bioturbation in deep-sea Pacific sediments. *Journal of the Geological Society of London*, **151**, 361–375.

——, ——, WOOD, D. M. & MURRAY, J. M. H. 1994. Microbiological effects on slope stability: an experimental analysis. *Sedimentology*, **41**, 423–435.

——, REICHELT, A. C., MEADOWS, A. & WATERWORTH, J. S. 1994. Microbial and meiofaunal abundance, redox potential, pH and shear-strength profiles in deep-sea Pacific sediments. *Journal of The Geological Society of London*, **151**, 377–390.

MEHTA, A. J. & RAO, P. V. 1985. Angle of repose of selected bivalve shell beds. *Journal of Coastal Research*, **1**, 365–374.

MITCHENER, H. J. & DAMGAARD, J. S. 1997. *Erosion of dry areas: recession experiments under current-only conditions*. HR Wallingford Ltd, Oxford. Report TR 23.

MUIR WOOD, D., MEADOWS, P. S. & TUFAIL, A. 1990. Biological strengthening of marine sediments. *In:* HOWSAM, P. (ed.) *Microbiology in Civil Engineering*. Chapman and Hall, UK, 306–316.

——, MEADOWS, A., MEADOWS, P. S. & MURRAY, J. M. H. 1994. Effect of fungal and bacterial colonies on slope stability. *In:* BARKER, D. H. (ed.) *Vegetation and Slopes – Stabilisation, Protection and Ecology*. Institution of Civil Engineers, Thomas Telford, London, 46–51.

NASH, D. 1987. A comparative review of limit equilibrium methods of stability analysis. *In:* ANDERSON, M. G. & RICHARDS, K. S. (eds) *Slope Stability*. John Wiley, Chichester, 11–75.

PATERSON, D. M. 1987. Sediment stabilisation by diatoms in the field: fact or fiction. Abstract of paper read at the winter meeting at the University of Durham. *British Phycological Journal*, **22**, 309.

——1989. Short-term changes in the erodability of intertidal cohesive sediments related to the migratory behaviour of epipelic diatoms. *Limnology and Oceanography*, **34**, 223–234.

—— & DABORN, G. R. 1991. Sediment stabilisation by biological action: significance for coastal engineering. *In:* PEREGRINE, D. H. & LOVELESS, J. H. (eds) *Developments in Coastal Engineering*. University of Bristol, Bristol, 111–119.

PENDER, G., MEADOWS, P. S. & TAIT, J. 1994. Biological impact on sediment processes in the coastal zone. *Proceedings of The Institution of Civil Engineers-Water Maritime and Energy*, **106**, 53–60.

PERLA, R. I. & MARTINELLI, M, JR 1976. *Avalanche Hand Book*. US Department Of Agriculture Forest Service, Washington.

PIPER, D. J. W., SHOR, A. N., FARRE, J. A., O'CONNELL, S. & JACOBI, R. 1985. Sediment slides and turbidity currents on the laurentian fanside scan sonar investigations near the epicentre of the 1929 Grand banks earthquake. *Geology*, **8**, 538–541.

PLATT, H. M. & WARWICK, R. M. 1980. The significance of free-living nematodes to the littoral ecosystem. *In:* PRICE, J. H., IRVIN, E. E. G. & FARNHAM, W. F. (eds) *The Shore Environment 2. Ecosystems*. Academic Press. Systematics Association Special Volume, **17**, 729–759.

RIECHELT, A. C. 1991. Environmental effects of meiofaunal burrowing. *In*: MEADOWS, P. S. & MEADOWS, A. (eds) *The Environmental Impact of Burrowing Animals and Animal Burrows*. Symposium of the Zoological Society of London, **63**, 33–52.

RHOADS, D. C., YINGST, J. Y. & ULLMAN, W. J. 1978. Sea floor stability in central Long Island Sound. Part 1. Temporal changes. *In:* WILEY, M. L. (ed.) *Esturine Interactions*. Academic Press, New York, 221–224.

RHOADS, D. C. & BOYER, L. F. 1982. The effects of marine benthos on physical properties of sediments. A successional perspective. *In:* MCCALL, P. L. & TEVESZ, M. J. S. (eds) *Animal–Sediment Relations*. Plenum Press, New York, 3–52.

SCOFFIN, T. P. 1970. The trapping and binding of subtidal carbonate sediments by marine vegetation in Bimini Lagoon, Bahamas. *Journal of Sedimentary Petrology*, **40**, 249–273.

SNEDECOR, G. W. & COCHRAN, W. G. 1980. *Statistical Methods* (7th edn). The Iowa State University Press, Iowa.

TUFAIL, A. 1987. Microbial communities colonising nutrient-enriched sediment. *Hydrobiologia*, **148**, 245–255.

UNDERWOOD, G. J. C. & PATERSON, D. M. 1993. Seasonal-changes in diatom biomass, sediment stability and biogenic stabilization in the Severn estuary. *Journal of the Marine Biological Association of The United Kingdom*, **73**, 871–887.

VAN RHEE, C. & BEZUIJEN, A. 1992. Influence of seepage on stability of sandy slope. *Journal of Geotechnical Engineering*, **118**, 1236–1240.

WARME, J. E., SCANLAND, T. B. & MARSHALL, N. F. 1971. Submarine canyon erosion: contribution of marine rock burrowers. *Science*, **173**, 1127–1129.

Mussels and mussel beds (*Mytilus edulis*) as stabilizers of sedimentary environments in the intertidal zone

PETER S. MEADOWS, AZRA MEADOWS, FRASER J. C. WEST,
PETER S. SHAND & MASROOR A. SHAIKH

*Biosedimentology Unit, Division of Environmental and Evolutionary Biology, IBLS,
Graham Kerr Building, University of Glasgow, Glasgow G12 8QQ, UK*

Abstract: Coastal zone protection of the intertidal zone is of great importance in view of the threats of sea level rise around the globe. Environmentally-friendly methods involving biological control may offer a solution. This paper studies mussels (*Mytilus edulis*) as stabilizers of the intertidal zone because they form beds that armour some intertidal sediments, hence reducing erosion. In field experiments we seeded high energy lower intertidal and low energy upper intertidal environments with isolated mussels and pre-formed clumps of mussels. More animals were lost from the higher energy site. Those that remained were transported landward for significant distances. Clumping protected animal loss at the low energy but not at the high energy site. Gravel placed under mussels improved their stability because mussels attached threads to them. Laboratory experiments show that mussels form clumps by attaching to other mussels, and when available to gravel which has to be at the sediment surface. Flume studies show single mussels decrease the critical erosion velocity of sediment near them. Similar effects are seen in the field at the edge of small mussel beds.

Mussels are common organisms in the intertidal zone attaching to both rocky and sedimentary environments. On sediments they form beds that can range in size from one or two square metres to half a square kilometre (Scott 1896; White 1937; Kuenen 1942; Verwey 1952; Theisen 1968; Seed 1976; Frechette & Bourget 1985). These mussel beds are significant features of intertidal environments around European coasts, and can occur on shorelines that are exposed to high energies as well as in the more sheltered sedimentary environments found in bays and the lower reaches of estuaries (Field 1922; Maas Gesteranus 1942; Havinga 1956; Asmus & Asmus 1991; Svane & Ompi 1993). Furthermore there is a developing interest in the use of environmentally-friendly biological methods of coastline protection as conventional engineering methods become less acceptable in the 21st century.

The main species of bivalve mollusc that forms these beds on European coasts is *Mytilus edulis*. The species forms clumps at the sediment surface by attaching its byssus threads to other mussels, other organisms in the bed, and to larger particles at the surface of the sedimentary column. The development of beds is therefore likely to modify and alter the sedimentary environment by decreasing erosion and hence stabilizing sediment beneath. However, the beds can occasionally be reduced or even destroyed by heavy storms or strong currents (Maas Gesteranus 1942; Baird 1966; Theisen 1968; Dare 1971, 1976). As a result, there has been considerable interest in the biology of the species, especially in the factors affecting byssus thread production and the influence of water currents on mussel attachment and thread strength (Glaus 1968; Harger 1970; Van Winkle 1970; Allen *et al.* 1976; Smeathers & Vincent 1979; Price 1980, 1982; Waite 1983; Young 1983, 1985; Witman & Suchanek 1984; Vincent *et al.* 1988; Meadows & Shand 1989; Lee *et al.* 1990; Shand 1991; Dolmer & Svane 1994). However, there appear to be no studies that attempt to understand the means by which mussel beds form in the field by *in situ* seeding experiments.

The work reported in this paper was stimulated by the observation that small mussel beds of the order of half to one square metre had become established in parts of the lower intertidal and upper intertidal zone on an intertidal bay, Ardmore Bay in the Clyde Estuary, Scotland.

The bay faces westward into the prevailing winds, and there is a clear differentiation on the beach between the lower intertidal area which is a relatively high energy area, and the upper intertidal area that is more sheltered and hence a lower energy area.

Our general objectives were to study naturally seeded groups of mussels on the shore, and their behaviour in the laboratory. We firstly describe field seeding experiments in the bay in the upper and lower intertidal areas which tested the ability of single mussels and groups of mussels to maintain their position on the shore with and without the presence of gravel beneath them as an anchor. We then describe laboratory experiments that investigate the responses of mussels to sand and gravel in terms of the numbers of byssus threads produced, and report the behaviour of sediment around mussels in a flume in terms of its critical erosion velocity.

Materials and methods

Animals and sediment for the field seeding experiment and for laboratory experiment 1 were collected from an intertidal bay, Ardmore Bay, in the Clyde Estuary (Latitude: 55°58′32″N Longitude: 4°41′29″W: British National Grid Reference: NS 321 792). Animals and sediment for laboratory experiments 2 and 3 were collected from an intertidal beach on Loch Long (Latitude: 56°12′15″N Longitude: 4°44′57″W: British

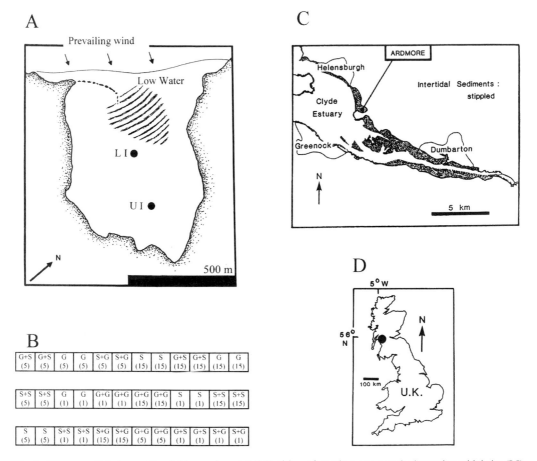

Fig. 1. Diagram of Ardmore Bay field experiment. (**A**) Position of quadrat array at the lower intertidal site (LI) and the upper intertidal site (UI). (**B**) Quadrat array used for both the LI and the UI sites. The diagram is to scale. Each quadrat was one metre square, and there was a one metre strip between each of the three rows of quadrats. 1, 5, 15 = single animals, clumps of five animals, clumps of 15 animals. The notation in (**B**) of G, S, G + G, G + S, S + G, and S + S refers to pre-seeding in the laboratory followed by seeding in the field. G = directly seeded onto gravel in the field. S = directly seeded onto sand in the field. G + G = pre-seeded onto gravel in the laboratory then seeded onto gravel in the field. G + S = pre-seeded onto gravel in the laboratory then seeded onto sand in the field. S + G = pre-seeded onto sand in the laboratory then seeded onto gravel in the field. S + S = pre-seeded onto sand in the laboratory then seeded onto sand in the field. (**C**) Location of Ardmore Bay in the Clyde Estuary. (**D**) Location of the Clyde Estuary in the UK.

National Grid Reference: NN 295 047). The Ardmore bay site was slightly more exposed than the Loch Long site, but apart from that there were no major differences. Sediment (fine sand) was wet sieved through a 500 µm British Standards sieve to remove coarser material. The sediment was stored in sea water until needed. Gravel particles for both the field seeding experiment and laboratory experiment 1 were sieved from coarse sediment collected from a high energy area of Ardmore Bay. Coarse gravel for laboratory experiments 2 and 3 were sieved from sediment from a high energy intertidal area on Loch Long. The particle size of the gravel used in all the experiments was 4–8 mm diameter. This size range was obtained by using an 8 mm and a 4 mm British Standards sieve. In the laboratory, animals were scraped clean of attached organisms, their byssus complexes were cut close to the shells, and they were maintained in clean sea water before use. Animals and sediment were used within four hours of being collected. Gravel was stored dry and then immersed in sea water before use.

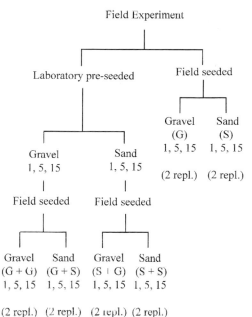

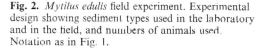

Fig. 2. *Mytilus edulis* field experiment. Experimental design showing sediment types used in the laboratory and in the field, and numbers of animals used. Notation as in Fig. 1.

Design and conduct of field experiment

Animals were seeded into two sites at Ardmore Bay (Fig. 1). These were in the lower intertidal region and the upper intertidal region (Fig. 1A, LI and UI, respectively). The following procedure was used for both the upper intertidal and the lower intertidal sites. Field collected animals were either pre-seeded in the laboratory, or seeded directly back into the field (Fig. 2). One group of animals was seeded directly into the field. These animals were seeded onto gravel that had been placed onto sand in the field (G) or seeded directly onto the field sand (S). A second group of mussels was pre-seeded onto either gravel or sand in the laboratory. The animals pre-seeded in the laboratory were either seeded onto gravel (G + G or S + G) or onto sand (G + S or S + S). They were seeded as individual animals, groups of five animals or groups of 15 animals. The pre-seeded animals in the laboratory were allowed to form clumps for three days and then seeded into the field. Two replicates of each treatment were included. This is illustrated in Fig. 1b.

The single animals and clumps of animals were seeded onto a matrix of quadrats at the upper intertidal site and at the lower intertidal site (Fig. 1b). The animals were marked with a small paint coding unique to each quadrat. The matrix consisted of three rows of twelve 1 m² quadrats whose corners were identified by thin

bamboo sticks. The quadrats to which the laboratory and field seeded mussels were assigned, were determined using random number tables. Replicate quadrats were situated next to each other in the matrix. Gravel was placed in the centre of the appropriate quadrats beforehand. Single animals, clumps of five animals and clumps of 15 animals paint-coded were then placed in the centre of the appropriate quadrats. The bay was visited every three days and measurements taken of numbers of animals lost from each quadrat, distance travelled and the direction in which the mussels had been transported. The experiment was terminated on day 18. This time was chosen because preliminary experiments showed that the most rapid changes in animal movement and animal loss occurred within a week. It would have been interesting to continue the experiment further, but this was not feasible.

Design and conduct of the laboratory experiments

Experiment 1. Nine glass dishes (internal diameter 20 cm, depth 9 cm) were set up, three containing sand (particle size <500 µm), three containing a 1:1 mix of sand + gravel and three containing only gravel (particle size 4–8 mm). The dishes were filled with sea water and then 5 cm depth of the designated sediment was added. Five *M. edulis* were then seeded into each dish and the experiment run for 96 hrs. At the end of the experiment the animals were narcotized and preserved *in situ*, using Propylene Phenoxitol and Steedmans solution, respectively. This enabled accurate counting of the number of threads and the number of stones attached to threads to be subsequently conducted, after the animals with attached particles were removed from the dishes.

Experiment 2. Eight clear perspex tanks (30 × 20 × 20 cm) were filled with sediment (particle size >2 mm) and gravel with combinations of three different layers of gravel. These were as follows, Tank one gravel at 0–1 cm (layer A); Tank two gravel at 3–4 cm (layer B); Tank three gravel at 6–7 cm (layer C); Tank four gravel at 0–1 cm and 3–4 cm (layer A + B); Tank five gravel at 0–1 cm and 6–7 cm (layers A + C); Tank six gravel at 3–4 cm and 6–7 cm (layers B + C); Tank seven gravel at 0–1 cm, 3–4 cm and 6–7 cm (layers A + B + C); Tank eight control tank gravel 15–16 cm layer only. Sea water was added and two mussels were added to each tank (at least 6 cm apart). The experiment was terminated on day 12. At the end of the experiment measurements of numbers of threads and numbers of grains attached to threads were recorded.

Experiment 3. Ten glass dishes (30 cm diameter and 12.5 cm deep) were filled with sediment which had one of five different particle size ranges. The ranges were 2–4 mm (A), 1–2 mm (B), 0.5–1.0 mm (C), 0.25–0.5 mm (D) and <0.25 mm (E). Eight *Mytilus edulis* were added to five of the dishes, the remaining five were control dishes containing no animals. The eight animals were arranged in eight orientations from 0° to 315° at 45° angles. The animals were placed in one of these orientations, chosen using random number tables and positioned with a one animal width spacing. Tanks were filled with sea water and after a 12 day period were placed one at a time into the flume. The tanks had been marked at the 0° point and this was positioned to face upstream. Movement was recorded using video equipment while the flume ran. Velocity profiles were taken along the mid-line of the dish, and 8 cm in front and behind the mid-line. The profiles ranged from the centre, 2, 4 and 8 cm to the left and right sides. Profiles were taken at depths of 0.25, 0.5, 1.0, 2.0, 4.0 and

8.0 cm above the sediment surface at all positions. The design and operation of the flume is described in detail by Girling (1984).

Results

The results are divided into two sections. The first section describes results of the field seeding experiment. In this we demonstrate that the upper intertidal area and lower intertidal area of Ardmore Bay are very different in terms of the distance mussels move, the effects of clump size, the numbers of mussels lost and the attachment of mussels to gravel by byssus threads.

The second section describes results of the three laboratory experiments. These experiments investigate (i) the degree to which mussels attach threads to gravel, gravel and sand, and sand, (ii) whether mussels will attach byssus threads to gravel beneath the sediment surface, and (iii) the effect of different water velocities on erosion of sand around mussels.

Field experiment

The results of the field seeding experiments are shown in Fig. 3 and Tables 1–5. We firstly describe the differential movement of mussels at the upper intertidal and lower intertidal sites, then describe the loss of mussels, and lastly the attachment of mussels to gravel particles.

Transportation of mussels in the field

Figure 3 shows the distances and direction of transportation of mussels in the two environments. It is clear that animals were transported considerably further at the lower intertidal site than at the upper intertidal site (maximum distance: 380 cm, 80 cm, respectively). There was also a strong directional movement at the lower intertidal site, in the direction of the prevailing wind and wave energy (low tide → high tide). In comparison, the movement at the upper intertidal site was essentially random.

Loss of seeded mussels in the field

Tables 1 and 2 document and statistically analyse the loss of the seeded mussels at the end of the 18 day experiment. At the upper intertidal site, fewest animals were lost from clumps of 15 (6%), more from clumps of five (15%) and most from

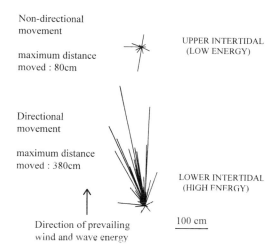

HIGH TIDE

Non-directional
movement

maximum distance
moved : 80cm

UPPER INTERTIDAL
(LOW ENERGY)

Directional
movement

maximum distance
moved : 380cm

LOWER INTERTIDAL
(HIGH ENERGY)

100 cm

Direction of prevailing
wind and wave energy

LOW TIDE

Fig. 3. *Mytilus edulis* field experiment. Distances and direction of transportation of *Mytilus edulis* showing the contrast between the upper and lower intertidal sites.

single animals (42%). This difference was significantly different ($\chi^2 = 18.19***$). At the lower intertidal site there was no significant difference (Table 1 rows 4–6. 67%, 77%, 84%, $\chi^2 = 3.337$). We then compared the numbers of animals lost at the upper intertidal and lower intertidal sites. Clumps of 15 animals and five animals lose more animals at the lower intertidal than at upper intertidal site (Table 1: 84%/6%, $\chi^2 = 220***$, 77%/15%, $\chi^2 = 45.95***$).

Effect of gravel on mussel loss. Table 2 compares the loss of animals that had been previously exposed to gravel in the laboratory then seeded onto either gravel or sand in the field (G + G, or G + S), animals previously seeded onto sand in the laboratory then on to either gravel or sand in the field (S + G or S + S), and animals seeded directly onto gravel or sand in the field (G or S).

The χ^2 analyses in Table 2 shows clearly that at both the upper and lower intertidal sites, animals exposed to gravel in the laboratory before seeding lost significantly fewer animals than those exposed to sand in the laboratory beforehand, or those directly seeded into the

field (Table 2: UI: 2% compared with 14% and 13%, $2 \times 3\chi^2 = 8.08*$; LI: 6% compared with 31% and 19%, $2 \times 3\chi^2 = 17.31***$). The $2 \times 2\chi^2$ in Table 2 substantiates this conclusion.

Loss and gain of gravel particles by seeded animals in the field

Tables 3–5 document the loss and gain of gravel particles by the end of the 18 day experiment, and assess by χ^2 any differences between numbers lost from different size clumps and from the upper intertidal and lower intertidal sites. Clumps of animals seeded onto gravel in the field picked up significant numbers of gravel particles (Table 3 column 10), clumps of 15 animals picking up the greatest number. Animals at the lower intertidal site, whether single animals, clumps of five animals or clumps of fifteen animals, picked up significantly fewer particles of gravel than those at the upper intertidal site, ($1 \times 2\chi^2$s on an upper intertidal/lower intertidal comparison: one animal $\chi^2 = 30.0$, $P < 0.001***$; five animals $\chi^2 = 32.00$, $P < 0.001***$; 15 animals $\chi^2 = 266.5***$, $P < 0.001$ table not presented). These statements were also true for animals seeded onto sand in the laboratory. Animals seeded directly onto sand in the field (Table 3 column 11) and pre-seeded onto sand in the laboratory then seeded onto sand in the field (Table 3 columns 8 and 9) picked up virtually no particles of gravel size.

G + G and G + S animals. Comparisons between single animals, clumps of five animals and clumps of 15 animals. We then considered the animals pre-seeded onto gravel in the laboratory and then seeded in the field onto either gravel (G + G) or sand (G + S) (Table 3 columns 1–4). At both the upper and lower intertidal sites there were significant differences in the numbers of grains remaining attached to the animals between the different clump sizes. Clumps of 15 animals had the largest number of gravel particles followed by clumps of five animals with the single animals having the least (Table 3 columns 1–4). This was obvious at both the upper and lower intertidal sites. The data was then analysed by $2 \times 3\chi^2$s comparing the numbers of gravel particles before and after field seeding for the numbers of the single animals, five animals and 15 animals. These χ^2s were applied to the G + G data at the upper intertidal site, the G + G data at the lower intertidal site, the G + S data at the upper intertidal site and the G + S data at the lower

Table 1(a). Mytilus edulis *field experiment. Numbers of mussels lost at the upper and lower intertidal sites. Effect of clump size (1 animal, 5 animals, and 15 animals)*

	Clump size		
	1 animal	5 animals	15 animals
Upper intertidal site			
Remaining	7	51	169
Lost	5 (42%)	9 (15%)	11 (6%)
Total	12	60	180
Lower intertidal site			
Remaining	4	14	29
Lost	8 (67%)	46 (77%)	151 (84%)
Total	12	60	180

Significant probabilities in statistical tests are asterisked in this and all subsequent tables as follows: $0.05 > P > 0.001*$; $0.001 > P > 0.001**$; $P < 0.001***$. All unasterisked probabilities are not significant.

Table 1(b). *Statistical analysis of data by* χ^2

		χ^2	d.f.	P
UI site	R/L vs 1/5/15	18.19	2	$P < 0.001***$
LI site	R/L vs 1/5/15	3.337	2	$0.20 > P > 0.10$
Single animals	R/L vs UI/LI	1.510	1	$0.30 > P > 0.20$
Clumps of 5	R/L vs UI/LI	45.95	1	$P < 0.001***$
Clumps of 15	R/L vs UI/LI	220.0	1	$P < 0.001***$

R/L = numbers remaining/numbers lost. d.f. = degrees of freedom. P = probability. UI = Upper intertidal site. LI = Lower intertidal site.

intertidal site (Table 3 columns 1–4). All four χ^2s were statistically significant (Table 4). This means that the proportion of gravel particles being lost or gained in each of the four categories differed between single animals, five animals and 15 animals. We have expressed this as a percentage of the gravel particles before and after field seeding (Table 3). In all four cases single animals lose gravel particles in the field (83%, 53%, 47%, 74%). Most of the clumps of five animals lose gravel particles in the field (162%, 56%, 68%, 65%), and all of the clumps of 15 animals gain gravel particles (221%, 228%, 117%, 137%).

Comparisons between G + G and G + S animals. A further set of χ^2s were applied to the data. These $2 \times 2\chi^2$s tested whether there was any difference in the number of gravel particles lost or gained by G + G and G + S animals. The χ^2s were applied to the single animals at the upper and lower intertidal sites and the clumps of five animals and fifteen animals at the upper and lower intertidal sites (Table 5). Neither of the single animal χ^2s were significant, and one of

the two five-animal clump χ^2s was significant. These mean that clumps of five animals at the upper intertidal site gain gravel if seeded onto gravel, and lose gravel if seeded onto sand (162%, 68%). Both the 15-animal χ^2s were highly significant. This means that at both the upper intertidal site and at the lower intertidal site clumps of 15 animals gain more gravel if they are seeded onto gravel than if they are seeded onto sand (UI: 221%, 117%; LI: 228%, 137%).

G + G and G + S animals. Differences between the upper and lower intertidal sites. The last set of χ^2s applied to the same data consisted of six $2 \times 2\chi^2$s comparing the number of grains before and after field seeding at both the upper and lower intertidal sites. These χ^2s were applied to single animals, clumps of animals and clumps of 15 animals, pre-seeded onto gravel in the laboratory then seeded onto gravel in the field, and pre-seeded onto gravel in the laboratory then onto sand in the field. The results of this analysis are not quoted here. Only one of these χ^2s was significant (clumps of five animals G + G: 162% (UI), 56% (LI)). This means that except in this

Table 2(a). Mytilus edulis *field experiment. Numbers of mussels lost at the upper and lower intertidal sites. Effect of presence or absence of gravel (1 animal, 5 animals and 15 animals)*

	Gravel treatment		
	G + G and G + S	S + G and S + S	G and S
Upper intertidal site			
Remaining	82	72	73
Lost	2 (2%)	12 (14%)	11 (13%)
Total	84	84	84
Lower intertidal site			
Remaining	79	58	68
Lost	5 (6%)	26 (31%)	16 (19%)
Total	84	84	84

G + G and G + S = laboratory gravel then field gravel and laboratory gravel then field sand.
S + G and S + S = laboratory sand then field gravel and laboratory sand then field sand.
G and S = field gravel and field sand.

Table 2(b). Mytilus edulis *field experiment. Statistical analysis of data by* χ^2

	χ^2	d.f.	P
Upper intertidal site			
R/L vs G + G and S + S/S + G and S + S/G and S	8.082	2	0.05 > P > 0.01*
R/L vs G + G and S + S/S + G and S + S	7.792	1	0.01 > P > 0.001**
R/L vs S + G and S + S/G, S	0.050	1	0.9 > P > 0.8
R/L vs G + G and G + S/G and S	6.753	1	0.01 > P > 0.001**
Lower intertidal site			
R/L vs G + G and S + S/S + G and S + S/G and S	17.31	2	P < 0.001***
R/L vs G + G and G + S/S + G and S + S	17.45	1	P < 0.001***
R/L vs S + G and S + S/G and S	3.175	1	0.10 > P > 0.05
R/L vs G + G and S + S/G and S	6.585	1	0.05 > P > 0.01*

R/L = numbers remaining/numbers lost. d.f. = degrees of freedom. P = probability. Other notations as above.

case there is no significant difference between the losses or gains of gravel at both the upper intertidal and lower intertidal sites for animals which had been pre-seeded onto gravel in the laboratory. Specifically for the single animals 83% (UI) is not different from 53% (LI), and 47% (UI) is not different from 74% (LI). For the clumps of five animals 68% (UI) is not different from 65% (LI), and for the 15-animal clumps 221% (UI) is not different from 228% (LI), and 117% (UI) is not different from 137% (LI).

Laboratory experiments

Experiment 1

The results of the experiments shown in Fig. 4, and analysed in Table 6, show that there are highly significant differences in the pattern of thread production by the animals on sand, sand + gravel and gravel. The following statements are based on the four one-way analyses of variance in Table 6 all of which were statistically significant. The lowest number of threads was produced by animals on sand, intermediate numbers by animals on sand + gravel mix and highest numbers on gravel, (Fig. 4a and Table 6: $F = 17.08$, $0.01 > P > 0.001$**).

Animals attached the greatest number of threads to shells when on sand, fewer on sand + gravel and fewest on gravel (Fig. 4b and Table 6: $F = 5.69$, $0.05 > P > 0.01$*). More threads were attached to gravel than on sand + gravel and no threads were attached to sand (Fig. 4C and Table 6: $F = 75.38$, $P < 0.001$). The same is true for grains attached to threads (Fig. 4D and Table 6: $F = 81.14$, $P < 0.001$).

Table 3. Mytilus edulis *field experiment. Numbers of grains before and after an eighteen day field seeding period. Percentages calculated as (After/Before) × 100*

| | Prior laboratory clumping followed by field seeding | | | | | | | | Field seeding | |
| | Lab gravel then field gravel (G + G) | | Lab gravel then field sand (G + S) | | Lab sand then field gravel (S + G) | | Lab sand then field sand (S + S) | | Field gravel (G) | Field sand (S) |
	Before	After	Before	After	Before	After	Before	After	After	After
Upper intertidal site										
1 animal	36	30 (83%)	43	20 (47%)	0	11	0	0	30	0
5 animals	50	81 (162%)	47	32 (68%)	0	105	0	0	45	8
15 animals	146	322 (221%)	163	191 (117%)	0	208	0	3	425	1
Lower intertidal site										
1 animal	32	17 (53%)	46	34 (74%)	0	5	0	0	0	0
5 animals	66	37 (56%)	62	40 (65%)	0	39	0	0	5	0
15 animals	134	306 (228%)	114	156 (137%)	0	117	0	0	64	0

Table 4. Mytilus edulis *field experiment. Statistical analyses of differences in number of gravel particles lost or gained by 1 animal, clumps of 5 animals and clumps of 15 animals*

Comparison	χ^2	d.f.	P
Upper intertidal site			
G + G			
B/A vs 1/5/15	14.66	2	$P < 0.001$***
G + S			
B/A vs 1/5/15	13.26	2	$0.01 > P > 0.001$**
Lower intertidal site			
G + G			
B/A vs 1/5/15	54.88	2	$P < 0.001$***
G + S			
B/A vs 1/5/15	12.94	2	$0.01 > P > 0.001$**

Chi-square (χ^2) tests. B/A = number of gravel particles attached to mussels after laboratory clumping prior to field seeding/number of gravel particles attached to mussels at the end of the 18 day field seeding. 1/5/15 = 1 animal/5 animals/15 animals. d.f. = degrees of freedom and P = probability.

Experiment 2

The results of this experiment are shown in Table 7 and analysed in Table 8. It is clear from Table 7 that single animals only attach to gravel particles when they are in the top layer, whether or not there are gravel particles beneath the surface as well (Table 7 tanks 1, 4, 5 and 7).

They do not attach threads to gravel particles below the surface even though there are no gravel particles at the surface (Table 7 tanks 2, 3 and 6). Animals attached virtually no threads in the control sediment (Table 7 tank 8) that contained no gravel particles. Table 8 shows the number of threads per animal (mean ± SD = 31.13 ± 11.09), the number of gravel particles per

Table 5. Mytilus edulis *field experiment. Statistical analyses of differences at the upper and lower intertidal sites for number of gravel particles lost or gained by clumps of 1 animal, 5 animals and 15 animals*

Data	Comparison	χ^2	d.f.	P
1 animal UI	B/A vs G + G and G + S	2.552	1	$0.20 > P > 0.10$
1 animal LI	B/A vs G + G and G + S	0.775	1	$0.50 > P > 0.30$
5 animals UI	B/A vs G + G and G + S	9.017	1	$0.01 > P > 0.001$**
5 animals LI	B/A vs G + G and G + S	0.237	1	$0.70 > P > 0.50$
15 animals UI	B/A vs G + G and G + S	18.94	1	$P < 0.001$***
15 animals LI	B/A vs G + G and G + S	10.19	1	$P < 0.001$***

Chi-square (χ^2) tests. UI = upper intertidal site. LI = Lower intertidal site. B/A — numbers of gravel particles attached to mussels at the end of the prior laboratory clumping/numbers of gravel particles attached to mussels at the end of the 18 day field seeding.
G + G = laboratory gravel then field gravel, G + S = laboratory gravel then field sand, d.f. = degrees of freedom and P = probability.

animal (mean ± SD = 5.625 ± 2.264) and the number of threads per gravel particle (mean-± SD = 6.237 ± 3.089), for the animals in tanks 1, 4, 5 and 7 Inspection of the data in the table indicates that there were no significant differences in any of these variables between the four tanks. This is substantiated by the three non-significant one-way analyses of variance in the lower half of Table 8.

Experiment 3

The results for experiment 3 are shown and statistically analysed in Table 9. The table shows firstly that tanks containing sediment of a smaller particle size (Table 9 rows 6–9 C and D) show decreased critical erosion velocities except for the finest particle size. This is to be

expected. In general finer sediments erode at lower velocities, except where cohesion is present in very fine grained sediments. The table also shows that tanks with animals show decreased critical erosion velocities compared to their control tanks. The statistical analyses of the data by Student's t-tests showed that in all cases the comparison between the control tanks and the tanks containing animals were significant (A: $t = 6.112$***), (B: $t = 13.51$***), (C: $t = 14.54$***) and (D: $t = 19.45$***), (Table 9 columns 4 and 6). The calculated mean bed shear stresses paralleled the critical erosion velocities. They ranged from 6.290×10^{-3} kPa to 1.851×10^{-3} kPa.

An inspection of the critical erosion velocity data showed that the presence of mussels in the water flow produced erratic velocity profiles which we interpret as being caused by increased

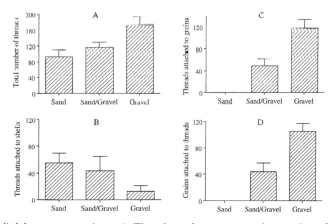

Fig. 4. *Mytilus edulis* laboratory experiment 1. Thread attachment onto various surfaces for three distinct substrates, Sand, Sand + Gravel mix and Gravel. (**A**) Total number of threads attached, (**B**) number of threads attached to shells, (**C**) number of threads attached to grains, (**D**) number of grains attached to threads.

Table 6. *Laboratory experiment 1. Groups of five* Mytilus edulis. *One-way analyses of variance comparing the numbers of threads attached to different surfaces for three types of sediment*

Comparison	Source of variation	d.f.	Sum of squares	Mean squares	F	P
Total number of threads	S/SG/G	2	10 156	5 078	17.08	$0.01 > P > 0.001$**
	Error	6	1 784	297		
	Total	8	11 940			
Threads to shells	S/SG/G	2	2 918	1 459	5.69	$0.05 > P > 0.01$*
	Error	6	1 539	257		
	Total	8	4 457			
Threads to grains	S/SG/G	2	21 073	10 536	75.38	$P < 0.001$***
	Error	6	839	140		
	Total	8	21 912			
Grains to threads	S/SG/G	2	16 805	8 402	81.14	$P < 0.001$***
	Error	6	621	104		
	Total	8	17 426			

S/SG/G = sand/sand plus gravel mix/gravel. d.f. = degrees of freedom. F = variance ratio and P = probability.

turbulence. A representative series of profiles are shown in Fig. 5. We also noted the development of characteristic trough and ripple bed forms immediately adjacent to the mussels at higher water velocities ($0.33 \, \mathrm{ms}^{-2}$). Samples of sediment from these troughs and ripples showed that when compared with control sediment, the sediment from troughs on either side of the animals and especially sediment that built up behind animals, had a coarser particle size distribution (Fig. 6). The presence of mussels therefore makes the surface sediment in their

Table 7. *Laboratory experiment 2. Single* Mytilus edulis. *Number of byssus threads attached to gravel particles at different depths in experimental tanks with gravel present or not present at each depth*

Tank	Animal	Gravel layer present	Number of byssus threads attached to gravel particles		
			0–2 cm	2–5 cm	5–8 cm
1	1	a	33	0	0
	2		37	0	0
2	1	b	0	0	0
	2		0	0	0
3	1	c	0	0	0
	2		0	0	0
4	1	a + b	15	0	0
	2		47	0	0
5	1	a + c	38	0	0
	2		31	0	0
6	1	b + c	2	0	0
	2		0	4	0
7	1	a + b + c	33	0	0
	2		15	0	0
8	1	control	0	0	0
	2		0	4	0

Gravel layers (a) = 0–1 cm, (b) = 3–4 cm, (c) = 6–7 cm and control = 15–16 cm only.

Table 8(a). *Laboratory experiment 2. Single* Mytilus cdulis *laboratory experiment. Numbers of threads/animal, gravel particles/animal and threads/gravel particle, in tanks 1, 4, 5 and 7*

Tank	Animal	Number of threads/animal	Number of particles/animal	Number of threads/particle
1	1	33	5	6.60
	2	37	7	5.286
4	1	15	3	5.000
	2	47	9	5.222
5	1	38	3	12.67
	2	31	4	7.750
7	1	33	6	5.500
	2	15	8	1.875
mean ± s.d.		31.13 ± 11.09	5.625 ± 2.264	6.237 ± 3.089

Table 8(b). *Single* Mytilus edulis *laboratory experiment. Statistical analyses of above data by three one-way analyses of variance comparing the number of threads per animal, the number of gravel particles per animal and the numbers of threads per particle between tanks 1, 4, 5 and 7*

Comparison	Source of variation	d.f.	Sum of squares	Mean squares	F	P
Threads per animal	Factor	3	154.00	51.00	0.29	$P > 0.75$
	Error	4	706.00	177.00		
	Total	7	861.00			
Particles per animal	Factor	3	13.38	4.46	0.79	$0.75 > P > 0.50$
	Error	4	22.50	5.63		
	Total	7	35.88			
Threads per particle	Factor	3	47.28	15.76	3.22	$0.25 > P > 0.10$
	Error	4	19.56	4.89		
	Total	7	66.84			

vicinity coarser. This is presumably caused by a winnowing effect produced by turbulent eddies around and behind animals.

Discussion

Mussel beds are known to form in a wide range of intertidal environments in the coastal zone, ranging from sheltered estuarine conditions to relatively high energy sandy shores on open coastlines. In fact, it is unusual to find isolated individuals unless they are dead. The mechanisms by which these beds form, are maintained and periodically destroyed, are therefore of considerable importance. This is particularly topical in view of the potential significance of mussel beds as an environmentally-friendly shoreline protection device. In this paper we have investigated various aspects of the behaviour of mussels in the laboratory and in the field and the way in which these behaviours are modified by contrasting high energy and low energy environments.

A number of authors have studied the behaviour of *Mytilus edulis* in relation to the formation and strength of byssus threads under field and laboratory conditions, and these are relevant to our own results. Animals form threads quickly both in the laboratory and in the field. Typically, animals can produce anything from 5 to 40 threads per day (Allen *et al.* 1976; Meadows & Shand 1989; Dolmer & Svane 1994; personal observations of authors). The rate of production is affected by animal size, salinity, oxygen and temperature (Reish & Ayers 1968; Allen *et al.* 1976). Our own observations show that the species can attach its first thread within an hour of being placed in a new environment, either in the laboratory or in the field. Byssus threads are then continuously produced, thus increasing the strength of attachment of the animal to the substrate as time progresses. However, older threads are weaker than those more recently formed (Price 1981) and thus will contribute less to the overall strength of the attachment. Byssus thread complexes are also periodically shed, and new

Table 9. Mytilus edulis *laboratory experiment 3. Groups of eight single animals. Critical erosion velocities and mean bed shear stress in tanks with different particle sizes (A, B, C, and D)*

Tank		Critical erosion velocity (ms⁻¹) mean ± s.d.	t	d.f.	P	Mean bed shear stress (kPa)
A	*M. edulis*	0.273 ± 0.007 (94%)	6.112	46	$P < 0.001***$	5.641×10^{-3}
	Control	0.290 ± 0.008				6.290×10^{-3}
B	*M. edulis*	0.165 ± 0.010 (75%)	13.512	46	$P < 0.001***$	2.279×10^{-3}
	Control	0.2200 ± 0.01				3.825×10^{-3}
C	*M. edulis*	0.154 ± 0.008 (77%)	14.539	46	$P < 0.001***$	2.013×10^{-3}
	Control	0.199 ± 0.007				3.193×10^{-3}
D	*M. edulis*	0.147 ± 0.007 (72%)	19.451	46	$P < 0.001***$	1.851×10^{-3}
	Control	0.203 ± 0.007				3.309×10^{-3}

Percentages shown in brackets (*M. edulis*/control × 100). A = 1.0–2.0 mm, B = 0.5–1.0 mm, C = 0.25–0.50 mm, D = <0.25 mm. t = t-test critical value, d.f. = degrees of freedom, P = probability.

complexes produced. The number and strength of byssus threads that animals produce varies in relation to changing environmental conditions. Greater numbers of byssus threads are produced

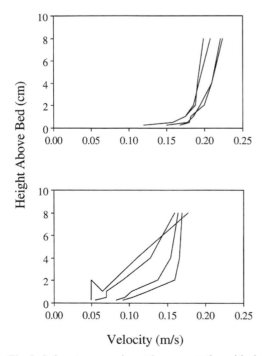

Fig. 5. Laboratory experiment 3 representative critical erosion velocity profiles. Upper graph, control sediment containing no mussels. Lower graph, experimental tank containing mussels. Each of the four lines in each graph represents one run.

in higher water velocities (Glaus 1968; Dolmer & Svane 1994), and the strength of attachment of animals is greater in exposed habitats with greater wave energy than in sheltered habitats (Price 1982; Witman & Suchanek 1984). It is interesting to note in this context that calculations by Smeathers and Vincent (1979) suggest a mussel with 50 byssus threads would be able to resist all but the most severe winter storms. Seasonal variation also occurs. Byssus threads are strongest in summer and autumn, and weakest in winter and spring (Price 1982 p.150 fig. 2). In addition, more threads are produced at higher salinities (Reish & Ayers 1968; Allen *et al.* 1976), and so mussel attachment will be stronger further down an estuary where higher wave action is more common.

The upper and lower intertidal zones on Ardmore Bay are very different in terms of their exposure to wave energy (Tufail *et al.* 1989). This is because the prevailing winds blow directly into the bay from the west. The lower intertidal zone is a relatively high energy area, and the upper intertidal is a relatively low energy area. This is most noticeable with a strong prevailing wind, because white capped waves occur over the lower intertidal zone but are not present in the upper intertidal zone. Figure 3 shows the very marked effect that this difference has on the transport and transport direction of field seeded animals. Over a three-day period animals in the lower intertidal are transported shoreward to a maximum of 3.8 m, while in the upper intertidal animals are transported randomly to a maximum of 0.8 m. These differences in transport are almost certainly caused by the

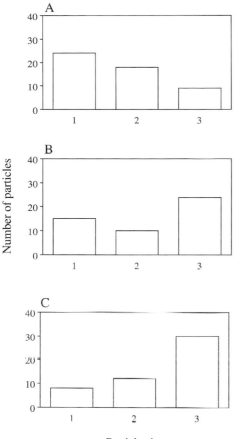

Number of particles

Particle size

Fig. 6. Differential particle size sorting around mussels in a flume. (**a**) Control sediments containing no animals. (**b**) Sediment from troughs beside animals. (**c**) Sediment from just behind animals. Particle size 1: $<100 \mu m$. 2: $100-200 \mu m$. 3: $>200 \mu m$.

different energy regimes and water currents at the two sites. In addition, by the time the experiment was terminated after 18 days considerably more animals were lost at the lower intertidal site (Table 1). In this context it is interesting to note that at the lower intertidal site there was no advantage to be gained from being in a clump. Here, 84%, 77% and 67%, respectively, of animals were lost from clumps of 15, five and single animals. There was no statistically significant difference between these. In contrast, at the upper intertidal site animals gained a significant advantage from being in a clump. Only 6% were lost from clumps of 15 animals compared with 15% from five animals and 42% from single animals. This difference was highly significant. From these results therefore animals

in clumps are protected from being lost in low energy intertidal environments but not in high energy intertidal environments. This result is somewhat surprising.

Animals that attach to larger particles such as gravel in sediments are likely to be less at risk from being washed away. This proved to be the case in our field experiment (Table 2). Animals that had been allowed to attach to gravel in the laboratory before field seeding were less likely to be lost than animals seeded directly into the field onto either sand or gravel. At the upper intertidal site 2% of the former and 14% of the latter were lost. The equivalent percentages at the lower intertidal site were 6% and 31%.

We also analysed the number of gravel particles lost or gained by animals during the field experiment (Tables 3–5). In general, single animals and clumps of five animals lost significant numbers of gravel particles while clumps of 15 animals gained significant numbers of gravel particles. Clumps of 15 animals gained gravel particles at both the upper and lower intertidal sites. This is interesting because more animals are lost from clumps of 15 animals at the lower intertidal site than at the upper intertidal site. The animals which survive at the lower intertidal site never-the less increase the number of gravel particles which they pick up, to the same degree as the larger numbers of animals at the upper intertidal site. Perhaps the higher energy environment at the lower intertidal site stimulates the animals to seek more frequently for gravel particles which will then provide them with greater anchorage.

We conducted two laboratory experiments under static water conditions to investigate the responses of mussels to gravel and sand, in which the gravel was both at the surface of the sediment and below the sediment surface. On sand in the absence of gravel, animals form clumps by attaching byssus threads to other individuals. In the presence of sand + gravel mix or pure gravel, they produce more threads in total while attaching fewer threads to other animals (Fig. 4 and Table 6). We have illustrated these effects in Fig. 7. Animals only attach threads to gravel when the gravel is at the surface, gravel particles in the sedimentary column are not searched for even if they are within 2–5 cm of the sediment surface. These results have important implications for the way that animals behave in the field. Clumps will form on sand but these clumps will be bound together solely by threads attached to animals shells in the clump. Clumps that form onto sand containing gravel or gravel alone will be anchored *in situ* to the sedimentary bed by threads being attached to gravel particles as well as to the shells of the animals themselves. Under field conditions these will have a great adaptive importance. Anchoring is needed mostly in high energy environments, which is where gravel is found.

Our last laboratory experiment investigated the erosion of sediment around animals in a flume. Surprisingly, our results show that the presence of isolated mussels tends to increase erosion over a range of particle sizes (Table 9). As is to be expected, coarser particle sizes had higher critical erosion velocities and higher mean bed shear stresses. However, in each of the four particle size ranges tested the presence of animals decreased the critical erosion velocity and mean bed shear stress. The velocity profiles with animals present were much more variable than those of control sediments (Fig. 5). This implies that animals cause a localized increase in turbulence. There was also a differential sorting of sediment immediately beside and behind mussels. Fine particles were winnowed out leaving a coarser sediment bed (Fig. 6). This is probably caused by the increase in turbulence. We have observed similar effects on the shore. Patterns of sediment erosion and transport are clearly visible around small mussel beds in the intertidal zone at Ardmore Bay (Fig. 8). Our laboratory results, combined with our qualitative field observations, mean that mussel beds will stabilize sediment underneath them but that there will be an erosional element at their edges.

Conclusions

The intertidal zone is an area of the coastal zone that is becoming progressively more at risk as we approach the 21st century and encounter the potential effects of global warming and sea level rise. As a result there is now a considerable interest in the use of environmentally friendly methods of coastal zone stabilization especially by using populations of naturally occurring living organisms.

The mussel *Mytilus edulis* forms naturally occurring beds at the surface of intertidal sediments that clearly act as barriers to coastal erosion, and also increase biodiversity of the intertidal community by offering additional habitats for invertebrate infauna and macro-algae. It is therefore of great importance to understand the way in which mussel beds form, maintain themselves, and are sometimes destroyed in different intertidal sedimentary ecosystems. In particular we need to establish any differences in behaviour of single and

Mytilus edulis byssus thread production

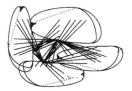

M. edulis on Sand

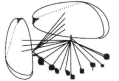

M. edulis on Gravel

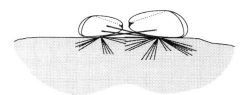

M. edulis on Rock

Fig. 7. *Mytilus edulis* laboratory experiment 1. Various attachment forms of *Mytilus edulis* on different substrates showing differing spatial relationships between animals on different substrates. Animals on sand clump closer and attach threads only to their own shells and other shells. Animals on gravel attach threads to gravel and to shells. Animals on rock attach threads to shells and rock.

clumped mussels when seeded into low and high energy environments, and to understand the erosional environments that are likely to affect the success otherwise of natural seeding programmes. These questions are best answered by combined field and laboratory investigations that attempt to provide a scientific background to the future use of mussels for seeding on a commercial scale, although this would be a major operation.

Our research has been directed towards these ends. We chose an intertidal bay in the Clyde Estuary that offered contrasting low and high

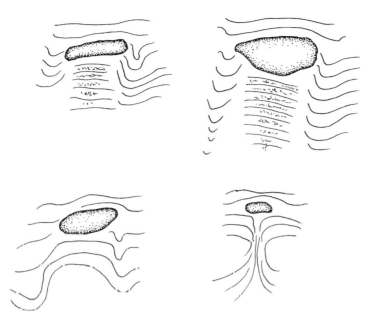

Fig. 8. Erosional wave form patterns from original drawings of mussel beds (stippled islands) made in the field at Ardmore Bay. The largest bed (top right) is *c.* 1.5 m across. The bottom of the figure points towards the low tide region. Note detritus in troughs of waves in upper diagrams

energy environments in the upper intertidal and lower intertidal zone, respectively. We then conducted field seeding experiments at these two sites with single animals, clumps of five animals and clumps of 15 animals. We also tested the effects of allowing the mussels to form clumps on gravel and sand in the laboratory before field seeding. The field seeding showed that animals in the higher energy environment were transported further by water action, and were more likely to be lost. Clumps of animals were less likely to be lost than single animals, and the presence of gravel further reduced losses. Mussels tend to pick up gravel under field conditions, clumps of 15 mussels being most effective in doing this. There were, however, no differences in this tendency between the high energy and low energy sites.

The field experiments were followed by controlled laboratory experiments that tested the ability of mussels to attach to gravel and to sand, and to determine whether animals could attach to gravel below the sediment surface. Mussels formed clumps by attaching byssus threads to each other whether on sand, on a mix of sand and gravel, or on gravel alone. When gravel was present at the sediment surface, mussels always attached byssus threads to gravel particles as well as to each other. This

will clearly have a stabilizing influence in the field. Mussels were unable to attach byssus threads to gravel below the sediment surface. We also investigated the erosion of sediments around mussels in a laboratory flume. Erosion of sediment was more likely to occur when mussels were present, and this erosion has been noticed under field conditions around small mussel beds in the field.

Our field and laboratory experiments taken together show that if field seeding of the intertidal zone is to be attempted on a large scale it will be necessary to do so using specific seeding protocols. It is likely that clumps of mussels will need to be preformed in the laboratory, and that the sediment surface will require the addition of gravel below the clumps before seeding. Clumps that become established in the intertidal zone by seeding will probably induce an element of erosion around their edges, but we do not consider that this will have any major destabilizing influence as it has been noticed around small naturally occurring mussel beds in the intertidal zone.

F. J. C. West wishes to thank his parents for their continued moral support and the Carnegie Trust for the Universities of Scotland for financial support. P. Shand wishes to thank N.E.R.C. for financial support. M. A. Shaikh wishes to thank the Ministry of

Education, Government of Pakistan (EG/2436 1993) and the Committee of Vice-Chancellors and Principals of the Universities of the United Kingdom (CVCP) (ORS/C20/4 1996) for their financial support.

References

ALLEN, J. A., COOK, M., JACKSON, D. J., PRESTON, S. & WORTH, E. M. 1976. Observations on the rate of production and mechanical properties of the byssus threads of *Mytilus edulis* (L.) *Journal of Molluscan Studies*, **42**, 279–289.

ASMUS, R. M. & ASMUS, H. 1991. Mussel beds – limiting or promoting phytoplankton. *Journal of Experimental Marine Biology and Ecology*, **148**, 215–232.

BAIRD, R. H. 1966. Factors affecting the growth and condition of mussels. (*Mytilus edulis*. L.). *Fishery Investigations. Ministry of Agriculture, Food and Fisheries. London*, (Ser. 2), **25**(2), 1–33.

DARE, P. J. 1971. Preliminary studies on the utilisation of the resources of spat mussels, *Mytilis edulis* L. occuring in Morecambe Bay, England. *International Council on the Exploration of the Sea Commitee Meeting* (Shellfish and Benthos Comm.). **K11**, 1–6.

DARE, P. 1976. Settlement, growth and production of the mussel *Mytilus edulis* L. in Morecambe Bay. *Fishery Investigations. Ministry of Agriculture, Food and Fisheries. London*, (Ser. 2), **28**, 1–25.

DOLMER, P. & SVANE, I. 1994. Attachment and orientation of *Mytilus edulis* (L.) in flowing water. *Ophelia*, **40**, 63–74.

FIELD, J. A. 1922. Biology and economic importance of the sea mussel, *Mytilus edulis*. *Bulletin of the Bureau of Fisheries. Washington*, **38**, 127–260.

FRECHETTE, M. & BOURGET, E. 1985. Energy flow between the pelagic and benthic zones: Factors controlling particulate organic matter available to an intertidal mussel bed. *Canadian Journal of Fisheries and Aquatic Science*, **42**, 1158–1165.

GIRLING, A. E. 1984. *Interactions between marine benthic macroinvertebrates and their sedimentary environment*. PhD Thesis, University of Glasgow.

GLAUS, K. J. 1968. Factors influencing the production of byssus threads in *Mytilis edulis*. *Biological Bulletin. Marine Biological Laboratory, Woods Hole, Mass*, **135**, 420.

HARGER, J. R. E. 1970. The effect of wave impact on some aspects of the biology of sea mussels. *Veliger*, **12**, 401–414.

HAVINGA, B. 1956. Mussel culture in the Dutch Wadden sea. *Rapport et procés-verbaux des réunions. Conseil permanent international pour l'exploration de la mer. Coppenhague*, **140**, 5–6.

KUENEN, D. J. 1942. On the distribution of mussels on the intertidal sand flats near Den Helder . *Archives néerldaises de Zoology*, **6**, 8–158.

LEE, C. Y., LIM, S. S. L. & OWEN, M. D. 1990. The rate and strength of byssal reattachment by blue mussels (*Mytilus edulis* L.). *Canadian Journal of Zoology*, **68**, 2005–2009.

MAAS GESTERANUS, R. A. 1942. On the formation of banks by *Mytilus edulis*. L. *Archives néerldaises de Zoology*, **6**, 283–326.

MEADOWS, P. S. & SHAND, P. 1989. Experimental analysis of byssus thread production by *Mytilus edulis* and *Modiolus modiolus* in sediments. *Marine Biology*, **101**, 219–226.

PRICE, H. A. 1980. Seasonal variation in the strength of byssal attachment of the common mussel *Mytilus edulis* (L.). *Journal of the Marine Biological Association of the United Kingdom*, **60**, 1035–1037.

—— 1981. Byssus thread strength in the mussel, *Mytilus edulis*. *Journal of Zoology, London*, **194**, 245–255.

—— 1982 An analysis of the factors determining seasonal variation in the byssal attachment strength of *Mytilus edulis* (L.) *Journal of the Marine Biological Association of the United Kingdom*, **62**, 147–155.

REISH, D. J. & AYERS, J. L. JR. 1968. Studies on the *Mytilus edulis* community in Alamitos Bay, California. III. The effects of reduced dissolved oxygen and chlorinity concentrations on survival and byssus thread formation. *Veliger*, **10**, 384–388.

SCOTT, A. 1896. Mussels and mussel beds. *Report of the Lancashire Sea-Fish Labs*, 21–32.

SEED, R. 1976. Ecology. *In*: BAYNE, B. L. (ed.) *Marine Mussels*. Cambridge University Press, Cambridge, 13–65.

SHAND, P. 1991. Sediment movement around mussels flume experiments on critical erosion velocities and sorting. *In*: MEADOWS, P. S. & MEADOWS, A. (eds) *The Environmental Impact of Burrowing Animals and Animal Burrows*. Symposium of the Zoological Society of London, **63**, 313–316.

SMEATHERS, J. E. & VINCENT, J. F. V. 1979. Mechanical properties of mussel byssus threads. *Journal of Molluscan Studies*, **45**, 219–230.

SVANE, I. & OMPI, M. 1993. Patch dynamics in beds of the blue mussel *Mytilus edulis* L.: effects of site, patch size, and position within a patch. *Ophelia*, **37**, 187–202.

THEISEN, B. F. 1968. Growth and mortality of culture mussels in the Danish Wadden Sea. *Meddelelser fra Danmarks Fiskeri -og Havundersøgelser (New Series)*, **6**, 47–78.

TUFAIL, A., MEADOWS, P. S. & MCLAUGHLIN. 1989. Meso- and microscale hetrogeneity in benthic community structure and the sedimentary environment on an intertidal muddy-sand beach. Topics in marine biology. *In*: ROSS, J. D. (ed.) *Scientia Marina*, **53**, 319–327.

VAN WINKLE, JR, W. 1970. Effect of environmental factors on byssus thread production. *Marine Biology*, **7**, 143–148.

VERWEY, J. 1952. On the ecology of distribution of cockle and mussel in the Dutch Wadden Sea, their role in sedimentation and the source of their food supply. *Archives néerldaises de Zoology*, **10**, 171–239.

VINCENT, B., DESROSIERS, G. & GRATTON, Y. 1988. Orientation of the infaunal bivalve *Mya arenaria* L. in relation to local current direction on the tidal flat. *Journal of Experimental Marine Biology and Ecology*, **124**, 205–214.

WAITE, J. H. 1983. Adhesion in byssally attached bivalves. *Biological Reviews*, Cambridge, **58**, 209–231.

WHITE, K. M. 1937. Mytilus(L) *Liverpool Marine Biology Committee Memoirs on typical British Marine Plants and Animals*. The University Press of Liverpool, **31**, 1–117.

WITMAN, J. D. & SUCHANEK, T. H. 1984. Mussels in flow: drag and dislodgement by epizoans. *Marine Ecology Progress Series*, **16**, 259–268.

YOUNG, G. A. 1983. The effect of sediment type upon the position and depth at which byssal attachment occurs in *Mytilus edulis*. *Journal of the Marine Biological Association of the United Kingdom*, **63**, 641–651.

——1985. Byssus thread formation by the mussel *Mytilus edulis*: effects of environmental factors. *Marine Ecology Progress Series*, **24**, 261–271.

Microscale biogeotechnical differences in intertidal sedimentary ecosystems

PETER S. MEADOWS[1], JOHN M. H. MURRAY[1], AZRA MEADOWS[1],
DAVID MUIR WOOD[2] & FRASER J. C. WEST[1]

[1] *Biosedimentology Unit, Division of Environmental and Evolutionary Biology,
Graham Kerr Building, IBLS, University of Glasgow, Glasgow G12 8QQ, UK*
[2] *Department of Civil Engineering, Queen's Building, University of Bristol,
University Walk, Bristol B58 1TR, UK*

Abstract: Intertidal sediments are inhabited by organisms that can modify the geotechnical
and sedimentological properties of the sediment. We have analysed small scale differences in
these properties at four closely adjacent sites on Ardmore Bay, Clyde Estuary, Scotland. The
sites were an *Enteromorpha* algal mat site (EAM), a *Corophium volutator* site (CV), the head
shafts of *Arenicola marina* (AMHS) and the tail shafts of *Arenicola marina* (AMTS) burrows.
Three replicate cores were taken from each site. We measured load resistance, particle size
parameters of mean particle size, sorting, skewness and kurtosis, and total organic matter
(TOM) and carbonate. Load resistance was measured with a newly developed microscale load
resistance penetrometer which measured load resistance of the sediment at 1 mm intervals
through the sediment core from the surface to 100 mm. Sediment cores were then sectioned
every 10 mm and particle size, total organic matter and carbonate content measured. *In situ*
shear strength measurements were also taken at the four sites. The data were analysed by
bivariate correlation analysis and multivariate cluster analysis. There was a number of
significant positive and negative correlations between the parameters at the four sites.
Significant down-core changes in the sediment parameters and their correlations were noted.
These differed between the four sites. The CV site had the largest number of significant
correlations, the EAM site had the least. Cluster analyses of the sites showed that in general the
sites clustered separately, although there were a number of overlaps. The EAM site showed
distinct clusters for its three separate replicate cores, while the CV site clustered into a top part
and a bottom part of the core. Cluster analyses of the depths across all the sites identified a
break in the data at depths of between 40 and 70 mm. There was a linear relationship between
field shear strength and laboratory penetration resistance. The results are discussed in relation
to the fine-scale geotechnical and sedimentological heterogeneity of intertidal sediments, and
the effects of biological activity.

The intertidal zone is of considerable interest in
terms of its role in recreational use, industrial
development and human habitation. It also
contains sites that have high levels of biodiversity
in its constituent animal and plant communities
(Mitsch 1994). As a result, there is a wide range
of investigations that describe or analyse the
engineering, geological or biological properties
of intertidal, nearshore and offshore environments (Lutenegger & Timian 1986; Meadows &
Meadows 1991; Baltzer *et al.* 1994; Stoll *et al.*
1994; Akal & Stoll 1995; Joshi *et al.* 1995;
Wheatcroft & Butman 1997). Many of these
centre on sedimentary ecosystems, partly because
sediments constitute the dominant part of the
intertidal zone on most coastlines, but also
because there is so much small scale spatial
variation in both their physical and biological
properties (Holland *et al.* 1974; Anderson &
Meadows 1978; Grant & Gust 1987; Meadows &
Tait 1989; Tufail *et al.* 1989; Paterson *et al.* 1990;
Muir Wood *et al.* 1990; Jones & Jago 1993;
Underwood & Paterson 1993) .

One of the major problems in such investigations, is the lack of any proper understanding of
the interactions between the properties and
functions of the physical and biological parts of
these ecosystems. It is only recently that the
necessary cross-disciplinary work has been successfully attempted. Biological interactions with
geotechnical variables such as shear strength,
slope stability, permeability, erodability and
sedimentation have all been investigated both
in the field and laboratory (Meadows & Tufail
1986; Meadows & Tait 1989; Paterson 1989;
Tufail *et al.* 1989; Meadows *et al.* 1990; Dade
et al. 1991; Shand 1991; Jones & Jago 1993;
Meadows *et al.* 1994). What is now required is
the development of innovative fine scale measurements of both geotechnical and biological
parameters under field and laboratory conditions (Muir Wood *et al.* 1990), which are then
analysed by multivariate statistical protocols.

With this background we have developed a
new microscale approach to assessing the
relationships between biological activity and

MEADOWS, P. S., MURRAY, J. M. H., MEADOWS, A. *ET AL.* 1998. Microscale biogeotechnical differences in
intertidal sedimentary ecosystems. *In*: BLACK, K. S., PATERSON, D. M. & CRAMP, A. (eds) *Sedimentary Processes
in the Intertidal Zone*. Geological Society, London, Special Publications, **139**, 349–366.

sedimentary parameters. We describe the use of
a penetrometer that provides a continuous load
resistance profile of a sedimentary core at a
millimetre scale (Muir Wood *et al.* 1990), and
relate this to changes in particle size parameters
of the sediment and to biologically derived
organic matter and carbonate at four closely
adjacent sites in the upper intertidal area of
Ardmore Bay in the Clyde Estuary, Scotland.
Application of correlation analysis and multivariate cluster techniques to this data has
revealed unexpected down-core and between-
site differences in intertidal areas dominated by
Enteromorpha algal mats (EAM), by populations of the mud burrowing crustacean *Corophium volutator* (CV), and by the head shafts
(AMHS) and tail shafts (AMTS) of burrows of
the polychaete lugworm *Arenicola marina*. The
results should lead to a more holistic understanding of the way in which intertidal sedimentary ecosystems function on different temporal
and spatial scales.

Materials and methods

An intertidal sampling area at Ardmore Bay
in the Clyde Estuary, Scotland (Latitude
55°58′32″N, Longitude 4°41′29″W; British
National Grid Reference NS 322 792) was chosen because it provided spatially heterogeneous
sedimentary ecosystems and infaunal communities (Tufail *et al.* 1989). The bay is divided into
a sheltered environment with less wave energy in
the high tide region as compared with the low
tide region which experiences a higher energy.
The bay is largely populated by a number of
burrowing polychaetes, bivalves and crusta-
ceans. An important feature of the high tide
region is the presence of the green macro-alga
Enteromorpha spp. which forms dense mats
especially in the summer and may cover areas
of 1–5 m^2 of the sediment surface (Tufail *et al.*
1989). These highly contrasting features of the
bay provided a unique opportunity to study the
microscale differences in the biogeotechnical
properties of closely adjacent but different
sites. Four sites were selected in the upper
intertidal region (Fig. 1). The first site was
covered by dense algal mats of *Enteromorpha*
spp. (EAM), the second was dominated by the
burrowing amphipod *Corophium volutator* (CV),
and the third and fourth sites included the head
shaft (feeding funnel end) (AMHS) and the tail
shaft (faecal cast end) (AMTS) of burrows of the
polychaete *Arenicola marina*. All the four sites
were within 10 m distance of each other.

Three replicate cores were collected from each
site using a 100 mm I.D. polyethylene corer. The

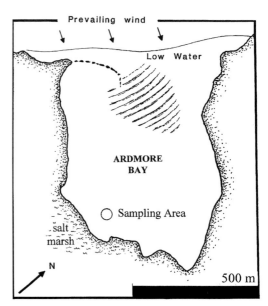

Fig. 1. Map of Ardmore Bay, Clyde Estuary,
Scotland. The sampling site where the cores were
collected, and where the *in situ* vane and cone shear
strength was measured is encircled.

distance between the three cores at each site was
500–800 mm. Cores were taken when the sites
were not covered by the tide. The corer was
gently inserted into the sediment to a depth of
200 mm and left in place to settle for ten minutes
prior to being carefully dug out. A flat base plate
held the recovered sediment core in position.
The cores were securely packed in an upright
position and immediately transported to the
laboratory for subsequent analyses. No internal
pistons or liners were used as the corers
produced negligible compaction or disturbance
of the sediment.

In situ *surface shear strength measurements.*
Three replicate readings of surface shear strength
were taken at the four sites using a Geonor fall-
cone apparatus (Hansbo 1957).

In situ *subsurface shear strength measurements.*
Two replicate sets of vane shear strength profiles
were taken at each of the four sites. Subsurface
shear strength was measured at 50 mm depth
intervals to a maximum depth of 200 mm using a
Pilcon Direct Reading Hand Vane Tester. The
apparatus consists of a torque head with a direct
reading scale, which is turned by hand. A non-
return pointer indicates the reading in kPa on
a scale on the torque head. A 33 mm vane is
attached to the head by extension rods. This
allows profiles of sediment shear strength to be

obtained by progressively inserting the vane into the sediment, stopping and turning the torque head to obtain shear strength readings at the appropriate depths. The apparatus has a high sensitivity to low shear strengths of field sediments such as those obtained in the present study. 290° of turn of the head is equivalent to 32 kPa, with an expanded scale at the lower end of the range (115° ≡ 10 kPa). An accuracy of 0.1 kPa was routinely obtainable in the field. At a given depth, the peak shear strength was obtained by rotating the vane until the sediment sheared, and then recording the reading on the torque head. The residual shear strength was obtained by rotating the vane a second time at the same depth, again noting the reading on the torque head when the sediment sheared. Care was taken to rotate the torque head at a constant rate, thus ensuring good replicability between replicate profiles of shear strength.

Laboratory processing of sediment cores

The cores were processed as follows. Load resistance profiles were conducted on each core followed by sediment analyses for particle size parameters, total organic matter and carbonate content.

Load resistance profile measurements. A 100 N load cell was connected to a cylindrical (100 × 10 mm) aluminium penetrometer. The load cell was supplied by Force Measurement Systems Ltd. It consisted of a low profile, full bridge copper foil resistance with an excitation voltage of 10 VDC, an output of 0.1437 mV/V at full scale deflection, and an output resistance of 700 Ω. The penetrometer-load cell assembly was fitted to a modified triaxial testing rig. The rig was a standard one, manufactured by Wykeham Farrance Eng Ltd (Model 56, fixed pillar cross beam loading jack). The rig was employed to drive the sediment core vertically upwards onto the penetrometer-load cell assembly at a constant speed of 1.6 mm min⁻¹. Data from the load cell was recorded by a data capture card fitted to a 386 IBM compatible PC. Data was recorded to disk and print-out simultaneously during profiling. The sediment core to be profiled was placed in a glass container which was gently filled up with 17.5% seawater (this matched the *in situ* salinity) until the core was completely saturated. The container was then placed on the platform (Fig. 2). Load resistance measurements were recorded at every 0.8 mm interval (equivalent to every 30 s) down the core. The data acquisition system was switched off either when the load resistance measured 100 N (the operational limit

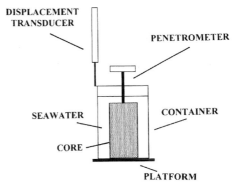

Fig. 2. Micro-scale load resistance penetrometer (MLRP) as set up on a sediment core.

of the load cell) or when the penetrometer reached 100 mm sediment depth (the operational limit of the displacement transducer). At the end of the load resistance profiling the sediment core was removed from the container and drained before being sectioned for further analysis.

Core sectioning. Cores were extruded and sectioned every 10 mm from the surface to a depth of 100 mm. The sediment sections were first air dried for one week and then oven dried at 100°C for 48 hrs. The dried samples were stored in a desiccator until sediment analyses were conducted.

Sediment analyses. Sediment samples were taken from the dried sections for particle size analysis, total organic matter and carbonate content analysis. Particle size analysis was carried out by dry sieving using a half phi (ϕ) scale interval (BS 1377 1975). These included sieve sizes of 2 mm ($-1\,\phi$), 1.4 mm ($-0.5\,\phi$), 1 mm (0 ϕ), 710 μm (0.5 ϕ), 500 μm (1 ϕ), 355 μm (1.5 ϕ), 250 μm (2 ϕ), 180 μm (2.5 ϕ), 125 μm (3 ϕ), 90 μm (3.5 ϕ), 63 μm (4 ϕ) and a receiver. The results from this analysis provided information on mean particle size, sorting, skewness and kurtosis. From here onwards these variables will be referred to as particle size parameters. Total organic matter was determined by loss on ignition at 480°C for four hours and carbonate content by loss on ignition at 950°C for one hour (Byers *et al.* 1978).

Statistical analyses. Seven sediment parameters were measured: load resistance at 0.8 mm intervals, and mean particle size, sorting, skewness, kurtosis, total organic matter and carbonate content at 10 mm intervals down to a depth of 100 mm. Since the MLRP generated a set of continuous load resistance readings down the core, the central value from each successive 10 mm interval was used in the statistical analyses. Bivariate and multivariate statistical analyses were conducted on the data from the four sites (EAM, CV, AMHS and AMTS). Two series of correlation coefficients were calculated between the sediment parameters. The first dealt with depth specific correlations while the second looked at site specific correlations. Multivariate cluster analyses were then applied to the data using correlation coefficients as distance measure and average linkage (Everitt 1980).

Results

The differences between the *Enteromorpha* algal mat dominated sediment (EAM), the *Corophium* dominated sediment (CV), the *Arenicola* head shaft sediment (AMHS) and the *Arenicola* tail shaft sediment (AMTS) are illustrated diagrammatically in Fig. 3. The surface of the EAM sediment contained a layer of *Enteromorpha* intermingled with sand to a depth of *c.* 30 mm. There were layers of decaying *Enteromorpha* below the surface, which became progressively less obvious to *c.* 60 mm. The top 20–50 mm of the *Corophium* sediment contained the burrows of *Corophium volutator*. The integrity of the U-shaped burrows is maintained by extracellular polymeric material produced by the animals. The sediment in this layer is usually aerobic and the sediment below is often anaerobic. The burrows of *Arenicola marina* extend much deeper into the sediment, and often reach a depth of 150–200 mm in the area of the beach where the samples were taken. The head shaft has a small depression which represents the area over which surface sediment is taken down the shaft to be ingested by the animal as it lies in the feeding chamber at the bottom of the burrow. The tail shaft is capped by a pile of faecal material whose integrity is loosely maintained by extracellular polymeric material secreted by the

animal as it voids its faeces. Although there is sediment in the head shaft and the tail shaft, their walls are distinct entities in the sedimentary column, and are held together by extracellular polymeric material secreted by the animals.

The remainder of the results is divided into five sections. The first section describes down-core changes in load resistance, particle size parameters, total organic matter and carbonate in the cores from the four sites. The second section describes the results of correlation analyses between load resistance, particle size parameters, total organic matter and carbonate at the different sites and at different depths. The third and fourth sections describe the results of multivariate cluster analyses of the data at the four sites. The clusters described in the third section identify specific groupings of sites and cores within sites. The clusters described in the fourth section identify distinct upper and lower depths of the sedimentary column sampled. The last section describes the field shear strength data, its difference between the sites, and its relationship to load resistance measured under laboratory conditions.

Down-core changes in load resistance, particle size parameters, organic matter and carbonate

Figure 4 illustrates the down-core changes for the sediment parameters measured at the four sites – EAM, CV, AMHS and AMTS. There are a number of distinct patterns and differences between the four sites, which we now describe.

EAM site

Load resistance increased down the core (Fig. 4 first row). However, there were marked changes in load resistance caused by the penetrometer coming into contact with and then moving

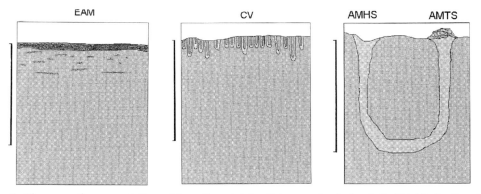

Fig. 3. Diagrammatic representations of the sediment at the *Enteromorpha* algal mat site (EAM), the *Corophium volutator* site (CV), and the *Arenicola marina* site (head shaft AMHS and tail shaft AMTS). Scale bar = 200 mm.

through layers of algal mat. This is most obvious in core 1 and core 2 where increases in load resistance followed by decreases in load resistance can be identified on the profiles. Mean particle size (MPS), sorting, skewness and kurtosis all showed considerable down-core variation, and this variation was different between the three cores. These differences may represent different layering of the algal mat in the three cores. In all three cores there were high levels of total organic matter and carbonate in the top 20 mm.

CV site

Load resistance increased smoothly down the core (Fig. 4 second row). Mean particle size, sorting and kurtosis decreased and skewness increased at deeper depths. Total organic matter remained constant while carbonate showed slight changes. All of the data show much less scatter between the cores and down each core than is present in the EAM cores.

AMHS site

Load resistance increased smoothly down the core (Fig. 4 third row) in a broadly similar way to the CV site data. Mean particle size decreased, while sorting, skewness and kurtosis all remained fairly constant, as did the total organic matter and carbonate. The data show about the same scatter between cores and down each core as at the CV site.

AMTS site

Load resistance increased smoothly down the core (Fig. 4 fourth row), but to a lesser degree than at any of the other sites. There was a large variation in mean particle size, skewness and kurtosis down the cores, but with no obvious trend. In contrast the sorting showed little variation. Total organic matter and carbonate remained constant down the cores and there was little variation between the cores.

Correlation coefficients between load resistance, particle size parameters, TOM and carbonate

Depth specific correlations (correlations across the four sites and three replicate cores at each of the ten depths)

Each correlation at each depth was calculated from 12 data pairs; one pair for each replicate core at each site (3 replicates × 4 sites = 12 data pairs). For a given correlation coefficient graph, load resistance with mean particle size for example, ten correlations are plotted; one for each depth. Figure 5 shows the change in a given correlation coefficient with depth. The 0.05 (5%) probability level of significance for the correlation coefficient values are indicated by the dashed lines in each graph.

There are significant changes in many of the correlations with depth. The correlation between load resistance and sorting is slightly positive at the surface and then significantly negative except for a non-significant value at 40–50 mm. The correlation between mean particle size and sorting shows a similar effect. There are also significant correlations between load resistance and skewness, and between load resistance and kurtosis at the same depth. The correlations between load resistance and TOM, and between load resistance and carbonate are significantly positive at the surface, but then fall to about zero. The correlations between mean particle size and skewness are significantly negative at the surface and at 60–70 mm but not elsewhere. The correlations between mean particle size and kurtosis were significantly positive at almost all depths. The correlations between sorting and TOM were significantly negative at 10–20 mm and at 20–30 mm and significantly positive at 50–60 mm. A similar reversal occurred in the correlations between sorting and carbonate at 20–30 mm and at 60–70 mm. TOM was positively correlated with carbonate, and these correlations were significant near the surface and then again from 60 mm downwards.

Site specific correlations (correlations across the depths and replicate cores at various sites)

Table 1 shows the site specific correlations. The top set of correlation coefficients are calculated for all the four sites combined. Each of these correlations was calculated from 120 data pairs: one pair for each depth from each replicate core at each site (10 depths × 3 replicate cores × 4 sites = 120 data pairs). The lower four sets of correlation coefficients are calculated for each of the sites separately. Each correlation in these sets was calculated from 30 data pairs: one pair for each depth from each replicate core (10 depths × 3 replicate cores = 30 data pairs).

The top set of correlation coefficients in Table 1 shows that load resistance is negatively correlated with sorting but is not correlated with any of

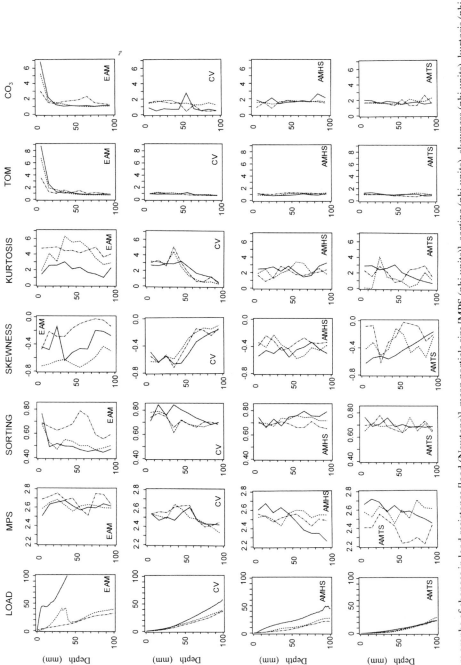

Fig. 4. Down-core graphs of changes in load resistance [load (Newtons)], mean particle size [MPS (phi units)], sorting (phi units), skewness (phi units), kurtosis (phi units), total organic matter [TOM (% dry sediment weight)], and carbonate [CO₃ (% dry sediment weight)]. The horizontal scales are in the appropriate units. The vertical scale in each case is depth (mm) from the sediment surface. EAM = *Enteromorpha* algal mat site; CV = *Corophium volutator* site; AMHS = *Arenicola marina* site head shaft; AMTS = *Arenicola marina* site tail shaft. The three lines on each graph represent the profiles from the three replicate cores at each site (——— = replicate core 1; ------- = replicate core 2; ·—·—·— = replicate core 3).

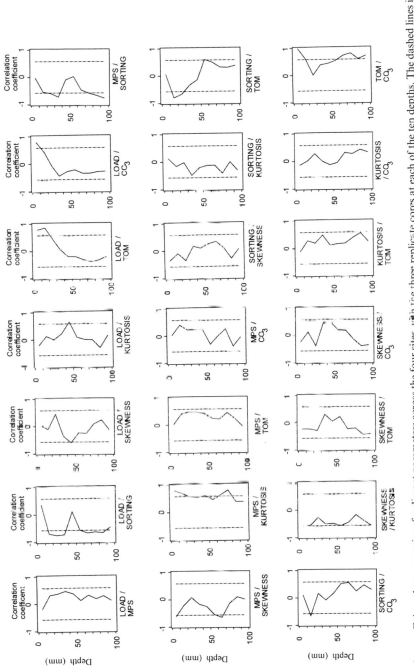

Fig. 5. Correlation coefficients between pairs of sediment parameters across the four sites with the three replicate cores at each of the ten depths. The dashed lines indicate the 0.05 (5%) significance level. Points outside these lines represent significant correlations at the 5% level.

the other parameters. Mean particle size is negatively correlated with sorting and skewness and positively correlated with kurtosis. Sorting is positively correlated with carbonate. Skewness is negatively correlated with kurtosis, and total organic matter is positively correlated with carbonate. Comparing the lower four sets of correlation coefficients, the CV site had the highest number of significant correlations (76%), and the EAM site had the lowest number of significant correlations (24%). Both the AMHS and AMTS sites had the same number of significant correlations (48%).

A detailed inspection of the correlation coefficients in the lower four sets shows important differences and similarities between the sites. There is a significant negative correlation between load resistance and sorting at the EAM and CV sites, but the same correlation at the AMHS site is significantly positive. Similarly, load resistance is negatively correlated with carbonate at the CV site but positively correlated with carbonate at the AMHS site. Load resistance is negatively correlated with all the other six variables except skewness at the CV site but with none of the variables at the AMTS site.

Table 1. *Correlation coefficients for all the four sites,* Enteromorpha *algal mat (EAM),* C. volutator *(CV),* A. marina *head shaft (AMHS), and* A. marina *tail shaft (AMTS)*

	Load	Mean particle size	Sorting	Skewness	Kurtosis	Total organic matter
All four sites						
Mean particle size	0.048					
Sorting	−0.617***	−0.395***				
Skewness	0.118	−0.348***	−0.054			
Kurtosis	−0.096	0.594***	−0.148	−0.536***		
Total organic matter	−0.044	0.120	0.070	−0.188	0.042	
Carbonate	−0.155	0.033	0.206*	0.134	0.064	0.848***
***Enteromorpha* algal mat**						
Mean particle size	−0.251					
Sorting	−0.613***	−0.057				
Skewness	0.055	0.262	0.356			
Kurtosis	−0.677***	0.326	0.315	−0.054		
Total organic matter	−0.245	−0.306	0.519**	−0.209	−0.291	
Carbonate	−0.306	−0.333	0.636***	−0.099	−0.235	0.982***
C. volutator						
Mean particle size	−0.623***					
Sorting	−0.414*	0.045				
Skewness	0.804***	−0.687***	−0.605***			
Kurtosis	−0.755***	0.762***	0.336	−0.949***		
Total organic matter	−0.655***	0.628***	0.345	−0.703***	0.681***	
Carbonate	−0.381*	0.469**	0.005	−0.339	0.396*	0.718***
***A. marina* head shaft**						
Mean particle size	−0.648***					
Sorting	0.529**	−0.453*				
Skewness	−0.213	−0.235	−0.602***			
Kurtosis	0.296	0.114	0.384*	−0.865***		
Total organic matter	−0.035	0.037	0.007	−0.054	0.046	
Carbonate	0.577***	−0.324	0.447*	−0.402*	0.516**	0.062
***A. marina* tail shaft**						
Mean particle size	−0.184					
Sorting	−0.281	0.079				
Skewness	0.273	−0.753***	−0.542**			
Kurtosis	−0.198	0.654***	0.458*	−0.942***		
Total organic matter	−0.177	0.684***	0.288	−0.660***	0.580***	
Carbonate	0.197	0.023	0.267	−0.257	0.362*	0.390*

Probabilities: $0.05 > P > 0.01$*; $0.01 > P > 0.001$**; $P < 0.001$***; d.f. = 118 for all four sites, d.f. = 28 for (EAM), (CV), (AMHS) and (AMTS) sites.

Mean particle size is negatively correlated with skewness and positively correlated with kurtosis and total organic matter at both the CV and AMTS sites. Sorting is positively correlated with carbonate at the EAM and the AMHS sites. This means that poorly sorted sediments having a high standard deviation of particle size contain high levels of carbonate. Sorting is negatively correlated with skewness at the CV, AMHS and AMTS sites. This means that well sorted

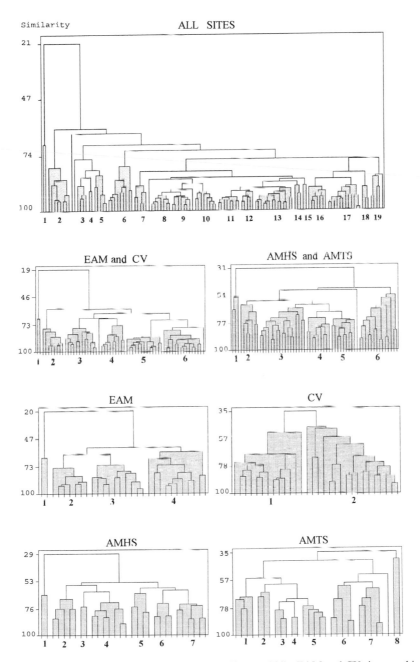

Fig 6. Clusters of sites and cores. Top: all sites combined. Upper middle: EAM and CV sites combined; AMHS and AMTS sites combined; Lower middle: EAM site; CV site. Bottom: AMHS site; AMTS site.

Table 2. *Clusters of the four sites, three replicate cores per site, ten depths per core using the seven sediment parameters*

Cluster number	Similarity level	Site	Core	Number of observations in cluster	
				Depth (0–50 mm)	Depth (60–100 mm)
1	68.51%	*Enteromorpha* algal mat	1, 2	2	–
2	78.39%	*Enteromorpha* algal mat	1	3	5
3	88.19%	*Enteromorpha* algal mat	2	2	2
4	90.66%	*C. volutator*	2, 3	2	–
5	83.23%	*Enteromorpha* algal mat	2	2	3
6	79.01%	*Enteromorpha* algal mat	3	4	5
7	88.11%	*C. volutator*	1	5	–
8	92.66%	*C. volutator*	2, 3	7	–
		A. marina tail shaft	3		
9	92.91%	*A. marina* head shaft	1, 2	4	3
		A. marina tail shaft	1, 2		
10	91.00%	*A. marina* head shaft	1	7	1
		A. marina tail shaft	1, 2		
11	93.74%	*C. volutator*	2	7	1
		A. marina head shaft	2, 3		
		A. marina tail shaft	1, 2		
12	91.29%	*A. marina* head shaft	1, 2	–	5
		A. marina tail shaft	2		
13	89.91%	*A. marina* head shaft	2, 3	6	8
		C. volutator	2		
		A. marina tail shaft	1, 2, 3		
14	88.59%	*C. volutator*	3	2	1
		A. marina head shaft	3		
15	88.32%	*A. marina* tail shaft	2	–	2
16	89.30%	*C. volutator*	1, 3	–	7
17	88.79%	*C. volutator*	2, 3	4	8
		A. marina tail shaft	1, 2, 3		
18	89.30%	*A. marina* tail shaft	3	–	3
19	84.64%	*A. marina* head shaft	1	–	4

sediments having a low standard deviation of particle size have a high skewness. At both the AMHS and AMTS sites sorting is positively correlated with kurtosis. Skewness is negatively correlated with kurtosis, and kurtosis is positively correlated with carbonate at the CV, AMHS and AMTS sites. Total organic matter is positively correlated with carbonate at the EAM, CV and AMTS sites.

Clusters of sites and cores

Figure 6 shows the clustering of sites and cores within the sites. The details of the clusters are shown in Table 2. The dendrogram at the top of Fig. 6, containing data from all the sites, identifies 19 clusters at similarities of 69% to 94%. Clusters 1, 2, 3, 5 and 6 contain solely EAM data. Clusters 4, 7 and 16 contain solely CV data. Cluster 19 contains solely AMHS, and clusters 15 and 18 contain solely AMTS data. Clusters 9, 10 and 12 contain AMHS and AMTS data. Cluster 14 contains CV and AMHS data.

Clusters 8 and 17 contain CV and AMTS data. Clusters 11 and 13 contain CV, AMHS and AMTS data.

Some of the clusters contained data almost entirely derived from the top 50 mm of the core (Fig. 6, clusters 1, 4, 7 and 8). Some of the clusters contained data almost derived solely from the bottom 50 mm of the core (clusters 12, 15, 16, 18 and 19). The latter group of clusters contained no data from the EAM site. All the clusters containing EAM data except one contained data from both the upper 50 mm and the lower 50 mm of the core (clusters 2, 3, 5 and 6). Cluster 1 contained data from the top 10 mm of EAM cores 1 and 2.

The dendrograms in the upper middle of Fig. 6 are for EAM and CV combined, and AMHS and AMTS combined. Table 3 shows that in the EAM and CV dendrogram clusters 1–4 are mainly EAM, and clusters 5 and 6 are solely CV. Clusters 1, 2 and 4 mainly represent EAM cores 1, 2 and 3. Cluster 5 consists of data from the 60–100 mm depth, and cluster 6

Table 3. *Clusters of sites* Enteromorpha *algal mat and* C. volutator, *and of* A. marina *head shaft and* A. marina *tail shaft for cores and depths*

Cluster number	Similarity level	Site	Core	Number of observations in cluster	
				Depth (0–50 mm)	Depth (60–100 mm)
Enteromorpha algal mat and C. volutator					
1	66.96%	*Enteromorpha* algal mat	1, 2	2	–
2	76.86%	*Enteromorpha* algal mat	1	3	5
3	76.70%	*Enteromorpha* algal mat and *C. volutator*	2, 2, 3, 1	7	5
4	74.21%	*Enteromorpha* algal mat	3	4	5
5	85.37%	*C.volutator*	1, 3, 2	–	13
6	78.93%	*C. volutator*	1, 2, 3	13	1
A. marina head shaft and tail shaft					
1	54.95%	Head shaft and tail shaft	1, 3	–	3
2	61.41%	Head shaft	1, 2	3	4
3	64.12%	Head shaft and tail shaft	1, 2, 3	11	6
4	72.94%	Head shaft and tail shaft	1, 2, 3	8	1
5	74.12%	Head shaft and tail shaft	2, 3, 1	–	9
6	53.29%	Head shaft and tail shaft	2, 3	8	6

Table 4. *Clusters of replicate cores and sediment depths for the* Enteromorpha *algal mat,* C. volutator, A. marina *head shaft and* A. marina *tail shaft sites*

Cluster number	Similarity level	Core	Number of observations in cluster	
			Depth (0–50 mm)	Depth (60–100 mm)
Enteromorpha algal mat				
1	64.91%	1, 2	2	–
2	74.73%	1	2	5
3	72.15%	2	5	5
4	59.56%	3, 1	6	5
C. volutator				
1	52.03%	1, 2, 3	–	13
2	48.02%	1, 2, 3	15	2
A. marina head shaft				
1	64.39%	1	–	2
2	68.30%	1, 2	1	4
3	74.94%	1	2	–
4	71.23%	1, 2	4	3
5	63.28%	2, 3	4	–
6	72.25%	1, 2	4	–
7	72.81%	3, 2	0	6
A. marina tail shaft				
1	69.69%	1, 2, 3	3	1
2	66.08%	1, 2	1	2
3	80.00%	1	–	3
4	86.13%	2, 3	2	–
5	77.23%	1, 2	5	–
6	61.54%	1, 3	–	5
7	63.83%	2, 3	4	1
8	40.74%	3	–	2

consists of data mainly from the 0–50 mm depth at the CV site. In summary, the EAM site clusters by cores and the CV site by depths. This is borne out by the single site dendrograms for the two sites shown in the lower middle part of Fig. 6. The CV dendrogram is particularly distinct in separating into two large clusters both of which contain data from cores 1, 2 and 3. Cluster 1 contains data solely from the 60–100 mm depth. Cluster 2 contains data almost entirely from the 0–50 mm depth (Table 4).

The dendrogram for the AMHS and AMTS data combined does not show such distinct clustering (Fig. 6, AMHS and AMTS dendrogram; Table 3). All of the clusters except cluster 2 contain both head shaft and tail shaft data. The same is true for the dendrograms for the AMHS and the AMTS sites shown separately at the bottom of Fig. 6 (Table 4).

Clusters of depths

Figures 7–10 show the results of clustering of the data to show depth clusters. In each figure, the top dendrogram represents all the sites, the second dendrogram represents the EAM site, the third dendrogram represents the CV site, the fourth dendrogram represents the AMHS site, and the bottom dendrogram represents the AMTS site. The most obvious clustering divided the upper part of the sedimentary column from the lower part of the sedimentary column. This unexpected result is clear in all but one of the dendrograms in Figs 7–9. The one exception is the dendrogram for the AMHS site using sediment parameters (Fig. 9, fourth dendrogram). The split between the upper and lower part of the column occurs either between 40 and 50 mm, 50 and 60 mm, or 60 and 70 mm. The effect is not present in the dendrograms produced by using TOM and CO_3, except for the top dendrogram for all the sites and the CV site. There may be a number of explanations for the split, including the effect of different types of biological activity, past and present depositional environments, and input from the water column or the sediment below the core. The other unexpected result from the clusters is that in some instances the top 10 mm band of sediment does not cluster with the remaining data. This occurs in the top two dendrograms in Figs 7, 9 and 10.

In situ sediment shear strength

Field measurements of peak and residual shear strength taken with the Pilcon Direct Reading Hand Vane Tester increased with increasing

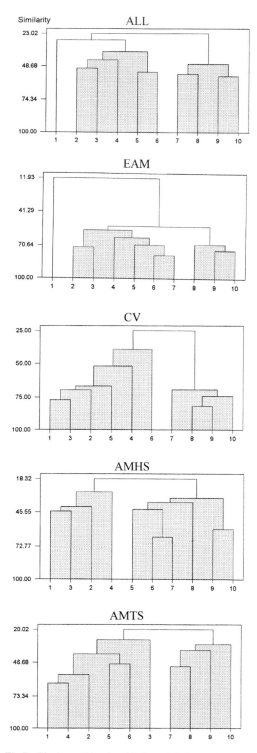

Fig 7. Clusters of depths. All data. All sites; EAM site; CV site; AMHS site; AMTS site.

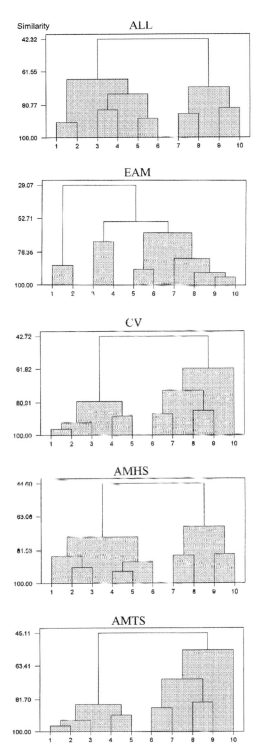

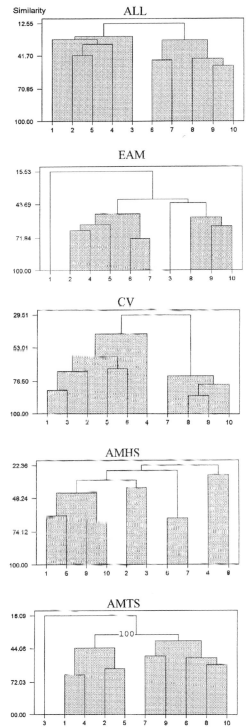

Fig. 8. Clusters of depths. Load data only. All sites; EAM site; CV site; AMHS site; AMTS site.

Fig. 9. Clusters of depths. Particle size parameter data only. All sites; EAM site; CV site; AMHS site; AMTS site.

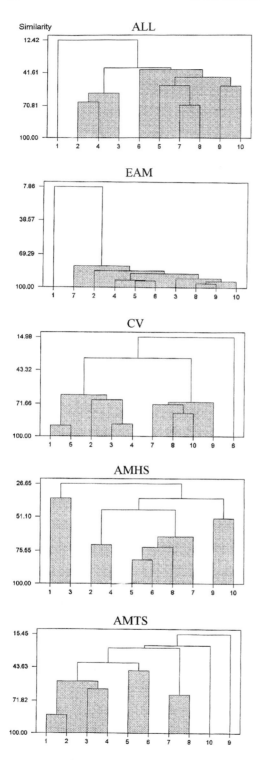

Fig. 10. Clusters of depths. TOM and CO_3 data only. All sites; EAM site; CV site; AMHS site; AMTS site.

depth into the sediment (Fig. 11). Surface sediment shear strength was also measured with a Geonor fall cone apparatus. The surface readings of the peak and residual vane shear strength roughly agree with the cone surface sediment shear strength. Vane peak shear strength was always higher than vane residual shear strength with increasing depth. There is some indication that peak shear strength increased more rapidly in the top 100 mm and less rapidly from 100 mm to 200 mm at the AMHS site than at the AMTS site. The changes in peak shear strength with depth are similar in the CV and AMTS site.

Relationship between laboratory load resistance and *in situ* sediment shear strength

By analogy with common geotechnical practice, load resistances were converted to penetration resistances (q) by dividing the load resistances (kN) by the cross sectional area of the cylindrical penetrometer (10 mm diameter, surface area $7.854 \times 10^{-5} m^2$). This allowed a direct comparison to be made between the laboratory load resistances (now transformed to penetration resistances) and the field shear strengths, using the same units ($kN\,m^{-2}$). The slope of the regression line relating *in situ* shear strength to laboratory penetration resistance is likely to be a useful index for future studies in similar sediments.

Peak and residual shear strengths measured in the field with the Pilcon Direct Reading Hand Vane Tester were therefore plotted against laboratory penetration resistances, and the data submitted to linear regression analysis. Figure 12 shows there is a positive linear relationship between peak vane shear strength and penetration resistance, and between residual vane shear strength and penetration resistance. These positive relationships, both of which are statistically significant (Fig. 12 legend), are important because the laboratory and field measurements were taken using different techniques and under different conditions. The field measurements of shear strength were taken using the Pilcon Vane when the tide was out and the water was at the level of the sediment. The laboratory measurements of load resistance were taken using the laboratory penetrometer on sediment cores covered with water.

Discussion

Intertidal environments show high levels of spatial heterogeneity. This heterogeneity is present in sedimentary environments on many

Shear Strength (kN.m^{-2})

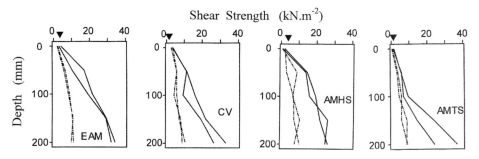

Fig. 11. *In situ* falling cone and vane shear strength profiles at the EAM, CV, AMHS and AMTS sites. The cone measurements (inverted triangle) were taken on the surface of the sediment, and the vane measurements were taken down the sedimentary column. (——— = peak shear strength; ·—·—·—·— = residual shear strength, two replicate profiles in each case).

intertidal beaches and can sometimes be recognized by differences in sediment topography over relatively short distances. On Ardmore Bay, for example, the large sand waves in the lower intertidal area and the patches of algal mat in the upper intertidal area are clearly distinguishable,

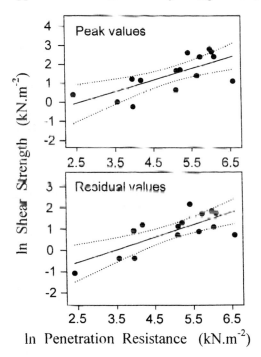

Fig. 12. Linear regression relationship between ln (penetration resistance in kN m^{-2}) and ln (shear strength kN m^{-2}) at the four sites. Top: peak shear strength. $y = 0.6111x - 1.603$, $F_{1,13} = 13.58$, $0.005 > p > 0.001$. Bottom: residual shear strength. $y = 0.5915x - 2.075$, $F_{1,13} = 17.05$, $0.005 > p > 0.001$.

and also contain different communities of infaunal invertebrates (Tufail *et al.* 1989). Here, spatial heterogeneity is operating at distances of 1–50 m, and can be quantified by suitably-designed field protocols. However, there is almost certainly smaller scale patterning at a centimetre or even millimetre scale that has received little attention because it is so difficult to measure (Anderson & Meadows, 1978; Jørgensen *et al.* 1979; Revsbech & Jørgensen 1981; Meadows & Tufail 1986). This was the starting point of the present investigation. Ardmore Bay provided us with a wide range of sedimentary environments and contrasting biological communities at different scales. This enabled us to test the potential relationships between geotechnical and sedimentological properties at a very fine scale, and how these relationships might be altered by the activities of different organisms living in the sedimentary column.

Our approach has been to sample four contrasting sediments that are not more than 10 m apart: an *Enteromorpha* algal mat site, a site dominated by the mud burrowing crustacean *Corophium volutator*, and sites containing the headshafts and tail shafts of the large infaunal polychaete *Arenicola marina*. Results from our new microscale load penetrometer, which can detect differences in sediment fabric down to a scale of a millimetre, have been combined with conventional field measurements of shear strength, and with sediment particle size parameters, total organic matter and carbonate content obtained from 10 mm thick slices of sediment. The analysis of this data by bivariate correlation coefficients and multivariate cluster analyses have revealed an unexpected degree of complexity both between the four sites and at a fine scale down the sedimentary column. Furthermore, the linear relationship between field shear strength and laboratory measured penetration resistance (Fig. 12), provides a potentially useful link between the fine scale vertical structure that we have detected and the results of more conventional field studies of shear strength (Lunne *et al.* 1976; Robertson 1990; Décourt 1992).

Correlation coefficients

The correlation coefficients (Table 1, Fig. 7) show a number of significant relationships. We first discuss the correlation coefficients for the four sites (Table 1). When the sites are considered together, load resistance is negatively correlated with sorting (particle size standard deviation). This is not what would be expected from theoretical and laboratory studies on particle packing (Sohn & Moreland 1968; Allen 1982), which predict a positive relationship between the number of particle–particle contacts and particle size standard deviation. One possible explanation is the role played by biological activity in relatively poorly sorted sediments such as those that are present at Ardmore. Another explanation is that natural sediments behave differently from artificial sediments. It is interesting in this context that during cone penetration tests, cone penetration resistance decreases but friction on the side of the cylinder above the cone increases, as one moves from sands to silts to silty clays (Meigh 1987, pp. 24–25).

The numbers of significant correlations and their patterns are radically different between the sites. In some instances the patterns are so different that the correlation coefficients reverse their sign. For example, load resistance is negatively correlated with sorting at the EAM and CV site, but positively correlated with sorting at the AMHS site. Both *Corophium* and *Enteromorpha* tend to stabilize the surface either by producing extracellular polymeric material (Meadows & Tait 1989; Meadows *et al.* 1990), or by acting as a biological geotextile respectively (cf. Bathurst 1967; Muir Wood *et al.* 1990; Meadows *et al.* 1994). In this context it would be interesting to know how the behaviour of *Enteromorpha* algal mat compared with man-made geotextiles (Theisen 1992; Athanasopoulos 1993; Di Prisco & Nova 1993). In contrast to the EAM and CV sites however, sediment in the head shaft of *Arenicola* burrows (AMHS) is almost continuously funnelling down the head shaft towards the animal's head and hence is intrinsically unstable. These differences between the EAM and CV site on the one hand and the AMHS site on the other, may account for the difference in sign between the coefficients.

At three out of the four sites total organic matter is positively correlated with carbonate. This may be due to the carbonate and the organic matter originating from the same source, possibly the sediment/water interface. At Ardmore, we have observed terrestrial organic material from a nearby salt marsh and fragments of bivalve shells from the intertidal and subtidal zone accumulating at the sediment/water interface in the area on which we were sampling.

Clustering of sites

The clusters identified in the dendrograms illustrated in Fig. 6 and described in Table 2 show distinct patterns that are associated with spatial heterogeneity between the sites and between the three replicate cores at each site. This is evident in the top dendrogram in Fig. 6 where many of the clusters are made of data from one of the four sites only. The variables that we have measured are therefore able to distinguish between the sites. However, there is an added level of complexity. A consideration of the clusters in the dendrograms in the middle and lower parts of Fig. 6 shows that the data clusters in different ways at the four sites. There is a clear distinction between the three replicate cores at the EAM site which must be caused by significant differences between the cores (Fig. 6 upper middle; EAM and CV dendrogram). In contrast, in the same dendrogram the replicate cores at the CV site cluster together, and hence are more homogeneous, but the clusters distinguish between an upper and lower part of the sediment sampled. The AMHS and AMTS dendrogram (Fig. 6 upper middle; AMHS and AMTS dendrogram) does not show clusters that differentiate between the sites. Each cluster except one contains data from both sites. Furthermore, when these two sites are clustered separately (Fig. 6 bottom two dendrograms), most of the clusters contain data from more than one replicate core, and are therefore homogeneous in a similar way to the cores at the CV site.

Clustering of depths

The clusters identified in Figs 7–10 show very significant down-core spatial heterogeneity. In most cases this consists of a dichotomy in the data, which clusters either side of the 50–70 mm depth. The effect is clearly evident when all the variables are used in the clustering, and when load resistance data and particle size parameters are used separately (Figs 7–9). However, it is less so when only total organic matter and carbonate are used (Fig. 10). Geotechnical and particle size parameters therefore identify the dichotomy between the upper and lower parts of the sediment core better than do TOM and carbonate. It is difficult to identify what factors might be causing this pattern. It might be caused by biological activity within the sediment, or by input from the water column across the sediment/water interface, or by input from deeper in the sedimentary column. Unfortunately, neither water content nor bulk density were measured down-core. It is therefore not possible to identify potential differences in compaction across the discontinuity. However, if compaction is responsible for the transition across the discontinuity, the compaction may still be a result of biological reworking.

The clustering of the upper and lower part of the sediment at the CV site shown in Figs 7–10 might suggest that *Corophium volutator* is playing a major role. The species might be turning over the top layer of the sediment by its burrowing activities (Meadows & Reid 1966) hence producing a differential packing of the sediment and causing spatial heterogeneity in the particle size parameters. The pattern is also present when TOM and carbonate are used to cluster the depths at this site. The transitional zone between 50 and 70 mm may correlate with the lower limit of biological reworking by *Corophium volutator*. This reworking may produce lower shear strength sediment which nevertheless remains stable to erosive forces due to the presence of extracellular polymeric material.

The dendrograms of the AMHS and AMTS depths using load resistance indicate that here also there is a clear distinction between the upper and lower part of the sediment core. The distinction is probably caused by patterns of ingestion (AMIIS) and defaecation (AMTS) that produce differential packing. Differential packing and spatial heterogeneity produced in this way would probably be detected by the load penetrometer. It is interesting that dendrograms for the same two sites using only particle size parameters show a distinction for the AMTS site but not for the AMHS site. The defaecation of sediment by *Arenicola marina* therefore produces a difference in the particle size parameters between the upper and lower parts of the core that is not produced by the feeding activities of the species. The dendrograms showing clustering of the depths at the EAM site are distinctive in a different way. The top 10 mm of the sediment does not cluster with any of the other depths in Fig. 7 (all parameters), Fig. 9 (particle size parameters only) and Fig. 10 (TOM and carbonate). This is because the algal mat biomass is concentrated in the top 10 mm. The pattern of clusters in Fig. 9 (load resistance) is different. The top 20 mm cluster together, followed by a cluster made up of the 20–40 mm depths. We suggest that the top cluster represents the load-bearing capacity of the intact algal mat, and the second cluster represents the change in load as the penetrometer ruptures the mat. The third and deepest cluster (50–100 mm depth) represents the underlying sediment whose properties are not affected by the overlying algal mat.

Part of this work was conducted during a Marine Technology Directorate grant (MTD: FOU 29, SERC: GR G 24446) to David Muir Wood (then in the Department of Civil Engineering at the University of Glasgow) and Peter Meadows, during which the microscale load penetrometer was developed. Fraser West is very grateful to the Carnegie Trust for the Universities of Scotland for partial financial support. All the authors are very grateful to Pat McLaughlin for considerable help at data preparation and writing up stage, without which the paper would not have been completed for submission to the Symposium volume.

References

AKAL, T. & STOLL, R. D. 1995. Expendable penetrometer for rapid assessment of seafloor parameters. *Oceans Conference Record*, **3**, 1822–1826.

ALLEN, J. R. L. 1982. *Sedimentary Structures. Their Character and Physical Basis*, Vol. 1. Elsevier, Amsterdam.

ANDERSON, J. G. & MEADOWS, P. S. 1978. Microenvironments in marine sediments. *Proceedings of the Royal Society of Edinburgh*, **76B**, 1–6.

ATHANASOPOULOS, G. A. 1993. Effect of particle size on the mechanical behaviour of sand-geotextile composites. *Geotextiles and Geomembranes*, **12**, 255–273.

BALTZER, A., COCHONAT, P. & PIPER, D. J. W 1994. In-situ geotechnical characterisation of sediments of the Nova Scotian slope, Eastern Canadian Continental-Margin. *Marine Geology*, **120**, 291–308.

BATHURST, R. G. C. 1967. Subtidal gelatinous mat, sand stabiliser and food, Great Bahama Bank. *Journal of Geology*, **75**, 736–738.

BS 1377. 1975. *Methods of Test for Soils for Civil Engineering Purposes*. British Standards Institution, London.

BYERS, S. C., MILLS, E. L. & STEWART, P. L. 1978. A comparison of methods of determining organic carbon in marine sediments, with suggestions for a standard method. *Hydrobiologia*, **58**, 43–47.

DADE, W. B., DAVIS, J. D., NICHOLS, P. D., NOWELL, A. R. M., THISTLE, D., TREXLER, M. B. & WHITE, D. C. 1991. The effects of bacterial exopolymer adhesion on the entrainment of sand. *Geomicrobiology Journal*, **8**, 1–16.

DÉCOURT, L. 1992. The standard penetration test, state-of-the-art report. *Proceedings of the 12th International Conference on Soil Mechanics and Foundation Engineering, Rio de Janeiro*. Vol. 4. A. A. Balkema, Rotterdam, 2405–2416.

DI PRISCO, C. & NOVA, R. 1993. A constitutive model for soil reinforced by continuous threads. *Geotextiles and Geomembranes*, **12**, 161–178.

EVERITT, B. 1980. *Cluster Analysis*, 2nd edn. Halsted Press, New York.

GRANT, J. & GUST, G. 1987. Prediction of coastal sediment stability from photopigment content from mats of purple sulphur bacteria. *Nature*, **330**, 244–246.

HANSBO, S. 1957. A new approach to the determination of the shear strength of clay by the fall-cone test. *Proceedings of the Royal Swedish Geotechnical Institute*, **14**, 1–49.

HOLLAND, A. F., ZINGMARK, R. G. & DEAN, J. M. 1974. Quantitative evidence concerning the stabilization of sediments by marine benthic diatoms. *Marine Biology*, **27**, 191–196.

JONES, S. E. & JAGO, C. F. 1993. *In situ* assessment of modification of sediment properties by burrowing invertebrates. *Marine Biology*, **115**, 133–142.

JØRGENSEN, B. B., REVSBECH, N. P., BLACKBURN, T. H. & COHEN, Y. 1979. Diurnal cycle of oxygen and sulphide microgradients and microbial photosynthesis in a cyanobacterial mat sediment. *Applied Environmental Microbiology*, **38**, 46–58.

JOSHI, R. C., ACHARI, G., KANIRAJ, S. R. & WIJEWEERA, H. 1995. Effect of aging on the penetration resistance of sands. *Canadian Geotechnical Journal*, **3**, 767–782

LUNNE, T., EIDE, O. & DE RUITER, J. 1976 Correlations between cone resistance and vane shear strength in some Scandinavian soft to medium stiff clays. *Canadian Geotechnical Journal*, **13**, 430–441.

LUTENEGGER, A. J. & TIMIAN, D. A. 1986. Flat-plate penetrometer tests in marine clays. *Proceedings of the 39th Canadian Geotechnical Conference, Ottawa*. Canadian Geotechnical Conference, Canadian Geotechnical Society, Montreal, 301–309.

MEADOWS, P. S. & MEADOWS, A. 1991. The geotechnical and geochemical implications of bioturbation in marine sedimentary ecosystems. *In*: MEADOWS, P. S. & MEADOWS, A. (eds) *The Environmental Impact of Burrowing Animals and Animal Burrows*. Zoological Symposium No. 63, Clarendon Press, Oxford, 157–181.

—— & REID, A. 1966. The behaviour of *Corophium volutator* (Crustacea: Amphipoda). *Journal of Zoology, London*, **150**, 387–399.

—— & TAIT, J. 1989. Modification of sediment permeability and shear strength by two burrowing invertebrates. *Marine Biology*, **101**, 75–82.

—— & TUFAIL, A. 1986. Bioturbation, microbial activity and sediment properties in an estuarine ecosystem. *Proceedings of the Royal Society of Edinburgh*, **90B**, 129–142.

——, TAIT, J. & HUSSAIN, S. A. 1990. Effects of estuarine infauna on sediment stability and particle sedimentation. *Hydrobiologia*, **190**, 263–266.

MEADOWS, A., MEADOWS, P. S., MUIR WOOD, D. & MURRAY, J. M. H. 1994. Microbiological effects on slope stability: an experimental analysis. *Sedimentology*, **41**, 423–435.

MEADOWS, P. S., REICHELT, A. C., MEADOWS, A. & WATERWORTH, J. S. 1994. Microbial and meiofaunal abundance, redox potential, pH and shear strength profiles in deep sea Pacific sediments. *Journal of the Geological Society of London*, **151**, 377–390.

MEIGH, A. C. 1987. *Cone Penetration Testing*. Butterworths, London.

MITSCH, W. J. (ed.) 1994. *Global Wetlands Old World and New*. Elsevier, Amsterdam.

MUIR WOOD, D., MEADOWS, P. S. & TUFAIL, A. 1990. Biological strengthening of marine sediments. *In*: HOWSAM, P. (ed.) *Microbiology in Civil Engineering*. E. & F. N. Spon, University Press, Cambridge, 306–316.

PATERSON, D. M. 1989. Short-term changes in the erodability of intertidal cohesive sediments related to the migratory behaviour of epipelic diatoms. *Limnology and Oceanography*, **34**, 223–234.

——, CRAWFORD, R. M. & LITTLE, C. 1990. Subaerial exposure and changes in the stability of intertidal estuarine sediments. *Estuarine, Coastal and Shelf Science*, **30**, 541–556.

REVSBECH, N. P. & JØRGENSEN, B. B. 1981. Primary production of microalgae in sediments measured by oxygen microprofile, bicarbonate fixation, and oxygen exchange methods. *Limnology and Oceanography*, **26**, 717–730.

ROBERTSON, P. K. 1990. Soil classification using the cone penetration test. *Canadian Geotechnical Journal*, **27**, 151–158.

SHAND, P. 1991. Sediment movement around mussels: flume experiments on critical erosion velocities and sorting. *In*: MEADOWS, P. S. & MEADOWS, A. (eds) *The Environmental Impact of Burrowing Animals and Animal Burrows*, Zoological Symposium No. 63, Clarendon Press, Oxford, 313–316.

SOHN, H. Y. & MORELAND, C. 1968. The effect of particle size distribution on packing density. *Canadian Journal of Chemical Engineering*, **46**, 162–167.

STOLL, R. D., BAUTISTA, E. & FLOOD, R. 1994. New tools for studying sea-floor geotechnical and geoacoustic properties. *Journal of the Acoustical Society of America*, **96**, 2937–2944.

THIEISEN, M. S. 1992. The role of geosynthetics in erosion and sediment control: an overview. *Geotextiles and Geomembranes*, **11**, 535–550.

TUFAIL, A., MEADOWS, P. S. & MCLAUGHLIN, P. 1989. Meso- and microscale heterogeneity in benthic community structure and the sedimentary environment on an intertidal muddy-sand beach. *Scientia Marina*, **53**, 319–327.

UNDERWOOD, G. J. C. & PATERSON, D. M. 1993. Seasonal changes in diatom biomass, sediment stability and biogenic stabilisation in the Severn Estuary. *Journal of the Marine Biological Association of the United Kingdom*, **73**, 871–887.

WHEATCROFT, R. A. & BUTMAN, C. A. 1997. Spatial and temporal variability in aggregated grain-size distributions, with implications for sediment dynamics. *Continental Shelf Research*, **17**, 367–390.

Spatial heterogeneity in an intertidal sedimentary environment and its macrobenthic community

AZRA MEADOWS, PETER S. MEADOWS & PAT McLAUGHLIN

Biosedimentology Unit, Division of Environmental and Evolutionary Biology, IBLS, Graham Kerr Building, University of Glasgow, Glasgow G12 8QQ, UK

Abstract: The intertidal sedimentary environment is an extremely varied one in which marked differences in habitats and animal communities occur over very short distances. This study reports small scale heterogeneity of an intertidal macrobenthic community and its sedimentary environment in large sand waves in a bay in the Clyde Estuary, Scotland. Three 50 m transects ran across sand waves along a peak (P), along a trough (T) and across a peak and trough (P/T). Five sediment parameters [redox potential (Eh), organic carbon, particle size, shear strength and water table] and abundance of 14 macrobenthic species were measured in contiguous 1 m² quadrats along each transect. There were more positive and negative significant correlations along the P/T transect than the P and T transects. Thirteen correlations were common between pairs of transects. Multivariate cluster and principal component analyses were conducted on the data. The results of the two techniques were broadly in agreement. Distinct clusters of macrobenthic species and sediment parameters were identified. Some species clustered with sediment parameters. Others clustered only with species. These analyses may imply important causal relationships some of which are physically controlled and some of which are biologically controlled. Some clusters contained solely species that were deposit feeders. Clusters of quadrats along the P/T transect grouped quadrats on the peaks, in the troughs and on the slopes of the sand waves. These show that the peaks, troughs and slopes are significantly different sedimentary microenvironments. Clusters of quadrats along the P and along the T transect grouped quadrats that were spatially adjacent. These clusters indicate significant small scale spatial variability along the peaks and along the troughs of the sand waves.

The coastal zone is an area of dynamic change and spatial heterogeneity. This is particularly true of the intertidal zone where sedimentary environments are alternately exposed to air and water as the tide falls and rises. In addition, winds, currents and river input produce a wide variety of salinity and hydraulic energy regimes. As a result, sedimentary environments together with their infaunal species show marked temporal and spatial heterogeneity (Schäfer 1972; Anderson & Meadows 1978; Reineck & Singh 1980; Gray 1981; Thiery 1982; Reise 1985; Tufail *et al.* 1989; Mackie *et al.* 1995; Lindsay & Woodin 1996). As compared to the subtidal zone, this heterogeneity is often on a relatively small scale that is detectable over distances of metres.

There has been considerable interest in these phenomena in subtidal continental shelf and deep sea communities which has centred on the functional relationships between biological communities and their physical and chemical environment (Sanders 1968; Rhoads & Young 1970; Dayton & Hessler 1972; Grassle & Sanders 1973; Jumars 1975; Gray 1977; Peterson 1980; Warwick & Uncles 1980; Josefson 1981; Ambrose 1984; McGuiness 1984; Commito & Ambrose

1985; Meadows & Tait 1985; Wildish 1985; Marques & Bellan-Santini 1993). Few authors, however, have attempted to analyse these interactions in intertidal sedimentary environments (Reise 1985; Tufail *et al.* 1989; Thrush *et al.* 1994; Lindsay *et al.* 1996; McLachlan *et al.* 1996).

In this paper we analyse small scale heterogeneity in a macrobenthic community and its sedimentary environment on an intertidal bay in the Clyde Estuary, Scotland. The sediment in the lower intertidal region of the bay is formed into large sand waves by prevailing westerly winds, and is a relatively high energy environment. The bay provides a unique opportunity to assess variability in sedimentary environments and in their associated infaunal macrobenthic communities. We established three 50 m transects, one across and two along the peaks and troughs of the sand waves, and used correlation coefficients and multivariate cluster analysis and principal component analysis on data from contiguous 1 m² quadrats. This allowed us to measure small-scale variability in both the sedimentary environment and its associated infaunal macrobenthic community, and to relate physical variability with community structure.

MEADOWS, A., MEADOWS, P. S. & McLAUGHLIN, P. 1998. Spatial heterogeneity in an intertidal sedimentary environment and its macrobenthic community. *In*: BLACK, K. S., PATERSON, D. M. & CRAMP, A. (eds) *Sedimentary Processes in the Intertidal Zone*. Geological Society, London, Special Publications, **139**, 367–388.

Study area and methods

The study site was a bay at Ardmore Point in the Clyde Estuary (Latitude 55°58′32″N, Longitude 4°41′29″W) (British National Grid Reference NS 322 792). The intertidal muddy sand beach is divided into a number of visually distinct areas (Fig. 1). Towards the low tide area there are sand waves with a wavelength of *c.* 25 m that run at right angles to the prevailing winds. 1–3 cm of water usually remain in the centre of their troughs after the tide recedes. These sand waves are almost certainly maintained by the prevailing winds acting on the water while the tide covers the beach, and they persist in size and position throughout the year. This is a relatively high energy erosional area of the beach and often receives much wave action. Part of the high tide area is covered by algal mats of between 1 and 5 m² that are interspersed with bare sediment. Here also, parts of the bare sediment remain covered with water after the tide has receded. The mats die down in winter but maintain their approximate position and size from year to year. These mats have spread towards the middle area of the beach during the last ten years. There are also small boulders scattered in the upper intertidal zone. Between the low and high tide areas there is an area of flat sediment on the left hand side of the bay. The overall geomorphological areas of the beach, including the sand waves have been permanent features of the beach at Ardmore for at least 20 yr.

Three 50 m transects were established in the sand wave area of the lower intertidal zone during October. The first transect was at right angles to the sand waves and is referred to as the peak/trough (P/T) transect. The second transect ran along a peak of one of the sand waves and is referred to as the peak transect (P). The third transect ran along the trough of an adjacent sand wave and is referred to as the trough transect (T). The peak/trough transect (P/T) crossed the peak transect (P) and the trough transect (T) at right angles. The exact position at which the P/T transect crossed the P transect was 573 m from high tide (SE), 286 m from the left hand side of the bay (SW), and 313 m from the right hand side of the bay (NE). Figure 2 shows that the P/T transect consisted of two half peaks (P1 and P3), one complete peak (P2) and two full troughs (T1 and T2). It also contained four slopes, two between P1 and P2, and two between P2 and P3. The P transect intersected the first half peak (P1) of the P/T transect, and the T transect intersected the first trough (T1) of the P/T transect. The P and T transects were *c.* 6 m apart at the point where the P/T transect

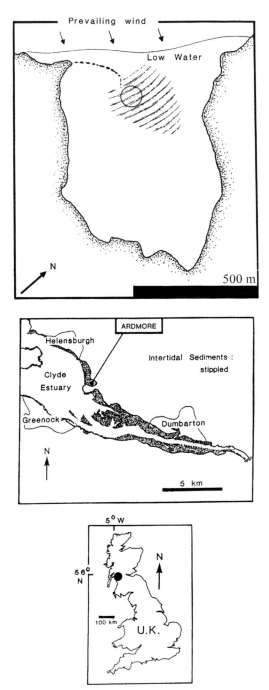

Fig. 1. Study area at Ardmore Bay in the Clyde Estuary, Scotland, UK. Upper diagram: Ardmore Bay showing the Low Tide site of the three (P/T, P and T) transects (encircled). Middle diagram: position of Ardmore Bay in the Clyde Estuary. Bottom diagram: position of the Clyde Estuary (●) in Britain.

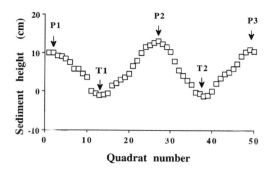

Fig. 2. Peak/trough (P/T) transect: sediment height (cm) above the water table level (0 cm) along the transect. The positions of the first, second and third peaks (P1, P2, P3), and the first and second troughs (T1, T2) are indicated by arrows. The peak (P) transect crossed the P/T transect at P1 and the trough (T) transect crossed the P/T transect at T1.

intersected them, which was at the centre of their lengths, in other words at about quadrat 25 on the P transect and quadrat 25 on the trough transect.

Measurements of five sediment parameters: shear strength, redox potential (Eh), water table, particle size, organic carbon content, and of the abundance of 14 macrobenthic species were made on contiguous 1 m² quadrats along the three transects. Shear strength was measured with a Geonor fall cone apparatus and redox potential with standard Eh electrodes (Platinum, Calomel). Four readings of shear strength and four of redox potential were taken in each quadrat. The shear strength readings were taken at the surface of the sediment, and the redox potential readings at a depth of 0.25–0.5 cm, which was the minimum depth of penetration of the electrodes.

The vertical depth of the water table below the sediment surface was measured by digging a hole in each of the quadrats and measuring the depth of the water below the sediment surface after the hole had filled up to its equilibrium position. Hence, larger positive values (cm) mean that the water table was further below the sediment surface. If the water was above the sediment surface the depth of water was measured and then recorded as a negative value. Measurement of the water table also allowed us to construct the profile shown in Fig. 2. Surface sediment samples were collected from each quadrat and air-dried for particle size and organic carbon analysis. Particle size was measured by dry sieving, using 1 mm (0 ϕ), 500 μm (1 ϕ), 250 μm (2 ϕ), 125 μm (3 ϕ), 63 μm (4 ϕ) sieves and the receiver (BS 1377 1975; Buchanan

1984). Organic carbon content was determined by the chromic acid wet oxidation method (Walkley & Black 1934; Buchanan 1984).

The abundance of the animal species in each quadrat was measured in two ways. *Arenicola marina* (Linnaeus) abundance was measured by counting numbers of casts, since it is known from previous work on this shore (Girling 1984) that the number of casts and number of animals are linearly related. Similar relationships have also been reported from other shores (Holme 1949; Longbottom 1970; Cadée 1976). The abundance of the remaining species was measured by taking one core of sediment 10.4 cm diameter and 15 cm deep from the centre of each 1 m² quadrat, and then sieving the sediment through a 500 μm sieve. The 15 cm depth was selected after preliminary tests with a 50 cm long core divided into 5 cm sections showed that all the individuals of the infaunal species occurred within the top 15 cm of sediment column. The infaunal species were classified according to their feeding modes into the following five groups: deposit feeders (D), carnivores (C), herbivores (H), omnivores (O) and suspension feeders (S) (McCall & Tevesz 1982; Fish & Fish 1989; Hayward & Ryland 1995).

The species were as follows: *Arenicola marina, Eteone longa, Hediste diversicolor, Nephtys hombergi, Pygospio elegans, Phyllodoce maculata, Scoloplos armiger*, a tubificid, *Cerastoderma edule, Hydrobia ulvae, Macoma balthica, Bathyporeia pilosa, Crangon* spp. and *Idotea* spp.

Statistical analyses

Bivariate statistics and multivariate statistics were applied to the data as follows. Correlation coefficients were calculated between species and sediment parameters, between species, and between sediment parameters, for each transect separately.

Multivariate cluster analysis and principal component analysis were then applied to the data from each transect (Maxwell 1977; Everitt 1980; Shaw & Wheeler 1985; Krebs 1989). Correlations were used for both multivariate analyses. Average linkage was used in the cluster analysis. The cluster analyses are divided into two major categories (Fig. 3): (1) clustering of species and sediment parameters using the quadrats and (2) clustering of the quadrats using the species and sediment parameters. Each of the categories was applied firstly to the peak/trough transect, secondly to the peak transect, and thirdly to the trough transect. In category 1, the species and sediment parameters

CLUSTER ANALYSES

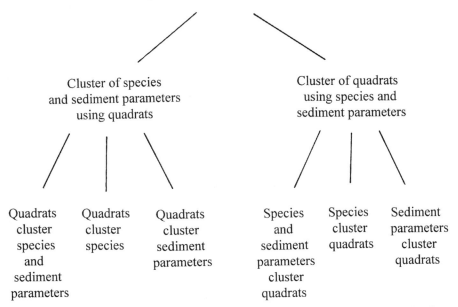

Fig. 3. Flow diagram showing two categories of cluster analyses conducted on the species and sediment parameter data from the peak/trough (P/T) transect, the peak (P) transect, the trough (T) transect. Each transect contained $50 \times 1\,\mathrm{m}^2$ quadrats.

were firstly clustered together, then the species were clustered separately, and lastly the sediment parameters were clustered separately. This was done using the quadrats. In category 2, the quadrats were firstly clustered using the species and sediment parameters together, then the quadrats were clustered using the species only, and finally the quadrats were clustered using the sediment parameters only. Principal component analyses were applied to the macrobenthic species and sediment parameter data for each transect in turn.

Results

The results are divided into three sections. The first describes the correlation analyses, the second the cluster analyses and the third the principal component analyses.

Correlation analysis

Peak/trough transect

There were a number of significant correlations along the P/T transect (Table 1). *A. marina* was positively correlated with *E. longa*, *P. elegans*, water table, redox potential and shear strength, but negatively correlated with *H. diversicolor*, *P. maculata*, *S. armiger*, *M. balthica*, *B. pilosa* and organic carbon. This indicates that *A. marina* was more abundant in more aerobic sediment with a higher shear strength where the sediment height above the water table was high. *E. longa* and *P. elegans* were positively correlated with the water table, while *H. diversicolor*, *P. maculata*, *S. armiger*, *H. ulvae*, *M. balthica*, *B. pilosa* and *Crangon* spp. were negatively correlated with the water table. The abundance of *E. longa* and *P. elegans* was higher where shear strength was high (positive correlations), while *H. diversicolor*, *P. maculata*, *S. armiger*, *M. balthica* and *B. pilosa* were negatively correlated with shear strength. *P. maculata*, *C. edule*, and *N. hombergi* were more abundant in regions with a high organic content (positive correlations). *B. pilosa* was the only species which was significantly correlated with particle size and was more abundant in finer sediment (positive correlation with particle size in phi units). There were three negative and three positive correlations between pairs of sediment parameters. Organic carbon was negatively correlated with sediment height above the water table, with redox potential, and with shear strength.

Table 1. Correlation coefficients for the peak/trough (P,T) transect

	Am	El	Hd	Nh	Pe	Pm	Sa	Tu	Ce	Hu	Mb	Bp	Cran	Ido	O.C.	Par.S	W.T	Eh
El	0.647***																	
Hd	−0.274*	−0.064																
Nh	−0.136	−0.396**	−0.024															
Pe	0.348*	0.343*	−0.132	−0.019														
Pm	−0.512***	−0.181	0.255	0.053	−0.053													
Sa	−0.475***	−0.307*	0.136	−0.010	−0.136	0.411**												
Tu	−0.065	−0.053	0.005	−0.232	0.061	−0.095	−0.081											
Ce	−0.138	−0.025	0.002	0.389**	0.286*	0.121	0.073	0.020										
Hu	−0.177	−0.267	0.038	0.121	−0.261	−0.22	0.123	0.355*	−0.085									
Mb	−0.516***	−0.278*	0.231	0.009	−0.221	0.781***	0.795**	0.104	−0.108	0.219*								
Bp	−0.424**	−0.374**	0.013	0.227	−0.057	0.373**	0.564**	0.131	0.290*	−0.026	0.174							
Cran	−0.239	−0.077	0.108	0.099	−0.290*	0.036	−0.068	−0.095	−0.208	−0.087	0.046	0.157						
Ido	−0.023	0.036	0.423**	−0.016	0.163	0.208	−0.009	0.025	0.009	0.408	0.230	−0.053	−0.082					
O.C.	−0.351*	−0.155	0.096	0.091	−0.190	0.342*	0.238	0.101	0.274*	0.039	0.213	0.289*	0.154	0.079				
Par.S	−0.004	0.080	−0.013	0.170	0.011	−0.001	−0.042	−0.082	0.212	−0.195	−0.176	0.279*	0.026	0.076	0.040			
W.T	0.785***	0.434***	−0.391**	−0.189	0.455***	−0.554***	−0.474***	0.020	−0.149	−0.320*	−0.59C***	−0.364**	−0.291*	−0.075	−0.456***	−0.029		
Eh	0.316*	0.155	−0.471***	−0.031	0.108	−0.305*	−0.123	−0.095	−0.195	−0.137	−0.346*	−0.135	−0.121	−0.278*	−0.413**	0.077	0.619***	
S.st	0.587***	0.286*	−0.368**	−0.230	0.348*	−0.526***	−0.419***	0.057	−0.247	−0.261	−0.493***	−0.454***	−0.265	−0.118	−0.566***	−0.136	0.876***	0.634***
	Am	El	Hd	Nh	Pe	Pm	Sa	Tu	Ce	Hu	Mb	Bp	Cran	Ido	O.C.	Par.S	W.T	Eh

Correlations are between the 14 species (*Arenicola marina*, *Eteone longa*, *Hedste diversicolor*, *Nephtys hombergi*, *Pygospio elegans*, *Phyllodoce maculata*, *Scoloplos armiger*, a tubificid, *Cerastoderma edule*, *Hydrobia ulvae*, *Macoma balthica*, *Bathyporeia pilosa*, *Crangon* spp. and *Idotea* spp.) and five sediment parameters (organic carbon, particle size, water table, redox potential (Eh) and shear strength). The transect was divided into $50 \times 1\,m^2$ quadrats.
Probabilities: $0.05 > P > 0.02$*, $0.02 > P > 0.01$**, $P < 0.01$***. d.f. = 48.

Table 2. *Correlation coefficients for the peak (P) transect*

	Am	El	Hd	Nh	Pe	Pm	Sa	Tu	Ce	Hu	Mb	Bp	Cran	Ido	O.C.	Par.S	W.T	Eh
El	0.257																	
Hd	0.229	0.053																
Nh	0.307*	0.247	0.037															
Pe	0.230	0.043	0.234	0.284*														
Pm	0.149	0.093	−0.070	0.339*	0.316*													
Sa	−0.416**	−0.185	−0.122	−0.150	−0.183	0.185												
Tu	0.062	−0.045	−0.107	−0.054	−0.043	−0.076	−0.107											
Ce	−0.043	0.376**	0.034	0.012	−0.099	−0.042	0.065	−0.093										
Hu	−0.097	−0.191	−0.108	−0.093	−0.243	−0.133	−0.102	0.099	0.065									
Mb	0.042	−0.004	−0.068	0.043	−0.225	−0.187	0.130	0.014	−0.023	0.086								
Bp	−0.086	−0.118	−0.014	0.045	0.011	0.094	0.187	0.026	0.044	−0.068	0.093							
Cran	0.007	−0.031	−0.068	−0.080	−0.140	−0.057	−0.059	−0.096	−0.074	−0.071	−0.058	0.328*						
Ido	0.194	0.173	−0.068	−0.080	0.174	−0.057	−0.059	0.045	−0.074	−0.071	−0.058	−0.052	−0.020					
O.C.	−0.226	0.015	−0.295*	−0.263	−0.072	−0.034	0.004	0.287*	0.111	−0.053	−0.061	−0.067	−0.067	−0.110				
Par.S	0.026	−0.028	−0.020	−0.159	0.167	0.052	−0.229	−0.156	−0.047	0.033	−0.326*	0.010	−0.080	−0.131	−0.015			
W.T	0.487***	0.065	0.175	0.004	−0.037	−0.017	−0.292*	0.094	−0.146	−0.052	0.042	−0.520***	−0.126	0.088	−0.142	0.067		
Eh	−0.145	−0.084	0.120	0.179	0.119	−0.003	−0.119	−0.021	0.005	−0.005	−0.326*	−0.089	0.065	0.076	0.011	0.106	0.088	
S.st	0.143	0.122	0.057	0.407**	0.276*	−0.038	−0.361**	−0.019	−0.019	0.022	−0.070	−0.008	0.091	0.057	−0.088	0.016	−0.197	0.115
	Am	El	Hd	Nh	Pe	Pm	Sa	Tu	Ce	Hu	Mb	Bp	Cran	Ido	O.C.	Par.S	W.T	Eh

Note: details as in Table 1.

Table 3. *Correlation coefficients for the trough (T) transect*

	Am	El	Hd	Nh	Pe	Pm	Sa	Tu	Ce	Hu	Mb	Bp	Cran	Ido	O.C.	Par.S	W.T	Eh
El	-0.056																	
Hd	-0.033	0.021																
Nh	0.120	-0.049	-0.251															
Pe	-0.075	0.346*	-0.000	-0.247														
Pm	-0.048	0.002	-0.221	0.035	0.107													
Sa	0.113	0.061	-0.028	-0.117	0.267	0.566												
Tu	-0.081	-0.087	-0.129	-0.170	-0.119	-0.154	-0.235											
Ce	0.263	-0.071	0.113	0.114	-0.064	0.019	0.160	-0.197										
Hu	-0.109	-0.042	0.101	0.164	-0.170	-0.090	-0.218	-0.069	-0.208									
Mb	0.051	0.217	0.130	-0.058	0.249	0.154	0.346*	-0.093	-0.050	0.160								
Bp	0.138	-0.135	0.083	-0.032	-0.021	-0.335*	-0.192	0.218	-0.217	0.276	-0.077							
Cran	-0.231	0.195	-0.289*	0.134	-0.075	-0.041	-0.041	-0.175	-0.098	-0.033	-0.313*	-0.042						
Ido	-0.102	-0.006	-0.220	0.075	0.336*	0.125	-0.117	0.151	-0.143	-0.118	0.024	-0.112	-0.069					
O.C.	0.056	-0.151	0.315*	0.077	-0.351*	0.122	-0.131	0.115	0.029	0.170	-0.172	0.051	0.104	-0.066				
Par.S	-0.116	0.100	-0.261	0.165	-0.071	0.060	0.127	0.087	0.185	0.018	0.002	0.068	-0.044	0.064	-0.223			
W.T	-0.077	-0.029	-0.210	-0.203	-0.083	-0.053	-0.210	0.202	-0.483***	-0.035	-0.322**	0.369**	-0.044	-0.085	-0.061	-0.072		
Eh	0.126	0.074	-0.137	0.074	0.174	-0.001	-0.003	0.154	-0.065	0.035	0.026	0.231	-0.135	0.161	-0.090	0.004	0.177	
S.st	0.065	-0.083	-0.164	0.029	-0.359**	-0.305*	-0.295*	0.158	-0.159	0.182	-0.290*	0.551***	0.160	-0.053	-0.087	0.066	0.499***	0.001
	Am	El	Hd	Nh	Pe	Pm	Sa	Tu	Ce	Hu	Mb	Bp	Cran	Ido	O.C.	Par.S	W.T	Eh

Note: details as in Table 1.

Peak transect

There were fewer significant correlations along the P transect (Table 2). *A. marina* was more abundant where *N. hombergi* numbers were high (positive correlation), but *A. marina* was negatively correlated with *S. armiger*. *A. marina* showed a similar positive correlation to the water table as it did in the P/T transect. *E. longa* was positively correlated with *C. edule*, *N. hombergi* was positively correlated with *P. elegans* and *P. maculata*, *P. elegans* was positively correlated with *P. maculata*, and *B. pilosa* was positively correlated with *Crangon* spp. *H. diversicolor* was less abundant in regions where organic carbon was high (negative correlation). *N. hombergi* and *P. elegans* were more abundant where the sediment shear strength was high (positive correlation), while the reverse was true of *S. armiger* (negative correlation). *M. balthica* was less abundant in sediment which was more aerobic and had a finer particle size (negative correlations with redox potential and particle size in phi units). *B. pilosa* was more abundant where the water table was at or above the sediment surface (negative correlation). There were no significant correlations between pairs of sediment parameters along the peak transect.

Trough transect

The total number of significant correlations along the T transect was the same as for the P transect (Table 3). *P. elegans* was positively correlated with *E. longa* and *Idotea* spp., *H. diversicolor* was negatively correlated with *Crangon* spp. *P. maculata* was negatively correlated with *B. pilosa* and *S. armiger* was positively correlated with *M. balthica*. *P. elegans* was more abundant where organic carbon was low (negative correlation). *P. elegans*, *P. maculata* and *S. armiger* were more abundant where shear strength was low (negative correlations). *B. pilosa* was more abundant where the water table was at or below the sediment surface and where the shear strength was high (positive correlations), while *M. balthica* and *C. edule* were more abundant where the water table was at or above the sediment surface. *M. balthica* was more abundant where shear strength was low (negative correlation). The only significant correlation between pairs of sediment parameters was for shear strength with water table (positive correlation).

Table 4 summarizes the number of positive and negative significant species/species correlations, species/sediment parameters correlations, and sediment parameters/sediment parameters correlations for the P/T transect, P transect and the T transect. There were more significant correlations along the P/T transect (26% species/species; 40% species/sediment parameters; 60% sediment parameters/sediment parameters) as compared with the P transect (8%; 14%; 0%) and the T transect (7%; 14%; 10%). There were more positive than negative species/species correlations for the P/T transect and P transect (14 vs 10, 6 vs 1), while there were more negative

Table 4. *Number of significant positive and negative correlation coefficients along the peak/ trough transect (P/T), the peak transect (P) and the trough transect (T), between pairs of species/species, species/sediment parameters and sediment parameters/sediment parameters*

Transect	Peak/trough	Peak	Trough
Species/species correlations (91 correlations)			
Positive correlations	14	6	3
Negative correlations	10	1	3
Total	24	7	7
Percentage	(26%)	(8%)	(7%)
Species/sediment parameters correlations (70 correlations)			
Positive correlations	11	4	3
Negative correlations	17	6	7
Total	28	10	10
Percentage	(40%)	(14%)	(14%)
Sediment parameters/sediment parameters correlations (10 correlations)			
Positive correlations	3	0	1
Negative correlations	3	0	0
Total	6	0	1
Percentage	(60%)	(0%)	(10%)

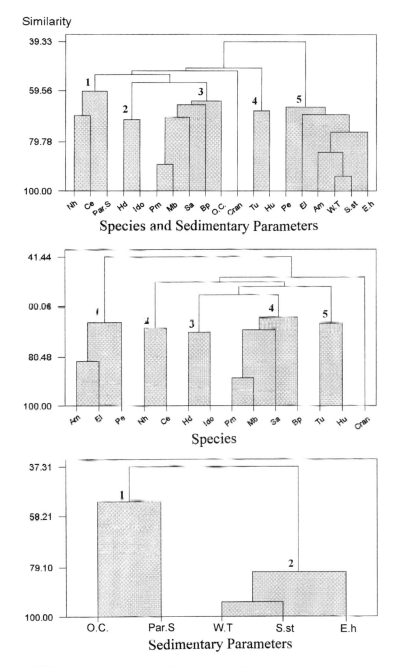

Fig. 4. Peak/trough (P/T) transect. Dendograms of species and sediment parameters clusters. Upper dendogram: clusters of species and sediment parameters. Middle dendogram: clusters of species. Bottom dendogram: clusters of sediment parameters.

than positive species/sediment parameter correlations for the three transects (17 vs 11, 6 vs 4, 7 vs 3).

Multivariate analysis: cluster analysis

Clustering of species and sediment parameters using quadrats

Peak/trough transect.

Species and sediment parameters. Figure 4 gives the dendograms with clusters for the P/T transect and Table 5 gives a detailed description of these clusters (with their similarity level) and

the feeding habits of the species in the cluster. This format, consisting of a figure followed by a table, will be also used in the subsequent description of the cluster analyses.

The P/T cluster analysis of species and sediment parameters produced five clusters (Fig. 4 upper dendogram, Table 5). Three of these were made up of species and sediment parameters, and two contained species only. In cluster 1 particle size grouped with *N. hombergi* and *C. edule*. Cluster 3 contained organic carbon and four species, *P. maculata*, *M. balthica*, *S. armiger* and *B. pilosa*. The first of these species was a carnivore and the remaining ones were deposit feeders. Cluster 5 contained the following sediment parameters, water table, shear strength

Table 5. *Clusters of sediment parameters and species with their feeding habits along the peak and trough (P/T) transect. C = carnivore; D = deposit feeder; H = herbivore; O = omnivore; S = suspension feeder*

Cluster number	Similarity level	Sediment parameter	Species	Feeding habit
Species and sediment parameters				
1	59.54%	Particle size	*N. hombergi*	C
			C. edule	S
2	71.14%	–	*H. diversicolor*	D, O
			Idotea spp.	H, O
3	63.52%	Organic carbon	*P. maculata*	C
			M. balthica	S, D
			S. armiger	D
			B. pilosa	D
4	67.59%	–	Tubificid	D
			H. ulvae	D
5	66.02%	Water table	*A. marina*	D
		Shear strength	*E. longa*	D
		Eh (redox potential)	*P. elegans*	D
Species				
1	67.25%	–	*A. marina*	D
			E. longa	D
			P elegans	D
2	69.43%	–	*N. hombergi*	C
			C. edule	S
3	71.14%	–	*H. diversicolor*	D, O
			Idotea spp.	H, O
4	65.20%	–	*P. maculata*	C
			M. balthica	S, D
			S. armiger	D
			B. pilosa	D
5	67.59%	–	Tubificid	D
			H. ulvae	D
Sediment parameters				
1	51.99%	Organic carbon	–	–
		Particle size		
2	81.33%	Water table	–	–
		Shear strength		
		Eh (redox potential)		

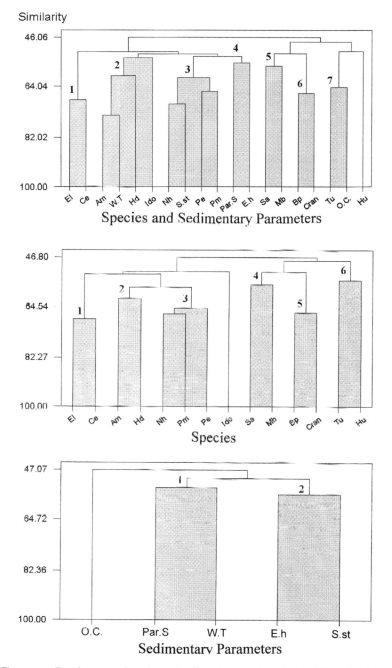

Fig. 5. Peak (P) transect. Dendograms of species and sediment parameters clusters. Upper dendogram: clusters of species and sediment parameters. Middle dendogram: clusters of species. Bottom dendogram: clusters of sediment parameters.

and redox potential, and the deposit feeders *A. marina, E. longa* and *P. elegans*. Clusters 2 and 4 contained pairs of species, *H. diversicolor* and *Idotea* spp., and the tubificid and *H. ulvae*, respectively.

Species only. This analysis also contained five clusters (Fig. 4 middle dendogram, Table 5). Cluster 1 contained all deposit feeders *A. marina, E. longa* and *P. elegans*. Clusters 2–5 contained species showing different feeding habits. It is interesting to note that all five clusters of species were also present in the previous cluster of species and sediment parameters (see above), except that clusters 1, 3 and 5 also included sediment parameters.

Sediment parameters only. The analysis produced two clusters (Fig. 4 bottom dendogram and Table 5). The first contained organic carbon and particle size. The second cluster contained water table, shear strength and redox potential, and was similar to cluster 5 of species and sediment parameters (see above) excluding the species.

Peak transect.

Species and sediment parameters. The analysis produced seven clusters (Fig. 5 upper dendogram, Table 6). Three of these contained species and sediment parameters (clusters 2, 3 and 7), three contained species only (clusters 1, 5 and 6) and one contained sediment parameters

Table 6. *Clusters of sediment parameters and species with their feeding habits along the peak transect (P). C = carnivore; D = deposit feeder; H = herbivore; O = omnivore; S = suspension feeder*

Cluster number	Similarity level	Sediment parameter	Species	Feeding habit
Species and sediment parameters				
1	68.78%	–	*E. longa*	D
			C. edule	S
2	53.57%	Water table	*A. marina*	D
			H. diversicolor	D, O
			Idotea spp.	H, O
3	60.77%	Shear strength	*N. hombergi*	C
			P. elegans	D
			P. maculata	C
4	55.32%	Particle size Eh (redox potential)	–	–
5	56.50%	–	*S. armiger*	D
			M. balthica	S, D
6	66.42%	–	*B. pilosa*	D
			Crangon spp.	C
7	64.34%	Organic carbon	Tubificid	D
Species				
1	68.78%	–	*E. longa*	D
			C. edule	S
2	61.44%	–	*A. marina*	D
			H. diversicolor	D, O
3	65.00%	–	*N. hombergi*	C
			P. maculata	C
			P. elegans	D
4	56.50%	–	*S. armiger*	D
			M. balthica	S, D
5	66.42%	–	*B. pilosa*	D
			Crangon spp.	C
6	54.93%	–	Tubificid	D
			H. ulvae	D
Sediment parameters				
1	53.35%	Particle size Water table	–	–
2	55.77%	Eh (redox potential) Shear strength	–	–

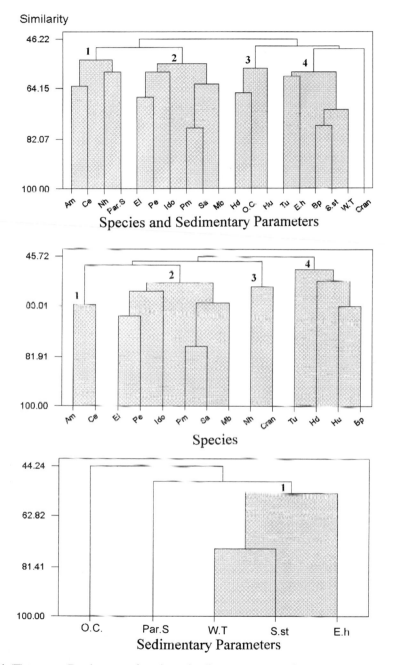

Fig. 6. Trough (T) transect. Dendograms of species and sediment parameters clusters. Upper dendogram: clusters of species and sediment parameters. Middle dendogram: clusters of species. Bottom dendogram: clusters of sediment parameters.

only (cluster 4). Cluster 2 showed that *A. marina,* *H. diversicolor* and *Idotea* spp. were grouped with water table. Cluster 3 contained two carnivores *N. hombergi* and *P. maculata* and one deposit feeder *P. elegans* grouped with shear strength. In cluster 7 the Tubificid clustered with organic carbon confirming that this deposit feeder is also dependent on organic matter for food. Cluster 4 contained particle size with redox potential. Clusters 1, 5 and 6 grouped pairs of species with differing feeding modes.

Species only. The analysis produced six clusters (Fig. 5 middle dendogram, Table 6). Four of these (clusters 1, 3, 4 and 5) contained similar groups of species to those in clusters 1, 3, 5 and 6 in the above analysis of species and

sediment parameters (see above). The remaining two (clusters 2 and 6) contained pairs of deposit feeder species.

Sediment parameters only. There were two clusters (Fig. 5 bottom dendogram, Table 6). One contained particle size and water table (cluster 1) and the other grouped redox potential and shear strength (cluster 2).

Trough transect.

Species and sediment parameters. The analysis produced four clusters (Fig. 6 upper dendogram, Table 7). Three of these (clusters 1, 3 and 4) contained sediment parameters and species and one (cluster 2) contained six species with varying feeding habits. In cluster 1 particle size

Table 7. *Clusters of sediment parameters and species with their feeding habits along the trough transect (T). C = carnivore; D = deposit feeder; H = herbivore; O = omnivore; S = suspension feeder*

Cluster number	Similarity level	Sediment parameter	Species	Feeding habit
Species and sediment parameters				
1	53.78%	Particle size	*A. marina*	D
			C. edule	S
			N. hombergi	C
2	55.19%	–	*E. longa*	D
			P. elegans	D
			Idotea spp.	H, O
			P. maculata	C
			S. armiger	D
			M. balthica	S, D
3	56.80%	Organic carbon	*H.diversicolor*	D, O
			H. ulvae	D
4	58.22%	Eh (redox potential)	Tubificid	D
		Shear strength	*B. pilosa*	D
		Water table		
Species				
1	63.16%	–	*A. marina*	D
			C. edule	S
2	55.19%	–	*E. longa*	D
			P. elegans	D
			Idotea spp.	H, O
			P. maculata	C
			S. armiger	D
			M. balthica	S, D
3	56.69%	–	*N. hombergi*	C
			Crangon spp.	C
4	50.33%	–	Tubificid	D
			H. diversicolor	D, O
			H. ulvae	D
			B. pilosa	D
Sediment parameters				
1	54.54%	Water table	–	–
		Shear strength		
		Eh (redox potential)		

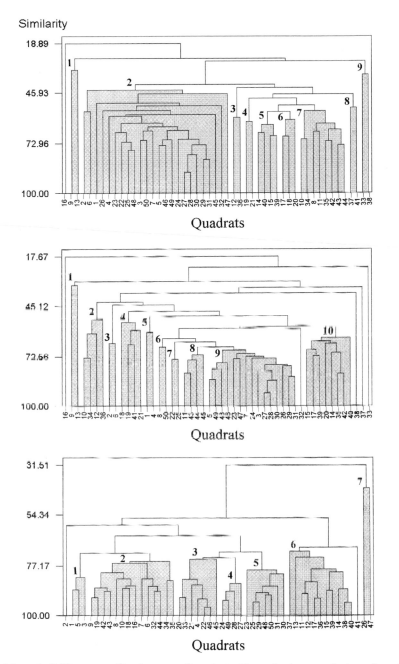

Fig. 7. Peak/trough (P/T) transect. Dendograms of quadrats. Upper dendogram: clusters of quadrats using species and sediment parameters. Middle dendogram: clusters of quadrats using species. Bottom dendogram: clusters of quadrats using sediment parameters.

grouped with *A. marina*, *C. edule* and *N. hombergi*. Cluster 3 contained organic carbon and two deposit feeders *H. diversicolor* and *H. ulvae*. Cluster 4 grouped redox potential (Eh), shear strength and water table with the Tubificid and *B. pilosa*.

Species only. The analysis produced four clusters (Fig. 6 middle dendogram, Table 7). Cluster 2 contained six species and was identical to cluster 2 in the previous analysis of species and sediment parameters. Clusters 1 and 3 contained pairs of species, *A. marina* and *C. edule* in the former and the carnivores *N. hombergi* and *Crangon* spp. in the latter. Cluster 4 grouped four species which are chiefly deposit feeders.

Sediment parameters only. There was one cluster in the analysis (cluster 1), which grouped water table, shear strength and redox potential (Fig. 6 bottom dendogram, Table 7). Organic carbon and particle size did not form a cluster.

Clustering of quadrats using species and sediment parameters

Peak/trough transect.

Species and sediment parameters. This analysis produced nine clusters (Fig. 7 upper dendogram, Table 8) which grouped the quadrats into peak, slope, trough, slope and peak, and slope and trough regions along the P/T transect. Cluster 2, the largest cluster, was made up of 24 quadrats all from the peak regions. Cluster 7 contained 8, and cluster 6 contained 3 slope region quadrats. Cluster 5 contained 4 and cluster 3 contained 2 quadrats from the trough region. Clusters 1, 8 and 9 all contained 2 slope and trough quadrats.

Species only. There were ten clusters in this analysis (Fig. 7 middle dendogram, Table 8). Cluster 9 contained the largest number of quadrats of 15, while clusters 3, 5, and 7 contained 2 quadrats each, all in the peak region. Clusters 1,

Table 8. *Clusters of quadrats along the peak and trough (P/T) transect. The clusters classify the transect into: peak, slope, trough, slope and peak, or slope and trough regions along the transect*

Cluster number	Similarity level	Number of quadrats	Region along the transect
Species and sediment parameters			
1	33.46%	2	Slope and trough
2	44.28%	24	Peak
3	59.24%	2	Trough
4	61.26%	2	Slope
5	63.30%	4	Trough
6	60.47%	3	Slope
7	55.57%	8	Slope
8	53.95%	2	Slope and trough
9	35.99%	2	Slope and trough
Species			
1	33.35%	2	Slope and trough
2	52.46%	4	Slope and trough
3	65.49%	2	Peak
4	54.06%	4	Slope
5	59.67%	2	Peak
6	67.58%	2	Slope and peak
7	74.22%	2	Peak
8	71.86%	4	Slope and trough
9	69.40%	15	Peak
10	62.53%	8	Slope and trough
Sediment parameters			
1	82.65%	3	Peak
2	75.34%	14	Slope
3	74.42%	7	Slope and peak
4	85.48%	4	Peak
5	79.51%	7	Peak
6	70.80%	11	Trough
7	42.12%	2	Peak

2, 8 and 10 contained 2, 4, 4 and 8 slope and trough quadrats, respectively. Cluster 4 was made up of 4 slope quadrats and cluster 6 contained 2 slope and peak quadrats.

Sediment parameters only. This analysis gave 7 clusters (Fig. 7 bottom dendogram, Table 8). Cluster 2 was the largest cluster with 14 slope region quadrats. Clusters 1, 4, 5 and 7 were made up of 3, 4, 7 and 2 peak quadrats, respectively. Cluster 3 contained 7 slope and peak quadrats and cluster 6 contained 11 trough quadrats.

Peak transect and trough transect. These analyses produced a number of clusters on both transects. The clusters, which are not illustrated, were examined to determine whether closely adjacent quadrats along the transects clustered together. This proved to be the case along both the peak and the trough transect. It is more obvious when species and sediment parameters are used to cluster the quadrats than when either species or sediment parameters are used separately. The phenomenon indicates a spatial patchiness along both the peaks (P) and troughs (T) of the sand wave system.

Multivariate analysis: principal component analysis

Grouping of species and sediment parameters

The results of the principal component analyses are shown in Fig. 8. The first principal component (y axis) has been plotted against the second principal component (x axis) for the species and sediment parameters in each of the three transects. In this figure, we have identified the clusters of species and sedimentary parameters which were obtained by cluster analysis (Figs 5, 6 and 7 upper dendograms). In clusters containing two items, the items are joined by a single line.(e.g. clusters 2 and 4, P/T transect: Fig. 4 upper dendogram; Fig. 8 upper plot). In clusters containing more than two items, the outer items are joined by lines forming a polygon within which the items of the cluster lie (e.g. clusters 1 and 5, P/T transect: Fig. 4 upper dendogram; Fig. 8 upper plot).

Peak/trough transect. The 5 clusters of species and sediment parameters identified in the cluster analysis for the P/T transect (Fig. 4 upper dendogram) can also be identified in the upper plot of Fig. 8.

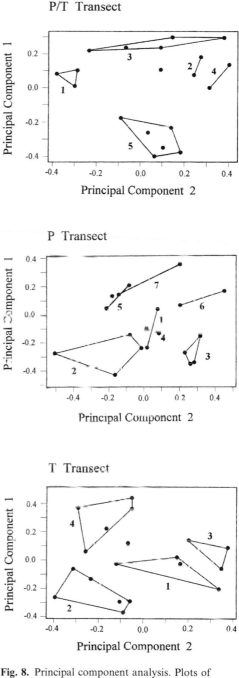

Fig. 8. Principal component analysis. Plots of principal component 1 (y axis) and principal component 2 (x axis) showing clusters of macrobenthic species and sediment parameters. Upper plot: peak/trough (P/T) transect. Middle plot: peak (P) transect. Bottom plot: trough (T) transect.

Peak transect. The 7 clusters of species and sediment parameters identified in the cluster analysis for the P transect (Fig. 5 upper dendogram) can also be identified in the middle plot of Fig. 8. In Fig. 8, clusters 5 and 7, and also clusters 1 and 4, are closely related to each other.

Trough transect. The four clusters of species and sediment parameters identified in the cluster analysis for the T transect (Fig. 6 upper dendogram) can also be identified in the lower plot of Fig. 8.

These results show that the two types of multivariate analyses, cluster analysis and principal component analysis, produce similar results when applied to the data from the three transects. Clusters of species and sedimentary parameters identified in the cluster analyses shown in Figs 4–6 can be readily identified in the principal component analyses plots in Fig. 8. In Fig. 8, most of the clusters are distinct from each other. In only two instances do clusters identified by the cluster analysis overlap in the principal component analysis plots, clusters 1 and 4, and clusters 5 and 7 for the P transect (Fig. 8 middle plot). Overall, therefore, these analyses show that the two multivariate techniques are consistent between themselves, and are robust when applied to our data.

Discussion

Ardmore Bay is unusual in having clearly differentiated areas in its intertidal zone that are visible to the casual observer. Furthermore, the prevailing winds give a symmetry to the lower part of the beach in the form of regular sand waves that appear to maintain their position year in and year out. A detailed inspection of these sand waves when the tide has receded shows that their peaks are dry and well drained, whereas their troughs are usually covered with water and sometimes contain fine detrital material. It is also obvious that at least one species has a patchy distribution that matches the peaks and troughs. Casts of the lugworm *A. marina* show that it is more abundant on the peaks. There are therefore *a priori* reasons for expecting the peak/trough system to impose a symmetry on sediment structure and on the macrobenthic community. This symmetrical patchiness if it existed, may also overlay other forms of patchiness that are present in both the sediments and their infauna that are not related to the sand waves. It was these initial observations and hypotheses that provided the starting point for our work. We used a peak/trough transect, intersected by a peak transect and a trough transect, together with correlation analyses, and multivariate cluster and principal component analyses on the data from the contiguous 1 m² quadrats. These highlighted associations and patterns of spatial patchiness within the sedimentary environment and the macrobenthic community in the area.

Associations between species and sediment parameters along the transects

There are a number of interesting associations along and between the transects that have been brought to light by the correlation analyses, and the multivariate cluster and principal component analyses. These concern differences between the numbers of positive and negative correlations and between the ways in which the multivariate analyses identified groupings of the species and sediment parameters.

There are a larger number of positive and negative significant correlations along the P/T transect than along the P or T transects. It is not immediately obvious why this should be so. It could be caused by the increased spatial heterogeneity along the P/T transect compared with the less heterogeneous environment along the P and T transects. It could also be related to the inclusion in the P/T transect of the data from quadrats on the slopes of the peaks and troughs. These observations may mean that in a spatially more heterogeneous environment, such as along the P/T transect, there are likely to be a greater number of interactions between species and sediment parameters as a whole. Conversely, in a spatially less heterogeneous environment, like the P and T transects, less variable conditions prevail, which may be responsible for the fewer significant correlations.

One of the important points to arise from the cluster analyses and the principal component analyses was the groupings between species and sediment parameters. For example, four species, two species and one species, respectively, clustered with organic carbon along the P/T transect, T transect and P transect. In the same way, three species (P/T) and two species (T), respectively, clustered with a group of sediment parameters consisting of redox potential (Eh), shear strength and the water table. It is also significant that the species associated with the sediment parameters are different on the different transects. There are no species associated with organic carbon that are common between the P/T, T and P transects.

These clusters imply either that sediment parameters are causally important in determining the abundance of the associated species or that the species are modifying some of the sediment parameters. In cluster 1 of the species and sediment parameters on the P/T transect, *N. hombergi* and *C. edule* cluster with particle size. The two species may prefer and hence be abundant in sediment of a particular particle size. However, it is also possible that the burrowing activities of both species transport certain particle sizes preferentially in the sediment column, thus modifying the local particle size distribution. Similar reasoning can be applied to the species clustered with organic carbon, shear strength and redox potential (Eh). Species may prefer sediments having a particular level of organic carbon, shear strength or redox potential. But it is well known that a number of species can themselves modify sediment properties. They can alter organic carbon, shear strength, redox conditions and sediment mixing by burrowing, selective feeding or the production of extracellular polymeric material (Rhoads 1963; Cadée 1976, 1979; Eckman *et al.* 1981; Aller 1982; Atkinson *et al.* 1982; Thayer 1983; Meadows & Tufail 1986; Meadows & Tait 1989; Meadows & Meadows 1991; Jones & Jago 1993).

Some species were not associated with any of the sediment parameters. There were four, six and four species, respectively, that fall into this category on the P/T, T and P transect. Presumably the abundance and distribution of these species are largely determined by biological interactions such as predation and competition, and less by the nature and properties of the sediment itself (Rhoads & Young 1970; Grassle & Sanders 1973; Woodin 1974, 1978; Peterson 1980; McCall & Tevesz 1982; Ambrose 1984; Commito & Ambrose 1985; Reise 1985; Wilde 1991; Woodin & Marinelli 1991; Lindsay & Woodin 1996; Lindsay *et al.* 1996).

We considered whether some of the clusters formed by species either on their own or with sediment parameters might be related to their mode of feeding. We therefore classified the species into carnivores, deposit feeders, herbivores, omnivores and suspension feeders. Only the deposit feeders clustered together, and these clustered with water table, shear strength, redox potential and in one case with organic carbon. These clusters can be identified on the cluster analysis of the P/T transect and the T transect (Table 5: species and sediment parameter clusters 4 and 5; species cluster 1 and 5. Table 7: species and sediment parameter clusters 3 and 4; species cluster 4). The effect was not so marked on the peak transect.

We regard the finding that macrobenthic species separate into those that are associated with sediment parameters and those that are not, as being of considerable significance in terms of understanding interactions between these species and their sedimentary environment. It is important to test whether this is a feature that is unique to Ardmore Bay or is a common feature of intertidal and subtidal macrobenthic communities and sedimentary environments in general.

A comparison of the species groupings in the species/sediment parameters clusters (Tables 5–7 upper section) and the species groupings in the species clusters (Tables 5–7 middle section) shows striking similarities. In Table 5 (P/T transect) compare cluster 3 in the species and sediment parameters with cluster 4 in the species-only clusters. Exactly the same four species are included: *P. maculata*, *M. balthica*, *S. armiger* and *B. pilosa*. A comparison of the upper sections of Tables 5–7 with the middle sections shows that the pattern occurs with almost every group of species. This could be interpreted as indicating that biological interactions are more important than sediment parameters in determining community structure. On the other hand other evidence suggests that sediment parameters may be equally significant in controlling the abundance and structure of those species that cluster with them. A comparison of the clusters containing sediment parameters only (Tables 5 and 7 lower sections) show that the cluster containing the water table, shear strength and redox potential (Eh) is also present in the species/sediment parameter cluster analyses shown in Tables 5 and 7 upper sections. Clearly there are complex interactions taking place between clusters of species with sediment parameters, clusters containing only species, and clusters containing only sediment parameters. These interactions require further investigation in other intertidal sedimentary environments to establish their generality.

Associations between quadrats along the transects

There were obvious spatial clusters of the quadrats along the P/T transect. These consisted of groups of quadrats that were either on the peak of the sand waves, or in the troughs of the sand waves, or on the slopes of the sand waves (Fig. 7 and Table 8). This clustering indicates that the peaks, slopes and troughs of the sand wave system represent distinctive sedimentary environments each with its own characteristic species grouping. When both species and sediment parameters were used to cluster the quadrats (Fig. 7 upper dendogram; Table 8 upper section, cluster 2), almost all of the peak quadrats formed one very large cluster containing 24 quadrats. This cluster divided into four clusters when clustered by species alone and when clustered by sediment parameters alone.

There were also less obvious but distinct clusters of quadrats along the peak transect and along the trough transect. These clusters contained quadrats that were close to each other. This highly significant finding means that there is small-scale spatial patchiness in the sedimentary environment and associated infauna in addition to that produced by the sand waves.

Common correlations between transects

There were 13 correlations that were common between the transects. Three were species/species correlations, nine were species/sediment correlations, and one was a sediment parameter/sediment parameter correlation. Five of these were between the P/T and P transects and seven were between the P/T and T transects. The common correlations between pairs of transects are as follows. *A. marina* was negatively correlated with *S. armiger*, and positively correlated with the water table, both at the P/T and P transects. *E. longa* and *P. elegans* were positively correlated at P/T and T transects. *P. elegans* was positively correlated with shear strength at the P/T and P transect. *P. maculata* was negatively correlated with shear strength at the P/T and T transects. *S. armiger* was negatively correlated with the water table at the P/T and P transects, but positively correlated with *M. balthica* at the P/T and T transects. *M. balthica* was negatively correlated with redox potential (Eh) at the P/T and P transects, and with the water table and shear strength at the P/T and T transects. *B. pilosa* was negatively correlated with the water table at the P/T and T transects. The water table was positively correlated with shear strength at the P/T and T transects. There was one correlation that was common in all three transects. This was a negative one between *S. armiger* and shear strength. Overall, the common correlations are important reflections of relationships between infauna and sediment parameters that occur irrespective of the spatial heterogeneity imposed by the sand waves or of the less obvious spatial heterogeneity along the P and T transects.

Conclusions

Our study of a small intertidal bay shows that the sedimentary environment together with its macrobenthic community shows significant levels of spatial heterogeneity on a relatively small scale. The spatial patterns are associated with the peaks, troughs and slopes of the sand waves found on the beach. Multivariate cluster analysis of quadrats along the peak and trough transects and between the peak and trough transects has shown that there is less spatial heterogeneity in the distribution and abundance of species and the levels of sediment parameters along the peaks and along the troughs than between the troughs and peaks. There is, however, a less obvious spatial clustering along the peaks and troughs. It would be very interesting to ascertain whether similar patterns of spatial heterogeneity exist on beaches where the sedimentary environment is less obviously heterogeneous.

The application of multivariate cluster analysis and principal component analysis to the relationships between sediment parameters and the abundance of macrobenthic species has revealed some remarkable patterns. Some species tend to cluster with sediment parameters, implying that either the organisms are affecting the properties of the sediment or that sediment properties are influencing the abundance of the species. Both interactive processes may be at work. Other species cluster only with species, suggesting that in those cases biological interactions such as competition for space or prey predator relationships are the main determinants of species abundance. In addition, some clusters consist of species that are specifically deposit feeders.

In summary, our study has shown that multivariate analyses of sedimentary parameters and abundance of macrobenthic species obtained from carefully designed field transects are powerful tools for benthic ecology and intertidal sedimentary ecosystems. Our approach offers a new methodology for the study of interactive processes between macrobenthic species and their sedimentary environments, and for the quantification of spatial heterogeneity in these environments and their macrobenthic communities.

References

ALLER, R. C. 1982. The effects of macrobenthos on chemical properties of marine sediment and overlying water. *In*: MCCALL, P. L. & TEVESZ, M. J. S. (eds) *Animal–Sediment Relations*. Plenum Press, New York, 53–103.

AMBROSE, W. G. 1984. Role of predatory infauna in structuring marine soft-bottom communities. *Marine Ecology Progress Series,* **17**, 109–115.

ANDERSON, J. G. & MEADOWS, P. S. 1978. Microenvironments in marine sediments. *Proceedings of the Royal Society of Edinburgh,* **B76**, 1–16.

ATKINSON, R. J. A., MOORE, P. G. & MORGAN, P. J. 1982. The burrows and burrowing behaviour of *Maera loveni* (Crustacea: Amphipoda). *Journal of Zoology,* **198**, 399–416.

BS 1377. 1975. *Methods of Test for Soils for Civil Engineering Purposes.* British Standards Institution, London.

BUCHANAN, J. B. 1984. Sediment analysis. *In:* HOLME, N. A. & McINTYRE, A. D. (eds) *Methods for the Study of Marine Benthos,* 2nd edn. IBP Handbook 16. Blackwell Scientific Publication, Oxford, 41–65.

CADÉE, G. C. 1976. Sediment reworking by *Arenicola marina* on tidal flats in the Dutch Wadden Sea. *Netherlands Journal of Sea Research,* **10**, 440–460.

——1979. Sediment reworking by the polychaete *Heteromastus filiformis* on a tidal flat in the Dutch Wadden Sea. *Netherlands Journal of Sea Research,* **13**, 441–456.

COMMITO, J. A. & AMBROSE, W. G. 1985. Predatory infauna and trophic complexity in soft-bottom communities. *In:* GIBBS, P. E. (ed.) *Proceedings of the 19th European Marine Biology Symposium.* Cambridge University Press, Cambridge, 323–333.

DAYTON, P. K. & HESSLER, R. R. 1972. Role of biological disturbance in maintaining diversity in the deep-sea. *Deep Sea Research,* **19**, 199–208.

ECKMAN, J. E., NOWELL, A. R. M. & JUMARS, P. A. 1981. Sediment destabilisation by animal tubes. *Journal of Marine Research,* **39**, 361–374.

EVERITT, B. 1980. *Cluster Analysis,* 2nd edn. Halsted Press, New York.

FISH, J. D. & FISH, S. 1989. *A Students's Guide to the Seashore.* Unwin Hyman, London.

GIRLING, A. E. 1984. *Interactions between marine benthic macroinvertebrates and their sedimentary environment.* PhD Thesis, Glasgow University.

GRASSLE, J. F. & SANDERS, H. L. 1973. Life-histories and the role of disturbance. *Deep Sea Research,* **20**, 643–659.

GRAY, J. S. 1977. The stability of benthic ecosystems. *Helgoländer wissenschaftliche Meeresuntersuchungen,* **30**, 427–444.

——1981. *The Ecology of Marine Sediments.* Cambridge University Press. Cambridge.

HAYWARD, P. J. & RYLAND, J. S. (eds) 1995. *Handbook of the Marine Fauna of North-West Europe.* Oxford University Press, Oxford.

HOLME, N. A. 1949. The fauna of sand and mud banks near the mouth of the Exe estuary. *Journal of the Marine Biological Association of the United Kingdom,* **28**, 189–237.

JONES, S. E. & JAGO, C. F. 1993. *In situ* assessment of modification of sediment properties by burrowing invertebrates. *Marine Biology,* **115**, 133–142.

JOSEFSON, A. B. 1981. Persistence and structure of two deep macrobenthic communities in the Skagerak

(west coast of Sweden). *Journal of Experimental Marine Biology and Ecology,* **50**, 63–97.

JUMARS, P. A. 1975. Environmental grain and polychaete species diversity in a bathyal benthic community. *Marine Biology,* **30**, 253–266.

KREBS, C. J. 1989. *Ecological Methodology.* Harper Collins, New York.

LINDSAY, S. M. & WOODIN, S. A. 1996. Quantifying sediment disturbance by browsed spionid polychaetes – implications for competitive and adult-larval interactions. *Journal of Experimental Marine Biology and Ecology,* **196**, 97–112.

——, WETHEY, D. S. & WOODIN, S. A. 1996. Modeling interactions of browsing predation, infaunal activity and recruitment in marine soft-sediment habitats. *American Naturalist,* **148**, 684–699.

LONGBOTTOM, M. R. 1970. The distribution of *Arenicola marina* (L.) with particular reference to the effects of particle size and organic matter of the sediments. *Journal of Experimental Marine Biology and Ecology,* **5**, 138–157.

McCALL, P. L. & TEVESZ, M. J. S. 1982. *Animal-Sediment Relations. The Biogenic Alteration of Sediments.* Plenum Press, New York.

McGUINESS, K. A. 1984. Equations and explanations in the study of species-area curves. *Biological Reviews,* **59**, 423–440.

McLACHLAN, A., DeRUYCK, A & HACKING, N. 1996. Community structure on sandy beaches – patterns of richness and zonation in relation to tide range and latitude. *Revista Chilena de Historia Natural,* **69**, 451–467.

MACKIE, A. S. Y., OLIVER, P. G. & REES, E. I. S. 1995. *Benthic Biodiversity in the Southern Irish Sea. Studies in Marine Biodiversity and Systematics from the National Museum of Wales.* BIOMÔR Reports, 1/263.

MARQUES, J. C. & BELLAN-SANTINI, D. 1993. Biodiversity in the ecosystem of the Portuguese continental shelf: distributional ecology and the role of benthic amphipods *Marine Biology,* **115**, 555–564.

MAXWELL, A. E. 1977. *Multivariate Analysis in Behavioural Research.* Chapman & Hall, London.

MEADOWS, P. S. & TAIT, J. 1985. Bioturbation, geotechnics and microbiology at the sediment-water interface in deep-sea sediments. *In:* GIBBS, P. E. (ed.) *Proceedings of the 19th European Marine Biology Symposium.* Cambridge University Press, Cambridge 191–199.

——& ——1989. Modification of sediment permeability and shear strength by two burrowing invertebrates. *Marine Biology,* **101**, 75–82.

——& TUFAIL, A. 1986. Bioturbation, microbial activity and sediment properties in an estuarine ecosystem. *Proceedings of the Royal Society of Edinburgh,* **B90**, 129–142.

——& MEADOWS, A. 1991. The geotechnical and geochemical implications of bioturbation in marine sedimentary ecosystems. *In:* MEADOWS, P. S. & MEADOWS, A. (eds) *The Environmental Impact of Burrowing Animals and Animal Burrows.* Zoological Society of London Symposia, 63. Clarendon Press, Oxford, 157–181.

PETERSON, C. H. 1980. Predation, competitive exclusion and diversity in the soft-sediment benthic communities of estuaries and lagoons. *In*: LIVINGSTONE, R. J. (ed.) *Ecological Processes in Coastal and Marine Systems*. Plenum, New York, 233–264.

REINECK, H. E. & SINGH, I. B. 1980. *Depositional Sedimentary Environments*. Springer, Berlin.

REISE, K. 1985. *Tidal Flat Ecology*. Springer, Berlin.

RHOADS, D. C. 1963. Rates of reworking by *Yoldia limulata* in Buzzards Bay, Massachusetts, and Long Island. *Journal of Sedimentary Petrology*, **33**, 723–727.

—— & YOUNG, D. K. 1970. The influence of deposit-feeding organisms on sediment stability and community trophic structure. *Journal of Marine Research*, **28**, 150–178.

SANDERS, H. L. 1968. Marine benthic diversity: a comparative study. *American Naturalist*, **102**, 243–282.

SCHÄFER, W. 1972. *Ecology and Paleoecology of Marine Environments*. Oliver & Boyd, Edinburgh.

SHAW, G. & WHEELER, D. 1985. *Statistical Techniques in Geographical Analysis*. John Wiley & Sons, Chichester.

THAYER, C. W. 1983. Sediment-mediated biological disturbance and the evolution of marine benthos. *In*: TEVESZ, M. J. S. & McCALL, P. L. (eds) *Biotic Interactions in Recent and Fossil Benthic Communities*. Plenum Press, New York, 479–625.

THIERY, R. G. 1982. Environmental instability and community diversity. *Biological Reviews*, **57**, 691–710.

THRUSH, S. F., PRIDMORE, R. D. & HEWITT, J. E. 1994. Impacts on soft-sediment macrofauna – The effects of spatial variation on temporal trends. *Ecological Applications*, **4**, 31–41.

TUFAIL, A., MEADOWS, P. S. & McLAUGHLIN, P. 1989. Meso- and micro-scale heterogeneity in benthic community structure and the sedimentary environment on an intertidal muddy-sand beach.

Proceedings of the 22nd European Marine Biology Symposium, Barcelona. Scientia Marina, **53**, 319–327.

WALKLEY, A. & BLACK, I. A. 1934. An examination of the Degtajareef method for determining soil organic matter, and a proposed modification of the chromic acid titration method. *Soil Science*, **37**, 29–38.

WARWICK, R. M. & UNCLES, R. J. 1980. Distribution of benthic macrofauna associations in the Bristol Channel in relation to tidal stress. *Marine Ecology Progress Series*, **3**, 97–103.

WILDE, P. A., W. J. DE 1991. Interactions in burrowing communities and their effects on the structure of marine benthic ecosystems. *In*: MEADOWS, P. S. & MEADOWS, A. (eds) *The Environmental Impact of Burrowing Animals and Animal Burrows*. Zoological Society of London Symposia, 63. Clarendon Press, Oxford, 107–117.

WILDISH, D. J. 1985. Geographical distribution of macrofauna on sublittoral sediments of continental shelves: a modified trophic ratio concept. *In*: GIBBS, P. E. (ed.) *Proceedings of the 19th European Marine Biology Symposium*. Cambridge University Press, Cambridge, 335–345.

WOODIN, S. A. 1974. Polychaete abundance patterns in a marine soft-sediment environment: the importance of biological interactions. *Ecological Monographs*, **44**, 171–187.

——1978. Refuges, disturbance and community structure: a marine soft-bottom example. *Ecology*, **59**, 274–284.

—— & MARINELLI, R. 1991. Biogenic habitat modification in marine sediments: the importance of species composition and activity. *In*: MEADOWS, P. S. & MEADOWS, A. (eds) *The Environmental Impact of Burrowing Animals and Animal Burrows*. Zoological Society of London Symposia, 63. Clarendon Press, Oxford, 231–250.

The role of vegetation in determining patterns of the accretion of salt marsh sediment

L. A. BOORMAN[1], A. GARBUTT[2] & D. BARRATT[2]

[1] LAB Coastal, The Maylands, Holywell, Cambs PE17 3TQ, UK
[2] Institute of Terrestrial Ecology, Monks Wood, Huntingdon, Cambs PE17 2LS, UK

Abstract: Vegetation contributes to the stability of the salt marsh surface both through the soil reinforcement provided by the root mass and by the ability of the aerial component of plant growth to increase the rates of sediment deposition. Salt marsh vegetation is variable in height, thickness and also in stiffness. These characteristics can all modify the role of the vegetation in trapping sediment. As the height of the vegetation increases so also does Manning's 'n', coefficient of roughness, but the taller vegetation is more easily flattened by moving water. It is not necessarily, therefore, more effective in slowing water flow and increasing sediment deposition. Shorter vegetation (mean height = 50 mm) has been shown to be quite effective, particularly if it is stiff enough to resist being flattened by the water at the rates of flow experienced.

The interplay of rates of sediment deposition is discussed with reference to data relating vegetation structure and pattern to local variations in accretion rates in salt marshes at Stiffkey, Norfolk, and Tollesbury, Essex, over a period of three years. At Tollesbury the mean annual rate of accretion was estimated to be 4.27 mm a^{-1} but there was no correlation between the vegetation height (mean height = 148 mm) and changes in surface level. At Stiffkey however the annual rate of accretion was estimated to be 3.08 mm a^{-1}, but there was a significant positive correlation between vegetation height (mean height = 75 mm) and accretion.

There is evidence that the relationship between effective vegetation height and the process of sediment accumulation is complex. Factors that can affect the relationship include the nature of the sediment, the height and composition of the vegetation and the microtopography and elevation of the marsh itself.

Salt marshes have been defined as intertidal areas of fine sediment that has been transported by water and stabilized by vegetation (Boorman 1995). Once a cover of vegetation has become established the rate of sedimentation (accretion) frequently increases as more of the incoming sediment is intercepted and trapped as the increased surface roughness decreases the velocity of water flow (Stumpf 1983; Stevenson et al. 1988). In addition, the vegetation also reduces the re-suspension of deposited material and, at the same time, organic matter is added to the marsh surface in the form of plant litter and to the marsh soil by below-ground productivity (Allen & Pye 1992).

The relationship between surface erosion from the soil, as a result of the runoff of surface water, and the extent of vegetation cover has been described by Rickson & Morgan (1988). They showed that even a 20% canopy cover could halve the loss of soil while a complete vegetation canopy could reduce the soil loss five-fold. The erosive power of water depends on the mean flow velocity (Morgan 1980) and the vegetation reduces the flow velocity in proportion to the increase in surface roughness that it creates (Rickson & Morgan 1988). The surface roughness can be characterized by a parameter such as Manning's 'n' coefficient (Copping & Richards 1990). This hydraulic roughness depends on the morphology of the plant as well as the height of the vegetation and the flow retardance also depends on the depth of the water flow.

This approach has been shown to be useful in analysing a variety of situations where water flow is modified by the presence of vegetation (Howard-Williams 1992). Once the vegetation is completely covered there is usually a rapid decline in roughness as the vegetation bends over with increasing velocity of water flow (Ree 1949). At low flow velocities the retardance of water flow by the vegetation is proportional to the height of the vegetation but with increasing velocities the retardance of tall vegetation can be less than that of shorter vegetation. Recent studies have indicated that there are some questions regarding the validity of the Manning's 'n' approach in the case of shallow flows (Makeshwari 1992) but in general it remains the best approach currently available. Studies in the United States on the relationship between the retardance of water flow and grass height showed that over a range of velocities a height of 50–150 mm was the most effective. The retardance at 50 mm showed that relatively short grass was effective. Grass taller than 150 mm

BOORMAN, L. A., GARBUTT, A. & BARRATT, D. 1998. The role of vegetation in determining patterns of the accretion of salt marsh sediment. *In*: BLACK, K. S., PATERSON, D. M. & CRAMP, A. (eds) *Sedimentary Processes in the Intertidal Zone*. Geological Society, London, Special Publications, **139**, 389–399.

showed a greater retardance only at low velocities (USSCS 1954). The erosion resistance of grass also depends on the degree of ground cover; good cover significantly increases the resistance to erosion by moving water (Hewlett *et al.* 1987). Clearly, where the vegetation is not composed solely of grasses but is made up of a mixture of broad-leaved and grassy species the picture will be considerably more complex although the same principles should apply.

The studies described above have all been concerned with the retardance of the water flow and the consequent reduction of erosion of sediment from the soil surface following the retardance of water flow. While this is of importance in the salt marsh situation the increased interception of sediment particles from the water column is of equal if not greater importance. From the point of view of the vertical growth of the salt marsh the net balance between the two processes is the key factor. This net balance can be defined in terms of the net addition of material to the marsh surface per tide or per annum. The latter time interval is perhaps the more useful as both accretion and erosion can vary greatly from tide to tide so that short term measurements (days, weeks or even months) are variable and potentially misleading if considered in isolation.

The studies described in this paper attempt to examine some aspects of the spatial variation in net rates of accretion observed in two East Anglian salt marshes and to consider the role played by the height and architecture of the vegetation cover. Consideration is also given to the various other environmental factors which influence the processes of accretion and erosion. The two salt marsh sites are located at Stiffkey, Norfolk and Tollesbury, Essex and have for several years been the subjects of detailed investigations into salt marsh processes (Boorman 1996). These studies used filter papers to catch the sediment from a single tide and they showed that while at Tollesbury, Essex the deposition of sediment is fairly evenly distributed across the marsh there are considerable variations across the marsh in the net deposition during a single tide at Stiffkey, Norfolk.

Processes that increase or reduce the accretion of sediment are clearly of importance to salt marsh development but the increasing influence of sea level rise resulting from global warming is greatly increasing the significance of any changes in the rate of accretion (Boorman 1992*a*). For example, Cundy & Croudace (1996) showed that the salt marshes of the Solent, southern England, were accreting at a rate of $4.0–5\,mm\,a^{-1}$. Viewed against a past rate of sea level rise of $1.2\,mm\,yr^{-1}$

it provides for healthy marsh growth. But current estimates of effective sea level rise are also between $4.0–5.5\,mm\,a^{-1}$ (Cundy & Croudace 1996). This brings the long-term future of these salt marshes into question.

Methods

Changes in surface level of the marsh were determined by the use of permanent 'Feno' markers. These are plastic blocks that were anchored at a depth of 700 mm in the marsh surface by the extension of stiff wire anchors. The depth of anchorage was considered to be sufficient to provide a permanent and stable reference point from which changes in the surface level of the marsh could be measured with no risk of the marker being disturbed by trampling or bioturbation. The changes in marsh surface level were determined by setting the markers in pairs each 2.2 m apart and by resting an aluminium alloy beam across the pairs of markers. The beam was marked at intervals of 100 mm and at each of these points the distance to the ground surface and the height of the nearest item of vegetation was determined. For every transect of 20 points the three plant species contributing the greatest vegetation cover were also recorded. Ground surface levels were recorded to the nearest millimetre while vegetation heights were recorded to the nearest five millimetres. The studies were conducted at Stiffkey, Norfolk and at Tollesbury Essex. The marsh at Tollesbury was an intricate mosaic with overall a mixture of *Atriplex portulacoides* and *Puccinellia maritima*. At Stiffkey the marsh was at a rather higher level and there were distinct patches where various different species were dominant notably, *Triglochin maritima*, *Puccinellia maritima*, *Limonium vulgare*, *Plantago maritima* and *Salicornia europaea* (nomenclature is according to Stace 1991). At each of the two study sites three parallel rows each of four transects were used to cover the study area. The 240 measurements at each site were repeated at monthly intervals from May 1993 to June 1995.

Results

The mean monthly changes in surface level of the marsh site at Tollesbury showed fluctuations of up to 6.2 mm erosion and 4.1 mm accretion (Fig. 1). The largest changes were during the winter months. During two years of parallel observations the mean rate of accretion at Tollesbury was estimated, by regression, to be

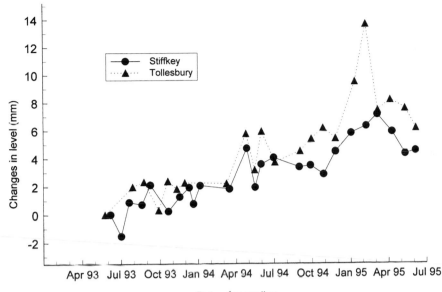

Fig. 1. Changes in salt marsh surface level at Stiffkey, Norfolk and Tollesbury Essex, 1993–1995. Each point represent the mean of 240 values and the standard errors, omitted for clarity, are all between 0.43 and 0.54 mm.

$4.27 \, \text{mm a}^{-1}$. The surface of the marsh level at Stiffkey also showed variations from month to month but these were generally smaller than those at Tollesbury, rarely exceeding 3 mm (Fig. 1). Some of the changes in surface level observed at Tollesbury were also observed at Stiffkey but other changes were only observed

at Stiffkey. The mean accretion rate at Stiffkey was estimated to be $3.08 \, \text{mm a}^{-1}$.

The data sets were then examined to see if there were any interactions between the overall change between May 1993 and June 1995 at individual points and the corresponding mean vegetation heights. At Tollesbury the vegetation

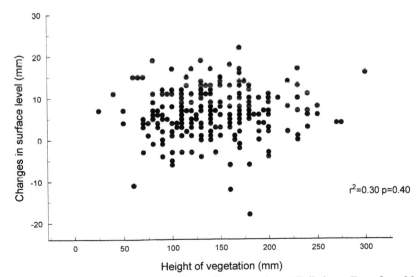

Fig. 2. Effect of height of vegetation on rates of accretion or erosion at Tollesbury, Essex from May 1993 to June 1995.

height varied from almost zero to 300 mm but there was no correlation ($r^2 = 0.30$, $p = 0.40$) between the mean vegetation height (148 mm) and the change in surface level (Fig. 2). At Stiffkey the mean and the maximum vegetation heights were very much less (75 and 180 mm) but there was a significant correlation ($r^2 = 0.67$, $p = 0.01$) between the vegetation height and changes in surface level (Fig. 3). Given that the apparent relationship was seen at Stiffkey but not at Tollesbury the data from Stiffkey were examined further.

Over the period of the study there were, at Stiffkey, considerable variations in both monthly accretion rates and in monthly vegetation heights (Fig. 4). The maximum period of accretion was between August and October 1995 following the summer period of vegetation growth. However, in 1994 and 1996 there were similar peaks of vegetation growth but with little accretion. Significant periods of erosion occurred in October 1993, May 1994, July 1995 and November 1995. The vegetation heights were relatively low at all these times with the

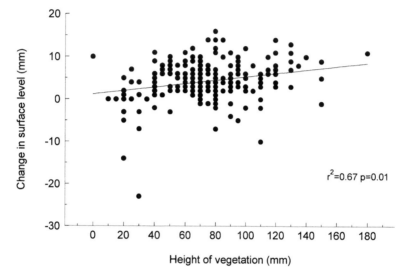

Fig. 3. Effect of height of vegetation on rates of accretion or erosion at Stiffkey, Norfolk from May 1993 to June 1995

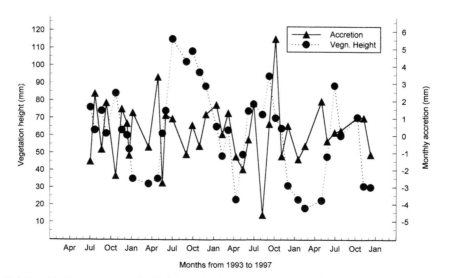

Fig. 4. Relationship between vegetation height and salt marsh accretion at Stiffkey, Norfolk 1993–1997.

exception of July 1995. The erosion at this time was subsequently followed by a marked period of accretion with a net gain overall from July to October.

The impact of vegetation cover on the rate of accretion is likely to depend on complex inter-actions between the plant architecture and its ability to reduce flow velocities and entrap sediment. It was considered that the biomass of the standing crop might give some measure of the effectiveness of the vegetation in this respect. Data collected during studies on salt marsh productivity at Stiffkey (Boorman 1996) show that the standing crop is at a minimum from January to March and that it is at a maximum between May and September (Fig. 5). It should also be noted that during this period the biomass of plant litter covering the ground surface is also at its maximum. This might also indicate suitable conditions for accretion of sediment.

When the results from each of the 12 tran-sects were examined there is a weak correlation between the mean vegetation height in Decem-ber 1995 (mean $= 33$ mm, $r^2 = 0.19$, $p = 0.16$)

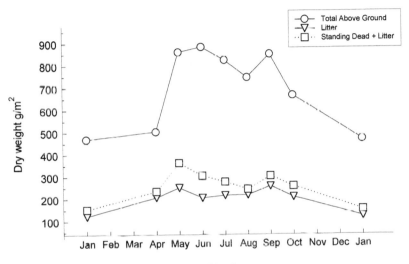

Fig. 5. Seasonal changes in the components of the standing crop in the Middle Marsh at Stiffkey, Norfolk, 1993.

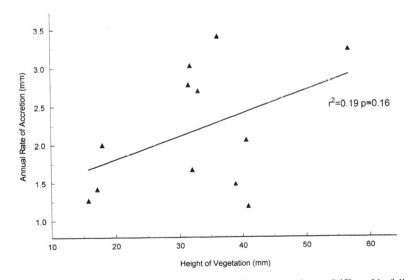

Fig. 6. Effect of the height of the vegetation in December 1995 on accretion at Stiffkey, Norfolk.

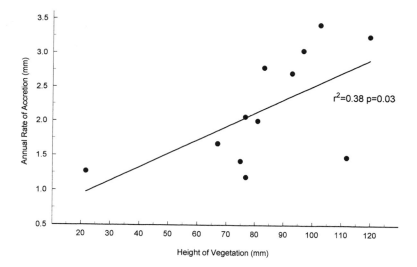

Fig. 7. Effect of the height of the vegetation in June 1995 on accretion at Stiffkey, Norfolk.

and the annual rate of accretion (Fig. 6) but there is a much stronger link between the mean vegetation height in June 1995 (mean $= 84$ mm, $r^2 = 0.38$, $p = 0.03$) and the annual rate of accretion (Fig. 7). The data would seem to suggest that accretion is only aided by plant growth when there is a vegetation cover in which the height is in excess of 80–90 mm.

While recording the heights of the vegetation, the species' dominance was recorded along each of the 12 transects and so it is possible to consider the seasonal changes at each of the transects in relation to the salt marsh plant species that dominated the plant cover. Because of the limited number of replicates for the

different plant species involved it was not possible to make a statistical assessment, nevertheless, there were indication of some specific differences. There were five different species that were dominant along the recorded transects, *Triglochin maritima* (mean June vegetation height $= 106$ mm; see Table 1), *Plantago maritima* (92 mm), *Limonium vulgare* (92 mm) *Puccinellia maritima* (88 mm), and *Salicornia europaea* (28 mm). *Triglochin*, the species that had the tallest June vegetation height, was associated with the highest rate of accretion (3.01 mm), although most of the accretion was during the summer of 1993 (Fig. 8a). Nevertheless, over the period of the observations, although accretion was rather variable there was very little erosion at any time. The heights and growth form of *Plantago*, *Puccinellia* and *Limonium* are similar but there were some apparent differences in the associated patterns of accretion. The one transect of *Puccinellia* was notable for the steady pattern of accretion throughout the period of observations (Fig. 8b). However, the pattern of accretion with the three transects with *Plantago* showed considerable variability (Fig. 8c). This effect was even more marked in the case of *Limonium* (Fig. 8d). The one transect where *Salicornia* was the dominant species not only showed the lowest overall accretion but it was also the most variable (Fig. 8e). *Salicornia* is an annual species in which the plant dies in the late autumn and the remains of the plant, although persistent for a while, gradually decay in the late winter leaving little or no cover over the ground surface in these areas.

Table 1. *Vegetation heights (±SE, n = 20) and the dominant species in each of the 12 transects in June and December 1995 at Stiffkey, Norfolk*

Transect no.	Dominant species	June height (mm)	December height (mm)
2	*Triglochin*	124 ± 6	59 ± 6
11	*Triglochin*	87 ± 7	25 ± 3
4	*Plantago*	112 ± 7	48 ± 6
6	*Plantago*	96 ± 8	33 ± 4
8	*Plantago*	69 ± 6	34 ± 6
7	*Puccinellia*	88 ± 27	27 ± 5
1	*Limonium*	67 ± 5	25 ± 4
3	*Limonium*	107 ± 7	28 ± 4
5	*Limonium*	120 ± 6	28 ± 4
9	*Limonium*	83 ± 6	19 ± 3
10	*Limonium*	81 ± 5	35 ± 3
12	*Salicornia*	28 ± 3	3 ± 2

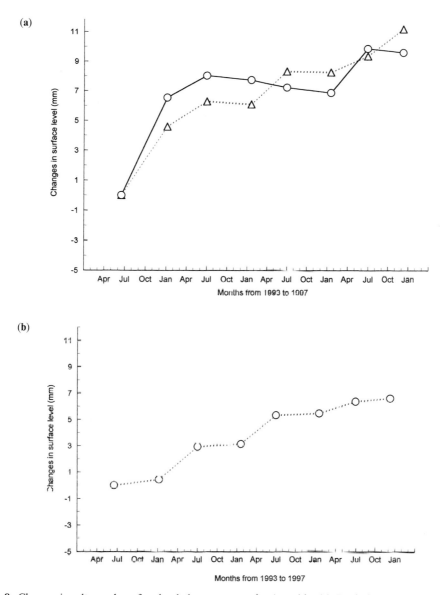

Fig. 8. Changes in salt marsh surface level along transects dominated by (**a**) *Triglochin maritima*, (**b**) *Puccinellia maritima*, (**c**) *Plantago maritima*, (**d**) *Limonium vulgare* and (**e**) *Salicornia europaea*, 1993–1997.

Studies had previously been made on sediment exchanges at both Tollesbury and Stiffkey (Boorman 1996). These have shown that the mean concentration of suspended solids at Tollesbury is generally low, averaging $18 \, \text{mg} \, l^{-1}$. The input of sediment only occurs when there is sufficient wave action to stir up the mud on the outer mud flats at the beginning of the flood tide. The mean concentration of suspended sediment at Stiffkey is only marginally higher

than that at Tollesbury ($23 \, \text{mg} \, l^{-1}$), however, at Stiffkey there is a much higher frequency of suspended sediment in excess of $150 \, \text{mg} \, l^{-1}$. These high sediment loads occur only during spring tides when there is a sufficiently high water velocity to pick up the larger size particles. The sediment loads are reduced with significant surface accretion occurring as soon as the high velocities that are needed for the transport of such materials are themselves reduced.

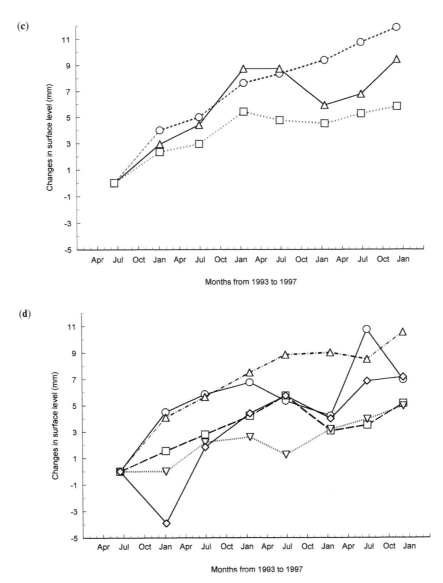

Fig. 8. (*continued*)

Discussion

For salt marsh accretion to occur there has to be a net import of sediment which, in effect, means that there has to be both a source of sediment and a means of transport. The sediment source itself will determine the availability of sediment for transport under the influence of tidal water movements. The actual sediment load that is carried will depend on both the particle size of the sediment available and on the water velocities experienced. The particle size of the

sediment depends on the sediment source itself. The magnitude of the transport of the sediment depends on the water velocities experienced; the larger the sediment particles the higher the velocities that are needed for sediment transport to occur. The proportion of the imported sediment that is deposited will depend on the magnitude of the reduction in the water velocity as it passes over the marsh surface.

At Tollesbury the sediments are generally finer than those found at Stiffkey and therefore lower velocities are required for transport of

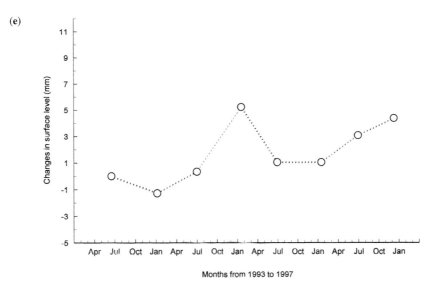

Fig. 8. (*continued*)

suspended sediment. Because of the smaller particle sizes at Tollesbury significant sediment settlement and deposition will only occur at very low water velocities, these are effectively only experienced during the short period at high water between flood and ebb tide. This has the effect of giving a relatively even pattern of accretion across the whole of the marsh surface. It also means that the effect of the generally tall vegetation is relatively uniform. Where the particle sizes of the incoming sediment are small, sediment can be deposited on the vegetation itself as well as directly on the marsh surface. The salt marsh plants themselves can thus act as a secondary sediment source (Stumpf 1983). After one particular storm tide it was observed that the leaves of salt marsh plants at Tollesbury were covered with sediment layer several millimetres thick. This was washed off by subsequent tides and by rainfall during the following week.

There is little apparent correlation between vegetation height and accretion at Tollesbury and it appears that the vegetation has little direct effect on accretion. It may be that the vegetation can ensure that once the sediment is deposited subsequent re-erosion is kept to a minimum. Visual evidence from Tollesbury indicated an association between erosion and limited plant cover (Boorman 1992*b*). Certainly the absence of vegetation would itself only have a small effect on the magnitude of sediment deposition. This lack of vegetation would, however, result in a great increase in subsequent erosion (even

though there might be a subsequent deposition occurring elsewhere) and thus a lowering in accretion overall (net accretion rate).

The larger sediment particles that occur at Stiffkey require higher minimum current velocities for their transport and conversely relatively small reductions in the water velocity can result in sediment deposition. The stiffness of the shorter vegetation growing on the Stiffkey marshes could produce these changes in water velocity. They can thus have a significant impact on the pattern of sediment deposition. However, the beneficial effects of increased vegetation stiffness can be offset by increased turbulence if the height of the vegetation is uneven (Hewlett *et al.* 1987). It appears that uniformity in the vegetation cover, both across the surface of the marsh and with time through the year, is the most important factor. In this respect the perennial salt marsh species such as *Limonium*, *Plantago*, *Triglochin* and *Puccinellia* are more effective that the annual *Salicornia*.

The study area at Stiffkey was small and its surface was relatively level, permitting direct comparisons to be made between the effects of these different plant species. On a more general scale the interactions between the various salt marsh plant species and sediment accretion have to be considered in relation to differing marsh levels. These elevations themselves are an important determinant of which species will grow in particular areas as the various salt marsh species each have their own characteristic tolerances to tidal immersion (Adam 1990). The elevation of a particular marsh surface determines the duration of tidal cover for a particular tidal level and thus determines the length of time that is available for sediment deposition. The elevation of the marsh surface will also determine the maximum depth of the water that can occur over the marsh surface. This height of the water column determines the maximum amount of sediment that is available for deposition. The effect of the vegetation on reducing water velocities is not simply a function of vegetation height or vegetation density. It is rather a function of vegetation height and vegetation density taken together with the relative stiffness of vegetation. As water velocities increase tall vegetation may bend in the current and thus become less efficient than vegetation that is initially rather shorter but stiffer.

Clearly, vegetation can only trap what sediment there is in the affected part of the water column. However, the process is more complex than it first appears in that the influence of the vegetation has, itself, been shown to vary with the magnitude of the sediment. In experimental studies Brueske & Barrett (1994) showed that when the sediment load was high sediment deposition rates were entirely determined by the velocities of flow with the vegetation having no significant effect. In contrast when the sediment load was low the vegetation had a highly significant effect on sedimentation. It has to be noted that even the low sediment load used in these experiments were such that it was resulting in rates of sedimentation that was at least two orders of magnitude larger than that observed at Stiffkey or Tollesbury. In view of this upper limit to the interaction of sediment load and vegetation it would be interesting to determine whether there is also a lower threshold limit to the interaction.

There is a further factor that could influence the degree of this interaction of vegetation on sediment deposition and that is the magnitude of wave energy experienced at a particular marsh situation. The marshes at Stiffkey, like all the north Norfolk marshes, are open to the North Sea and wave energy might be expected to be a major factor across the marsh surface. However, in the area that was involved in this study that was located towards the landward edge of the marshes, wave action does not appear to have a major effect. Salt marshes are extremely effective in buffering wave energy under the conditions in this area (Moeller *et al.* 1996). This reduction in wave energy provides a low energy environment in which vegetation can play a significant role in the trapping and stabilizing of sediment.

Conclusions

The correlation between vegetation height and the rate of accretion at Stiffkey suggests that there are certain circumstances under which vegetation can affect patterns of sediment accretion across the salt marsh. For there to be an interaction of the vegetation has to be able to increase the marsh surface roughness and thus to reduce the water velocities to values at which sediment can be deposited. The vegetation at Tollesbury was taller than at Stiffkey and there was no significant correlation between vegetation height and accretion. Tall vegetation often has less effect than might be expected as the flow of water over the marsh surface can flatten the vegetation and thus reduce its roughness. Short stiff vegetation is likely to have the greatest effect on surface roughness and the consequent decrease in water velocities although unevenness in the vegetation cover can cause local turbulence. Sediment particle size is also important. With fine sediment, settlement effectively only occurs when the water velocities approach zero and under these conditions the effect of the vegetation cover is small. With rather coarser sediments small reductions in flow rates can have a significant effect on the magnitude of sediment deposition.

The authors would like to thank all those colleagues in the wider salt marsh research programme at other institutes in England, the Netherlands, France and Portugal and especially those who assisted in the field work and without whose enthusiastic co-operation the project would not have been possible. We should particularly like to acknowledge the support of DG XII of the Commission of the European Community for their financial support under Grants EV4V-0172F and EV5V-CT92-0098.

References

ADAM, P. 1990. *Saltmarsh Ecology. Cambridge Studies in Ecology*. The University Press, Cambridge, UK.

ALLEN, J. R. & PYE, K. 1992. *Saltmarshes: Morphodynamics, Conservation and Engineering Significance*. The University Press, Cambridge, UK.

BOORMAN, L. A. 1992a. The environmental consequences of climate on British salt marsh vegetation. *Wetlands Ecology and Management*, **2**, 11–21.

——1992b. *Studies of salt marsh erosion in Essex*. Final Report to NRA. Contract Report. Institute of Terrestrial Ecology, Huntingdon, UK.

——1995. Sea level rise and the future of the British Coast. *In*: JONES, N. V. (ed.) *Coastal Zone Topics 1. The Changing Coastline*, 10–13.

——1996. Results of the Institute of Terrestrial Ecology, England. *In*: LEFEUVRE, J. C. (ed.) *The effects of environmental change on European salt marshes: structure, functioning and exchange potentialities with marine coastal waters*. Volume 5. University of Rennes, France.

BRUESKE, C. C. & BARRETT, G. W. 1994. Effect of vegetation and hydraulic load on sediment patterns in experimental wetland ecosystems. *Ecological Engineering*, **3**, 429–447.

COPPING, N. J. & RICHARDS, I. G. 1990. *Use of Vegetation in Civil Engineering*. Butterworths, London.

CUNDY, A. B. & CROUDACE, I. W. 1996. Sediment accretion and recent sea level rise in the Solent, Southern England – inferences from radiometric and geochemical studies. *Estuarine Coastal and Shelf Science*, **43**, 449–467.

HEWLETT, H. W. M., BOORMAN, L. A. & BRAMLEY, M. E. 1987. *Design of reinforced grass waterways*. C.I.R.I.A. London.

HOWARD-WILLIAMS, C. 1992. Dynamic processes in New Zealand land-water ecotones. *New Zealand Journal of Ecology*, **15**, 91–98.

MAKESHWARI, B. L. 1992. Suitability of different flow equations and hydraulic resistance parameters for flows in surface irrigation – a review. *Water Resources Research*, **8**, 2059–2066.

MOELLER, I., SPENCER, T. & FRENCH, J. H. 1996. Wind wave attenuation over salt marsh surfaces: preliminary results from Norfolk, England. *Journal of Coastal Research*, **12**, 1009–1016.

MORGAN, R. P. C. 1980. Field studies of sediment transport by overland flow. *Earth Surface Processes*, **5**, 307–316.

REE, W. O. 1949. Hydraulic characteristics of vegetation for vegetated waterways. *Agricultural Engineering*, **30**, 184–187.

RICKSON, R. J. & MORGAN, R. P. C. 1988. Approaches to modelling the effects of vegetation on soil erosion by water. *Proc. EEC Workshop on Erosion Assessment for the EEC. Methods and Models*, Brussels, 237–253.

STUMPF, R. J. 1983. The process of sedimentation on the surface of a salt marsh. *Estuarine and Coastal Shelf Science*, **17**, 495–508.

STACE, C. 1991. *New Flora of the British Isles*. The University Press, Cambridge, UK.

STEVENSON, J. C., WARD, L. G. & KEARNEY, M. S. 1988. Sediment transport and trapping in marsh systems: implications of tidal flow studies *Marine Geology*, **80**, 37–59.

USSCS 1954. *Handbook of channel design for soil and water conservation*. Publication SCS-TP61. US Department of Agriculture, Washington, DC, USA.

Index